COUNSELLING

DATE DUE FOR RETURN

This book may be recalled before the above date.

COUNSELLING

The BACP *Counselling* Reader

Volume 2

EDITED BY
Pat Milner *and* Stephen Palmer

British Association for
Counselling and Psychotherapy

SAGE Publications
London • Thousand Oaks • New Delhi

SAGE Publications Ltd
6 Bonhill Street
London EC2A 4PU

SAGE Publications Inc.
2455 Teller Road
Thousand Oaks, California 91320

SAGE Publications India Pvt Ltd
32, M-Block Market
Greater Kailash – I
New Delhi 110 048

British Library Cataloguing in Publication data

A catalogue record for this book is available
from the British Library

ISBN 0 7619 6419 3
ISBN 0 7619 6420 7 (pbk)

Library of Congress control number available

Typeset by SIVA Math Setters, India
Printed in Great Britain by The Cromwell Press Ltd, Trowbridge,
Wiltshire

Contents

Contents

Part Two **Counselling Contexts and Practice**

Contents

Part Three **Counselling Issues**

Contents

Contents

Contents

Foreword

Change is inevitable. As individuals we may embrace or resist change, but we cannot escape from this fundamental fact of our existence. A second volume of BAC readings confronts the reader with how our field of work is changing, with an emphasis on the practical work of counselling in a wide variety of contexts, some of them novel. We are used to interacting as counsellors and psychotherapists face to face with our clients. Emergent ways of working using the new technologies extend that format as stand-alone computers provide powerful interactive facilities that clients can access in their own time, and e-mail and the Internet support real-time and time-framed interaction at a distance.

Another theme is that of how to work to best effect in diverse settings. Theoretical models compete for the counsellor's affiliation. Off-stage and coming to centre-stage is the evaluative dimension of evidence-based practice. In time there may be critical evaluations of theoretical models, which will guide counsellors in their choice of approach. For now, this volume presents more descriptive accounts of service delivery in settings as diverse as primary care and prison.

Cutting across the theme of special context is a more general dimension of the dilemmas of counselling practice, from confidentiality to ending counselling. Supervision, accreditation and training are discussed as vital supports for good practice.

I commend this volume as a way of keeping up to date. The points raised will surely prompt practitioners to debate issues and the detail of their practice. Now that the BAC has changed its name to the British Association for Counselling and Psychotherapy, I wonder what consequent change we may see in Volume 3 of the *Reader*. I look forward to that day.

Mark Aveline
Past President
British Association for Counselling and Psychotherapy

Acknowledgements

The editors, publisher and BACP would like to thank the various authors for agreeing to the reproduction of their material in this book.

Every effort has been made to trace all authors to seek permission to republish their work. Some difficulty was encountered. We would like to thank executors for granting permission in certain instances. If any parties have been inadvertently overlooked we shall be pleased to include an acknowledgement at the next available opportunity.

Introduction

BAC has become the British Association for Counselling and Psychotherapy; its journal *Counselling* was relaunched in 2000 as the monthly professional journal for counsellors, and the editorship of various publications has been diversified. The BACP office in Rugby employs an increasing number of paid staff as its structures and organization are reshaped. Much has changed, much remains the same. The publication of the *BACP Counselling Reader*, Volume 2, as a companion volume to the 1996 *Reader*, Volume 1, bridges old and new, preserving tradition and supporting transition. The Association is referred to as BAC throughout the text since this was its designation when the chapters were originally written.

In compiling a selection of articles appearing between 1992 and 2000, and inviting authors to update their work, the editors, Pat Milner and Stephen Palmer, reflect a major aim of the journal between those years – to balance some legitimate aspirations to being a professional and academic journal with a responsibility to offer a forum for debate and disagreement, and a mouthpiece for members. Journal readers are an intriguingly diverse group of practising professional and volunteer counsellors, academically inclined writers and teachers of counselling psychology, trainers emphasizing experiential learning, integrators of counselling skills and philosophies with other work, self-helpers, and those who from the beginning have been supportive of, interested in, and critical of the activity we call counselling. We were established as the British Association *for* Counselling and (although we are now the British Association *for* Counselling *and* Psychotherapy) it is still important to include in our remit not only counsellors and therapists but also supporters of our work. The book is written by and aimed at this diverse readership, but students of counselling, their trainers, experienced counsellors and supervisors in particular will find in its wide range of topics, and the discussion issues included in each chapter, stimulation for reflection, debate and perhaps material for essay subjects.

The *Reader* begins with a foreword from the BACP Past President, and is organized into six parts: Counselling Approaches, Counselling Contexts and Practice (including Practical Approaches), Counselling Issues (including Counselling and Practice Dilemmas), Counselling and Research and Future Trends. The final part, The Last Word, is a view of the future of BACP from its former Chief Executive. The book's 92 chapters are a representative selection from and a celebration of *Counselling* in the 1990s.

Through the *Reader* and as an organization we in BACP want to continue, as Sheila Dainow, an editor of the journal and of the first *Reader* suggested, 'to provide a framework which holds members with the same kind of care with which we aim as therapists to hold clients; safe and trustworthy; powerful and empowering; challenging and supportive; uncompromising of integrity and creatively flexible' (Dainow 1992).

Reference

Dainow, S. (1992) Features Editorial, *Counselling*, vol. 3, no. 2, p. 80 (May), Rugby: British Association for Counselling.

In memory of my mother,
Edith Milner (nee Evans),
'a gradely Lancashire lass'.
Born in Bolton (1908) she died in Blackheath, London (2000)
in her 92nd year,
thus matching the number of chapters in this, her book.

Pat Milner

To Maggie for her support

Stephen Palmer

PART ONE

COUNSELLING APPROACHES

Introduction to Part One

On re-reading all the articles relating to therapeutic approaches published in *Counselling* over the past ten years, it is easy to notice the general trend in the latter part of the decade towards the publication of papers on brief forms of counselling or psychotherapy. In particular, solution-focused, problem-solving and cognitive behavioural therapies dominate. Has the focus on brief counselling been led by consumers, counsellors or trainers? Or, perhaps, it is external factors such as financial restraints, for example within the National Health Service, that are mainly driving the interest in these approaches. Nevertheless, research has indicated that the majority of clients are in counselling for about six to eight sessions, suggesting that counselling could be seen as brief by default.

If we consider the vast number of articles that have been published in *Counselling*, only a small percentage focus specifically on approaches, and the same authors seem to have had several of these published. What is behind the reluctance to submit this type of article? Perhaps it is the fear of writing about what is already known and is now written about more extensively in book form. We can only guess at the reasons.

Part One includes chapters on the three main counselling approaches – person-centred, psychodynamic and cognitive forms of therapy – as well as on more recently developed models such as solution-focused therapy. Colin Feltham begins with a challenge to the idea of a core theoretical model of training. He asserts that there are serious philosophical and clinical objections which lead to the conclusion that training in, and support for, a core theoretical model are ultimately untenable and even oppressive. Sue Wheeler, however, drawing on her experience as Co-chair of the BAC Courses Accreditation Group and as a counsellor trainer, argues for an appropriate core theoretical model which evolves as a function of the counselling course's staff team. These two chapters may seem almost out of place in a section devoted to approaches, yet they set the scene before we focus specifically on any particular form of counselling.

Ivan Ellingham is still on his quest for a person-centred paradigm and reflects on the work of Rogers as well as of others. Earlier articles had raised responses that he continues to address in this chapter. Christina Saunders' shares her personal experience of solution-focused therapy, demonstrating how she has used scaling, the miracle question and exceptions with a client by providing us with a therapy transcript. She highlights how

1

solution-focused therapy can be used for longer-term counselling when a client has a variety of problems. In a companion piece to Saunders' earlier journal articles on solution-focused therapy, Jonathan Hales shows how he has incorporated the solution-focused concepts and methods within a person-centred approach. There are a surprising number of similarities between the two approaches, although he does include a number of apparent differences too. He believes that both approaches hold the same core beliefs and values. A chapter on problem-solving counselling by Michael Neenan and Stephen Palmer illllustrates how they have integrated both the seven-step problem-solving model with the ABCs of rational emotive behaviour therapy. Although this brief therapeutic approach predates solution-focused therapy, there are similarities between them, although interestingly the main proponents often write about the differences. Problem-solving therapy tackles both the practical and emotional problems a client may be encountering when dealing with difficulties.

Psychodynamic therapy is the focus of two different chapters. John Lees shares with us an erotic countertransference and notes that his subsequent attempts to process the experience contained elements of therapist defensiveness, anxiety and transformation. Even when the therapy had finished, he could not stop thinking about the woman who had been his client. How often do we as counsellors experience therapeutic relationships that play on our minds in this manner? The published literature itself does not indicate that this is an acknowledged common experience. Or is it only psychodynamic therapists who write about such an intimate topic? John O'Brien discusses a psychodynamic approach to mentoring derived from Freud's early descriptions of the workings of the psyche and from post-Freudian formulations. He was involved in a mentoring programme that was an integral part of a change programme for a company employing 60,000 staff.

Integration is the theme of Richard Nelson-Jones's attempts to reconcile the strengths of the humanistic and cognitive-behavioural counselling approaches. In suggesting that cognitive-humanists hold humanistic values, which include the belief in rationality and in humanitarianism, he observes that both humanistic and cognitive-behavioural approaches have insufficiently emphasized the concept of the mind. Ten guidelines for counselling practice undertaken within a cognitive-humanistic framework are provided. This contrasts with the next chapter by Michael Neenan and Windy Dryden on rational emotive behaviour therapy, although similarities between the two approaches can be seen. One of the interesting aspects of rational emotive behaviour therapy is that it has a vocabulary of unhealthy and healthy negative emotions such as anxiety versus concern, and depression versus sadness. Neenan and Dryden briefly mention that the approach has a number of conceptual and methodological flaws and additional research is required, which may be true for the majority of approaches commonly practised in Britain.

Diana Whitmore considers psychosynthesis an approach with a soul. Apparently, psychosynthetic work differs from psychodynamic work in that the former delves into the past in a focused way about particular life issues, and indiscriminate delving into the unconscious is discouraged. Of course, whether psychodynamic therapists would agree with this view is debatable. One of the longer-term goals of psychosynthesis therapy is the fostering of a stable sense of identity. The individual identity leads to a recognition of interdependence within the context of society and a complex network of relationships.

'In the Counsellor's Chair' was a popular section in the 1990s version of *Counselling*. In Chapter 12, Stephen Palmer interviews Arnold Lazarus on multimodal therapy.

Developed by Lazarus, this approach has become one of the best known systematic and technically eclectic forms of therapy. The approach uses an assessment procedure that focuses on seven modalities. Interestingly, Lazarus argues that although a multimodal framework exists, multimodal therapy itself does not exist! He also raises the issue of clients who do not receive appropriate treatment suing their therapists, and shares his fantasy of established therapeutic techniques having to be used for particular disorders.

The creative approaches of art therapy and writing as therapy bring a change of emphasis from models, paradigms and theories to practical, experiential counselling. Sydney Klugman, in his work with young offenders, reveals how art can enable our inarticulate selves to find expression and help understanding of the personal implications of what we have created. Gillie Bolton's workshops provide a group space, in which the powerful impact of writing as therapy is able to be realized. Both chapters call for the healing power of the arts to receive fuller consideration and due recognition as counselling and psychotherapeutic approaches.

In the B.Sc. (Hons) Therapeutic Counselling programme in Leeds, the challenge for the course staff was to find the concepts that offered an integration of their common ground and to develop a shared framework. Geoff Pelham, Stephen Paul and Peter Holmes discuss the relational model of counselling that evolved from this exciting process. More recently they have developed a post-qualification MA in Therapeutic Counselling in which the participants can explore the approach in greater death. This highlights how counsellors working together can build bridges and move beyond the boundaries set by different therapeutic approaches. This brings to an end the counselling approaches section and leaves it on a positive note.

1

Challenging the Core Theoretical Model

Colin Feltham

The British counselling world differs from much of the rest of the world in insisting not only on career-long clinical supervision, but also on identified core theoretical models in training. (I shall mainly refer to models, although the terms approach, school, orientation, etc. are also used more or less synonymously in the literature.) Although the United Kingdom Council for Psychotherapy (UKCP) differs structurally from the British Association for Counselling (BAC), it too is organized around identified, distinct models of psychotherapy. The British Confederation of Psychotherapists (BCP) accepts only traditional psychoanalytically oriented organizations as members.

For a training course to be recognized by BAC, it must in effect show that it adheres to well-established psychodynamic, person-centred or, slightly more tenuously, to a variety of humanistic, integrative or systematically eclectic approaches. There are said to be in excess of 450 theoretical models of counselling and psychotherapy and, officially at least, BAC, UKCP and the European Association for Psychotherapy (EAP) support diversity and do not discriminate against any reputable approach. In Britain, most BAC-recognized courses are psychodynamic or person-centred, a few are based on transactional analysis or psychosynthesis, or an acceptable integration of one of these and other humanistic and skills-based or cognitive-behavioural approaches.

Why a core theoretical model?

Arguments in favour of some sort of identified core theoretical model appear to run as follows:

1 It is important that trainees are exposed to at least one coherent model and its implications. The model's parts may be described in terms of its world-view and concept of human beings or image of the person; learning, developmental and motivational concepts; conceptualization of psychological disturbance and health; acquisition and perpetuation of psychological disturbance; treatment goals; therapeutic strategies and techniques; expected change process; limitations; etc. (Wallace 1986; Dryden 1996). A training should demonstrate internal consistency; that is, the core theoretical model should be reflected in theoretical seminars, skills practice, personal growth work and supervision. Failure to embrace one model in depth results in practitioners who are confused, lacking in rigour, and whose knowledge base is thin.

2 Trainees must learn and hone the practical and clinical attitudes, skills and techniques associated with a particular approach if they are to become competent practitioners.

This chapter was first published in *Counselling*, Journal of the British Association for Counselling, vol. 8, no. 2, pp. 121–5 (1997).

Attempts to learn a mish-mash of skills from various models results in ineffective or dangerous clinical practice by counsellors who are merely syncretistic dilettantes rather than adept at systematic assessment, technique selection, timing, and so on. Also, theoretically inconsistent counsellors risk transmitting their confusion to clients.

3 It is expected that as counsellors become mature practitioners they will develop a personalized model or approach that maximizes their skills and best meets the needs of their clients (Skovholt and Ronnestad 1992; Spurling 1993). They cannot achieve such maturity without first having had a thorough grounding in a coherent model. *After* this, they may choose to develop some form of theoretically consistent eclecticism (Dryden 1991) or thoroughgoing integration of two or more models (Wilkins 1997). Although it is widely believed that theory should never overshadow or distort the actual therapeutic encounter, paradoxically practitioners should hold strong theoretical positions (Karasu 1992: 8).

Why are core theoretical models untenable?

A *prima facie* case for core theoretical models certainly exists. My own objections are obviously not intended to commend confusion or incompetency in training. Rather, I have come to believe that there are serious philosophical and clinical objections which lead to the conclusion that training in and support for a core theoretical model are ultimately untenable and even oppressive. This is admittedly a change from my previous position in Dryden and Feltham (1994). My objections in summary form are as follows.

1 Since the advent of multiple therapeutic theories, there never has been a clear front runner among psychotherapies (that is, one which consensually commands intellectual or scientific respect, or popular support); nor has there been any school without its dissidents. Those schools whose leaders have made political attempts to demean or exclude their own dissidents may have appeared to possess internal solidarity. The costs of dissent are high, as Karen Horney discovered when the New York Psychoanalytic Institute demoted her in 1941 with the following curious rationale:

> The Educational Committee is fully in favour of free and unhampered discussion of all points of view existing in psychoanalysis. Such discussions are possible and most fruitful only if the preparatory analyses and preliminary, theoretical fundamentals are such as not to prejudice the student in advance to the basic principles of psychoanalysis. (Cited in Quinn 1987: 348)

This position of dogma preceding and disingenuously silencing free inquiry has persisted into our own professional training bodies today, of course.

2 It is difficult to defend the position that *any* one model, arbitrarily singled out from 450 (or even from a mainstream 10 or 20) and offered as an in-depth training, can adequately prepare therapists to help most clients referred to them. It is well known that many psychoanalysts consider behaviour therapists to hold absurd views, and vice versa; indeed the field is full of dispute. On what basis, then, is any one model to be selected as the foundation of a professional training (Feltham 1997)? Is not the field itself confused and incoherent? Karasu (1992) cites Smith et al. (1980: 185): 'Although all therapies are equally effective, one must choose only one to learn and practice.' Must one? Why?

3 There are no core psychotherapeutic models older than a few decades (classical Freudian psychoanalysis may be the exception but even that has been largely torn into

many divided schools) and none has been shown to yield consistently excellent results or to be decisively clinically superior to others (Luborsky et al. 1975; Smith et al. 1980). Some models have seen their reputations wax and wane, and some have already become virtually extinct. In his own ambitious personality theory, Gooch (1975) acknowledged that all theories are provisional and that turnover in psychological theories is especially rapid. 'The turnover arises, among other things, from the complex and peculiarly nebulous nature of psychological material, and not least from our own inevitable involvements with it' (Gooch 1975: 527).

4 When human nature and behaviour are themselves the object of study, psychotherapists and counsellors must realize that they share the field with philosophers, theologians, political scientists, psychologists, anthropologists, historians and others. It must surely be conceded that no one appears to be any closer than anyone else in arriving at answers to radical and perennial questions about human suffering and deliverance from it (see, for example, Stevenson 1987).

5 Insistence on a core model perpetuates a tradition-driven practice of psychotherapy rather than one based on empiricism, on listening to clients' needs and views, on research findings and rational clinical innovation. The therapy world is characterized by competing theories and practices generated by charismatic leaders, defended by enthusiastic followers and orthodox institutes. In fact we appear to insist on core counselling models without even knowing what we mean: 'There has been no thorough examination of what actually constitutes an adequate theory of counselling' (Bayne et al. 1994: 150).

6 The argument that trainees who are not equipped with particular, theoretically mediated competencies but arbitrarily and dangerously use a mixture of techniques requires examination. It has not been demonstrated explicitly what the specific skills and techniques of each model are, exactly how they are taught and how long this training must take, whether they actually differ fundamentally from the skills espoused in other models and exactly how counsellors practise dangerously with 'inadequate' training in them. Paradoxically, a great deal of resistance exists among therapists to the systematization of such therapy training, for example by devising and using technical treatment manuals; instead, much training seems shrouded in mystique. The possibility must be considered that proponents of each model unintentionally exaggerate the uniqueness and complexity of their skill base, and exaggerate the alleged dangers of misapplication.

7 It is quite likely that training in a highly specific model may lead the practitioner to dispense that model to all and sundry inappropriately, fitting clients to the theory and associated techniques rather than the reverse. For example, everyone gets long-term, insight-promoting therapy or non-directive therapy, cognitive restructuring or therapy focusing on ego states, regardless of their actual presenting problem, personality, circumstances and wishes. This might be particularly true of therapists in training and those who are relatively inexperienced, who are so anxious to 'do it right' that this preoccupation becomes more determining than the client's welfare. This is an especially serious problem for defenders of the core theoretical model position, because the reality often is that clients with a wide array of clinical needs are seen by trainees or beginners, or are seen in settings where a narrow, traditional approach is being used.

Robertiello and Schoenewolf (1987: 266) discuss the case of a client abused in one such traditional setting. 'The approach taught at this institute and practiced by its training analysts, control supervisors, and the like, contained a built-in resistance to emotional ventilation.' To scream was exactly what the client indicated he needed to do, but the analyst would not and could not permit it because of his training. There is a strong case for saying that each theoretical model magnifies – indeed, capitalizes on – certain aspects of human behaviour and neglects others, and that a rigorous training would actually attend holistically and equally to past and present behaviour, affect, sensation, imagery, cognition, and psychosocial, biological, cultural and spiritual factors. As far as I am aware, no such training exists.

8 There is a case for saying that it is not particular core theories that have any significant effect on clients; rather, a combination of non-specific factors is responsible for successful therapy (Frank 1974). Many of these are about the client's *belief* in the therapist, confidence in the status of the therapist, therapist qualities (including those built by ordinary life experiences), working alliance, the protected setting, etc. Some are about simple human needs for attention, warmth and acceptant interest (Howe 1993). Karasu (1992: 27) argues that the therapist's passionate belief in his or her theories and methods is crucial, since the aura of conviction conveys itself to clients. Conviction, not theoretical correctness, is what counts according to Karasu's argument.

9 We might also consider that reports of advanced practitioners' reflections on their initial training tend to identify clinical work and supervision as of far more formative significance than core theory (Dryden and Spurling 1989). Goldberg's (1992: 49) interviewed master practitioners reported a high degree of retrospective dissatisfaction with 'misguided clinical theories'. Even before training, the intuition possessed by many individuals (that therapy is essentially interpersonal and atheoretical) manifests in a reluctance to opt for and be moulded by any narrow model, but unfortunately candidates for training have little choice but to accept one circumscribed model or another. Individual clinical giftedness, so overlooked as a factor in therapy, may well be more significant than any pedagogic theory:

> Traditionally, it has been common for senior analysts to teach the kind of orthodoxy that is expected which essentially repeats the party line. They have been reluctant or unable to really articulate what they actually do in practice. Many of our most gifted clinicians are successful because of the way they actually work, not for the reasons they declare in pedagogic situations. (Corbett 1995: 77)

10 Another argument against core models is that they are self-evidently productions of a patriarchal society. To date, all have been founded by charismatic white men, initially of mid-European origin but now almost entirely American. (Anna Freud, Melanie Klein, Karen Horney and other women contributors have been modifiers rather than founders.) The awe in which leading figures – even Carl Rogers, the founder of non-directive, think-for-yourself, person-centred therapy – are held closely resembles religious and political phenomena of reverence, obedience and discipleship. The common aim of psychotherapy – autonomy – is belied by the reality of training institutes which demand conformity from trainees (Masson 1990) and by psychotherapy which either mystifies clients (McLellan 1995) or subtly converts them to belief in the tenets of the particular approach (Levenson 1983).

Virtually all current psychotherapeutic theory reflects white, Western psychology and implicit assumptions about the universal correctness or desirability of autonomy, assertiveness, insightfulness and emotional freedom – qualities which are not in fact valued by all individuals in all cultures at all times. Core theoretical models in psychotherapy and counselling encourage monolithic, ethnocentric and patriarchal thinking and tacitly discourage and marginalize (even forbid) any kind of anarchic (Feyerabend 1994), personalistic (Smail 1978), radically feminist (McLellan 1995), politicized (Newman 1991) and dialogical (Sampson 1993) accounts of human functioning, distress and healing.

11 All psychotherapeutic models are predicated on the assumption that human nature and behaviour is understandable, classifiable, adaptable and even predictable. Most clinical practice operates on the assumption that the client's new insights, attitudes and behaviours will act upon his or her environment with automatic benefits. Of course, it can also be argued that our environment is often indifferent or hostile to us and that our efforts to conceptualize, control and order our lives are susceptible to constant frustration. All therapeutic models are partly fictions and inadequate because they de-emphasize or even deny the role of chance, complexity, macro changes outside our control, and chaos generally. Perhaps inadvertently, they promote their methods as almost infallible. Beneath the promised orderliness of therapeutic valhalla there may always be a necessarily ragged, imperfect, vulnerable and unimprovable or ungovernable self (Vicinzey 1969; Rose 1989; Feyerabend 1994).

Acknowledging differences

Let me try to combine and present these arguments differently by comparing two approaches to studying and addressing the matter of individual problems in living.

Approach number one goes like this. My own problems were greatly helped by therapy x: I have now trained rigorously in therapy x and I see daily the benefits it brings to people; I continue to study and refine my technical grasp of therapy x which I believe to have an edge over other therapies; I don't believe researchers have grasped the subtleties of therapy x; I don't believe it can be readily integrated with other therapies; it is essential that trainees themselves have therapy x and dedicate many years to learning its complexities; it is essential that all practitioners operate from a secure theoretical base.

Approach number two goes like this. I see that people have a wide variety of problems and that society itself is hardly a sanity-generating milieu; I see that hundreds of explanations are held up and as many solutions proposed, none of which seems wholly satisfactory or unequivocally effective; I believe there is some sense and nonsense in most therapies and I strive hard to see how each individual can best be helped by the more sensible bits from each (or indeed by bits of religion, education, philosophy, etc.); I do not believe the pursuit of theoretical or technical purity and separatism is healthy or credible; I think such tendencies are tribalistic, wasteful and ultimately detrimental to mental and social health.

The first approach is quite common and often flows from personal experiences of perceived salvation or need for certitude and ultimate meaning. Many of us cling to an ideological object, such as a particular religion, political view or psychotherapy, which we cherish and can never let go of. Arguably, all such ideologies act as opiates and their true function is to infuse us with a reassuring but defensive sense of certainty and direction in an unpredictable and frightening world. It is comforting to think that Freud, like Jesus, heroically explored the psychic wilderness singlehandedly and has passed on the hard-won answers to us lesser mortals. But why – in psychotherapy and religion especially – do we invest so much faith in such figureheads? And how can we distinguish between crazy and/or mistaken cult leaders and reputable discoverers and master practitioners (Storr 1996)? The tendency towards emotional investment is quite evident in this approach.

The second approach is perhaps less common and is characterized by a mixture of pragmatism, restless truth-seeking, agnosticism, scepticism, and distaste for or avoidance of certainties and in-groups. Positively, this approach echoes the message of mystics and philosophers through the ages to avoid the traps of thinking that you have finally understood, and to embrace instead the *via negativa*, eliminating all illusory solutions. Negatively, those attracted to this approach may be pathologically avoiding belonging to any group, casting themselves romantically as outsiders, heroic and lonely defenders of unpalatable truths. They may simply be manifesting a naughty child/rebellious adolescent archetype, or a negative transference towards theory (Rangell 1985). The tendency towards nihilism, cynicism, arrogance and empty relativity is obvious in this approach.

I cannot pretend to *know* that I am right about core theoretical models being untenable. Indeed, sometimes I shudder a little when I read a student's incoherent essay displaying a grasshopper-like predilection for jumping from one unrelated theme to another, or magpie-like attraction to glittering, gimmicky techniques unanchored in any solid understanding. Sometimes I read eloquent and persuasive passages in the literature of some deeply traditional psychotherapy and doubt my own scepticism. On the other hand, students who are poor writers or ill-disciplined thinkers can be very warm, intuitive and effective healers, and many therapeutic encounters remind me how ill-fitting most generalized theory is to real individuals. I find some untrained carers or supposedly superficially trained therapists more human and insightful than some highly trained practitioners who may be steeped in one or another core theoretical model.

Implications

If my scepticism about core theoretical models has some validity or interest, where might it lead? I propose the following possibilities.

1 BAC, UKCP and similar professional bodies might consider the pleas of trainers who wish to base their syllabus not on traditional core models (nor, obviously, on sloppily constructed programmes) but on a range of responsibly critical, intuitional, eclectic, systemic, trans-theoretical, atheoretical, interdisciplinary, dialogical or pluralistic perspectives (Samuels 1993). This questions the widespread developmental view that a first training must treat (adult) trainees as babies to be spoon-fed traditional material (however stodgy or toxic), and that only advanced trainees or mature practitioners can handle a rich diet of pluralistic perspectives, real debate and critical analysis. It is often said that therapists must be able to tolerate ambiguity in clients – but not in the theoretical content of courses?

2 Researchers might investigate further the comparative effectiveness of practitioners trained in conventional traditions with core theoretical models and those trained differently (experimentally, eclectically, minimally, informally, autonomously, etc.).

3 Trainers and theoreticians dissatisfied with the prescriptive positions of existing professional bodies might risk launching themselves as independent commentators, critics and creators of new therapeutic cultures and methods, thus challenging the assumption that the only alternatives to traditional models are flimsy, illegitimate hybrids.

4 Academic departments of counselling and psychotherapy might further develop the function of questioning the field and its assumptions, becoming what critical and philosophical psychologists now are in relation to classical psychology. Such study might include detailed historical and sociological analysis of the roots of therapeutic ideologies and of the ways in which therapeutic enthusiasms regularly swell and fade in their efforts to capture conceptually and clinically the elusive rhythm of human suffering, aspirations and limitations.

5 There is no reason to abandon the search for a grand unified theory of human suffering and psychotherapy. Although ambitious and unfashionably counter-postmodernist, it is possible to conceive of an overarching, interdisciplinary conceptual structure which might accommodate and reinterpret diverse therapeutic theories (e.g. Stevens and Price 1996).

6 Continuing identification of the active ingredients of effective therapy (that is, placebo factors, relational qualities and distinctive techniques) could lead to a fruitful pragmatics of psychotherapy divorced from speculative aetiological, personality and clinical theories (Lazarus 1990; Thompson 1996).

Finally we might (but we won't) inject some humour and humility into our debates about training by admitting that our knowledge base is still insubstantial and our techniques are pretty fallible. We might (but we won't) inject some ontological seriousness into our thinking and training, shifting the axis from received wisdom and 'conceptual imperialism' (Goldfried et al. 1992) to live, urgent, owned and shared analysis of the human condition (Bohm 1994). As still relatively young and status-hungry professions, counselling and psychotherapy are probably in no mood for any radical revision of their theories and practices. This is regrettable, since not only do they thereby defend untenable orthodoxies, but unwittingly and oppressively place an obstacle in the path of real inquiry and growth.

Readers interested in an updated version of this argument with a response from Sue Wheeler, should consult Feltham (1999: 182–205).

References

Bayne, R., Horton, I., Merry, T. and Noyes, E. (1994) *The Counsellor's Handbook*, London: Chapman and Hall.

Bohm, D. (1994) *Thought as a System*, London: Routledge.

Corbett, L. (1995) 'Supervision and the mentor archetype', in P. Kugler (ed.), *Jungian Perspectives on Clinical Supervision*, Einsiedeln, Switzerland: Daimon.

Dryden, W. (1991) *Dryden on Counselling*, vol. 1: *Seminal Papers*, London: Whurr.

Dryden, W. (ed.) (1996) *Handbook of Individual Therapy* (3rd edn), London: Sage.

Dryden, W. and Feltham, C. (1994) *Developing Counsellor Training*, London: Sage.

Dryden, W. and Spurling, L. (eds) (1989) *On Becoming a Psychotherapist*, London: Routledge.

Feltham, C. (1996) 'Beyond denial, myth and superstition in the counselling profession', in R. Bayne, I. Horton and J. Bimrose (eds), *New Directions in Counselling*, London: Routledge.

Feltham, C. (ed.) (1997) *Which Psychotherapy? Leading Exponents Explain Their Differences*, London: Sage.

Feltham, C. (ed.) (1999) *Controversies in Psychotherapy and Counselling*, London: Sage.

Feyerabend, P. (1994) *Against Method*, London: Verso.

Frank, J.D. (1974) *Persuasion and Healing: A Comparative Study of Psychotherapy*, New York: Schocken.

Goldberg, C. (1992) *The Seasoned Psychotherapist*, New York: Norton.

Goldfried, M.R., Castonguay, L.G. and Safran, J.D. (1992) 'Core issues and future directions in psychotherapy integration', in J.C. Norcross and M.R. Goldfried (eds), *Handbook of Psychotherapy Integration*, New York: Basic Books.

Gooch, S. (1975) *Total Man: Notes Towards an Evolutionary Theory of Personality*, London: Abacus.

Howe, D. (1993) *On Being a Client: Understanding the Process of Counselling and Psychotherapy*, London: Sage.

Karasu, T.B. (1992) *Wisdom in the Practice of Psychotherapy*, New York: Basic Books.

Lazarus, A.A. (1990) 'Can psychotherapists transcend the shackles of their training and superstitions?', *Journal of Clinical Psychology*, 46: 351–8.

Levenson, E. (1983) *The Ambiguity of Change*, New York: Basic Books.

Luborsky, L., Singer, B. and Luborsky, L. (1975) 'Comparative studies of psychotherapies: Is it true that "everyone has won and all must have prizes"?', *Archives of General Psychiatry*, 32: 995–1008.

Masson, J. (1990) *Final Analysis: The Making and Unmaking of a Psychoanalyst*, London: HarperCollins.

McLellan, B. (1995) *Beyond Psychoppression: A Feminist Alternative Therapy*, North Melbourne: Spinifex.

Newman, F. (1991) *The Myth of Psychology*, New York: Castillo.

Quinn, S. (1987) *A Mind of her Own: The Life of Karen Horney*, London: Macmillan.

Rangell, L. (1985) 'On the theory of theory in psychoanalysis and the relation of theory to psychoanalytic therapy', *Journal of the American Psychoanalytic Association*, 33: 59–92.

Robertiello, R.C. and Schoenewolf, G. (1987) *101 Common Therapeutic Blunders: Countertransference and Counterresistance in Psychotherapy*, Northvale, NJ: Aronson.

Rose, N. (1989) *Governing the Soul: The Shaping of the Private Self*, London: Routledge.

Sampson, E.E. (1993) *Celebrating the Other: A Dialogic Account of Human Nature*, New York: Harvester Wheatsheaf.

Samuels, A. (1993) 'What is a good training?', *British Journal of Psychotherapy*, 9 (3): 317–23.

Skovholt, T.M. and Ronnestad, M.H. (1992) *The Evolving Professional Self: Stages and Themes in Therapist and Counsellor Development*, Chichester: Wiley.

Smail, D.J. (1978) *Psychotherapy: A Personal Approach*, London: Dent.

Smith, M.L., Glass, G.V. and Miller, T.I. (1980) *The Benefits of Psychotherapy*, Baltimore, MD: Johns Hopkins University Press.

Spurling, L. (ed.) (1993) *From the Words of my Mouth: Tradition in Psychotherapy*, London: Routledge.

Stevens, A. and Price, J. (1996) *Evolutionary Psychiatry*, London: Routledge.

Stevenson, L. (1987) *Seven Theories of Human Nature*, Oxford: Oxford University Press.

Storr, A. (1996) *Feet of Clay: a Study of Gurus*, London: HarperCollins.

Thompson, R.A. (1996) *Counseling Techniques: Improving Relationships with Others, Ourselves, our Families, and our Environment*, Washington, DC: Accelerated Development.

Vicinzey, S. (1969) *The Rules of Chaos*, London: Macmillan.

Wallace, W.A. (1986) *Theories of Counseling and Psychotherapy*, Boston: Allyn & Bacon.

Wilkins, P. (1997) *Personal and Professional Development for Counsellors*, London: Sage.

Discussion issues

1 Do you agree that a core theoretical model is essential and, if so, why?
2 If the commitment to core theoretical models were abandoned, which do you consider would be the most promising ways forward for their replacement in training and practice?
3 Do you agree that our knowledge base is still insubstantial and our techniques are pretty fallible?
4 Has the commitment to core theoretical models by the professional bodies stifled the development of eclecticism?

2

A Sound Foundation for Counsellor Competence

The case for a core theoretical model

Sue Wheeler

In the May 1997 edition of *Counselling*, Colin Feltham (1997) challenged the notion of a core theoretical model of counselling being a requirement for counsellor training courses seeking BAC course accreditation, and argued that this leads to adherence to 'untenable orthodoxies' which 'place an obstacle in the path of real inquiry and growth' (p. 124). This reply to his treatise draws on my experience as Co-chair of the BAC Courses Accreditation Group and inevitably on my experience as a counsellor trainer. I could have chosen to go through Feltham's article point by point, refuting or agreeing with the issues that he raises, but that would not make for interesting reading, and instead I have chosen to give my own account of why I believe that counsellor training courses should define and then adhere to a core theoretical model that influences all aspects of the training, without being prescriptive about what that model should be. In developing my argument in favour of a core theoretical model, I shall take a pragmatic approach, presenting a realistic appraisal of the art of the possible in counsellor training. I will also argue that the core theoretical model will evolve as a function of the staff team, which may or may not be coherent. This will lead to a discussion about the development of an appropriate core theoretical model.

What is the pattern of counsellor training in Britain?

Various studies of counsellor training in Britain reveal that there are probably more integrative or eclectic training courses than any other, Wheeler (1997) conducted a survey of counsellor training courses and of the 39 courses that responded 9 were described as person-centred, 9 as psychodynamic, 2 adhered to another single model and 19 were either integrative or eclectic. Counting the current courses accredited by BAC, 36 in total, 11 are person-centred, 8 are psychodynamic, 2 are other single models and the remaining 15 are integrative and eclectic. Hollanders (1997) surveyed counsellors, asking about their training and subsequent practice, and found a substantial interest in eclecticism/integration: 'The evidence gathered in this study is both clear and strong, showing a reported preference by a great majority of the participating practitioners for working with concepts and techniques that span a number of orientations

This chapter was first published as 'Challenging the core theoretical model: a reply to Colin Feltham', in *Counselling*, Journal of the British Association for Counselling, vol. 9, no. 2, pp. 134–8 (1998).

and approaches' (p. 455). Hunt (1995) collected prospectuses of counsellor training courses in the north-west of Britain and reported that the majority seemed to be person-centred, many were described as integrative, although 38 per cent of the publicity material produced about courses failed to indicate which theoretical model was being offered.

Theoretical creativity and diversity is therefore alive and well in Britain, and there is no evidence to suggest that traditional purist mono-theory courses are the norm, nor that they dominate the list of courses that have gained BAC accreditation. Experience of working as a consultant to courses seeking accreditation suggests that counsellor training courses that present an integrative or eclectic model probably have to do more soul-searching and preparation for the accreditation process than those that adhere to a model that is supported by a body of literature.

What is a core theoretical model?

'Most approaches or models of counselling have in some way been spawned by one of the broad psychological schools of personality and are often regarded as synonymous with them' (Dryden et al. 1995: 26). Approaches to the understanding of personality vary widely and provide diverse explanations for the way in which psychological problems occur. Some theories have given rise to associated methods and techniques for treating distressed clients that have become known as psychotherapeutic interventions and are organized in schools of thought such as Rogerian or Kleinian, named after the prime protagonist for that school. The practice of counselling in Britain has been influenced by psychoanalytic theory, humanistic and person-centred theories and the behavioural school (McLeod 1993). A theoretical base for counselling might be labelled as an orientation, a school or model, and describes the nature of the theory, including theory of personality, that informs practice. Indeed, Mahrer (1989) suggests that it is the understanding of personality that is of prime importance for counsellors rather than the skills they use in the therapeutic process.

A narrow view of a core theoretical model would be one that was based on one of the three predominant paradigms – humanistic, psychoanalytic or cognitive-behavioural – made even more specific by being aligned with one of the major writers within these groups, such as Carl Rogers, Sigmund Freud or Aaron Beck. A broader view of a core theoretical model (and indeed the one embraced by BAC course accreditation) accepts that integration of theory and skills is possible, providing that the integrative process has been fully considered and documented.

The core theoretical model should be reflected in all aspects of a course, from theory to skills training, methods of and criteria for assessment, supervision and personal development, as well as the inclusion of 'equal opportunities' issues. It can be just as difficult to incorporate some of these elements into a mainstream core model as into an integrative model. Wheeler and Izzard (1997) discussed the challenge to integrating an approach to race, culture and sexual orientation issues into a mainstream psychodynamic course bearing in mind the classic psychoanalytic interpretation of homosexuality as a perversion (Davies and Neal 1996) and that tradition's complete disregard for social issues (Thomas 1992).

What are the components of a core theoretical model?

The BAC course accreditation scheme demands that 'there should be enough counselling theory, drawing on relevant social science disciplines, to enable students to make explicit the underlying assumptions, basic principles and elements, concepts, strategies and techniques of the core theoretical model' which the course espouses (BAC 1996: 13). Elsewhere the recognition booklet states that the core theoretical model should be reflected not just in theory, skills and practice of the students, but also in the way the course is structured, assessed, taught and administered. In other words the core theoretical model is evident throughout the course, providing coherence and internal consistency. This emphasis does not militate against eclectic or integrative courses, but it does demand that such courses regard their eclectic or integrative nature as their core theoretical model, exploring fully its philosophical, theoretical and practical implications. The model must have a rationale for the nature of psychological difficulties, a theoretical basis for understanding human growth and development, the nature of the therapeutic relationship and the change process, as well as an explanation for the way in which counselling techniques are employed to bring about change. Horton (1996) helpfully details the components of a model of counselling under the broad headings of process structures and themes, general principles of change, process of change and mechanisms of change.

So why should counsellor training courses adhere to a core theoretical model?

Time

The minimum number of taught hours for a counsellor training course to be accredited by BAC is 400. Applicants for individual BAC accreditation need to have completed 450 hours of counsellor training. Wheeler (1997) found in her survey of counsellor training courses in Britain that the average number of taught hours for diploma courses was 353. The trend, then, is towards courses of about 400 hours. Given the amount that there is to learn to take on the responsible role of professional counsellor, perhaps these hours are far too few. Some institutions offer more hours of training, but there are strong market forces and courses need to be economically viable to recruit. So time is limited. While it may be desirable that attention is paid to the question of 'What treatment suits what kind of client best?', and that all students are able to turn their hand to the preferred model or technique for a particular complaint, how realistic is it that competence can be achieved in a broad range of counselling approaches in such a short time? Surely it is preferable that given time limitations students develop skills that fit within an identifiable framework within which they feel confident to practise, even if it means that they cannot meet everyone's needs all of the time.

Assessment

'Student assessment should be congruent with the core theoretical model' (BAC 1996: 14). It is only fair that students embarking on a course of study know what is expected of them and how they will be assessed. An assessment procedure should be comprehensive and reflect all aspects of a student's learning. Students also need to know the criteria by which they are to be assessed, which will include criteria developed to determine whether they meet the required standard of the course in maintaining a counselling relationship, creating a climate of understanding conducive to the work, interacting with a client to bring about change and understanding the process of change. In other words, reflecting on Horton's components of the counselling model, it is about whether they have achieved competence in the model. If there is a lack of clarity in what the model is, this will be reflected in the criteria for assessment, which will in turn leave students unclear about what is expected of them. Excessively broad outcome statements about competence will now be put to shame by the publication of NVQ (National Vocational Qualification) standards, developed over five years using the skill and expertise of hundreds of counsellors and therapists. While the NVQ scheme for awarding qualifications in counselling is subject to considerable criticism and scepticism (Frankland 1996), the competency statements are both clear and comprehensive across a range of counselling models and will almost certainly be adopted by counselling trainers for use as assessment tools on courses. Clarity about the core theoretical model will then be even more important.

Supervision

Supervision of clinical work has often been described as the forum in which the most powerful learning about practice takes place (Carroll 1996). Courses will engage or work alongside a number of supervisors providing supervision for their students. Unless there is some coherence to a core theoretical model, how can students best use their supervisory experience to achieve the competence that the course requires? While a psychodynamic supervisor may provide help and support to a trainee, if the course is antithetical to psychoanalytic ideas, how will the student be assessed if they have adopted ways of thinking about their work in tune with their supervisor? Inskipp and Proctor (1994) argue that if a working contract is agreed between counsellor and supervisor as a result of negotiation, a mismatch of theoretical orientation is possible, but supervisors must know what the students are expected to achieve by the end of their course. If the objectives related to the model are clear then supervisors can decide whether they are suited to working with the course and can provide appropriate feedback to their supervisees.

Stance of the therapist and relationship with the client

One of the crucial ways in which theoretical models differ is in the stance that the therapist takes with the client. This might mean, for example, that in a person-centred model the counsellor exhibits warmth and empathy towards the client, and perhaps sometimes discloses things about themselves. In a psychodynamic model, the counsellor takes a more neutral role and holds back from self-disclosure. Using a behavioural model, the counsellor will be quite directive with the client and suggest activities that may help to alleviate symptoms, which is quite different from an approach that expects clients to develop through self-actualization. Students need clarity about how they are expected to be with clients and how they are expected to behave, which a coherent model provides. Kahn (1991) is optimistic that a 'new harmony' can be brought about in providing a relationship that can be therapeutic that is not entrenched in the dogma of traditional models, but that can only happen as a result of painstaking work on the process of integration.

Staff are more likely to work as a cohesive team

The development of a counsellor training course is an interesting phenomenon. A training course is either designed by the staff engaged to teach it, or is inherited from others. There are often either constraints imposed by the institution they work in, which might include finance, staffing, accommodation, existing courses within the institution, the mission statement of the organization, or with regard to local competition from other counselling courses, or even local employment opportunities. Some courses are developed by individuals who 'grow' an organization to support the training that they design. The staff group may choose each other, based on their prior acquaintance and knowledge of their professional interests, or they may be thrown together with little or no regard for their compatibility. Hence, sometimes courses are conceived with a shared vision of an ideal training course, but more often are created with the ideas generated by individuals, which are modified and transmuted as others join the team. Consequently, counselling courses reflect the knowledge and belief systems of the people who design them, which works well as long as those people stay in post, but becomes more problematic when they move on. When new staff are appointed, either they must fit in with the course as it is, or be proactive in bringing about change. Greater job satisfaction will ensue if staff feel that there is congruence with their competence and expertise. In essence, the core theoretical model will be influenced by the people teaching it, who will provide a more consistent training for their students if they are in harmony.

How is a core theoretical model chosen?

Larsen (1996) claims that all psychological theories can be viewed as stories, which reflect the life experiences of their authors. Counsellors and therapists are influenced by their own experience or story as they develop or adopt their theoretical stance. It is interesting to trace how many of the therapeutic theoreticians have been influenced by the environment that fostered their development. Freud was influenced by Charcot and began to develop his theories of the unconscious from his experience of hypnotism; Rogers was influenced by his psychology background to use an experimental approach to understanding the helpful aspects of therapeutic relationship (McLeod 1993). Counsellor trainers are similarly influenced by their life experience, training, environment, friends and colleagues, as well as responding to demands from students and employers which may or may not harmonize and synthesize into a coherent whole when a package of training is offered. A theoretical model may stretch to accommodate individuals, or may be distorted by individuals. Hence, it could be argued that it will be easier to recruit staff to teach a course that has a well-known and well-documented core theoretical model about which there will be some level of agreement. On the other hand, from a diverse and creative staff group, particularly one that has ample time for developmental activities and discussion, an innovative and comprehensive new and unique core model may evolve.

What sort of training objectives does a counsellor training course have?

Given a training course of about 450 face-to-face teaching hours, such that might be eligible for BAC course accreditation (BAC 1996), the objectives of such a training course will vary but may include something like the following:

By the end of the training course students will:

- be competent to practise as counsellors in an agency that offers counselling to a generic client group;
- be able to distinguish between those clients for whom counselling as practised by the student is appropriate and potentially helpful and those for whom it is not;
- be able to make appropriate referrals to other agencies, having knowledge of other services available;
- be competent to manage the therapeutic frame for counselling with due regard to the *Code of Ethics for Counsellors* (BAC 1997);
- be aware of cross-cultural, disability, sexual orientation, gender, age and social class/economic issues that affect clients and settings and be able to interact with clients appropriately;
- be able to manage the boundary between their own interpersonal and intra-personal processes and those of their clients;
- have a clear understanding of the theoretical background to their practice;
- be able to monitor and evaluate their own practice;
- be willing and able to engage in a supervisory relationship with an appropriately experienced and qualified practitioner who will be involved with the continued professional development of their practice.

How can such objectives be met?

A lot is required from a relatively short course to meet such objectives as described above. A curriculum that incorporates theory, practical skills training, ethics and professional practice, social awareness, personal awareness, understanding and co-operation with other helping agencies, research and evaluation, specific issues related to client groups and contextual issues, supervision, preparation for assignments, community meetings, etc., as well as methods of assessment, and criteria for assessment, is a challenge. The therapy literature is rich, counselling models proliferate and for those enthralled by therapeutic process, the attraction to incorporate a wide range of diverse theories and ideas is great. It is like being confronted with a sumptuous feast. The choice is whether to eat as much as possible with its inevitable consequences or whether to choose a discreet amount that is complementary and digestible. Curriculum development is a complex and skilled process. Making choices about what should be included in the syllabus to ensure that the learning objectives are met and that competent counsellors emerge is an exacting task. Time must be carefully allocated to ensure that all crucial aspects of counsellor training are covered. A core theoretical model provides a framework for the syllabus, within which all the elements of training can be contained.

What is acceptable to BAC as a core theoretical model?

Given the discussion about the amount of time available to deliver a viable course, it follows that the most important consideration is that trainees are provided with an experience that meets the aims and objectives of the course. The onus is on the trainers to put together a package that best meets that need. Students need a comprehensive and digestible model that provides a foundation for their practice. This may be an integrative model, but the BAC accreditation criteria require that the integration is clarified by the staff offering the training rather than left to the students. Of course counsellors evolve and develop their own integrative style of working with experience, but the initial training should provide clear guidelines about how pieces fit together. It is this that is so often lacking in courses that apply for accreditation, not the fact that they claim to be integrative *per se*.

What is the essence of an integrative course?

This leads to a discussion about integration and how it is managed successfully. There are integrative models that are well documented and comprehensive, providing detailed information about theory and practice (Egan 1982; Kohut 1984; Ryle 1990; Prochaska and Diclemente 1992). Egan is a popular choice for courses in Britain. Integrative models that are more questionable are those idiosyncratic ones that evolve largely as a result of the mix of current or previous staff teaching the course. At best, an integrative course has been rigorously thought through and documented. Attention is given to an understanding of human growth and development, development of psychological problems, therapeutic and theoretical frame, the nature of the therapeutic relationship, skills and techniques, assessment of client difficulty, congruent means of pursuing personal development and complementary methods of organizing the course and assessing progress and final competence. At worst, the course is constructed around what staff are available and what they are best qualified to teach. Dialogue between staff about the theoretical model is problematic and students are given conflicting messages. Assessment procedures are woolly because there is no internal consistency. The rationale offered for such a course is that students can make of it what they will and find their own style.

Ideally a course should offer students a map of the journey on which they are about to embark. The map should not be rigidly drawn so that no deviations from the path can be made, but needs to be colourful enough to provide opportunities to stop and admire the view on the way, or to take minor detours. The journey is time limited and cannot include too many deviations or the ultimate destination will not be reached. The journey needs to be planned in such a way that the trainees arrive at the destination feeling stimulated and rewarded by their travel, enriched and matured through the experience and hungry for more, but feeling adequately equipped to manage the tasks that a professional counsellor faces. A spirit of adventure and creativity should unite the trainers rather than pull them in opposite directions. Students need to be able to articulate how their interventions and strategies in working with clients are rooted in their theoretical understanding (Orlinsky et al. 1994).

What about eclecticism?

If we define eclecticism in the context of counselling as a collection of techniques from different theoretical models, there is no reason why a training course should not offer training in two or more models, providing that sufficient time (probably in excess of 400 hours) is given to the training. The problem arises when an eclectic course offers a taster of a range of distinct models, applying none of them in any depth. Students may then be expected to draw on their skills in a particular model to work with a relevant client or to synthesize the training into a coherent whole – a lot to ask of inexperienced trainee counsellors. Another way in which an eclectic model might be acceptable would be if it is offered as an established model, such as multimodal therapy (Lazarus 1992). At least there is some documentation to refer to that explains the rationale for the model. One course accredited by BAC offers a parallel psychodynamic and person-centred training. Two trainers are present at all sessions and the perspective of both models are presented throughout the course. Students tend to choose one model or the other, while consistent dialogue takes place, and Kohut's work is discussed as a possible point of integration. Perhaps this offers some hope for eclectic courses that seek BAC accreditation, but there is probably a book to be written about how the theory and the practice taught on each course hang together and constitute a training of sufficient depth.

Is this not all rather paternalistic and dogmatic?

Yes, it is a bit, but perhaps it is helpful to see counsellor training as akin to the process of growing up. Consistent parenting that provides a containing environment in which the child feels nurtured and safe is a blueprint for healthy emotional development (Winnicott 1986). Children like to know where they are and what is expected of them. Parents do provide some kind of life map and set of rules that guide and provide security. Parents cannot provide children with specific knowledge to deal with every situation they meet, but they can provide a template for thinking about and managing life. Good parenting provides a good foundation on which a child can build their own identity. It is not infinitely malleable and flexible. Parents adhere to their values and beliefs and pass them on to their children. As young people mature they hold these in mind while perhaps experimenting with new ideas and making adjustments to their beliefs. This seems like a helpful metaphor for counsellor training, a process of growing and developing intellectually, emotionally and professionally, with a sound core theoretical model. The model provides the framework in which the learning takes place, a secure base to which the counsellor can return, or from which new paths can be explored.

References

BAC (1996) *Recognition of Counsellor Training Courses*, Rugby: British Association for Counselling.
BAC (1997) *Code of Ethics for Counsellors*, Rugby: British Association for Counselling.
Carroll, M. (1996) *Counselling Supervision: Theory, Skills and Practice*, London: Cassell.
Davies, D. and Neal, C. (eds) (1996) *Pink Therapy*, Buckingham: Open University Press.

Dryden, W., Horton, I. and Mearns, D. (1995) *Issues in Professional Counsellor Training*, London: Cassell.

Egan, G. (1982) *The Skilled Helper* (2nd edn), Monterey, CA: Brooks/Cole.

Feltham, C. (1997) 'Challenging the core theoretical model', *Counselling*, 8 (2): 121–5.

Frankland, A.M. (1996) 'Accreditation and registration', in R. Bayne, I. Horton and J. Bimrose (eds), *New Directions in Counselling*, London: Routledge.

Hollanders, H. (1997) 'Eclecticism/Integration among counsellors in the UK in the light of Kuhn's concept of paradigm formation', unpublished Ph.D. thesis.

Horton, I. (1996) 'Towards the construction of a model of counselling', in R. Bayne, I. Horton and J. Bimrose (eds), *New Directions*, Routledge: London.

Hunt, P. (1995) 'Regional training audit: a survey of counselling, psychotherapy and related trainings within Merseyside and adjacent regions' (unpublished and obtainable from the Administrator, Merseyside Psychotherapy Institute, c/o 26 Barchester Drive, Liverpool L17 5BZ).

Inskipp, F. and Proctor, B. (1994) *Making the Most of Supervision*, Twickenham: Cascade.

Kahn, M. (1991) *Between Therapist and Client: The New Relationship*, New York: W.H. Freeman and Co.

Kohut, H. (1984) *How Does Analysis Cure?*, Chicago: University of Chicago Press.

Larsen, D.J. (1996) 'Eclecticism: psychological theories as interwoven stories', paper given to the IRTAC Conference. Vancouver, Canada, May.

Lazarus, A.A. (1992) 'Multimodal therapy: technical eclecticism and minimal integration', in J.C. Norcross and M.R. Goldfried (eds), *Handbook of Psychotherapy Integration*, New York: Basic Books.

Mahrer, A.R. (1989) *The Integration of Psychotherapies: A Guide for Practicing Therapists*, New York: Human Science Press.

McLeod, J. (1993) *An Introduction to Counselling*, Buckingham: Open University Press.

Orlinsky, D.E., Grawe, K. and Parks, B.K. (1994) 'Process and outcome in psychotherapy – noch einmal', in A.E. Bergin and S.L. Garfield (eds), *Handbook of Psychotherapy and Behaviour Change*, New York: Wiley.

Prochaska, J.O. and Diclemente, C.C. (1992) 'The transtheoretical approach', in J.C. Norcross and M.R. Goldfried (eds), *Handbook of Psychotherapy Integration*, New York: Basic Books.

Ryle, A. (1990) *Cognitive-Analytic Therapy: Active Participation in Change: A New Integration in Brief Psychotherapy*, Chichester: Wiley.

Smith, M. (1996) 'Response to "Does psychotherapy need NVQ's?" by Rosemary Randall', *British Journal of Psychotherapy*, 12 (4): 536–8.

Thomas, L. (1992) 'Racism and psychotherapy: working with racism in the consulting room: an analytical view', in J. Kareem and R. Littlewood (eds), *Intercultural Therapy: Themes, Interpretations and Practices*, Oxford: Blackwell Scientific.

Wheeler, S. (1996) *Training Counsellors: The Assessment of Competence*, London: Cassell.

Wheeler, S. (1997) 'Issues and trends in professional counsellor training', paper presented to the BAC Counselling Research Conference, Birmingham, June.

Wheeler, S. and Izzard, S. (1997) 'Training counsellors: integrating difference', *Psychodynamic Counselling*, 3 (4): 401–17.

Winnicott, D.W. (1986) *Home is Where we Start From*, Harmondsworth, Penguin.

Discussion issues

1 How do theories of personality influence core models?
2 How much training in counselling is sufficient to ensure competent practice?
3 What are the advantages and disadvantages of eclecticism?
4 Which models of counselling are compatible?

3

On the Quest for a Person-Centred Paradigm

Ivan Ellingham

> We need to examine some of the reasons why our intellectual culture is itself so sceptical
> about the kind of large-scale theories which alone might serve to displace psychoanalysis.
>
> (Richard Webster 1995: 441)

In an article in *Counselling* (Ellingham 1995), I made use of Thomas Kuhn's (1970) description of a scientific paradigm for the purpose of illuminating the relationship between the person-centred and psychodynamic approaches to counselling/psychotherapy.[*] I sought to clarify in particular the two schools' disagreement over whether 'counselling' and 'psychotherapy' are the same or different – the person-centred view being that the two terms refer to a unitary phenomenon; the psychodynamic that the terms refer to different phenomena, albeit interrelated along a continuum.

What I said in my paper caused a certain amount of consternation among some psychodynamic practitioners (cf. *Counselling*, vol. 7, no. 1, pp. 10–11; Naylor-Smith 1996). This I took to be hardly surprising as I had dared to suggest that a future paradigm (i.e. 'global theory') of counselling/psychotherapy would be based not upon the psychodynamic framework of thought but the person-centred. In the present article I revisit and elaborate upon ideas put forward in my earlier piece.

On presuming a paradigm

According to Kuhn, the mark of scientific understanding is the possession by members of a particular discipline of a common framework of ideas, a unitary theory or 'paradigm' by which to define the discipline's proper subject matter and legitimate methodological procedures. While the great pioneers of the field of c/p aimed to generate scientific understanding, it is patently obvious that the field still lacks a paradigm in the Kuhnian sense. What it boasts instead, as colourfully described by Hans Eysenck, is 'a mish-mash of theories, a hugger-mugger of procedures, a gallimaufry of therapies, and a charivari of activities having no proper rationale' (1970: 145). Thus the more deeply a person becomes immersed 'in the study of the dozens of theories and approaches to counselling and psychotherapy', the more, avows Cecil Patterson, 'he or she ... develops the feeling of being in a jungle. Differences, inconsistencies, and contradictions appear at all levels, from philosophy to techniques' (1986: 532).

This chapter was first published in *Counselling*, Journal of the British Association for Counselling, vol. 8, no. 1, pp. 52–5 (1997).

[*] Throughout this article, in accord with the person-centred tradition I shall treat the terms 'counselling' and 'psychotherapy', and their cognates, as referring to a unitary phenomenon. I employ the composite 'counselling/psychotherapy' – 'c/p' for short – to emphasize this point.

Does such a state of affairs matter? In my view, yes, very much! What kind of scientific undertaking is it that can't agree on how best to make sense of a particular person's psychological difficulties, or how best to help that person? Go to one counsellor saying you're depressed and you are told to think positive thoughts; to another and you are encouraged to unearth the negative; to a third and you are allowed to focus on what you like; to a fourth and you are taught how to plan your day; to a fifth and you are expected to bare your soul to an empty chair, etc., etc.

Such a disconnected application of disparate procedures would be remedied with the establishment of a paradigm. But is it simply pie in the sky to dream of developing one? Some authorities in the field of c/p certainly suggest that it is. The authors of *The Counsellor's Handbook* (Bayne et al. 1994), for instance, define 'counselling' on the basis of what they term 'an integrative process model' (p. 35). But the non-integrative nature of such a model is made only too plain in their confession that it is based on the assumption that 'people are too complex to be explained by any one theory' (p. 35).

And then again there is John McLeod's puzzling pronouncement that '[c]ounselling is in many respects an unusual area of study in that it encompasses a set of strongly competing theoretical perspectives, a wide range of practical applications and meaningful inputs from a number of contributing disciplines' (1993: 7). McLeod's assertion is puzzling to me because, having acknowledged these 'competing theoretical perspectives', he goes on to declare that, '[t]he field of counselling and psychotherapy represents a *synthesis* of ideas from science, philosophy, religion and the arts' (my italics). 'It is an interdisciplinary area', he contends,

> that cannot appropriately be incorporated or subsumed into any one of its constituent disciplines. Any approach to counselling which was, for example, purely scientific or purely religious in nature would soon be seen not to be counselling at all, in its denial of key areas of client and practitioner experience. (pp. 7–8)

Why I find McLeod's avowal puzzling is because (a) 'a synthesis of ideas' is a theory, so that having been told the field is made up of competing theories we then seem to be informed that there is nevertheless a single overarching theory, i.e., a paradigm; (b) McLeod seems to be suggesting that what common sense takes to be disparate aspects of human mental functioning – scientific, philosophical, religious and artistic thought – can never be understood scientifically, i.e., interpreted in terms of a unitary paradigm, the achievement of which, in my view, constitutes the goal and *raison d'être* of a scientific psychology.

Given, therefore, that both McLeod and the authors of *The Counsellor's Handbook* have a background in academic psychology, what appears to be showing through in their opinions is the unease with which psychologists regard the notion of a scientific paradigm in relation to psychology.

For the field of c/p may fairly be said to be a sub-field or daughter discipline of the overall domain of psychology; while the parent is concerned with scientific understanding of 'behaviour and mental processes' *per se*, the daughter discipline of c/p aims to achieve such understanding with respect to certain aspects of human behaviour and mental processes. It is not surprising to learn, therefore, that the diverging and competing theoretical perspectives which fragment the daughter are part and parcel of theoretical perspectives which fragment the parent (namely the behavioural, cognitive, humanistic, psychodynamic, physiological perspectives). In consequence, as McLeod recounts, behind the debate concerning the development of a unitary theory of c/p lies the question 'of whether it is even in principle possible to create a universally acceptable framework for understanding human behaviour [and mental processes]' (1993: 99) – whether, that is, it will ever be feasible to generate a scientific paradigm for psychology.

Thus, unless a unitary and authoritative scheme of thought can be generated, that is, a scheme in terms of which genuine scientific understanding can be fabricated, both psychology and the field of c/p will remain made up of quasi-religious cliques exhibiting divergent beliefs. It is little wonder that Arnold Lazarus admonishes those within the field of c/p '[to] step out of the field of theology and enter the realm of science' (1990: 45).

On presuming a person-centred not a psychodynamic paradigm

'Revolution' is a key notion of Kuhn regarding the advance of scientific understanding and the emergence of paradigms: revolution in terms of the fundamentally different view of the world which a novel paradigm introduces compared to previous paradigm or to competing pre-paradigm theories. Kuhn likens such a revolution to switches of visual gestalt: the switch from the chalice to the two faces, from the young woman to the old lady.

Perhaps from what I have said already, it has become clear just how revolutionary it would be for a paradigm of c/p to be developed: for a unitary theoretical perspective to be formulated which truly synthesized the field of c/p's present cacophony of 'ideas from science, philosophy, religion and the arts', one which grasped in a single frame not only the variety of procedures employed in c/p, but also the diverse aspects of the counselling client (the physical, chemical, biological, animal, mental, spiritual, whatever).

It is not only psychologists but individuals in general who are likely to say that a vision of this kind is beyond the bounds of common sense. But that is exactly the point! Such a unitary vision must of necessity be beyond the bounds of contemporary conception, because current common sense cannot contain it. To sense a comprehensive order and unity to things beyond the confines of present conceptualization is the mark of a mystic, which is why in my earlier article I spoke of a paradigm for the field of c/p coming about through 'the further articulation of a truth which mystics such as Carl Rogers have previously intuited' (1959: 290). For, I would claim, it was Rogers – the originator and main architect of person-centred theory – who not only sensed an ultimate pattern to things but who in his formulation of it articulated it in a manner suitable for development into a bona fide paradigm.

Rogers' vision is part of 'a deep collective vision' in terms of which others, not necessarily psychologists, have formulated ideas congruent with his. Descriptive terms such as 'holistic', 'organismic', 'process', 'field theory' and 'systems theory' identify the formulation of individuals thus in tune with Rogers' person-centred theorizing. It is, I would claim, by comparison with the theoretical expositions of these other like-minded theorists that we will be able to hone and augment current person-centred ideas and so move towards the development of a paradigm for the field of c/p. Particular thinkers I have in mind in this regard are Ernst Cassirer, Susanne Langer, Fritz Perls, Jean Piaget, Michael Polanyi, Rupert Sheldrake, Heinz Werner and Alfred North Whitehead.

Allow me to suggest, therefore, what in my view are likely to be some key features of such a paradigm:

1 *The person will be defined in process terms, part and parcel of a universe so defined.* What this means is that patterned activity, process, constitutes the fundamental concept by which to make scientific sense of ourselves and the world in which we dwell. In 'Rogers' anthropology', writes Harry Van Belle (1980), 'man [*sic*] is first of all a tendency, a process, an activity or functioning rather than an entity. ... Originally man is an organism, and remains this however he might change and however complex his activity may become' (p. 71).

What other process thinkers can bring to person-centred theory in this regard is a deeper understanding both of what it means to view the person as an organism, a complex pattern of activity, and of how the oneness of the human organism can be conceptualized as one with the overarching 'organism' of the universe. In particular, the oneness of the human organism can be expressed in conceptual terms, with 'body', 'mind' and 'spirit' conceived as manifestations of different patterns of process.

2 *More specifically, the person and the universe will be defined in terms of the process of growth, of becoming.* Thanks in large measure to Darwin and Einstein, the contemporary scientific paradigm already envisages the physical universe as a structural field of evolving processes. Rogers' conceptualization of the person in terms of a growth process (the 'actualizing tendency') which is an aspect of a universal process of becoming (the 'formative tendency') fits harmoniously into such an overall scheme.

3 *Like all organisms, the structure of the human organism will be interpreted as a hierarchy of increasingly complex patterns of process, patterns which have emerged over the course of evolution.* According to Rogers, thanks to the workings of 'a strong formative tendency in our universe, which is evident at all levels' (1980: 134), 'every form that we see or know emerged from a simpler, less complex form' (p. 125). Other process theorists make explicit that a corollary of Rogers' hypothesis is that each organism possesses a hierarchical structure related to the different forms or patterns of process from which it evolved. One person with much to contribute to person-centred theory in this regard is Michael Polanyi. For not only does Polanyi speak of 'the hierarchy of levels found in living beings' and avow that '[w]e can see all the levels of evolution at a glance in the individual human being' (1966: 36), but he also elucidates the logical principles linking such levels to each other and how disorder may be interpreted – this last a particularly important notion in relation to understanding psychological dysfunction as 'incongruence', a key person-centred concept (cf. Rogers 1959).

4 *Consciousness and unconsciousness will be defined in relative terms as aspects of process.* As Rogers writes:

> The ability to focus conscious attention seems to be one of the latest evolutionary developments of our species. This ability can be described as a tiny peak of awareness, of symbolizing capacity, topping a vast pyramid of non-conscious organismic functioning. (1980: 127)

Psychodynamic theory treats the categories of conscious and unconscious as fundamental categories of conception. Such an interpretation derives from Descartes' identification of consciousness with 'mind', one of his two basic and unmixable categories of reality, 'mind' and 'matter'. In a paradigm which treats 'process' as fundamental, both mind and matter, consciousness and unconsciousness, are manifestations of patterns of activity. One cannot ask what 'stuff' or 'substance' process is comprised of, for it is fundamental. As Whitehead puts it, 'The reality is the process' (1925: 72). On such a scenario, what is conscious or unconscious is a relative affair, relative to the character of the pattern of process comprising the human individual and to the character of the processes comprising the surrounding field. On the one hand, like Lancelot Whyte, we may postulate a single realm of processes 'continuous and mainly unconscious, of which only certain transitory aspects or phases are accessible to immediate conscious attention' (1960: 18); on the other, posit that in association with the different levels of process comprising the human organism there exist different levels or degrees of consciousness. Such a view is in accord with not only Rogers (cf. Evans 1975: 6), but also Erich Fromm when he declares that:

> There is no such thing as 'the conscious' and no such thing as 'the unconscious'. There are degrees of consciousness-awareness and unconsciousness-unawareness. ... Unconsciousness ... represents the plant in him [man], the animal in him, the spirit in him; it represents the past down to the dawn of human awareness. (1986: 62 and 58)

It is a view which allies, too, with the 'new paradigm' in psychology championed by Rom Harré, that is, 'discursive psychology' – according to which,

> discursive phenomena, for example, acts of remembering, are not manifestations of hidden, subjective, psychological phenomena. They *are* the psychological phenomena. Sometimes they have subjective counterparts; sometimes they do not. (Harré and Gillett 1994: 27)

What, though, of Freud's 'primary processes', those processes whose 'paradoxical logic' constitutes the hall-mark of the psychodynamic unconscious? That such processes can be fitted into a person-centred process paradigm has been made plain by Charles Rycroft when he 'argues that Freud's theory of the non-verbal "primary processes" of the unconscious ... is better expressed by [Susanne] Langer's concept of "non-discursive" symbolism' (Lomas 1987: 42). Langer, of course, is a process theorist. For her non-discursive symbolization represents a type of process: that which marks the evolutionary appearance of the first humans (cf. Langer 1982). By thus regarding the human being as the symbolizing animal, or 'animal symbolicum', as Ernst Cassirer (1944: 28) puts it, we are able to augment current person-centred theory when it postulates that positive personality change involves accurate symbolization to awareness (cf. Rogers 1959).

Conclusion

Kurt Lewin was fond of observing that '[t]here is nothing as practical as a good theory' (Marrow 1969: 128). As the best theory for its time, that theory which becomes a paradigm is the most practical of all. I would like to think that this article has made some contribution, however small, to the generation of such a theory.

References

Bayne, R., Horton, I., Merry, T. and Noyes, E. (eds) (1994) *The Counsellor's Handbook*, London: Chapman & Hall.

Cassirer, E. (1944) *An Essay on Man*, New York: Bantam, 1970.

Ellingham, I.H. (1995) 'Quest for a paradigm: person-centred counselling/psychotherapy versus psychodynamic counselling and psychotherapy', *Counselling*, 6 (4): 288–90.

Evans, R.I. (1975) *Carl Rogers: The Man and His Ideas*, New York: E.P. Dutton.

Eysenck, H.J. (1970) 'A mish-mash of theories', *International Journal of Psychiatry*, 9: 140–6.

Fromm, E. (1986) *Psychoanalysis and Zen Buddhism*, London: Unwin.

Harré, R. and Gillett, G. (1994) *The Discursive Mind*, London: Sage.

Kuhn, T. (1970) *The Structure of Scientific Revolutions* (2nd edn), Chicago: Chicago University Press.

Langer, S.K. (1982) *Mind: An Essay on Human Feeling*, Baltimore, MD: Johns Hopkins University Press.

Lazarus, A.A. (1990) 'Why I am an Eclectic (not an Integrationist)', in W. Dryden and J.C. Norcross (eds), *Eclecticism and Integration in Counselling and Psychotherapy*, Loughton, Essex: Gale Centre.

Lomas, P. (1987) *The Limits of Interpretation*, Harmondsworth: Penguin Books.

McLeod, J. (1993) *An Introduction to Counselling*, Buckingham: Open University Press.

Marrow, A.J. (1969) *The Practical Theorist: The Life and Work of Kurt Lewin*, New York: Basic Books.

Naylor-Smith, A. (1996) 'Counselling and psychotherapy: a reply by Alan Naylor-Smith', in S. Palmer, S. Dainow and P. Milner (eds), *Counselling: The BAC Counselling Reader*, London, Sage.

Patterson, C.H. (1986) *Theories of Counseling and Psychotherapy* (4th edn), New York: Harper & Row.

Polanyi, M. (1966) *The Tacit Dimension*, Garden City: Doubleday.

Rogers, C.R. (1959) 'A theory of therapy, personality, and interpersonal relationships', in S. Koch (ed.), *Psychology: A Study of a Science*, vol. 3, New York: McGraw Hill.

Rogers, C.R. (1980) *A Way of Being*, Boston: Houghton Mifflin.

Van Belle, H. (1980) *Basic Intent and Therapeutic Approach of Carl R. Rogers*, Toronto: Wedge.

Webster, R. (1995) *Why Freud Was Wrong*, London: HarperCollins.

Whitehead, A.N. (1925) *Science and the Modern World*, New York: Free Press, 1967.

Whyte, L.L. (1960) *The Unconscious Before Freud*, London: Tavistock.

Discussion issues

1 Is the generation of scientific understanding in the field of counselling/ psychotherapy a meaningful aim?

2 How far would you agree with the author that the field of counselling/ psychotherapy is 'made up of quasi-religious cliques exhibiting divergent beliefs'?

3 If, like the author, you believe it will be possible to integrate the various combinations of the diverse schools of counselling and psychotherapy, on what basis do you think this can be achieved?

4 In your view, are there irreconcilable differences between the person-centred and psychodynamic approaches?

4

Solution-Focused Therapy in Practice

A personal experience

Christina Saunders

In 1994 I went to America for an advanced training course in Solution-Focused Brief Therapy (SFBT) and then wrote an article (Saunders 1995). Many of you responded with interest, wanting to know more, and someone suggested I write a follow-up. How am I using the SFT model eighteen months later? (I have renamed it 'Solution-Focused Therapy' (SFT) because I have found the model to be useful in long-term work as well as brief therapy.)

My work consists of 80 per cent counselling and 20 per cent training. The counselling work (individuals and couples) consists of about one-third short-term therapy (3–8 sessions) with clients who are self-referred via EAP (Employee Assistance Programme) providers, and two-thirds long-term therapy (25–40 sessions), with clients who are usually self-referred, via a variety of sources including word-of-mouth. In my short-term counselling work I am using SFT as my primary model, sometimes exclusively, sometimes in concert with TA, Gestalt and person-centred. In long-term counselling, I work eclectically or perhaps integratively using person-centred, Gestalt, TA, transpersonal and SFT. My training work is concerned with management development and personal development courses and, as a consequence of the above-mentioned article, some workshops on SFT lasting from 2½ hours to a day. I have noticed that SFT finds a natural place in my training work.

Purpose of this article

My intentions are, first, to share my progress with those of you who contacted me and those who already know something about SFT; second, to inspire those of you who know a little or would like to know more, to go to a workshop and find out what SFT has to offer you.

SFT model

As a reminder, this is my interpretation of the model. *Solution* means behavioural and/or perceptual changes which therapist and client construct to resolve the problem/difficulty. *Solution-focused* therapists believe that only a small change in one person's (the client's) behaviour can lead to profound and far-reaching differences in the behaviour of all the

This chapter was first published in *Counselling*, Journal of the British Association for Counselling, vol. 7, no. 4, pp. 312–16 (1996).

persons involved, and that one small change can lead to other changes and therefore further improvement. Further, that change in one part of the system leads to change in the whole, be it a couple, family, work, school, etc.

This therapy model is at all times respectful of the client and is highly interactive, with the therapist always working within the client's framework, using the client's language. It is based on a series of appropriate and well-thought-out open questions, designed to help the client find more useful ways of perceiving their world and/or ways of behaving which will work better for them.

A first session begins with some informal conversation, confidentiality and boundary setting and an explanation of how the therapist works. This is followed by:

1 *What brought you here today?*
   Supplementary: *Why now?*
2 *How can I help?*
   Supplementary: *What would need to happen for you not to want/need to come here any more? Or what would need to happen here today for it to have been worth your while coming?*
   This is a way of setting short- and long-term goals/objectives.
3 The Miracle Question: the therapist asks: *Suppose that after we talk here today you go home and while you are asleep a Miracle occurs and the problem which brought you here today disappears, is resolved, and because you are asleep you do not know the Miracle has happened. What would be the first sign for you after you wake up that will tell you the Miracle has happened?*
   Supplementaries: *What else? What else? What else? What would your partner/ mother/children/friends/work colleagues notice that would tell them the Miracle has happened? (Bringing in other people* one at a time *is important in building up a picture of change.) When they see you doing [whatever the client has mentioned they will be doing differently] what do you think they will do? When they do that, what will you do? (... and so on).*

The therapist needs to work back and forth building up the picture of change. The more information on what will be different the better, because it gives the client a choice of things to do differently when they come to the first small step.

Clients will often return to problem talk. When this occurs, the therapist needs to listen and respond with respect and then go back to 'Tomorrow, *when* the Miracle has occurred, what you will notice is ...' (repeating what the client has already said will be different) and continue with 'What else?'

When the client describes negative behaviour, the therapist asks what will they be doing instead:

Client: I won't be angry
Therapist: What will you be doing instead of being angry?

This type of intervention can turn the conversation back to positives easily and painlessly.

In SFT there is a lot of going back over what clients have said, so the therapist really does need to take notes. With practice I have found that my ability to listen, make eye contact and take legible accurate notes simultaneously has become very good.

4 Finding exceptions: exceptions are parts of the Miracle which are already happening now or happened in the past.

When was the most recent time all or some of these things were happening? (referring to the Miracle).

Supplementary: *How come? How did you make that happen? What were you doing differently?*

The word 'differently' is a very important one and can be used over and over and over again.

Finding exceptions helps clients see that they have some control over what is happening to them. They can see what works, what is helpful and then choose which course to take.

5 Scaling questions: scaling is very useful especially for ascertaining degrees of discomfort, commitment and movement. It creates a shorthand for therapist and client: *Where are you today? How did you get from 4 to 5?* and so on.

6 Coping questions: complimenting clients on how well they are coping or have coped empowers them and gives them useful information about their strengths, skills and resources.

7 Normalizing: this reassures the client that they and/or their circumstances are part of life (if they are) and that they are doing as well as can be expected. Normalizing will be used when the therapist thinks it would be helpful/useful.

8 Break: the therapist leaves the room for a few minutes (having explained this to the client at the beginning of the first session) to gather his/her thoughts and prepare a summing up which includes:

Compliments – appropriate and genuine, which may be direct or indirect, referring to things the client has done or is doing which are remarkable and/or work for them.

Bridging – a statement which explains the link between the client's goal and the task.

Task – this could be a *thinking task,* an *observation task* or a *behavioural/ doing task.*

Humour is useful when setting tasks; so is being tentative. The therapist sets the tasks with the co-operation of the client – sometimes asking them to suggest what they might do differently during the week that would be useful.

It is not useful to set a task if the client is unlikely to do it, as this means failure; above all SFT is trying to promote success.

The rules I took from America were:

- Keep it simple.
- If it works do more.
- If it does not work, try something different.
- There are no mistakes: everything is useful.

Useful phrases were:
- And so?
- Suppose that …
- How come?

- What will you have to do differently?
- What else?
- How will you do that?
- What is different?
- What is the first small step?
- How is that helpful?
- WOW!

I am using all of these and have noticed how useful a tentative 'suppose' can be. I also notice that I use 'amazing', 'fantastic', 'wonderful' and other encouraging words (my 'wow') a great deal, appropriately and to good effect.

SFT in my practice

The Miracle Question is the pivot of the model, on which all further sessions turn. I have found that most clients believe in miracles. However, some do not. In such circumstances I have successfully used 'Well, just *suppose* a miracle could happen', or 'Something magical occurs', or 'Just indulge me for a moment and suppose it were possible', said with humour. Once they become immersed in the differences they will notice after the miracle, it does not seem to matter whether they believe in miracles or not.

The timing of the Miracle Question is very important. I remember a client getting very angry and saying 'I didn't come here for solutions: I came for you to *do* something.' What I had to *do* was listen and sympathize, and I had not done *enough*. When I had done enough, the client was ready to hear the Miracle Question and find solutions.

It is not always straightforward, as with a couple who had come because they could not agree about access to their child. When asked the Miracle Question, he described a situation where they could talk, agree, have a good working relationship. Her Miracle was that 'he would be dead'. I was so shocked that I lost my concentration, felt total panic, and resorted to reflecting back and silence instead of continuing with 'How will that help you?' I have since role-played this situation twice, and learnt a lot. Given similar circumstances now, I think I would do better.

The important lesson for me is to hang on, stay calm and keep asking the questions in different ways. Good advice is given by Steve de Shazer to both therapists and clients: 'If it doesn't work, try something different.'

Here is a brief example where I have used Scaling, the Miracle Question and Exceptions:

Client

Alan (not his real name), aged 32, self-employed, married to R. They have known each other since they were about 15, and have been married 11 years.

Presenting problem: depressed, mood-swings, affecting his work and relationship. Counselling suggested by his doctor. Self-referred.

Immediate goal: for him to get a balance in his moods so that he can work effectively.

The following are extracts taken from my notes, an abridged version of what the client said.

Second session

Therapist: If zero is the worst you've ever felt and ten is the best, where were you before you came to see me?

Client: Oh, minus one – well, zero.

Therapist: After our first session?

Client: Two.

Therapist: And now?

Client: Five

Therapist: Wow. So you've gone from zero to two to five in two sessions – that's amazing! How did you do that?

Client: Hanging on in there, not panicking.

Therapist: How do you do that?

Client: By making decisions and sticking to them. For example, the house, family, job. Recognizing that I have control. Telling myself. It's not easy.

Therapist: Well that's amazing and I hear it's not easy. I'm wondering what a seven or eight looks like and I'd like to ask you a strange question. Suppose … [*Miracle Question*]?

Client: I'll be living somewhere else, where it is quiet, less people. [*Miracle Question is too big.*]

Therapist: Yes, it will be wonderful when you are living somewhere else, and I'm wondering what the Miracle will look like tomorrow?

Client: I'll be happier, laughing, eating less – well, normal meals, playing golf, socializing, playing sport, reading, talking more, listening to music, going out doing things.

Therapist: What kind of things?

Client: Walking, sport – things like that.

Therapist: Doing things *you enjoy*?

Client: Yes.

Therapist: What else? [*Long pause. Time to change tack.*] So after the Miracle you will be … [*repeat all the above*] and what will your wife notice that will tell *her* something amazing has happened?

Client: That I'm more fun.

Therapist: How will she see that?

Client: I'll be smiling, joking, talking, even more loving. [*Pause.*] Thinking about pleasing her, making food.

Therapist: You'll be more attentive, more focused on her?

Client: Yes.

Therapist: What will she do differently when you are more fun, more attentive, more focused on her?

Client: She'll be happier, motivated, doing sport, going to the gym. [*Pause.*] She'll laugh more.

Therapist: What else?

Client: She'll be lighter. We'll do fun things in the evening.

Therapist: What kind of fun things?

And so on, constantly repeating the Miracle, I went on to ask what colleagues, friends, clients would notice, and what they in turn would do differently. We agreed the Miracle was a ten and he would settle for eight.

Therapist: When was the last time you were at eight?

Client: 1984 – university.

Therapist: What was happening that made it an eight? What was different?

Client: Sharing a house with P [*male best friend*] and involved with R [*now his wife*]. It was of the moment. [*Pause – pensive.*]

Therapist: Of the moment?

Client: Yes, we were talking about ourselves. Oh, and involved with music. I was a stage-hand. This was before we formed the band.

He went on to described a carefree existence, having fun, living his life from day to day. 'Of the moment' was an important clue for him. We went on to look at how he could get from five to six.

During the *break* I made the following notes for use in my summary:

Compliments: Tenacious, hanging on in there, intelligent, caring.

Bridging: Having experienced the Miracle in 1984, knows what it feels like.

Task: Try a Miracle day this week.

Fourth session

By now he was at seven and had had a Miracle week.

> *Therapist:* How come?
> *Client:* Make up my mind each day I am going to enjoy it. Set aside things that bother me.
> *Therapist:* How do you do that?
> *Client:* Decide the night before, have a conversation in my head. What will I gain, what will I lose? The miracle comes from inside me. I can decide.

His mood swings decreased; he and his wife were talking about themselves, their feelings, their life, instead of work, and they were doing more fun things.

Sixth session

The focus of this session was their forthcoming holiday and how to make it a success. He was very anxious about it because he said all their holidays were a 'disaster', and he was left feeling upset, unsatisfied and resentful.

We concentrated on what he would need to do differently to ensure success. Conclusion: negotiate with his wife, before they went, for time on his own to read, as well as time together to play sport, walk, have fun and do things they both enjoyed.

We also looked at the future, viz., his work, having a family (the bigger Miracle).

Follow-up session (nine weeks later)

The holiday was 'fantastic'. He and his wife had done a lot of talking about themselves, their feelings, their future. They had had time alone and time together. They made friends with another couple in their hotel (something they had never done before on holiday). They played sport, read, swam and had fun.

They were both surprised to discover how far apart they had drifted and he was shocked to find how strongly she felt about his work intruding into their lives, and how resentful she felt about having to help him with his work after doing her own full-time job.

They made some big decisions: to move house and buy a separate building for offices. They had already made offers on both and put their house on the market. They decided to start a family; she has since become pregnant, and they have agreed that she will take six months' maternity leave and that she will not join him in his work.

Conclusion

The solution-focused therapy model can appear simple, even simplistic. In fact it requires a great deal of skill on the part of the therapist. Getting the balance right, when to move on, how light or heavy to be with humour, when to be quiet and wait, when to repeat a question – all require sensitivity and an aptitude for making quick judgements. The pace is often fast, with the therapist being proactive in order to move the client along and, as I mentioned earlier, listening, thinking, writing and paying attention require a lot of practice.

I believe that the solution-focused therapy model works well and gets results, when used exclusively, particularly in fixed, short-term work (3–8 sessions), for example in an EAP (Employee Assistance Programme) or in a GP practice. And it is also very helpful when used as a part of a 'tool kit' to clarify, motivate, enthuse, focus and empower the client.

Understandably there is scepticism as to whether solution-focused therapy can be used with all 'presenting problems' and any client. Steve de Shazer would say that since solution-focused therapy does not label the client, or pathologize the client, the answer is yes. Having watched him and Insoo Berg and others working with clients where I would have thought the model unsuitable, I have come to the conclusion that their expertise allows them to work with all types of problems so long as the client is a 'customer', that is, the client really wants to find a solution.

When I am working I try to set aside my doubts, and I am aware that the model works best when I feel confident. I have also noticed this when training others. Once the counsellor is convinced that solution-focused therapy is effective, the clients respond. I realize that these are prerequisites for most therapies.

Another issue which has been brought to my attention is whether the 'positive emphasis of the therapy might miss emotional states in the client'. This is not my experience. With this model, as with others, the therapist is at all times aware and respectful of the client's feelings. However, I can understand this concern from counsellors who have not seen the model in action.

Finally, it is important to re-state that only one problem can be dealt with at any one time. Therefore therapy using the solution-focused therapy model could continue for some time with someone who has a variety of problems.

Following my last article I received a letter from a consumer (that is, a client), which was published in *Counselling*, in which, she describes her experience of solution-focused therapy used in an integrative way. I think her letter explains what I am trying to say perfectly.

It suits longer term clients too.
I went into therapy because of a phobia. It took so few sessions of Solution-Focused Therapy to understand and cure it, that I've stayed on to tackle a range of limitations of mind, body and spirit, including:

- identity and self-esteem problems;
- relationship and work issues;
- coping with disease (MS) and pain;
- learning to relax and enjoy.

It's a framework, not a strait-jacket.
My therapist uses the Solution-Focused techniques to transform my wurbling [*sic*] whinges into positive goals, so that we know what I want and how I'll know when I've got it. *How* we then achieve it – using for instance Ericksonian hypnotherapy, NLP, TA or a behavioural or cognitive route – depends on my goal. There's flexibility to adapt to my current needs.

It's generative and empowering.
Solution-Focused Therapy feels like equal-power team-work: my therapist maintains the focus while I work towards a solution. Each success increases my belief in my own resources. Because it's all open and clear, I learn skills to take away with me to adapt to other situations. Christina Saunders describes Solution-Focused work with short-term/EAP clients, with family therapy and in team-therapy, for general problem-solving. I think it can be more than that. The final item on my own 'shopping list' will be Jungian-type individuation, and from my experience so far I see Solution-Focused Therapy as a way to get there.

After 18 months' practice on my own I now feel at ease with the model and can trust the process. I can be myself, relaxed, intuitive, and the results are often dramatic.

Short-term counselling is on the increase (EAP and GP referrals). Solution-focused therapy is versatile, adaptable and gets results which are measurable. Increasingly therapy is to be audited and we will be held accountable for results. I hope this sharing of my experiences will contribute to your involvement in these developments.

Update

Four years on from the original publication of this article I notice that my average number of sessions with private clients is 12, the range being 6–30, and that I am using the SFT model in all areas of my life. As a supervision tool it is invaluable, and can also be adapted for use in training – in fact with any group.

Having successfully found solutions, some clients do return at a later date for one or two sessions, with a different problem/difficulty and very occasionally clients come back because of a particularly bad relapse. However, I discovered that discussing the probability of relapse (in the second or third session) and exploring in detail how they will recover and get back on track, generally eliminates the need to return.

I learned a useful formula from Steve de Shazer at one of his seminars, which I would like to pass on as I have found it particularly helpful when I am feeling 'stuck' or 'lost'.

1   What does the client want?
2   What does the client need to do (differently) to get what they want?
3   What needs to happen so that clients can do what they need to do (differently) to get what they want?

In fact, it helps me, to keep this in mind at all times!

Reference

Saunders, C. (1995) 'Berg, de Shazer and friends: an American training experience', *Counselling*, 6 (2): 128–31.

Discussion issues

1 Should counsellors be client-led, that is, give clients what they want in the therapy room?
2 Is it helpful for clients to use their counsellor in the way they use their GP?
3 Is too much emphasis put on the Miracle Question?
4 Solution-focused therapy is a simplistic approach.

5

Person-Centred Counselling and Solution-Focused Therapy

Jonathan Hales

I read with great interest Christina Saunders' articles about solution-focused therapy in recent issues of *Counselling*, because I think the approach represents a 'carrying forward' of many ideas fundamental to counselling in general, and to person-centred counselling in particular (Hales 1989). However, a number of the methods and techniques of solution-focused work, coming as they do from family therapy (Cade and O'Hanlon 1993), can appear alien or difficult to counsellors like myself from a person-centred background.

With this in mind, I thought it might be useful to write a companion piece to Christina's articles (Saunders, 1995, 1996 [see Chapter 4], 1998), to demonstrate similarities between solution-focused brief therapy and person-centred counselling. I believe that the fundamental philosophy of both approaches is very similar. On a practical level, I hope to show that it is possible to take a 'selective approach' to solution-focused methods, within an overall framework of thinking. There is no 'set menu' in solution-focused work. I have seen demonstrations by a number of leading practitioners of the approach, and they all seem to work rather differently (as one would hope, in an approach that stresses flexibility and imagination!). In my own work I have learned to incorporate a range of solution-focused concepts and methods within what I still regard as a fundamentally person-centred approach.

In this article I will describe what I see as the shared underlying philosophy of the two approaches. I will then consider some apparent areas of difference. Then I will illustrate how this works out in practice, using a recent case example. My hope is that this might serve as encouragement to other counsellors who find the solution-focused approach interesting but who are looking for a 'bridge' to their own accustomed counselling style.

Person-centred and solution-focused – the similarities

I see a number of similarities between person-centred thinking and solution-focused therapy.

The emphasis on the client's strengths and resources

There is a saying within the Samaritans that 'We are all callers (clients) in some part of our lives.' When someone has problems or difficulties, there is always more to their life than

---

This chapter was first published in *Counselling*, Journal of the British Association for Counselling, vol. 10, no. 3, pp. 233–6 (1999).

just the problems, no matter how extensive and painful these may be. This person has other parts of their life in which they have accomplished things, in which they have strengths and skills and personal resources. This person might be in pain and difficulty right now, and those difficulties might be extensive and long-standing, but it is highly likely that they have faced and overcome other difficulties in other parts of their life. They may have made partially successful attempts to resolve the difficulties; or they may have managed with strength and determination to bear the things that they have not been able to change.

As a person-centred counsellor I often valued the concept of the client's strengths and resources. I believed that people have a fundamental capacity to move in a growthful direction – what Rogers (after Maslow) calls 'the self-actualising tendency' (Rogers 1961). Solution-focused therapy has shown me how to make full and explicit use of this concept in the therapy sessions. I now deliberately pick up and play back to clients any reference they make to their success and achievements, to difficulties resolved or coped with, and to the personal strengths and skills that enabled them to do this. Often this amounts to reminding the client about a part of her life experience that she has almost forgotten, since most of us are much more aware of our 'failures' than our successes! Being reminded of an achievement in some other part of her life is not only likely to boost the client's self-esteem, it may well be that this previous achievement contains 'transferable skills' that will help the client deal with her present difficulties.

Looking at the whole picture of the client's situation

Person-centred counselling places emphasis on valuing the whole person. In a similar way, solution-focused work is interested in the whole context of a person's life. What are the achievements as well as the failures? What are the times when things go better, as well as the times when they go badly? Solution-focused work asks about 'exceptions to the problem'. If a client consistently has trouble in some aspects of his life, when are the times when that issue is *least* difficult? What makes the difference between 'most difficult' and 'least difficult'? What is the client doing that makes a difference? In thinking about these differences clients often notice aspects of their lived experience that they had not fully noticed before. These things can often provide keys to the door of change.

As part of looking at the whole picture, there is the method in solution-focused work of 'normalizing' the problem. Some problems and distress that clients have can be seen as natural and 'normal' reactions to particular life stages or life events. A parent feeling depressed when his or her children have grown up and left home is going through a process that is known to affect many parents (of course, that does not stop it being intensely painful and upsetting). Someone with post-traumatic flashbacks is not 'going mad', but is going through a process that is known to be a common reaction to traumatic events. In solution-focused work it is seen as helpful to the client to point out this wider context to their difficulties, though not in a way that belittles those difficulties.

The emphasis on the client making the decisions

Person-centred therapy likes to think of the client as the person in charge of the therapy process. The client is the person who explores and evaluates her various thoughts and feelings. It is the client who makes judgements about her felt experience, and takes decisions. It is the client who puts those decisions into action. Rogers writes about 'the locus of evaluation' being with the client (Rogers 1951). Once again, solution-focused therapy takes this concept and uses it in a direct and explicit way. Clients are seen as 'customers', who can be asked quite explicitly what they want to get out of counselling, what changes they want to see happen in their lives, and how they will know when the job is done and the need for counselling is over. My experience is that clients generally respond well to this encouragement to make choices and take decisions, both in the counselling sessions and in their wider lives.

The emphasis on future directions and goals

The concept of a 'self-actualizing tendency' – that people have an innate capacity to change and grow – carries with it the idea of ending up different from how you started. In person-centred work this is an implicit understanding. In solution-focused work the implicit is made explicit. Clients are often asked, 'What do you think life will be like when you have got through these difficulties?' 'When you have found a way to overcome these troubles, what kind of things do you see yourself doing then?' There are two advantages to this. One is that as the client thinks about these questions they become clearer about what they want and where they want to arrive by the end of the counselling. The second advantage is that describing the desired outcome in this way actually seems to bring it closer. In some rather mysterious way, spending time imagining and thinking through how you would like things to be – life beyond the problem – seems to release reserves of creative energy and enthusiasm to bring it about. Jumping ahead to a future beyond the problem often frees things up when people are feeling stuck in the circumstances of the present. Solution-focused therapy is probably best known for the 'miracle question': 'If a miracle were to occur overnight, and the miracle was that you had somehow overcome all these difficulties we have been talking about, what are the first things you would notice that would tell you that life is different?'

The concrete details of a person's experience

This takes us to a further similarity, namely that both approaches value the concrete, specific details of lived experience more than abstract labels or explanations. Clients often begin counselling by saying, 'Things are awful and I want them to get better.' But what is 'better'? 'Better' is an abstract idea. In both approaches the counsellor encourages the client to translate abstract ideas into specific details. 'Do you have a particular "better" in mind?' 'What exactly will be different when things are better?'

These specific details of lived experience include what a person thinks and how he feels about things, but also what he does. Often a person's inner thoughts and feelings show themselves through his outward actions. Solution-focused work goes further than person-centred work in explicitly linking inner and outer. If the client says 'I want to feel more contented', a solution-focused response might be, 'What will "more contented" look like? What will you be doing differently in your life when you are more contented?'

If the client says 'I want to be less depressed', a response might be, 'What might you notice yourself doing when you become less depressed?'

These then are ways in which the two approaches are very similar. Solution-focused therapy and person-centred counselling seem to share a set of beliefs and values about a person's inner resources to develop, grow and create new solutions to old problems. Some of the most important person-centred ideas and values are made explicit in the solution-focused approach and put into action through particular techniques and methods of working.

Let us now consider some of the apparent differences between the two approaches.

The apparent differences

Is there less empathy in solution-focused work?

One apparent difference is that in solution-focused work there seems to be less emphasis on listening to the client's feelings, particularly their feelings of pain and distress. There seems to be less time spent emphathizing with and reflecting back the client's felt experience. You certainly get this impression from some of the early books about solution-focused brief therapy, which seem to show solution-focused therapists discouraging their clients from talking at length about their problems and distress, and making efforts to get them to talk 'solution talk' instead. But more recently solution-focused writers have pointed out that this is a misrepresentation of what they actually do (Cade and O'Hanlon 1993). Most solution-focused therapists actually spend considerable time in sessions listening to and acknowledging the pain and distress that people feel from their problems and difficulties. Once this has been done sufficiently, they move on to a discussion of aspects that might build towards 'solution' strategies. Jane Lethem says that 'acknowledgement is the hidden ingredient of solution focused therapy' (Lethem 1994).

Some schools of therapy hold that if you feel painful feelings enough, you come through to the other side. My own experience of therapy is that sometimes this is profoundly true, and sometimes it is not. Sometimes the most helpful thing to do is to feel and experience the feeling as fully as possible, particularly with new feelings that are just coming into awareness. But sometimes the feeling is just that same old painful feeling again, going round and round, and feeling it one more time does not get the client any further. A solution-focused response would be to point out the choice and ask the client which would seem to them the most helpful thing to do. I have found this approach particularly helpful with people who have experienced abuse and neglect in their childhoods, and who have picked up a message that in counselling you are 'supposed' to go over those painful experiences again and again. This is not necessarily the wrong thing to do, but it may be that it would be more helpful to the client to concentrate on changes that she would like to make to her life in the present. I think that the client should be given power over the choice.

Does being more active mean being more 'directive'?

In solution-focused work the counsellor seems to be steering or shaping the conversation more than in person-centred counselling. When you look at videos of some of the leading practitioners working with clients, they seem to ask a lot of questions. Some of what the client says gets ignored in favour of other things they say. Some directions get followed up and other directions are not. It looks very different from person-centred therapy. But is it? I remember that Rogers himself said that he did not see himself as completely 'non-directive' (Rogers 1980). He would choose what things from the client to feed back and give emphasis to. He would to some extent steer the conversation towards the client's clearest and fullest expression of his or her feelings and 'felt meanings' (Hales 1989).

Nowadays in my own work I ask questions rather more than I used to and I 'reflect back' rather less, but I do not think this makes me more 'directive'. What I pick up on and comment about still comes from what the client is saying about their felt experience. I am responding to things that the client has said or at least implied. I keep in mind the focus that we have agreed for the work, and the particular difficulties that the client has said he wants to overcome. The client is still the leader in the process – the 'locus of evaluation' remains with him. What I am very definitely *not* doing is giving the client suggestions about what I think he should do. In this I think solution-focused work is very different from some types of cognitive-behavioural work, with which it is sometimes compared.

Now let us look at some of these similarities and differences in action.

Case example: a man with post-traumatic stress symptoms

James was a man in his twenties who came to counselling because of post-traumatic stress symptoms. He had been attacked and robbed while walking in the park near to his place of work. He told me that he had felt in danger of his life and at the same time completely helpless and out of control. Since the incident he had taken extended sick leave from work. He had in effect retreated to his home, rarely venturing out of the front door. He had lost interest in his leisure activities. His wife was very supportive, but was worried about how deeply his life had been affected. James felt anxious and depressed much of the time. He had nightmares that woke him up in terror and made him fearful of going to sleep. James told me in our first session that he wanted all these things to stop and for his life to return to normal, and especially he wanted to return to work. This felt almost impossible because his job involved a great deal of contact with members of the public, and James had become fearful of strangers.

Much of my work with James consisted of person-centred listening and acknowledging, but there were particular solution-focused features to the work that seemed to make a tremendous difference for him:

1 *Normalizing*. In our first session James was describing all the things that were happening in his life and he repeatedly said that he could not understand why he was reacting in this way. He said that he was seriously worried that he was 'going mad'. Since he did not seem to know about post-traumatic stress I told him about it, and said that it is now known to be a common reaction for people who have had the kind of life-threatening experience that he had. I said that many of the feelings and reactions he had described were ways in which many other people were known to respond, although of course that did not make them any the less painful and distressing. I was 'normalizing' James's experience, saying that it is very normal for people to react in the way he had reacted,

and that this seemed to me something very different from 'going mad'. James looked visibly relieved as I said this. He said that it made a huge difference to feel 'that it was not just him'.

2 *Noticing small improvements*. Later in the first session James was telling me that his nightmares seemed to come in phases, and that in the recent phase they had been a little less frightening. I commented that this seemed to be a small change for the better. James agreed with me. He then paused for thought, and said that actually he supposed that there *had* been some changes from the very worst times. Six months earlier he would just not have been able to talk with me about the incident without becoming deeply upset and tearful. Now there seemed to be a distinct 'felt moment' for James. His eyes glistened with emotion as he realized that, yes, in fact there had been some improvements. He said that he suddenly felt that he had hope; for the first time in a long time he had some optimism that things could get better.

3 *Identifying the next small steps*. James stayed with this 'felt meaning' some minutes longer. He then said that he could think of some things that he could go out and do now that he had been afraid to do before. He said that he wanted to try going out of the house more, to see if he could get over his fears of being in places where there would be strangers and where things would not be totally predictable and within his control. He wanted to try going out to his local shops, where there would be strangers, but not too many of them. I could see that this was directly relevant to one of James's main goals: going to the shops might represent the first steps towards going back to work. The remainder of the first session was spent discussing which shop he would like to go to first, what would be the easiest way to go about it, and what things he could think of that might help him in going through with his plan. In all this I was asking him questions to encourage him to think through his plan. I was not making suggestions myself. James was doing the 'task setting' for himself.

4 *Relapse prevention*. At the beginning of the second session two weeks later I asked James how he had got on with his plan. He had done even better than he had expected. He had gone into many more shops than he had originally planned. He had ventured out of his neighbourhood a number of times, and he now wanted to advance to the centre of town where there would be more strangers and more bustle. His wife had commented a number of times on signs of his increasing confidence and happiness. His nightmares were now less frequent and much less frightening. Hearing all this I felt like praising James for his progress (which I did), but I also thought that he was doing so well that he might become very disappointed if he encountered a setback. I wanted to 'normalize' setbacks and relapses. I said to James that for many of the people I work with progress seems to happen 'three steps forward and two steps back'. I did not want to assume that it would be the same for him, but if he was to hit a setback, how would he like to cope with it? There was another long felt moment, and James said that he was glad I had asked the question. He said that he was the kind of person who got very upset if there was a setback, and of course there might be. But he knew that if he was expecting possible setbacks, they would not be too much of a problem. He would just tell himself that everyone has bad days, and remind himself of all the good changes that had happened since the very bad times.

Our work together continued in much the same way, with James consistently reporting successes in putting himself into situations where there were lots of strangers, lots of bustle and lots of unpredictability. He eventually took himself to Oxford Street for a morning.

James began making detailed plans about how to help himself through starting back at work. During this time the nightmares stopped, James found himself taking a renewed interest in his hobbies and he began to spend more time going out on trips with his wife. I worked with James for a total of five sessions, by the end of which time he was just about to go back to work. I later heard from him that he had accomplished this successfully.

Conclusion

I think that this case example shows the powerful effect of encouraging the client to explore the whole picture of the problematic situation, with particular emphasis on signs of the client's strengths and resources, and focusing on any small improvements and achievements. 'Normalizing' James's responses to the trauma seemed to allow him to sidestep his feelings of failure and inadequacy and to access instead his energy and determination. This I would argue is person-centred empathy, done in a particular (solution-focused) way. James had his own ideas about the next small steps to take towards his ultimate goal; the 'locus of evaluation' remained very much with him.

It is my belief that solution-focused therapy holds the same core beliefs and values as person-centred counselling. The methods of solution-focused work are many and varied, and they represent a range of choices from which counsellors can make their own individual selection. I would maintain that, used appropriately, they constitute person-centred counselling in action.

References

Cade, B. and O'Hanlon, W.H. (1993) *A Brief Guide to Brief Therapy*, London: W.W. Norton & Co.

Hales, J. (1989) 'Feeling and meaning in client-centred therapy', *Counselling*, no. 67 (February).

Lethem, J. (1994) *Moved to Tears, Moved to Action: Solution Focused Brief Therapy with Women and Children*, London: BT Press.

Rogers, C. (1951) *Client-Centred Therapy: Its Current Practice, Implications, and Theory*, Boston: Houghton Mifflin.

Rogers, C. (1961) *On Becoming a Person: A Therapist's View of Psychotherapy*, Boston: Houghton Mifflin.

Rogers, C. (1980) *A Way of Being*, Boston: Houghton Mifflin.

Saunders, C. (1995) 'Berg, de Shazer and friends: an American training experience', *Counselling*, 6 (2): 128–31.

Saunders, C. (1996) 'Solution focused therapy in practice: a personal experience', *Counselling*, 7 (4): 312–6.

Saunders, C. (1998) 'Solution focused therapy: what works?', *Counselling*, 9 (1): 45–8.

Discussion issues

1 Which plays the largest part in facilitating change – exploring the origins and development of the problem or exploring the 'exceptions to the problem'?

2 Is talking about a desired problem-free future merely wishful thinking? Does it ignore the reality of difficulties and distress?

3 'If you feel painful feelings enough, you come through to the other side.' Do you agree?

4 Which is more important to a person-centred counsellor – what a client feels, or what she thinks and what she does?

6

Problem-Solving Counselling

Michael Neenan and Stephen Palmer

Problem-solving counselling is a structured and systematic method of teaching clients to identify current problems or stressors in their lives and then learn a series of graduated steps or skills in order to tackle these difficulties. Programmes designed to teach individuals social, workplace or interpersonal problem-solving skills have increased in the last three decades (e.g. D'Zurilla and Goldfried 1971; D'Zurilla 1986; Palmer 1997). These problem-solving approaches have in common a number of sequential steps that include problem definition, generation of alternative problem-solving methods, decision-making and evaluation of the chosen course(s) of action.

The problem-solving counselling we describe here is double-headed or dual systems approach, namely one which tackles the emotional and practical aspects of a problem. As Walen et al. (1992: 52) observe: 'Dealing with the emotional problem is necessary, but *not necessarily sufficient*: resolving emotional problems gets rid of emotional disturbance; dealing with *practical* problems leads to self-actualization and improvements in the patient's quality of life. Both are important.'

The emotional problem is tackled first as clients are not usually effective practical problem-solvers when they are emotionally disturbed. For example, a man who is depressed (emotional problem) about his lack of friends (practical problem) fails to develop a social network. This is because his view of himself as unlikeable and unattractive militates against making any successful social overtures. By helping him to challenge and change his negative self-image and depressogenic thinking, he is then able to focus his restored energies on initiating the necessary practical measures (such as joining a singles group, or adventure weekends) in order to provide opportunities to find a suitable partner.

The dual systems approach to problem-solving we practise is essentially a cognitive-behavioural one because it emphasizes the significant impact our thinking has on our emotions and behaviour. The specific cognitive – behavioural model we employ for emotional problem-solving is Ellis's (1994) rational emotive behaviour therapy (REBT); the model for practical problem-solving is the one proposed by Wasik (1984). The ultimate aim of this dual systems approach is to teach clients to become their own counsellors or problem-solvers (Milner and Palmer 1998).

Emotional problem-solving

The cornerstone of REBT rests on the assumption that individuals are not so much disturbed by events as by the views they take of these events (Ellis and Bernard 1985). For

---

This chapter was first published in *Counselling*, Journal of the British Association for Counselling, vol. 11, no. 8, pp. 482–5 (2000).

example, two people fail the same job interview; the first person is disappointed but realizes that nobody has to give him a job and therefore he keeps on applying for other ones; the second person becomes depressed and angry because he believes he absolutely should have got the job and the interview panel have revealed his worthlessness by not appointing him – he now concludes that it is futile to apply for any more jobs. The ABCDE model of emotional disturbance and change presents clients with a means of understanding and tackling their emotional problems:

A = activating event (past, present or future, internal or external)
Being passed over for promotion.
B = beliefs in the form of rigid and absolute musts, shoulds, have-tos, got-tos, oughts
'I absolutely should have been promoted; it's not fair.'
C = emotional and behavioural consequences
Hurt and withdrawal ('sulking') leading to both decreased productivity and interpersonal contact at work.
D = disputing the client's rigid beliefs that produce her emotional and behavioural reactions at C
'Just because I very much wanted the promotion there is no reason why I have to get it. Too bad that I didn't. I'd better stop moping about and get on with the job I have got.'
E = a new and effective rational outlook based on flexible thinking which reverses the workplace decline and ameliorates the disturbed feelings noted at C.

From the REBT viewpoint, it is B rather than A that determines C (though it is important to emphasize the significant contribution that A brings to C). This is known as *emotional responsibility*, whereby the individual accepts that her emotional problems are largely determined by her rigid beliefs. In order to achieve E, the client usually has a lot of hard work (homework) to carry out through the disputing (D) process. This is known as *therapeutic responsibility*. The use of the ABCDE model is illustrated in the following case study.

John – a case study

John had been referred by his GP for anxiety and stress. He was a 32-year-old single man who lived in a block of flats. He worked part-time in a local supermarket and described his life as 'quiet and uneventful' with few friends and little social life. However, his 'quiet' life was frequently shattered by the couple in the next flat who played their music loudly and for long periods. He described himself as 'always being on edge' when at home and felt ashamed that he was not able to confront the couple in the next flat. The therapist was keen to find out what prevented him from doing this:

Client: I'd get anxious if I went next door.
Therapist: Because …?
Client: They wouldn't pay any attention to me. They'd laugh at me or tell me to 'get lost'.
Therapist: And if they said or did those things, what then?

Client: Well, all the sneering and horrible looks I'd get from them on the stairs, meeting them in the hallway or in the car-park outside. I did once ask them to turn the music down and that's how they responded.

Therapist: And what are you anxious about if they do behave like that?

Client: I'd feel very uncomfortable knowing how much they dislike me or that they're laughing at me. I don't want to feel like that. I try to avoid any arguments or unpleasantness in my dealings with other people.

Therapist: Is that what you are most anxious about: that you wouldn't be able to cope with the intense personal discomfort you would experience if you confronted them?

Client: Yes, that's it. I just want a quiet life.

Therapist: That seems to be precisely what you're not getting at the moment.

The therapist has located the reason John's anxiety (C) blocks him from taking any effective action with his noisy neighbours (A) – his avoidance of interpersonal tension or conflict. In REBT, this is hypothesized as *low frustration tolerance* (LFT) or *discomfort anxiety*, that is, the worry individuals experience when anticipating pain, discomfort, agitation, unpleasantness, etc.

Implicit or explicit in this anxiety is a demand that the anticipated discomfort must not be too great, otherwise it will be unbearable. This point of view is offered to the client:

Client: That sounds a lot like me. I'm always trying to avoid unpleasantness in my life because I believe I can't cope with it but avoidance doesn't make me any happier.

Therapist: So how would you state your belief in precise terms so we are both clear what it is that you want to change?

Client: I must avoid at all costs any unpleasantness or conflict with other people because I just can't cope with it (B)

Therapist: In the case of your noisy neighbours, would you be interested in working with me to lower your anxiety and increase your ability to cope with this difficult situation by challenging and changing that belief?

Client: I suppose I need to do something about this situation but I just can't go round there now and have it out with them.

Therapist: I'm not asking you to do that. Let's first deal with the ideas that drive your anxiety because they prevent you from taking effective action with the couple next door.

Client: OK, I've got nothing to lose but my mind if that music doesn't stop.

During subsequent sessions John agreed to undertake a variety of homework or self-help assignments in order to weaken his disturbance-producing beliefs and strengthen his newly emerging emotional problem-solving beliefs ('I don't like these unpleasant situations or feelings but I can learn to deal with them better'):

Cognitive tasks – compiling a list of the advantages and disadvantages of not tackling his problem and then revisiting the advantages to examine whether they were genuinely advantageous; reading a self-help book which encourages individuals to court and tolerate discomfort in order to achieve their goals (Dryden and Gordon 1993).

Behavioural tasks – undertaking a series of 'stay-in-there' exercises (Grieger and Boyd 1980) which consisted of remaining in situations he usually avoided in order to work through his disturbed thoughts and feelings, for example visiting his parents who nearly always criticized him for not 'getting on in life', going to the dentist for a much delayed check-up.

Emotive tasks – engaging in shame-attacking exercises (Ellis 1969). As John said, he felt ashamed of himself – 'I'm weak and pathetic for not standing up to them.' These exercises teach clients to expose themselves to public disapproval or criticism in order to learn to accept themselves for their perceived defects and to distinguish between criticizing a behaviour or trait but not condemning themselves on the basis of it. Exercises that he carried out included asking directions to the local railway station while standing outside it and walking down the road with an umbrella open when it was not raining. After eight sessions of tackling successfully the emotional aspects of his problem, John then focused on its practical aspects.

Practical problem-solving

John said that he wasn't always sure what to do when he had practical problems to deal with and this often meant he ended up with more rather than fewer problems. The model taught to him was Wasik's (1984) seven-step problem-solving approach which includes self-questioning:

Steps	Questions/Actions
1 Problem identification	What is the concern?
2 Goal selection	What do I want?
3 Generation of alternatives	What can I do?
4 Consideration of consequences	What might happen?
5 Decision-making	What is my decision?
6 Implementation	Now do it!
7 Evaluation	Did it work?

Step 1

John's obvious problem was his noisy neighbours who made his home life unpleasant. This was the biggest current problem in his life (if he had a multitude of difficulties to be addressed then a problem list would have been drawn up).

Step 2

His goal was to find some means of influencing his neighbours to reduce their music playing to a more tolerable level – 'so that I no longer feel I'm living in the same flat as them'.

Step 3

Here John was encouraged to come up with as many possible solutions to his problem no matter how ludicrous or unrealistic some of them initially appeared; in other words, to brainstorm. At first, he had trouble suggesting solutions, so the therapist offered some as a means of prompting him and then he produced these:

a. Ask the council for a transfer.
b. Let their car tyres down.
c. Knock on their door every time they play their music too loud and ask them to turn it down. Be persistent.

d. Find out the council's rules and regulations regarding the playing of music and what enforcement powers they have.
e. Ask the other neighbours if they are upset over the music levels and try to get up a petition.
f. Blast them out with my music!
g. Let the noisy couple know what my plan of action will be if they ignore me.

Step 4

This involved John considering the advantages and disadvantages of each solution produced from the brainstorming session. The client may wish to rate the plausibility of each possible solution on a scale of 0–10: 0 = the least plausible … 10 = the most plausible:

a. 'It's running or, literally, moving away from the problem. I've done too much of that in my life.' (1)
b. 'Too childish and may make the situation worse.' (1)
c. 'This sounds more like it. It will be hard for me to do that but if I don't, I'm never going to get any peace. Stand up and be counted.' (8)
d. 'This is a very sensible step and I will contact them if the couple don't turn down their music.' (7)
e. 'If there are other people in the block who are also fed up with the music, then force of numbers either through a petition or knocking on their door might prevail.' (6)
f. 'A non-starter. Then I'll get a double dose of loud noise.' (0)
g. 'I'll certainly use this tactic if I get no satisfaction from them.' (6)

Step 5

John now chose which solution to pursue based upon the calculus of probable success decided in the previous step: 'I'll start with c, and fall back on d, e and g if the going gets really tough.'

Step 6

This involved role-play: the therapist took on the role of one of the neighbours while John made repeated requests to him to turn the music down. John's voice faltered at times and he often looked down at the floor. Coming out of the role-play, the therapist commented upon John's indecisive manner and changes were made in his interactional approach. John then practised the new behaviour in the session as well as agreeing to act it out in imagery for a homework task. The therapist can also prompt the client to suggest ways of handling the situation if setbacks occur (they usually do).

Step 7

At the next session, which is after the client has carried out the agreed solution, therapist and client evaluated its outcome:

Therapist: How did you get on?
Client: They're still playing their music too loud but the good news is that every time they do that I've been straight round there to complain.

Therapist: And how did they respond?

Client: As expected: rude, slammed the door in my face sometimes and, at other times, didn't even bother answering it.

Therapist: Any threats of physical violence?

Client: No, but if there are, I will immediately call the police which I didn't put on last week's list.

Therapist: Were there any moments or times when you wanted to forget the whole thing?

Client: On several occasions. The old ideas came back.

Therapist: Such as … ?

Client: 'I can't stand all this unpleasantness. Why won't it go away? I just want a quiet, uneventful life.'

Therapist: How did you deal with those ideas?

Client: As you taught me in the earlier part of therapy – vigorously dispute them.

Therapist: Did it work?

Client: Yes, it did. I told myself to stop running away when things become unpleasant or difficult in my life and see the problem through to the bitter end. I think I'm beginning to get some backbone.

Therapist: It's good to hear you're making progress. So what's the next step with the noisy neighbours?

Client: Well, I told them yesterday that I've had enough and I'm officially complaining to the council and demanding that action be taken. I'll also be seeking the views of other residents.

Therapist: How does it feel to be doing all that?

Client: To be honest, I feel quite proud of myself. At last I'm really carrying something through.

In the following weeks, John reported that the music level of his neighbours had dropped appreciably. 'They still give me icy stares when they see me but I can live with that.' Another benefit he enjoyed was that he finally got to know and became friendly with other residents in the block of flats: 'We were strangers until I knocked on their doors.'

The practical problem-solving section of counselling had lasted for five sessions. To return to step 7, if the proposed solution(s) has been successful, the client can then pick another problem from his list and follow steps 1–6 again.

Ending

Now that he had success in one area of his life, John said he had experienced a 'sea change' in his outlook and wanted to do more with his life such as leaving his part-time job in the supermarket and pursuing 'a career that will be interesting and challenging for me in ways which the supermarket has never been'. He also wanted a more exciting social life and now felt he had the confidence to meet people and make more friends. Follow-up appointments were arranged for three, six and 12 months to monitor his progress in maintaining his therapeutic gains as well as finding out about the other developments in his life.

In conclusion

Problem-solving counselling is a psychoeducational approach that teaches clients how to remediate their present problems and prevent or reduce the occurrence of future ones. It is an approach that can be used in a variety of clinical settings (e.g. in- and out-patient environments, community mental health teams, group therapy) as well as non-clinical ones (e.g. schools, colleges, industry). Problem-solving counselling is ideally suited to brief therapy regimes used in, for example, employee assistance programmes and general practice. Whether the emphasis is on emotional problem-solving or practical problem-solving, or both, we believe that this approach has a great potential for helping individuals to accelerate the process of change in their lives and adapt more effectively to the increasing demands of a complex society.

References

Dryden, W. and Gordon, J. (1993) *Beating the Comfort Trap*. London: Sheldon Press.

D'Zurilla, T.J. (1986) *Problem-Solving Therapy: A Social Competence Approach to Clinical Intervention*, New York: Springer.

D'Zurilla, T.J. and Goldfried, M.R. (1971) 'Problem-solving and behaviour modification', *Journal of Abnormal Psychology*, 78: 107–26.

Ellis, A. (1969) *Suggested Procedures for a Weekend of Rational Encounter*. New York: Albert Ellis Institute for Rational Emotive Behaviour Therapy.

Ellis, A. (1994) *Reason and Emotion in Psychotherapy* (2nd edn), New York: Birch Lane Press.

Ellis, A. and Bernard, M.E. (eds) (1985) *Clinical Applications of Rational-Emotive Therapy*, New York: Plenum.

Grieger, R. and Boyd, J. (1980) *Rational-Emotive Therapy: A Skills-Based Approach*, New York: Van Nostrand Reinhold.

Milner, P. and Palmer, S. (1998) *Integrative Stress Counselling: A Humanistic Problem-Focused Approach*, London: Cassell.

Palmer, S. (1997) 'Problem focused stress counselling and stress management training: an intrinsically brief integrative approach' (Parts 1 & 2), *Stress News*, 9 (2): 7–12; 9 (3): 6–10.

Walen, S.R., DiGiuseppe, R. and Dryden, W. (1992) *A Practitioner's Guide to Rational-Emotive Therapy* (2nd edn), New York: Oxford University Press.

Wasik, B. (1984) 'Teaching parents effective problem-solving: handbook for professionals', unpublished manuscript. University of North Carolina, Chapel Hill.

Discussion issues

1 The structure of problem-solving counselling is too restrictive for effective therapy.

2 Is problem-solving counselling an example of two therapeutic approaches being successfully integrated?

3 For which clients or settings would problem-solving counselling be suitable?

4 Solution-focused therapy is just a variation of problem-solving counselling.

7

On Becoming a Psychodynamic Counsellor

Learning about countertransference

John Lees

Introduction

Several years ago – before I had completed my formal training as a counsellor – I had an experience with a client which is still clear to this day. Indeed it is easy to remember because of its gratifying nature: in psychodynamic terms I experienced an erotic counter-transference. There have been several references to such experiences in the literature recently (mostly, it appears, by men): Samuels (1985, 1993), Hirsch and Kessel (1988), Mearns and Thorne (1988), Thomas (1991), Mann (1994, 1997), to name a few. However, there have also been some important contributions by women: for instance, O'Connor and Ryan (1993) and Schaverien (1997, 1998). Furthermore, some psycho-dynamic authors have asserted that the failure to pick up eroticism in the therapeutic rela-tionship is a therapeutic failing. O'Connor and Ryan (1993) refer to therapeutic defensiveness in regard to working with homosexual clients, possibly as a result of the arousal of homosexual erotic feelings in the therapist (ibid.: 185). Schaverien (1997) con-siders that the failure of therapists to pick up the erotic transference and countertransfer-ence may result in some clients leaving therapy too soon. Finally, Mann (1997: 11) refers to the 'therapist's anxiety about the erotic heating to boiling point and dangerously over-flowing'. Others have spoken about the positive nature of the erotic in human develop-ment: Samuels (1993: 154) speaks about a healthy 'erotic playback' in childhood, that is, 'an optimal erotic relation' between parent and child, while Mann (1997) talks about the transformative aspects of the erotic in therapeutic work. However, when I saw my client, I was only dimly aware of these perspectives and the experience of eroticism presented me with a dilemma as it does for many inexperienced counsellors (and experienced ones too). My subsequent attempts to process the experience contained elements of therapist defensiveness, anxiety and transformation. Indeed, writing about it is part of an attempt to transform it into a useful professional developmental experience in the light of some of the recent thinking on the subject.

The account concentrates on the aftermath rather than the clinical work itself, but it is necessary to mention a few basic facts. The client was a woman with striking blue eyes. I was inexperienced at the time and poorly supervised. The client was about 20 minutes late for this particular session and, knowing that she lived nearby, I phoned her. She seemed surprised and embarrassed, but immediately came round. At first the session

This chapter was first published in *Counselling*, Journal of the British Association for Counselling, vol. 5, no. 4, pp. 299–301 (1994).

was rather low-key. Then she mentioned a doctor who had behaved 'rather unprofessionally'. A few moments later I was overwhelmed by feelings of desire and excitement, which made it difficult for me to remain calm. I did not interpret or refer to what was happening. All my energy went on maintaining my 'sangfroid' for the rest of the session. But, afterwards I was still affected. In order to distract myself – or perhaps maintain the exciting feelings – I listened to an early seventies album by The Who called *Who's Next?* on my car stereo (a rather crude and rhythmic piece of rock music). I played one track, called 'Behind Blue Eyes', several times.

In due course the therapy ended – apparently satisfactorily. My client's condition had apparently improved. But I could not get her out of my mind and I felt uneasy about this.

First stage of learning and becoming

I later wrote a dissertation on countertransference as part of my counselling training. In retrospect I think this was partly an attempt to come to terms with such experiences. While studying the subject I considered the possibility that the pioneers of depth psychology had also had difficulties with similar feelings. Joseph Breuer, for example, became fascinated – one could even say preoccupied – with Anna O whom he treated between 1880 and 1882. For a time he visited her daily and took extensive notes. Freud, too, was powerfully affected by his clients. What, for instance, was he feeling when he wrote as follows about Elizabeth von R? '... if one pressed or pinched the hyperalgesic skin and muscles of her legs, her face assumed a peculiar expression, which was one of pleasure rather than pain. She cried out – and I could not help thinking that it was as though she was having a voluptuous tickling sensation' (Freud 1895: 204). Why, towards the end of the treatment, did he break confidentiality and reveal one of her secrets to her mother? And what was he thinking when, some time after the treatment ended, he 'heard that she was going to a private ball for which I was able to get an invitation, and I did not allow the opportunity to escape me of seeing my former patient whirl past in a lively dance' (ibid.: 230)?

It has been suggested that one of the reasons for Freud's self-analysis was 'to investigate himself, both in the light of his discoveries with his patients and in respect of his emotional responses to his patients' (Meltzer 1973: 6). Yet it wasn't until 1910 (almost 30 years after first hearing about Anna O and almost 20 years after treating Elizabeth von R) that he publicly acknowledged that analysts have to struggle to manage strong feelings in the consulting room. In that year he said that countertransference 'arises in him [the analyst] as a result of the patient's influence on his unconscious feelings' (1910: 144). His subsequent references to the subject urged caution and restraint, since 'the experiment of letting oneself go a little way in tender feelings for the patient is not altogether without danger' (Freud 1915: 164–6). He also recommended that therapists should model themselves 'on the surgeon' and exercise 'emotional coldness' (1912: 115): the so-called rule of abstinence. Other references – few in number – seem to suggest that therapists should 'cure' themselves of their countertransferences before entering the consulting room.

This was reassuring for me. In view of Breuer's abandonment of analysis, Freud's need for his self-analysis, his reluctance to speak about countertransference, and his difficulty in shaking off the memory of some of his clients, I felt in good company. They both obviously had difficulties as well. I even imagined that Freud's case studies may have helped him to come to terms with these experiences, just as writing this paper helped me, and I wondered whether the long time lapse before Freud spoke openly about countertransference was because, like me, he felt uneasy about his feelings.

It was edifying to compare myself with Freud. To some extent I also modelled myself on him, inasmuch as I cultivated clinical detachment. Yet the similarities were superficial. There was one fundamental area where we differed – although I was not aware of this at the time. He advised practitioners to refrain from encouraging 'the patient to suppress, renounce or sublimate her instincts'

> ... just as though, after summoning up a spirit from the underworld by cunning spells, one were to send him down again without having asked a single question. One would have brought the repressed into consciousness, only to repress it once more in fright. (1915: 164)

I had manifestly failed to do this with my client. On the contrary I 'urged' her to 'sublimate her instincts'. I was neither sufficiently experienced, knowledgeable, or confident enough to sustain the powerful erotic feelings. Consequently I did not bring them to my client's awareness and missed the opportunity to explore what was taking place. Indeed the remaining sessions were uneventful – even desultory.

Moving to the second stage of learning

Of course Freud was referring to the client's feelings, not the therapist's: he felt that the therapist should exercise 'emotional coldness'. At this point I read some of the recent literature on countertransference and eroticism, and I realized that his approach to countertransference had been superseded. Many people today take the view that the therapist should sustain both his/her feelings as well as the client's. For example, the psychoanalyst Racker said that the therapist should not 'deny (or even inhibit), in front of the patient ... [his/her] ... interest and affection towards him. For only Eros can originate Eros' (Racker 1968: 31). Similarly, the Jungian analyst Samuels remarked that: 'There is always a level at which Eros as a presence in analysis and psychological change in the patient implies and requires an erotic involvement on the part of the analyst though not a physical enactment of this undeniably real experience' (Samuels 1985: 207). Such papers drew my attention to the fact that I had not only supressed the client's feelings but also my own. This again reassured me that I need not feel guilty or ashamed. I could now 'own up' to my own erotic countertransference. It happened to others as well as me. And so I still felt that I had helped the client and that the therapy had ended satisfactorily.

My perspective on my countertransference was further enhanced when I read Heimann's (1950) seminal paper on the subject: 'The analyst's countertransference is an instrument of research into the patient's unconscious ... the emotions roused in him are much nearer to the heart of the matter than his reasoning' (pp. 81–2). In other words the therapist's countertransference is an important 'tool' for understanding the patient: better, in many ways, than his/her thinking. With this fresh understanding in mind I now asked myself: what did my countertransference tell me about my client that couldn't be expressed in words? In order to understand this question I contemplated my client's history. I remembered that her parents had divorced when she was approaching puberty and that, after an unpleasant custody battle, she had lived with her father while her brother had lived with her mother. I also recalled that, in adult life, she had never had a lasting relationship with a man – a fact that had always puzzled me considering that she was attractive and had had a succession of admirers. I concluded that her relationship with her father had been too close for comfort. She had become the 'little wife' and the relationship had probably had sexual undertones, although there was no evidence of any overt abuse. I imagined that she had learnt to be flirtatious in order to attract his attention and that this had hindered her experience of puberty, leaving her sexually immature as an adult. In consequence she could now only relate to her admirers in a flirtatious manner and was incapable of forming a deeper union. I imagined that she easily provoked her admirers' erotic arousal, thus raising their expectations, but that she then rejected them when faced with the possibility of intimacy, sexual or otherwise, and that this led to a great deal of suffering and dissatisfaction in her life. I assumed that this had happened to the doctor 'who had acted unprofessionally' and that it had also happened to me.

However, as these reflections were retrospective they were no use to the client – assuming, of course, that they were true. So they were largely for my benefit. They left me with mixed feelings about the work I had done with her. On the one hand I felt that it had been limited. But I also felt that by resisting the urge to flirt with her I had broken a pattern of reacting that seemed to have become a problematic feature of her life. Had I responded like other people in her life I would have been 'brought down to the level of a lover' (Freud 1915: 163) and thereby rendered useless as a counsellor. But by resisting this urge I felt I had helped her, since I had not reacted in the way that people usually did. Perhaps I had given her the opportunity to think twice about her behaviour, which in turn gave her the opportunity to begin to modify it. Consequently I did not feel too displeased with the work that I had done. Yet I still could not rid myself of her memory. I was troubled, not least because the memories often turned into erotic fantasies.

Stage three: return of doubt and uncertainty

Early on in my counselling course I had mentioned the case in a supervision group. The supervising tutor asked me about the telephone call. Could it have given the client the wrong message? (By this she meant: Did I encourage her in some way?) This put me on the spot, but I managed to brush aside the question and subsequently forgot all about it. Now it resurfaced. I began to have doubts and uncertainties once again. I contemplated Segal's words (1977: 36): 'the major part of the countertransference, like the transference, is always unconscious'. Maybe a major part of this 'countertransference experience' had remained unconscious all this time and was still troubling me? I began to conduct an internal debate with myself. *Had I done something wrong?* ... Surely not. I'd handled myself professionally in the session and had helped the client ... I then recalled some of the events which followed the session. *'I still felt excited'*? ... Well that wasn't so surprising. It just showed how involved I had been with the client. *'I listened to an early seventies album by The Who called "Who's Next?"'* ... Well the title certainly had a seductive undertone. But surely that reflected the client's pathology? It couldn't possibly have anything to do with mine. '*I played one track – called "Behind Blue Eyes" – several times.*' ... And then I remembered. The client had blue eyes. The realization startled me. I re-evaluated my work. I felt that I may have precipitated the events in the session because I was attracted to the client and – recalling the communicative psychotherapy of Robert Langs – perhaps the client's reference to the 'doctor who acted unprofessionally' was an indirect reference to me, since I had 'acted unprofessionally' by phoning the client. Hitherto in my career I had focused on other people's neuroses and problems. Now I began to focus on my own. Like Freud I now felt that 'the main patient who pre-occupies me is myself' (1895).

As I read more of the recent literature on countertransference and eroticism in the therapeutic relationship I realized that 'neurotic' countertransferences are not necessarily harmful. We are, after all, human. But they become harmful if they are unobserved, and even more harmful if they are acted out. Because of this the centre of gravity of my work changed. Originally my 'clinical attitude' could be summed up by the question: How can I help this client to understand his/her pathology? Now it was something like: How can I manage my own so as to give my clients a living example of how to manage theirs? To understand my client's inner worlds I began to look at my own. Taking this a step further I imagined my clients were unconsciously saying: 'Well I'm unable to deal with this problem. So I'll sit back and see how he deals with it.' The question of who precipitated what was of secondary importance. The important point was how we dealt with it once it happened.

This period of my professional development was a time of turmoil and uncertainty for me. I no longer felt like a 'god descending from Olympus' to sort out the affairs of human beings, but a fallible human being helping other fallible human beings, albeit – I hoped – with some degree of insight and understanding. In the case of this client, however, I realized that – while working with her – my understanding had been limited. I had succeeded in 'summoning up a spirit from the underworld' but then I took fright. So what happened to the 'spirit?' It certainly did not go away. Indeed it seemed that to the extent that I was unable to confront the feelings in the session I was haunted by them outside. The 'spirit from the underworld' ran amok: the feelings persisted and were uncontained. And I can only surmise that it was the same for the client. After the treatment had ended she sent me a Christmas card, and numerous letters. She also conveyed her greetings via a mutual acquaintance, thereby fuelling my fantasies even more.

The fourth stage: an alternative approach

An alternative – more therapeutic – approach would, I believe, have been to do what Freud suggested; namely, to be more courageous and ask the 'spirit' some questions. Or – to put it differently – to give the client the opportunity to express, and thereby explore and understand, her unmanageable feelings in the subsequent sessions. But how could I have done this? In the first instance I would have had to struggle to sustain 'the feelings which ... [were] ... stirred in ... [me] ... as opposed to discharging them (as does the patient), in order to subordinate them to the analytic task in which he functions as the patient's mirror reflection' (Heimann 1950: 82). By sustaining my own 'neurotic' reactions to the client in the sessions I would have helped her to sustain and examine her own.

This would then have given us some time and space to understand them. Such an understanding, however, would not have been easy. It would have required, in the first place, empathizing with the client's pain – not running away from it out of fear or letting my own erotic feelings overwhelm me. In other words it would have involved sustaining the feelings even when the client resisted this. Yet this would not have been enough. To preserve myself – to maintain my own identity and capacity to function as a professional – I would have had to maintain my capacity to think. And this is where training, theoretical understanding, and experience are indispensable. However, the skill and effort involved in maintaining both empathy and understanding cannot be underestimated. As Noonan (1983: 66–7) has said: 'It requires emotional effort to become so immersed in another person's system and even more effort to remain involved but detached: it requires the apparently contradictory actions of letting go of yourself and remembering who you are.'

I believe that the benefits of such an undertaking would have been potentially great for this client – as much of the recent writing on countertransference and eroticism suggests. It would have given her hope by showing her that her feelings were not completely unmanageable. Ideally she would have then felt less threatened and confused by them. By confronting the 'spirit' in the session and grappling with it I would have had the opportunity to 'hold' and 'contain' the client which would have, in turn, given her the opportunity to take responsibility for her feelings. Both her feelings – and mine – could have been put back where they belonged instead of taking on a life of their own.

The latter course of action was clearly beyond my capacities at the time. But, assuming my understanding of this scenario has some truth, I now have the possibility to learn from the experience and do better next time because I have learned more about the power of the counselling relationship and our responsibility as counsellors.

References

Freud, S. (1895) 'Fraulein Elizabeth von R', in S. Freud and J. Breuer, *Studies in Hysteria*, Harmondsworth: Penguin Books, 1988.

Freud, S. (1910) 'The Future Prospects of Psycho-Analytic Therapy', in S. Freud, *The Standard Edition*, vol. 12, London: The Hogarth Press, 1958.

Freud, S. (1912) 'Recommendations to Physicians Practising Psycho-Analysis', in S. Freud, *The Standard Edition*, vol. 12, London: The Hogarth Press, 1958.

Freud, S. (1915) 'Observations on Transference Love', in S. Freud, *The Standard Edition*, vol. 12, London: The Hogarth Press, 1958.

Heimann, P. (1950) 'On counter-transference', *International Journal of Psychoanalysis*, 31: 81–4.

Hirsch, I. and Kessel, P. (1988) 'Reflections on mature love and countertransference', *Free Associations*, 12: 60–84.

Mann, D. (1994) 'The psychotherapist's erotic subjectivity', *British Journal of Psychotherapy*, 10 (3): 344–55.

Mann, D. (1997) *Psychotherapy: An Erotic Relationship*, London: Routledge.

Mearns, D. and Thorne, B. (1988) *Person-Centred Counselling in Action*, London: Sage Publications.

Meltzer, D. (1973) *Sexual States of Mind*, Perthshire: Clunie Press.

Noonan, E. (1983) *Counselling Young People*, London: Routledge.

O'Connor, N. and Ryan, J. (1993) *Wild Desires and Mistaken Identities*, London: Virago.

Racker, H. (1968) *Transference and Counter-Transference*, London: The Hogarth Press.

Samuels, A. (1985) 'Symbolic dimensions of Eros in transference–countertransference: some clinical uses of Jung's alchemical metaphor', *International Review of Psycho-Analysis*, 12: 199–213.

Samuels, A. (1993) *The Political Psyche*, London: Routledge.

Schaverien, J. (1997) 'Men who leave too soon: reflections on the erotic transference', *British Journal for Psychotherapy*, 14 (4): 3–17.

Schaverien, J. (1998) 'Alchemy and the erotic transference: a Jungian approach', *Psychodynamic Counselling*, 4 (2): 149–69.

Segal, H. (1977) 'Countertransference', *International Journal of Psychoanalysis*, 6: 31–7.

Thomas, P. (1991) 'A therapeutic journey through the Garden of Eden', *Counselling*, 2 (4): 143–5.

Discussion issues

1   Have you experienced eroticism in the therapeutic relationship? If so, how have you dealt with it?

2   Do you think it is therapeutically beneficial to work with erotic feelings or should they be left alone?

3   Do you think countertransference is merely an observational tool or can we also work with it therapeutically?

4   Are there any clinical experiences from your early work as a counsellor which you can clearly remember several years later? Has writing about them helped you to work through the experience?

8

Mentoring as Change Agency

A psychodynamic approach

John O'Brien

The growth of mentoring programmes in the UK and USA is now prolific. Approaches vary from 'caring, nurturing relationships' designed to 'maximise potential' (Hamilton 1994), to coaching, and even to clairvoyancy (Smith 1993). While mentors are often trained counsellors, mentoring is clearly distinguishable from counselling at work. Counselling at work is usually located within an employee assistance function, its focus can be wide ranging, and the scope of intervention is usually limited to the individual. By contrast, mentoring is located within the mainstream of line management, its focus is on the overlap between individual and organizational interests, and the scope of intervention may often include the individual, the team and the organization as a whole. Mentoring in corporations is typically conducted through a series of one-to-one consultations either with a senior employee of the organization, or with an external consultant specifically trained for the purpose. This article outlines the work of a consultancy currently operating with a major UK corporation. The approach is unusual, in so far as intrapsychic and systemic approaches have been combined to create a win/win situation for individuals and the organization which is undergoing rapid culture change.

Rapid organizational change often causes distress and turbulence for individuals and organizations alike and this can manifest in dysfunction at all levels. The consultancy has found that individual and group methodologies firmly rooted in psychodynamic theory and practice have been most useful in understanding and transforming potentially damaging dynamics into positive action. It is perhaps the extent and rapidity of change experienced by large contemporary institutions which determine the necessity for depth psychology to most effectively understand and manage the complexities of the human dimension.

A brief description of the current programme is given, followed by a theoretical exposition of some of the more useful concepts which have been applied to, or which have emerged from practice. Finally, comment on the programme is provided and individual and organizational benefits are noted.

Overview

The mentoring programme was commissioned early in 1993 as an integral part of the Change Programme of a company employing some 60,000 staff. Initially open to the top 60 managers, including the Chief Executive, the programme has now been extended to

This chapter was first published in *Counselling*, Journal of the British Association for Counselling, vol. 6, no. 1, pp. 51–4 (1995).

134 managers, and additionally includes extensive group work throughout the organization. The programme is designed to last two years and aims to embed a 'mentoring attitude' within line management. The business objective is to help the organization through a process of rapid change towards a culture where high-level skills in human relations are not only valued, but acknowledged as a source of competitive advantage in a mature service industry.

The use of psychodynamic and phenomenological approaches to human relations is still leading edge, as industry has a stronger tradition of empirical measurement deriving from its dominant accounting methodology. The discipline of robust challenge to major investment decisions is of course essential for any sound business needing to demonstrate return on equity through rigorous cost management. Hence behavioural psychology, with its emphasis on measurable outcomes, found ready acceptance in the business arena. None the less, in the organization in question, approaches to mangement development derived from this field (e.g. 'management competencies') have now been complemented by the mentoring programme which acknowledges and values the inner world of the mentee and its power in the construction of corporate reality. Direct indications of success of the mentoring programme are largely qualitative, which signifies an important additional perspective in a large corporation strongly grounded in empirical quantitative methodology. The growing awareness of the importance of phenomenological approaches to organizational management is perhaps reflected not only in providing 'warmer' customer service but also in the recognition of the necessity to develop 'transformational leadership' skills in senior managers (Howell and Avolio 1993).

In order to operate a personal mentoring programme in a corporate context, boundary conditions must be clearly stated. In the case of the project in question, potential mentees sign a constract with their mentor and the employing organization which binds the mentor to confidentiality and commits him/her to the Code of Ethics of the British Associa-tion for Counselling. Thereafter, hourly sessions are conducted weekly. The freedom of the individual to decline participation in the programme is explained by the Chief Executive in written communication prior to launch. Furthermore, mentors interview each potential mentee in some depth, again emphasizing the voluntary nature of the scheme before engaging. In the organization described, approximately 5 per cent of the initial group preferred not to participate. The process can be terminated by individual mentees at any time and specific agendas are chosen by the mentee. Occasionally mentees may get in touch with painful personal material which requires a therapeutic environment for full working through and a system exists whereby mentees, with their consent, may be referred to the British Association for Counselling and/or psychotherapists known to the organization. It is noteworthy that during the project in question there have been no referrals, and it is possible that the rigorous psychodynamic underpinning has, in many cases, enabled anxieties to be contained within the mentor/mentee relationship. While the programme itself is defined in broad stages, the pace is set by mentees who will use the process to varying degree of depth. Where appropriate, mentors will help mentees examine connections between the different areas of experience depicted in Figure 8.1.

Mentors are typically Masters level counsellors, counselling psychologists, or psychotherapists, with dual business qualifications and experience. All are required to attend supervision one and a half hours weekly, training four hours per week, offsite training one day per month and one residential week per quarter. Additionally, all mentors are encouraged to continue personal growth and professional development, and each must

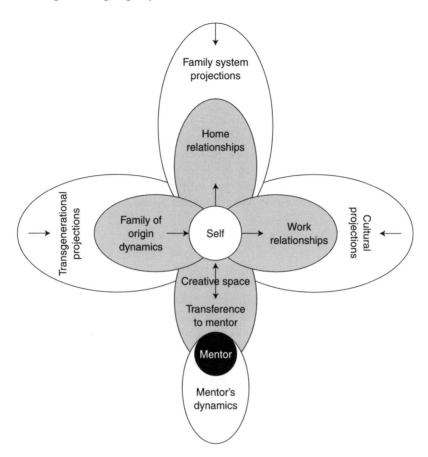

Figure 8.1   *The mentor as a change agent*

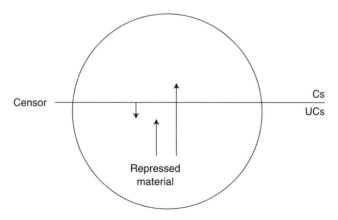

Figure 8.2   *Individual mentoring*

subscribe to the relevant professional body. The consultancy has group membership of the British Association for Counselling.

Clearly, a major investment in the programme is made by both the individual concerned and the corporation, particularly taking into account opportunity costs of staff time. Where mentees wish to communicate business issues up the line anonymously, business data is gathered for presentation in the form of a Mentor Action Report. This identifies themes and issues which are often disconfirming of senior management beliefs about organization performance and provides invaluable feedback which forms as basis of improved decision-making. This has proved useful for the organization concerned, which, because of its size, and despite flat structures, has a long line of communication between senior executives and front line managers. Individual mentoring, mentor action reporting, and group work ensure that culture change is driven top-down, horizontally, and bottom-up.

Individual mentoring

Individual change through this particular kind of mentoring is underpinned by a dynamic process of bringing to awareness some of the unconscious factors which drive perception, beliefs and behaviours. This typically enhances strategic capability at the conscious level as the individual gains greater understanding and control of behaviours which may have been dysfunctional. Progress is characterized by a greater sense of 'personal mastery', greater choice and an increased repertoire of behaviour, improved strategic decision-making capability, and an openness to new learning. There is predictably significant reduction in reality distortion and a move from repetition to generativity. The process can be simply represented as shown in Figure 8.2.

The model is essentially psychodynamic and derives from Freud's early descriptions of the workings of the psyche (Freud 1953). In practice, ideas derived from Freud's later work have also proved helpful, as well as from the formulations of the post-Freudians. Much energy is often wasted in unnecessary 'intrapsychic conflict' where unacceptable impulses and unpleasant feelings and memories are constantly being censored. Perception can be distorted, behaviour can become 'stuck' and world-views can become fixed. Through the mentoring relationship, unconscious material is brought into the arena of conscious action. 'Material' can be analysed and decoded in terms of its 'unconscious' or 'latent' meaning. A range of interactive dynamic techniques is employed in the mentoring relationship to transform dammed-up energy into creativity.

Through interpretation of the transference (see Figure 8.1), mentors can help mentees understand not only the extent to which family of origin dynamics replay in the work context (Argyris and Schon 1980) but also the phenomenon of transgenerational projection, where themes and situations replay throughout the history of generations (Pitt-Aikens and Ellis 1988). Central to the process is the use of the relationship between mentor and mentee, which operates in the context of past relationships, present family and work relationships and future. The fundamental aim is to help the mentee become aware of themes and situations which are likely to replay, often contrary to the mentee's well-being or conscious intention. The working approach derives from Freud's (1920) notion of repetition compulsion (Freud 1957b).

Consider for a moment the hypothetical example of a senior manager who, physically and psychologically distanced from his/her own team, experiences all relationships

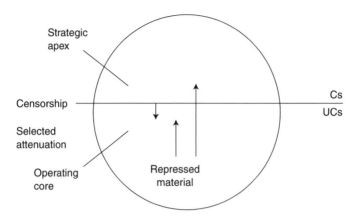

Figure 8.3 *Organizational change*

with seniors as hostile and persecuting, and whose team experiences his/her management style in a similar fashion. Insight into earlier relationships with an abusive parent, and further insight into that parent's childhood difficulties can often bring about realization of the transgenerational and family of origin introjects, and awareness of some of the reasons for difficulties with the manager's own team. The sense of grappling with such awesome material is often followed by an appreciation of the power of cultural influence and the contribution of the unconscious projection of others to family and work. Gains made in this area can often yield substantial benefits in the area of the mentee's life. In the work arena, patterns of troubled relationships with bosses, peers, and team members can be transformed. Such is the substance of culture transformation.

Similarly, a mentee may discover through the relationship with his/her mentor, tendencies to unwittingly coach the mentor to behave in certain ways, such as to abandon or to behave punitively. Mentor countertransference in this respect is monitored through close supervision and mentees are thereby helped to examine the relationship. The individual may well find that this brings to mind hitherto forgotten uncomfortable memories from his/her family of orientation, which might also be replaying in present relationships at work. Greater control over aspects of work life which may relate to repeated family of orientation dynamics can often be gained in this way.

Organizational change

At the organizational level, the culture transformation process operates in a similar way. The aim is to improve strategic capability by promoting the flow of undistorted valid data (Schein 1992) up through the system to the strategic apex (Mintzberg 1983). This can be conceptualized as bringing the organizational unconscious to awareness, in the same manner as the mentoring programme promotes individual growth, see Figure 8.3.

Information must of course be attenuated as it flows towards the strategic apex (Mintzberg 1983; Beer 1985), but all large corporations select out anxiety-provoking, disconfirming data according to the 'ego strength' of the top team. This material, however, contains information of both operational value and of dynamic importance. It is characterized by the anxieties which often drive the organization into repetitive behaviour and fixed belief systems.

Through the mentoring programme, latent material of significance to the business is elicited, decoded and presented to the strategic apex in the form of the Mentor Action Report. This enables the strategic apex of the organization to function with greater choice, creativity and competitive strength in relation to the business environment.

Mentor Action Reporting might typically involve the recording and presentation to senior managers of a number of related issues by mentees from different parts of the organization. For example, if the organization is moving towards staff empowerment, one might expect a large number of questions and concerns expressed about the clarification of boundaries. At the same time, anxiety might be manifest in 'splitting' (them and us) as the organization works through its rapprochement issues.

The critical need for clear communication at such times can be expressed through the Mentor Action Report to senior managers who become increasingly aware of the dynamic impact of their own behaviour, and who are thereby enabled to manage more effectively. More simply, several mentees may report a similar problem with a technical function of the business, which direct information may be invaluable and otherwise not available to senior managers, who, strongly invested in the success of the area in question, might be susceptible to denial.

Team change

At the team level, again the aim is to improve group strategic capability by bringing awareness to those unconscious aspects of group life which drive behaviours towards 'off task' goals (Bion 1959). At the same time, the creative power of the group unconscious can be harnessed and employed to bring about a quantum leap in performance.

Group ego strength is built to enable it to successfully manage increasing levels of disconfirming data both from within the group 'repressed area' and from the organizational area. Group cohesiveness is engendered through the development of high-level trust, intimacy, and self-regard through success orientation. From this base, non-critical mistakes can be reviewed as learning opportunities, and respectful challenge and disagreement can be encouraged as contributions to learning (Short 1991). Emphasis on task orientation ensures that 'group think' phenomena (Bernthal and Insko 1993) are minimized.

Consider a typical team locked into process at the expense of task. The group may enjoy being together and may be strongly creative, but produce little of value to the organization as a whole, and may become increasingly marginalized. Refocus on the task of the group within its organizational context might help the team consider its outputs, as well as its creativity. It could be that the team is behaving as though its purpose is to provide an opportunity for the members to engage in creative activity rather than to produce any particular outputs ('basic assumption pairing' mode – Bion 1959). Awareness of this phenomenon can provide the first step towards the team understanding how it processes anxiety, and can help the team focus its creativity in a functional direction.

Conclusion

While methodology in each area is quite different, the overall shape of the culture transformation process is, as described, contained in each component, as well as in the whole. The integrity of design accelerates the change process as it is experienced simultaneously at all levels of the organization – as a whole, group systemic, and individual.

The mentoring programme is now regarded as an essential component of the culture transformation process, and is being extended to include a wider range of group work and facilitation training. Many senior managers in the organization feel that their self-knowledge, interpersonal skills, and business performance have increased as a result of mentoring, and many are beginning to apply a mentoring approach to their own staff management. Independent Audit findings report that mentees are highly appreciative of outcomes which result in a greater sense of personal mastery in their lives, and in observably enhanced interpersonal functioning and decision-making at work.

The indirect link of the mentoring programme to improved business performance is acknowledged, and there has been a shift from a 'power' culture towards a 'humanistic' approach which has been independently measured by a culture inventory. The quality of service experienced by the customer has correspondingly improved, as have all quality indicators used by the organization to measure its performance. Similar quantitative measures of staff pride and morale have also risen.

Areas in which participants have experienced direct benefits from the programme are listed in the independent audit as: performance improvement, leadership skills, personal growth and change management activities. A key finding is that managers feel more able, not only to empower, facilitate and listen, but also to set appropriate boundaries and to insist on results. This aspect of management may appear one of the more difficult facets to integrate within the overall culture change, but is usefully addressed dynamically from the perspective of the exercise of good authority based on positive parent introjects (Pitt-Aikens and Ellis 1988).

In conclusion, it has been greatly encouraging to note the ready acceptance of applied psychodynamics by a major corporate employer and to be able to demonstrate clear added value through enhanced organizational capability and business performance. The programme has been particularly relevant in the context of a mature service industry where competitive advantage is sought through improving customer service, staff development, and strategic decision-making capability.

References

Argyris, C. (1957) *Personality and Organisations*, London: Harper Press.
Argyris, C. and Schon, D. (1980) *Theory in Practice: Increasing Organisational Effectiveness*, San Francisco, CA: Jossey Bass.
Beer, S. (1985) *Diagnosing the System for Organisations*, Chichester: John Wiley.
Bion, W.R. (1959) *Experiences in Groups*, London: Tavistock.
Freud, S. (1953) 'The Interpretation of Dreams' (1990). *Standard Edition*, vols. 4 and 5, London: Hogarth Press.
Freud, S. (1957a) 'Papers on Metapsychology' (1915). *Standard Edition*, vol. 14, London: Hogarth Press.

Freud, S. (1957b) 'Beyond the Pleasure Principle' (1920). *Standard Edition*, vol. 17, London: Hogarth Press.

Mintzberg, H. (1983) *Structure in Fives*, Englewood Cliffs, NJ: Prentice Hall.

Pitt-Aikens, T. and Ellis, A. (1988) *The Secrets of Strangers*, London: Pelican.

Schein, E.H. (1992) *Organisational Culture and Leadership*, San Francisco, CA: Jossey Bass.

Short, R. (1991) *A Special Kind of Leadership*, Seattle, WA: The Leadership Group.

Journals

Bernthal, P. and Insko, C. (March, 1993) 'Cohesiveness without groupthink', *Group and Organisations Management*, 18 (1).

Hamilton, R. (June 1994) 'Caring for success', *Training Management*.

Howell, J. and Avolio, B. (1993) 'Transformational leadership, transactional leadership, locus of control, and support for innovation: key predictors of consolidated business-unit performance; *Journal of Applied Psychology*, 8 (6).

Smith, L. (December 1993) 'The Executive's New Coach', *Fortune*.

Discussion issues

1 What is your understanding of mentoring?
2 In what ways are mentoring and counselling similar, and yet different?
3 What can counselling learn from mentoring?
4 Mentoring is a passing fad.

9

Towards Cognitive-Humanistic Counselling

Richard Nelson-Jones

How can you counsel using both your heart and your head? One of the principal dilemmas facing many counsellors is that of reconciling the strengths of the humanistic and the cognitive-behavioural counselling approaches. Each working day numerous counsellors attempt the task of combining the humanity and whole-person focus of the former approaches with the clarity and technical precision of the latter. The same holds true for counsellor trainers and counselling students. This paper articulates some theoretical and practical principles of cognitive-humanistic counselling that draw upon and possibly add to the strengths of existing humanistic and cognitive-behavioural approaches.

Humanistic values

The Concise Oxford Dictionary defines humanism as 'a belief or outlook ... seeking solely rational ways of solving human problems, and concerned with human beings as responsible and progressive intellectual beings' (Thompson 1995: 661). Embedded in this definition is a cognitive approach to humanism.

Values are the principles that guide your life. Cognitive-humanists hold humanistic values. Humanistic values include a belief in the value both of rationality and of humanitarianism. Humanitarians seek to promote human welfare and to practise humane actions, such as being benevolent and compassionate. Such humanistic values are espoused not only by Western humanistic psychology, but also by Eastern religions, such as Buddhism.

Counsellors tend to hold humanistic values. In his national survey of American counsellor values, Kelly reported his findings on a final sample of nearly 500 randomly selected members of the American Counseling Association (Kelly 1995). Of the ten value types derived from the Schwartz Universal Values Questionnaire (Schwartz 1992), respondents scored highest on the value types of benevolence (a concern for the welfare of others with whom one is in frequent personal contact in everyday interaction), self-direction (an aspiration toward independent thought and action and being curious and creative), and universalism (an appreciative concern for the welfare of all people and of nature). Though British data are unavailable, probably most British counsellors share similar humanistic values.

Humanistic values are based on the notion of people being able to improve themselves to show the better qualities of humankind, for example altruism, self-transcendence and co-operation. Though cognitive-behavioural counselling approaches contain humanistic

This chapter was first published in *Counselling*, Journal of the British Association for Counselling, vol. 10, no. 1, pp. 49–54 (1999).

values, possibly such values receive less emphasis than in the humanistic approaches. For example, rational emotive behaviour counselling heavily stresses the value of hedonism, albeit long-range as well as short-range (Ellis 1980, 1996). Also, if anything, cognitive-behavioural counsellors, especially those with a leaning towards traditional behaviourism, value environmental determinism more than humanistic counsellors.

Creating mind

As people think, so they become. Cognitive-humanism stresses the primacy of mind. A basic assumption is that people's minds influence and create their communication, actions and feelings. People's minds are powerful tools that they always have at their disposal. A simple analogy is that of driving a car: barring unforeseen circumstances, how skilfully you think determines how well you drive.

The concept of mind provides a superordinate construct in which various mental processes take place. People have minds that they can create for good or ill. The word brain is a possible synonym for mind. One way to view your mind is that it is the psychological component of your brain.

People create their minds and thoughts within three important contexts: biological, socio-cultural, and the influences of prior learning. Biological influences include: evolutionary traces and instincts; individual differences, such as in intellectual intelligence and emotional intelligence (Goleman 1995); and sexual and affectionate orientation. Throughout history, people's minds have been influenced by contextual considerations such as the time in history in which they live, technological change, culture, race, social class, amongst others. In addition, family-of-origin influences and how individuals continue to process these prior influences affect how they create their minds.

To date, humanistic and cognitive-behavioural counselling approaches have insufficiently emphasized the concept of mind. For example, neither Rogers, Ellis nor Beck uses the concept of mind as a central part of his theoretical statements. This omission is surprising given that the term mind is commonly used in everyday language: for example, using your mind or losing your mind. Furthermore, cognitions, cognitive processes and the experiencing of feelings take place within the context of mind.

How can counsellors and clients control their minds to influence positively how they communicate and act? First, they can understand that they have a mind with a capacity for super-conscious thinking – or thinking about thinking – that they can develop. Second, they can become much more efficient in thinking about their thinking if they view their mental processes in terms of skills that they can train themselves to control. A skill can be viewed as a sequence of choices in a particular area: good choices make for good skills and poor choices for poor skills, though often people make a mixture of good and poor choices in specific skills areas.

Third, counsellors and clients can not only improve their minds to handle current problems but develop their minds to become more effective and loving persons. Fourth, in daily life, they can assiduously practise using their mind skills to influence how they communicate and act.

Below are brief descriptions of six central mind skills. These skills are derived from the work of leading cognitive-behavioural counsellors, such as Beck (Lazarus 1984, 1995;

Beck and Weishaar 1995 and Ellis 1995, 1996). The concept of mind skills enables counsellors to 'surf' different cognitive approaches to counselling without getting trapped in their separate languages. I describe both these six central and other mind skills more fully elsewhere (Nelson-Jones 1997a, 1997b).

- *Creating self-talk*   Instead of talking to yourself negatively before, during and after specific situations, you can acknowledge you have choices and make coping self-statements that assist you to stay calm and cool, establish your goals, coach you in what to do, and affirm the strengths, skills and support factors you possess.
- *Creating visual images*   You can use visual images in ways that calm you down, assist you in acting competently to attain your goals, and help you to resist giving in to bad habits.
- *Creating rules*   Your unrealistic rules make irrational demands on yourself, others, and the environment: for instance, 'I must always be approved of by my others'; 'Others must not make mistakes'; and, 'Everything in my life must be fair.' Instead, you can develop realistic rules: for instance, 'I prefer to be approved of by others, but it's unrealistic to expect this all the time.'
- *Creating perceptions*   You can avoid perceiving yourself and others either too negatively or too positively. You distinguish between fact and inference and make your inferences as accurate as possible. Also, you work on reducing your uncalled-for self-protective tendencies.
- *Creating explanations*   You can explain the causes of events accurately. You avoid assuming too much responsibility by internalizing, 'It's all my fault', or externalizing, 'It's all your fault.'
- *Creating expectations*   You are realistic about the risks and rewards of future actions. You assess threats and dangers accurately. You avoid distorting relevant evidence with unwarranted optimism or pessimism. Your expectations about how well you will perform tasks and about the outcomes of your performance are reasonably accurate.

In reality, some of the mind skills overlap. For instance, all of the skills, even visualizing, involve self-talk. To distinguish the skill of using self-talk I stipulate a definition by stating that mostly it refers to self-statements relevant to coping with specific situations. Interrelationships between skills can also be viewed on the dimension of depth. Arguably, people possessing the rule 'I must always be approved of by others' are more prone to perceiving cues of rejection than those not possessing such a rule.

Inner strength is a way to describe the well-developed mind. People with such minds have a sound sense of what values are important to them, yet are open to new experiences and information. They feel centred and yet allow themselves to be influenced by the experiencing and feedback of others. At the same time as having a mind of their own, their minds incorporate the emotions, preferences and needs of others. They are neither easily threatened nor psychologically self-protective when there is no realistic need for this. They are capable of relating to others on the basis of mutual respect rather than needing to control or be controlled by them. If anything, I adopt a secular approach to mental development and maturity. Undoubtedly, some readers will wish to add a spiritual dimension: namely, that by purifying your mind you become more in touch with the underlying spiritual core of your nature. Christians might say 'The kingdom of God is within', as Jesus did (Luke 17.21), and Buddhists might refer to revealing one's innate Buddha nature.

Mind and communication

Here communication is used as a general term to encompass all externally observable actions. When thinking of any area of communication, there are two main considerations: first, what are the components of skilled behaviour and, second, what interferes with enacting such behaviour? For instance, take the area of creating happier relationships by improving people's partner skills. Seven key partner skills areas are: becoming more outgoing, listening better, showing you care, sharing intimacy, enjoying sex together, managing anger and communicating assertively, and managing relationship problems (Nelson-Jones 1999). Each of these partner skills areas can be viewed as consisting both of communication skills, what to do, and of mind skills, how to allow your mind to enhance rather than to get in the way of your communication.

Many communication skills are relatively straight-forward, for instance, using good attending behaviour when listening or taking turns in pleasuring one another during sexual foreplay. The question then becomes: 'If these skills are so easy, why don't people just do them?' The answer is that mind drives communication and that, unless people successfully address their poor mind skills, frequently they just repeat their poor communication skills.

Mind and feelings

Feelings represent people's animal nature and are not skills in themselves. Physical reactions, for instance muscular tension, both represent and accompany feelings and, in a sense, are indistinguishable. Whereas mind may not drive feelings, it certainly can influence them. As illustrated below, three important areas in which mind can influence feelings are: experiencing feelings, expressing feelings, and managing feelings.

Regarding experiencing feelings, people can use their minds to come to their senses. For instance, they can create self-talk that acknowledges the importance of listening to and understanding their feelings. Also, people can use their minds to help express feelings: for instance, transcending sex-role stereotypes about which feelings men and women should communicate. In addition, skilful use of mind is important in managing unwanted feelings, such as harmful anxiety, and encouraging wanted feelings, such as happiness. For instance, people can question the reality of their anxiety-evoking perceptions to see how closely they fit available facts.

Ten guidelines for counselling practice

Just like there are humanistic approaches and cognitive-behavioural counselling approaches, so there may be cognitive-humanistic approaches, rather than a single approach. Here I offer ten guidelines for counsellors wishing to work within a cognitive-humanistic framework. The guidelines reflect my lifeskills counselling approach

(Nelson-Jones 1997a), but are stated more generally. Without losing the spirit of cognitive-humanism, some counsellors may want to adapt these guidelines to arrive at a way of counselling that is both comfortable for themselves and effective for clients.

Guideline 1: Empower your own mind

Cognitive-humanistic counselling starts at home. Counsellors require a willingness to develop their own minds. Talking the talk without walking the walk is not good enough. Furthermore, you are unlikely to understand the mind skills properly unless you have successfully learned to use them to create your own thoughts skilfully. The Buddhist tradition emphasizes mental development on a daily basis (Thitavanno 1988). Though counsellors need scarcely be Buddhist monks engaging in daily meditation, they require a daily commitment to using and developing their minds. Furthermore, similar to many religious traditions, cognitive-humanistic counsellors require a daily commitment to purifying their minds, something insufficiently emphasized in contemporary cognitive-behavioural counselling approaches. Living a life based on humane values, such as altruism and compassion, requires a daily struggle to confront and cope with harmful anxieties and areas of ignorance that can diminish oneself and one's clients.

Guideline 2: Take pride in your humanistic values

Maslow (1971) observed that many people are inhibited in expressing their 'higher potentials'. He thought that humans repressed the highest just as they repressed the lowest within themselves. Living a life based on humanistic values requires counsellors to acknowledge, express and take pride in their own and their clients' higher potentials. Compassionate and tender hearts, especially if accompanied by tough and humane minds, are very positive attributes.

Possibly counselling is more grounded in humanistic values than either psychiatry or clinical psychology. In the latter professions, sometimes narrow scientific values prevail over humanistic values. In addition, unlike psychiatrists and clinical psychologists, who mainly work in hospitals, counsellors working with a broad range of clients are in a better position to focus on developing mental wellness rather than overcoming mental illness. Cognitive-humanistic counsellors can combine cognitive insights with humane values to develop interventions that help their clients bring out the best in themselves and others or, in Maslow's words, to express their 'higher potentials'.

Guideline 3: See the goal of counselling as that of empowering clients to develop their own humanity

Counsellors empower clients by strengthening their ability to assume personal responsibility for developing their humanity. When people are being personally responsible they are in the process of making the choices that maximize their own and others' happiness and fulfilment (Nelson-Jones 1995). Personal responsibility is a positive concept whereby you are responsible for making your own choices and affirming your own and others' lives. It contrasts with a common meaning of responsibility, namely that of responsibility to others, including living up to their standards. Though the process of personal responsibility is difficult, it also liberates. It frees counsellors and clients to concentrate on how they can be most effective.

Where possible, cognitive-humanistic counselling aims to help clients adopt and implement a fundamental attitude of personal responsibility for becoming more effective and humane persons. In reality, most counselling work is of a shorter-term nature than that required to bring about what for many clients is a fundamental attitudinal change. Nevertheless, even within the constraints of focusing on specific problems and problematic situations, counsellors can do their best to impart the idea that clients are personally responsible for developing and using the relevant mind and communication skills to manage these problems and situations better and more humanely in future.

Guideline 4: Share a common language with clients

Since humanism is an outlook that is 'concerned with humankind as responsible and progressive human beings', cognitive-humanistic counsellors should treat their clients this way. It is unnecessary to develop theories about clients in one language and then to conduct the counselling conversation in another. For example, central concepts of person-centred theory, such as conditions of worth and self-actualizing tendency, are not shared with clients. Instead the counselling conversation takes place in language similar to the clients' everyday language.

Because counselling's main purpose is to encourage personal responsibility, it is important that clients know how they have been contributing to their problems and how they might assume responsibility for thinking and acting more effectively in future. Consequently, the language both of counselling theory and practice needs to be simple and functional. For example, clients have thoughts rather than cognitions and they deal with situations rather than with activating events.

Furthermore, counsellors may need to teach clients how to think about their problems. The language in which counsellors theorize about problems in private can still be the same as that with which they discuss the same problems with clients in counselling, In successful cognitive-humanistic counselling, clients learn to talk themselves through problems on their own. During counselling, a transfer of thinking takes place. The result of this transfer is that both counsellors and clients now think in the same language about the problems with which clients came for counselling. Since in future clients are going to be the guardians of their own humanity without counselling assistance, they require a functional language for guiding themselves in performing this task.

Guideline 5: Value and vary the counselling relationship

The counselling relationship is the quality and strength of the human connection that counsellors and clients share. A compassionate and humane counselling relationship is fundamental to this approach. Listening and showing understanding skills are central to building quality relationships with clients.

I endorse Lazarus's view that skilled counsellors adapt their counselling relationships to their clients (Lazarus 1993). For instance, when starting counselling, highly anxious and vulnerable clients may require a more gentle approach than seemingly more resilient clients. Also, though a simplification, a useful distinction exists between counsellors possessing relationship orientations and task orientations. Effective counsellors focus both on relationships and on the tasks of helping clients develop mind and communication skills. They go beyond establishing *talking* relationships, where the relationship overshadows the task, to forming supportive *working* relationships, where the relationship facilitates the task. The counselling relationship can support clients as they learn mind and communication skills for self-support.

Guideline 6: Develop clients' assessment and monitoring skills

To foster personal responsibility, it becomes important that not just counsellors but also clients develop good assessment and monitoring skills. At the very least clients can learn to understand how they may be perpetuating the problems and problematic situations which caused them to come for counselling. Cognitive-humanistic counselling focuses on assisting clients to become self-reliant. One of the reasons that clients sustain problems is because they possess insufficient insight into how they think and act.

Developing clients' capacity to understand their contribution to problems not only lays the groundwork for interventions during counselling, but provides the basis on which clients can regulate their mind and communication skills after counselling ends. Though such insights and realizations may come bit by bit as clients become less defensive, more aware and more knowledgeable, counsellors can hasten this process by tactfully sharing their assessments of clients' skills strengths and deficiencies and encouraging clients to assess and monitor themselves. In addition, counsellors can assist clients to become more aware of how, through anxiety and ignorance, they may block experiencing and expressing compassionate and altruistic tendencies.

Guideline 7: Develop a repertoire of counselling interventions

Counsellors require a repertoire of interventions or intervention skills to cover a range of clients' mind and communication skills deficiencies. Such counselling interventions assist clients to nurture and develop their own and others' humanity. Because of the enormous range of clients' problems and areas of poor skills, counsellors may need to specialize in the most useful interventions for the client populations with which they deal.

The object of all counsellor interventions should be to strengthen clients' self-reliance: 'I as a counsellor am of most use to you as a client if I help you to intervene, at first with my assistance but later on your own, to develop and maintain *your* skills to manage *your* problems now and in future.' In general, the better clients are able to manage their psychological pain and problems both during and after counselling, the more energy and love they have available for enhancing their own and others' lives.

Guideline 8: Counsel as though you are a client-centred coach

Cognitive-humanistic counselling asserts that you can be of more assistance to clients if you not only assist them to experience their feelings, but coach them in relevant mind and communication skills as well. Clients as learners require counsellors as trainers or coaches to guide their learning. Counsellors as trainers require not only knowledge of what interventions to provide, but also skills for delivering interventions. The *what* of intervening needs to be supplemented by the *how* of intervening.

Counsellors require the ability to draw on the client's resources as they explain, demonstrate and coach the client in relevant mind and communication skills. For example, when discussing how to approach a forthcoming situation, counsellors can ask clients for their suggestions first. Also, counsellors can encourage client self-assessment before they provide any feedback on how well a client performs a particular skill. Even then, clients are encouraged to assess the validity of the counsellor's feedback from their own viewpoints.

Guideline 9: Engage in developmental education

When counselling individuals, one way to look at the role of cognitive-humanistic counsellors is as developmental educators. In addition, frequently counsellors can create opportunities to work as developmental educators with groups of people. Sometimes, they may run counselling groups based on cognitive-humanistic principles in helping-service settings. On other occasions, counsellors may run developmental education courses outside helping-service settings. For instance, assisting young people to develop partner skills is an important area for developmental education. Some such courses may be run as part of the curriculum in schools, colleges and universities. Also, voluntary agencies, be they church-related or otherwise, can run their own partner skills courses. Elsewhere, I have presented the possible content of a partner skills course based on cognitive-humanistic principles (Nelson-Jones 1999). Part of the importance of successfully training people in partner skills is that such courses lay the foundation for more humane and compassionate family life. Thus partner skills courses can lay the seeds for future generations to possess better mind and communication skills.

Guideline 10: Monitor and evaluate your counselling

Cognitive-humanistic counselling is essentially a learning or educational approach to assisting clients to develop the mind and communication skills they require to fulfil more of their human potential. Eysenck (1994) makes a strong case for the success of approaches to counselling and psychotherapy based on learning principles, such as reinforcement and modelling. However, possibly unlike the behaviour therapies about which Eysenck writes, cognitive-humanism is a philosophy of life in addition to being a counselling approach to clients' problems and problem situations.

Individual counsellors can also, either on their own or with peers or supervisors, evaluate their counselling. Here relevant questions are: 'How good am I at empowering my mind?' 'How skilled am I in the different processes of empowering my clients?' 'How do I know that my clients are becoming more empowered?' McMahon (1998) suggests some simple and practical methods for counsellor self-evaluation.

Concluding comments

Clients, counsellors and all humans have both hearts and heads. For some time now, humanistic writers such as Rogers (1980) and Frankl (1988) have been warning us against dehumanizing and reductionist influences in counselling, psychotherapy and education. Increasingly, in modern technologically advanced societies, people may reduce themselves and one another to become objects or things rather than sentient human beings.

Counselling within a cognitive-humanistic framework provides a 'middle way' between two of the great traditions of counselling, the humanistic and the cognitive-behavioural approaches. The cognitive-humanistic approach addresses a major challenge for counsellors in the new millennium, namely how to increase their effectiveness in assisting clients and others to develop their full humanity. Though I have only presented an overview or vision rather than a detailed description, I hope that many counsellors can identify with the cognitive-humanistic approach to counselling outlined here.

References

Beck, A.T. and Weishaar, M.E. (1995) 'Cognitive therapy', in R.J. Corsini and D. Wedding (eds), *Current Psychotherapies* (5th edn), Itasca, IL: Peacock, pp. 229–61.

Ellis, A. (1980) 'Overview of the clinical theory of rational-emotive therapy', in R. Grieger and J. Boyd (eds), *Rational-Emotive Therapy: A Skills-Based Approach*, New York: Van Nostrand, pp. 1–31.

Ellis, A. (1995) 'Rational emotive behaviour therapy', in R.J. Corsini and D. Wedding (eds), *Current Psychotherapies* (5th edn), Itasca, IL: Peacock, pp. 162–96.

Ellis, A. (1996) *Better, Deeper and More Enduring Brief Therapy: The Rational Emotive Behavior Therapy Approach*, New York: Brunner/Mazel.

Eysenck, H.J. (1994) 'The outcome problem in psychotherapy: what have we learned?', *Behaviour Research and Therapy*, 32: 477–95.

Frankl, V.E. (1988) *The Will to Meaning: Foundations and Applications of Logotherapy*, New York: Meridian.

Goleman, D. (1995) *Emotional Intelligence: Why It Can Matter More Than IQ*, London: Bloomsbury.

Kelly, E.W. (1995) 'Counselor values: a national survey', *Journal of Counseling & Development*, 73: 648–53.

Lazarus, A.A. (1984) *In the Mind's Eye: The Power of Imagery for Personal Enrichment*, New York: Guilford Press.

Lazarus, A.A. (1993) 'Tailoring the therapeutic relationship, or being an authentic chameleon', *Psychotherapy*, 30: 404–7.

Lazarus, A.A. (1995) 'Multimodal therapy', in R.J. Corsini and D. Wedding (eds), *Current Psychotherapies* (5th edn), Itasca, IL: Peacock, pp. 322–55.

Maslow, A.H. (1971) *The Farther Reaches of Human Nature*, Harmondsworth: Penguin.

McMahon, G. (1998) 'News editorial', *Counselling*, 9: 89.

Nelson-Jones, R. (1995) 'Lifeskills counselling', in R. Nelson-Jones, *Theory and Practice of Counselling* (2nd edn), London: Cassell, pp. 349–84.

Nelson-Jones, R. (1997a) *Practical Counselling and Helping Skills: Text and Exercises for the Lifeskills Counselling Model*, London: Cassell.

Nelson-Jones, R. (1997b) *Using Your Mind: Creative Thinking Skills for Work and Business Success*, London: Cassell.

Nelson-Jones, R. (1999) *Creating Happy Relationships: A Guide to Partner Skills*, London: Cassell.

Rogers, C.R. (1980) *A Way of Being*, Boston: Houghton Mifflin.

Schwartz, S.H. (1992) 'Universals in the content and structure of values: theoretical advances and empirical tests in 20 countries', *Advances in Experimental Psychology*, 25: 1–65.

Thitavanno, P. (1988) *Mind Development*, Bangkok: Mahamakut Buddhist University.

Thompson, D. (ed.) (1995) *The Concise Oxford Dictionary* (9th edn), Oxford: Clarendon Press.

Discussion issues

1 What is your understanding of cognitive-humanistic counselling?
2 Is cognitive-humanistic counselling just another form of cognitive-behaviour therapy?
3 In what ways can a coach be client-centred?
4 Counselling within a cognitive-humanistic framework provides a 'middle way' between two of the great traditions of counselling, the humanistic and the cognitive-behavioural approaches.

10

Rational Emotive Behaviour Therapy

An overview

Michael Neenan and Windy Dryden

Background

Rational emotive behaviour therapy (REBT) was founded in 1955 by an American clinical psychologist, Albert Ellis. Ellis (1994) originally practised as a psychoanalyst but became increasingly disenchanted with this approach as he considered it to be long-winded, time-consuming, anti-scientific, needlessly passive and fundamentally wrong in its view that present emotional problems have their roots in early childhood experiences. Having abandoned psychoanalysis in 1953, Ellis, now calling himself a 'psychotherapist', experimented with active-directive approaches to therapy informed by his abiding interest in philosophy, particularly the Stoics, Epictetus and Marcus Aurelius. It is a quote from Epictetus that forms the cornerstone of REBT: 'People are disturbed not by things, but by the views which they take of them.' In other words, emotional distress is largely determined by our perceptions, meanings, evaluations of events rather than by the events themselves. REBT is primarily concerned with how individuals maintain their problems through their belief systems, rather than how these problems were acquired. Since its inception, REBT (called rational-emotive therapy until 1993) has evolved into a sophisticated model of psychotherapy and is one of the leading approaches within the cognitive-behavioural movement.

Basic theory

REBT sets out a primarily cognitively orientated theory of emotions through its ABCDE model of emotional disturbance and its amelioration (Ellis and Dryden 1997). In the model:

A = activating events (actual or inferred past, present or future occurrences; internal or external);
B = evaluative beliefs which mediate the individual's view of these events;
C = emotional and behavioural consequences largely determined by the individual's beliefs about these events;
D = disputing disturbance-producing ideas, particularly irrational beliefs;
E = a new and effective rational outlook.

REBT hypothesizes that rigid and absolute beliefs in the form of musts, shoulds, have tos, got tos, oughts are usually to be found at the core of emotional disturbance, e.g. the

This chapter was first published in *Counselling*, Journal of the British Association for Counselling, vol. 7, no. 4, pp. 317–21 (1996).

anxiety-inducing belief 'I must never make a mistake otherwise I'm pathetic.' Flowing from these primary musts, shoulds, etc., are three major derivatives: awfulizing – defining negative events as so terrible that they cannot be comprehended within a human and therefore realistic scale of grimness; low frustration tolerance (LFT) – the perceived inability to endure discomfort or frustration in one's life and to envisage any happiness while such conditions exist; damnation of self or others – assigning a global negative evaluation to oneself and/or others based on a particular action or trait as in the above example. These rigid beliefs are called irrational (self-defeating) because they are illogical, unrealistic, block or interfere with individuals realizing their goals for change and generate a good deal of emotional disturbance. By forcefully and persistently disputing these distress-inducing ideas through a variety of multi-modal (cognitive, behavioural, emotive, imaginal) methods a rational and effective philosophy of living can be internalized.

Beliefs based on flexible preferences, wishes wants, desires are seen as rational (self-helping) because they are logical, realistic, aid goal-attainment and usually reduce the individual's specific or general level of emotional disturbability, for example the concern-producing belief 'I would greatly prefer not to make a mistake, but there is no reason why I must not do so. If I do make one. I can acknowledge the mistake without condemning myself on the basis of it.' Flowing from these primary preferences, wishes, etc., are three major derivatives and constructive alternatives to the above: anti-awfulizing – negative events are evaluated along a continuum of badness that lies within the realm of rational comprehension; high frustration tolerance – the ability to tolerate or withstand a great deal of difficulty or discomfort in one's life and still achieve some measure of happiness or stability; acceptance of self and others – human beings are seen as fallible and in a state of flux, therefore it is futile to assign to them a single, global rating (though they can rate their individual traits or actions if they so choose).

Two types of disturbance

REBT posits two types of emotional disturbance that underpin most, if not all, neurotic problems: ego and discomfort (Ellis 1979a, 1980). The former type relates to demands made upon oneself, others or the world, and the resulting self-depreciation when these demands are not met, for example 'As I can't have your love, which I must have, this means I'm no good.' The latter type involves demands made upon oneself, others or the world that comfortable life conditions must exist and the consequent frustration when they do not, for example 'I can't stand any longer this turmoil in my life. It shouldn't be this way!' Ego and discomfort disturbance are discrete categories but frequently overlap in emotional distress as when, for example, a man berates himself as weak for being unable to cope with a stressful work environment.

Constructing an emotional vocabulary

Dryden (1995) suggests that emotional reactions to adverse life events can be divided into unhealthy and healthy negative feelings with their cognitive correlates of, respectively,

Table 10.1   *A vocabulary of unhealthy and healthy negative emotions*

Unhealthy	Healthy
Anxiety	Concern
Depression	Sadness
Guilt	Remorse
Shame	Regret
Hurt	Disappointment
Damning anger	Non-damning anger
Jealousy	Concern about one's relationship
Envy (malicious)	Non-malicious desire to possess another's advantages

demands and preferences (see Table 10.1). This is not meant to be prescriptive in the sense of telling clients how to feel but a means of establishing which emotions may require therapeutic attention in order to alleviate the client's suffering, for example focusing on a woman's prolonged damning anger and depression over being rejected by her partner rather than on her non-damning anger at queue-jumpers. Transforming unhealthy negative emotions into healthy ones through attitudinal change can help individuals to bear what they perceive to be unbearable and thereby help them to adapt constructively to harsh or grim reality.

Practice

REBT therapists teach clients two forms of responsibility: (1) emotional – that they largely construct their emotional disturbance which they may blame on others for causing; and (2) therapeutic – that in order to overcome their problems they need to carry out a variety of tasks often on a lifelong basis if they wish to maintain their therapeutic gains (Dryden and Neenan 1995). In order to help clients absorb these responsibilities, REBTers use an active-directive approach that sorts out clients' presenting problems into their ABC components and which includes encouraging them to move away from A–C thinking (e.g. 'He makes me anxious') to embracing B–C thinking (e.g. 'How do I make myself anxious about him?'). Such a paradigmatic shift in understanding emotional causation can come as a shock to some clients as well as act as a major reason for them to terminate therapy prematurely. The following case example illustrates some of the steps in the REBT counselling sequence.

Early problem-solving focus

While REBT therapists pay attention to developing a therapeutic alliance through warmth, empathy and unconditional acceptance of their clients, they also wish to encourage them to start tackling their problems as quickly as possible. This can often engender a sense of empowerment as clients bring clarity to chaos, order to confusion. In the following interchange we show how the REBT therapist helps the client to do this:

Therapist: Which problem would you like to start with?

Client: I get knots in my stomach every time I have to do any public speaking.

Therapist: Can you describe a specific example?

[REBT therapists argue that analysing specific examples helps clients to be clear about self-defeating emotions and behaviours and the irrational beliefs that underpin them.]

Client: Yes, I had to give a presentation to some senior managers and my stomach was churning, heart racing, my head was spinning … that sort of thing. I felt physically sick. I don't know how I got through it. It's always the same.

Therapist: So you were highly anxious, bordering on panic.

[Early on in the therapeutic process REBTers help their clients to identify their unhealthy negative emotions.]

Client: Exactly.

Therapist: Do all of your colleagues experience similar anxiety when they give presentations?

Client: A few do but most of them don't. Some of them are as cool as a cucumber. That's how I want to be, if possible.

Therapist: We can say then that it isn't the talks themselves that make you anxious otherwise all your colleagues would be, but some ideas that you bring to these talks that really are the culprits. Would you agree with that assessment?

[Here the REBT therapist helps the client to understand that it is not A (that is, giving a talk) that determines his anxiety, but the beliefs he holds about giving the talk at A.]

Client: Yes, I would but I don't know what these ideas are. My panic just seems to descend upon me and I can't do anything about it.

Therapist: Well, let's find out what's going on.

What is the client most disturbed about and how to start dealing with it?

At the core of the client's anxiety is, REBT hypothesizes, a rigid and unqualified irrational (self-defeating) belief in the form of a must or should. At this stage of the assessment, the therapist is unclear as to what the client is most disturbed about at A (known as the critical A) and seeks to elicit it through a process known as inference chaining, that is, linking the client's personally significant assumptions about giving presentations. This process combines speed with depth in moving the client from the periphery to the centre of his anxiety by encouraging him to assume the worst:

Therapist: Now close your eyes and imagine standing in front of your senior managers. How are you feeling?

Client: Very anxious!

Therapist: Now what is anxiety-provoking in your mind about giving the presentation?

[Here the therapist initiates the inference chain.]

Client: I might make a mistake.

Therapist: Let's assume that you do. Then what?

[In inference chaining, the therapist does not challenge the client's inference; rather she uses it to go deeper into the chain.]

Client: They might think I'm incompetent.
Therapist: And if they do …?
Client: [starting to panic] Oh! God. I can see them rejecting me.

[This seems like the critical A because the client begins to panic.]

Therapist: So you are standing there alone and rejected. What's going through your mind at that very moment?
Client: I'm totally unlikable, useless, no one wants me. I might as well kill myself.
Therapist: Okay, open your eyes now. Out of those things that you fear might happen to you, which is the most fearful?

[Here the therapist double checks with the client concerning the nature of the critical A.]

Client: That I'll lose their approval and end up worthless.
Therapist: In their eyes or yours?
Client: Ultimately mine. But none of this has happened yet.
Therapist: But it might do and that's what drives your anxiety.

At this point the therapist might contrast, among other options, the emotional and behavioural outcomes of a philosophy based on demands with one based on preferences and ask the client which one is present in his thinking:

Therapist: What do you think you are demanding at this point?
Client: I'm demanding that I must have their approval otherwise I'll see myself as worthless.

[Having identified the critical A, the therapist helps the client to identify his major demand about this A.]

Therapist: Now if you want to be, as you said earlier, 'as cool as a cucumber' when you give these presentations, what do you need to change?
Client: That rigid belief of mine. It hasn't done me much good over the years.
Therapist: Well, we'll do something about that through a variety of disputing methods which will encourage you to examine this belief in great detail. Now let me start by asking you how, in your mind, does losing their approval through a poor presentation make you worthless?

[Here the therapist begins to dispute the client's self-downing derivative from his demand.]

Client: I've always been like that – looking to others to make me feel good about myself.
Therapist: Okay, so you've subscribed to this belief for a long time. In REBT, we believe it is more important to focus on how the belief is being maintained rather than how it was originally acquired in order to start dismantling it as soon as possible. So let me ask you again, how are you a worthless person because you've lost their approval?
Client: Well, no one wants to be disliked, do they?

[In disputing, it often happens that the client responds to a question about his irrational belief with the evidence in favour of his rational belief. The therapist notes this and then returns to the original inquiry.]

Therapist: Probably not, but not every person condemns him- or herself on the basis of being disliked by others. You're giving power to others, whether they know it or not, to control your feelings rather than you controlling them.
Client: But I can't seem to have faith in myself that I'm still okay if others reject me. I've nothing inside of me to fall back on.

Therapist: That's because self-esteem, which REBT sees as based on conditional self-worth, often vanishes when things go wrong or people reject us, whereas unconditional self-acceptance, which I want to teach you, is an enduring means of support irrespective of how others are treating you and is always something 'to fall back on' as well as the basis for addressing the problems in your life.

[In disputing clients' irrational beliefs, REBTers often use a blend of Socratic questions (with which the therapist in this interchange began) and short didactic explanations about rational concepts as in the above therapist response.]

Client: I can see how that would be a better way but I don't think I could ever be like that. I'm too set in my ways.
Therapist: That may be true, but shall we put it to the test and review the situation after six sessions?
Client: Okay, I'll give it a try.

The therapist outlines some of the potential problems involved in the process of change, such as feeling strange or unnatural as individuals start to undergo personality change – called the 'I'm not me' syndrome or cognitive emotive dissonance (Grieger and Boyd 1980), and a major reason why some clients may drop out of therapy at this point. Also that sustained hard work and practice will be needed to effect such change and can trigger low frustration tolerance (LFT) beliefs, such as 'Change is too hard, as it must not be, and I can't stand it!' Ellis (1979b) advises clients that force and energy rather than milk-and-water methods are usually required to remove irrational ideas and internalize rational ones. This can be difficult for clients to achieve who believe that they have to go very slowly in tackling their problems and therefore may actually reinforce their emotional disturbance, for example 'I'm so fragile I have to go at this pace.'

At the end of the first session, as at the end of every session, homework tasks (or whatever term the client prefers to use) are negotiated with the client in order for him to practise strengthening his rational beliefs and weakening his irrational ones and thus developing both competence and confidence in facing his problems as well as minimizing the potential for him to become dependent upon the therapist. The therapist is also alert to the client seeking her approval which, when it occurs, she challenges and places within the context of his presenting problems. The therapist elicits sessional feedback from the client to determine which aspects of counselling he finds both helpful and unhelpful. This will assist her to tailor therapy to his requirements, but not if the client's suggestions appear to exacerbate his psychological problems, for example the client seeking continual reassurance that the therapist likes him.

Course of therapy

In striving for unconditional self-acceptance as a fallible human being, the client found the following methods instrumental in realizing this goal. Bibliotherapy – reading self-help literature such as Paul Hauck's *Why Be Afraid?* (1981) and *Hold Your Head Up High* (1991). Imagery – for example, feeling highly anxious as he imagines, being rejected for giving a poor presentation and then, with no alteration of details, feeling concerned about what has occurred but without rejecting himself. Behavioural – such as giving as many presentations as possible in order to habituate himself to the discomfort involved in carrying them out, as well as developing his public speaking skills. Emotive – principally, shame-attacking exercises (Ellis 1969) in which he acts in a 'shameful' way (for example taking an imaginary dog for a walk) in order to invite public ridicule, criticism or disapproval and distinguish between condemning an action but refraining from condemning himself on the basis of it. Such exercises helped him to remove the 'horror' (emotional disturbance) of losing others' approval. All these methods were used in the service of cognitive change as the client repeatedly and forcefully chipped away at his irrational ideas.

The client's approval needs were present in other areas of his life (such as with his partner, friends, neighbours) and tackling his core belief enabled these other problem areas eventually to be addressed concurrently rather than consecutively. The client stayed beyond the agreed six sessions and actually attended for twelve. At the end of therapy, his anxiety had greatly reduced because he was striving to be much more self-accepting in the face of potential or actual rejection. Practical benefits experienced in developing a rational outlook included delivering presentations in a highly competent manner as he was much less afflicted by performance-diminishing anxiety.

At the follow-up appointments (three, six and twelve months), he said he felt a greater sense of autonomy in his life which enabled him to take hitherto avoided risks, such as seeking promotion and leaving his unsatisfactory relationship. He realized that maintaining and deepening his therapeutic gains would be a lifelong commitment which would continue to include relapses but 'using the ABCDE of REBT usually gets my life back on the rails again'. The client had become his own therapist, which is the ultimate aim of REBT.

Applications of REBT

Ellis and his colleagues have produced many books on REBT including a growing number on its clinical application to specific emotional and behavioural problems such as substance abuse (Ellis et al. 1988), anxiety (Warren and Zgourides 1991), and those experienced in childhood and adolescence (Ellis and Bernard 1983; Bernard and Joyce 1984). REBT is applied in various treatment modalities: individuals (Dryden and Yankura 1993), couples (Ellis et al. 1989), and families (Huber and Baruth 1989). REBT is used non-clinically in business and industry where the word 'therapy' is dropped and the 'focus in [industrial] training is always on the relation of self-defeating thinking to low productivity, not on irrationality and emotional consequences' (DiMattia 1991: 309).

Research findings

Silverman et al. (1992) in a review of 89 outcome studies of REBT carried out between 1982 and 1989 supported earlier research (DiGiuseppe and Miller 1977; McGovern and Silverman 1984) that REBT 'has constantly verified its role as an efficacious therapy applicable in a variety of problem situations' (p. 169). However, a number of conceptual and methodological flaws in REBT research need to be addressed if REBT is to improve its scientific status as an empirically based psychotherapeutic approach. This task is under way as REBT seeks responsible criticism, from both within and without, in order to increase its therapeutic efficacy (Kendall et al. 1995).

References

Bernard, M.E. and Joyce, M.R. (1984) *Rational-Emotive Therapy with Children and Adolescents*, New York: John Wiley & Sons.

DiGiuseppe, R.A. and Miller, N.J. (1977) 'A review of outcome studies on rational-emotive therapy', in A. Ellis and R. Grieger (eds), *Handbook of Rational-Emotive Therapy*, New York: Springer.

DiMattia, D.J. (1991) 'Using RET effectively in the workplace', in M.E. Bernard (ed.), *Using Rational-Emotive Therapy Effectively: A Practitioner's Guide*, New York: Plenum Press, pp. 303–17.

Dryden, W. (1995) *Preparing for Client Change in Rational Emotive Behaviour Therapy*, London: Whurr.

Dryden, W. and Neenan, M. (1995) *Dictionary of Rational Emotive Behaviour Therapy*, London: Whurr.

Dryden, W. and Yankura, J. (1993) *Counselling Individuals: A Rational-Emotive Handbook* (2nd edn), London: Whurr.

Ellis, A. (1969) *Suggested Procedures for a Weekend of Rational Encounter*, New York: Institute for Rational-Emotive Therapy.

Ellis, A. (1979a) 'Discomfort anxiety: a new cognitive-behavioral construct', Part 1, *Rational Living*, 14 (2): 3–8.

Ellis, A. (1979b) 'The issue of force and energy in behavior change', *Journal of Contemporary Psychotherapy*, 10: 83–97.

Ellis, A. (1980) 'Discomfort anxiety a new cognitive-behavioral construct', Part 2, *Rational Living*, 15 (1): 25–30.

Ellis, A. (1994) *Reason and Emotion in Psychotherapy* (2nd edn), New York: Carol Publishing.

Ellis, A. and Bernard, M.E. (eds) (1983) *Rational-Emotive Approaches to the Problems of Childhood*, New York: Plenum Press.

Ellis, A. and Dryden, W. (1997) *The Practice of Rational-Emotive Therapy* (2nd edn), New York: Springer.

Ellis, A., McInerney, J.F., DiGiuseppe, R. and Yeager, R.J. (1988) *Rational-Emotive Therapy with Alcoholics and Substance Abusers*, New York: Pergamon Press.

Ellis, A., Sichel, J.L., Yeager, R.J., DiMattia, D.J. and DiGiuseppe, R. (1989) *Rational-Emotive Couples Therapy*, New York: Pergamon Press.

Grieger, R. and Boyd, J. (1980) *Rational-Emotive Therapy: A Skills-Based Approach*, New York: Van Nostrand Reinhold.

Hauck, P. (1981) *Why Be Afraid?*, London: Sheldon Press.

Hauck, P. (1991) *Hold Your Head Up High*, London: Sheldon Press.

Huber, C. and Baruth, L. (1989) *Rational-Emotive Family Therapy: A Systems Perspective*, New York: Springer.

Kendall, P.C., Haaga, D., Ellis, A., Bernard, M.E., DiGiuseppe, R. and Kassinove, H. (1995) 'Rational-emotive therapy in the 1990s and beyond: current status, recent revisions, and research questions', *Clinical Psychology Review*, 15: 169–86.

McGovern, T. and Silverman, M. (1984) 'A review of outcome studies on rational-emotive therapy', *Journal of Rational-Emotive Therapy*, 2: 7–18.

Silverman, M.S., McCarthy, M. and McGovern, T. (1992) 'A review of outcome studies of rational-emotive therapy from 1982–1989', *Journal of Rational-Emotive and Cognitive-Behavior Therapy*, 10 (3): 111–86.

Warren, R. and Zgourides, G. (1991) *Anxiety Disorders: A Rational-Emotive Perspective*, New York: Pergamon Press.

Discussion issues

1   What do you think of the REBT view that emotional disturbance is largely self-induced?
2   Does disputing a client's irrational beliefs seem too confrontational?
3   Why are homework tasks a crucial part of therapy?
4   What are some of the differences between self-esteem and self-acceptance?

11

Psychosynthesis

A psychology with a soul

Diana Whitmore

Initial motivation: freedom from pain

'It hurts.' 'I want to feel better.' 'I want to know what is happening to me.' 'I want to be free.' Every good therapist will want to respond sensitively to what is motivating a client in the moment. Nearly always our initial motivation involves a deep pain we are experiencing which usually reflects a much deeper need contained within the pain and the problem. People seek therapy because they are in pain. Pain in this context is one of the most powerful motivating forces for change. The good news is that, although seemingly negative, this step provides a healthy, energizing and life-affirming force for the beginning of the therapeutic work.

Psychosynthesis maintains that when an individual seeks to enter therapy, there is invariably more lying beneath the immediately obvious. We could question whether our problems in life are 'distractions to be got rid of' – the result of inadequacy – or psychological wounding from childhood experiences. Alternatively, we could entertain the hypothesis that problems and obstacles at their deepest level are inherently meaningful, evolutionary, coherent and potentially transformative. Perhaps it is no accident that various conflicts become foreground issues at particular times in our lives. Old psychological forms die in order for new ones to be born. The energy of conflict is the energy of transformation.

Reframing pathology: the creative use of pain and crisis

Psychosynthesis hypothesizes a model of 'emerging purpose' which provides a progressive context within which the client can experience herself and make choices, rather than merely mend brokenness. A client will report many experiences which will prompt the psychosynthesis therapist to speculate as follows: What is trying to emerge through these difficulties, and what potential for growth is contained within them? If the client was unconsciously seeking a step forward, what might it be? What old behaviour pattern is dying in order for something new to be born? This attitude provides a way of 'reframing' experience, enabling the creative potential within a problem to be actualized.

This chapter was first published in *Counselling*, Journal of the British Association for Counselling, vol. 7, no. 2, pp. 127–31 (1996).

The existential crisis

Also among those who seek therapy are many who are basically healthy and able to function well, but who experience a sense of dissatisfaction with the quality of life and long for greater fulfilment. There may be a need, conscious or unconscious, to expand individual identity beyond personal existence. The choice to enter counselling can reflect a life-affirming impulse which transcends the confines of conventional life – a search for meaning, for purpose and a deeper identity leads to this choice.

Although a person may appear to be integrated and to live a more or less successful life with many goals achieved, her life can lose its lustre and become somewhat grey and meaningless. The things in life that were once rewarding may become no longer so. This is not neurosis, for often the individual has attained a level of functioning readily called 'normal' by modern mental health standards. But once an individual can stand on her own two feet, what does she do then? Just stand there? She may ask herself questions like: 'What am I here for?' 'What is the meaning of my life?' 'What is my place in the world?' 'There must be more to life than this!' These pertinent questions may drive a person to seek therapy.

The process of therapy

Assagioli likens the three principal stages of psychosynthesis therapy to Dante's *Divine Comedy*: first there is the descent into the Inferno, which represents the psychodynamic phase of descent into the lower unconscious; then the journey through Purgatory which resembles working with the client's existential reality; and finally the ascent to Paradise which symbolizes exploring the transpersonal dimension of the psyche.

The past: assessment of the unconscious

Psychosynthesis has its roots in psychoanalysis. Before founding psychosynthesis, Dr Roberto Assagioli (1888–1974) was a member of the Freud Society in Zurich in 1910 and, together with various other pioneers of the psychoanalytic movement, was among the first to bring psychoanalysis to Italy.

The first step in psychosynthesis is the attainment of a certain level of self-knowledge, the ability to move within one's inner world with some degree of awareness. The influence of our childhood is multi-dimensional, often indirect and pervasive. It profoundly affects our capacity for love and intimacy, for assertion and self-affirmation; it determines our perception of life, and colours our deepest attitudes and values. Unless we are to remain puppets to the past, our neurotic elements must be brought into consciousness and transformed.

Psychosynthesis counselling begins by assessing the client's blocks and potentials to allow for a purposeful exploration of the unconscious. In order to reach the roots of psychological complexes, childhood experiences are uncovered with particular regard to the impact they currently have on the client's life. Our past, our history, our childhood experiences do not sit quietly in the basement of our psyche. Repression, suppression or denial of feelings creates emotional stress, Psychosynthesis works extensively to release the grip of the past and to learn to express real, but buried feelings in the present. When a natural capacity for expression of feelings is redeemed, emotional health can be re-established.

Our perception is also conditioned and coloured by our history. From past experiences, defence mechanisms are formed, which preserve the stability of the personality but do so at the expense of distorting reality. They lower anxiety in order to maintain a stable level of functioning. Initially these defences serve us well, but later they may restrict our quality of life. These 'loyal soldiers' must be acknowledged for how they have served us in the past, but then released as obsolete.

Psychosynthesis contends that the past may have an even deeper function in determining the quality of our life as adults. Our inner life and world may be incongruent with our outer life, which contributes to a sense of inauthenticity. As a result, the integrity of feeling at home in the world may be lacking. Mentally too, our history influences our attitudes, beliefs and philosophies about life. We may, for example, unconsciously believe that people cannot be trusted, or that we will never get our needs met. These basic attitudes will in turn condition our image of reality.

The main difference between psychodynamic work with the unconscious and psychosynthetic work is that psychosynthesis delves into the past in a focused way on particular life issues. Indiscriminate delving into the unconscious is not encouraged. The client's 'presenting problem' will evoke a further exploration into the roots and historical background. The principle in psychosynthesis is for awareness to be expanded into the unconscious regarding an issue in the client's life and then for that awareness to be integrated in a controlled manner. This work with the unconscious will include attention to the dynamics of transference and countertransference. The transferred childhood pattern which clients unconsciously 'live again', in their relationship with the therapist, needs also to be addressed.

The present: exploration of subpersonalities and identity

Experiences which are familiar and repetitious are often to be found in the client's presenting problems. It is as if some uncontrollable force is conditioning both inner and outer experience. Recurring situations, seemingly out of the client's control, result in predictable and limited behavioural responses. Every chronic life pattern has its historical base, its biography, often traumatic, around which many other painful experiences accumulate. Whether positive or negative, the core experience tends to repeat itself again and again, forming a generalized behaviour pattern which in similar situations evokes similar responses. Eventually the client will perceive her whole world through this 'psychological system' and it will colour vividly her attitudes and expectations.

The memories belonging to such a life pattern will have a similar basic theme and carry a strong emotional charge of the same quality. For example, a pattern of low self-esteem will contain the client's memories of past experiences, of the humiliating and degrading situations that damaged it. These life experiences will form identities which form autonomous configurations within the personality. They are discrete psychological identities, co-existing as a multitude of lives within one person; each with its own specific behaviour pattern and corresponding self-image, feelings and beliefs. Their unique characteristics form a relatively unified whole.

Each of our identities has an exclusive way of experiencing and responding to life. We are often different when we are with our children compared to when we are in our workplace; or in certain challenging situations we quickly lose the calm, self-assured demeanour that we display most of the time. When we shift our identifications in this way it is often in reaction to the demands of the situation and in response to the unconscious feelings evoked. We are unaware of the expectations from the environment and the demands of our inner world that control us. We are caught in ambivalence, confusion or conflict.

These identifications are usually unconscious and largely beyond our control. Our identifications will change in response to the demands of both inner and outer conditions, much more than our desire and will. If we identify too closely with any one aspect of our personality, we lose accessibility to the rest of our personality. We need to free ourselves from the limited and dominating behaviour of any one particular identity.

Self-identification and psychological freedom

A longer-term goal of psychosynthesis therapy is the fostering of a stable sense of identity. Exploring the unconscious, working with chronic life patterns and specific identities foster the recognition that our true identity is beyond the contents of our consciousness. We all have within us an element which is permanent, consistent and unchanging. Little by little we can acquire an internal point of reference, a centre of identity which is psychologically free, uncluttered and available at will. A goal of psychosynthesis is to detach and free ourselves in order to access more of our personality, resolve conflicts and become more self-determining and autonomous. This will provide access to a wider range of experience and choice.

The above, longer-term work of psychosynthesis therapy is not the same as 'distancing' or suppression. We too often live submerged in a particular identity, role or behaviour. We are lost in an unconscious way of being. Liberating ourselves from an identification does not mean rejecting or abandoning it. On the contrary, to be conscious brings more aliveness.

The future: the transpersonal dimension of therapy

As previously mentioned, establishing a stable centre of identity and a degree of inner mastery is an aim of psychosynthesis therapy. A balanced emphasis on the development of self-identity provides the psychological stability for an awakening and exploration of the transpersonal domain. The revival of interest in the transpersonal today is triggered by an increasing dissatisfaction with competitive materialism, the pursuit of immediate gratification, as well as by a conscious or unconscious search for different and higher values and activities, a longing for what is sometimes termed 'spiritual'.

Few would deny that people are hungry for truth, goodness, beauty, but in our culture, and in psychology, it is difficult to talk about this transpersonal dimension. Our spiritual lives have become as embarrassing to us as sexual lives were to the Victorians. Until recently our scientific bias has limited us to quantitative and statistical exploration. In spite of accounts of experience of a higher reality found in all ages, we are reluctant to admit the existence or experience of spiritual values.

Freud saw the desire for something beyond the personal as neurotic – a regressive tendency to return to the undifferentiated primal unity of our mother's womb; or as a sublimation of drives and instincts. Assagioli criticized Freud for labelling our higher values and achievements as adaptations of these lower instincts and drives. Assagioli maintained that these higher impulses, desires and motives exist in their own right, develop whether or not the aggressive and sexual drives are satisfied and have their own source – a spiritual centre of identity.

Transpersonal work in therapy is not a substitute for psychological work, but rather a vivifying and practical complement. A therapist working in a transpersonal context will be committed to a particular set of assumptions which are not absolute, but are useful as 'working hypotheses'. A few commonly adopted contexts are:

- In each of us there exists a spiritual centre of identity, the Self, which includes the personal dimension, but goes beyond it, and both the experience and expression of this Self fosters growth and well-being.
- Pain, crisis and pathology are opportunities and challenges for growth and creative steps forward, and are intimately connected with our self-realization.
- We can benefit from identifying a purpose in life which is meaningful and potentially fulfilling.
- Spiritual drives are as real, fundamental and indispensable as the basic psychological ones, and these needs must be met for optimum health. A goal of psychosynthesis is to enable the client to meet physical, emotional, mental and spiritual needs appropriately in accordance with individual temperament. Hence, no one principle, method or technique is correct for everyone.
- It is therapeutically valuable to explore experiences of superconscious content, with those descending into the client's field of consciousness or those found in the process of transcendent levels – creativity, intuitive insight, spiritual revelation, mythical and archetypal realms and altruistic imperatives.

Transpersonal experiences can arise at any time, often spontaneously and when least expected. There are various modalities through which the contents of the superconscious emerge into consciousness: through intuitive insight into one's problems, through the imagination and images which carry a positive charge, through inspiration and its subsequent creative expression, or through illumination which reveals the essential nature of life and its true unity. The therapist who holds a transpersonal context will use these moments to further the client's work on herself by responding to them and encouraging their elaboration.

The Self

The Self can be described as a person's most authentic identity, the deepest experience of Being. It can be a conscious experience for some, while for others it may be latent until superconscious experiences stimulate awareness of its existence. Experiences of beauty, of creative intelligence, of illumination, of insight into life, and of altruistic imperatives can awaken the individual to this deeper identity.

The yearning for unity or the lack of connection to Self/soul can underlie many psychological symptoms: a chronic feeling of isolation; self-destructive behaviours such as alcohol or drug consumption, which dull reality and create a false sense of unity; suicidal impulses which may suggest an unconscious desire to return to security and the primal unity of the womb; existential despair and hopelessness.

It is also worth noting that the awakening of the Self may also be stimulated by crisis and negative experiences. For one client the death of a loved one stimulated a search for meaning which led her to the experience of the Self; another, overwhelmed by a mid-life crisis, found relief through deep acceptance of her Being, which altered her priorities and life direction. For an over-stressed businessman, the loss of his valued career shocked him into a transcendent experience of his true identity far beyond his role as a businessman. These insights are often gained through psychospiritual work in therapy. In times of stress or trauma, people in therapy may be more able to take a wider perspective of life and maintain a greater sense of proportion.

A transpersonal context

A therapist working in a transpersonal context recognizes the pivotal role of consciousness in determining the outcome of therapy. Consciousness is both the instrument and the object of change, and the therapist will be less concerned with 'problem-solving' than with enhancing the conditions in which the client can address the challenge creatively. The emphasis is upon learning 'how' to deal effectively with problems as they arise, rather than resolving a particular situation in the client's life.

Most essentially, working from a transpersonal context means that, regardless of method or technique, the therapist has taken a firm stand for basic human goodness, placed her trust in the client's fundamental 'all-rightness' and is willing to accompany her on her journey to wholeness.

The therapeutic relationship

Working from a transpersonal context also creates a transpersonal element in the therapist's and client's relationship – so essential for sincere and successful work. The ground on which they stand together is rich with the necessary components for the client to both heal herself and move progressively forward. There is no doubt that the quality of the human relationship has a profound influence on determining the outcome of therapy. Without a 'bifocal vision' – one which sees both the light and the shadow in clients – and without a context which sees the client as more than her pathology, the therapist reduces greatly the effectiveness of the work.

Assagioli spoke of the relationship being the very heart of the therapeutic process. He believed that without authentic human relating, trust would not be established between therapist and client, and without this essential ingredient little growth was possible. He further elaborated the dangers of both dependency and projection of the sublime without a genuine relationship. The client might remain dependent upon the authority figure of the therapist for answers to her problems and guidance towards normative psychological health. Autonomy and a healthy separation from the therapist then become immensely difficult. Projection of the sublime occurs when the client perceives the therapist as more intelligent, more creative, more in possession of all the positive qualities for which she yearns.

Transference and countertransference

Assagioli did not see transference as the centre of gravity around which the therapy revolves in the way that Freud did. However, he did acknowledge transference and countertransference as tremendously important factors to be conscious of. A psychosynthesis psychotherapist aims to dissolve the transference *as* it emerges, rather than encourage it to build into a full transference. A full transference neurosis is not encouraged or discouraged, nor is it seen as the core of the therapeutic process.

The psychosynthesis attitude towards transference is to treat it *as* it arises as one of *many* ways to help the client confront her issues. *Much* of the 'intrapsychic' work in psychosynthesis, which actively and experientially engages the client, attains the same goal as transference work – to deal with unconscious neurotic conflict and to strengthen the ego.

Erich Fromm said that, after all, it is the child in the client who is transferring. Hence, any work done with the *inner child* of the client will address the same basic level as working with transference. Psychosynthesis uses 'active techniques' like subpersonality work and guided imagery to access 'inner-child levels' in therapeutic work. Working experientially with parental relationships can also address transference issues. Re-living and re-experiencing parental relationships can release past trauma and profoundly affect transference dynamics. Basically, psychosynthesis will address transference intrapsychically by work with the *inner child* and parental work, as well as interpersonally, in more traditional interpersonal work.

Assagioli also stressed that the therapist must not lump all client responses into the transference construct, but must use discrimination to examine and assess their validity. The therapist is wise to work within herself for her own affective response to the client. For instance, if the client feels judged, the therapist must look within herself for these feelings towards the client. In the safety of the therapeutic situation, the client may also be 'trying out' new behaviours that are being learned. For example, if she has previously conformed in order to win approval, the first place where she may begin to be assertive is in her relationship with the therapist (as a prelude to doing so in life).

Some but not all of the countertransference may belong to an earlier part of the therapist's life. As with transference, countertransference is not always pathological, but can be an authentic human response to the client. On the other hand, it can also be a sign of the unconscious dynamics that are being played out and are pulling the therapist into a repetitive response. Analysing countertransference helps to detect and evaluate the transference.

Our interface with society

Finally, just as treating the symptoms of disease brings relief but does not heal the whole person, therapy without exploring the client's relationship with the larger whole would be limited and unreal. We do not exist in isolation, but within the context of the larger whole of society and of an intricate network of relationships. With its emphasis on purpose and meaning, psychosynthesis therapy places a high value on this area. Individual identity is not the end-result but leads to a recognition of interdependence and to a more creative response to life.

At any time the client may naturally begin to question and want to explore the nature of values and how she chooses to relate to her world. This idea is congruent with Maslow's 'hierarchy of needs', which proposes that, as personal survival, safety and self-esteem needs are fulfilled, the individual will move towards a more universal orientation, a natural expansion of ego boundaries and a desire to make life choices that are consistent with this large identity.

Bibliography

Assagioli, R. (1993) *Psychosynthesis: A Manual of Principles and Techniques*, London: HarperCollins.
Assagioli, R. (1994) *The Act of Will*, London: HarperCollins.
Assagioli, R. (1991) *Transpersonal Development*, London: HarperCollins.
Ferrucci, P. (1990) *What We May Be*, London: HarperCollins.
Ferrucci, P. (1990) *Inevitable Grace*, Wellingborough: Thorsons.
Hardy, J. (1989) *Psychology With a Soul*, London: Penguin Books.
Parfitt, W. (1994) *The Elements of Psychosynthesis*, Shaftesbury: Element Books.
Whitmore, D. (1994) *Psychosynthesis Counselling in Action*, London: Sage.

Discussion issues

1 How important do you think it is for the counsellor to recognize and affirm that the client is essentially a soul or spiritual being and is *more* than his or her pathology, and what are the implications of not doing so?
2 What does it mean to you to validate and explore the realm of an individual's potential as well as their existential reality?
3 Do you recognize the fundamental human need for meaning and yearning for unity with one's own Self?
4 How do you experience your own need for unity, both with your Self and with others?

12

In the Counsellor's Chair

Multimodal therapy

Stephen Palmer interviews Professor Arnold A. Lazarus

Arnold, why did you decide to enter the world of psychotherapy and counselling?

There are many different reasons, but I suppose the main one was tied up with the fact that even as a youngster of 14 or 15 I was the neighbourhood shrink. I was quite sensitive and caring, at least that was the feedback I received from my peers and there was gratification in being able to help. I became fascinated with the mind. I was never interested in organic medicine which was why I never went to medical school and only entered the field of psychology when I was told I didn't have to become a medical doctor or a physician to practise psychotherapy. I actually started university with a view to becoming a journalist but the English department at my *alma mater* was very boring and I found the psychology books more interesting than the professors! I read them with my eyeballs bulging with excitement and gravitated towards the notion of helping people psychologically and emotionally. It dovetailed with the way I had always been, even as a youngster. I can think of no other profession for which I would be better suited.

How did you come to develop multimodal therapy?

Largely because I was disappointed with the follow-up information I had gathered when using other approaches. I found that a lot of people tended to relapse, not only with problems such as weight, but even with anxiety and depression. I kept feeling that somehow more could be done. The operative term is 'more' – more could be done. Now there's obviously a point of diminishing returns. I mean, two aspirins are good for you, but ten are not five times better! So you've got to have a cut-off point somewhere. But as I looked at what therapies were doing I realized they were focusing on pet areas, pet theories, pet problems and missing the spectrum. I saw therapists doing excellent work in a rather narrow way. I would see people who would come away after many years of psychoanalysis with insights to spare but no one had ever taught them to stand up for their rights; they were very unassertive. No one had ever taught them any interpersonal skills so they were often critical, demanding, inept and getting into trouble. And that's what I meant when I said more could be done and that's when I started using what I described as 'broad spectrum methods' using the analogy of broad spectrum antibiotics. I was also aware that one had to be extremely systematic. It wasn't enough to just have a broad range of techniques.

We had to categorize them, prioritize them; this was the thinking behind it and this was what led to the eventual development of multimodal therapy.

Can you explain what is meant by the phrase 'a systematic and technically eclectic approach' which is often used to describe multimodal therapy?

The term 'eclectic' can mean anything. It can mean people borrowing bits and pieces from divergent systems and often ending up with a mish-mash of incompatible ideas. So just to be eclectic doesn't make sense. Also to try to blend different theories that might be incompatible doesn't add up to much. So technical eclecticism means taking techniques, preferably empirically validated techniques, and using them as required. And it doesn't matter who gave birth to the techniques; as long as they are effective we can explain it by any theory that we may prefer to resort to. So the emphasis was on techniques, and 'systematic' means that you don't just do what feels right, you don't play by intuition but you have a rationale for what you do. If somebody says 'Why did you choose that particular technique for psychodrama and Gestalt therapy?', you don't say, 'Well it made sense' or 'It felt right.' You say, 'Well, data have shown that under conditions X, Y and Z, this type of strategy is likely to be effective, that's why it was chosen.' And then 'Why did you add a de-sensitization to it?' Again, because the literature shows that if you de-sensitize under these conditions you attenuate the anxiety. So we try to be very systematic and empirically conscious of what is available experimentally, and we do not just haphazardly fly by the seat of our pants.

Maybe at this point you could tell us a little more about the BASIC I.D.

The BASIC I.D. is an acronym. B = Behaviour, A = Affect (the psychological term for strong feelings or emotions), S = Sensation, I = Imagery, C = Cognition, I = Interpersonal, D = Drugs/Biology. Descriptively, we are beings that act and move (Behaviour), have strong emotions (Affect), see, hear, taste, smell and feel (Sensation), picture events in our mind's eye (Imagery), think and plan (Cognition), relate to one another (Interpersonal), and at base we are neurophysiological entities, wherein the most usual treatment is the use of psychotropic medications (Drugs/Biology). These seven modalities are interactive; this is not a linear thing. I am referring to a reciprocal, circular interaction. However, we can stop at any point artificially to examine any one modality, asking, 'Well, what are you picturing? What's going on in your imagery and what specific sensation are you aware of? How do you behave when you 'image' and sense that way? And how does that impact on what you are doing with people?' This kind of flux and interaction is very important. The BASIC I.D. serves as a template to be sure that we don't leave out something that can be very important in people's lives. If you look at other systems, most of them leave out sensation and imagery. They talk about A, B, C – Affect, Behaviour, Cognition. My view is that if you don't separate out sensation from affect, imagery from cognition, left from right brain, and you don't emphasize the interpersonal and the biological elements, therapists are apt to overlook them in their treatment and their clients don't get thorough treatment.

Are there are other unique features of multimodal therapy?

Apart from the BASIC I.D. there is a 'Second Order' method. That's a strategy to be used when you are having trouble resolving a problem in one area, and you take the problem area and run it through another BASIC I.D. So let's say the person has had terrible trouble with assertiveness and you've gone through assertiveness training to no avail. So you say 'Let's look at behaviour, B. If you were assertive, how would you be acting? How would you feel, what would be your main sensations? What pictures come to mind if you visualize yourself being assertive? What are the cognitions, etc.?' And then, bingo, you might just hit on something and the person says, 'Well I get the picture of my father, I see him struggling', and you go into it. Taking a fairly simple view, what comes out of it is that that person resisted being assertive because he felt that he was not entitled to be a truly assertive person. He had already accomplished a lot more than his own father and for him now to become even more assertive would be to make such a mockery of his own dad that he'd rather stay 'somewhat crippled', as he put it. He said, 'Now I realize why I was struggling.' He did not have access to that information at the beginning. It's not as if he could say: 'Look, forget about the assertiveness training because I don't want to supersede my father.' He knew that he was having a block, but the Second Order BASIC I.D. gave us an insight into the reasons.

We also use a technique called tracking which means we have a look and see which modalities people prefer or favour. When some people make themselves anxious they first do so by thinking something, then imagining it and then getting the sensations. That is a C (cognition), I (imagery), S (sensation) pattern. Other people respond differently; they may start with behaviour, they may do something. And from the behaviour they'll get a sensation, and from the sensation they get an image, so that's a different sequence. The value of tracking is that we can the more easily deduce the right techniques to help this person overcome his or her problem. So two people can have an identical sounding problem but their firing order, their tracking, is different and if you use the same technique on both you are unlikely to be successful in both cases, whereas you would be if you tailored the techniques to their particular modalities.

The other is bridging. If you want to talk about the person's feelings, for instance, and they keep giving you intellectual material, this is perhaps a sign that they are not ready to talk about this heavy-duty emotion. So you go into their cognitive modality, you talk about cognition, and then you can bridge to something a bit less frightening, such as sensation. Then you talk about their sensations, moving across to their feelings a little later. Those kind of tactics are used only by multimodal therapists in a systematic way. Other good therapists will use things similar to this but it's not the same, because it's not systematic. It's not well thought out in advance.

What's the Deserted Island fantasy?

Many years ago a client said to me, 'Gosh, I'd like to take you to a deserted island' and I said, 'Well what would happen?' and she ran off on a fantasy that opened up all kinds of vistas that I would never have thought of. I decided to use it with other people by saying to them, 'Tell me what would happen if you were on a deserted island with someone of your choice, if you are gay it would be a same-sex person, if you are heterosexual an opposite sex person.' It's amazing to see how people come up with such different interpretations, and give you ideas you might not have thought of prior to this intervention. Suddenly you see how competitive they are, how territorial they are, how anxious they are, how controlling they are. Running with this particular fantasy opens up all kinds of information that sometimes would not otherwise be readily accessible.

What are the main advantages of multimodal therapy over the other major approaches?

In a certain sense I would argue that there's no such thing as multimodal therapy. There's not a particular therapy that's multimodal. But the multimodal approach is systematic and broad; it lets you use many interactive techniques and zooms in on various strategies that each individual is most likely to benefit from. In most other therapies if they're following a particular school, the person gets what the therapist uses. That is to say, whether or not they need what that therapist is offering, they will get that. The analogy I've often used is that somebody needs a tonsillectomy but happens to go to a urologist and so they get a prostatectomy because that's what the urologist does. Many people will go to a therapist and they need somebody, for example, who is very active and directive but they happen to see someone who is very laid back and just listens, or vice versa. In multimodal therapy, we will try to match the therapist to the client. I've spoken about being an authentic chameleon and that means you really try to blend in and if you cannot, you refer on to someone who might be a better resource than you are. You see, the client's welfare is what you have at stake. I've had people come to me and although they could afford my full fee, I've referred them elsewhere because I felt that someone else might be better for them than I would. I don't hang on to them for the money.

I remember reading one of your books and you mentioned referring someone for colonic irrigation.

That was a story about a woman with whom I was unsuccessful, as were about six or seven other therapists. She went to some quack naturopath who irrigated her colon and gave her all kinds of pseudo-scientific explanations and she did well. My whole point was, you never know what will help certain people. Keep an open mind.

You mentioned earlier, in passing, integration. Obviously the current trend is towards integration of therapies. Can you be a bit more specific about your views on this?

Yes, integrating what? It's a catch-all term. You would sometimes want to integrate individual with couple therapy, individual with group therapy, psychotherapy with drug therapy. I oppose the idea of blending theories with the idea of getting a more robust technique and strategy. There is no evidence that this has ever happened. The blend of two or more theories, to my knowledge, has never produced a better strategy or technique. So it doesn't make much sense. It's good on the one hand that people are stopping the proliferation of schools of thought. Instead of saying, 'I'm a primal therapist and we have all the answers to universal problems', people are saying that there's something to be learned from other approaches which is good. There are also booby-traps. These are blending things that really cannot be blended. If you take good wine and good beer and blend them, you're not going to have a very good concoction. If you toss in some whisky and brandy you're really going to have a mess. Whereas individually, you might have some really good booze if you're into that sort of thing, there are some other juices that really just don't go together.

You mentioned the proliferation of therapies and at the moment there's some 450, maybe increasing by the day. How do you see the field of counselling developing over the next 50 years?

I'm hoping that it'll self-destruct in the sense of 'enough of this nonsense' Organic medicine at one time had as many theories as there were doctors practising and this is what's happening in our field. I'm hoping that what will happen is that people (and I think this is happening in some circles) will pay respect to empirically established therapies and methods. By the way, in America some people have been sued for not using the appropriate methods. A very famous case was of a man who was a doctor, was very depressed and was in a very prestigious institution called Chestnut Lodge. He was treated with psychoanalytic psychotherapy but just got worse and worse. Finally, the family admitted him to another hospital called Silver Springs where they gave him anti-depressants and in a matter of weeks he was turned around. The family sued Chestnut Lodge (who settled out of court) for not using the proper techniques. Now more and more empirically validated techniques are coming up and I think that many therapists will be in jeopardy if they don't use the right technique. I can just imagine the court case, 'Excuse me, doctor, did you or did you not use response prevention and participant modelling? No. Well, why not? Because this is what the data show, this is what you treat obsessive compulsives with before anything else. And with this panic disorder what did you do? And with this Post-Traumatic Stress Disorder, did you use the established methods of therapy and if so did you use them correctly?' And this is my fantasy of what it would sound like. I don't think I'm far off the mark. I'm hoping that practitioners of the future will be taught all the empirically validated methods, will know when to use them and how to use them and when there are gaps one can fill in with some artistry. But first and foremost let's use what we know works for specific conditions. That would be a boon and a blessing for the consumer.

If you could take one book to your Deserted Island, which one would it be?

One of my big complaints of trying to keep up as much as possible with the field of psychology and therapy, is that I don't get time to read novels. So I get told about Stephen King and Ann Tyler or these other people who are writing these great novels, and I don't get a chance to read them. So if I could take any one author's works I would go for one of those and really get into some exciting novels. I don't want psychiatry books, or medical books, or psychology books on my island. I don't want the *Encyclopaedia Britannica* which is, I think, what Albert Ellis chose; I want good novels that I can enjoy.

Is there anything else you'd like to add to this interview?

Well, I think that the basic message I'd like to get across is that I wish people would stop using systems like religion and understand that therapy and life require flexibility. Flexibility in thought and action are the most important ingredients. If we can teach that to other therapists and we can learn that ourselves, I think we and those that associate with us will be a lot better off.

Discussion issues

1. How does multimodal therapy differ from eclectism as practised by many therapists?
2. What are your views about the use of the BASIC I.D. to assess clients and their problems?
3. There is no such thing as multimodal therapy.
4. Why is keeping an open mind in therapy important? Have you any examples from your practice that illustrates this view?

13

From Education to Art Therapy

Sydney Klugman

All good therapy leads to both education and growth.

Naumberg (1966)

Background

There are many art therapists working in prisons, some in their official capacity and many as art teachers. For art therapists the key issue is under which umbrella they practice, for a great many of them are working in the education department. After disturbances at Strangeways and other institutions the Home Office set up a working party to consider art therapy for prisoners in an attempt to provide them with an emotional outlet. A conference on 'The Visual Arts in Prisons' attended by 140 delegates, in April 1990, produced a report in September 1990 (Riches 1994). In 1992 an Arts in Prison working party was set up to see if the profile of art therapy could be raised within the prison environment and amongst its distinguished members was Judge Tumin, who professed a great respect for the value of the arts in general. Included in their agenda was a desire to create guidelines for employers and ways of setting up support networks to combat feelings of isolation and poor communication.

A number of important issues emerged which still need to be worked through. The types of environment that constitute prisons throughout the country have their own idiosyncrasies which need to be taken into account. Some prisons have the education department separate from the main prison block which means that the communication network is less effective. Art therapists have a tendency to work in isolation and therefore need to find ways of communicating their needs and providing information about their role. Supervision for art therapists is essential, and its provision, together with issues of confidentiality and methods of referral, need to be addressed. Finally, how do we as art therapists know that what we do is effective? This questions the validity of art therapy and highlights the need for research to consider questions such as whether art therapy alongside other services within the prison system can help prevent recidivism.

Many young offenders once in the confines of prison not only abandon their education, despite education being offered to them, but also lose access to treatment and counselling. A report from the Social Work Development Unit, University of East Anglia highlighted the gaps in the treatment of young offenders and described the levels of therapeutic intervention as 'sporadic and extremely limited in adult prisons' (Boswell 1993).

This chapter was first published as 'From education to therapy: art therapy in a young offenders' institute', in *Counselling*, Journal of the British Association for Counselling, vol. 6, no. 2, pp. 132–5 (1995).

Introduction

This article is a short account of the sessional work of an art therapist in a Young Offenders' Institute under the umbrella of the education department and with the invaluable support of the education officer. Although there were counsellors at the institute, there had never been any art therapists working in this setting. This was a new venture for this institute and it was felt that art offered another form of expression to complement the work of the counselling team, because words at times were unable to satisfy the youngsters' needs. Some counsellors take an integrative approach as their model of working, trying to contact the client at a physical, verbal, or creative/non-verbal level. As an art therapist I constantly shift between the verbal and non-verbal in an effort to forge a creative alliance with my clients. As a trainer of rehabilitation counsellors at the West London Institute of Higher Education I ensure that creativity forms an important part of their programme.

Liesl Silverstone (1993: vi) a counsellor and art therapist observed that 'psychotherapy often attached undue importance to the spoken word and other modes of expression need to be found'. She argues that there is a need to work with the right side of the brain, quoting Roger Sperry (1973: 116) in his research conducted in California Institute of Technology: 'the right side of the brain is non-verbal, spacial, spontaneous, intuitive, creative and non-judgemental. There is an argument that at times the left hemisphere mode of thinking; analytical, judgemental and verbal can limit the potential for change.' Silverstone (1993) also suggests that as a counsellor she needs to work with both modes, since talking about problems can keep the client in his or her left side of the brain, and not connected with repressed material on the right side of the brain — the very material needed for integration. Working with art materials as well as working on emerging issues in counselling can allow the client to address painful and frightening experiences in a safely contained and symbolic way.

Edith Kramer, an art therapist working with children, says: 'Forbidden wishes and impulses can be symbolically expressed. Painful and frightening experiences that had to be endured passively can be assimilated by actively reliving them on a reduced scale' (Kramer 1973: 8). Several authors, among them Halgood (1994) and Nowell-Hall (1987: 157), raise some interesting observations around this issue. Halgood (1994: 201) describes how the marriage of art therapy and counselling could prove effective and challenging: 'clients loved the art therapy because they could actually see their problems in front of them instead of only talking about them'. There were times when counsellors would refer offenders for art therapy, as they found the clients' need to place the emphasis on the non-verbal creative part of their being.

Halgood (1994) also makes the point that, paradoxically, those resistant to words are often able to talk about issues quite naturally after painting. Nowell-Hall (1994) describes the essential healing power of art therapy as beyond words and suggests that 'experiencing is perhaps the best way of knowing'. For me the tension between the image and the blank paper is like the silences in counselling, full of possibilities. Thomson (1989: 21) writes 'There is never nothing happening.' Sometimes verbalizing gets in the way and the process becomes too intense and exhausting. Playing with art materials, watching the paint transform the paper can give real pleasure and often can be a link to those thoughts and feelings for which words are hard to find. Winnicott (1971: 44) describes 'bringing the patient from a state of not being able to play into a state of being able to play'.

Working as an art therapist in this particular setting requires an acute awareness of boundaries and adaptive skills, for one of the aims of coming into the prison setting is to provide a link between inside prison and the outside world. Prison life is often seen in isolation from the community even though the majority of offenders, who come from large inner-city environments and are often products of poor education and social problems, will after serving their sentences, return to that same environment. For prisons to be effective, strong links between inside prison and the outside world need to be forged.

Art therapy and the prison environment

Art therapy is an interplay between the conditions imposed by the setting and its particular population, which means that a prison setting is interesting and challenging for the therapist. There is a perception of prisons as grey and intimidating despite various attempts to brighten them up. First impressions of the prison environment can be daunting, with its security and barbed wire surrounds. Eileen McCourt, an art therapist working in Northern Ireland said at a lecture on Art Therapy in Prisons, 'At first glance it would appear that a prison environment cannot be anything but anti-therapeutic. It is ostensibly geared towards rehabilitation, but the atmosphere and emphasis on security militates against privacy and confidentiality required for therapeutic space' (1992: 19). The peculiar factors that make up a prison environment make the need for therapy all the greater. We cannot, however, wait for the ideal environment, for the need is with us now.

From my discussions with education officers around the country there would seem to be a consensus that there is a great deal of anger and frustration among prisoners, which punishment cannot deal with, and one of the functions of the art therapist is to provide an outlet for this destructive energy. Art is an act of behaviour, and not only that which is painted but also the manner in which the art object is made can offer release of strong emotions. Art can be a means of channelling anti-social behaviour in a socially acceptable way and within safe boundaries. 'When speech is impaired/underdeveloped or for some reason rejected as the normal means of communication, art activity can provide a most valuable substitute' (Dalley 1992: 8).

An example of work

To illustrate some of the points raised above, an example of work with an inmate Dan (suitably disguised) is discussed.

Dan, a young man of 20, was referred for art therapy by the Education Officer who had observed his behaviour in education classes and on the prison wing. It was the perception of the Education Officer that Dan's self-esteem was low and that the views he was expressing were self-destructive. She had seen a number of his paintings and felt he would benefit from art therapy. The officer had hoped that because of his interest in art he might be motivated to explore his destructive behaviour towards himself and others. Dan had a history of petty thefts and drug abuse. While under the influence of drugs he had committed arson and was sentenced to two years at a Young Offenders' Institute.

My initial meeting with Dan took place in the education department with the Education Officer present. Dan showed his work painted over the last six months, consisting of a series of stark empty landscapes using board chalks on black paper, work which had been a major form of contact between the Education Officer and himself. After he had shown his pictures I suggested that Dan came to art therapy. The atmosphere suddenly changed. Dan bundled his work up, apologized and said he had to go. The officer explained that because of Dan's negative history of therapy he had become frightened and she offered to talk to him.

Three weeks later he started art therapy and we contracted to meet one afternoon a week in the education department. There were a number of rooms available within the education department and a small room was offered with enough space to put a table and two chairs. There was no water available but this could be accommodated. My main concern was that the space available was practical and perceived as ours. Winnicott (1971) maintains the environment has special importance and the more disturbed the client the more reliable the setting has to be, for the setting does much of the work.

Initially Dan had a great fear of therapy based on previous therapeutic input in a drug dependency unit, which had been highly confrontational and was perceived by him as a negative experience. He also had a vested interest in presenting a certain face to the rest of the inmates as he had formed a resentment of authority and anything that represented middle-class values. However I, as the therapist, was from outside the prison system and represented someone neutral in whom Dan could confide. It became evident that Dan needed to have someone he could trust outside the prison walls.

Dan said he resented the labels people put on him and it was a measure of his desperation that he agreed to have art therapy. Two painting sessions illustrate some of his difficulties and also something about prison life.

The island painting

Dan arrived and said that he had been in solitary for a week as he had sworn at an officer in charge. He described himself as quite drained and flustered. He described his week as solitary and like being on an island. I asked him if he could visualize the island and the feelings he had, being there. Just as Dan was drawing the island the sun came out and cast a shadow of the window bars which looked like prison bars. Around the outside of the island he drew a sun and a smudge of red, yellow, green and black. He also drew a tree which looked like an arrow and some triangles to represent mountains. When he elaborated on the painting he described the island as representing an emptiness and also a feeling of claustrophobia which he said he was experiencing. The colours and shapes he described as part of the outside world; the red he described as anger. He began to speak of his anxiety about what would happen to him when he left the prison and the strong fear he had that he would go back to drugs and the life from which he had come. We spent some time reflecting on what light the bars had metaphorically thrown on his picture and by implication his life.

This session raised issues which were unique as well as more universal. It highlighted Dan's difficulties in containing his anger within the session and the consequences if he did not. It highlighted the importance of our addressing his leaving behind the illusory safety of being locked up and the problems of readjusting to the outside world. It also raised the question of prison as punishment. In Dan's particular case it demonstrated his inability to cope with his feelings and his desire to escape from the concrete reality facing him. The metaphor of a deserted island followed the therapy for a long time. The importance of this session was the opportunity for Dan to find an outlet to express his thoughts and fears in a safe place and to be given genuine and honest attention. The art image had allowed the schism between thoughts and feelings to be tentatively bridged.

Striving for wholeness

The second painting arose out of the changes taking place and the conflicts of staff directed at the art therapist. A number of teaching staff began to feed back to the art therapist that Dan's behaviour had become worse, he was speaking more openly about drugs and had stopped doing any art work outside the therapy sessions.

When Dan arrived for this particular session he was quite pleased with himself and spoke about his ability to manipulate the system. I wondered who he was manipulating? The discussion focused on being inside and outside — inside the therapy and outside, inside the prison and outside. He then said he had an idea and painted a mandala image of the Yin–Yang symbol. He spoke about how wicked he had been and how he would have to meet his maker, and spoke about how he would like to visit his father's grave. In his picture he painted some flowers, a syringe, an image of cannabis and a ban the bomb sign. Schaverian (1992) describes the picture as an embodiment to house all the good and bad feelings. By externalizing the imagery perhaps he would then begin to find a way of acceptance.

In this session there were many tears, which was a breakthrough for Dan, as until now he had been well defended in order to survive in the prison. He had said, 'In this place it is the fittest that survive.' Dan went on to speak about his mother and their relationship. There was a great sadness present. It was getting towards the end of his sentence and his family was becoming more important. The future was becoming the key issue.

Closure

Endings are extremely important as they contain the seeds of the separations that have happened in the past and the potential for growth and movement into the future and new relationships. There has been much written on this aspect of art therapy and therapy in general. Wood (1990) comments on the painful separation issues for many of her clients and the need to engage in the task of mourning which needs to be 'undertaken with humility'. For Dan endings were painful. He tore up picture after picture, and there was a silent anger which he put into art and disposal. There was much we could have explored, particularly his anger towards me, but prison decides when therapy is over and suddenly he was gone. In this sense the uncertainty of the future was mirrored by the uncertainty of when he would cease to attend.

Conclusion

Murphy (1994: 21) describes the art therapist as a bridge between the conscious and unconscious and the many physical chasms that need to be bridged in prison: between staff and prisoners, between community and prison. She asks, 'Is the bridge the therapy or the therapist?'

The story of Dan illustrates the effects of the context on art therapy. It illustrates the uncertainties of place, time and continuance. Trust and containment are essential if any intra-personal work is to be entered into. Dan's well-being mirrored part of the dynamics taking place and without the support and openness of the Education Officer the therapeutic interventions would have been much less effective. Three months after his release, there was a message to the Education Officer to say that Dan had phoned to thank the therapist and that he was now back home with his mother and off drugs.

I have tried to show that art therapy can provide a space for prisoners to look at themselves and a chance to revalue themselves. From my point of view Dan had a period of time where he could form a trusting relationship, where he could express feelings which he had long buried under a blanket of guilt and abandonment. The art therapy and our relationship filled part of this gap, but in addition a great deal of effort by the Education Officer and the education staff went into Dan's well-being. He had also had a period of counselling and this too provided stepping-stones to work from. How long-lasting the effects of therapy will be is unknown, but a start has been made.

Liebmann (1994) stresses the importance of this type of work in prisons: 'While restriction of liberty prevents offending by external control, there is a recognition that, in the longer term, it is only when offenders "resolve personal difficulties and acquire new skills" that offending is really prevented. … Art therapy with all it has to offer could also be made available more widely as part of probation services provision.'

References

Dalley, T. (1992) *Art as Therapy*, Tavistock/Routledge.

Halgood, M. (1994) 'Group art therapy with adolescent sex offenders', in M. Liebmann (ed.), *Art Therapy with Offenders*, London: Jessica Kingsley.

Kemp, E. (1984) *Fostering Creativity: A Practical Guide for Group Training, or Self-Development*, London: Pavie.

Kramer, E. *Art as Therapy with Children*, London: Elek.

Liebmann, M. (ed.) (1994) *Art Therapy with Offenders*, London: Jessica Kingsley.

McCourt, E. (1992) 'Art in Prison', 'Proceedings' at Conference, Royal College of Art, London: Visual Arts.

Murphy, J. (1994) 'Mists in the darkness', in M. Liebmann (ed.), *Art Therapy with Offenders*, London: Jessica Kingsley.

Naumberg, M. (1966) *Dynamically Orientated Art Therapy*, New York: Grune & Stratton.

Nowell-Hall, P. (1987) 'Art therapy: a way of healing', in T. Dalley et al., *Images of Art Therapy*, London: Tavistock Publications.

Riches, C. (1994) 'The hidden therapy of a prison art education programme', in M. Liebmann (ed.), *Art Therapy with Offenders*, London: Jessica Kingsley.

Robinson, M. (1984) 'A Jungian approach to art therapy based in a residential setting', in T. Dalley (ed.), *Art as Therapy*, London: Tavistock.

Schaverien, J. (1992) *The Revealing Image*, London: Routledge.

Silverstone, L. (1993) *Art Therapy – The Person-Centred Way*, London: Autonomy Books; 2nd edn (1998) London: Jessica Kingsley.

Sperry, R. (1973) *Lateral Specialization of Cerebral Function in the Surgically Separated Hemispheres*, New York: Academic Press.

Thompson, M. (1989) *On Art and Therapy: An Exploration*, London: Virago.
Winnicott, D.W. (1971) *Playing and Reality*, London: Penguin Books.
Wood, C. (1990) 'The triangular relationship', *Journal of British Association of Art Therapists* (1).

Discussion issues

1 Do you think the use of art as a non-verbal form of communication can be used within the counselling process?
2 Many of our clients are limited in finding words to express what they feel. Is there room to introduce art media into the counselling process in order to supply the means for them to be heard?
3 What is your reaction to the notion that 'Art may explore at a deeper level without the necessity to manipulate language' (Robinson 1984)?
4 What is your response to the idea that art is spatial and has no time element? A picture can portray many aspects of life at once, whereas verbalization is a linear form of communication.

14

Writing – a Therapeutic Space

Opening the box

Gillie Bolton

Safe

> She drags
> darkness over her head
> and arms curled
> around knees folded to breasts
>
> the clock ticks
> but she is in the centre
> where a still nail pins the hands

Jo couldn't talk about her experiences, it hurt too much; she needed to attempt to make sense of her life on her own. Luckily she was literate enough to use a paper and pencil as her therapist, otherwise she might still be a tight ball of denial. This poem is a distillation of pages of her writing.

Jo's writing slipped between the bars she had erected around herself; her pencil wrote things she did not know, could not consciously remember from the seemingly halcyon days of her little girlhood. She wrote things, then wrote their opposite – trying and testing. At first she thought her story was something her sick mind had invented, until its intensity and clarity forced her to face the truth her pencil was telling her. The jigsaw pieces, which her blank conscious memory refused to supply, fitted together. She faced her trauma and recovered.

Writing as therapy – an explanation

The 'Talking Cure' is helpful for many, but others need something else as well or in its place. Personal or expressive writing can run alongside work with a therapist – keeping a daybook or journal for example. For those who find talking difficult or impossible, or those who too readily 'intellectualize', writing can be a solution. The integrity and confidentiality of the diary or journal cannot be doubted. The writers can change their minds, state seeming opposites, try things out, express the experiences of a flayed mind, without the pain or awkwardness of anyone else knowing. And writing need not be shared.

This chapter was first published under the title 'Taking the thinking out of it: writing a therapeutic space', in *Counselling*, Journal of the British Association for Counselling, vol. 6, no. 3, pp. 215–18 (1995).

A spoken communication can never be unsaid or unheard. Writing can be privately kept in a locked drawer, or even torn up – an important part of the process for some. Some ask – 'Writing seems so laborious, and anyway, I was no good at English, why can't I just think this through?' But thought tends to go round and round, only to slip away with the ghost of a laugh, or else ungraspably merge with the next thought.

Writing *can* be an effective form of communication, when and if the writer is ready. Sharing a poem with another, or developing a dialogue, can be a vivid and dynamic process, quite different from talking.

Learning how to write for therapy

'The diary I have is therapeutic and feels like a friend that I confide in … [but] the style and method of writing in my diary will be very different and hopefully more useful from now on. *I'll be taking the thinking out of it!*' was a reflection made near the end of a Writing as Therapy dayschool. The 18 group members came from many branches of the helping professions and were either counsellors, or in training. We spent the day writing as if we were clients ourselves; discussing the process; and the applicability within their very varied counselling work.

Many of the group expressed anxiety to begin with. Negative memories of school, a view that only writers/academics can write, and a natural nervousness at being exposed, all combined to create apprehension. But I'm used to this, just as I'm used to the intense excitement afterwards when course members realize what they have created and discovered. They only way to overcome this fear is not to think or talk about writing, but to *do* it.

This was what we did. First we wrote whatever came into our heads for six minutes, to clear the brain of clutter such as traffic frustrations. This has two additional benefits – the rule is to write something, so the paper swiftly becomes no longer frighteningly blank. Also, vital fleeting ideas and images can be captured and expressed – to be considered and built on later. People must know this six-minute writing is not for sharing, unless they choose to do so. I always say: today you can't write the wrong thing; whatever you write is of value.

I then scattered all sorts of containers between us: an egg, a sheep's skull, a tom-tit's nest, a police officer's helmet, a Victorian ink bottle. Everyone had to choose something and begin to write straightaway – continuing the free-flow style. First we described the look, feel, smell, etc., of the object, then what it would be like to be *inside* it. Everyone would be invited to read a bit of this writing out, but of course there was no compulsion. About 25 minutes later the intensity of the scribbling seemed to be slackening off; hopefully anyone who wished to write more would continue in their own time.

Next we silently studied our writings. This is a vital stage as you do not always know what you have written until you read it; also intriguing connections and areas needing further exploration appear, to be marked for further attention. We each choose a part to share with the group, though many felt their material was too private. But everyone did (including me), emboldened by each other. Verna chose a big and a little seahorse:

Some writings

> Why no comforting presence, no warmth, no eyes which
> shine with love and pride,
> Only father leads the little one, who follows,
> confused, empty and alone.
> Yet go it must, for to be alone in the great ocean is to die.
> The child must follow the man longing, yearning, hoping
> for recognition, but none comes …
> Who is here to find and hold?
> Who is there to love and comfort?
> No one emerges from the quietness, the blackness.
> There is only silence, more profound than death,
> Silence and nobody there.

Joan felt the empty coffee box would be straightforward:

Why did I pick the bright box which had held coffee? Well, I used my 'ordered' mind to realize we were going to be asked to write about it. Then, Gillie has told us not to be 'ordered' and let our thoughts and feelings rule the writing. Very difficult sat round a group of tables with thirteen other pens all scribbling at the same time!

The box is bright, descriptive and instructional, like parts of my life, the decoration is ornate but represents, for the coffee maker, something they wish to impart to everyone. Are we like that? Do we have a part of us that represents to the outside world what is acceptable and what we think it wishes to see? Yes, of course.

And what happens when I open the lid? That it's plain inside, dark grey and empty. There is a side to me that is like that. Unfulfilled dreams and hopes. How then can I expect or think that anyone can cope with death better because of my input! How clever do we think we are that we can be trained to make things better. Walking alongside is what we can do best. Having someone to walk with is so important. What about the Franks of this world who had no one and died with only the love of us to save his loneliness? Second chances. We don't get one really. Life is like the box, looks bright, descriptive and has instructions, take it off the shelf and claim it as yours, and the brightness will dull and the instructions fade if not preserved and loved …

After reading this Joan felt amazed, shocked even: 'I didn't even realize I'd written about Frank (a patient) until I read it back.' She'd thought this death had been thoroughly dealt with at the funeral and in supervision. She enjoyed writing, despite her emotion on reading it out.

Sue too had written and written breathlessly, only to realize how vital it was on reading it back. She wrote in her summative evaluation: 'I was shocked by the impact the exercises had on me. There are a number of issues I realize I have not dealt with as well as I'd thought.'

Unlike many of the others, Doreen's writing brought only happy memories – suggested by a tiny lidded basket:

When I was seven or eight I had the most beautiful Christmas present. It was a basket-work sewing box – with a lid. Perfectly round, the basket weave could be followed round to a point in the middle of the base and a point in the middle of the lid. My mother had lined it with white taffeta. The basket had a wonderful smell, and half the joy of it was burying my head in its soft interior and savouring this smell …

From time to time the pins fell out – a tangled mass upon the floor. Then we fetched the magnet and created a stream of shiny, shimmering connected pins, stuck even more closely together than they were before …

Everyone gave a part of themselves when they read. One expressed what we probably all felt: 'It's been a privilege.' The remainder of the day was spent discussing the uses of writing within counselling or therapy.

Writing myself?

The benefits of this kind of writing are clear. Yet it seems to be an indulgence for the therapists/counsellors themselves. Writing in an attractive folder or book with a special pen or pencil is facilitative, but – can we allow ourselves? When? Someone might *need* us just as we've settled.

The best time and place might be away from telephone, family and clients. Amazing things can happen at a time of low barriers such as the very early morning, or in an unusual place. But we must feel safe enough: bed alone in the private middle of the night might be perfect. And then – how do I begin to cover this blank paper? Many many writers, even the most successful, suffer from this. Yet another cup of coffee is needed first, this letter must be replied to, I'm not really ready to write yet. All these prevent us from setting out on this explorative, possibly dangerous journey. But – you need only write for six minutes in the first instance, and can always throw it away afterwards.

Once started, the initial writing must be allowed to flow – without anxieties about grammar, making sense, or subject. There may well be later stages of more structured writing, threads may emerge to be followed diligently. Follow them without a *why*? or *this is rubbish*!

And now for my client

Writing can be self-therapy, as for Jo; therapist and client can collaborate; or a professional writer can work with a group, as with this dayschool. Writing can become an integral part of a therapy process, or used intensively when appropriate. The therapist can suggest tactics, or write alongside the client; or leave the client to keep a journal. This helps the client to continue therapeutic work between sessions.

Privacy is important. A student counsellor told us of a client's mother who had read and destroyed her diary, forbidding her to write another.

Although writing as therapy is different from other approaches, there are similarities. Like art therapy it offers direct access to a client's creativity (Milner 1950). 'Art as therapy is a mirror that the patient makes to find his (*sic*) own self reflected' (Simon 1992). 'The image is … often an external expression of some unconscious internal state which has yet to emerge into consciousness' (Waller and Dalley 1992). Anyone can gain from this kind of writing, including professionals: 'Writers end up writing about their obsessions. Things that hurt them; things they can't forget; stories they carry in their bodies wanting to be released' (Goldberg 1986).

Working with my clients – what about me?

Writing can be a support for the caring professional. Focusing on work experiences (particularly ones that have caused anxiety or fulfilment) can be self-educative and releasing.

Patricia Benner (1984) advocates building on the huge body of knowledge embedded in experience in nurse training. Here is a nurse writing about the death of a patient fifteen years before:

> She had felt troubled by the memory of Ashiko, that she had not done enough to help her, that 'there was still unresolved business between us when she died'. Writing about her made it clear, however, that things had been resolved, since (she now realized) they had both learned from each other: 'As I was writing, I thought, No, I really think we came to some agreement at the end.' (Landgrebe and Winter 1994)

How to start

The dayschool discussed many different pathways for our clients: dialoguing with parts of oneself, perhaps the inner child with the parent; writing unsendable letters to mother or schoolteacher; rewriting an event with a different ending …

- Dreams can be endlessly rewritten: relocating the 'I' in each of the characters or objects; dialoguing between characters; rewriting the ending, and so on.
- Myths, nursery rhymes or fairy stories explore facets of our everyday experience. Retelling from a novel angle (such as 'Buttons' or 'a little kid') be be powerful.
- Soap-box writing: shout your pain or rage on to the page with a thick red felt-tip pen.
- Reminiscence work is useful with the elderly and the dying, a holistic experience, helping them come to terms with difficult episodes, and re-experience happy memories. It's also a record for loved ones to keep. Many more ideas for therapeutic creative writing, and reports of practice can be found in Birren and Deutchman (1991), Bolton (1999 a, b, c) and Bolton et al. (2000). We heard about a beautiful book created for her daughter by one hospice patient. At a previous workshop we'd heard about birth mothers writing letters to their children about to be adopted: a difficult and heartwrenching task.

Then we turned to some of the many ways to actually start writing. Shells can, like containers, lead to thoughts of safety or enclosedness, or of holiday memories. Clients' precious mementoes or old photographs, buttons or plastic animals to sort and arrange, well-known tunes or playground games can all be triggers. Key words (such as stockpot, burrow, apple) introduce free association.

> '*I like the idea of lists,*' a hospice worker said, '*I shall use this with bereaved relatives – asking them to write positive and negative feelings.*' Or: things that make me feel squirmy and uncomfortable/warm and happy/rage. (Morris 1971)

Listing can deal with *should I?* or *should I not?* dilemmas, pros and cons being listed separately, possibly in different colours. These then can be re-ordered and weighted with numbers from one to ten. The answer is now there in front of your client – but don't be surprised if she chooses the opposite one! The answer is not as important as the process of examining and weighing.

The *spider* is a dynamic form of listing. The initial problem word goes in the middle – *writing block*, for example. Everything relating to this theme clusters around according to their relationship to each other. *Lack of time/no space in the house*, and *Miss Jones/spelling* might be two clusterings.

Final word

The group were astonished writing had offered such accurate expression; they'd felt able to share it and even shed tears; the group had offered support and interest and even 'gave me permission to be human'.

The writing itself, moreover, had been so enjoyable! The reading aloud had brought the shock of the content.

Writing does seem to offer a direct path to an inner voice, bypassing some blocks and shutting up that inner critic. An intense therapeutic journal-writing method has been developed in America (Progoff 1975). 'Slowly the argument about the healing power of the arts has begun to be considered more widely' (Senior and Croall 1993). Writers-in-residence are being employed in hospices, hospitals, old people's homes, prisons, doctor's surgeries and schools (Alexander 1990; Hague and Barnett 1991; Corner 1992; Senior and Croall 1993).

The urge or need to create is strong in us all. It doesn't have to be perfect but it is our own. Joan, the coffee box writer, said:

As a carer you have to give 80–90 per cent of yourself. So you have to protect that last part of you, keep that bit back.

But that didn't happen with the writing. And then when I started reading that back I thought 'hell, did I write that? Oh yes I see, oh gosh that's interesting.' What happens when I open the lid, and then off I went …

When you said ten minutes I thought ten! Give me two! But by the end of the 25 minutes I wanted longer. It isn't until you actually do it that you realize what it costs the writer. You realize counselling's deep and important and might think writing's easy and cosy, but it's not! Did I write that? Was that really me? When you sit and role-play in the training you can pick something safe, but you can't with the writing. I suppose it's because you're not listening to yourself as you write.

Writing takes you out of control. It should be trained for like the counselling.

Opening the box – it's like a jack-in-a-box, isn't it?

References

Alexander, L. (1990) *Now I Can Tell: Poems for St John's Hospice*, London: Macmillan.

Benner, P. (1984) *From Novice to Expert: Excellence and Power in Clinical Nursing Practice*, California: Addison Wesley.

Birren, J. and Deutchman, D. (1991) *Guiding Autobiography Groups for Older Adults*, Baltimore, MD: Johns Hopkins University Press.

Bolton, G. (1994a) 'Stories at work: writing for professional development', *Issues in Social Work Education*, 14 (2): 21–33.

Bolton, G. (1994b) 'Stories at work: fictional-critical writing as a means of professional development, *British Educational Research Journal*, 20 (1): 55–68.

Bolton, G. (1999a) *The Therapeutic Potential of Creative Writing: Writing Myself*, London: Jessica Kingsley.

Bolton, G. (1999b) 'Stories at work: reflective writing for practitioners', *The Lancet*, 354: 243–5.

Bolton, G. (1999c) 'Every poem breaks a silence which had to be overcome: the therapeutic power of poetry', *Feminist Review*, 62 (Summer): 118–33.

Bolton, G. Gelipter, D. and Nelson, P. (2000) 'Keep taking the words: therapeutic writing in primary care', *British Journal of General Practice*, 50 (450): 80–1.

Corner, L. (1992) *Pyramids of Light and Other Stories: The Arts and Mental Health*, Dewsbury: Yorkshire and Humberside Arts.

Goldberg, N. (1986) *Writing Down the Bones: Freeing the Writer Within*, Boston: Shambhala.

Hague, I. and Barnett, J. (1991) *The Arts and Terminal Care*, Dewsbury: Yorkshire and Humberside Arts.

Landgrebe, B. and Winter, R. (1994) 'Reflective writing on practice: professional support for the dying?', *Educational Action Research*, 2 (1): 83–94.

Milner, M. (1950) *On Not Being Able to Paint*, London: Heinemann Educational.

Morris, I. (1971) *The Pillow Book of Sei Shonagon*, London: Penguin.

Progoff, I. (1975) *At a Journal Workshop*, New York: Dialogue House Library.

Senior, P. and Croall, J. (1993) *Helping to Heal: The Arts in Health Care*, London: Calouste Gulbenkian.

Simon, R. (1992) *The Symbolism of Style: Art as Therapy*, London: Routledge.

Waller, D. and Dalley, T. (1992) 'The theoretical perspective', in D. Waller and A. Gilroy (eds), *Art Therapy*, Buckingham: Open University Press.

Discussion issues

1 Creative writing can be a useful tool for any therapist or counsellor to use.
2 There are a very large number of ways writing can be used with a client.
3 Writing can help a client be more independent in therapeutic work.
4 Writing can be a confidence-building and enjoyable creative process.

15

A Relational Model of Counselling

Geoff Pelham, Stephen Paul and Peter Holmes

For a number of years the trainers on the B.Sc. (Hons) Therapeutic Counselling (a consortium of Leeds Metropolitan University, Park Lane College Leeds and Wakefield College) have struggled to define a shared framework. Although we come from different backgrounds (humanistic-existential, psychodynamic) *our areas of agreement outweigh the differences*. The challenge has been to find the concepts that genuinely offer an integration of our common ground. The desire to develop a shared framework has, in part, been fuelled by the BAC requirement that courses wishing to be recognized define a core theoretical model which informs all aspects of the theory and practice of the course (Dryden et al. 1995). We believe that we are developing such an approach, calling it a 'relational model' of counselling. Though it is at an early stage of development we believe that it offers a framework for training that others may find interesting, helpful and a stimulus for debate.

The relational model

The past decade has seen the clarification of a new paradigm in therapeutic theory. This is the relational paradigm. It has one central defining assumption: that relations between people are the basis of individual and social life, and relational concepts are used to understand human life in all its complexity.

Stephen Mitchell (1988, 1993; Greenberg and Mitchell 1983) is a key figure in the articulation of this paradigm. Working from within the psychodynamic tradition, he argues that the paradigm integrates object relations, interpersonal and self psychology. These are all approaches that take relations as the central concept in the theory and practice of therapy.

Though it has its origins in the psychodynamic tradition, the relational paradigm provides a framework for integrating (or reinterpreting within a relational framework) concepts and practices across the spectrum of counselling theory. Such integration is possible through a shared common vision, viz. the centrality of relations in the development of personality, the origin and persistence of psychological problems, and the process of counselling. We shall expand upon the fundamental assumptions below.

For the purposes of providing a coherent and manageable framework for diploma-level students (which does not overburden them with complexity and controversy) the relational model will offer a view of the person and the counselling process that integrates primarily the existential-humanistic (mainly person-centred) and psychodynamic

---

This chapter was first published in *Counselling*, Journal of the British Association for Counselling, vol. 7, no. 3, pp. 229–31 (1996).

(object relations and interpersonal theory) traditions. In this we will be following the work of Michael Kahn (1991). His book will be a basic text for the course. The books by Mitchell (1988, 1993), though of fundamental importance, are at too high a level of sophistication for diploma-level students. As the students near completion of their diploma, Mitchell's books will be recommended for future study.

Students will also be alerted to the way cognitive and cognitive-behavioural thinking can be understood from a relational perspective (this will be expanded upon below).

Assumptions about human nature

A person is born with the potential which develops through relations with other people. Physical and psychological dependency in infancy and childhood ensures the crucial importance of care-givers. But in addition to dependency, relating to others (to know and be known, to love and be loved) is an essential, defining part of being human across the life span. Paradoxically it is through relations with others that the person develops, maintains and changes a sense of self. Identities are intertwined (Rogers 1961; Stern 1985; Winnicott 1990; Brazelton and Cramer 1991).

The importance of relations in the development of the self offers both opportunity and risk. When developmental needs are met in an appropriate way then a strong and positive sense of self evolves along with an ability to establish close intimate relations and a sense of inner direction and creativity. Such a person will not be free of conflict because human relations by their very nature embody tension and potential conflict (for example, the child striving for autonomy while retaining secure bonds with parents; parents lovingly attending to the child while pursuing their own distinct interests). But the strong positive sense of self gives a secure foundation for experiencing and working through the conflicts. People have the potential, through relations with others, to become fully functioning individuals utilizing their inner resources to maximize their interpersonal relations.

How do psychological problems develop?

The relational model accepts that the individual has the potential to develop as a person and that life experiences influence this developmental process.

'Significant others' (parents, siblings, friends, teachers, etc.) do not exist simply to provide optimal experience for the self. Each has his/her own personal agendas, illusions, conflicts and needs through which they relate to others.

For example, a parent experiences a newborn infant through a life history that significantly determines how he/she 'meets' the child (Bowlby 1988). Parental fantasies, hopes, fears, conflicts and needs are expressed in the relationship and profoundly influence the developing sense of the child (Stern 1995). The interpersonal dynamic will be assimilated and become part of the self. Emotional states that were not attuned to, or were forbidden, are lost or disavowed (Stern 1985). Needs that were not met or disdained (e.g. for closeness or separation) are repressed and projected (Bowlby 1988). Emotional states, behaviours and achievements that are 'required' (being a 'good' child, academic success, etc.) produce a 'false self' (Winnicott 1990). If love is conditional, then the child will strive to meet those conditions (Rogers 1951).

Experience of not 'good enough' relations with important others produces a host of problems for the self: lack of self-esteem, fear of intimacy, repressed 'unacceptable' feelings (often generating anxiety), lack of inner direction and creativity, and so forth.

Throughout a person's life events occur that can cause trauma. This trauma may be exacerbated by previous life experiences or may be focused around the traumatic event itself – the death of a relative or experience of redundancy, for example. Similarly, traumatic and oppressive experiences can trigger distortions in a person's perception of self and others.

Mechanisms that perpetuate psychological problems

The various therapeutic traditions have explored and described a host of ways the person protects him/herself from psychological distress and unmet needs. These have been described as defence mechanisms, or organizing principles. They include such strategies as repression, displacement, splitting, denial, and so forth. Breakdown of these defensive manoeuvres leads to pain, chronic anxiety, depression, etc.

The person develops patterns of relating to others, based upon his/her sense of self, that tend to ensure the world conforms to preconceived expectations and defensive strategies. For example, the person expecting rejection tends to be very vigilant for signs of rejection by others, interprets ambiguous situations to meet expectations, and acts in ways that generate rejection by others (Rogers 1951; Casement 1985; Bowlby 1988).

Interpersonal dynamics tend to perpetuate problems. It frequently happens that a person establishes close relations with others that embody and recreate the familiar disturbed relations. Thus the person expecting rejection enters a relationship with a partner who is rejecting. This recreation of the original disturbed relational dynamic is particularly resistant to change, as the person's fantasies and expectation about close relationships are borne out by current experience.

Therapeutic change

Clients bring to counselling issues which arise out of their current sense of self (embodying as it does the previous history of relating) and relations with others. Therapeutic change involves a transformation of the sense of self, and, along with this, changes in forms of relating to others. The transformations involve a move away from constrictions, distortions, defences, debilitating inner fantasies, and self-defeating repetitive patterns of relating, toward a positive sense of self, recognition of self-chosen life choices, and the ability to establish freely chosen forms of relating to others, including intimate relations (if so desired).

These changes occur as the client explores in counselling his/her way of relating to self and others. The counselling relationship itself provides the secure base that creates the possibility for the client to recognize, challenge and change his/her way of relating.

Range of therapeutic interventions

To enable trainees to work with this model they first need to develop the attitudes and skills defined by the person-centred approach. Unconditional positive regard, empathy and congruence facilitate the mutual meeting that is the heart of the counselling and all genuine growth-promoting relationships (Buber 1923; Rogers 1951, 1961).

Alongside the core conditions, trainees develop and use generic counselling skills (Dryden et al. 1995) to enable the client to explore more deeply his/her experience of relationships past and present (including the client's relationship with her/himself) and the experience of the counselling relationship itself. Building on these generic skills trainees develop the ability to identify and work with persistent relational themes in the client's material (e.g. client repeatedly feeling rejected or judged).

The relational approach anticipates that the client's problems will be re-experienced within the counselling relationship. The client may seek to recreate familiar patterns of relating and project into the counsellor an expectation for a particular role response (Casement 1985). The counsellor has to be aware and skilled enough to work with this process. Developing the self-awareness of the counsellor is at the heart of this model of counselling as is the ability to explore authentically the dynamics of the counselling relationship (Maroda 1991). Trainees will be introduced to and work with the framework offered by Michael Kahn (1991) for facilitating a re-experiencing by the client of her/his relational difficulties as they re-emerge within the counselling relationship.

The counselling 'frame' is a crucial site for the unconscious expression of the client's relational difficulties (Casement 1985). Trainees will learn the importance of establishing a secure counselling frame (often a particular challenge to trainees working in institutions), through, for example, initial contracting, and the relational implications of holding or changing the frame.

Trainees on a diploma course need to learn knowledge and a set of interventions to put the core model into practice. At the same time, we do not believe that the relational approach prescribes a defined set of interventions. The model gives clearer structure and direction to the counsellor. Within the context of a secure base of theory and practice the counsellor may wish to further develop her/his range of interventions, perhaps drawing upon skills and techniques from other approaches.

The relational model and other approaches to counselling

The basic assumption of the centrality of relationships marks this approach off from other approaches. So, for example, it does not accept the drive model of classical psychoanalysis, nor does it accept the empiricist methodology and environmentalist approach of operant behaviourism.

At the same time, the relational model is able to reinterpret within its own paradigm many of the theoretical and technical gains of alternative approaches. Mitchell (1988, 1993) has explored psychoanalytic concepts from the relational perspective. The wide range of humanistic therapies has developed concepts and practices that are congruent with the relational approach. For example, transactional analysis embodies a fully relational approach that in many ways (and in its own language) parallels the position developed here. Behaviourist themes can fruitfully be explored by understanding the crucial importance of behaviour in the creation and maintenance of relational patterns (Stern 1985, 1995). Similarly, cognitive approaches have developed important therapeutic tools for exploring and changing the ways clients interpret their world. The relational approach provides a context for understanding the development and function of cognition in the life of the client (Bowlby 1988; Stern 1995).

The relational model and the social/political

By its very nature a relational approach invites us to consider wider social/political relations and their implications for counselling. The counselling relationship develops out of, is permeated by and embedded within social processes that have to be understood and addressed. For example, class, gender, race, sexual preferences, disability, power and control are issues that challenge us at the societal level, but also go to the very heart of the counselling relationship. Trainees will be invited to explore and confront the reciprocal influence of relations at the macro level.

Conclusion

We have described here a model that as both practitioners and trainers we can own and work with, that is not limited to one theoretical school and yet is *integrative* and not *eclectic*. The process of integration produces something new. Our model is not psychodynamic plus person-centred (where purists of both traditions will be outraged), but rather it generates its own *relational perspective* that invites us to highlight and explore particular issues (e.g., the *mutuality* of the counselling relationship). It also offers its own stance on familiar dilemmas (e.g., whether or not to hold the therapeutic frame, to give the tape to clients after recording, to self-disclose) by inviting the counsellor to consider the *relational meaning* for counsellor and client of any such intervention.

The relational model has been taught on our professional course for over five years now and has received excellent feedback from external examiners, supervisors and students. We have developed a post-qualification MA in Therapeutic Counselling in which participants can explore in depth the philosophical basis, therapeutic concepts and practice which underpin this approach. Paul and Pelham (2000) have further developed the model in a recent publication with particular reference to both its theoretical underpinnings and practical application.

References

Bowlby, J. (1988) *A Secure Base*, London: Routledge.
Brazelton, T.B. and Cramer, B.G. (1991) *The Earliest Relationship*, London: Karnac Books.
Buber, M. (1923) *I and Thou*, Edinburgh: T. & T. Clark.
Casement, P. (1985) *On Learning from the Patient*, London: Tavistock.
Dryden, W., Horton, I. and Mearns, D. (1995) *Issues in Professional Counsellor Training*, London: Cassell.
Greenberg, J.R. and Mitchell, S.A. (1983) *Object Relations in Psychoanalytic Theory*, Cambridge, MA: Harvard University Press.
Heron, J. (1990) *Helping the Client*, London: Sage.
Kahn, M. (1991) *Between Therapist and Client*, Oxford: W.H. Freeman & Co.
Maroda, K.J. (1991) *The Power of Countertransference*, Chichester: Wiley.
Mearns, D. and Thorne, B. (1988) *Person Centred Counselling in Action*, London: Sage.

Mitchell, S.A. (1988) *Relational Concepts in Psychoanalysis: An Integration*, Cambridge, MA: Harvard University Press.

Mitchell, S.A. (1993) *Hope and Dread in Psychoanalysis*, New York: Basic Books.

Paul, S. and Pelham, G. (2000) 'A relational approach to therapy', in S. Palmer and R. Woolfe (eds), *Integrative and Eclectic Counselling and Psychotherapy*, London: Sage.

Rogers, C.R. (1951) *Client-Centred Therapy*, Boston: Houghton Mifflin.

Rogers, C.R. (1961) *On Becoming a Person*, Boston: Houghton Mifflin.

Stern, D.A. (1985) *The Interpersonal World of the Infant*, New York: Basic Books.

Stern, D.A. (1995) *The Motherhood Constellation*, New York: Basic Books.

Winnicott, D.W. (1990) *The Maturational Processes and the Facilitating Environment*, London: Karnac Books.

Discussion issues

1 In what ways does this model place the relationship as central to change?

2 How does this paradigm enable humanistic and psychodynamic concepts to be applied within a common framework?

3 What are the advantages and disadvantages of this approach?

4 Many approaches consider the relationship to be important in therapy. What specific contributions does this model make to understanding the importance of the relationship?

PART TWO

COUNSELLING CONTEXTS AND PRACTICE

Introduction to Part Two

In contextualizing the practice of counselling and psychotherapy Part Two presents a selection of journal writings offering breadth and quality, reflecting the current challenge of finding ways to incorporate new thinking with traditional ways of working and relating directly to practice. Authors' work and perspectives embrace a multiplicity of human experiences in various cultural, social and organizational settings. Their chapters attempt to be specific and focused in addressing the particular issues and problems encountered in counselling within the context and practice of difference. Such difference may be found in the realms of culture, race, sexuality, gender or disability, in the myriad common human experiences which characterize our lives and in the diversity of settings to which counselling contributes.

A quartet of chapters representing intercultural awareness begins with Irene Bloomfield's account of work with those who survived the Holocaust of the Nazi concentration camps. Long after the events and toward the ending of their lives, survivors are seized by the duty and the pain of remembering and of telling the remembrance, lest we forget. 'We have learned that the long-term damage to severely traumatized people is increased considerably if the world stands by and goes into denial for the next 30 or 40 years.' In a personal experience presaging the 'outing' of institutionalized racism, Tuck-Chee Phung gives a gentle account of positive remedial counselling, yet reminds us how much we still need to do to create an intercultural society within our counselling world. Sitting 'in the counsellor's chair' Lennox Thomas tells Aisha Dupont-Joshua of his life's journey from Grenada to become one of the first black psychotherapists in the UK. Nelson Mandela put his international stature behind the fight to combat Aids, transmitted mainly through heterosexual contact, in Africa, describing it, at the Labour Conference, 2000, 'as a crisis of a dimension which I cannot support in words'. He asked for help from the cultures of the world to meet this crisis. In sub-Saharan Africa, despite malaria, tuberculosis and war, Aids is the biggest killer (UNAIDS 2000). When a dire economic climate results in totally inadequate finances for expensive drugs to treat the condition, what chance palliative care? This question is posed by Tomás Campbell, Tashisho Chabala and Gita Sheth, an intercultural team, in their account of a counselling support group for HIV people at Hope House, Kara Counselling and Training Trust in Zambia.

In contrast, but continuing the group work theme, two companion pieces describe counselling with women university students who sought help with difficulties concerning eating, weight and food. Cathy Richards and Catherine McKisack illustrate the progress of a group based on Susie Orbach's work, Peter Ross charts that of a largely cognitive-behavioural group approach based on a foundation of insight psychology. Both chapters focus on counselling being offered quietly in a difficult area, now considered – like many of our problems – to have a genetic component.

Richard House gives a bravura account of his opinions and experience of General Practice counselling, presenting not so much a plea as a storming of straw bastions, or using controversy and dissent to move counselling and psychotherapy forward in a positive and constructive way.

People experiencing a temporary state of sadness or feelings of short-term misery, may consider that they feel depressed. Virulent depression generates deep despair, total unhappiness and utter desolation. With depression now affecting 10 per cent of the population the World Health Organization (WHO) suggests that in 20 years it will be the world's second most burdensome condition (BBC 2000a). Janet Boakes, a psychiatrist and psychotherapist first shared her wisdom and experience in 1992, when calling for a two-pronged remedy in which insight and drugs together help people to overcome this insidious experience. However, when depression is relieved by suicide the painful and destructive legacy bequeathed to friends and family often creates further victims, as shown by Alice Middleton and David Williams. It is courageous to suggest that our current understanding of bereavement and grief supported by notable practitioners has limitations, but Peter Farrell gives a pertinent reminder that grief's spiritual aspects remain an intriguing search for the ineffable.

The Sydney Paralympic Games 2000 provided a valiant two-fingered victory salute to our attitudes to impairment of many kinds, plus gold medals galore, and silver, and bronze! Three authors write from personal experience of counselling in the context of impairment and disability. Tony Makin, wearing his activist's hat, introduces a social model of disability alongside the traditional medical one. The components of the medical model do not cause people's impairment, but it is enlightening to be faced with their disabling effects. Pauline Monks and Linda Martin share clearly the rare experience of being a deaf counselling trainee and her tutor, respectively, without forgetting the endurance needed by fellow students.

Disability has been likened to imprisonment, but two writers focus on therapy with women and men whose behaviour can actually bring them into direct conflict with the law. Angela Devlin brings out the counselling aspect of her research on conditions in women's prisons and Calvin Bell provides some straight talking about the need to acknowledge the safety of parters in his work with men seemingly addicted to domestic violence. Can we doubt their addiction when police receive, on average, a call for help from families every minute (BBC 2000b)?

The Trades Union Congress (TUC) Lesbian and Gay Conference 2000 focused on the institutional discrimination faced by lesbians and gay men at work, in the home and socially. Cordelia Galgut and Lyndsey Moon both follow this theme, highlighting the potential pitfalls arising from the attitudes (conscious and unconscious) of counsellors which this minority group often faces in the therapeutic world, where they might reasonably expect to be better understood. They suggest that we have work to do before this is the case for clients, or for those counsellors themselves who do not by nature form part of the binary gender system.

Journal articles on counselling with children are rare but we offer a piece on adoption and one on counselling children in an adult mediation centre, both from 1995. Lesley Marks wrote candidly of the emotional challenge facing people who were adopted as children (as she was), when they decide to search for their birth parents. The current work of the Post-Adoption Centre provides an update. The impact on children of warring parents engaged in a bitter battle of divorce or separation is Birgit Carolin's focus. She outlines the mediation help for parents to help them to work out and hold a measure of middle ground in an adversarial arena, and the creation of a complementary counselling service for children, offering individual counselling in the Family and Divorce Centre and group work with students in co-operative local schools.

Disasters arising from travel on railway trains or by Concorde aircraft are shocking reminders that the world can be dangerous. Life's nature is such that it is interrupted by smaller, but also traumatic, events. The place of counselling in both large and smaller tragedies has changed; it is made available to families and 'counsellors' are called in to support survivors. What happens when the counsellors have gone home after unlawful deaths at schools or multiple casualties from train failures or maritime tragedies like the loss of the *Herald of Free Enterprise* at Zeebrugge? The work of the Dover Counselling Centre (McLeod et al. 2000) and support networks in some schools, such as the one at Kidbrooke School Greenwich (Hudson 2000), suggest that there can be positive ongoing outcomes to tragedy. Frank Parkinson describes a particular kind of help 'debriefing' and warns of some of the dangers associated with the misunderstanding and misuse of this method of work. A historical overview of post-traumatic stress disorder, with interesting literary asides, is provided by Suzanna Rose. Media attention has raised the profile of stress management and counselling during the past decade and BACP itself now offers regular training courses on managing stress. Six-figure compensation sums are being paid to stressed employees and the Trades Union Congress (TUC) reports that over 500 stress case claims have been proceeding through the courts since the beginning of this millennium. Seldom does a month pass without a new study showing how stressed we are as a nation, or yet another stress compensation case is reported. Our contribution to the literature comes from Michael Neenan and Stephen Palmer who offer a choice of five cognitive-behavioural ways of tackling stress.

It is significant that the chapters following trauma, stress and debriefing concern the effects of child abuse. Moira Walker has edited the paper she presented at the 1993 ASC conference (now Association for University and College Counselling [AUCC]), describing the aftermath of sexual abuse for both clients and their counsellors. Without diminishing the deep trauma often resulting from child sexual abuse, Colin Crawford and Billy McCullough attempt to contextualize the impact of such abuse to counter a certain media and professional morbidity which they perceive as damaging to clients.

If children receive small mention in our journal, older people are even less well represented. Perhaps we need to question a possible age bias? Although we become older each day, becoming more *elderly* is a qualitatively different experience and Yvonne Craig considers the contribution of mediation in helping us as we age.

In couple work Jane Robins uses the patterns absorbed from childhood relationships with parents to suggest ways of helping adult intimate relationships to thrive in the intricacies and pressures of twenty-first-century life.

Part Two ends with an innovative series of chapters from articles initiated by Gladeana McMahon, news editor of the journal, in August 1994, and continuing until 1999. Originally published under the heading of 'Practical Approaches' (currently titled 'Managing your Practice'), five chapters offer guidance on practical aspects of counselling and activities supporting the work of counsellors, such as note-taking, which training courses do not necessarily address. Gladeana McMahon herself introduces the idea of reflective practice, Gabrielle Syme delineates important areas of assessment and contracting and Sue Warren-Holland provides useful hints on writing letters referring clients to other sources of help. The art of composing case studies is looked at in some detail by Mary Parker, and Gladeana McMahon contributes the final chapter on note-taking for counselling supervisors.

The diversity arising from contextualizing counselling and its practice offers an opportunity to confront our attitudes and prejudices through understanding others. Reading which is always tailored to reflect our own experience is comforting, but it tends to confirm our established views rather than challenging us to reflect upon, rethink and expand our counselling and life horizons.

References

BBC (2000a) Check-up programme, BBC Radio 4, 29 September.

BBC (2000b) Six o'clock news, BBC One, 25 October.

Hudson, P. (2000) *Kidbrooke Counselling and Personal Development Programme. All-in-Success*, 11 (2) (Spring): 6–8.

McLeod, J., Johnston, J. and Griffin, J. (2000) 'A naturalistic study of the effectiveness of time-limited counselling with low-income clients', *European Journal of Psychotherapy, Counselling and Health*, 3 (2) (August): 263–77.

UNAIDS (2000) *Report on the Global HIV/AIDS Epidemic*, United Nations.

16

Counselling Holocaust Survivors

Irene Bloomfield

The term 'Holocaust' means large-scale destruction, but since the end of the Second World War it has come to stand for the attempted annihilation of the Jews of Europe. The war ended more than 50 years ago, and the number of people who survived Nazi concentration camps is shrinking fast. Those who are still alive are getting old. There has, nevertheless, been a revival of interest in the Holocaust in recent years, because after 40 years of virtual silence on the subject there has been a spate of books, films, plays, documentaries and Holocaust art. There have also been international gatherings of particular groups of survivors in the late 1980s and early 1990s, when their stories and experiences were heard for the first time.

Who is a survivor?

A survivor is one who has been threatened with death, touched or witnessed death, but has remained alive. Concentration camp survivors were constantly surrounded by death and suffered from dehumanisation, degradation and constant terror. (Lifton, 1976)

Holocaust survivors are not a homogeneous group. Those who were young adults and adolescents at the time of their imprisonment had the best chance of surviving, especially if they were able to stay together with a relative or close friend. Babies, young children and the old and sick were mostly killed immediately on arrival, as they would not have been able to work the required ten to twelve hours per day on starvation diets. A few younger teenagers survived, because they were warned by more seasoned prisoners to pretend that they were older and had a trade or special skill.

Rabbi Hugo Gryn, whose death was commemorated throughout the UK, was one of them. An obituary written by the historian Martin Gilbert (1996) is not only a tribute to a much respected and loved man, but also illustrates the total arbitrariness of life and death in the camps:

Hugo was one among ten thousand Jews who were deported to Auschwitz from the ghetto in Carpathia in March 1944. When the doors of the train were opened after a long time, Hugo saw some people in striped uniforms moving along the train taking hold of the prisoners' few possessions. 'One of them saved my life,' said Hugo. 'He kept muttering in Yiddish: "You are 18 and you have a trade." It sounded like the ravings of a lunatic, but my father took it seriously and when an SS man asked my age, I said: "I am 19, and I am a carpenter." My brother, who was 3 years younger, could not pretend that he was 19, so he was sent with the old people in the wrong direction. That was the last time I saw my brother.'

This chapter was first published in *Counselling*, Journal of the British Association for Counselling, vol. 8, no. 1, pp. 42–6 (1997).

Kinder transportees

A group which has come to notice in recent years are the 10,000 children who came to Britain on the eve of the Second World War. Their parents recognized that it was the children's last chance of escape, for the parents themselves it was already too late. The children were bundled on to trains, waved goodbye to their parents and set off into an unknown future in what has become known as the *Kindertransport* ('children's transport'). Some were no more than five years old. The vast majority never saw their parents again. Their stories are told in two books: ... *And the Policeman Smiled* by Barry Turner (1990), and *I Came Alone: The Story of the Kindertransport* (1990) by Berta Leverton. A recently revived play called *Kindertransport* describes very poignantly what some of the short-term and long-term effects of these abrupt and mostly permanent separations were.

Hidden children

Finally, there were the 'hidden children':

> They hid wherever they could for as long as it took the Allies to win the War, often separated from their families for months or even years. They lived in sewers, cupboards, barns, attics or woods – any place that might provide shelter. They had to grow up overnight, behave as adults, fabricate new identities and sacrifice their childhood to save their lives. They could not cry, and it was perilous to be sick. They were innocent victims of a world gone mad.

Their story is told by Jane Marks in *The Hidden Children* (1993). It is only very recently that they finally broke their silence and began to talk of their experiences in hiding. In 1991 a gathering of 1,600 of the 'hidden children' took place in New York, where for the first time they began to tell their stories. They had remained in 'emotional hiding' for almost half a century.

Lessons for our time

With the vast number of recent human catastrophes, mass murders and genocides, it has become particularly important to learn all we can from the experience of the survivors of 50 years ago, from mistakes made at the time, and from lessons learned from victims of more recent atrocities in Somalia, Rwanda, Bosnia, Zaire and elsewhere.

This was brought home to me quite poignantly at a joint meeting of the Medical Foundation for Victims of Torture and a recently formed organization called PCSR (Psychotherapists and Counsellors for Social Responsibility). The purpose of the meeting was to look at counsellors' and therapists' work with refugees and survivors of torture, and it highlighted the consequences of persecution, exile, loss of home, country, language, culture, profession, status, relationships and everything that had been familiar. We heard from the refugees about the permanent and severe damage to whole families and communities. Contrary to government protestations about 'bogus refugees', those who actually make it to our shores are a very tiny proportion of the estimated 27 million people currently living in exile or refugee camps. Figures of millions, however, lose their meaning. We cannot empathize with millions, but the personal stories of a few refugees who have managed to escape recently from persecution, torture and imprisonment bring home the pain and grief, which remain part of the refugees' lives, even when they integrate and become established professionally and socially in their host country.

At the PCSR meeting it struck me how important and valuable it would be to make more use of the vast body of knowledge and information about survivors of the Holocaust which has been gathered since the end of the Second World War. No previous genocide has been studied, researched and documented as thoroughly as the Holocaust. This material also provides information about the second and third generation and the profound effect of living with parents who have been so severely traumatized, and helps us to recognize the considerable contribution which refugees can and have made to their host societies, a fact which is frequently ignored.

The survivor syndrome

There is a range of symptoms which are common to people who have been exposed to massive traumatization, such as somatic symptoms, sleep disturbances, flashbacks, nightmares, ruminations and depression. A sense of guilt for having been spared is also common, but is particularly pronounced in Holocaust survivors. They frequently suffer from an overwhelming sense of sadness and isolation and from intense fear of separation. Even a very brief separation from an adult son or daughter can cause intense anxiety, amounting to panic. At the same time, they generally find it hard to acknowledge weakness and illness since these meant instant death in the camps. Ensuring safety for their families, extreme vigilance regarding danger, and making sure that the larder is always filled, can be constant preoccupations. In some cases pieces of bread were hidden in secret places for years after the liberation. Eating problems are common in the children of survivors, and many suffer from anorexia, which causes even greater anxiety in survivor parents than in Jewish parents normally. Often even a morsel of food could make the difference between living for another day or dying.

One of the defences which was essential for survival in the camps was a cutting off from all feelings, a feature of post-traumatic symptomatology:

> All feelings ceased to be. One could not exist and at the same time live with such feelings of abhorrence, disgust and terror. There was an automatisation of the ego which produced robot-like numbness and a psychological closure. This was a necessary strategy for survival during imprisonment, but frequently created difficulties in the survivors' relationships with spouses and children later in their lives. Some remained frozen in their grief and unable to enjoy anything. (Lifton 1976)

Another ongoing after-effect of the Holocaust experience was the survivors' suppressed rage. It would have been fatal to weep or lament as a prisoner, and any expression of rage would have resulted in instant death.

Professional responses

The concept of concentration camp or survivor syndrome was not identified as a syndrome with specific characteristics in the early years after the war, and doctors and psychiatrists were frequently trying to fit the patients' symptoms into organic or psychiatric categories which were inappropriate and did not match.

Camp survivors themselves rarely asked for counselling or therapy in the early years after their liberation, but when they were seen for physical or psychological conditions the doctors' or psychiatrists' reports from this period generally contained just one sentence about the fact that the patient had been in a concentration camp. Very little notice was taken of the impact of the intense and prolonged traumatization suffered by these survivors. There was a distinct reluctance on the part of the general population, as well as of medical and psychiatric services, to become closely involved with such severely traumatized people. It was as if the survivors were tainted in some way.

It was also enormously difficult for survivors to put into words experiences which defy description, and there seemed to be a feeling that only exceptional writers such as Primo Levi and Elie Wiesel could do justice to the experience of living in the hell of the camps. They both received the Nobel Prize for their work. It is only during recent years that others have begun to write autobiographical accounts of their lives in the camps.

Some survivors longed to talk to a sympathetic listener, but there was a good deal of reluctance to do so because of shame and guilt as well as mistrust and the conviction that it was utterly impossible for anyone who had not experienced life in the camps even to begin to understand. This applies largely even today, although in recent years survivors have begun to speak out both publicly and privately. There is now a sense of urgency about letting the world know what really happened, before it is too late and there is no one left to remember. There is also a wish to combat the earlier as well as the more recent denial of the Holocaust.

For the relatively small number of psychiatrists, counsellors and psychotherapists who attempted to work with survivors therapeutically, there was often a reaction of: 'It can't be true: it is impossible and inconceivable.' Dr William Niederland (1976) writes: 'The denial is not just the defence of the patient, but also of the one who listens and there was frequently a kind of tacit agreement between patient and doctor to gloss over and thereby ignore the traumatic data.'

Today counsellors are just beginning to wonder whether we have been overdoing the rushing in to offer counselling for any one-off trauma, yet for the survivors of the concentration camps there was very little help on offer at the time – it came only several decades later.

The survivors themselves soon got the message that the world did not want to know about the Holocaust, but they were also primarily concerned with making new homes and creating new families and new lives. They mostly kept themselves very busy and active, which was also a way of keeping painful memories at bay. This worked quite well up to a point, until they began to age and were forced to slow down because of retirement, illness, and fewer demands from family and careers. Old age is generally a time for reflection rather than hyperactivity, but for survivors it meant that this escape from painful memories became less possible, and old memories and nightmares began to re-surface. With more time on their hands, greater physical weakness and ill-health, old fears returned: any sign of weakness would have led to instant selection for the gas chambers in the camps. These associations still haunt them. There are also fears that they may lose their hard-won independence, become dependent on others, and will no longer be in control of their own lives. The need to be in control was especially important because in the camps they had no control whatsoever and were totally at the mercy of brutal, sadistic and unpredictable guards.

Delayed mourning and survivor guilt

Ageing also means the inevitable loss of spouses, other relations, contemporaries and friends. Most people find such losses hard to bear, but for survivors they can be catastrophic, because they reactivate feelings about all the other losses during their imprisonment. Many survivors lost all their family members. In some cases, especially for those from eastern Europe, this could mean 60 or 70 people. There was no way in which they could mourn for all those who were killed or who starved or just disappeared. There were no graves, no rituals, no prayers for the dead, no bodies even, and, of course no possibility of expressing grief.

Dr Joost Merloo in 'Delayed mourning in victims of extermination camps' was 'amazed and surprised to find that with all the horror of the camps peoples' greatest complaint was that they had not been premitted to mourn' (1976). It was not the torture, nor the starvation, humiliation or degradation which kept them down even many years later, but the lack of any ceremonial. In the midst of the hell of death the survivors felt themselves to be as guilty as the Nazi murderers. This survivor guilt frequently remained with them for the rest of their lives, because one of the hidden thoughts of virtually every inmate had been: 'If my neighbour gets killed before me, I get another chance of survival.' Elie Wiesel, a survivor of several camps, said in connection with this hidden wish: 'If the figure for killings on any particular day was 10,000, and I was 10,001, I would live another day.' Many former inmates continue to reproach themselves for surviving when all their loved ones died, and go on asking: 'Why did I not save them? Why did I survive when my brother, sister, parent or wife who were so much better than I, had to die?' And when it was a child who died, there is the extra guilt of a parent not able to protect their son or daughter.

Delayed mourning and identification with the murdered victims is often triggered by the actual death of relatives or friends, and being helped to mourn those they could not mourn at the time is an essential part of therapy or counselling with survivors.

Loss of independence

I mentioned already how utterly terrifying the prospect of having to go into hospital or a home can be for the elderly survivor. It triggers memories of being taken by the Gestapo and never seeing their home or their families again. It can even cause mental breakdowns which resemble psychotic episodes with paranoid features. This may happen even where there has been no sign of mental instability during the previous 40 or 50 years, during which they have been relatively symptom-free. Samuel A., a man in his early 70s, had come to Britain in 1947, having spent several years in concentration and displaced persons' camps after the war. He had made an apparently good adjustment, had married and had two grown-up children with whom he had a somewhat distant relationship, but no major problems. He had suffered from insomnia, occasional flashbacks, and some depression, especially at the time of year when his parents had been killed, and he himself was taken but there had been no major health problems until he had a heart attack and had to be admitted to hospital. He became extremely panicky when two ambulancemen collected him from his home. He was adamant that he was not going into hospital in spite of his condition and the threat to his life if he did not receive treatment. The ambulancemen somehow managed to get him into the ambulance, but he became more and more disturbed. It emerged later that the uniforms of the ambulancemen had revived memories of the uniformed Nazis in the camps, and being carted off in an ambulance brought back memories of the train which had taken him away from his home, which he never saw again. Being helpless again, and, as it seemed to him, at the mercy of others, obliterated present reality, and he felt as if he were back in that terrifying past.

It is not only uniforms which can trigger flashbacks but also sounds of cars backfiring, reminding survivors of the constant and indiscriminate shootings in the camps. Smells too can trigger memories of the stench of death all around and of the gas ovens working overtime.

Survivors themselves can still be reluctant to talk about their Holocaust background, even though in recent years there has been much greater openness on their part, but once suspicions have been aroused, as was the case with Samuel A., they will clam up. To trust strangers, especially non-Jewish ones, can still at times be difficult. Trust of the non-Jewish world was totally lost during their Holocaust experience, although there were also people in several European countries who risked their own lives by hiding individuals and occasionally whole families. The Dutch couple who hid Anne Frank and her family ended up in a concentration camp themselves, and were killed. Only Anne's father survived. There were a few really heroic people such as Raoul Wallenberg and Frank Foley who each saved 10,000 Jews, but for those who experienced only the Nazi persecutors and none of the rescuers, suspicion can still be aroused even now, and, like Samuel A., they easily feel threatened.

A Jewish counselling service

It was partly with this in mind that a Jewish counselling service was established in 1978. It was called the Raphael Centre after the Angel of Healing mentioned in the Hebrew Bible. As the centre became known, the number of survivors who applied to it increased steadily, and through case discussions and supervision we came to learn more about this special group of clients and to discover some of their particular difficulties.

Many of the survivor clients told us that they could not have 'taken the risk' of going to a Health Service department or other non-Jewish clinic. It was very important for them to know that their counsellor would understand their background and history, even if it took them quite some time before they were able to talk of their experiences with some degree of openness. For the counsellors it was often a most distressing and difficult experience and it was hard not to become overwhelmed by what they heard. There was a danger of over-identification, and a wish to protect the client from the pain of remembering. Counsellors who had no Holocaust background themselves sometimes experienced feelings of irrational guilt because they had not suffered or lost members of their families. Others felt they had not done enough to fight the 'evil'. For all these reasons it was particularly important for the counsellors to meet regularly for case discussion and supervision, to enable them to look closely at the feelings triggered in them, and to regain their professional distance.

For some clients the Raphael Centre represented an idealized 'Jewish mother' who would provide for all their needs, and as a result they became excessively demanding. One client, who was never actually seen, telephoned frequently to demand that we should contact the Polish authorities and ask them to restore his parents' property. Although a slight misunderstanding of our function, it was an expression of the expectation that as a Jewish Centre we should be ready and able to meet every need.

Other transference and countertransference reactions

The tendency on the part of some survivor clients to see anyone in authority as a potential Nazi can evoke hostile feelings as well as compassion in the counsellor/therapist.

> Many of the survivors have a masochistic character problem which brings out sadistic impulses in authority figures with whom they interact. They experience the examiner who makes them recall the painful events of the persecution as their enemy, who in the immediate transference can be experienced as a new edition of an SS or Gestapo officer. The unconscious tendency to form an aggressive, authoritarian, degrading or over-indulgent counter-transference can create a special problem. It is important therefore to be constantly aware of these counter-transference reactions. (Krystal 1976)

Undetected countertransference can lead to loss of empathy, as happened with the German doctors and psychiatrists who had to see survivors after the war to assess the degree of damage which was due to their wartime experience, in order that survivors could claim their pensions. These psychiatrists tended to be cold and distant and looked only at organic damage, ignoring psychological effects, so that in most cases the claims for pensions were rejected by the German authorities, irrespective of the damage to claimants. This was generally due to unrecognized and unacknowledged negative transferences, and was not very helpful to the patients. Countertransferences which are recognized and acknowledged can be used constructively and make a positive contribution to the therapeutic process. Dora was one of very few survivor patients referred to me during nearly 30 years in the Health Service. She was 69 years old, married, with two sons who had done well socially and professionally. Dora had seen me for a few weeks when she was due to have her house redecorated. All the arrangements had been made for her and her husband to move out for a couple of weeks while the decorating was proceeding, but as the date for their temporary move drew near, Dora went into a state of acute anxiety and felt quite unable to contemplate this move. My initial reaction was of mild irritation, as it had taken a good deal of work and preparation to get Dora to this point, but my reaction seemed to be uncalled for, since as therapists we have to be prepared to work with extreme or irrational behaviour much of the time. I had the impression that Dora was deliberately withholding information and I was puzzled until she began to talk about the time she had spent away from home with friends only to discover that during her absence the Gestapo had called at her home and taken her parents and her younger sister. She alone had escaped. Once we were able to make this connection between her absence from the parental home and the current anxiety about her temporary absence, my irritation disappeared, and Dora was able to go ahead with the decorating and the temporary move. It was an important insight for both of us.

Recent reactions to survivors

In 1980 an international conference on the survivor syndrome was organized by Caroline Garland and Earl Hopper under the auspices of the Tavistock Clinic. It brought together a large number of people with a special interest in survivors of the Holocaust as well as of other genocides. It was an outstanding conference, evoking strong passions, which is still remembered vividly by those who attended it, but it did not result in a great increase of referrals. In 1988 there was another, much larger, international conference, organized by Elisabeth Maxwell, which took place in Oxford and was called 'Remembering for the Future'. It attracted several hundred participants and a vast number of experts from many fields who had studied the effects of massive trauma. In addition to the experts, there were also a number of quite vocal survivors, no longer prepared to remain silent.

I recall vividly how angry and misunderstood many of them felt about what they saw as 'being pathologized' and fitted into medical categories of sickness, which they rejected vehemently. They pointed out that they had, on the whole, made reasonable adjustments, and many had successful careers and had created new families. Few of them had consulted psychiatrists, therapists or counsellors, and they had long periods of being virtually symptom-free. Their children and grandchildren might not quite agree, but the experience of the second and third generation, although very relevant, is another story.

What is most helpful for survivors?

Following the Oxford conference a few counsellors, therapists and social workers met together with some of the survivors who had also attended, in order to look at the kind of provision which would meet the survivors' needs and wishes. This resulted in the establishment of a Holocaust Survivors Centre in 1992. The Centre provides an opportunity for its members to meet informally for a variety of activities. It is a place where survivors can be with others with whom they can share memories and experiences, and who will understand them as no one else can. This often helps to reduce the sense of isolation which many of them still feel in the company of people who did not share the camp experience.

Activities and therapies which are of help to survivors

There are no treatments or activities which are of help to all survivors, and it is particularly important for those attempting to counsel, to offer therapy or groups, to be as flexible as possible. Clients have much to teach as well as to learn. With Holocaust survivors this is even more important, because of their special sensitivities. Counsellors need to learn from them about activities and approaches which they can make use of as well as those that are unhelpful. Judy Hassan, Director of the Survivors Centre, emphasizes that 'many survivors need their defences to cope with their lives and may not wish to look at their past even now'. It is necessary to find a medium that is possible for them.

> This can take the form of art or music as well as dialogue. Some join self-help groups in which they share what they can. These groups can create a sense of community and belonging. Some

survivors write their stories, some make tapes for their grandchildren and future generations, others give interviews for historical archives.

All this can help survivors to feel that there is still something important they can do, a contribution they can still make to the society they live in and a way of fighting those who even now deny that the Holocaust ever happened. There are others who act as 'educators' and are invited by schools and other educational institutions to talk of their own memories and experiences. To have an actual survivor in their midst, one who was there, is generally a powerful experience for the listeners.

What counsellors and therapists can offer

For most survivors there is a great deal of 'unfinished business'. This applies particularly to the mourning, which was not possible at the time their major losses occurred. Talking of and remembering a murdered relative can make it possible to express some of the suppressed grief, pain and rage, and enable them to be more in touch with other emotions. Being cut off from feelings and frozen in their pain and grief often led to total emotional inaccessibility, especially in relation to their own children. For many it may be too late to undo years of silence caused by the mistaken desire to protect their children from the impact of such horror and the children's wish to protect parents from the pain of remembering.

Improvement in communication between the generations, however, is still possible, and can be promoted by groups in which members of both generations (not belonging to the same family) come together. Once they can begin to listen to each other and recognize the pain and difficulties each of them experienced, dialogue can take place between them and lead on to dialogue within their own families. This was particularly important and helpful a few years ago, but many survivors now find it easier to talk to their grandchildren. The most important issue for many survivors now is how to face old age, the deaths of spouses and contemporaries, and their own death. They fought hard for survival, and death can have the connotation of victory for the Nazi perpetrators.

What, if anything, have we learned from the Holocaust and its aftermath?

Looking at the many horrific genocides, civil wars and violence in the world today, we may be justified in thinking that as societies we have learned pathetically little. But that is not altogether true. We have learned that the long-term damage to severely traumatized people is increased considerably if the world stands by and goes into denial for the next 30 or 40 years. It is said that we have to repeat what we don't want to remember. Is it possible that the increase in violence and atrocities in so many parts of the world today are a consequence of this denial? There is no definitive answer to this question at present, but what we can say is that future generations may be spared some of the pain and suffering of the survivors of the Holocaust and their children if we apply the knowledge we have gained from our work with them. Education and information can play an important part in this, and survivors themselves often make the best educators, as indicated earlier. It may also require a conscious effort on the part of all of us – victims, prepetrators, counsellors and clients – to become informed and pool our knowledge.

References

Frankl, V. (1959) *Man's Search for Meaning*, London: Allport.

Gilbert, M. (1996) 'Recollections of Rabbi Hugo Gryn', in *Jewish Chronicle*, 20 August.

Krystal, H. (1976) 'Clinical observations on the survivor syndrome', in H. Krystal (ed.), *Massive Psychic Trauma*, New York and London: International Universities Press, pp. 327ff.

Leverton, B. (1990) *I Came Alone: The Stories of the Kindertransports*, Sussex, England: The Book Guild Ltd.

Lifton, R.J.M.D. (1976) 'Similarities and differences between survivors of the Hiroshima disaster and Nazi persecution', in H. Krystal (ed.), *Massive Psychic Trauma*, New York and London: International Universities Press.

Marks, J. (1993) *The Hidden Children*, London: Piatkus.

Merloo, J. (1976) 'Delayed mourning in victims of extermination camps', in H. Krystal (ed.), *Massive Psychic Trauma*, New York and London: International Universities Press.

Niederland, W. (1976) 'The problem of the survivor', in H. Krystal (ed.), *Massive Psychic Trauma.*

Oliner, S.P. and Oliner, P.M. (1988) *The Altruistic Personality*, New York: The Free Press, Collier Macmillan.

Turner, B. (1990) *... And The Policeman Smiled*, London: Bloomsbury Publishing.

Discussion issues

1 To bear witness to an accumulation of atrocious human behaviour and to testify to the individual sorrows and traumas of their own experience. Are these the redeeming needs of all survivors?

2 Children and grandchildren of survivors may choose not to be 'Jewish', perhaps to avoid potential persecution. If they prefer to work with non-Jewish counsellors what might be the resulting advantages and/or difficulties?

3 What do creative therapies offer those who find the trauma of being a survivor beyond spoken words?

4 Sharing the pain of survivors requires an enduring empathy. Does such empathy have limits? What might a counsellor do when they reach these?

17

An Experience of Intercultural Counselling

Views from a Black client

Tuck-Chee Phung

> This personal account is a response to Aisha Dupont-Joshua's article on Inter-Cultural Therapy, *Counselling*, vol. 5, no. 3, pp. 203–5 (August 1994).

About three years ago I decided to seek counselling to deal with the impact of racism on me. In my work I had become more aware of my racial identity, and with it the history of being Chinese in a British society. I had none the less continued to interpret what I now termed as 'prejudices' and 'discrimination' as unfortunate personal encounters with the world at large. This interpretation of such encounters was shattered by my experience as the only non-White participant in a two-day conference on anti-racism. Although two of the facilitators were Black, it was a struggle for me to be the only non-White participant in the conference. I found it difficult to accept what some White people were saying about racism, namely: 'There is no racism where we live', and 'Our organization cannot prioritize resources for this problem.' I became aware of two things. One, the unconscious collusiveness of group behaviour in denying the perspectives of the other and how disabling I found this. Two, that there was hostility in a silence that left things unsaid, therefore unchallenged. I struggled in the two days to present an alternative view, drawing examples from my own personal experiences.

The experience of invisibility

In these two days, I became aware of something larger than personal racism, in the shape of organizational or institutional racism by which the agenda and process were determined by the majority. And the experience of being a minority in such a setting was for me 'invisibility'. I was listened to but not really heard. I came away from this conference ungrounded and depleted, losing my sense of faith and hope that racism could be tackled in our society. I date the awakening of my political consciousness from this time and there were consequences arising from this experience. In addition to having to cope with my own emotions, I felt I had to re-evaluate my life and my relationships, both personal and professional, in the context of this new-found political awareness. The issues of power and stereotyping in race and culture were, for me, important features in my interactions with other people and these required some attention. The realization that I had colluded in situations and internalized racism was painful. It was in this context that I sought help from counselling.

This chapter was first published in *Counselling*, Journal of the British Association for Counselling, vol. 6, no. 1, pp. 61–2 (February 1995).

133

I wanted in particular to work with a Black counsellor, because of what I needed to explore. I had some sense that a Black counsellor might empathize with me better because of his/her own experiences of racism, and that they might have some shared history of colonialism. I did not wish to examine my pain of racism in front of a White person. However, the reality was that there were, and are, no Black counsellors in northeast Scotland. Inquiries produced two names of accredited White counsellors and I made an appointment to see one of them. I was nervous because I was not sure how we would respond to each other within the context of what I wanted to explore. He said two things at this meeting which enabled me to make some perceptual shift in recognizing that it was all right to work with him in spite of my initial intention: he acknowledged that he was a second choice for me and also that we needed to look at our differences. I felt good about this insightfulness which I reckoned was an important starting point.

At about this time I also made contact with a group of Black people working in my profession in Scotland and was able to meet with them and maintain some contact between meetings. This was an important parallel development to my work with the counsellor. I found the meetings with this group supportive and affirmative. I was understood in this group without having to explain and justify my experiences of racism. I adopted the political term 'Black', because it provided me with a framework to deal with racism. This is not an easy definition for me to hold, because I did not see myself as a political person and the term in itself produced some startling reactions from people around me. Most important of all, I found it empowering to be in contact with other Black people, and this indirectly facilitated my work with the counsellor because it clarified for me what I needed to look at.

The experience of counselling

The counselling relationship was essentially interactive – challenging and being challenged, reflective and supportive, enabling me to explore a range of situations. An essential aspect of the interaction was the counsellor's capacity to deal with structural and organizational issues, as well as personal ones. Too often counselling deals only with personal issues without acknowledging structural concerns, which in itself can be oppressive, and clients are then in danger of being pathologized. Certainly racism is not only a personal perception of an experience but is also a reality of the society we live in, and this needs to be acknowledged in any counselling relationship involving a Black client.

The counsellor, in acknowledging his own racial identity and his status of being White, acknowledged the difference in our world. I learned that our interest in racism could be similar, as we both believe in justice. I had a sense that he was an ally. On reflection, I think his openness and absence of defensiveness created a bridge of understanding for me. I was touched by his humanity. Our work together lasted for about two years, and the gift in it was that it partly restored my faith that there were people who cared enough to want to heal the damage caused by racism.

There is of course no guarantee that I will not again be ungrounded by what I encounter in the world. And racism will exist. There is a probability that, in being more aware, I will be more open to my feelings when I encounter prejudice and discrimination. There may be a better chance that I will cope more effectively with racism because

I am clearer about my own agenda. I think as a result of counselling I have also emerged as a better worker in my job because I have become more integrated as a person.

As a way of ending our work together, the counsellor asked me to consider not just what I had gained from counselling but what I had not. As an answer to the latter, I said that working with a Black counsellor would have offered me a different experience. The starting point would perhaps have focused on similarities rather than differences. This answer does not diminish in any way for me the valuable work I have done with an extremely skilled White counsellor. I was fortunate to have one and I am aware that Black clients have a limited choice from counselling services. Yes, there need to be more Black counsellors, and White counsellors need to take on board the reality of racism experienced by their Black clients. (See Chapter 88.)

Discussion issues

1 What do you think might be the issues in intercultural counselling in the article for (a) the counsellor and (b) the client?
2 How as a counsellor can you prepare to work across race and culture? What aspects of your counselling training and experiences have helped you in intercultural counselling?
3 In the interests of promoting equal opportunities and eradicating 'institutional racism', examine the organizational and counselling context in which you work as a counsellor and identify ways you could make an improvement in offering counselling to clients from a different racial and cultural background.
4 Can you outline some anti-racist principles which are essential to your counselling practice?

18

In the Counsellor's Chair

Intercultural counselling

Aisha Dupont-Joshua interviews Lennox Thomas

At the time of this interview Lennox Thomas was the Clinical Director of the Nafsiyat Inter-Cultural Therapy Cenre in London. Originally from Grenada, he was one of the first black psychotherapists in Britain, and is a leading figure in the ideas of intercultural therapy. A member of the British Association of Psychotherapists and a member of the Group for Advancement of Psychotherapy and Psychodynamics in Social Work, he was joint course director of the UCL M.Sc. in Intercultural Psychotherapy and is a visiting teacher at the Tavistock Centre. Involved in race and gender equality training since 1981; a training therapist and supervisor to three organizations with UKCP membership, Lennox Thomas works in private practice in London with individuals, couples and families.

How do you come to be heading the Nafsiyat Inter-Cultural Therapy Centre?

I have been involved with Nafsiyat since its beginning in 1982, with Jafar Kareem. I was one of the first therapists who worked here sessionally and then as a supervisor. Jafar and I first met because we both trained as psychotherapists with the British Association of Psychotherapists and we became friendly as a result of one of the papers he gave to the United Anglo-Caribbean Society, in the early 1980s, on working therapeutically with people from ethnic minorities. We became quite friendly and I learned about Nafsiyat which was about to be established. I then came to work here. I worked in the evenings as a therapist, two or three evenings a week, and then we went away and spent time working on the ideas, looking at the principles that we thought would be needed in order to run the organization.

Now you are directing, how did that come about?

It happened sadly because my dear friend, colleague and mentor, Jafar Kareem, died in 1992, and although it would have seemed perfectly obvious that I would have applied for the post that became vacant after his death, it really didn't occur to me until quite some time after, that maybe it was one of the things that I'd care to do. I'd actually been working in the probation service for 19 years, and after working in the public services for that length of time you'd have to be crazy to want to leave, because of all the pension rights and all the kind of security that one got as a result of that, which I certainly don't get in

---

This chapter was first published in *Counselling*, Journal of the British Association for Counselling, vol. 6, no. 3, pp. 180–2 (1995).

this job. I thought that it was worth a change. Nineteen years in the same organization was probably too long, and I thought that maybe I should take a risk.

Tell us a bit about your background – your upbringing, education experience and a bit about the passage of your life.

Well let's start at the beginning. I was born in the Caribbean, on the island of Grenada, and was raised there until I was seven years old before coming to this country. My brother, parents and I settled in a very small town, not quite a village but a very small town in Derbyshire. We lived there for a few years and then moved to the nearby city of Nottingham. I left Nottingham when I was 18 to come to London to study.

Why did your family move to England?

In the late fifties and early sixties people in the Caribbean thought that they probably wanted to take a risk, some people wanted to have a change, and do something different. Some came for economic reasons and others came because friends were coming. In my father's case, he came to this country with two friends who were not married and didn't have any responsibilities. My parents married quite young. My father's friends were travelling to England and they said 'Why don't you come and join us – it'll be nice, and good for your children, they'll enjoy the opportunity.' They came reluctantly; my father wasn't keen and my mother wasn't all that interested in leaving her life in the Caribbean. They weren't badly off, they weren't poor, they were secure, had employment, a home and prospects. They came, and as soon as they arrived decided they were going back. They didn't stay in this country for more than ten years. As soon as we were big enough to get on with education they went back.

How did you get on in school – how did racial issues affect you?

I loved school, I enjoyed it. As far as the system is concerned I don't know that I actually understood quite what was going on in the system until I was a little older. But there was some discrimination that I observed when I was seven, you know, being called names by some children, but that actually subsided and then I began to notice that it was the teachers who discriminated, were off-hand, racist, or made negative comments.

Towards you?

Yes towards me personally and to black people collectively. You know the usual thing – like when I was able to give a correct definition of the use of the words 'where' and 'were' and give a description of the different usage, one English teacher told the rest of the class that they should be ashamed of themselves because Thomas is a foreigner, and came from a country that didn't speak English properly and that he knew the definition better than they did. And that was the kind of thing that was done to undermine me as a person, and my relationship with classmates. Other things that were not done to me, but these are stories of people that I know – being told in the convent school, that black people couldn't get to heaven as easily as white people. So there was a lot of subtle racism that actually belonged to the professionals, in whose care we are entrusted, and you know that does undermine children. Fortunately one of the good things for me was that my father was very affirming and Pan-Africanist. He was the person that I could talk to about these things.

Your family's belief system seems to have been very important to you.

Religion had been quite a big part of our lives as a family, as well as socialism – I mean the things went side by side.

How come they went side by side?

Well they did – for some people they do. Socialist-Christians – in fact there are groups of Socialist-Christians, and they were side by side. And I think that they were side by side because I think that religion is something that is actually quite traditional. Christianity is quite traditional in a lot of the Caribbean islands as a representation of a spiritual life, which had probably replaced an African spiritual life, that most of the people would have had and experienced. So for us it was Christianity.

Do you find that socialist ideas go along with social work? That the two are interlinked?

Yes, it's about redressing social wrongs, redressing balances in society and helping the least privileged in our society to make changes through social and psychological changes in their lives.

Would you see that your social work and probation work linked up with your work in psychotherapy? Do you see that they overlap?

They always did. The type of social work that I was taught would be indistinguishable from psychotherapy. In fact during the period of the 1940s and 1950s in the social work profession, we were influenced by psychoanalysis and we influenced psychoanalysis in turn. People like Helen Harris-Perlman, Elizabeth Irvine, Kathleen Feraud and Noel Honeybun have been pioneering social workers. Florence Hollis, writer on psychosocial therapy, has actually worked very closely to understand people's social conditions, people's social motivations as connected to their psychological states – very connected.

Would you see yourself as a pioneer? You must have been one of the first black men to do counselling and social work in Britain.

I certainly felt that I had to be a trail-blazer – and I had to be conscious of the fact that I was being watched. Right from the start I became involved in advancing services for black users, black clients.

Why do you think that you chose counselling and psychotherapy as ways of working with race and culture?

I think that counselling and psychotherapy are ways of working with race and culture – there's lots of other ways of working with racial and cultural issues, but this organization is specifically looking at ethnicity and cultural ideas. I think that every profession has to look at itself and examine how its practices don't discriminate, and furthermore how its practices could actually enhance differences, and actually help people to a better under-standing of their position – if they're white or black or of mixed parentage or whatever. I felt that I couldn't actually practise as a psychotherapist and pretend that race wasn't an issue in psychotherapy. It was only during the course of my training that I realized how little colleagues considered issues of race in psychotherapy.

Did you voice this and if so what was the reaction?

I can't remember, but I suppose it would have been a blank or a bland response. But then I realized, as I also realized when I trained as a social worker, that if I want to find this sort of thing out, I have to get about it myself – and that's precisely what I did. I scoured the references, tried to find books, made contacts with people I had known – I had fortunately known psychoanalysts in America, and managed to get information. I needed to do this just for the purpose of the paper that I wrote at the end of my psychotherapy training.

Was that to do with black issues?

Oh yes – it was to do with clinical issues, and since I was the clinician, it had to involve issues about black people. The patients that I treated were white and for one of them our racial difference was significant.

And that was accepted? Well received or not?

It was received – I don't know if it was well received, but I know that a couple of members of the association that I belonged to became very interested, spoke to me about it, and wanted to read what I had written. A couple of people said 'This is very interesting because I am also working with a black man or woman in therapy – and this is quite interesting for me to hear.'

Did you feel isolated in your training?

No I didn't – maybe that's something to do with the person that I am. To a large extent I don't have any great expectations. I know that I can be taught so much and the rest I have to do for myself – I have to learn for myself. So there is no great disillusionment or any great disappointment that I hadn't been given what I wanted.

I have talked with some black trainee counsellors/therapists and they have been very distressed when bringing up racial and cultural issues on their training courses especially in therapy groups – it's brushed away – and they feel very isolated with their feelings.

Well you see if I hadn't trained fifteen years ago and I was in training now, then I probably would feel like that.

Why?

Because training institutions should know more about those issues now. And you see I was probably among the first black psychotherapists in training, so as a trail-blazer yet again I didn't expect that people knew anything about how to teach me, what was going to be pertinent to my clinical practice, how transference or countertransference would be affected by the fact that I was working with white people and I was a black person. So I found those things out for myself and I had no expectations – but I think now a trainee should have expectations of the training organization or a supervisor.

Do you still enjoy your client work?

I do, immensely. In fact that's probably one of the reasons why I decided to leave the probation service, because it was no longer possible – you know one was being a manager, not a practitioner. And I liked working with clients.

How do you see the current situation in intercultural ideas, in Britain at the moment, and the taking on of racial and cultural issues.

Well certainly the people who are from the minorities will take them up. Those who have become counsellors and psychotherapists will take them up and some other people will.

Are or will?

Are, some people are. You see one of the interesting things about Nafsiyat was that it was seen as quite an oddball sort of place, because people couldn't quite understand how psychotherapy could have a particular focus on cultural or racial difference. How could it be? Psychotherapy was neutral, wasn't it? That was a silly question, but people actually are able to see that therapists have to prepare themselves, have to be armed with some knowledge to receive and understand the differences that people present them with, and have the courage to work with those differences. Before Nafsiyat and other intercultural ideas developed, black people weren't considered to be psychologically minded enough for psychotherapy. They were considered to have too many gross social problems to overcome for psychotherapy to have any influence in their lives, and I thought that was very discriminating.

Do you feel comfortable about talking about clients' reaction to you, as an individual and as a black man?

Yes – well all of the clients that I see at Nafsiyat are usually very positive. They have this kind of sense of relief that they've come to a place – a lot of the Caribbean, Asian and people from other minorities feel a sense of relief, and it's interesting that while people have said things like they're really pleased that there is a place like Nafsiyat, I think that there is still a difficulty in actually getting to transference issues. At the same time as being really pleased that I'm a black person and that I can listen to them and I will give them a chance, there is still sometimes a suspicion that actually lies at the root of black people, and black people together. That kind of fear that I've talked about earlier, about the kind of negative self-identity, and self-hatred which works itself out quite efficiently in a black therapist/black client's transference relationship. Sometimes we don't get that far because people are in a brief therapy, but in longer therapeutic pairings you can't escape it. People have internalized such negative images and negative ideas about themselves as black that it is then projected on to me as being not much good, not of any use – 'can't be good because he's not white' – in order to regulate their own internal processes they will regulate their comfort or discomfort by the use of projection. There's a white person that I'm seeing at the moment who actually came through the door for the first meeting – he is actually married to a black woman – he came through the door with an immense surprise and I couldn't help but comment on it during the assessment session with him. I said 'You seemed quite taken aback when you saw me at the front door', and he said, 'Well I was so pleased that you were black because if I really were asked who I wanted to have as a therapist I would have said a black man.' And you see I couldn't disbelieve him because I know from the experience of working with him that it's true. In much the same way I made a point of having a white male analyst the second time. I can see that he probably did the same. People make certain connections in their minds about what they want to confront in themselves, which can be an image of 'the other' and they go and find that situation in order to work.

Lennox, how do you see the condition of counselling and psychotherapy at the present time, especially in Britain?

I think counselling and psychotherapy is going to broaden its base, to take on board issues of race, gender, sexuality, culture and disabilities. It has to – because I think counselling has grown as a profession and is now probably a very strong profession. People actually counsel on particular issues or particular problems. I think that counsellors have a particular skill in being much more specific about the focus of their work, and I think that to a large extent counsellors are going to be able to address some of those contextual differences of race, gender, sexuality or culture, because they are much more focused. Systems-thinking people largely working with families are also becoming very interested in these issues. (See Chapter 88.)

To conclude, Lennox, do you feel that on a national counselling organizational level racial and cultural issues are being written into their constitutions?

The BAC has a section, the United Kingdom Council for Psychotherapy (UKCP) has a section, and this Inter-Cultural Committee looks at race/cultural issues, gender and disabilities issues – it's been an expanded role for that committee since January 1995 – so it is beginning to be written into the constitutions at an organizational level.

Lennox, thank you for sitting in the Counsellor's Chair

Discussion issues

1 Why are cultural identity and family history important avenues of exploration for non-English clients?
2 Explore some of the transference and countertransference issues that might occur with a black therapist and a white client.
3 Why might black students on counselling courses say that these courses are not relevant to them?
4 How could the 'mixed raceness' of counselling dyads be a creative element in the relationship?

19

Issues Raised in a Counselling Support Group for HIV+ People in Zambia

Tomás Campbell, Tashisho Chabala and Gita Sheth

HIV infection is a major health problem in sub-Saharan Africa and Zambia has not escaped its devastating consequences. In 1992 it was reported that 6.18 per cent of the Zambian population was infected (Msiska 1992). The actual figure is likely to be much higher. HIV infection may bring many difficulties to the individual concerned of a physical, emotional, financial, social and psychological kind. Until recently HIV infection was not discussed in public in Zambia, resulting in a situation where people with HIV (PHIV) often do not have the opportunity to talk about their status in an environment which is confidential and non-judgemental. As a result it seems that many infected people feel isolated and stigmatized because of their status (Campbell et al. 1994). Support groups have been used in both Western style cultures and in Zambia (Hedge and Glover 1990; Campbell et al. 1994) to provide information about HIV/AIDS, to encourage mutual support and to help people cope with the emotional difficulties that being HIV+ may bring. This article describes a counselling support group for PHIV and discusses the issues within a Zambian context.

The Zambian context

The use of counselling techniques to help deal with health crises is a relatively new phenomenon in a developing country such as Zambia. Evidence from studies in developed countries suggests that provision of social support can have a positive effect on the course of disease in people with a terminal illness (Blazer 1982; Cohen and Syme 1985) and the work of Campbell et al. (1994) in Zambia seems to suggest that people *feel* better when they can talk to others about their problems and experiences. Counselling theories developed within a Western socio-economic framework cannot readily be transplanted into developing countries but it does seem that allowing people time, space and respect coupled with some professional expertise can be of great value.

Great care must be taken to understand the cultural and economic framework within which people with HIV are living in order for any counselling intervention to be successful. For example, most people in Zambia (including PHIV) are extremely poor and are not well educated. Women have low status and are even more disadvantaged than men in financial and educational terms (Central Statistical Office 1991). For counselling to be useful in such a context counsellors must be realistic about what can be achieved.

This chapter was first published in *Counselling*, Journal of the British Association for Counselling, vol. 6, no. 3, pp. 211–14 (1995).

Sometimes when people are offered counselling they see this as an opportunity to ask for other kinds of help such as financial, educational or medical. It is important for any counsellor in such a situation to be aware of his/her limitations and to have clear boundaries. Most counsellors are not in a position to help with financial and educational problems. These boundaries may be different from the usual therapeutic boundaries that counsellors in Western countries might use and may have to take into account cultural, social and economic factors that are unique to the culture. For example, it is very important that younger people display respect to older people whether or not the two people are in a counselling relationship; women might only attend for counselling with a male counsellor accompanied by a female relative; issues of confidentiality are different in a culture where all those in a family are entitled to know all medical details of a family member.

Other important cultural dimensions which need to be understood are that childbearing is extremely important in Zambia for both women and men. Fertility is high and women begin bearing children at a young age. By the age of 19 over 60 per cent are mothers or are pregnant for the first time (Demographic and Health Survey 1992). The practice of men (in particular) having more than one sexual partner is not uncommon. Within some of the ethnic groups polygamy is a traditional practice. These cultural dimensions of sexuality may be important when it comes to deciding such issues as protected sex and whether to have a family or not.

Kara Counselling and Training Trust is a non-governmental organization (NGO) established in 1991 and committed to the care of people with HIV/AIDS in Zambia. It has four main activities: (a) the provision of counselling services to PHIV or people who are worried that they may have been exposed to the virus; (b) counselling training; (c) community outreach education; (d) skills re/training for PHIV. It is a Lusaka-based organization but provides training to health workers from all over the country. The skills training scheme is based in Hope House which also operates as a community and activity centre for PHIV in Lusaka. It is a centrally based facility which also houses an autonomous organization named PALS (Positive And Living Squad) which is an informal network and campaigning organization for PHIV.

Counsellors working in Kara Counselling come from a variety of professional backgrounds such as social work, psychology, nursing and teaching. All the staff counsellors have a professional qualification and have received in-service training within the organization. A small number of the counsellors have trained on a professional full-time training course (diploma in counselling) established under the auspices of Kara Counselling by the first author. This was the first full-time professional counselling training course to be established in Zambia and currently attracts students from the wider central African region.

Why offer a group?

This article presents a case study of a support group for PHIVs in Lusaka, the capital of Zambia. All participants were attending a 12-week skills training course for PHIV in Hope House. They were being trained in such skills as batik, tailoring, wood and stone carving. The training course aimed to equip people with skills which they could use to generate an income through the sale of their work. While attending the training scheme, trainees were given a small amount of money each week as a transport allowance and had a cooked lunch every day. They also had access to medical help if they had any health problems while on the course. All the trainees were poor people who lived in shanty compounds in Lusaka. Most had never had a job and those participants who had been employed had worked in casual and unskilled jobs. Money was a big problem for everyone. In practical terms this meant that they would have enough money for one meal a day and very little spare for educating their children or buying medicines.

Previous skills training courses had established that many trainees had difficulty in coming to terms with their HIV+ status and in an attempt to meet the psychological and emotional needs of the trainees a counselling support group was established which they were invited to join. Membership of the group was restricted to those on the skills training scheme.

Aims and membership of the group

There were ten participants in the group: six women ranging in age from 23–34 years and four men ranging from 25–35 years. Most were married or widowed and those who were widowed had lost their spouses through AIDS. Only one member did not have children. Four participants had not informed their current sexual partner of their status. Most had discovered their HIV status within the 12 weeks prior to joining the skills training scheme.

The aims of group counselling were:

- to facilitate discussion about the problems they were facing as a result of their status;
- to encourage them to provide emotional and psychological support to each other;
- to identify and put into practice practical strategies to cope with their problems.

Facilitator's role

The facilitator conceptualized his role in two basic ways: (a) to create a safe environment where people could feel free to express themselves without censure or criticism, and (b) to encourage the participants to support each other by asking participants who had dealt with HIV-related problems in the past to share their experiences with the group. In this way members could learn and discuss how strategies could be adapted for their own particular circumstances. The facilitator also used brainstorming techniques to generate possible approaches, strategies or solutions to the difficulties that participants brought to the group. The participants were at different stages of their lives, with some being older and some younger, and the facilitator also tried to use this as a strength to help participants look at their situations from different perspectives. The facilitator did not adopt an expert stance in the group. Rather, he encouraged the group to rely on its own ingenuity, capacity to cope, and resourcefulness.

What happened in the sessions?

The hour-long group was run over eight consecutive weeks by a Zambian counsellor who was familiar with several of the local languages. A semi-structured interview was conducted before the group began which focused on members' feelings about their status and their current concerns. The aims of the support group were explained and the importance of maintaining confidentiality was stressed. Membership of the group was completely voluntary. At the end of the group members were invited to provide feedback about how helpful the group had been. This took place within the last session.

The group began by sharing their experiences of having a positive HIV test. All but two had been tested because of poor health and said that they felt they had not received adequate pre-test counselling. Of the others, one was forced by her husband to be tested and another was tested when her husband died of AIDS. The participants reported feelings of denial, anger, shock, hopelessness, guilt and depression when informed of their test result.

The areas of concern for the group members which emerged were the following.

Children

The future of their children was a major worry for all participants who were parents. All were aware that their HIV status would probably lead to deterioration in their health and this would affect their ability to provide financially for their children. They had difficulties in planning for their children's educational and financial future as well as their physical and psychological well-being. They reported they could not trust their families to take care of the children. They hoped that through using their new skills they would make enough money to make provision for their children's future.

Many participants felt guilty that their children would suffer as a result of their HIV status. The women felt they were victims (of their partner's infidelity) and their children had to suffer the consequences. Most reported that their relatives would be unwilling to take care of the children either because of the stigma attached to children whose parents died of AIDS or because of poverty. Others were afraid of asking relatives because it would inevitably mean talking about their HIV status.

Isolation and stigma

Everyone identified rejection by others and fear of the stigma of being labelled HIV+ as a major worry. Four had not told their sexual partners of their HIV status because they were afraid of negative reactions such as physical violence, gossip or divorce. Others had not told parents, siblings or the wider family network.

Many found it difficult to trust people. This was demonstrated within the group itself by a small number of participants who were quite reluctant to share their experiences. They were not sure how the others would react to them. They were afraid of criticism and condemnation which seems to reflect a wider concern about societal attitudes in general. They opened up with the help of the older members.

The future

Nearly all group members were worried about what would happen after the support group had ended and they had graduated from skills training. They wanted the group to continue because they felt supported both financially and emotionally. One member who was single and childless was worried about dying without a child. She didn't feel comfortable 'dying without leaving her own mark for people to remember her'. She realized the possible health implications of pregnancy for herself and the child but felt that it might be worth the risk. She felt that to remain childless was to mark her as different in a society where it is considered very important for a woman to bear children.

Sexual relationships

The participants with sexual partners felt that they had a responsibility to inform them. After discussing practical ways of doing so, some members later reported that they had successfully informed their partners without any adverse consequences. The issues of safer sex were discussed. Some participants said that they were using condoms with their partners yet were also considering the possibility of having further children. Some women said that they did not feel that they could insist on their partners using condoms, saying that within Zambian culture women are expected to be sexually submissive. Many agreed that condoms reduced sexual pleasure.

Illness and death

During the course of the group some members became ill. This stirred up some very difficult and contradictory feelings for everybody. The participants acknowledged that death was a part of life and should be accepted but at the same time they were very unwilling to talk about their feelings about their own death. Participants said they didn't want to go through a long painful illness. They would rather become ill and die quickly. One person said he would rather die in a road accident than of AIDS.

Ending

As the end of the support group drew nearer attendance at the group began to fall. The facilitator attempted to explore with the remaining members why this might be so. It seemed that they were feeling very fearful of the future and how they would cope by themselves without the emotional support of the other members and the financial support they received from the training scheme. The participants said that they did not want the group to end, as it had provided them with an opportunity to speak about issues that might not have been otherwise addressed. Some talked about the end of the group as the break-up of the 'family'.

Did the group help?

The feedback received from the clients was that the group was helpful in bringing issues into the open for discussion. Many had never talked about their own death before or what would happen to their children and families, and while these were distressing topics they had the effect of helping the participants feel somewhat more in control of their lives.

The concerns which emerged from the support group reflect the very concrete problems faced by PHIV in a developing country. Most PHIV in Zambia will not have access to adequate orthodox (that is, Western style) health care because it is scarce and expensive and many were afraid of long-drawn-out painful illnesses. It is somewhat surprising that this issue was not more prominent in the support group because of the extreme lack of health care. However, in a society where health care is usually not available whatever the illness, it may be that people have grown to accept the situation.

The participants relied on Hope House not just for emotional and psychological support but also for financial support. When the training course was approaching its conclusion many were fearful of the future. While attending Hope House they had a small income but when they finished this would cease. The participants were being trained in skills which should allow them to generate their own incomes, and while in the short term this would be useful there was the question of what would happen when they were no longer able to work. In developed countries there is usually some kind of social welfare system to resort to but in Zambia this does not exist.

While participants felt stigmatized by their status it seemed that as the work of the group progressed this became less of an issue. It seems to have been helpful for people to hear how other members dealt with stigma, and as a result they were able to develop their own strategies to deal with this important issue.

Some participants expressed the desire for (more) children even though they were aware that this might have serious consequences for their own health (as a woman) or the health of the child. This reflects the importance that childbearing has in Zambian society. It is important to remember that all participants were HIV+ and maybe felt that changing sexual behaviour was of limited value. However, there was still the potential to infect others. Another aspect to this issue may be that sexual behaviour change in a context of poverty may be too difficult to achieve. Participants may have felt that there were other priorities such as adequate nourishment and housing. This may be an important issue for counsellors working with people from underdeveloped countries in the UK. It may be hard for a counsellor from a Western style country to understand why a person with a terminal illness would choose to have a child.

Conclusion

The use of formal counselling approaches in Zambia is taking place often in very difficult circumstances. This article demonstrates that the use of counselling as an intervention is helpful in providing support for people who feel stigmatized and isolated and who are living with a terminal illness. Such work needs to be acknowledged and encouraged.

Update

After I left Kara Counselling and Training Trust in 1994 the therapeutic work of the groups continued for some months. However, the other trained counsellor left for a new post in Tanzania the following year, resulting in a situation where there was nobody with sufficient training and experience to carry on the work or to supervise it. Kara Counselling remained committed to providing HIV counselling within an HIV-testing context but this was mainly individual and sometimes couple based. Psychological and emotional support continued to be provided to HIV+ people by a self-help group of people living with HIV. This situation in Kara Counselling reflects a wider problem in Zambia and in most sub-Saharan African countries in that psychological interventions are not well supported by governments, donor agencies, and health-care systems. Often this is a result of ignorance of the benefits and effectiveness of counselling/therapeutic interventions but sometimes it reflects the power of the medical establishment to dismiss the importance of emotional and psychological health and to focus resources (often scarce) exclusively on medical issues. Counselling can be beneficial and this message needs to be made repeatedly to those with the power to decide how scarce resources are allocated.

Tomás Campbell

References

Blazer, D.G. (1982) 'Social support and mortality in an elderly community population', *American Journal of Epidemiology*, 115: 684–94.

Campbell, T., Chanda, C., Phiri, M., Mukosha, M. and Sheth, G. (1994) 'Group counselling of people with HIV, Lusaka, Zambia,' Presentation at the 10th conference on AIDS, Yokohama, Japan.

Central Statistical Office (1991) *Women and Men in Zambia: The Facts*, Lusaka, Zambia.

Cohen, S. and Syme, S.L. (eds) (1985) *Social Support and Health*, New York: Academic Press.

Demographic and Health Survey (1992) Central Statistical Office, Lusaka, Zambia.

Hedge, B. and Glover, L.F. (1990) 'Group intervention with HIV seropositive patients and their partners', *AIDS Care*, 2 (2): 147–54.

Msiska, R. (1992) *Overview of the HIV/AIDS Situation in Zambia*, Lusaka, Zambia: Ministry of Health.

Discussion issues

1 How can counselling theories which evolved within a Western socio-economic framework be helpful in developing countries?

2 How are issues of confidentiality different in a culture where all those in a family are entitled to know all medical details of another family member?

3 Is it hard to understand why a person with a terminal illness would choose to have a child?

4 What kind of care must be taken to understand the cultural and economic framework within which people with HIV are living in order for any counselling intervention to be successful?

20

Group Therapy for Women with Eating Problems

Cathy Richards and Catherine McKisack

The high incidence of food-related difficulties experienced by women is well documented (Bloom 1987; Lacey 1985), as is the increasing incidence of eating problems in student populations (Pertschuk et al. 1986). Various treatment approaches have been developed to enable women to overcome their distress associated with eating and/or not eating, for example group therapy for bulimia has been found to be effective, both in controlled and uncontrolled trials (Mitchell 1991; Fettes and Peters 1992; Hartmann et al. 1992). One influential intervention is the eclectic self-help package developed by Susie Orbach in 1978. This approach emphasizes the influence of culture and early experiences on the development of eating difficulties. The group described in this article explored and developed many of the ideas proposed by Orbach two decades ago.

Why offer a group?

The group was offered to female undergraduates aged 19–22 whose main reason for seeking counselling concerned difficulties with eating, weight and food. Some of these women had symptoms of bulimia, others of anorexia. We decided to offer group treatment to this diverse group for several reasons: due to the high level of requests for counselling from this population it seemed sensible to run a group; both authors were interested to see how effective a group approach would be; we suspected that university students already familiar with seminar groups would be readily able to make use of such a format; and we were aware of the possible advantages of group interventions such as a decrease in feelings of isolation and shame (Rorty et al. 1993). Alongside these feelings of purposefulness and hope we experienced anxiety and fear. Other therapists had spoken about the difficulties of such groups – stating for example that they as therapists had developed heightened sensitivity concerning their own weight as a consequence of facilitating eating disorder groups.

What happened in the sessions?

Each student was seen twice for assessment during which they had an opportunity to meet both of us, ask questions and were informed that the group was being evaluated.

This chapter was first published in *Counselling*, Journal of the British Association for Counselling, vol. 4, no. 4, pp. 270–1 (1993).

Eight women were offered eight weekly sessions lasting 90 minutes. To facilitate cohesion and to enable us to start and end promptly, each session began and ended with a round. During the rounds the group members and facilitators spoke in turn. Examples of rounds are:

'One thing I like about myself is ...'
'If I were a colour what would I be ...?'
'One thing I do well is ...'

Sessions consisted of a mixture of group exercises, group discussion, exercises in pairs and triads, as well as individual exercises such as a pictorial representation of their journey through the group and fantasy exercises based on those in *Fat is a Feminist Issue* (Orbach 1978). Care was taken to achieve a balance between giving individuals freedom to speak, without pressurizing anyone to speak if they preferred to be silent. We gave a number of short talks lasting about twenty minutes with interruption and discussion being encouraged. Topics included cultural pressures on women to conform to a passive, thin, polite and food-producing role; family influences on eating behaviour and feelings about our bodies; assertiveness and emotional experience and expression; and the meaning of bingeing.

From session one we were amazed at the openness of the group members, their willingness to participate and the positive impact that the group seemed to be having on them.

The role of women in society

We spent the first sessions and parts of most subsequent sessions looking at the pressures on us as women to conform. We explored the link between conforming and food and we tried to emphasize the way in which these conflicts were part of every woman's experience, not just those who identified themselves as having difficulty with eating, thus highlighting the tendency many of us have to judge the success of a day upon how we had eaten or exercised.

One revealing exercise was a round beginning 'As a woman I am expected to ...' Responses included 'to be thin', 'to eat up all my food', 'to be neat', 'to be nice and polite', 'not to get angry' and 'to be attractive'. During this and later exercises we began to explore the feelings of anger surrounding these pressures and some members began to acknowledge their difficulty in becoming angry. We reviewed the way we express, or don't express, our feelings. Some of the women commented that they often ate when they felt angry, lonely or bored, acknowledging that, in a sense, during a binge, they were 'stuffing down' or avoiding their negative feelings.

Later sessions moved on from this insight to discuss assertive methods of expressing positive and negative emotions, and developing the skills for meeting emotional needs constructively. One of the most painful exercises for the group was a round beginning 'One thing I like about x is ...'. Some of the women seemed to find accepting positive comments almost impossible, although at our final meeting several of them said they would have liked to repeat this exercise.

Early experiences

A second theme, which seemed to run throughout the group, was the impact of early experience and relationships with parents. We spoke about the ways that gender roles are learnt during childhood, exploring how these roles seem to be an integral part of the mother–daughter relationship mentioning research which indicates daughters are often fed less and fed less sensitively than baby boys (Belotti 1975).

Such issues were explored via fantasy exercises, for example focusing on family meals (Orbach 1991), and in discussion following these exercises the group shared a wealth of material. One woman, realizing that she had always taken seconds as a means of silently supporting her mother at the meal table, found herself more able to decide whether or not to take more food, and in what way she wanted to support her mother. Two of the women realized that as children thay had returned home from school to find nothing to do and so filled up their time with biscuits to escape the feelings of emptiness, boredom and loneliness until their parents returned home from work. Both young women were able to connect why the times between lectures and mealtimes were still so difficult because historically they had always felt bad and eaten at those times.

Was the group effective?

The two standardized measures (Self-Esteem Scale, Rosenberg 1965; Eating Disorder Inventory, Garner et al. 1983) and the progress described by members suggests the group was a very successful intervention. It was particularly pleasing to see the significant improvement in the self-esteem and body dissatisfaction scales. Six months after the end of the group only one participant had been re-referred to the counselling service, suggesting that, for most of the students, the improvement had been maintained for six months. This progress is a significant change after years of obsession with food.

Despite our early fears we found the experience of working with the group to be very positive. We also enjoyed the chance to prepare, facilitate, review and evaluate a piece of counselling work together, rather than alone as is often the case with individual work.

Update

One of us, enthused by this experience, went on to run and evaluate three further groups working with an NHS population (McKisack and Waller 1996), concluding that treatment was shown to be moderately effective, even when correcting for the bias due to women dropping out of the groups. The level of symptom reduction found suggested that other treatments would often be required to supplement the group.

References

Belotti, E.G. (1975) *Little Girls*, London: Arrow Books.
Bloom, C. (1987) 'Bulimia: a feminist psychoanalytic understanding', in M. Lawrence (ed.), *Fed up and Hungry*, London: The Women's Press.

Fettes, P.A. and Peters, J.M. (1992) 'A meta-analysis of group treatments for bulimia', *International Journal of Eating Disorders*, 11: 97–110.

Garner, D., Olmstead, M. and Polivy, J. (1983) 'Development and validation of a multidimensional Eating Disorder Inventory for anorexia nervosa and bulimia', *International Journal of Eating Disorders*, 2: 15–34.

Hartmann, A., Herzog, T. and Drinkmann, A. (1992) 'Psychotherapy of bulimia nervosa: what is effective? A meta-analysis', *Journal of Psychosomatic Research*, 36: 159–67.

Lacey, J.H. (1985) 'Time limited individual and group treatment for bulimia', in D. Garner and P. Garfinkel (eds), *Handbook of Psychotherapy for Anorexia Nervosa and Bulimia*, London: Guilford Press.

Mitchell, J.E. (1991) 'A review of the controlled trials of psychotherapy for bulimia nervosa', *Journal of Psychosomatic Research*, 35: 23–31.

McKisack, C. and Waller, G. (1996) 'Why is attendance variable at groups for women with bulimia nervosa? The role of eating pathology and other characteristics', *International Journal of Eating Disorders*, 20: 205–9.

Orbach, S. (1978) *Fat is a Feminist Issue*, London: Arrow Books.

Orbach, S. (1991) *Fat is a Feminist Issue* (2nd edn), London: Arrow Books.

Pertschuk, M., Collins, M., Kreisberg, J. and Fagers, S. (1986) 'Psychiatric symptoms associated with eating disorders in a college population', *International Journal of Eating Disorders*, 5 (3): 563–8.

Rorty, M., Yager, J. and Rosotto, E. (1993) 'Why and how do women recover from bulimia nervosa? The subjective appraisals of forty women recovered for a year or more', *International Journal of Eating Disorders*, 14: 249–60.

Rosenberg, M. (1965) *Society and Adolescent Self Image*, New Jersey: Princeton University Press.

Discussion issues

1 What would you see as the advantages/disadvantages of group treatment for eating disorders in comparison with individual treatment?

2 When assessing suitability for such a group what would you be looking for as inclusion/exclusion characteristics?

3 Do you agree with the suggestion that a group approach might be more suitable for a student population than a more general one? State reasons.

4 How would you feel about running such a group? How many facilitators would the group need and what support would you want to have in place for yourself before beginning?

21

A Further Look at Group Therapy for Women with Eating Disorders in a University Setting

Peter Ross

The high incidence of eating disorders both in the female general population and in the female student population are well known. Less well known, perhaps, is the gradual spread of eating disorders into the male population (variously put at between 25 to 100 per 1,000), the increasing incidence of early (age 10–15) onset of presentation, and the large number of sub-clinical cases – often distressed enough to seek help, but not severe enough to come above formal threshold definitions. This means that by typical university age (18–25) eating disorders are often well established at both clinical and sub-clinical level even if well hidden from others. The latter is especially true of those who are bulimic rather than anorexic. The DSM III (R) diagnostic criteria for bulimia (American Psychiatric Association 1987) include: a minimum of two episodes of binge eating per week for three months; feelings of lack of control over eating, regular self-induced vomiting, dieting, exercise, laxatives etc.; and persistent over-concern with body image and weight. Although diagnosis of bulimia almost always requires the client to be about average or greater weight (derived from frequent over-eating) and diagnosis of anorexia almost always requires greatly reduced weight (even to the point of starvation until death) it will readily be seen that many features overlap. The primary overlap feature is extreme concern and preoccupation about diet, shape and weight. In other words, the primary overlap feature is distorted ideas, perceptions and images about the self, particularly about how the self is valued in terms of 'looks' rather than IQ or skill or anything else. This should not surprise us: much of popular culture is permeated by distorted values and images. One has only to consider that every university counselling service in the UK is consulted by some three women to every two men, to see evidence of the way women are expected and expect themselves to carry a greater burden of responsibility (over-concern themselves with?) for feelings and relationships than do men, at present.

Therapy: individual or group?

Various kinds of therapy have been used with these clinical and sub-clinical populations. At first sight, direct focus on the thinking and behaviour in question would seem sensible. Outcome studies of group work (Johnson et al. 1983; Lacey 1983; Mitchell et al. 1985; Schneider and Agras 1985) focusing directly on thinking and behaviour show promising results, as does similar individual work (Fairburn and Cooper 1989).

This chapter was first published in *Counselling*, Journal of the British Association for Counselling, vol. 4, no. 4, pp. 272–3 (1993).

Outcome studies using other orientations are either non-existent, or similarly mixed. None of them addresses the unique problems of dealing with eating disorders within a university culture.

Pertschuk et al. (1986) have evaluated the incidence and complexities of eating problems in a student population. However, probably the best attempt to develop a comprehensive understanding of eating problems within a US campus setting is the monumental work edited by Whitaker (1989). The approach advocated in this combines the structured focus of cognitive-behavioural work while emphasizing the importance of dealing with the reaction to the structuring through developing the client's comprehensive understanding of the meaning of their symptom. To this end, peer support and campus-wide awareness of the way competitive pressures impact on self-concept, are deemed invaluable. The group approach described in this article explores, develops and applies the above in a British campus setting. Early attempts to set up groups in this way simply collapsed. It was discovered that the huge concern and sense of burden of responsibility focused on those who were severely anorexic, inhibited all other work. Nowadays, all clinical anorexics are referred to a newly established local NHS Eating Disorder Unit. Current groups therefore screen in bulimics and sub-clinical anorexics. Any medium-sized university (about 10,000–12,000 students) using a term rather than semester structure, will find presentations erratic. A group for our purposes therefore now consists of beginning with one or two clients and expanding to a maximum of four as others present and are screened in individually. The sessions are ongoing, but clients contract for six one-hour weekly sessions, with two one-hour follow-up sessions at two-weekly intervals. Clients are encouraged to 'buddy up' for support outside the group.

The start of each group is a discussion period. The end of each group is marked by a handout of literature suitable for this intelligent client population (see References for some examples of these). Each client also gets a 'self-help' pack describing how to identify and change the thinking processes which trigger and/or maintain their behaviour. For details and worked examples of the cognitive-behavioural method applied to eating disorders see Fairburn and Cooper (1989). The primary focus of the group is therefore upon each client taking responsibility for helping themselves, with the support of counsellor and other group members. Naturally, much of the work revolves around the problems thrown up by personal application of the method, and integration of all this within their ever-expanding understanding of the meaning for them of what is going on in their lives.

Processes and content of group sessions

The content already described is perhaps less important than the way the package is put together, and the manner and atmosphere in which the sessions are conducted. This has been determined by research which has shown that clients with low self-esteem respond least well to many forms of intervention (Mahoney and Mahoney 1976) and that increasing self-esteem within treatment is important for maintenance of a positive outcome. The overall package is founded upon a self-esteem-giving assumption that clients can take responsibility for their own treatment, that they can read the research literature and use it to benefit themselves, that they can help others even as they get help. The atmosphere is therefore a deliberately respectful one, in which particular attention and respect is accorded to any feeling, such as anger, which vents or enhances self-care and assertiveness. Non-compliance with suggestions is especially respected as over-compliance is so clearly part of the underlying problem. The cognitive-behavioural interventions (Garner and Bemis 1982) work sufficiently quickly to overcome early on the frequent all-pervading sense of ineffectiveness and inability to control, so reinforcing positive self-concept. Maintenance of cognitive gains depends on this wider understanding and improved self-concept.

In the 'self-help' pack is a form for homework, repeated weekly, in which clients list positive things about themselves and others in the group. Of all the structures used, clients find this by far the most difficult – both to accept positives from self as well as others. Because of this, lots of reasons are typically found to try to avoid doing it. One of the most crucial functions of the counsellor is to prevent this avoidance, and to ensure that self-esteem statements are shifted from eating-orientated attributions ('I am good because I managed to stop eating after my initial binge mouthful by telling myself, "Yes, it really does matter"') to other ones ('I am good because I managed to hang on to my integrity when arbitrating between my flatmates').

Was the group effective?

At initial assessment, any client invited to the group completes an Eating Disorder Inventory (Garner and Olmsted 1984). It is also completed on termination. This superb scale was standardized on a college population (at the University of Toronto) and contains good sub-scales for 'ineffectiveness' (essentially a 'self-concept' scale), 'perfectionism' (essentially a measure of 'compliance') and 'maturity fears' (essentially a measure of 'responsibility taking'), as well as others. These three sub-scales in particular are crucial for our purpose. Before and after measures show the group to be very effective, and although clients have re-referred themselves, the re-referral has been 'to review progress' (confidence, etc.) and no evidence of continuing active bingeing has been seen. The subjective reports of clients have been both very positive and enthusiastic. The outcome has been sufficiently encouraging to continue in this format and the next stage will be to conduct really long-term follow-up studies.

Update

Since writing the original article, this work has evolved through three stages. In the first stage I continued to conduct the group as described but with constantly updated reading materials. At the same time I sent out a brief questionnaire plus another EDI to students who had left the group and graduated from university. It gradually became clear that much time and effort would be needed if long-term follow-up was to succeed. This work constantly got pushed to the bottom of the pile of priorities. Eventually I gave up on follow-up, frankly disheartened by the amount of work involved. A 20 per cent response from early follow-up was almost all good, but of course statistically meaningless. At about the same time Professor Peter Cooper (Cooper 1993) joined the staff of our Psychology Department and we began to use his small paperback self-help manual as a substitute for some of the literature mentioned above. This episode helped shape our views in preparation for the third and current stage.

The University Medical Practice (which shares a building with us) refers about 25 per cent of all clients, but of course a higher proportion of those with eating disorders. Both GPs and the psychiatrist became keen to be able to show that our mutual practice was evidence based. (See Roth and Fonagy 1996 for a good introduction to the whole area of evidence-based practice in counselling and psychotherapy.) At the same time the GPs wanted to be more involved in treatment rather than just refer and forget. After discussion and review over a period of some six months the entire team (psychiatrist, GPs, nurses, counsellors, physiotherapists) of about 35 people decided to adopt for both individual and group work what we saw as a more detailed and comprehensive version of the structured and self-help work we were already doing. Treasure and Schmidt (1997) contains a clinician's guide, lots of worksheets for clients to do homework calculated to enhance motivation, and of course the self-help guide for clients. We decided on this because of good evidence that it is effective, because it reduces counsellor contact time, because it ensures all staff are familiar with what others are trying to do as clients/patients consult, and because it appealed to a broad consensus of staff with very different backgrounds, training and interests. Are the results good? Yes. Better? Probably. But I suspect that this has got much more to do with the effect of integrated and committed cross-disciplinary teamwork rather than anything else. This then is the pragmatic outcome of ten years of evolution in working with bulimia at a University Counselling Service.

References

American Psychiatric Association (APA) (1987) *Diagnostic and Statistical Manual of Mental Disorders*, Washington, DC: APA.

Cooper, P.J. (1993) *Bulimia Nervosa – a Guide to Recovery*, London: Robinson Publishing.

Fairburn, C. and Cooper, P. (1989) 'Eating disorders', Chapter 8 in K.S. Hawton, P.M. Salkovskis, J. Kirk and D.M. Clark, *Cognitive Behaviour Therapy for Psychiatric Problems*, Oxford: Oxford Medical Publications.

Garner, D.M. and Bemis, K.M. (1982) 'A cognitive-behavioural approach to anorexia nervosa', *Cognitive Therapy and Research*, 6: 123–50. See also their article in D.M. Garner and P.E. Garfinkel (eds) (1985) *Handbook of Psychotherapy for Anorexia Nervosa and Bulimia*, New York: Guilford.

Garner, D.M. and Olmsted, M.P. (1984) *Manual for the Eating Disorder Inventory (EDI)*. Odessa, FL: Psychological Assessment Resources Inc.

Johnson, C., Conners, M. and Stuckey, M. (1983) 'Short-term group treatment of bulimia', *International Journal of Eating Disorders*, 2: 199–208.

Lacey, J.H. (1983) 'Bulimia nervosa, binge eating, and psychogenic vomiting: a controlled treatment study and long-term outcome', *British Medical Journal*, 286: 1609–13.

Mitchell, J.E., Hatsukami, D., Goff, G., Pyle, R., Eckert, E. and Davis, L.E. (1985) 'Intensive outpatient group treatment for bulimia', in D.M. Garner and P.E. Garfinkel (eds), *Handbook of Psychotherapy for Anorexia Nervosa and Bulimia*, New York: Guilford Press.

Mahoney, M.J. and Mahoney, K. (1976) *Permanent Weight Control: a Total Solution to the Dieter's Dilemma*, New York, NY: Norton.

Pertschuk, M., Collins, M., Kreisberg, J. and Fager, S. (1986) 'Psychiatric symptoms associated with eating disorders in a college population', *International Journal of Eating Disorders*, 5 (3): 563–8.

Roth, A., and Fonagy, P. (1996) *What Works for Whom? – a Critical Review of Psychotherapy Research*, New York: Guilford Press.

Schneider, J.A. and Agras, W.S. (1985) 'A cognitive behavioural group treatment of bulimia', *British Journal of Psychiatry*, 146, 66–9.

Treasure, J. and Schmidt, U. (1997) *Getting Better Bit(e) by Bit(e) – a Survival Kit for Sufferers of Bulimia Nervosa and Binge Eating Disorders*, London: Psychology Press.

Whitaker, L.C. (1989) *The Bulimic College Student: Evaluation, Treatment and Prevention*, New York: Haworth Press.

Handouts vary, but have included non-technical research articles of general stimulating interest such as:

Davis, E and Furnham, A. (1986) 'Body satisfaction in adolescent girls', *British Journal of Medical Psychology*, 59: 279–87.

Palmer, R.L. (1979) 'The dietary chaos syndrome: a useful new term?', *British Journal of Medical Psychology*, 52: 187–90.

Szmukler, G.I. and Tantam, D. (1984) 'Anorexia nervosa: starvation dependence', *British Journal of Medical Psychology*, 57: 303–10.

Wardle, J. (1987) 'Compulsive eating and dietary restraint', *British Journal of Clinical Psychology*, 26: 47–55.

Discussion issues

1 Women are expected and expect themselves to carry a greater burden of responsibility for (over-concern themselves with) feelings and relationships than do men, at present. Comment.

2 Do distorted ideas, perceptions and images about the self and how it is valued in terms of 'looks' rather than intelligence or skill or anything else, affect both young men and young women?

3 Why is it important for counsellors to ensure that students make positive statements about their achievements in areas of their lives other than eating?

4 What is your reaction to the recent suggestion that there is likely to be a genetic component to bulimia and anorexia?

22

General Practice Counselling

A plea for ideological engagement

Richard House

In discussing the ideological tensions and differences that exist between orthodox
medical and humanistic counselling approaches to mental ill-health, it is argued that the
theory and practice of humanistic (as opposed to cognitive-behavioural) counselling sit
uneasily in a medical setting in which, historically, the medicalization of mental health
problems has held sway. The way in which this ideological debate develops and is ultimately resolved may substantially determine the form that the future of GP counselling
takes in Britain. It is hoped that this deliberately provocative discussion will open up a
fertile and enlightening debate within the wider policy-making arena, as well as within
the doctor–counsellor nexus itself.

GP counselling in context

The rapid growth in the availability of counselling in primary care settings in recent
years has, I believe, masked a serious and fundamental ideological contradiction,
namely, that an approach to health care – counselling – which is typically humanistic,
person-centred, holistic and non-mechanistic in orientation, has grown up within an
orthodox medical system which is typically 'bits-of-person'-centred and increasingly
mechanistic and technocratic in its approach to medical treatment and health care. In the
case of the so-called 'depressive disorders', for example, even GPs who are enthusiastic about and supportive of counselling in General Practice still routinely, and sometimes almost automatically, reach for their prescription pad, *effectively* entailing the
implicit assumption that 'depression' consists in some kind of neurochemical 'dysfunction' in the brain that the appropriate chemical fix will cure. In contrast, many counsellors tend to hold the very different view that the experience of 'depression' is a result
of a highly complex interaction between emotional, social, environmental and physical/
biological factors, and that a sustainable and appropriate treatment for 'depression' must
take account of its complex and multi-faceted aetiology. On this latter view, then, to tinker
with the symptomatic chemical imbalance in the brain, which is merely the material end
result of a highly complex sequence and combination of factors, may in the short run
relieve some of the more troubling depressive symptoms, but will do little or nothing to

This chapter was first published in *Counselling*, Journal of the British Association for Counselling, vol. 7,
no. 1, pp. 40–4 (1996).

address the underlying aetiology and the factors that may be maintaining the person's depressive experience.

These seemingly incompatible approaches to mental ill-health have only been able to co-exist in primary care because of a thoroughgoing collusive denial of, and refusal openly to acknowledge and face up to the implications of, the ideological incompatibility of these disparate approaches to ill-health. Both parties, GPs and counsellors, have strong motivations for perpetuating such denial: the former because an acceptance of the values of humanistic counselling would threaten to undermine the core assumptions on which their medical practice is based; and the latter because of the fear that a full acknowledgement of the counter-cultural nature of their health care values and assumptions might well threaten their continued existence as professional practitioners in the primary care setting.

Humanistic counselling in general practice

In an editorial in the May 1994 issue of the *British Journal of General Practice*, Salinsky and Jenkins (1994) discussed the current status of counselling in the General Practice setting. Their thorough and succinct review referred to three 'major areas of concern in counsellor provision': namely, counsellor competency; lack of mutual understanding of each other's roles by the doctor and the counsellor; and the development of a working relationship between primary care and secondary mental health services. It is the second of these questions that I wish to address. As the authors write, 'different models of illness [constitute an] obstacle to effective collaboration' between counsellor and GP; but Salinsky and Jenkins do not develop this point further in their editorial. I will give detailed attention to the question of the ideological differences that stem from divergent models of ill-health, for I believe this issue to be of quite central importance in any consideration of the future shape and extent of counselling in the General Practice setting.

I am a professional humanistic counsellor working in General Practice in Norwich, and a founding member of the Norfolk Association of Professional Surgery Counsellors (formed 1994). The term 'humanistic' is used in a variety of different contexts, and has a quite specific meaning when used in the counselling field. There it refers to a holistic, person-centred conception of human ill-health and disease, which eschews mind–body dualism and mechanistic, symptom-preoccupied approaches to health care, and advocates instead a 'healing' approach which prioritizes the emotional and helps clients to mobilize their own internal resources for authentic and sustainable therapeutic change. It is implicit in such an approach that many of the health problems presented to GPs in general medical practice are in fact the surface manifestations of a deeper underlying spiritual or emotional malaise (Peck 1993), and that somatic symptoms are in some way associated with the patient's early pathological family experiences (McDougall 1989; Wilson and Mintz 1989), and/or with the patient's having repressed and denied very traumatic or painful past experiences (Krystal 1988). The advocacy of humanistic and psychodynamically informed clinical methods from *within* conventional medicine is by no means unheard of (Stein 1982; Gorlin and Zucker 1983; McWhinney 1989; Breggin 1991).

Differing ideologies

When I originally wrote this article (May 1995), counselling in General Practice was at a crossroads: would it be assimilated into the orthodox biomedical treatment model (Engel 1977; Mishler 1981), offering purely short-term, focused, cognitive-behavioural interventions with the prime motivation of symptom alleviation or removal (Fahy and Wessely 1993; House 1996a); or would humanistic counselling gain a sufficient foothold within the medical system such that its holistic values would begin to be accepted and perhaps even start to transform the practices of the medical profession towards more person-centred (as opposed to 'bits-of-person'-centred) conceptions of healing and therapeutic change (House 1994a)? While, in the year 2000, counselling seems to have a more secure foothold in General Practice than ever before (Lees 1999), I believe that an open and honest debate is still needed to inform public policy decisions as to the future of GP counselling. My concern is that crucial decisions of funding may well be made within this field without anything like a full airing of the fundamental issues at stake – in the mid-1990s there were disquieting signs that this was already happening (Jenkins 1995).

I attempt to open up the lines of such a debate in a deliberately provocative way because (along with William Blake) I believe that 'without contraries is no progression'; and that unless these difficult and challenging questions are fully addressed, there is a real danger that future decisions about the trajectory of GP counselling will be ill-informed and, as a result, quite possibly piecemeal and even dysfunctional.

It seems clear that modern Western medicine is still dominated by the primary goal of symptom removal, and remains largely untouched by humanistic or post-modern conceptions of illness and healing (House 2001). I stress that I have no particular investment in portraying Western medicine *per se* as some kind of 'baddie', at whose door can be laid all the blame for our current health care malaise, for it is clear that *any* system of medicine must reflect the culture and the associated set of assumptions about health within which it is embedded (Good 1994). Thus, patients who present with somatic complaints and expect a somatic diagnosis will unconsciously put great pressure upon their GP to provide such a diagnosis; they will tend to resist an approach which involves the threat of talking about underlying emotions; and they may well feel neglected or short-changed unless they leave the surgery carrying a prescription (Brook 1967; McKinstry 1992). The 'victim' frame of mind (Hall 1993) goes hand in hand with such an approach, and (to use Jill Hall's terminology) reflects the 'reluctant adult's' desire to blame an outside agency for one's own condition and state of health. And, of course, the pressure upon doctors to collude with this perspective on ill-health may typically be irresistible, not least because it coincides with the materialistic, and commonly deterministic assumptions underlying their own training and cultural experience.

As Howard Stein has persuasively argued in a book which should in my view be compulsory reading for all who work in medical settings (Stein 1985), it is only when we are able individually and collectively to face up to the *psychodynamics* of medicine and health care that we will begin to see what a non-pathological, fully human system of health care might conceivably look like. Such a process will also involve a radical and fearless deconstruction of the ways in which power, culture and ideology, *actively construct* human experience, and the (medical) linguistic categories we invoke to understand it (Parker 1995; House 2001). Until then, it seems that we are condemned to unconsciously 'acting out' (to use a psychoanalytic term) from our deepest fears and anxieties, which are in some sense rooted in repressed (and therefore unintegrated) pain and suffering (House 1996b). It seems that modern medicine is very unwilling fully to face the emotional or spiritual aspects of illness and disease (Zalidis 1994; Lawlis 1996), which fact in turn reflects a species-wide reluctance to integrate our own pain and suffering – what Scott Peck (1993) called 'the necessary pain of living'.

Ideologies in conflict: the cases of Prozac and Ritalin

With the recent high-profile coverage of the benefits or otherwise of the anti-depressant Prozac (BBC 2 Television 1994; Breggin and Breggin 1994; Kramer 1994; Leder 1994; McBride 1994), the selective serotonin re-uptake inhibitor, this seems to be a highly topical and pertinent example with which to illustrate the schism that exists between medical and humanistic approaches to emotional/mental problems (Freeling and Levenstein 1983). Leder (1994) has written of the fundamental unresolved question of what is a medical disorder or illness and what is normality (House 2001). What is dangerous in all of this is not our ignorance *per se* (for it is psychodynamically rooted *fear* that substantially drives our unease with non-understanding), but rather the assumption that we do possess a scientific understanding of 'mental disorder' or distress when, in reality, what we do understand is dwarfed by that of which we are ignorant (House 2001).

An extraordinary claim has been made for the so-called 'happy pill', Prozac, that science now enables, you 'to change your personality with a pill' and to 'cure' unhappiness (McBride 1994). From the viewpoint of humanistic counselling and post-modern perspectives on identity and selfhood, the idea that a pill can change the human personality in any predictable and beneficent way is both absurd and frightening: *absurd* because of its mechanistic assumption about what it is to be human, encouraging the idea that people are little more than biochemical machines, and that if only we could come up with the right chemical formula, the quite natural existential difficulties of living could be dispensed with. (Compare Maguire's (1984) discussion of 'bio-engineering ideology'. Note also that the deep philosophical or ontological problems involved in specifying what 'ill-health' and 'personality' actually consist in are completely ignored.) And it is *frightening* because of the way in which such a view is peddled with seemingly no awareness of the *necessary* function that the experience of human pain and suffering serves in our ability to live integrated, responsible and mature lives (Peck 1993).

A humanistic or transpersonal approach is highly sceptical of the attempt to medicalize so-called 'psychological' or 'emotional' problems. Historically, the medical and psychiatric professions have routinely prescribed medication for emotional difficulties, in part because the practitioners themselves are unable to contain the projected anxieties of their patients because of *practitioners' own* unintegrated pain. It is for this reason, among others, that Howard Stein (1985) has persuasively argued that the psychodynamics of medical practice should take a central role in the training and practice of medical professionals (Erskine and Judd 1994) – a view that, revealingly, has been virtually ignored by the medical profession, notwithstanding its convincing advocacy over 40 years ago in the pioneering work of Michael Balint (1964) and more recent support for the teaching of 'humanistic medicine' by Gorlin and Zucker (1983). This situation in turn reflects a pervasive, species-wide propensity to flee from our own psychic pain (House 1996b). The advocacy of Prozac as a medical treatment and panacea for depression should be seen in this wider cultural light. From a humanistic or transpersonal standpoint, it is only when we are individually and collectively able to embrace the full reality of living – including pain and suffering – that the idea of a 'happy pill' will be relegated (and rightly in my view) to the status of a minor footnote in medical history.

I have set out the dimensions of the Prozac debate in deliberately stark and challenging terms in order to highlight the difficulties that ensue when two philosophically incompatible and incommensurable ideologies come into conflict. As long as counsellors with humanistic principles or a post-modern world-view are working within a medical context which is founded upon a very different set of beliefs about human dis(-)ease and ill-health, there will be an inevitable tension in the work that counsellors do in the GP setting. This tension will manifest itself in a variety of ways: in counsellors who feel uneasy or guilty about the work they do, knowing that it is sometimes based on values which are antithetical to, and possibly undermining of, the views of their employers (the referring GPs); and doctors who feel threatened by a more holistic and less defensive approach to the difficulties and distress with which their patients present.

In a response to my original 1996 article, Totton (1997) argued that the non-medical values of humanistic/dynamic counselling cannot but be contaminated and compromised – perhaps fatally so – by being directly associated with the medical model values that dominate any medical setting.

Currently the medical model is very much alive and kicking, with recent and extraordinary reports of Prozac being prescribed to toddlers as young as three (*Daily Express*, 20 March 2000), and new drug-prescribing powers being proposed for the 'treatment' of children's so-called 'behavioural disorders' (*Observer*, 27 February 2000). For me these are criminally irresponsible approaches which miss the point completely. Rather than 'attention deficit' or 'hyperactivity' being routinely pathologized, and their sufferers subjected to normalizing biomedical treatment, I believe that such symptoms are far better understood as children's understandable response to, and unwitting commentary on, technological culture's ever-escalating over-stimulation, and its associated 'left-brain' distortions of early child development (House 2000a, b). Such flagrant misspecification of causality in 'diagnosing' people's suffering can indeed have catastrophic consequences for their well-being, with (medical) treatment easily becoming part of the dis(-)ease itself rather than part of the cure. Between 1993 and 1998, for example, the number of child Ritalin prescriptions in England rose by no less than 36 times, or 3,600 per cent (*Observer*, 27 February 2000). Clearly, there is no room for complacency merely because counselling seems to be gaining increasing professional legitimacy in general medical practice.

Acknowledging ideological conflict

I have heard it argued that these tensions should not exist and should actively be avoided, but it should be clear from the foregoing that I am very sceptical about such a (non) response to real conflict. Jenkins (1994) refers to

> rigidity of thought and practice, preciousness of behaviour and arrogance, often accompanying an antipathetic attitude to medical models of care.... Closer inspection of the problem sometimes reveals a counsellor who is unable to alter his or her method of working to fit into the working environment.

And a professional counsellor colleague of mine criticized the attitude which is sometimes prevalent in some counsellors, whereby the doctor and the 'medical model' in general are treated as 'the enemy', rather than as partners with whom to collaborate in health care.

Higgs and Dammers (1992) have written that 'in the moral field counselling and medical care work in opposite directions and may clash head on ... That they often do is a matter of common observation in many medical encounters.' If the reality is that there *does* exist an incompatibility of value systems between humanistic and medical conceptions of ill-health, then it is simply fudging and avoiding the issues to pretend that we can all work together in an integrated and harmonious way. It seems more likely that the kinds of polarized positions described by Jenkins and my colleague will tend to obtain and are more likely to have a destructive effect to the extent that the ideological divergences underlying those positions are fudged, denied or ignored. Whether both parties – doctors and GP counsellors – are in a position fully to engage with their differences in an open and mutually respectful way remains to be seen. But I sense that the way in which this question is resolved will go a long way to determining the future shape and trajectory of GP counselling in Britain.

A refusal, then, to acknowledge the incompatibility of broadly humanistic and medical-model views of emotional/mental problems when such differences are an undeniable aspect of the General Practice setting would surely constitute a flight from reality rather than a constructive engagement with it. And the problem is that flight from pain and conflict typically does not work. As Scott Peck (1993) so insightfully writes: 'much disease is the result of the attempt to avoid the necessary pain of living': I would argue that much of the 'dysfunctional' nature of organizational behaviour is a result of the avoidance and collusive denial of the real difficulties and conflicts that exist within organizations (Kets de Vries and Miller 1984; Hirshhorn 1998), whether such conflicts are rooted in interpersonal dynamics or in conflicting ideological viewpoints. The refusal openly to acknowledge the very real tensions that exist between orthodox medical and humanistic or post-modern approaches to human distress and ill-health cannot but lead to dysfunctional organizational dynamics and sub-optimal decision- and policy-making.

It might appear from the foregoing that my agenda is one of undermining the cause of GP counselling, but quite the reverse is the case. I am a professional counsellor in a General Practice, with a passionate belief in GP counselling and a commitment to the extension and availability of counselling to as many people as wish to receive this form of help. I am in full agreement with what Michael Balint (who did such pioneering work at the Tavistock Clinic on the dynamics of doctor–patient relationships) wrote many years ago: 'The more one learns of the problems of general practice, the more impressed one becomes with the immediate need for psychotherapy' (Balint 1964).

But I have an equally strong belief that unless the fundamental ideological conflicts that I have highlighted are fully, fearlessly and realistically addressed, the danger is that GP counselling will either be diluted beyond all recognition, becoming assimilated into a medical-model approach which demands short-term, focused, symptom-orientated, 'provenly' cost-effective cognitive-behavioural interventions (Fahy and Wessely 1993), thereby removing any pretensions to helping people towards deep and sustainable therapeutic change; or it will wither and die a slow death, as the orthodox approach to mental and emotional problems resists and ultimately rejects as a 'foreign body' humanistic, non-materialistic counselling approaches to human distress. 'It would be naïve to underestimate the resistance that is likely from within the medical profession to an approach (i.e. humanistic counselling) which, if widely adopted, might substantially undermine the very assumptions on which the medicalization of human ill-health rests' (House 1994b).

Jenkins (1994) writes: 'Mental health services … are going to alter radically if counselling services develop [in General Practice] … The traditional psychiatric model of classification, diagnosis and treatment is beginning to look threadbare' (cf. House 2001). But whether *in practice* the traditional model will be superseded by a more person-centred, humanistic approach to mental health problems is still very much an open question.

It might well be asked why GPs do seem to be enthusiastic about employing counsellors if there exists such an ideological tension between the value systems of the two approaches to ill-health, as I have argued forcefully. The answer to this question is highly complex; but, in general, I believe that GPs are at the same time both enthusiastic *and* deeply ambivalent about employing counsellors: enthusiastic, because, *inter alia*, it gives them the opportunity to offer at least some of their patients the kind of quality time and caring attention which their current working practices increasingly preclude them from offering, and, in some cases, gives them a welcome outlet for their erstwhile unhelpable 'heart-sink' patients; yet deeply ambivalent, because, at some level, GPs must surely know that a full acceptance of counselling as a valid means of health treatment would fundamentally question not only some of the central assumptions on which the medicalization of ill-health is predicated, but also the value system underlying the exhaustive training system through which they have all passed (Engel 1977; Gorlin and Zucker 1983; Stein 1985).

If articles by leading practitioners (Fahy and Wessely 1993) and the recent NHS trends towards audit and 'marketization' are anything to go by, then the omens for the future of humanistic and post-modern counselling approaches in general practice are not encouraging (Jenkins 1995; House 1996a). My strong conviction is that if we ignore the ideological conflicts discussed here, then it will be less likely that such a transformation of mental health problems will take place.

A call for open debate

I am fully aware that this discussion raises very fundamental questions for both GP counsellors and General Practitioners, and is likely to provoke strong responses from both quarters. Not least are the questions of efficacy and cost-effectiveness (Tolley and Rowland 1995; House 1996b) – and whether or not a humanistic approach is commensurable with the increasingly strident demands for audit and efficiency, and the associated managerialist ethos currently sweeping the NHS. Yet I believe that an open and honest dialogue on these differences and difficulties can only have a positive effect in contributing to the public policy debate over the future place of counselling and psychotherapeutic interventions within the developing health care system in this country. If this article helps provoke such a debate, it will have more than served its purpose.

References

Balint, M. (1964) *The Doctor, His Patient and the Illness* (2nd edn), London: Pitman Publishing.

BBC 2 Television (1994) *Everyman* series, 'Welcome to Happy Valley', 14 August.

Breggin, P. (1991) *Toxic Psychiatry*, New York: St Martin's Press (Fontana 1993).

Breggin, P.R. and Breggin, G.R. (1994) *Talking Back to Prozac: What Doctors Won't Tell You about Today's Most Controversial Drug*, New York: St Martin's Press.

Brook, A. (1967) 'An experiment in general practitioner/psychiatrist co-operation', *Journal of the Royal Society of General Practice*, 13.

Engel, G.L. (1977) 'The need for a new medical model: a challenge for biomedicine', *Science*, 196: 129–36.

Erskine, A. and Judd, D. (eds) (1994) *The Imaginative Body: Psychodynamic Therapy in Health Care*, London: Whurr.

Fahy, T. and Wessely, S. (1993) 'Should purchasers pay for psychotherapy?', *British Medical Journal*, 307: 576–7.

Freeling, P. and Levenstein, S. (1983) 'Psychotropic pills or psychotherapy?', in J. Fry (ed.), *Common Dilemmas in Family Medicine*, Lancaster: MTP Press.

Good, B.J. (1994) *Medicine, Rationality and Experience*, Cambridge: Cambridge University Press.

Gorlin, R. and Zucker, H.D. (1983) 'Physicians' reactions to patients: a key to teaching humanistic medicine', *New England Journal of Medicine*, 308: 1059–63.

Hall, J. (1993) *The Reluctant Adult: An Exploration of Choice*, Bradford: Prism Press.

Higgs, R. and Dammers, J. (1992) 'Ethical issues in counselling and health in primary care', *British Journal of Guidance and Counselling*, 20: 27–38.

Hirshhorn, L. (1998) *The Workplace Within: Psychodynamics of Organizational Life*, Cambridge, MA: MIT Press.

House, R. (1994a) 'Counselling in general practice – conflict of ideologies?', *Therapist*, 4: 40–1.

House, R. (1994b) 'The stresses of working in a general practice setting', in W. Dryden (ed.), *The Stresses of Counselling in Action*, London: Sage, pp. 87–107.

House, R. (1996a) 'Psychotherapy and counselling on the run', *Asylum: Magazine for a Democratic Psychiatry*, 9 (4): 33–5.

House, R. (1996b) '"Audit-mindedness" in counselling: some underlying dynamics', *British Journal of Guidance and Counselling*, 24 (2): 277–83.

House, R. (2000a) 'Ritalin v culture' (Letter), *Observer*, 5 March, p. 30.

House, R. (2000b) 'Psychology and early years learning: affirming the wisdom of Waldorf', *Steiner Education*, 34 (2): 10–16.

House, R. (2001) 'Psychopathology, psychosis and the Kundalini: post-modern perspectives on unusual subjective experience', in I. Clarke (ed.), *Psychosis and Spirituality: Exploring the New Frontier*, London: Whurr, pp. 107–25.

Jenkins, G.C. (1994) 'Service delivery, effectiveness in counselling: recent developments', Staines: Counselling in Primary Care Trust: in *CMS Newsletter of the BAC*.

Jenkins, G.H.C. (1995) 'Editorial: Does counselling work?' *Update*, 1 April, pp. 413–14.

Kets de Vries, M.F.R. and Miller, D. (1984) *The Neurotic Organization*, San Francisco: Jossey-Bass.

Kramer, P.D. (1994) *Listening to Prozac*, London: Fourth Estate.

Krystal, H. (1988) *Integration and Self-Healing: Affect–Trauma–Alexithymia*, Hillside, NJ: Analytic Press.

Lawlis, G.F. (1996) *Transpersonal Medicine*, Boston, MA: Shambhala.

Leder, M. (1994) 'Prozac – panacea or poison?', *British Medical Journal*, 309: 487.

Lees, J. (ed.) (1999) *Clinical Counselling in Primary Care*, London: Routledge.

McBride, G. (1994) 'America goes crazy for "the Happy Pill"', *British Medical Journal*, 308: 665.

McDougall, J. (1989) *Theatres of the Body: A Psychoanalytic Approach to Psychosomatic Illness*, London: Free Association Books.

McKinstry, B. (1992) 'Paternalism and the doctor–patient relationship in general practice', *British Journal of General Practice*, 42: 340–2.

McWhinney, I. (1989) 'The need for a transformed clinical method', in M. Stewart and D. Roter (eds), *Communication with Medical Patients*, Newbury Park, CA: Sage.

Maguire, P. (1984) 'Communication skills and patient care', in A. Steptoe and A. Mathews (eds), *Health Care and Human Behaviour*, London: Academic Press.

Mishler, E.G. (1981) *Social Contexts of Health, Illness and Patient Care*, Cambridge: Cambridge University Press.

Parker, I. (ed.) (1995) *Deconstructing Psychopathology*, London: Sage.

Peck, M.S. (1993) 'Salvation and suffering: the ambiguity of pain and disease', *Human Potential* (Summer): 15, 17, 24–6.

Salinsky, J. and Jenkins, G.C. (1994) 'Editorial: Counselling in general practice', *British Journal of General Practice*, 44: 194–5.

Stein, H.F. (1982) 'Toward a life of dialogue: therapeutic communication and the meaning of medicine', *Continuing Education for the Family Physician*, 16: 29–32, 37–8, 44–5.

Stein, H.F. (1985) *The Psychodynamics of Medical Practice: Unconscious Factors in Patient Care*, Berkeley, CA: University of California Press.

Tolley, K. and Rowland, N. (1995) *Evaluating the Cost-effectiveness of Counselling*, London: Routledge.

Totton, N. (1997) 'Inputs and outcomes: the medical model and professionalisation', in R. House and N. Totton (eds), *Implausible Professions: Arguments for Pluralism and Autonomy in Psychotherapy and Counselling*, Ross-on-Wye: PCCS Books, pp. 109–16.

Wilson, C.P. and Mintz, I.L. (eds) (1989) *Psychosomatic Symptoms: Psychodynamic Treatment for the Underlying Personality Disorder*, Northvale, NJ: Jason Aronson.

Zalidis, S. (1994) 'The value of emotional awareness in general practice', in A. Erskine and D. Judd (eds), *The Imaginative Body: Psychodynamic Therapy in Health Care*, London: Whurr.

Discussion issues

1 What are the assumptions, tacit and explicit, underlying 'medical-model' and humanistic/post-modern approaches to (ill-)health, and to what extent are they compatible in theory or in practice?
2 To what extent is it possible to stay true to humanistic, transpersonal or post-modern counselling approaches when working within a medical (GP) setting?
3 Will the institutional professionalization of (GP) counselling help, hinder or be neutral in relation to the challenging issues raised in this chapter?
4 Do your own experiences as a patient and/or counsellor support or contradict the views of the author?

23

Depression

Janet Boakes

Depression is the most common condition presenting both to doctors and to counsellors, and it is a killer. For everyone who actively commits suicide there are as many 'accidents'. If we include those whose suffering drives them to alcoholism, drug addiction or other forms of escape and relief the numbers rise astronomically. It is a life-threatening condition, sometimes a psychiatric emergency. Yet there can be few people who can truly say that they have never been depressed.

What causes depression? The medical view

This year [1992] the Royal College of Psychiatrists is mounting a major campaign against depression. Under the slogan, 'Define it, diagnose it, defeat it' the college seeks to broaden general understanding of this most disabling of conditions. Yet its cause is not well understood. Doctors think of it as an illness, to be treated like others with all the skills at their command. Others regard it as a normal reaction to life's difficulties and reject the 'medical model'. The truth probably lies somewhere between the two. Just as drugs may alter our emotions, for good or ill, so emotions may alter the chemistry of our body and our brain.

Psychiatrists distinguish two forms of depression – a more severe form called 'endogenous' meaning 'arising from within', to distinguish it from 'reactive' depression which is in response to an external event. Reactive depression is much easier to understand because it follows a clearly definable event or stress whereas the endogenous form can often appear 'out of the blue'.

Endogenous depression tends to run in families and is often severe and disabling. Sufferers experience a slowing of bodily and psychic function with loss of weight, energy, appetite and concentration. The mood is low, but with a distinct pattern over the twenty-four-hour cycle. This 'diurnal' variation, whereby a sufferer feels dreadful on first waking but improves in spirits as the day progresses, has led to some scientists linking depression to hibernation patterns in animals. Sleep patterns show distinctive changes. The patient has no difficult in getting to sleep, but wakes early, often around 3 a.m. when psychic energies are said to be at their lowest. The night hours pass in fruitless recriminations, hopelessness and despair until the sufferer drifts back to sleep around 6 a.m., to wake an hour or so later irritable and unrefreshed. In this type of depression the patient may become so severely depressed that s/he loses all touch with reality. Delusions of

This chapter was first published in *Counselling*, Journal of the British Association for Counselling, vol. 3, no. 4, pp. 210–11 (1992).

guilt, of having committed the unforgivable sin, or of one's insides rotting away or being eaten up from within are prominent. Ideas of this sort mark the onset of a psychotic illness and carry a high risk of suicide. Such suicides are planned in advance and these are the people who put their affairs in order, leave notes and in extreme cases may kill others under the influence of their delusion.

In 'reactive' depression there is almost always an identifiable crisis in the recent past. Often this is a loss of some kind. Physical symptoms are less marked, with normal energy levels or even restlessness. Crying is common and the individual feels better when helped to talk. Sleep is often long in coming but then the patient has difficulty in waking and facing the day. S/he seems to use sleep to escape the problems of living. There is not usually weight or appetite loss. Mood variation is less marked and depends on the presence of other people. In company depression lifts, only to fall again as the sufferer is once again alone. Suicide is a risk but is much more likely to be an impulsive act, born out of anger and despair. Such acts, called 'parasuicide' are often regarded as 'cries for help' but are likely to elicit a negative reaction from those around them.

To make things even more confusing, if we look back over the year preceding the onset of severe, endogenous type depression, we are likely to find a major life crisis. It is as if there has been a 'pause button' in operation to delay the onset of symptoms and give the impression of depression arising from nowhere.

In endogenous depression scientists have been able to show definite changes in brain chemistry, and this type of depression responds well to drug treatment. Reactive depression does not respond well to drug treatment, nor are there the same chemical changes, and such patients are likely either to present themselves, or to be referred, to counsellors. Indeed the majority of those seeking counselling are likely to be experiencing some form of depression, and in some the risk of suicide is ever present.

The role of the counsellor

But where does 'mind' fit into this? And what is the place and value of talking about one's experience, and of 'insight', which is psychological understanding?

'Insight' means 'sight within' or interior understanding. Understanding our inner world is necessary for major psychic change to occur. It is only through deep self-knowledge that a person is freed to make choices about his or her own life without blaming others for perceived failures.

A skilled counsellor can do much to help the depressed person and for most reactive depressions counselling is the best form of help.

When faced with a client, the counsellor tries to understand through the client's eyes: What is it like to be that person? How does it feel? How are things understood? What indeed has happened? People often come to a counsellor feeling very confused and muddled. In struggling to tell their story they may discover new ways of looking at it. It may be the first time such a person has been able to tell their story and have it listened to and respected. The experience of being deeply attended to is in itself healing, and for some that may be enough.

In other instances both client and counsellor may wish to go further and explore the past. It seems that our experiences as we grow up from childhood into adult life influence the way that we respond to the challenges and difficulties of life. In understanding how our upbringing has shaped us we learn how to give up old and outdated reactions and try new strategies to deal with painful experiences. For example, the child who was unsure of its parents' love can grow into an adult who desperately seeks to please others. Since it is impossible to please everyone all the time, this may lead to feelings of depression. If helped to see how this is a hangover from childhood and no longer appropriate to the present, such a person may grow in confidence and self-assertion, no longer judging everything by whether or not others will approve. (That usually has the effect of making the person much more likeable, or 'pleasing' as well!)

In coming to understand their past, clients are able to find new ways of coping with stressful events in the present and face the future with hope.

Counsellors need to recognize that for some people understanding alone is not enough. They need to be aware of the different forms of depression and know when to refer on for psychiatric help. It is perfectly possible to understand how someone's depression has come about and yet that person may still need anti-depressant treatment. Psychiatrists likewise sometimes need reminding that drugs alone seem arid and that their patients may be crying out for human understanding, for someone who will listen.

In this year of the 'Defeat Depression' campaign, we need a two-pronged attack in which drugs and insight work together to overcome this most insidious and debilitating condition.

Discussion issues

1   Do counsellors need to recognize that for some people understanding alone is not enough? Is it possible for someone to understand how their depression has come about and still need anti-depressant treatment?
2   Do psychiatrists sometimes need reminding that drugs alone seem arid and that their patients may be crying out for human understanding, for someone who will listen?
3   Is a two-pronged attack on depression in which drugs and insight work together a positive way forward?
4   What is your reaction to the views expressed in this chapter?

24

The Aftermath of Suicide

Alice Middleton and David I. Williams

Suicide involves much more than the destruction of the person. Very often, it destroys others in the family. The real victim, time after time, is not the body in the coffin, but the family.

Suicide is a major cause of death. In 1999 there were over 6,000 cases in the UK and, globally, 1,000 people a day take their own life. There may be many more suicides than statistics indicate, for death from suicide may be recorded as 'undetermined' in order to lessen the pain of those left behind. A coroner can bring in a verdict of 'death by mis-adventure', 'accidental death' or 'open verdict' and such verdicts are often passed when a coroner seeks to protect relatives.

Those left behind after a successful suicide have had many hardships to bear and many prejudices to face. In France it was customary until the eighteenth century for the body of the suicide to be desecrated and dragged through the streets to the great humiliation of the family. Family property and goods were forfeit to the government, leaving survivors with only their clothing. In England in the eighteenth century laws were changed with the intention of helping survivors. Verdicts of insanity were passed by the juries so that the element of crime – both civil and religious – was eliminated.

Yet the view of suicide as a disgrace and something to be kept secret remains and puts great strain on friends and relatives. Funerals are often hasty and hushed up, and these sudden deaths explained to family and friends as accidents; children are often not told until years later, if then. Their skeleton in the closet is often discovered by neighbours who then might assign the blame – those close to the deceased may be shunned by neighbours and taunted until they eventually leave, moving to an area where they are not known. Suicide still carries a stigma and a sense of shame.

It is only over the past 20 years that the issue of the effects of a suicide death on the family have been addressed. Those bereaved by a suicide are found to incur a particular intense and painful reaction (Cain and Fast 1972). They tend to be at higher risk of psychological impairment, and of having suicidal tendencies themselves (van Dongen 1988). Attitudes towards the bereaved tend to be far more negative than for other types of death (Rudestan 1977).

The coroner's court

Legal action can get in the way of the grieving process. In England and Wales deaths termed unnatural are subject to legal investigation. While still in the throes of bereavement

This chapter was first published in *Counselling*, Journal of the British Association for Counselling, vol. 6, no. 4, pp. 307–9 (1995).

survivors face various problems; there is the legal procedure and registration, there are funeral arrangements, issues of finance and insurance and benefit entitlements. The need for a coroner's inquest means that the procedure for obtaining a death certificate, registering the death and arranging the funeral is different from that of a 'normal' death.

Suicide is no longer a crime but police inquiries begin immediately. Personal loss becomes a matter for public scrutiny. Evidence will include the suicide note. Legally this is the property of the person to whom it is written. In fact, however, the suicide note is delivered at the discretion of the coroner. These investigative procedures are inevitably distressing and intrusive for the survivors. Coroners do try to balance public interest against private grief. The Brodrick Report (1971) made specific proposals to reform the inquest procedure for suicide, suggesting that coroners should have discretion to dispense with inquests in certain cases. So far these proposals have not been acted upon, although the Home Office (1999) has recently published a 'moral charter' for Coroners' courts recommending a more supportive approach towards bereaved families.

The inquest accounts for much of the distress experienced. However, it may be a positive and crucial event. It can be an opportunity for witnesses to put forward their own version of events, or, by actually hearing the evidence of others, to find out more about what actually happened at the time of the suicide. Obtaining accurate information – for example, about the actual circumstances of the death – can be a vital means of making the whole event seem more real. For those who have not seen the body, this can be particularly important.

Grief following a suicide

Bereavement is an accepted experience and grief is becoming a socially acceptable response, but suicide disrupts that which is socially acceptable. Those who are bereaved by suicide appear to be at greater risk of disturbed grief reactions. They face the triple loss of rejection, disillusionment and self-doubt. The effect is often hostility, which is turned inwards. How then does the pattern of grieving differ from the more 'normal'?

Feelings of *shock* and *disbelief* are likely to be greater and last longer than for other bereavements. The news may be received from strangers or the police. It is possible that the suicide act was committed away from the victim's home. Both these factors can increase the likelihood of survivors experiencing feelings of disbelief or *denial* – the first reaction to the news of a suicide death is 'It can't be, it must be a mistake, it's someone else.' Relatives often describe the death as natural or accidental. Avoiding the truth may virtually prevent the working through of mourning; limit opportunities for checking distorted fantasies against the realities of the suicide act; encourage a variety of gross misconceptions; and perhaps most important of all, arrest dealing with, and eventually resolving, the irrational guilt and anger felt towards the deceased. With suicide there are frequent requests by survivors to falsify death certificates.

Searching for meaning and cause is unique to those left behind after a suicide death. The search for 'why' may last for ever and is very important in work with survivors, working with it may be the key to resolving their grief.

Several studies have identified *guilt* as the most prevalent response. The guilt one feels for missing clues that were probably given; guilt that one is not good enough to share the feelings of the deceased; guilt that one may have contributed towards the suicide. If there was disharmony in the home and someone took their life, there is often the assumption that someone is to blame. There is a societal assumption of guilt which is part of the legacy of the taboo and stigma. Guilt after bereavement is common, but with a suicide it tends to be greater and more pervasive. If the individual who committed suicide intended to make the survivor suffer, then many succeed. This may explain why the search for explanations after suicide are less amenable to resolution than after natural or accidental death.

Wrobleski (1985) showed that 86 per cent of survivors felt guilty following the suicide and 22 per cent felt blamed by others for the death. So while sadness is the most obvious reaction and anger the most enduring, guilt is the most prominent. Anger and guilt are closely related. Survivors may feel angry for not doing more for the deceased and consequently feel guilty. The majority see suicide as the ultimate rejection, feeling responsible for the deceased choosing death rather than life with them.

Anger is common: anger towards the person who took their life; anger for their rejection; anger toward God and the world for allowing it to happen; anger at the professionals involved who failed to act; anger at friends for being unsupportive; and anger at themselves for not having been able to prevent the act. It is a common feature that while asking 'Why, why, why?' they usually mean, 'Why did s/he do this to me?' The anger felt towards the deceased is often not expressed out loud, nor is it even experienced as anger because the guilt is too great.

The most destructive guilt arises when survivors feel *responsibility* for the death, as when the deceased tried manipulation before the act. Feeling responsible can have devastating effects, especially on children – a parent commits suicide – the child is not told – so, the child may think that by becoming a 'perfect' child, not doing anything wrong, then the parent will return.

An emotion which probably often occurs, but has seldom been studied, is *relief*. Wrobleski and McIntosh (1987) in their research observed that 67 per cent of their sample were relieved because the person was no longer suffering, and 47 per cent expressed relief because the person had died. Yet sadly relief cannot be shown.

Depression can manifest itself following a suicide bereavement. The constant questions, anger, sleeplessness, lack of nourishment, sadness, along with other emotions all contribute. Another issue peculiar to suicide is preoccupation with the death scene. Those who found the body, or who witnessed the act, may have mental images that remain with them forever.

The bereavement process may be hindered by the amount of involvement the person had in the suicide act, for instance, if they discovered the body, or witnessed the death, or were affected by the suicide note. Only 15–30 per cent of people who commit suicide leave a written message behind and often if notes are found they are withheld from the authorities. The existence of a suicide note implies an intimate involvement. Some will place importance on the note as they search for meaning, yet these notes do not always provide the answer; the deceased only say what they want the reader to know. There are two types of notes – those which are hostile and those which attempt to exempt the survivor from blame. Note content affects the severity of distress experienced.

Relatives may feel that they are being actively avoided by many of those from whom they would normally expect and receive help. Even worse than the general lack of help is the active finger pointing. With the lack of social support it seems inevitable that many will remain silent. Against the silence which surrounds a suicide, a person may be limited in opportunities for catharsis, in checking distorted fantasies against the reality of the suicidal act, in clearing up a variety of gross misconceptions, or in dealing with irrational guilt and anger felt towards the deceased. This conspiracy of silence can hinder the grieving process; it may be important for healing and peace of mind that silence is broken. When trauma/crisis invades a family it is normally discussed and natural feelings can be expressed. In contrast to 'normal death', family and friends of someone who commits suicide often do not want to hear and be reminded that something awful has happened. When this happens the bargain of silence is a family's solution to the anger and blame they feel towards each other.

Ultimately, those bereaved by suicide death share common tasks with all those who are bereaved; they must accept the loss as final, give up the attachment, and learn to live without the deceased.

The needs of those bereaved by suicide

What are the needs of those left behind? Initially, the majority of friends and relations look for comfort and support, practical help, advice and guidance, particularly over financial/insurance issues. They may also look for religious counselling. A number of writers on the aftermath of suicide (see Dunne et al. 1987) suggest that help is more effective within the first 24 hours and suggest offering debriefing within a crisis intervention approach.

The psychological autopsy has been used as an investigative technique to aid in the determination of the intentionality of death. Information is gathered about the deceased under the headings of: brief life history; psychiatric-psychological data; research for clues to, or communications of suicide; recent life events; and miscellaneous data which may be relevant to this death, but not necessarily psychological in nature (Sanborn and Sanborn 1976).

Counsellors need to focus the client on three areas: (i) understanding of the event – this involves facing the reality of the suicide by asking for descriptions of the event and its effects; (ii) external resources; and (iii) inner resources. Working with this task in individual counselling or group work can enable survivors to look at alternatives and make choices. Keeping a journal or diary can also be beneficial, enabling survivors to separate the thoughts that bombard and occupy the mind. Writing a letter to the deceased asking the 'whys' and expressing guilt and anger is another way of overcoming feelings of helplessness. Because it is a private activity, previously denied relationship issues with the deceased can be expressed, obsessive thoughts may lose some of their obsessive qualities, and survivors may find they are recording thoughts of which they were not previously aware.

Counselling services can provide a safe and supportive environment where survivors may explore and work through the more complex issues of a suicide bereavement. A priority need for the survivor is for someone to listen in a caring non-judgemental way as they work through their feelings of anguish and confusion. The possibility of another suicide among survivors is very real (van Dongen 1988).

Suicide survivor groups

With the range and intensity of the emotions involved and the particular factors peculiar to suicide bereavement, it would appear that a group separate from those bereaved by other causes is essential. The goals of a support group are designed for survivors to learn collectively and individually to meet their own needs through the sharing of understanding, support and knowledge. Survivors share a common experiential bond, but some are further along in the grieving process and can offer hope and suggestions to the new survivor.

General counselling services for the bereaved may not be of great help to those bereaved by suicide. 'I went to a bereavement group, there was shock on their faces at the mention of suicide.... I could not face the shame....' Survivors feel they are blamed for the suicide, and this needs to be shared with others who have experienced a suicide bereavement. Others feel they do not deserve to be among other bereaved (normal) people.

At present there are only five suicide survivor groups in the United Kingdom (Belfast, Reading, Croydon, Norwich and Hull). In North America, some of the existing groups follow a strict programme. The Survivors' Support Programme in Marin County, Toronto, for example, has a non-professional, time-limited, structured programme of support and assistance specifically directed towards the understanding and resolving of stress that is unique to those bereaved by suicide.

Survivors of bereavement by suicide are an at-risk group for abnormal bereavement yet there is little support provided for them. A practical response to help survivors would be to enhance the role of a Coroner's Welfare Officer. It would also be invaluable if the Brodrick Report were implemented. There is no doubt that distress could be relieved by such a change through preventing the publication of reports of inquests, and by providing greater opportunity for discussion of contentious matters with the Coroner or a representative. This might also reduce some of the stigma felt by survivors. The legal system in Britain concerning the classification of death is, perhaps, unnecessarily formal, harsh and stigmatizing. It is crucial and urgent that there is a better support system for those bereaved by a suicide death. There is a clear need for a targeted, specialized support system which offers hope and compassion for those left behind.

Conclusion

Grief after suicide differs from that from other causes of death. The grieving process is exacerbated by police inquiries, the inquest, media attention and society's attitudes. As well as feeling rejected by the deceased, survivors may feel rejected by society. Few resources are available to help them. As long as suicide death is tabooed and stigmatized, survivors will continue to have unique problems and provision needs to be made to offer specific intervention and support.

References

Brodrick Report (1971) *Report of the Committee on Death Certification and Coroners*, London: Home Office.

Cain, A. and Fast, I. (1972) 'The rules of bereavement: are suicide deaths different?, *Journal of Community Psychiatry*, 116: 255–61.

Dunne, E.J., McIntosh, J.L. and Dunne, M.K. (1987) *Suicide and its Aftermath*, New York: Norton.

Home Office (1999) Coroners Service: Model Coroners' Charter, *Circular 46*.

Rudestan, K.E. (1977) 'Physical and psychological responses to suicide', *Family Journal of Consulting and Clinical Psychology*, 45: 162–70.

Sanborn, D.E. and Sanborn, C.J. (1976) 'Diseases of the nervous system', *Journal for Psychiatrists and Neurologists*, 37: 4–9.

van Dongen, C.J. (1988) 'The legacy of suicide', *Journal of Psychosocial Nursing*, 26: 8–13.

Wrobleski, A. (1985) 'The suicide survivors' grief group', *Journal of Death and Dying*, 15: 173–84.

Wrobleski, A. and McIntosh, J.C. (1987) 'Problems of suicide survivors: a survey report', *Journal of Psychiatry Related Science*, 24: 137–42.

Useful Contacts

SOBS (Survivors of Bereavement by Suicide) Helpline, Tel. 01482 826559.
SOBS National Headquarters, Tel. 01482 610728.
Compassionate Friends, Tel. 0117 953 9639 (parents only).

Discussion issues

1 What modern-day pressures are contributing to the increase in suicide?
2 Is the legal system a help or hindrance to survivors of bereavement by suicide?
3 What do you consider are the main differences between a 'normal' bereavement and a 'suicide' bereavement?
4 How might the needs of survivors of suicide be best served in the first 48 hours after the death?

25

The Limitations of Current Theories in Understanding Bereavement and Grief

Peter Farrell

An ancient Buddhist text, relates the story of Kisagotami, a mother distraught by her child's death. Seeking help, she found none, save one person who told her of a wise being who was currently giving teachings in the vicinity; it might be that he could help. Desperate, Kisagotami sought out the Master with her dead babe in her arms and begged him to restore life to her child. He listened to her pleading, then sent her to fetch a grain of mustard seed from a house where none had died. She searched in vain, but nowhere could be found where death had not entered.

The death of an individual, particularly a relative, with its associated traumas of mental and physical pain and disease, is perhaps the most profoundly destabilizing event with which *all* humankind must deal in the context of what may be considered normal daily experiences (normal as opposed to those who experience traumas such as abuse on a regular basis). The result of death for those left behind, as demonstrated in the story of Kisagotami, is grief, and to varying degrees avoidance strategies (Murray-Parkes et al. 1996; Rando 1986), which although not often as obvious as Kisagotami's, are in some way designed to reverse such an inexorable event. To understand this common affliction of humankind, there have been many attempts to establish biological, cognitive and behavioural reasons for grief resulting from bereavement (Freud 1917; Bowlby 1980; Raphael 1984). Others have sought to define characteristic patterns or stages that a bereft individual may experience so that counsellors who would assist fellow humans in their bereavement can recognize these stages should they present difficulties, and thus assist people in coming to terms with their grief (Worden 1982; Murray-Parkes 1986). I review some of the theory of grief and bereavement from which recognition and understanding of these stages has developed and question how far, and in what sense, this understanding contributes to the individual's progression, or whether it simply helps to place the individual firmly back in an ostensive sense of security until the next loss occurs. I suggest that the recognition of death is a foundation for progress beyond that of mundane daily living. In looking at the generally accepted understanding of the nature of bereavement, I believe that it is limited in its current view, and I suggest other reasons why grief is so great. It should be understood that I am concentrating only on what appears to be missing in the current understanding of bereavement and bereavement counselling. I do not question the undoubted beneficial results of it, nor criticize the magnificent progress that has been made in bereavement counselling, but merely suggest its limitations in understanding bereavement as it is *generally* currently presented.

This chapter was first published in *Counselling,* Journal of the British Association for Counselling, vol. 10, no. 2, pp. 143–6 (1999).

Bereavement counselling can be seen to derive from theories of bereavement and grief expounded by the researchers already mentioned. Bereavement is being deprived by death of a relative, friend or loved one (or thing), while grief describes the reaction of that person while in a state of bereavement (Wright 1992). This theory would appear to describe the process of bereavement as something that has an end, albeit, as Wright states further, an 'adaption' to loss. The implication of adaption is that there is no cure: we simply have to find methods of adjusting our being to an irreversible change. Of course we do this every moment of our waking lives; each moment we are bereft of the past, it is simply a memory. However, because each moment brings a new experience as a result of the past moment, we attribute a solid continuity to our existence. In a generally 'well-adjusted' existence this apparent continuity, when combined with the continuity of significant objects and others, provides us with a relatively solid and secure foundation from which we may develop and thus carry out the everyday tasks of living and survival with hopefully a reasonable degree of happiness. Murray-Parkes et al. (1996: 3) describe this continuity or binding of events aptly: 'The people we love become tangled up with us in a network of unique interlocking systems of thought and behaviour, which, over time, we take for granted.' For most of us, however, this recognition of the frailty of our existence, and the pain arising from it, becomes starkly apparent most often only in times of bereavement, particularly of loved ones. When this occurs, the pain and sense of loss and insecurity, particularly for those who have evolved a more sensitive nature, is unbearable. 'Bereavement cuts a swathe through these systems [of thought and behaviour] and multilates just as surely as surgeons multilate a person when they cut off a limb' (Murray-Parkes et al. 1996: 3).

Could it be that this adjustment to loss (which occurs each moment) allows us to establish a possibly erroneous yet powerful sense of security, which I describe as the appearance of intrinsic permanence or reality. Perhaps we have been inoculated with the relatively painless daily doses of impermanence and loss, allowing us to resist the stark reality of the disease that surrounds us and ultimately affects all existence, that of impermanence and death. Effectively we block out the disease temporarily, ignoring its existence, even though we can clearly see it and discuss it, and in consequence we impute the quality of permanence and solidity to our own lives and those of others. However, when the methods we use to enable this continual adjustment have been assaulted with a loss so great and obviously irreversible as death, it strikes at the very heart of this apparent continuity, in fact, at the very heart of our existence.

Many would agree that some form of security is damaged by bereavement. According to Bowlby (1980), the method of maintaining that security, that intrinsic reality, is attachment. Simplistically, attachment to significant others gives security to the individual's life; it is a basis for healthy, happy survival; it is the background to all other relationships. The nature or extent of any threat to this attachment (loss) determines the extent of the consequent behaviour (grief). The consequence of that behaviour is designed to ensure continuity of an emotional bond or attachment. However, this only explains bereavement or loss in terms of behavioural mechanisms of survival. What of the discerning intelligence involved that understands that such a bond or attachment can never return or be replaced? Clearly, due to intelligent recognition of the finality of the loss, it can no longer be thought of as just an animal survival mechanism, and so in theory it should no longer be necessary to display these emotions to maintain the continuity of that attachment.

Why do we continue to display these emotions when they are of no survival benefit to us?

Attachment and loss are undoubtedly a part of the story, but not the whole story. Yet this theory is mainly what most bereavement counselling is based on: that is, grief is the emotional response to loss (Murray-Parkes et al. 1996; Ward 1996). Undoubtedly, grief is the emotional response to loss and the stages of grief are empirical markers whereby counsellors may assess the progress, or the lack of progress, in those individuals working with their grief and as a result assist them in their journey of adapting. Yet, even with this knowledge something appears to be amiss, or at least not addressed fully. Why does grief cut so deep and in so many different ways? Why do we continue to grieve if, according to Bowlby (1980), it is an animal survival mechanism, particularly when that mechanism is not needed for our survival?

Grief is something to be worked with and through if we are to survive and maintain a reasonably happy existence. However, many of those who have studied bereavement, and from whose theories and writing bereavement counselling has developed, are only in part correct in their assumptions about grieving and its outcome. The methods of understanding individuals' grief *per se*, that is, attachment and loss, resistance to change, the tasks of mourning and the determinants of grief, and the phases of mourning (Bowlby 1980; Worden 1982; Lendrum and Syme 1992; Murray-Parkes et al. 1996) are not in question. They provide a means of understanding individuals' varied grief processes and supply counsellors with the means to assist clients in overcoming them, thus enabling clients to continue without their significant other. But can we ultimately be expected to believe that a loss so great can be overcome? Should it even be that we allow ourselves, arguably, to complete the process of grieving and then continue in our own way in the light of such a powerful revelation as death?

It appears that the working through of grief does imply some sort of end or completion of the grief process as mentioned earlier, even though this is clearly denied by current authors. 'In the reestablishement phase, there is a gradual decline of grief … the loss is not forgotten, but put in a special place, which, while allowing it to be remembered, also frees the mourner to go on to new attachments' (Rando 1986: 22). Humphrey and Zimpfer (1996) argue that the resolution of grief was in the past a task to be accomplished or got over without the healing of the void within us that has occurred due to loss, while Tatelbaum (1981: 94) describes recovery from grief as 'restoration'. Terms such as re-establishment, healing and restoration, while describing something more than an end, still contain the implication of completion or of returning to an original position where we can continue to forge secure attachments. While, thank goodness, individuals by themselves, and through the aid of those with counselling skills, can achieve this goal to varying degrees, by doing this many may have allowed a unique opportunity to pass them by: that is, the opportunity to 'evolve' (Tatelbaum 1981: 138) rather than continue.Whatever the state of recovery from grief, it can never be resolved if it is based on an incomplete understanding of bereavement and grief, and therefore will be as painful, if not more so, upon its return from the depths of the unconscious and subconscious in which it has been unknowingly placed. Why? Because the reasons for grief hold deeper meaning than can be understood on a biological, behavioural or cognitive level.

Tatelbaum (1981: 94) states: 'Recovery from grief is the restoration of our capacity for living a full life and enjoying life without feelings of guilt, shame, sorrow or regret', and so should it be. However, she and others would claim that such feelings are in relation to the individual who has died. While this is undoubtedly true for the reasons they give (Rando 1986; Murray-Parkes et al. 1996), I suggest that these feeling are also related to the recognition of other factors at deeper, possibly even spiritual, levels of consciousness, levels beyond behavioural mechanisms, from which arises the loving kindness that would bestow happiness on others and from which arises the compassion that would wish to remove others from the suffering that it has experienced itself. The impetus that would generate such love is not least of all the stark recognition that nothing, including ourselves, has any intrinsic permanence, because the notion of intrinsic permanence, when challenged, is one of the prime causes of such suffering.

Intrinsic permanence is a quality we bestow on life to help us maintain our continuity, our sense of reality of being, that enables us to continue our existence with some degree of happiness. Even though we can recognize intellectually that we are impermanent and subject to disintegration, our sense of self or being allows us to continue to maintain the notion of an apparent permanent entity. Death directly confronts our intellect, presenting us with our own lack of permanence and the relative brevity of our existence, thus threatening our reason to be. Is it any wonder that denial is a complication of grief-work. Lendrum and Syme (1992: 10) state that 'where early attachments are very anxious and insecure, the numbers and losses too frequent ... then the direct expression of feelings and needs becomes increasingly difficult and instead the true feelings are denied'. Why? Because they are deepening realizations of the lack of intrinsic reality or permanence. We are confronted with the plain truth and if we do not have the means – spiritual, philosophical or otherwise – to deal with it, the only other way is to suppress it by denial. Although the consequences of denial that may result (locked-in feelings for the individual) can be addressed temporarily with the aid of the counsellor, the stark reality remains to be dealt with, if not now then at some later stage.

In addition to the recognition of impermanence, the loss of something or someone provides the further recognition that, in fact, we have no power to interfere in the process of disintegration. In the case of a loved one, we are helpless: we cannot help them on whatever journey they may be about to undertake, we cannot guide them or give them words of love or encouragement; we cannot tell them they are safe; we cannot hold them or comfort them; we can no longer protect them. No longer do we have the power to interfere for the sake of their welfare. What greater reason for grief can there be than this, the knowledge that another being, particularly a loved one, even more so a child or dependant, is alone on a journey, where as far as we know there are no roads and no signposts? Perhaps the guilt we feel is due to more than such things as not doing something for the deceased or having ambivalent feelings toward the deceased (Worden 1982; Murray-Parkes 1986). Perhaps the guilt is due also, and possibly at a deeper level of consciousness, to the fact that we have allowed ourselves to become totally immersed in the search for happiness based on an erroneous sense of permanence. Consequently, we may have made little or no effort to confront impermanence and death while the loved one was alive, and thus have made no such provision for their welfare during their dying. In short, we are confronted with the knowledge that we have not found an answer to death and impermanence and we have not discovered any way in which we may assist our loved ones beyond this life.

The current understanding of bereavement and bereavement counselling is limited in its view, and the ultimate cause of grief has more to do with a deep spirituality that searches for meaning in life, than the search for the more practical answers suggested by Rando (1986). It is that search that many would toy with philosophically and academically, but in that search, achieve little because they only acknowledge impermanence in an intellectual, non-intuitive way that does not grasp its true nature. It is only in the face of such loss as death that the true intuitive awareness of impermanence is blindingly revealed to us. Yet, for many, that intuitive flash brought on by death is soon dimmed by many of the protective devices, such as denial, suggested by Freud (1917), Murray-Parkes (1986) and others. Although I would not deny that such theories have substance and are powerful tools in understanding and aiding the bereaved, these theories of bereavement are only related to the more gross aspects of our being. While bereavement counselling is a vital necessity, it lacks the ability to deal with the underlying, dare I say more noble, reasons I have described, that is, the profound questions that are presented to us when a death occurs.

Bereavement counselling helps individuals to deal with their loss and adapt to the changes occurring, but ultimately it falls short in its task – that of facilitating a greater, one might even say spiritual, healing. Such counselling may currently only help to place the individual firmly back in their ostensive sense of security until the next loss occurs or until that intuitive flash surfaces every so often when one's guard is lowered or one is reminded of one's loss. What then can be done to aid this problem if, as I have suggested, there is no ultimate help within the level currently understood by bereavement counselling? Perhaps what we do is the best we can do, at least without introducing values and beliefs. It may be that in society's general breaking away from organized religion we have lost that arena of counselling, if there was one, that would allow us to deal with the deeper spiritual reasons for grief. The advent of secular counselling may have allowed more openness and honesty, providing a transition to a more profound understanding of the nature of bereavement and death. If not allowed to stagnate in relatively limited theories, it may result in more profound and satisfactory counselling methods based on spirituality (not blind religious dogma) rather that on biological, cognitive and behavioural understanding alone.

Perhaps any answer to the deeper reasons for grief goes beyond any counselling in the sense that we would discuss here. To deal with bereavement fully may require, for some at least, the methods used by the Master to help the grieving mother in the story of Kisagotami to the absolute realization of death and impermanence; she sought long and in vain for a house where death had not entered. For her, realization came when, upon finding no such house, she returned to the Master and told him of her failure. At which the Master said:

> My sister thou hast found, searching for what none finds – that bitter balm I had to give thee. He thou lovedst slept dead on thy bosom yesterday: today thou knowest the whole wide world weeps with thy woe: The grief which all hearts share grows less for one. (Humphreys 1962: 82)

In offering this alternative view of understanding grief and coming to terms with it, I am not suggesting that counsellors should go round confronting the bereaved in such a way as the Master did Kisagotami, almost as though to say 'Look, that's the way it is, we must all face up to it.' This story alludes to the futility of looking for a cure where there is none. The fact that Kisagotami was brought to this truth led her to follow the spiritual path that aspires to cure all disease. I am suggesting that there is something more to the nature of bereavement, that it is beyond the understanding currently presented, and that the blinding light of realization of our impermanence should spur us on to a search that may ultimately help others in this state. Tatelbaum (1981: 138) advises that we can either 'succumb to adversity or use adversity to transform our lives'. That transformation may be the ability simply to adapt to the immense changes in our lives due to the death of another, or it may lead us to 'see life in a context that is larger than that which is concrete'. Kisagotami was led to this greater view by her Master, and through his teachings it is said that she achieved a state beyond suffering. Would that we could all meet with such a Master.

Something more than the current theories and understanding of grief underlies the suffering of those beings experiencing bereavement. The limitations of counselling methods, based on the current understanding of bereavement, and the healing resulting from bereavement counselling methods, may possibly inhibit and even suppress, at least in some, a more spiritual growth. Clearly, these points are part of a wider debate, possibly extending beyond the scope of the current understanding of bereavement and counselling which cannot extend to something that requires possible definitive beliefs, because then it might go beyond facilitating and enter the realm of dogma and advice-giving. It may be that bereavement counselling can only facilitate such things as restoration and personal growth beyond loss in the context of 'normal' everyday living and that the remainder of a person's journey, particularly into spiritual growth and the search for meaning, can only be addressed and realized in that individual's own natural evolution. Bereavement counselling cannot be said to lack necessity, efficacy or appropriateness, particularly for those who are currently unable to extricate themselves from pathological grief. However, a greater understanding of grief is required beyond that within which counselling currently operates and though a new framework might appear to present problems relating to counselling's whole ethos, it would be ignorant and cruel, in the face of the enormity of universal suffering, not to attempt to integrate a more spiritual understanding.

References

Bowlby, J. (1980) *Sadness and Depression: Attachment and Loss*, vol. 3, Harmondsworth: Penguin.

Freud, S. (1917) *Mourning and Melancholia*, Standard Edn, vol. XIV, London: Hogarth.

Humphreys, C. (1962) *Buddhism* (3rd edn), Harmondsworth: Penguin.

Humphrey, G.M. and Zimpfer, D.G. (1996) *Counselling for Grief and Bereavement*, London: Sage.

Lendrum, S. and Syme, G. (1992) *Gift of Tears*, London: Routledge.

Lindemann, E. (1944) 'Symptomatology and management of acute grief', *American Journal of Psychiatry*, 101: 141–9.

Murray-Parkes, C. (1986) *Bereavement: Studies of Grief in Adult Life* (2nd edn), Harmondsworth: Penguin.

Murray-Parkes, C., Relf, M. and Couldrick, A. (1996) *Counselling in Terminal Care and Bereavement*, Leicester: BPS Books.

Rando, T.A. (1986) *Parental Loss of a Child*, Illinois: Research Press Company.

Raphael, B. (1984) *The Anatomy of Bereavement: A Handbook for the Caring Professions*, London: Hutchinson.

Tatelbaum, J. (1981) *The Courage to Grieve*, Great Britain: Cedar Books.

Ward, B. (1996) *Good Grief* (2nd edn), London: Jessica Kingsley.
Worden, J.W. (1982) *Grief Counselling and Grief Therapy*, Cambridge: Cambridge Univeristy Press.
Wright, B. (1992) *Skills for Caring: Loss and Grief*, USA: Churchill Livingstone.

Discussion issues

1 Is the element of spirituality of fundamental significance in our understanding of bereavement and grief?
2 Are the ways in which people address their grief to be found only within the context of their own belief system?
3 Is it important for counsellors to have an understanding of a variety of belief systems?
4 When spirituality is an integral part of grief work and belief systems provide the bereaved with means of addressing their grief, is it within the brief of modern counselling, *per se*, to enter this arena? If so, do counsellors currently have a sufficient knowledge base and training to do this?

26

The Social Model of Disability

Tony Makin

There are many terms used to describe people and disability. As someone who is disabled I now understand what is meant by the terms 'medical model' and 'social model' and find the distinction between the two helpful in understanding the ways in which disabled people are disadvantaged in our society. I know that many counsellors, while feeling empathy for a client who is a disabled person have a limited level of awareness of the ways in which that person can feel overwhelmed and oppressed just by the terms which are used to describe them. In presenting the medical and social models of disability, in the hope of extending the awareness of counsellors, it is important that I also explain certain words in common use.

Disabled people themselves have looked for words and definitions which distinguish between the physical condition of an individual and the oppressive constrictions experienced by all disabled people because of the ways in which society is organized. One group, the Union of Physically Impaired Against Segregation (UPIAS) makes the following distinctions:

Impairment

Lacking all of or part of a limb; having a defective limb or mechanism of the body.

Disability

The disadvantage or restriction of activity brought about by contemporary social organization, which takes little or no account of people who have physical impairments and thus excludes them from participation in the mainstream of social activities. Physical oppression thus becomes a form of social oppression.

Disabled people

In this definition UPIAS focuses on disablement as a result of societal constrictions rather than on people's own individual conditions. It uses the social model to describe a person's oppression as their disability, rather than their individual problem, as the medical model tends to do.

Making a difference

Through stubbornness and determination I have managed to overcome much of my impairment, yet I was aware that something else was still disabling me. The explanation lay within my discovery of the social model which outlines how my capabilities and

This chapter was first published in *Counselling*, Journal of the British Association for Counselling, vol. 6, no. 4, p. 274 (1995).

opportunities were being restricted or curtailed by poor social organization. As a counsellor, this new awareness also gave me a new dimension into disabled clients' problems.

This new dimension suggests that disabled people's individual and collective disadvantage is due in large part to a complex form of institutional discrimination as fundamental to our society as sexism, racism or heterosexism. Most people have not been brought up to accept disabled people as they are. Through fear, ignorance and prejudice, barriers and discriminatory practices develop which are disabling to us. Therefore, in the eyes of the disabled people's movement, the 'cure' to problems of disability lies in the restructuring of society. It is their view that the position of disabled people and the discrimination against us are socially created and have little to do with our impairments.

In an attempt to raise awareness of the discrimination against disabled people the BAC Disability Issues Sub-Committee (DISC) first published ò *RAMPS Aren't Everything* (BAC 1996) which not only highlights how the design of the built environment exercises control over the lives of people with disabilities, but gives a detailed guide to physical access. It also offers a checklist of the needs of disabled people, guidance on helping blind and deaf people to participate and where to get services and information. Because the DISC publication included in its title the bureaucratic symbol for disability, a wheelchair, it was a good first step in disability awareness. Crow (1992) suggests that disability and impairment, in UPIAS terms, must interact because they play such a large part in determining our experiences in a world governed by the able-bodied.

As counsellors we need to pay particular attention to the fact that the problems that a client experiences may not always appear on the surface. I think that the medical model is focused on seeing the disabled person as 'the problem' and on disregarding society's contribution to the creation of problems for disabled people.

The two models of disability are illustrated in Figure 26.1 and 26.2.

In addition to the problems for which a client is seeking counselling, there may also be practical issues in their lives which require resolution. The following sources may be helpful.

Sources of help

British Council of Disabled People (BCODP) Litchurch Plaza, Litchurch Lane, Derby DE24 8AA. Tel. 01332 295551, www.bcodp.org.uk (Bimonthly newsletter *Update*).
Information Officer: Danny Start, tel. 01332 298288, danny@bcodp.org.uk
Assistant Information Officer: Lindsay Armstrong, info@bcodp.org.uk
Disability Alliance, Universal House, 88–94 Wentworth Street, London E1 75A. Rights Advice Line, tel. 020 7247 8763.

These two organizations can usually give advice and information immediately.
Local Coalitions of Disabled People can be contacted through BCODP and are also a valuable source of support and information.
Disability Now is a monthly newspaper dealing with disability issues, free to people receiving benefits, obtainable from Scope, 6, Market Road, London N7 9PW. Subscriptions Hotline 020 7619 7331. View on the Net at www.disabilitynow.org.uk

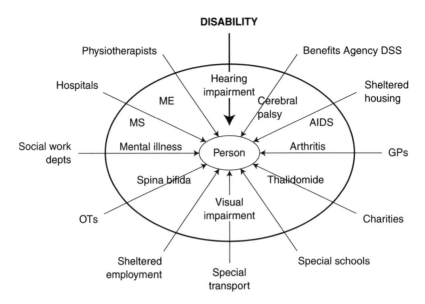

Figure 26.1 *Medical model*

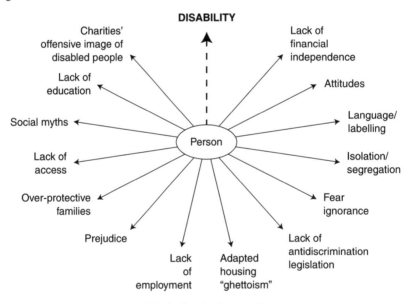

Figure 26.2 *Social model*

References and suggested reading

BAC (1996) *RAMPS Aren't Everything*, Rugby: British Association for Counselling.

Barnes, C., Mercer, G. and Shakespeare, T. (1999) *Exploring Disability: A Sociological Introduction*, Cambridge: Polity Press.

Barnes, C. (1991) *Disabled People in Britain and Discrimination*, Hurst & Calgary in association with BCODP.

Barnes, C. (1991) 'Institutional discrimination against disabled people: a case for legislation', paper, Derby: BCODP.

Barton, L. (ed.) (1996) *Disability and Society: Emerging Issues and Insights*, London: Longman.

Crow, L. (1992) 'Renewing the social model of disability', *Coalition Magazine* (July).

Disability Rights Handbook (2000) Disability Alliance, Universal House, 88–94 Wentworth Street, London E1 75A (issued annually).

Humphries, S. and Gordon, P. (1992) *Out of Sight: The Expression of Disability 1900–1950*, Plymouth: Northcote House.

Morris, J. (1993) *Community Care and Disabled People: Independent Lives*, London: Macmillan.

Oliver, M. (ed.) (1991) *Disabled People and Disabling Environments*, London: Jessica Kingsley.

Discussion issues

1 Do you counsel a client or their impairment? How do you know?
2 In what ways might the social model of disability empower and change the lives of clients and their counsellors?
3 Does the social model have relevance to the lives of people in other minority groups?
4 Which particular personal attitudes has this chapter challenged?

27

A Deaf Counselling Trainee

Can it work?

Pauline Monks and Linda Martin

The trainee's experience

I am deafened, which means I am not prelingually deaf. I started losing my hearing about 16 or 17 years ago. I have a genetic degenerative hearing loss: Initially I was categorized as partially deaf and then severely deaf and I am now registered as profoundly deaf. I have some residual hearing and wear a hearing aid, primarily because I need some sense of noise and use my 'memory' of the noise in conjunction with lip-reading. Lip-reading requires intense forms of concentration and is extremely tiring.

When I decided to embark on a Diploma course I investigated which courses would be suitable for me. There are, apparently, only two courses for deaf people, one at Westminster Pastoral and one at Manchester University. The Westminster Pastoral course is a Counselling Skills and Attitudes for Deaf Trainees. Both courses are run in British Sign Language. BAC had no information and it seemed, from contacts I was making within the deaf world, that I would have to undertake a mainstream course. I met with a deaf counsellor who had just completed the mainstream Diploma Course at WPF but had used an interpreter for the entire three-year course. This had been a very costly exercise, also bringing with it difficulties with the dynamics of an 'outsider' in the group. However, this was not a realistic option for me as, although I am learning BSL, it is not my first language and I am not adept enough to be able to utilize it within a learning experience.

I was interviewed at Crawley and West Kent colleges, and realized that both sets of tutors had little or no deaf awareness. I sensed at West Kent an interest and a desire to learn, and had two interviews at my request, one to discuss the deaf-specific issues I would be bringing to the course and its ensuing problems known and unknown. The second was my formal interview. Having been on a Certificate course elsewhere I was only too aware of the co-operation and support I would need and felt it was important to impress on the tutors my needs and the difficulties which lay ahead. They seemed to accept this and were prepared to work through it. We agreed that I would liaise with the college to set up a loop system and that on the first day I would introduce myself to the group explaining my disability, expressing my needs and asking for their co-operation. We also agreed that I would speak with a tutor at the end of each course day to check-in and keep close liaison as to how the course was working for me and whether any adjustments need be made or stronger support given.

This chapter was first published in *Counselling*, Journal of the British Association for Counselling, vol. 8, no. 4, pp. 263–5 (1997).

On the first day the loop system had not been correctly set up. Fortunately I had anticipated this and had brought with me radio aids which consist of a body-worn transmitter and receiver. It was apparent that as the loop was not in operation I needed to make adjustments to my requests to the group, and it was agreed with the tutors that the transmitter be left in the centre of the room, and each person when speaking was first to pick up the radio aid, return to their seat, speak, and then return the aid to the centre of the room. I was introduced to the group and then made my own personal introduction and request. This, of course, had a strong impact for many people: it was not what they had anticipated they would have to do for the next two years. It was a most harrowing day for me, having to make myself so vulnerable on the first day, feeling the brunt of others' anger, and the spotlight on me which I did not want, especially as we also have a disabled man on our course. I felt I was asking for all the support and attention, more than anyone else. However, I did feel very supported by the tutors and I sensed their interest and some excitement at the deaf-specific issues I was bringing to the course and how it would affect the dynamics. I liked that, as it gave me a feeling of acceptance from them, something I had not experienced on my Certificate course, where I had felt a nuisance who demanded more than anyone else. In consequence, because I had not had the support there, I had spent most of the year hearing very little indeed.

The loop was set up the following week, but in fact I was not able to hear with it, the system not being strong enough for my hearing loss. The tutors were very happy to continue with the radio aids, which suited me.

The college has since loaned another transmitter which enables the tutors to have one between them and one for the group. The system with the radio aids has worked very well for me and, despite the fears of some of loss of spontaneity, it has, I think, had a positive effect within the group. It has been interesting to observe, on different occasions, various people's behaviour in connection with the aid. People can hold it to themselves, a form of holding their thoughts in a tactile way. It brings out other issues for people, for some the embarrassment of walking to the centre of the room in such a large group. Positively it prevents interrupting and negatively it does halt spontaneity, but it enables me to do the course.

This is how it has continued for the past five months and it has worked extremely well for me. I feel satisfied that I have chosen well, relieved my fears were unjustified, and delighted for so much support and co-operation (a very new experience for me). And I have a sense of enabling others as well as myself with the deaf issues I have brought to the course. I feel a strong member of this course which has helped my self-acceptance.

Pauline Monks

The course leader's experience

I first met Pauline Monks, a profoundly deaf woman, at the Open Day for the Advanced Diploma in Counselling course at West Kent College in May 1996. I do not recall this meeting, which must have been very brief, but as Pauline had talked with Val Cunningham, a colleague on the course, I was aware from my later conversation with Val of the possibility of a deaf trainee joining the next intake.

Initially, I did not see how this could work. Counselling and psychotherapy are sometimes referred to as 'the talking cure' and I wondered how someone who could not hear others talking could work in this field. I had virtually no deaf awareness, having never worked with any deaf person, nor known anyone socially who was deaf. However, I had chanced to read Oliver Sack's *Seeing Voices*, so had some small theoretical knowledge of the issues of deaf people through this book.

I have participated in and led trainings on difference, concentrating largely on issues such as gender, sexual orientation and race and including work on disability. I had worked with a blind colleague on my first counselling training and had worked with students in wheelchairs, so I had some practical experience of the possibilities of working constructively with people with different needs. I had recently completed a year of training with Carl Hodges, from the New York Gestalt Institute; this training had centred on issues of difference. How do we respond to those who are different, whether racially, physically, culturally or in any other way? Do we seek to push them out, get rid of them, to keep ourselves pure and intact? Ultimately this can lead to the 'Final Solution' of the Third Reich, the 'ethnic cleansing' of the former Yugoslavia and Rwanda. These questions interested me, in my work as a group therapist and counselling trainer and in wider senses as well, in the areas of psychology, sociology, economics and politics.

In considering the possibility of working with Pauline on the course, I drew on my training on difference and challenged my initial response of 'it can't work'. I realized that part of my initial response had been a resistance to looking at ways in which it might be made to work. I thought about our Equal Opportunities statement which is included in the course brochure and thought – what does it mean? Is it just a meaningless, politically correct platitude? Or does it mean that I and the other tutors and the students might be prepared to work and think and maybe do some things differently, so that a disabled person can join the course? It was this challenging of myself which enabled me to meet with Pauline in (I hope) an open and constructive way. I and the two other tutors, Val and Sally Sugg, met with her to discuss the practicalities of her joining the course. This was prior to her interview.

It seemed as if large-group work would be impossible for Pauline to manage and I was back to 'it can't work', as large-group time is an important part of the training. I had to struggle with my own resistance again, which now took the form of thoughts which ran – 'I am busy enough already without having all these extra problems', and 'The course is carefully designed and effective as it is and you are not going to tell me how to run it and I am not going to change it.' So there was a kind of laziness on my part and also a wish not to be controlled. I found that once I was able internally to understand my resistance to what she was saying, I was able to listen to her more rationally. I found that I was willing to take on some extra tasks if they were necessary. The Equal Opportunities statement really was more than a platitude for me or, at least, I was willing to make it so. I found also that Pauline was very willing to listen to our point of view and was not saying that we should not have large-group time but was asking if there was any way she could be part of that experience. So, on both sides, there was good will and a willingness and ability to listen to each other.

The outcome was that we all approached Pauline's joining the course as an experiment. It was agreed with the college (who were more than helpful throughout) that a loop would be provided and we would see how that worked. The college agreed that Pauline would pay her fees termly and, if the experiment did not work for her, she would only be liable for the term or terms she had attended, rather than for the whole year. The college provided a specialist in deaf awareness who would visit and talk to the whole student and tutor group. We, the tutors, agreed to meet briefly with Pauline every week to check how things were going and to find out how we could best support her.

I now felt very excited by the prospect of Pauline's joining us. I read Marion Corker's book *Counselling: The Deaf Challenge* and viewed working with Pauline as a challenge rather than a nuisance. I do cringe rather at the word 'challenge' in this context as it has been so over-used in Equal Opportunities training: it has become both a cliché and a joke. Perhaps 'interesting' is a better word: I have found the prospect of working with Pauline interesting.

The loop system did not work well for Pauline and we used and continue to use radio aids. Pauline has a receiver and the tutors use one transmitter and the students another, so in large-group work people must get up and take the aid before they speak. Some people have difficulty with this – they feel embarrassed, inhibited and so on. I regard this as useful material with which to work, rather than a problem as such.

We have ceased to have weekly check-ins with Pauline as to how things are going because by now (after one and a half terms) she is so integrated into the group and clearly giving and receiving so much that this no longer seems necessary. Naturally, we continue to be available, should she have suggestions or requests. One recent request she made was that when we have specific training on disability next term the college will provide a lip-speaker. We have, at her suggestion, occasionally used non-verbal exercises to help all of us be more aware of how it might feel to be deaf and to experiment with communicating in different ways, such as by gesture and drawing.

I find it easy to forget about Pauline's needs and have to remind myself of them. For instance, Pauline uses lip-reading as well as the radio aid and so I need to remember to look at her when I speak and I often forget this. I ran a Saturday workshop recently and used music as part of the day, completely forgetting that Pauline could not hear it. Pauline is patient and considerate when people forget – sometimes people even forget to pick up the radio aid or make a joke or an aside which excludes her as she cannot hear it. I imagine I would feel very angry – but then, I suppose, if Pauline became angry every time people forgot, she would be angry all the time.

I am very glad Pauline chose to join the course. She happens to be a very able student; had she not been, then the experience would of course have been different, and I suppose it helps that she is gifted in many ways. I have found that my fears were groundless – it can work and work well, the course can benefit rather than suffer, no great amount of extra work ensued for the tutors, and a deaf person can work effectively as a counsellor. I have learned a lot about the needs of deaf people, about how to be flexible and creative and about my own attitudes to disability and difference.

I believe that all of us, both students and tutors, have gained from Pauline's joining us. I would wholeheartedly encourage other counselling courses to accept suitable deaf candidates: it really can work.

Linda Martin

Update

It is now three years since the article was first written. On re-reading it, I recall how determined I needed to be to succeed. As a first-year trainee, and having had only a few years of personal therapy, I was still struggling with my hearing loss and the stigma attached to that, and with my own self-acceptance, self-esteem, assertiveness and sense of 'difference'. It was not easy to disclose my vulnerability at the introductory stage, nor to stay with the ongoing challenging process of the deaf-specific issues. I am also mindful of how well and fully the group co-operated much of the time. Without the tutors' 'non-negotiable' thinking around the use of the radio aids, I believe the successful outcome would not have been possible for me.

The whole training was a challenge and a learning experience for us all, and we should all take credit for its success. The deaf-specific issues presented were an opportunity for others to address their personal difficulties and sense of difference, and prompted shifts which positively altered the dynamics of the group. Participating in the course experience was one of the best things I have done for myself.

I completed and graduated from the course, and now have my own private counselling practice, working with hearing and hearing-impaired clients. I give workshops and presentations to counsellors, agencies and other counselling Diploma courses on deaf awareness and difference. I am continuing my studies, and am a trainee in TA psychotherapy.

Pauline Monks

Pauline now visits the course as a guest tutor to teach a session on disability issues. We are both pleased at the awareness of disability issues which the inclusion of our article in this *Reader* represents. There is clearly more to be done: not from a sterile and joyless 'political correctness', but from a genuine and down-to-earth sense of decency that attempts realistically to tackle the needless limitations that disabled people continue to face in their lives.

Linda Martin

References

Corker, M. (1995) *Counselling: The Deaf Challenge*, London: Jessica Kingsley.
Sacks, O. (1991) *Seeing Voices: A Journey into the World of the Deaf*, London: Pan Books.

Discussion issues

1 What effect might the use of aids to enable deaf students to participate in counselling course groups have on the group dynamics?
2 Can political correctness counter a lack of that sense of decency which tries realistically to tackle the limitations faced by disabled people?
3 What advantages might there be in being the client of a disabled counsellor?
4 What is your reaction to the views expressed in this chapter?

28

Counselling Women in Prison

Angela Devlin

As part of my research for a book (Devlin 1998) on conditions in women's prisons, I spent five years interviewing prisoners and staff at 12 of the 17 establishments in the UK that take women. Many of the 150 prisoners I interviewed said they felt they needed counselling. A variety of prison-based professionals see counselling as part of their jobs, but how far it is possible for them to provide therapeutic help within regimes that are by definition punitive – especially if they hold keys to lock the women up? And how far can counselling work be reconciled with the duty, required of most prison staff, to 'tackle offending behaviour'?

Which women were asking for counselling?

Almost all women sent to prison suffer from situational depression and need support, but for many their incarceration is exacerbated by deep-rooted problems which have never been addressed. Sir David Ramsbotham, Chief Inspector of Prisons, in his comprehensive review of women's imprisonment (Ramsbotham 1997), deliberately chose to use the phrase 'women who become prisoners' – a sensitive recognition of the previous life histories of women in prison. Some of my interviewees realized this could be the first chance they had ever had to 'sort themselves out'. As a probation officer put it: 'It's no good looking at shoplifting in isolation. You have to look at the drugs habit that caused the shoplifting, and the sexual or physical abuse that may have led to the drug or alcohol abuse.'

Half of all women prisoners have dependent children, and separation causes deep distress and guilt, especially as many were not expecting a custodial sentence (Morris et al. 1995). Many also come into prison from abusive relationships and for those who have suffered years of domestic violence, the initial period in prison can feel like an empowering experience, giving them some space to work with a counsellor, if such help is available. As a prison psychologist explained:

> For so many women this will be the first time they have been removed from violence for years. For them, prison will seem like a haven. A woman may need time and space to stand back and evaluate what has gone on in her life – dangerous things she has got sucked into. All I can do is initiate a few things that may facilitate change, and be with them through the tangled mess of their lives. I listen to them and together we look at who they were before they came in, who they are now, who they would like to be. (Devlin 1998: 298)

This chapter was first published in *Counselling*, Journal of the British Association for Counselling, vol. 10, no. 2, pp. 101–4 (1999).

A high percentage of imprisoned women have been sexually abused as children. A professional woman counsellor who regularly works with Holloway prisoners emphasized how important it is to help such women move on:

> Women should not remain in the victim mode. If a woman comes to me and tells me she was abused from the age of 3 to the age of 16 I will then be able to say, 'Right, you were abused, and of course you were a victim. But now let's see how we can use this to generate energy to change your life.' It's a creative progression and I tell people how to come out of the past, to stop it corroding their future too. I would want to say that the abuse is something that can be worked *with*, not used as an excuse for illegitimate behaviour, or for being ineffective in your life. (ibid.: 299)

Many abused women habitually mutilate themselves. Three-quarters of the self-harming women in my sample had suffered childhood sexual abuse, and a third had suffered sexual abuse (mainly rape) as adults. Intrusive strip-searching for security reasons can trigger flashbacks of earlier abuse. Most were desperately seeking counselling: asked what would help them most, all the self-harming women I interviewed said they 'needed someone to listen'. But more often they found that their self-inflicted wounds were stitched up and they were given psychotropic medication or tranquillizers. One prisoner who had worked as an orderly in the prison health-care centre said, 'I would see women lining up one after another with slashed arms and the nurses would just stick tape over their wounds and send them away. There was no counselling, nothing for them at all.'

Some of these women told me they had been isolated in the segregation cells. Technically self-harm is still a punishable offence in prison, and much of this punitive approach still remains. Prison inspectors condemned the practice of isolating self-harming women as 'a simplistic response. Nobody engages in self-harm capriciously and the response needs to support the individual through that pain as well as dealing with the injury' (Ramsbotham 1997). The inspectors recommended support from a professional counselling service such as The Bourne Trust whose counsellors work with Holloway remand prisoners.

Other women in need of help were those experiencing doubts about their sexuality: many women seek lesbian relationships in prison out of a longing for physical affection and are aware this is temporary. But others realize that they have discovered their true sexual orientation: both groups may need counselling to come to terms with their feelings.

Many women I spoke to were addicts withdrawing from alcohol or drugs. Some were given medication or chemical substitutes like methadone to assist withdrawal; some suffered agonies, left alone to 'cold-turkey'. But few had received help from a trained counsellor as part of a planned detoxification/rehabilitation programme.

Research (Arnold 1995) has identified 'situational triggers' which may lead to suicide attempts. There could be a letter or phone call with tragic news from home. Women may be told that their children have been fostered or sent for adoption, or that a relationship with a trusted partner has broken down. Prison officers have adopted the expression 'anniversary syndrome' for certain days which plunge women into depression, such as the birthday of a loved one (maybe the victim, an abusive partner whom the woman nevertheless loved). One prisoner got a telephone call telling her that her 20-year-old son had been diagnosed as suffering from Hodgkin's disease. She had never heard of the illness, but just before locking her into her cell alone for the night, an officer told her it was potentially fatal. An education officer said women have been told they were HIV positive, then sent straight back to her classes: she felt strongly that counselling should have been in place ready for them. Some women elect to have their pregnancies terminated when they enter prison: they have the same right to this choice as any woman in the community, but probation staff told me that counselling is not always available as it would be outside. Then there are prison-induced stresses such as forthcoming review boards, women being told their sentence length, and parole refusals, as well as peer pressure caused by bullying (usually drug-related). If counsellors were immediately on call, some of these stresses could be alleviated before they get out of hand.

What counselling is provided, and by whom?

Provision seemed to me very patchy, and the Prison Service's approach to counselling confused and modelled on male prisoners' issues. Some managers were frankly sceptical: the governor of a male prison with a women's unit told me he did not agree with women having counsellors, 'raking over endlessly what goes on inside their heads. One week they will have one problem, the next week another.' There is no female equivalent of HMP Grendon, the men's therapeutic prison, and from my research it appears that counselling is provided in a fairly *ad hoc* fashion by prison-based professionals who are not given enough time to help the women, or who see counselling as only a peripheral part of their job. These include psychologists, probation officers, chaplains and some education staff.

The prison psychologists I interviewed (and not all prisons employ one) try their best, but often find their time taken up with emergency intervention. Dr J is the only psychologist for 170 women in a busy remand prison:

> What you have to realise is that in here we are meeting women first when they are in a state of crisis. It might be the day after a woman killed her husband. So all you can give them is basic support and crisis management. I do a lot of bereavement counselling. A woman may be a killer but we mustn't forget that she is suffering a bereavement as well. So often we are seeing the accumulation of traumas which culminated in the offence. (Devlin 1998: 30)

Most of the prison-based probation officers I interviewed said they regarded themselves as the last bastion of the Probation Service still working in terms of its original social-work base, and many try to provide counselling. But like the psychologists they find themselves under increasing pressure:

> Being in a state of crisis recalls other crisis situations for these women, especially previous abuse. I feel I can do some good in this prison because there is time for counselling, which there is no time for outside. I would like to get involved more, but at the same time I have to try and help women with all the practical problems of being in prison, mainly child care, accommodation and dealing with social services. I have been pulled off a lot of this work now and they are cutting back on probation officers seconded to prisons, I'm afraid I may be pulled out at any moment. (ibid.: 32–3)

Disciplinary officers may also be involved in counselling: every prisoner is now supposed to have a 'personal officer' – a prison officer who supports and supervises her through her sentence plan, and counsels her about choices in work, training, education and personal problems. But prisoners frequently mentioned their concerns about whom they could trust. An independent counsellor gave me her view:

There is no doubt about it – officers are the enemy. They are not just *perceived* as the enemy by prisoners, they *are* the enemy, because they are the ones locking the women up and stopping their freedom. They can stop a woman's visits, they can send her to the seg [punishment block]. Can we really expect an officer to say, 'I can do all this to you – now tell me about yourself'? Would *you* tell them anything? I sure as hell would not – because they have so much power over you. (ibid.: 300)

What works?

There are undoubtedly officers who overcome these concerns by the quality of the relationships they are able to establish with prisoners. And there are certainly examples of good practice which imprisoned women find helpful. My interviewees in Holloway and HMP Cookham Wood praised a new cognitive skills programme being piloted at these two prisons. It is called Reasoning and Rehabilitation and has been widely used in Canada. It focuses on appropriate criminogenic needs and is multi-modal in that it recognizes that offenders may have a wide variety of problems. It differs radically from other courses in that the prisoner's offence is never mentioned. The emphasis is on helping people learn to leave behind the impulsive behaviour which had led so many to commit crimes, to help them realize the likely consequences of their actions and to help them take responsibility for what they do. Alice, a lifer nearing the end of her sentence, says 'R and R' is the best course she has ever taken in the 17 years she has spent in prison:

> Some of us are murderers, some of us are kiters [those who pass forged cheques]. It doesn't matter. Today's session, for instance, was about failure. The best thing is that we learn that though something we may have attempted may have failed to happen, we are not ourselves failures. We learn to find another way to reach our goals, or how to move on to a different goal. (ibid.: 293)

Probation officers who work in men's prisons as well as women's say that women are much more receptive to this kind of group work:

> Women are very good at throwing out lifelines to each other. They are more supportive to each other than men in a group. Women challenge each other on why they behaved the way they did. Men are often quite anxious and will not let down their defences and talk about their offences. I find men will jump through the hoops necessary to get them through parole reviews, but they don't want to change their lives. Women do. (ibid.: 296)

So why the need for independent counsellors?

If so many prison-based professionals have an input into counselling women in prison, why is there a need to import independent counsellors from outside the establishment?

Prisoners may feel unable to trust those who hold the keys to their cells but the issue is in fact more complex. All the prison-based professionals mentioned above who might offer counselling, are also required to write parole reports which can have a direct effect on a prisoner's release date. This is bound to affect the relationship between a woman and her counsellor. Some of the more sceptical officers felt that prisoners would tell staff what they thought they wanted to hear, so as to obtain a good report. Any such strategy would of course make a nonsense of an effective counselling relationship.

Parole reports have to consider how far the prisoner has been successful in 'addressing her offending behaviour', and prison staff are expected to contribute to this process by making sure that she faces up to her crime. How does this square with the counselling relationship?

A private counsellor who works with female remand prisoners is at pains to distance herself from this requirement to 'tackle offending behaviour':

> What I do is therapy – and therapy is not tackling offending behaviour: the offence is peripheral to my work. But if therapy is effective then there will be less offending as a result. For instance a woman might say she's a shoplifter. She's addicted to shoplifting, she loves it, she loves the adrenaline. But she might also say she wants to give up shoplifting because she's fed up with being in prison, she misses her kids. *Then* I can say, 'Let's look at this, let's deal with it.' And I will roll up my sleeves. (ibid.: 289)

Prison inspectors acknowledge (Ramsbotham 1997) that 'custody is not the best setting for therapeutic work', and that to embark on the process of trying to address women prisoners' emotional needs can be like 'opening Pandora's box', especially as so many women are given very short sentences. This is another reason for bringing independent counsellors into prisons. Unlike prison-based professionals, whose work ends when a woman is released, private counselling services will be free to continue the work they have begun, though it has to be remembered that because there are so few female prisons, women are often sent far away from their homes and most will return to their own communities on release.

What of the future?

Whatever the ideal, how likely is it that more independent counsellors will be brought into women's prisons? In the last five years the number of women in prison has doubled. There are now more women prisoners than at any time since 1905 and the Prison Service clearly expects this increase to continue, although many staff openly acknowledge that most women prisoners pose no danger to the public and could be given community sentences. But at present there are few appropriate community alternatives available which can provide women with suitable work, accommodation, transport and child care.

The way things are going, it seems future initiatives are likely to be budget-driven, with governors spending on security rather than rehabilitation, on razor wire rather than counselling. But prison managers might be more receptive to counsellors backed by charitable funding who are able to offer a free or at least a heavily subsidized service. Kate Donegan, Governor of Cornton Vale, Scotland's only women's prison, brought in no fewer than ten voluntary organizations, including bereavement counsellors and marriage guidance advisors, in her attempt to 'ventilate' that prison in the wake of a spate of tragic suicides.

Another alternative favoured by many of the women I interviewed is for peer counselling by specially trained prisoners. Already in both male and female prisons the Samaritans train prisoners as 'Listeners' (known in Holloway as 'Befrienders'). Prison inspectors advise that these should be available to support all prisoners as part of the reception process. Many of my interviewees said they felt able to trust other prisoners, especially those women who had shared similar life experiences and had been successful in coming to terms with bereavement and overcoming addiction.

Most women coming into prison suffer from chronically low self-esteem, and by the time they leave it is lower still. Prison is not only expensive – it is also ineffective. Figures quoted by NACRO (1998) show that 53 per cent of all prisoners, and 75 per cent of young offenders, are reconvicted within two years of release. Yet appropriate counselling at the right time can change lives. As one of the Holloway counsellors says:

> These women have a history of people supposed to be dealing with their offending behaviour – and yet the recidivism still goes on. All we can do as counsellors is to give the women choices. Perhaps I could help a woman say no to things she doesn't want – for instance to say no to a man who is abusing her, or to say no to taking drugs, or to say no to carrying a packet of drugs on a plane. A good image is jumping over a cliff. A woman may think there are only two choices: to jump over the cliff or not to jump over it. I would try to show her there might be a path down that cliff. (ibid.: 292)

References

Arnold, L. (1995) A study of 76 self-harming women at the Bristol Crisis Centre for Women.

Devlin, A. (1998) *Invisible Women: What's Wrong with Women's Prisons?* Winchester, England: Waterside Press.

Morris, A., Wilkinson, C., Tisi, A., Woodrow, J. and Rockley, A. (1995) *Managing the Needs of Female Prisoners*, London: Home Office.

NACRO (1998) *Too Many Prisoners*, London: National Association for the Care and Resettlement of Offenders.

Ramsbotham, D. (1997) *Women in Prison: A Review*, London: HM Inspectorate of Prisons.

Discussion issues

1 The Samaritans train prisoners as 'Listeners' to support others in a peer counselling style network. What does this arrangement offer to listeners and those befriended?

2 What are the advantages of seeking counsellors from voluntary organizations to work with women (or men) who become prisoners? Are there drawbacks?

3 Is it possible to integrate a helpful cognitive skills programme such as Reasoning and Rehabilitation with a humanistic or psychodynamic approach to counselling?

4 How may women who become prisoners benefit from prison experience?

29

Counselling Intervention with Men Who Batter

Partner safety and the duty to warn

Calvin Bell

Clients who pose a risk of serious injury or death to others may be thought to be rare and unlikely to be present in our counselling rooms. However, given the ubiquity of domestic violence revealed by second-wave feminists and confirmed in recent government publications (e.g. Smith 1989; Hester et al. 2000; Home Office 2000), given that approximately a quarter of all violent assaults *reported* to the police (most domestic assaults are not) take place in the home (Morley and Mullender 1994; Mirrlees-Black 1999) and that annual Home Office figures typically reveal that virtually half of the women murdered in England and Wales are killed by their current or ex-partners, it is hard to imagine that most counsellors have not at some time, knowingly or not, worked with someone who has been physically violent behind the closed doors of his own home (see Harway et al. 1997). My use of the male pronoun here is intentional for, while there is evidence of domestic assault within lesbian and gay relationships (e.g. Jasinki and Williams 1998) and by women of their male partners (e.g. Magdol et al. 1997), there is little doubt that *battery* (systematic psychological abuse and repeated physical violence) is primarily a heterosexual male preserve (Mullender 1996). In the words of Gloria Steinem (1992), it is clear that: '*The most dangerous place for a woman is not the street but in her own home.*'

I contend that the assessment and management of risk and the prioritization of the safety of the female partners of prospective male clients referred because of relationship difficulties or violence should be fully adopted, despite its particular legal, professional and ethical dilemmas, if we are to avoid the delivery of counselling which is naive, collusive and potentially dangerous. Following recent references in *Counselling* to confidentiality, I shall also address the scope of counsellors' responsibility in disclosing otherwise privileged information in order to safeguard potential victims, once counselling has begun.

Current trends

Feminist and pro-feminist activists have urged counsellors working with violent heterosexual men to prioritize the protection of battered women over attempts to rehabilitate their abusers, arguing that the needs of their partners for safety should not be compromised

---

This is an edited version of an article first published in *Counselling*, Journal of the British Association for Counselling, vol. 9, no. 3, pp. 219–23 (1998).

by the therapeutic needs of the men who batter. Moreover, counselling, it is maintained, should also be evaluated from the perspective of whether, in attempting to provide help for the instigators of the violence, it does more to enhance or to endanger the safety of battered women (Hart 1988b). Some practitioners even advocate that the *victim* of violence be seen as the primary client in this context albeit that it is the 'perpetrator' who is the actual focus of clinical intervention.

Impact of counselling provision

Since the declared objective of leading projects providing counselling for men who batter is to put an end to victimization, then, clearly, recognition of the impact upon the partner's welfare of service provision is essential. This is especially so since the client's attendance alone is likely to be the most significant factor in his partner's decision to remain with him or even to return where she has already managed to leave (Gondolf 1988). Though recent research into the effectiveness of group counselling (the intervention of choice) with men who batter shows encouraging signs (Dobash et al. 1996; Burton et al. 1998), programmes have delivered mixed results (Hague and Malos 1993) and there is as yet little empirical knowledge as to what works: we continue to operate at the frontier of our understanding.

Some practitioners even maintain that information gleaned from rehabilitative interventions actually enables clients to enhance their regime of intimidation and control over battered women (Harris et al. 1990). Suggestions have also been made that beneficial outcomes of counselling may only be short term (Hart 1988b) and that, if not done well, therapy is best not done at all (Horley 1990). Therefore, however well-intentioned, the mere offer of counselling for the abusive man may well result in exposure of his partner to risk that would have otherwise been avoided by her leaving or staying away (see Bell 2001).

Current literature

Yet, despite a rapidly increasing volume of literature exploring the many facets of domestic violence, references examining risk assessment issues are few. However, there are some authors who do recognize that a proportion of abusive men may be too lethal to be treated on an outpatient basis (Stordeur and Stille 1989) or while not in custody (Hart 1988b) and I am of the view that counsellors should never make the assumption that a partner is safe. Others recommend that a man not be accepted for treatment before a reduction in what they claim to be high-risk markers (Sonkin et al. 1985). I believe there is, therefore, a strong case for counsellors to adopt this moral and, as suggested by Jenkins (1998), ultimately legal responsibility to victims if intervention is not to double as a confessional in which counselling inadvertently assists the maintenance of the man's violence rather than resolves it. (See Chapter 60.)

Dilemmas for counsellors

The assumption of this duty to predict responses to client engagement and to consider the safety of vulnerable others is not, however, without its dilemmas. Perrott (1994) describes how practitioners often face contradictory demands from a number of different groups: offenders, victims, the judiciary, government and society. In some professional settings, further tensions arise because of differences in ideological, theoretical or ethical perspectives. In the absence of any corporate risk-assessment protocols in the context of our work, it is, I believe, our individual responsibility to deliberate about the merit of imposing conditions or restrictions on the delivery of counselling (surrender of weapons, use of personal alarms for the victim, requiring the client to sleep away from home after using alcohol, temporary separation, compliance with criminal justice or civil law sanctions, etc.) or indeed, *whether to offer counselling at all*. The high ambivalence levels of many of the men referred (most are *(pre-)contemplative*) means that the insistence on contracting for partner safety easily repels a prospective client (though, as McNeil (1987) suggests, some clients who experience homicidal urges toward their partners often feel comforted in the knowledge that some external controls will be imposed to minimize the risk of their feelings being acted upon). Given the unlikelihood of custodial sentences and the minimal effect that criminal justice sanctions have with high-risk offenders anyway (Sherman 1992), and given the absence of any other service that addresses the man's violent behaviour, the decision to reject or delay a client because of his suspected or proven lethality is not always easily taken when this is the very client most in need of help. To do otherwise, however, is to accept an abusive man into treatment in the hope of facilitating change but in the knowledge that to do so may well, in the short term at least, collude with the exposure of his victim to potentially life-threatening risk.

First steps

Various studies (Monahan 1984; McNeil et al. 1988; Blomhoff et al. 1990) underpin the common assumption that the most reliable predictor of interpersonal violence is a history of previous violence: there can be no better assessor of a man's capacity for violation of his partner than the victim/survivor herself. She will more than likely be able to identify antecedents and cycles in her abuser's behaviour and may know best what measures to take to minimize her self-exposure. However, the victim can hardly be expected to be familiar with the process or content of the counselling her partner is about to undertake or to anticipate his response to it. Feminists have long emphasized battered women's need to be furnished with adequate information about therapeutic intervention with their partners; the importance of counsellors not making over-zealous claims of success has also been stressed. Arming a victim with accurate information about working styles and counselling paradigms and about the uncertainty of change, therefore, seems an essential first step in the fulfilment of any commitment to consider her safety, since the acceptance of her abuser into counselling makes at least a tacit statement that we deem him safe enough to be at large and that treatment has a reasonable chance of eliminating his violence.

Nevertheless, the product of what Ferraro and Johnson (1983) call the *process of victimization* for many battered women is the tendency to rationalize their partner's abusiveness especially in the absence of any institutional or cultural support. The denial of injury and of victimization itself is also cited as a consequence of subjection to long-term abuse which tends to leave the victim accepting responsibility for her partner's violence in the belief that her supposed provocation is synonymous with justification. The victim's interests may not therefore be best served by an ill-informed presumption that the provision of information in itself will necessarily empower the woman to act decisively to provide for her own safety, even assuming her access to appropriate resources.

Practice tensions

This elicits further dilemmas: do we assume that the partner is unable or unwilling to take some responsibility for her own welfare and, as it were, make (patronizing?) decisions on her behalf as to whether she will be at more or less risk by her abuser being offered counselling. Or, do we accede to her possible requests (that he remain with her in the matrimonial home, that he undertake counselling, etc.) in the knowledge that her comments may well have their origin in shame (Carden 1994), fear, denial, financial dependence or in the hope that he will change *this* time? Does she harbour conscious or unconscious hopes that a decision to prioritize her safety will in fact be made *for* her, despite her best protestations, in order to avoid the violent recriminations that could follow her efforts at self-determination? The tendency of men who batter to under-report the frequency and severity of their violence is well established (Ganley 1981; Sonkin et al. 1985; Stordeur and Stille 1989; Saunders 1992), as is clinicians' poor track record in predicting violence (Miller and Morris 1988; Gondolf et al. 1990). *Male* practitioners' proneness to collude with abusive men's minimization of their violence has also been researched (Hearn 1993). One obvious resolution to the predicament of assessing dangerousness would therefore be to actually interview the partner herself to enhance judgements as to the degree of her abuser's lethality and to attempt to ascertain and to cater for her reasonable wishes. However, to initiate such direct contact has often been condemned by women's organizations on the grounds that this approach in itself could well put the woman at further risk. She may receive violent admonishments, prior to any meeting, as a reminder to censor her contributions or face subsequent assaults as her partner seeks to elicit evidence of any 'indiscretion'. Also, any unpopular decision ultimately arrived at, perceived by her partner as consequential to the meeting, risks sentencing her to further reprisals. Parenthetically, O'Leary et al. (1992) also underlined that few abused women interviewed indicate that violence is a major problem in their relationships *unless directly questioned* about its presence.

In addition to providing the partners of prospective clients with the appropriate information, I suggest it is good practice therefore for counsellors to liase with local women's organizations (such as Women's Aid) in order to avoid direct contact with the battered woman herself. They seem best placed to help the victim assess what is actually in her best interests and to communicate the product of their collective appraisal in a way that minimizes risk and informs the design of any safety planning. Moreover, the inclusion of another agency, especially when added to by the corroboration of other third parties, can greatly enhance the accuracy of predicting further violence in the face of measures to prevent it (Werner et al. 1983; Prins 1988). Here, again, this domain is not without its tensions. Counsellors can often find themselves in receipt of sensitive material provided by women's advocates with the understandable request that it be treated confidentially. This frequently means arriving at a decision regarding counselling that is mainly informed by privileged information but in such a way that the prospective client may need to remain unaware of its existence. Apart from reflecting on the obvious ethical issues involved, there are of course concerns as to whether, despite our best endeavours, the client intuits its transmission either by our inadvertent disclosures or simply by the effect the possession of such information has *counter-transferentially* on our demeanour or attitude in the room.

The duty to warn

A counsellor's fundamental professional responsibility is to foster a client's autonomy and therefore not to interfere in her/his affairs. However, therapists working with clients who have a history of violence have begun to acknowledge an obligation to intervene where there is evidence of risk to potential victims. This *duty to warn* was first defined in the US courts in the landmark case Tarasoff v. The Regents of the University of California in 1976. It has since been largely ratified, if not extended, by numerous subsequent judicial rulings throughout the USA, where practitioners have been held liable for not exercising reasonable care to warn and to protect a person foreseeably endangered by a client's behaviour (Sonkin et al. 1985) and even potentially liable for not acting even when the victim is *not* identifiable (Gross et al. 1987). As Scoggins et al. (1997) (see Chapter 59) and Jenkins (1998) (see Chapter 60) point out, the scope of this responsibility has yet to be determined by the British courts but various UK professional bodies have already embraced these moral concerns in their codes of practice. The British Psychological Society's Code of Conduct, for example, is unequivocal in requiring that psychologists, ... '*where there is sufficient evidence to raise serious concern about the safety or interests of recipients of services, or about others who may be threatened by the recipient's behaviour, take such steps as are judged necessary to inform appropriate third parties without prior consent ...*' (BPS 1995: 4.3). The BAC's Code of Ethics also acknowledges ... '*exceptional circumstances may arise which give the counsellor good grounds for believing that the client will cause serious physical harm to others...*' (BAC 1997: B.4.4).

Nevertheless, advocates for women experiencing domestic violence maintain that, though increasingly recognized, this duty is rarely executed, in part because of counsellors' belief that for a danger to exist, the client must make a specific threat or disclose an actual plan to do harm (Hart 1988a, 1988b). Researchers contend, however, that a recognizable potential for imminent danger can in fact prevail (risk) despite the absence of declared intentionality by the client (threat). This concurs with McNeil (1987) who holds that a verbal threat to a given individual is not an essential criterion for warning if the counsellor can judge that a dangerous situation exists purely on the basis of the client's past behaviour and present circumstances. Here, then, responsible risk-management becomes a task of ongoing appraisal where counsellors are advised to review continually in supervision the abusive client's circumstances in the light of the risk factors identified in the initial assessment. The locating or return of a partner (and therefore the availability of a victim), the loss of employment, a financial crisis, the onset of psychosis, etc., when applied to the client's known history, especially if coupled with fantasy or the rehearsal of reprisal plans, may well constitute sufficient grounds to act. In most cases, my staff would inform clients of any disclosure before or after the event and good communication between counsellor and client may well result in agreement for disclosure to be made. However, circumstances frequently arise where to do so at all would put the likely victim at more risk.

The duty to protect

Furthermore, feminists insist that if the ultimate objective of counselling with men who batter is the cessation of violence, then agencies must also adopt the *protection* of victims as an interim goal. They advocate a much broader *duty to protect* which goes beyond the traditional confines of the obligation to give warning. Certainly, the commentary in the literature on US case law suggests that the reasonable exercise of responsibility to foreseeable victims should include giving notice not merely to the woman herself (assuming adequate records of her whereabouts are kept) but also to anyone else who might assist her in the receipt of that warning and who might afford some measure of protection (police, psychiatric and social services, Women's Refuges and perhaps members of her family) (Sonkin et al. 1985; Gross et al. 1987).

Practice tensions

Adoption of this practice produces inevitable tensions. First, at a practical level, for counselling to be effective it requires an environment in which clients feel able to take the risk of exploring issues which they may well have never previously discussed. Though client/counsellor confidentiality has never been absolute because of the requirements of the Children Act 1989 and the Prevention of Terrorism Act 1976 (as well as some archaic statutes relating to treason), and of the possibility of counsellors being required by the courts to disclose privileged information (I am frequently sub-poenaed to give evidence *against* my clients), the working precept of most generic counsellors is that the efficacy of the therapeutic alliance increases in proportion to the extent of confidentiality: honesty should be rewarded with privacy. In general practice it is held that these fundamental Rogerian principles will be overthrown by disclosure, resulting in alienation of the client. The BAC Code of Ethics (1998: B.4.1) in fact states: '*Any limitation on the degree of confidentially offered is likely to diminish the usefulness of counselling.*' Where then, in this context, is the interface at which the attempt to deliver effective counselling built upon confidentiality to a man who is violent is subsumed by the need to provide for the more immediate welfare of his victims by breaching it? At what point do the roles of counsellor and agent of social control conflict?

Paradoxically, perhaps, the limited confidentiality inherent in the adoption of this duty to protect does afford a compensatory educational benefit. It firmly establishes the counsellor's values and promotes a sense of personal responsibility and the unacceptability of violence by modelling the prioritization of partner safety over client comfort and by emphasizing that the use of violence is always a matter of choice. The educational value of this tenure also extends beyond the client himself and sends messages both to the victim/survivor and to statutory and voluntary agencies involved with the family. Interestingly, Hart (1988b) argues for pro-feminist services which are more educational than psychotherapeutic in nature and as such do not need to extend the degree of confidentiality usually reserved for the greater intimacy of counselling. Stordeur and Stille (1989) also maintain that a formal therapeutic contract must exist between client and counsellor before entitlement to confidentiality and that therefore assessments, at least, are deemed to be outside the scope of such contractual arrangements. At *Ahimsa* (*Ahimsa* is the Sanskrit word for 'non-violence' and the name given to our independent community safety initiative), our participation contract makes very clear to clients the limitations of confidentiality and the context of likely disclosures.

Second, this dissonance obviously also extends into the ethical frame. The mandate for confidentiality (Milner and Campbell 1995) and the client's right not to have privileged information disclosed is seen by some colleagues as a basic tenet of human privacy. McFarlane (1985) also alludes to how the breaking of confidence, particularly given practitioners' low predictive accuracy, can prejudice clients' civil liberties. Indeed, the Tarasoff ruling itself made it very clear that in some cases a warning to a threatened party may well be too radical an action to constitute 'reasonable care' (Gross et al. 1987). Again here, there seems to me to be no entirely satisfactory formula for resolving this tension other than by the use of informed judgement (after supervision, wherever possible) on a case-by-case basis.

Not all abusive clients have contact with their partners during counselling, some may not be in a relationship at the time and not all have a high potential for dangerousness. However, I have attempted to build a case for the need to identify those clients who do or may present a risk to vulnerable others in order to maintain professional standards which do not value an abuser's therapeutic needs over his victim's needs for safety.

References

BAC (1997) *Code of Ethics and Practice for Counsellors*, Rugby: British Association for Counselling.

Bell, C. (1999) '*Primum non nocere* ("First do no harm"): Developing corrective programmes for court-mandated perpetrators of domestic violence against women', in L. Keeler (ed.), *Recommendations of the Eu Expert Meeting on Violence Against Women,* Helsinki, Finland: Ministry of Social Affairs and Health.

Blomhoff, S., Seim, S. and Friis, S. (1990) 'Can prediction of violence among psychiatric in-patients be improved?', *Hospital and Community Psychiatry*, 41 (7): 771–5.

Burton, S., Regan, L. and Kelly, L. (1998) *Supporting Women and Challenging Men*, Bristol: Policy Press.

BPS (British Psychological Society) (1995) *Code of Conduct: Ethical Principles and Guidelines*, Leicester: BPS.

Carden, A.D. (1994) 'Wife abuse and the wife abuser: review and recommendations', in G. Stone (ed.), *The Counselling Psychologist: Wife Abuse*, 22 (4) (October): 539–97.

Dobash, R. et al. (1996) *Research Evaluation of Programmes for Violent Men*, Scottish Office Central Research Unit, HMSO.

Ferraro, K. and Johnson, J.M. (1983) 'How women experience battering', *Social Problems*, 30: 325–39.

Ganley, A.L. (1981) *Court-Mandated Counselling for Men who Batter. Participants' and Trainers' Manual*, Washington, DC: Centre for Women's Policy Studies.

Gondolf, E.W. (1988) 'The effect of batterer counselling on shelter outcome', *Journal of Interpersonal Violence*, 3 (3): 275–89.

Gondolf, E.W., Mulvey, E.P. and Lidz, C.W. (1990) 'Characteristics of perpetrators of family and non-family assaults', *Hospital and Community Psychiatry*, 41 (2): 191–3.

Gross, B.H., Southard, M.J., Lamb, R. and Weinberger, L.E. (1987) 'Assessing dangerousness and responding appropriately: Headflund expands the clinicians' liability established by Tarasoff', *Journal of Clinical Psychiatry*, 48 (1): 9–12.

Hague, G. and Malos, E. (1993) *Domestic Violence: Action for Change*, Cheltenham: New Clarion Press.

Harris, S., Holmes, M. and Goodwin, R. (1990) *Summary Report of Ontario Mens' Groups: Working Together to End Violence against Women*. Changing Ways (London) Inc. Ontario (A perpetrator programme).

Hart, B. (1988a) *Safety for Women: Monitoring Batterers Programs*, Harrisburgh, PA: Coalition.

Hart, B. (1988b) 'Beyond "duty to warn". A therapist's duty to protect battered women and children', in K. Yllo and M. Bograd (eds), *Feminist Perspectives on Wife Abuse*, London: Sage.

Harway, M., Hansen, M. and Cervantes, N.N. (1997) 'Therapist awareness of appropriate intervention in treatment of domestic violence: a review', *Journal of Interpersonal Aggression, Maltreatment and Trauma*, 1: 25–38.

Hearn, J. (ed.) (1993) 'Researching men and researching men's violences', Research Paper no. 4, University of Bradford (Research Unit on Violence, Abuse and Gender Relations).

Hester, M., Pearson, C. and Harwin, N. (2000) *Making an Impact: Children and Domestic Violence*, London: Jessica Kingsley.

Home Office (2000) *Multi-Agency Guidance for Addressing Domestic Violence*, London: HMSO.

Horley, S. (1990) 'Responding to male violence against women', *Probation Journal* (December): 166–70.

Jasinki, J.L. and Williams, L.M. (1998) *Partner Violence*, London: Sage.

Jenkins, P. (1998) 'From transference to false memory: counsellor liability in an age of litigation', *Counselling*, 9 (1) (February): 40–4. (See Chapter 60.)

Magdol, L., Moffitt, T.E., Caspi, A., Newman, D.L., Silva, P.A. and Fagan, J. (1997) 'Gender differences in a birth cohort of 21-year-olds: bridging the gap between clinical and epidemiological approaches', *Journal of Counselling and Clinical Psychology*, 65 (1): 68–78.

McFarlane, V.J. (1985) 'Clinical predictions on trial: a case for their defence', in C.D. Webster, M.H. Ben-Aron and D.J. Hucker (eds), *Dangerousness: Probability and Prediction. Psychiatry and Public Policy*, New York: Cambridge University Press, pp. 209–25.

McNeil, D.E., Binder, R.C. and Greenfield, T.K. (1988) 'Predictors of violence in civilly committed acute psychiatric patients', *American Journal of Psychiatry*, 145 (8): 965–70.

McNeil, M. (1987) 'Domestic violence and the skeleton in Tarasoff's closet', in D.J. Sonkin (ed.), *Domestic Violence on Trial: Psychological and Legal Dimensions of Family Violence*, New York: Springer.

Miller, J.S. and Morris, N. (1988) 'Predictions of dangerousness: an argument for limited use', *Violence and Victims*, 3 (4): 263–83.

Milner, J.S. and Campbell, J.C. (1995) 'Prediction issues for practitioners', in J.C. Campbell (ed.), *Assessing Dangerousness*, Thousand Oaks, CA: Sage.

Mirrlees-Black, C. (1999) *Domestic Violence: Findings from a New British Crime Survey Self-Completion Questionnaire*, Research Study 191, London: Home Office.

Monahan, J. (1984) 'The prediction of violent behaviour: toward a 2nd generation of theory and policy', *American Journal of Psychiatry*, 141: 10–15.

Morley, R. and Mullender, A. (1994) *Preventing Domestic Violence to Women. Police Research Group*, Crime Prevention Unit Series, Paper 48, London: Home Office Police Department.

Mullender, A. (1996) *Rethinking Domestic Violence*, London: Sage.

O'Leary, K.D. et al. (1992) 'Assessment of physical aggression against women in marriage: the need for multi-modal assessment', paper originally presented at the Annual Convention of the Association for Advancement of Behavior Therapy, San Francisco 1990.

Perrott, S. (1994) 'Working with men abusers', in C. Lupton and T. Gillespie (eds), *Working with Violence*, Basingstoke: Macmillan.

Prins, H. (1988) 'Dangerous clients: further observations on the limitation of mayhem', *British Journal of Social Work*, 18: 593–609.

Saunders, D.G. (1992) 'A typology of men who batter: three types derived from cluster analysis', *American Journal of Orthopsychiatry*,

Scoggins, M., Litton, R. and Palmer, S. (1997) 'Confidentiality and the law', *Counselling*, (November), 8 (4): 258–62. (See Chapter 59.)

Sherman, L.W. (1992) 'The influence of criminology on criminal law: evaluating arrests for misdemeanour domestic violence', *The Journal of Law and Criminology*, 83 (1): 1–45.

Smith, L. (1989) *Domestic Violence,* Research Study 107, London: HMSO.

Sonkin, D.L., Martin, D. and Walker, 1985. '*The male batterer: a treatment approach*', New York: Springer Publishing.

Steinem, G. (1992) 'Foreword', in K.L. Hagan (ed.), *Women Respond to the Men's Movement*, London: Pandora.

Stordeur, R.A. and Stille, R. (1989) *Ending Men's Violence against their Partners. One Road to Peace*, London: Sage.

Werner, P.D., Rose, T.L. and Yesavage, T.A. (1983) 'Reliability, accuracy and decision-making strategy in clinical prediction of imminent dangerousness', *Journal of Consulting and Clinical Psychology*, 51 (6): 815–25.

Discussion issues

1 The 1995 United Nations Beijing Declaration states that violence against women is a manifestation of historical unequal power relations between men and women and one of the social mechanisms by which women are forced into a subordinate position to men. As counsellors, how do we reconcile this with the traditional psychodynamic view of (men's) violence as a symptom of individual psychopathology?

2 At what point are a client's rights to privacy superseded by the needs of his victim?

3 To what extent do our own biases and assumptions based upon gender, class or race, for example, play a part in arriving at judgements?

4 Is denial the sole prerogative of our clients?

30

A Fair Deal for Lesbians in Therapy

A point of view and an ethical issue?

Cordelia Galgut

As part of my MA in counselling I investigated the knowledge, experience and attitudes of a sample of qualified counsellors and therapists concerning lesbians generally and their lesbian clients specifically. I sent out 172 questionnaires and had a very encouraging 65 per cent response rate. Although there were quite a lot of lesbian positive responses, I was concerned by a number of aspects highlighted by the research findings.

My sample comprised experienced counsellors – 41 per cent had more than 5,000 hours' counselling experience. Over 70 per cent of the total sample had knowingly counselled ten or fewer lesbians. Forty per cent did not ask about the client's sexual orientation if the client did not tell them; 20 per cent asked as a matter of course. Within these figures are different results for practitioners from different theoretical approaches. To quote the extremes: 70 per cent of person-centred counsellors do not ask about a client's sexuality if she does not refer to it; 14 per cent of integrative counsellors do not ask.

Of the counsellors surveyed, 44 per cent had read one or two books with lesbian themes; 22 per cent had seen one or two plays, films or television programmes with such themes; 22 per cent were unsure or negative about lesbians adopting children; 29 per cent were unsure or negative about lesbian access to artificial insemination. A number of respondents espoused pathologizing attitudes towards lesbians – 10 to 15 per cent, depending upon how pathologization is defined – for example, that lesbianism is a result of sexual abuse, nurturing that was negative, a fear of male sexuality.

Having broken down the results according to the age, experience, sexuality, religiosity and theoretical approach of the respondents, I found quite striking differences between these groups. For example, those espousing an integrative or person-centred approach were generally much more supportive of lesbians than those with a psychodynamic or psychoanalytic one. Older respondents (41+), heterosexuals and those with a religious belief were similarly less positive towards lesbians.

Since the sample is such an experienced one, the results raise some pressing questions. Seven out of ten of the practitioners in my sample have knowingly counselled only ten or fewer lesbians. *How can this be explained, given the estimates of the numbers of lesbians in society ranging from 10 per cent (Crooks and Baur 1990) to 25 per cent (Falco 1991), depending on how lesbianism is defined, together with the suggestion that lesbians seek counselling more than heterosexuals (Sorenson and Roberts 1997)?*

This chapter was first published as 'A fair deal for lesbians in therapy – a point of view', in *Counselling*, Journal of the British Association for Counselling, vol. 10, no. 4, p. 285 (1999).

Could some lesbians be going through therapy without revealing their sexuality and, if so, what implications are there for our practice as counsellors and for our lesbian clients?

Earlier studies seem to indicate that lesbians do want to reveal their sexuality, although they do not want that fact recorded (Lucas 1992). However, my data seems to indicate that practitioners often wait for a lesbian client to own her sexual orientation. I acknowledge that this is a tricky area for us as counsellors. Have we the right to ask a client this kind of question directly? *The trouble is, if we do not ask, or facilitate sexuality disclosure, to some extent at least, where does that leave our lesbian client?*

In the first instance, I believe that the counsellor/client relationship is a microcosm of society, in which homophobia and prejudice are rife (Nelson and Krieger 1997). A lesbian client may well want to disclose her sexuality but not feel confident enough – as was once my own experience in therapy. She may not wish to reveal her sexuality to a counsellor of whose attitudes she is not sure.

Would a statement of non-discrimination from a counsellor such as, 'If there's anything about yourself you'd like to tell me, please feel free to do so now, or at any time that feels comfortable for you', early in the relationship, help clients to embark on their therapeutic journey less fearfully and more fully?

While my own practice as a counsellor bears out the efficacy of such an enabling invitation, I acknowledge that none of us is entirely free of discriminatory impulses, such as homophobia. Indeed, some therapists may not be aware of these impulses within themselves and this raises other questions. Nevertheless, I consider that such a statement would, at the very least, be useful as an intention of good-will.

Since a significant number of my respondents were able to express pathologizing attitudes towards lesbians, do such attitudes go relatively unchallenged within the counselling and therapeutic community? If so, what implications does this have for us as counsellors and for our lesbian clients?

The number of my respondents who were unsure or negative about lesbians adopting children (22 per cent) and about them having access to artificial insemination (29 per cent) links with the evidence from my research data that some counsellors have limited experience of lesbian life-style and culture.

Do such attitudes and lack of exposure of counsellors limit their ability to meet and understand the needs of their lesbian clients (Gochros 1984)?

There is widening concern about the effectiveness of counselling (Roth and Fonagy 1996). In my work with clients, it has been helpful to acknowledge that sexuality and social context can influence the dynamics of our relationship in a way which, when not spoken about, can negatively affect an otherwise successful therapeutic outcome.

We are concerned about all clients in counselling. From my point of view, I wonder whether all lesbian clients are getting a fair deal in therapy.

References

Crooks, R. and Baur, K. (1990) *Our Sexuality*, Redwood City: Benjamin/Cummings.

Falco, K.L. (1991) *Psychotherapy with Lesbian Clients: Theory into Practice*, New York: Brunner/Mazel.

Galgut, C.N. (1998) 'Counsellors and therapists: an investigation of their experience, knowledge and attitudes concerning lesbians', unpublished MA thesis, University of East London.

Gochros, H.L. (1984) 'Teaching social workers to meet the needs of the homosexually oriented', *Journal of Social Work and Human Sexuality*, 2 (2/3): 137–56.

Lucas, V.A. (1992) 'An investigation of the health care preferences of the lesbian population', *Health Care for Women International*, 13 (2): 221–8.

Nelson, E.S. and Krieger, S.L. (1997) 'Changes in attitudes toward homosexuality in college students: implementation of a gay men and lesbian peer panel', *Journal of Homosexuality*, 33 (2): 63–81.

Roth, A. and Fonagy, P. (1996) *What Works for Whom? – A Critical Review of Psychotherapy Research*, New York: Guilford Press.

Sorenson, L. and Roberts, S. (1997) Lesbian uses of and satisfaction with mental health services: results from Boston lesbian health project', *Journal of Homosexuality*, 33 (1): 35–49.

Discussion issues

1 What is your reaction to the research findings outlined in this chapter?
2 As counsellors, do you think we have a responsibility to address the issues raised?
3 If so, how best do you think we can do this?
4 What factors do you think will affect a successful therapeutic outcome for a lesbian client?

31

Working with Lesbian and Gay Clients

Lyndsey Moon

For too long, a discussion focusing on the counselling needs of lesbian and gay male clients has remained in the therapeutic closet. Various reasons for this spring to mind:

I don't see many gay clients;

I don't see them as any different to other clients;

I've no problem working with lesbian/gay clients.

Religious and legal stigmatization and repression go mostly unchallenged, while the medical and helping professions have altered their position by declassifying homosexuality as a mental illness (American Psychiatric Association 1973), and accepting that people living with diverse sexual orientation exist and the existence of the diversity is not pathological. As a result of the latter, counsellors were, as Graham (Graham et al. 1983) points out, expected to shift their own attitudes and behaviours from a sickness model to a model whereby gay people would be helped to self-actualize as gay people. Despite this, research indicates a divergence of opinion among counsellors and psychotherapists regarding the acceptability of homosexuality – with as many as one-third in many samples expressing negative attitudes (Rudolph 1988). Added to this are results showing that counsellors with inadequate training and lack of information about lesbian and gay people are providing services to this population.

Garfinkle and Morin (1978) show that counsellors approach the task of counselling with 'in built maps of inference'. They conclude that counsellor attributions of psychological health towards their clients differed as a function of client sexual orientation and 'the decreased psychological health attributed to homosexual clients was a function of the perceivers'. As counsellors we are a part of the society in which we live, and cannot help but be affected by the attitudes, beliefs and values of our culture. According to Dworkin and Gutierrez (1989) these are 'carried into the counselling session and affect the definition, assessment and treatment of the problem presented'.

A small number of counsellors I questioned gave contradictory feedback. Although *all* counsellors had worked or were working with lesbian/gay clients none had received any specific training in issues related to counselling with lesbian, gay or bisexual clients. Also, despite counsellors accepting that their own sexual orientation, attitudes, or lack of knowledge would be relevant when working with lesbians or gay men, 80 per cent felt they had explored their own attitudes and feelings towards the gay community while only half of those asked felt they would have no difficulty in being obejctive when counselling with lesbians and gay men.

This chapter was first published in *Counselling*, Journal of the British Association for Counselling, vol. 5, no. 1, p. 26 (1994).

Some 25 per cent of gay people seek counselling at some stage in their lives while up to 50 per cent report discontent with their professional counselling experiences. For the lesbian or gay male client, Rudolph (1988) suggests that the source of dissatisfaction centres on counsellors' negative, prejudicial attitudes towards, and a lack of understanding of, homosexuality.

Prior to working with lesbians and gay male clients, counsellors need to work through their own myths, stereotypes and sexual feelings (including attractions and aversions) towards persons of the same or opposite sex. I wonder how many counsellors presently working with lesbian or gay clients have taken on this responsibility? In order to work with lesbian and/or gay male clients, counsellors need to be aware how the attitudes, beliefs and values of the client may differ from those of the counsellor and ask ourselves whether we can respect these differences.

Update

Recent research conducted with 30 counsellors answering unstructured interview schedules reported that none had received specific training in issues relating to lesbian and gay client work. Additionally, the view when working with those who are transgendered, transvestite or trans-sexual, was a highly medicalized approach to their well-being. This usually relied on a medical/psychological frame of reference being referred to initially, in order that these populations could be understood, rather than relying on the frame of reference of the client. From this it was noted that a general lack of knowledge surrounding some clients means that counsellors, lacking a challenging training where a multiplicity of approaches could be introduced, end up relying on knowledge via psychology or a small number of publications within the counselling field rather than being able to step outside of this (Moon, in progress).

More recently, a Gay Affirmative approach towards non-heterosexual clients has been suggested which indicates some degree of hope in the future both for counsellors who are non-heterosexual and for non-heterosexual client work. The series *Pink Therapy* has challenged a number of assumptions about working with those who are lesbian, gay, bisexual or transgender, while the British Psychological Society has taken a major step in allowing the Lesbian and Gay Psychology Section to be inaugurated. There is no doubt that, together, these initiatives will spur research into counselling and psychotherapy with lesbians and gay men. Milton (1998) suggested a number of recommendations for counselling psychologists which also apply to counsellors. If taken note of, these could influence the direction of therapeutic work with lesbian, gay, bisexual and transgender people. They include four main themes:

- **training**: questioning issues being taught; assessment of trainees' attitudes to difference; what does the course incorporate about non-heterosexual clients; how does the validating body set criteria around this?
- **further research**: to be conducted on and between models in relation to non-heterosexual clients; to increase the production of research in this field.
- **personal qualities**: to focus on the attitudes and prejudices of both trainees and qualified practitioners; using ongoing 'reflective' supervision.

- **professional structures and issues of sexual diversity**: that a 'Committee' be established to review and monitor practice around lesbian, gay and bisexual concerns.

Taking responsibility for the transformation of these measures into working practice will not only recognize the needs of non-heterosexuals, but will also show how those who are heterosexual are willing to take responsibility for proper therapeutic practice when working with those who represent sexual diversity and difference.

References

American Psychiatric Association (1973) *Diagnostic and Statistical Manual of Mental Disorders*, Washington, DC: APA.

Davies, D. and Neal, C. (1996) *Pink Therapy: A Guide for Counsellors Working with Lesbian, Gay and Bisexual Clients*, Buckingham: Open University Press.

Davies, D. and Neal, C. (2000) *Pink Therapy 2: Therapeutic Perspectives on Working with Lesbian, Gay and Bisexual Clients*, Buckingham: Open University Press.

Davies, D. and Neal, C. (2000) *Pink Therapy 3: Issues in Therapy with Lesbian, Gay, Bisexual and Transgender Clients*, Buckingham: Open University Press.

Dworkin, S.H. and Gutierrez, F. (1989) 'Counselors be aware: clients come in every size, shape, color and sexual orientation', *Journal of Counseling and Development*, 68 (September/October): 6–8.

Garfinkle, E. and Morin, S. (1978) 'Psychologists' attitudes toward homosexual psychotherapy clients', *Journal of Social Issues*, 34 (3): 102–12.

Graham, D.L.R., Rawlings, E.I., Halpern, H.S. and Hermes, J. (1983) 'Therapists' needs for training in counselling lesbians and gay men, *Professional Psychology: Research and Practice*, 15: 482–96.

Milton, M. (1998) 'Issues in psychotherapy with lesbians and gay men: a survey of British psychologists', British Psychological Society Division of Counselling Psychology Occasional Papers, Vol. 4.

Moon, L.T. (in progress) 'Working with lesbian, gay, bisexual and transgender clients: counselling and sexuality', unpublished Ph.D. dissertation.

Rudolph, J. (1988) 'Counsellors' attitudes toward homosexuality: a selective review of literature', *Journal of Counselling and Development*, 67 (November).

Discussion issues

1 How essential do you think it is to consider your feelings, actions and beliefs towards those with a different sexuality from your own?
2 How would you feel if a lesbian, gay or transgender couple say they want to consider raising children of their own?
3 What is the meaning of Gay Affirmative therapy for you?
4 Do you think non-heterosexual clients should have their own counselling services?

32

Adopted and at Home in the World

A message for counsellors

Lesley Marks

The subject of adoption, now talked about quite openly, has not always been so freely discussed. In the past, a policy of total confidentiality was seen as essential. Neither the biological nor the adopting parents knew more than a few basic particulars about one another. Sometimes even these details were kept from the adopted child whom everyone wanted to protect from unpalatable facts about his or her birth story. Consequently, many people who were adopted 30, 40 or more years ago have almost no details at all about their beginnings in the world.

The route to discovering birth information has been greatly facilitated by Section 51 of the 1976 Adoption Act. This demands that local authorities establish a counselling service for adoptees seeking information about their adoption and states:

> (4) Before supplying any information to an applicant under subsection (1) the Registrar General shall inform the applicant that counselling services are available to him –
>
> (a) at the General Register Office; or
> (b) from the local authority for the area where the applicant is at the time the application is made; or
> (c) from the local authority for the area where the court sat which made the adoption order relating to the applicant; or
> (d) if the applicant's adoption was arranged by an adoption society which is approved under section 3 of this Act or under section 4 of the Children Act 1975, from that society.

So far so good.

However, in a discussion paper entitled 'Feeding the hungry ghost', the Post Adoption Centre (PAC) suggests that many social services departments are not providing an appropriate service. Moreover, they point out that given the growing 'feedback from people who are affected by adoption ... the time is ripe to plan a more efficient, well published counselling service' (PAC 1990: 3–4) (see Update).

This discussion paper made it clear that the PAC wished to see better collaboration between the statutory authorities and voluntary agencies, as well as more comprehensive training for counsellors working in adoption.

While Section 51 is a move in the right direction, it is limited in that it provides for only one mandatory counselling interview, with the aim of enabling an adoptee to obtain her or his original birth certificate. ('Original', that is pre-adoption, certificates will usually give a birth relative's – most likely the birth mother's – name, address and occupation at the time of the birth, thus facilitating the process if and when the adoptee wishes

This chapter was first published in *Counselling*, Journal of the British Association for Counselling, vol. 6, no. 1, pp. 48–50 (1995).

to trace birth family members.) Ideally, adoptees' experience of this one-off counselling interview will be positive, encouraging them back to the same counsellor if they decide to take matters further.

Personal experience

My own interest in this subject stems both from the fact that I was adopted as a three-week-old baby, and from my work as a counsellor of adopted adults.

As a child, my need to understand the circumstances of my adoption, coupled with the evident distress displayed by others whenever I sought more information, led me to believe very early on that *adoption was not a subject that could be discussed*. It was simply too painful. In addition, at that time (some 40 years ago) little thought was given to a child's psychological need to know about his or her origins. In fact, confidentiality *vis-à-vis* the identity of birth parents was seen as essential to successful placement of children into adoptive families.

Simply put, I learned to keep it quiet. I did not talk about adoption though I often thought about my birth mother. I longed to know what she looked like, what features I'd inherited from her, whether she ever thought about me. (I have not yet come across another adopted adult – either in the literature or in the flesh! – who has not had the same yearning *to know*; and the same mistrust of other people's ability to listen well while they wonder out loud.)

About three years ago I decided to seek out my birth mother. As a trained counsellor myself, I went straight to a local agency and sought out counselling, mediation and advice. However, the most helpful tool I had during that time (and since) was a peer-counselling group which consisted of people who had hardly ever *thought* about adoption, much less studied the issues it raises. Their greatest gift to me was their willingness to listen; knowing they had much to learn, they listened with avid attention while I cried, raged and talked through some of the debilitating confusion I felt about having been separated from parents I'd never known.

By outlining some of the key issues identified by adoptees, I hope to open this area of work to debate amongst counsellors and within BAC. While the specialist agencies do their own excellent work in the field of adoption, I believe that counselling has some specialist skills of its own to offer, in particular the ability to listen 'actively', and an appreciation of the importance and value of such listening.

Counsellors and adoptees

Counsellors who are approached because of the legislative demands upon adoptees in search of their origins are in an unusual situation. On the one hand, clients may be considered self-referred because they will have *chosen* to search for birth information. On the other, there is no choice about whether or not to attend a counselling session; consequently, clients may well have approached the counsellor because they have to, and not because they want to or see any need for support.

Moreover, counsellor and client may meet only once or twice. The counselling may take place in the offices of local social services – inhibiting a client who has negative feelings about seeing a 'social worker'; and the client may be reticent about attending again once the information has been passed over, though unresolved issues may remain.

Adoptees will be aware that the counsellor holds the key to the information they seek. They may have strong feelings about pursuing the search independently, and may not be used to sharing personal information – especially with regard to their adoption. It is helpful to understand therefore, that the counsellor may be perceived initially by adopted clients as a barrier, rather than a resource.

Initially the counsellor's role is to help gain access to the client's original birth certificate and the name of the agency that handled the placement. It is likely that in the course of gaining information, or during the search, an adoptee will talk about the difficulties that arise out of the process. However, until the client makes it clear that s/he wishes to work through a specific problem, too much probing by the counsellor may be seen as intrusive rather than supportive.

Searches are often prompted by a newspaper article or television programme and many adoptees have little or no knowledge about their own rights of access to information, or about the rights of the other parties to their adoption. Some adoptees believe they must 'pass' in some way – concerned that they will not be considered ready to receive the information they seek. It is crucial that the counsellor clarifies that it is the client's *right* to receive the information, and that this issue, in turn, is quite clear in the mind of the counsellor.

Common themes

In discussions with adopted adults some common themes emerge: that adoption was seen by their adoptive parents as belonging to the past and 'not important any more'. For some, even mentioning it within the adoptive family did not feel right. Attempts at open discussion often provoked embarrassment and discomfort in the adults around them so that many adoptees came to believe that asking for information was hurtful and could be experienced as a betrayal by the adoptive family they loved so dearly.

Many people agree that the common response to their adoption was an assumption of illegitimacy, deprivation and abuse in the birth family, despite the fact that, in many cases, not one scrap of information was available. It was rarely (if ever) suggested that the child had been deeply loved and wanted, and that separating from him or her had been most painful to the birth parent(s).

Consequently people may experience feelings of blame regarding the birth parents or misinformation about the reasons for the adoption and possibly the adoption may be seen purely in terms of rejection and abandonment. Some clients will find it hard to connect with the enormity of the experience of gaining new information about a parent they have never seen, or (possibly distressing) details of the reasons for their adoption.

Considerations for counsellors

Counsellors will (hopefully) be fully aware of the significance of the information they are making available to clients and of the danger of having any arbitrary expectations about how a client should react. It is not unusual for clients to find it very difficult to react at all to information that has long been trivialized or deemed 'irrelevant' by others close to them.

Many adoptees have been told most of their lives how they should react to their birth story and adoption with comments such as 'Don't worry about it, it's all in the past'; 'But you've got us now!' The counselling, therefore, might be aimed at *asking* the client how it feels and normalizing the response, rather than predicting reactions that conform to an arbitrary set of standards.

Counselling possibly provides a unique opportunity for adoptees to consider the beliefs and feelings they have about why they were adopted. Information that emerges during the process of investigation and search may contradict much of what the clients have held true all their lives and adopted adults need the opportunity to re-evaluate their thoughts and emotions as each new piece of information comes to light.

Having rarely, if ever, had the opportunity to be listened to well in this regard, the client might benefit from being asked open questions such as, 'What was it like being adopted?' The answers will clue the counsellor in to the client's individual story and, if the tone is natural, light and lively, it will help dispel the notion that talking about adoption is unsafe or embarrassing. Many adoptees will probably never before have been asked what being adopted was like for them.

Some clients discover through the search process that their birth parents, far from having abandoned and rejected them, were deeply distressed by the separation and did not part from them willingly. Information like this necessitates a complete re-evaluation of that person's adoption story. In such a case, it might be helpful to simply remind clients from time to time that what was unthinkable before is in fact now true – that they were loved and wanted. Being wanted as opposed to being 'rejected' is going to be a massive contradiction to the client's beliefs about themselves and their beginnings in the world.

Apart from the ability to listen with interested and encouraging attention, the counsellor's key tool is time. This is a process which simply cannot be rushed and sometimes a great deal of time is needed for the information to be absorbed and for the feelings to emerge. Many clients will describe themselves as 'stunned' at the time of receiving birth details. The client needs to be allowed to set the pace of the counselling and of the search process. Weeks, months or even years may pass between stages of receiving information and taking things further – or not.

Adopted adult clients may have spent a lifetime keeping feelings about their adoption well hidden, and may experience nothing more than a sense of feeling completely blank. For my part, being asked how it felt, over and over, by someone who looked genuinely interested, someone who didn't back off when I was not immediately able to respond, helped me to appreciate the significance of this process, and allowed me to connect with my feelings of outrage, pain, excitement and apprehension.

This last point lies at the heart of the counselling process. The adoptee's experience may have been of people backing off all the time: from the earliest experience of losing the birth parents, to later experiences of people's embarrassment and distress around a subject that was considered taboo. The adopted client may well need the counsellor to demonstrate as often and as clearly as possible that s/he is there to listen *for as long as it takes*.

In the event of considering communication with a birth parent, adopted adults will undoubtedly benefit most from being empowered to take charge of the process themselves.

In early childhood adoptees were powerless to determine the course of events and helpless in the face of the separation which occurred. As adults they no longer need to feel like the victims of their own birth stories. Adopted adult clients can decide each and every detail: how to communicate (letter, phone, meeting), what to reveal, what to ask, what they want from the birth parent and what they themselves have to offer. This, too, will need time to work out for it is likely that any thoughts and fantasies of tracing a birth parent have begun and ended with seeing the person and recognizing the first traces of familiarity.

Finally, it is essential to keep in mind the prevailing stereotypes of family relationships – something many adoptees will have encountered throughout their lives. They are forced to confront the fact that the very people who were supposed to love them best relinquished them. They have to reconcile their feelings and fantasies with the message that, having been adopted, they shouldn't have any feelings for their birth parents. This is very confusing. It becomes even more confusing when, in the process of searching for more information about their origins, things they have always believed about why they were adopted are suddenly proved untrue.

We need to take care not to fall into the trap of believing the myth that blood is thicker than water. 'Real' parents are the ones the child identifies as his or her own mum and dad. The rest is something else; something we perhaps do not yet have a language to describe. I know what 'mum' means – I am still trying to discover what 'birth mother' means and where she fits.

Meeting a birth parent, seeking information from court records, or simply attending counselling sessions to talk through the experience of being adopted, are indicators of the need to know and the willingness to grow. Counsellors working with these clients are witnessing a manifestation of the child's natural need for self-knowledge. It will help to remember that the need to know more does not signify a need for love from, or even a relationship with, the birth family.

The notion of rejection, feelings of anger, pain, grief – all these are old hurts and emotions that need to be expressed and worked through. Once that is achieved, clients are left with space to celebrate their *own* identity, separately from the identity of any parent, and their own uniqueness in the world.

Update

The Post-Adoption Centre Director: Monica Duck

Founded in 1986 to meet the needs of adults and children experiencing problems arising from adoption, the Centre has developed a range of services reflecting the complexities of contemporary adoption, and offers support, counselling, advice and therapeutic input to individuals, couples and groups. The Centre's director and counsellors are professionally qualified, racially diverse, and have a wide range of experience and training in post-adoption work, with particular experience of working with black children and families and transracially adopted adults, as well as gay and lesbian adopted people. Their counselling rooms and washroom are wheelchair accessible. A contact and mediation service offers support for birth mothers, fathers or grandparents who have lost a child to adoption. Adoptive parents or professionals can also access support for all aspects of contact between adopted children and their birth relatives. Skilled mediators offer a neutral, confidential and supportive atmosphere where birth relatives, adoptive parents and carers can explore issues and reach their own arrangements, independent of statutory agencies.

For counsellors, therapists and social workers the centre runs the highly regarded post-adoption counselling training and skills (PACTS) course each year, together with a programme of specialist seminars and courses on post-adoption work.

The Post-Adoption Centre, 5 Torriano Mews, Torriano Avenue, London NW5 2RZ Tel. 020 7284 0555: Advice 020 7485 2931: Fax 020 7482 2367
Website: www.postadoptioncentre.org.uk
e-mail: advice@postadoptioncentre.org.uk

Reference

Post Adoption Centre (1990) 'Feeding the hungry ghost', discussion paper, London: PAC.

Discussion issues

1 How important is a focus on the past in counselling clients who were adopted as children?
2 Is believing that blood is thicker than water a myth? How might it be a trap for adoptees or for other children?
3 Birth parents and adoptive parents have a child in common, but rarely meet. How significant might this be for an adopted client, who has potentially four parents?
4 What particular learning do you take from this chapter?

33

Working with Children in a Family and Divorce Centre

Birgit Carolin

This chapter is based on a talk given at a conference entitled 'Divorce 1994', in Cambridge, before an audience of professionals working in the area of divorce: lawyers, court welfare officers, mediators and counsellors, among others. As one of two child counsellors working at that time at the Family and Divorce Centre in Cambridge, my aim was to give a brief history of the setting up of the Children's Service under its auspices, in 1993, and a summary of our principles and practice. I also tried to indicate what counselling young people actually involves, and how, in some ways, it differs from working with adults. My views are based on my own experience over the past 30 years of working with young people, initially as a teacher and then as a counsellor in secondary schools, a drop-in centre, a college and on the telephone at Child Line.

As in all successful counselling, much depends on the relationship of mutual trust and understanding established between the two individuals involved. Such a relationship rests upon good communication, which assumes a common language. This is not usually possible with very young children, whose vocabulary and comprehension may be limited, although their perceptions may well be sharper than those of most adults! Accordingly, the room in which we see most children is equipped with play – and drawing – materials: clay, sand-trays, a doll's house, glove-puppets, etc. My co-worker, a trained play-therapist, mostly works with those aged between 6 and 12, while I usually see those aged 13 to 18, although there is inevitably some overlap. Teenagers are apt to scorn any approach through play but may avail themselves of paper and felt-tips, given the opportunity to do so. They tend to have their own modes of expression, frequently bewildering to an adult, in addition to a commonly held mistrust of authority. To overcome these obstacles, a counsellor working with young people needs, perhaps even more than usually, to be willing to put aside the mantle of authority without abdicating adult responsibility; to adopt a vocabulary appropriate to that of the child or adolescent, without a trace of condescension; and most of all to observe and hear, with acute attention, whatever the child chooses to express by word or action, silently or noisily. It is rare, in the experience of many who are growing up today, to receive the undivided attention of an adult in this way; it is equally rare for a parent, teacher or other professional to be able to offer it.

Listening to the voice of the child

Of course much of my time in the counselling session is spent listening: listening in private, with a commitment to confidentiality; listening to words spoken sometimes with force

This chapter was first published in *Counselling*, Journal of the British Association for Counselling, vol. 6, no. 3, pp. 207–10 (1995).

and fluency, but more often with hesitation and doubt; listening also to the silences, which frequently express the inexpressible more eloquently than any words. At such times, I am aware that these children may not yet have words for their feelings, and so I try, without intruding, to trace those feelings in their faces, gestures, body language. The primary emotions are always present (the blues of sadness, sorrow and grief; the scarlet of anger and rage; the yellow of anxiety and fear) and many more complex and subtle variations besides. I try particularly to recognize the negative, normally unacceptable, feelings. In our culture, which places so much emphasis on success and achievement, the negative aspects of experience (especially those of a child) are not often openly revealed. By acknowledging that these very feelings do exist, though they are frequently unspoken (especially when family life has been fractured by separation and divorce) and by devoting my undivided attention to those young people who choose to come and talk to me, I hope to convey my genuine interest and respect and also to secure mutual trust and understanding.

Understanding is essential because when we feel understood – as child or adult – self-understanding and insight, increased trust and confidence may often follow naturally. Trust is also important, especially because, for most children nowadays, talking to a stranger is a forbidden and dangerous activity. Once young people can really believe that I accept them as they are, without criticizing or controlling, most welcome the chance to unburden themselves and to explore, with growing confidence, their relationships, their situation and, most important, those hidden aspects they rarely admit even to themselves. The crucial thing is that no one is ever coaxed, persuaded or forced in any way.

In his address to the Annual Meeting of Mediation in Divorce, its President, Sir John Balcombe, Lord Justice of Appeal, said in 1993:

> I am more and more convinced that even comparatively young children frequently have firm and sensible views to which we should pay attention; certainly no one ... should ever refuse to listen to the voice of the child who asks to be heard.

These words endorse the principles of the Children Act (1989) and echo those established by the Gillick Case (1986) and again by the Cleveland Report (1989). They also recall the UN Convention on the Rights of the Child (1989). Children are people in their own right, not merely objects of concern. If we want them to become mature and responsible adults, it makes sense to consider not only their opinions but also their feelings.

A counselling service for children

In order to pay special attention to the feelings of young people whose parents are splitting up (not in order to involve them directly in the process of mediation, nor to provide reports or recommendations to the Court based on their views), I began, in 1991, to work as a volunteer with the Cambridge Family and Divorce Centre. With the support and encouragement of its co-ordinator, Celia Dickinson, and one of the trustees, Martin Richards, I was asked to look into the possible need and viability of a permanent counselling service for children, to supplement the mediation offered to divorcing couples.

My previous experience of listening to children had alerted me to the potential impact of divorce, not least on their lives but on their emotions and their self respect. Feeling abandoned and bewildered, torn by the conflict within themselves and between their parents, overwhelmed by grief and sadness, furious and frustrated, it is not surprising that many lose heart. How they express – or often do not express – their feelings depends on age, gender, individual temperament and circumstance. In fact, for many children today, separation and divorce constitute an experience of loss equivalent to death – but without the comforting rituals of bereavement; and without the recognition of the disabling effects it may have, particularly the crippling of self-esteem and trust.

These days, divorce is much more likely to occur in a child's life than the death of a close friend or relative. Each year, in England and Wales, 160,000 children under 16 are affected by divorce. By the time they have left school, over 25 per cent of all children will have experienced at least once the dissolution of family life (HM Government Statistics 1994). The implications are sobering when we consider the long-term effects on children and on society. There is not much that we, as counsellors, can do to diminish the impact on children of warring parents. What we try to do is to build upon children's own strengths and to give them some experience, however brief but timely, of a trustworthy adult in whom they can confide. There is good evidence that, provided children are given the attention and support they need, they may not only recover from the shock of a fractured family but even find new benefits and advantages.

Consultation process

In the autumn of 1991, I consulted with a number of people: a school head, an inspector, teachers, social workers, a doctor, school nurse and educational psychologist, lawyers, mediators, parents and counsellors – not to mention a few children. All confirmed the impression that the need for suitable help was overwhelming but the provision of specialized support was virtually non-existent except in Scotland and Suffolk. Since then, the number of counsellors working with children in divorce settings has increased. In Scotland alone, thanks to more enlightened public funding, Aberdeen, Edinburgh, Strathclyde and Tayside all supply a service for children. Belfast, Greater Manchester, Northumberland, Swindon, Bromley and Ipswich also provide interesting variations in the models they have established. Whereas the principle at the Cambridge Family and Divorce Centre is to offer mediation to couples and counselling separately and directly to children, whether or not their parents are married or in mediation, other services link the provision of mediation for parents with counselling for children. Some provide groups for divorced and divorcing parents, while seeing their children in separate groups, in the hope that better understanding may develop on both sides. At present, our resources do not allow for this approach.

Funding

We submitted a proposal based upon my investigations in March 1992 to the BBC Children in Need Appeal, which set out specifically to offer direct help to children, individually and in groups, and to liaise with professionals, such as teachers, social workers and health visitors, rather than with parents.

In August 1992, we received a letter from the BBC awarding us 'a grant of £18,455 spread over three years, to provide 15 hours of direct counselling per week for under 18-year-olds'. The conditions stipulated that we 'monitor and evaluate' the project and requested the following information to be included in our annual report to them:

1 The number of under 18-year-olds consulted.
2 A breakdown by sex and age of these figures.
3 The major 'types' of problems encountered.
4 The average number of sessions per child.

We were also required to give a detailed account of expenses, together with income from any other source.

In December 1992 I was appointed as one of the two children's counsellors, to be joined one month later by my co-worker, Carol Dasgupta, and we worked together to establish the children's service.

Working with others who work with children

We raised additional funds from local firms to buy the necessary equipment and books. Leaflets were designed to advertise the new service, which was officially launched at a meeting in June 1993. There was an astonishing attendance and we were reluctantly forced to turn people away. The various professionals working with children were represented and, in an effort to meet the demand expressed by them, two half-day workshops were arranged the following November and January. These were designed to answer an overwhelming need for more up-to-date information on the incidence and effects of divorce and separation on children and, inevitably, on society as a whole. The doctors, nurses, teachers, social workers and counsellors, therapists and mediators who attended, also had the opportunity to make useful links and to share experiences. The speakers were both working within the University of Cambridge in the field of research, examining the effects of parental and family disturbance on children. Additional sessions for primary and secondary support staff, and for health visitors and school nurses have also been provided by Carol and myself, in response to specific invitations. Through these and school visits, we have begun to establish good links with professionals, who have been helped to work more effectively with children of divorce, or who have referred them to us.

Our main focus remains on the children, most of whom we see one-to-one at the Centre in a pleasant room, suitably equipped with a doll's house', sand-trays and other play materials.

Between June 1993 and February 1995 we saw individually:

73 children under 10 (32 male, 41 female)
46 children (11–15) (23 male, 23 female)
13 teenagers (16–18) (4 male, 9 female)
4 young people (18/19) (2 male, 2 female)

This amounts to a total of 136 young people, each seen on average between two and four times.

Work in schools

In addition, between us, we have met well over 100 children in three primary schools, at the invitation of teachers. Our message to these children is that divorce, though frequently painful and disruptive, is increasingly a fact of life; that it can be helpful to express feelings generated by separation and loss; and that we are available to help anyone who approaches the Family and Divorce Centre for counselling. In one primary school, my colleague has conducted three very successful ongoing groups of eight sessions each, during the past two years, seeing a total of 22 children. These groups were pre-selected by teachers, with parental permission, and met once a week in school time with the aim of giving the children a chance to share their feelings and experiences in a secure setting, with skilful support from my colleague and a voluntary assistant.

The final requirement by the BBC was a description of the major types of problems. I quote from our report:

All children seen encountered a combination of both practical and psychological problems, such as those described below:

Practical:

These included financial, contact, residence and holiday arrangements – all a frequent focus of confusion and conflict.

Psychological:

These included the general disturbance and physical strain associated with strong but largely suppressed emotions. These varied with each individual (even within the same family) but were almost always characterised by a conflict of loyalties, feelings of frustration and helplessness, sadness and grief, anger and aggression, guilt and poor self-esteem. Difficulties with parents and siblings, as well as with step-families were common and caused much distress and hostility. Frequently both school and social life suffered.

Guidelines and fundamental principles

The Children's Service is supported by a special Management Committee, which reports regularly to the main Management Committee of the Family and Divorce Centre. Our recently revised Guidelines are based on five fundamental principles:

1 No child is ever forced to come for counselling. At an initial assessment session, to which parents are also invited, they are given an opportunity to decide whether or not they want to come again.
2 If the child is under 14, the permission of both parents is requested before counselling can begin. If one parent explicitly refuses permission, we are not, unfortunately, able to offer help. We think that whatever absolute rights the Law may now accord to children, an umbrella agency such as the Family and Divorce Centre, which exists to mediate between parents for the benefit of their children, cannot take sides with one parent against the other, even if this might arguably be in the interests of the child. However, children over 14 may refer themselves without their parents' permission and are guaranteed confidentiality.
3 We do not feed back, either to the parents or to anyone else, what the child tells us (unless asked to do so by the child). However, no child under 14 is given a promise of absolute confidentiality. The child's safety is always the paramount principle and this is made clear to everyone present at the first meeting. So far, rarely has a child disclosed information which we have felt obliged to pass on.
4 We do not offer long-term 'treatment' or attempt to explore issues not directly arising from divorce. We are there only to help children come to terms with a difficult situation.
5 If any child appears to be suffering from some serious psychological problem, a referral to the local Child and Family Consultation Clinic would be considered. We have not yet made any such referrals.

Our practice is to offer children a maximum of up to six sessions, following the first assessment when parents may be present for at least some of the time. After the sixth session an occasional further session can be arranged, should the need arise. We have found this works well and avoids the necessity for a waiting-list. Most children are seen at the Centre but we will also see them in school, if they prefer and that is convenient.

Clearly, our Service is in its infancy and we have a long way to go before we can confidently say that it is well established. Adequate funding remains an anxiety and the future holds no secure promises. What seems certain is that there will continue to be a real need for services such as ours, providing help for children of divorce.

Update

The original conviction that helping children cope with separation and loss may prevent later suffering was reinforced by my subsequent work as a student counsellor, when I met many troubled, depressed, even suicidal young adults who had sustained serious losses in childhood through parental divorce, separation or death. My recent experience as volunteer co-ordinator of the Children's Service of Cambridge Cruse Bereavement Care confirms that the demand, from parents and professionals, for guidance, support and individual help for children affected by death, is rising steeply with increased understanding of their needs.

Since its inception in 1993, the Children's Service of the Cambridge Family and Divorce Centre (still funded mainly by BBC Children in Need) has continued to meet the demand for individual help for children whose parents are in the process of separating, or have separated and sometimes formed new relationships, further complicating the impact on the children. From 1997, the Service conducted a two-year research project for the Joseph Rowntree Foundation, which evaluated (with the help of the Winnicott Institute, Cambridge) positive outcomes of group and individual intervention for children in eight local primary schools. In addition, the Service is looking to develop group work with children, both in schools and at the Centre (possibly with parental involvement) as well as support to parents on children's issues connected with separation and divorce.

References

Balcombe, J. (1993) 'The voice of the child: an address to the Annual Meeting of Mediation in Divorce (The Twickenham Service)', *Family Mediation*, 4 (1).
The Children Act (1989) (came into force 1991) London: HMSO.
The Cleveland Report (1989) Lord Justice Butler-Sloss.
Gillick v. West Norfolk and Wisbech Health Authority (1986).
HM Government Statistics (1994).
United Nations Convention on the Rights of the Child (1989).

Recommended Reading

The Which? Guide to Divorce. Helen Garlick. Consumer Association/Hodder, 1992. ISBN 0340-5701-56.

Focus on Families: Divorce and its Effects on Children. The Children's Society, 1988.
Helping Children Cope with Divorce. Rosemary Wells. Sheldon Press, 1989. ISBN 0-85969-593-X.
Coping with Separation and Divorce. Ann Mitchell. Chambers, 1986. ISBN 0-550-20509-8.
Helping Children Cope with Separation and Loss. Claudia Jewett. Batsford, 1982. ISBN 0-7134-4707-9.
Step-Parents, Step-Children, Step-by-Step. Christina Hughes. Kyle Cathie Ltd., 1993. ISBN 1-85626-082-8.
To and Fro Children: A Guide to Successful Parenting after Divorce. Jill Burrett. Thorsons, 1993. ISBN 0-7225-2794-2.
Parenting Threads: Caring for Children when Couples Part. Erica De'Ath and Dee Slater (eds). Stepfamily Publications, 1992.
Time to Listen to Children: Pat Milner and Birgit Carolin (eds). Routledge, 1999.

Organizations

ADR (Family) Mediation
Grove House, Grove Road, Redland, Bristol BS6 6UN
Tel: 0117 9467180

Cambridge Family and Divorce Centre
Essex House, 71 Regent Street, Cambridge CB2 1AB
Tel: 01223 576308   Fax: 01223 576309

Family Mediators Association
PO Box No. 5, Bristol BS99 3WZ
Tel: 0117 9467062

National Family Mediation
9 Tavistock Place, London WC1H 9SN
Tel (Client Line): 020 7383 5993   Tel (Admin): 020 7388 9309
Fax: 020 7383 5994

Parentline Plus (Merger of Parentline and The National Stepfamily Association)
Third Floor, Chapel House, 18 Hatton Place, London EC1N 8RU
Tel: 020 7209 2460   Fax: 020 7209 2461

Discussion issues

1 How does working with children under 18 differ from working with adults?
2 What implications may these differences have for setting up a service specifically for children and young people?
3 How important is it to gain the agreement of both parents when accepting referrals of children under 14?
4 What potential impact may the splitting-up of parents have on their children?

34

Critical Incident Debriefing

Frank Parkinson

Any incident where there is an element of shock and trauma will result in reactions which can be anything from mildly disturbing and lasting a few moments, to symptoms which are persistent, terrifying and devastating. Where the incident is particularly distressing, reactions will usually be more intense, but these are usually normal and natural responses and not signs of weakness or inadequacy. If particular traumatic reactions intensify and persist for more than a month and severely disrupt the ability of an individual to cope with life, home, self and work, Post-Traumatic Stress Disorder might be diagnosed. The problem with PTSD is that it is not known exactly why it occurs, who will develop it or when. It is also very difficult to treat, some being helped to cope with their symptoms rather than being 'cured'. However, techniques have emerged in an attempt to help people to cope better when they have been involved in traumatic incidents, but because of the nature of PTSD, these methods are not claimed to counteract its development.

Defusing and critical incident debriefing

After traumatic events, professional rescue workers often have an operational debriefing, led by a senior officer, to discuss practical issues and make them aware of resources available should help be needed. However, because of their reactions, those affected are often least likely to ask for help and can believe that if they have reacted badly there must be something wrong with them. Partly because of these problems, in the 1980s Dr Jeffrey Mitchell, a psychologist working with the fire service in the USA, saw the need for a more structured approach by offering what he called 'defusing and critical incident stress debriefing'. The principle, of both defusing and debriefing, is not new but mirrors the natural response of one human being to another after a crisis: 'What has happened?' 'How are you and how has it affected you?' and 'What help do you want or need?' Parents, partners, friends and the best leaders have used this process without any formal knowledge of defusing or debriefing. The difference is that these techniques have a definite structure and can be offered within an organizational context.

Defusing

Defusing is an informal session with an individual or group conducted by a team or group leader soon after an incident. It usually lasts 30–40 minutes, and no longer than one hour at the most. A short *introduction* leads into an *exploration* stage *encouraging* people to

---

This chapter is a revised version of the article published in *Counselling*, Journal of the British Association for Counselling, vol. 6, no. 3, pp. 186–7 (1995).

talk about and discuss their experiences. The *information* stage which follows gives reassurance about the normality of reactions, explains about the possibility of other reactions and outlines what support is available.

Critical incident debriefing

Critical incident debriefing is the name given in the UK to Mitchell's American debriefing system. Dr Atlé Dyregrov developed a method of 'psychological debriefing' in Norway contemporaneously with Mitchell's work. In 1989, Dyregrov presented a paper on debriefing at the Tavistock Clinic, London. Debriefing techniques were largely influenced by four main areas of experience and treatment: war and combat, civilian disasters and traumas, crisis intervention theory and cognitive methods. When traumatized, individuals are often overwhelmed by their emotions, which can become detached from the practical events of the incident.

> I feel frightened and helpless so must be weak, pathetic and useless. Feelings are everything and they determine exactly who and what I am.

Reactions can be so powerful that it is often forgotten that the event triggered the reactions and not the other way around! The balance between the rational, thinking self and the feeling self is disturbed, with emotional reactions dominating. This is typified by the woman who blamed herself entirely for being raped by a total stranger in a park. The fact that he put a knife into her mouth at the time had been suppressed. Some who come for help seem to be saying, 'I want you to make this go away as though it has never happened.' But experiences do not 'go away'. You cannot change the past, but you can be helped to adjust or change the way you respond to it by gradually integrating the experience into your life so that it becomes part of who and what you are now.

Critical incident debriefing attempts to do this by:

- encouraging and initiating the process of integration;
- providing a safe environment to discuss and a structure in which to place 'unstructuring' experiences;
- restoring a cognitive–emotive balance;
- normalizing responses by giving reassurance and information about reactions;
- providing information about resources for support and referral;
- restoring the solidarity of groups;
- showing that organizations care.

Most importantly, within organizations *debriefing should be one element in a wide approach to coping with stress and trauma*. This should also include education, information and training for all personnel about possible reactions to stress and trauma, courses and training in stress-management, staff knowing how to recognize and cope with those who are traumatized, the use of techniques such as defusing and debriefing, support, monitoring and follow-up of personnel, and channels and resources for referral.

The general criteria for both Mitchell and Dyregrov are that debriefing should:

- be a single session, open-ended in time – three to four hours is common;
- not take place within the first two to three days, at the earliest, and in some cases much later;

- be conducted only by professionals trained in the cognitive–emotive model;
- be negotiated with debriefees and be voluntary.

It is an exploration not just of the 'there and then' but also of the effects 'here and now'.

Debriefing structure: Facts – Feelings – Future

Although both Mitchell and Dyregrov produced a debriefing model in seven almost identical stages, Dyregrov favours beginning the story of the event before it happened, then working through it until it is over. He also explores sensory impressions before looking at feelings and emotional reactions. The 'Facts – Feelings – Future' structure, now widely used, incorporates all the original Mitchell and Dyregrov stages. At the beginning of the three-stage structure the debriefer who, where possible, should have met the debriefees already and know what happened, gives a self-introduction. Then the *purpose* is explained, the *rules* outlined and the *procedure* of trying to separate the facts from the feelings made clear.

Stage one: Facts

Debriefees are then encouraged to talk through the incident from before it happened until it was over, concentrating on thoughts, expectations and impressions and on the 'facts' rather than the feelings. If feelings emerge, they are sensitively acknowledged, but not explored.

Stage two: Feelings

The aim of this stage is not, as some imagine, to create or encourage catharsis, but to further the general aims outlined above. The emphasis should be on the need for integration: to face reactions, to understand why they have emerged and what their effects have been and still might be.

Sensory impressions
The sights, sounds, smells, touches and tastes associated with the event are explored individually and located in the incident where they originated. Each one is then related to the feelings or emotions it generated at the time and whether or not the sense is still present. This is to create an understanding of why reactions took place and to suggest that such reactions were natural under the circumstances, for example, that it is normal to be frightened or to feel helpless when someone points a gun at you. Also, this fear might still be around now.

Emotions and feelings
The debriefer then looks separately at specific feelings and emotions. Fear, discussed in the sensory impression stage, generated by the sight of a knife or gun, might have emerged more strongly when the person went home and realized that they could have died. Hidden or expected feelings are also addressed.

Stage three: Future

This stage consists of three sections: a *normalizing* stage, explaining reactions; an *information* stage about present and future possible reactions; a *support* stage, discussing personal support and outlining what help is available within the organization and from outside agencies. Possible future issues such as identification parades, court appearances, funerals and inquiries are also discussed. Leaflets, booklets and information about resources can be provided.

The session concludes with a short statement from each person present about what they now think or feel, and if there are any who particularly need advice or help the debriefer can speak to them individually.

Questions about debriefing

Debriefing is now widely used in the emergency services and many other organizations, as well as by private counsellors and practitioners. However, some researchers have produced results which suggest that it does not work and might make people worse, and which have generated media headlines such as 'Intensive counselling may damage disaster victims.' The problems are:

- Some researchers do not understand what debriefing is and use the words 'debriefing' and 'counselling' interchangeably when they are very different methods.
- The belief is perpetuated that debriefing is about catharsis.
- Defusing is confused with debriefing.
- PTSD is confused with Post-Trauma Stress.
- Debriefing is referred to as an injection against PTSD.

All of these are incorrect. Debriefing is more about integration than catharsis and uses a cognitive–emotive balancing approach which attempts to help people to restructure and reframe their experiences and reactions. In addition, some researchers have ignored the criteria laid down by Mitchell and Dyregrov for debriefing and their 'debriefings' have been conducted by untrained people using sessions as short as 40 minutes, sometimes within the first 24 hours, and some have used one-hour sessions as standard. The researchers know this, but still say that debriefing does not work! An educational psychologist said, 'They take apples and pears and produce bananas!' It is totally unprofessional to make misleading statements, to claim to have done research into proper debriefing when this is clearly not the case, and then to suggest that it does not work (Dyregrov 1998).

Disturbingly, there seems to be an increase in the use of debriefing by people who are not trained, typified by the woman who said she was a qualified debriefer, but who eventually confessed that she had done her training on the telephone! An officer in the army also claimed to be a qualified debriefer, but said he had been trained to do it in 45 minutes. Furthermore, a number of organizations, practitioners and even EAPs are offering 'debriefing', when what they are providing are informal counselling sessions with counsellors who are not trained in any specific debriefing model, and are using a one-hour session with no preparation of personnel or follow-up. Little wonder there are claims that it might make people worse. It would be better if we had some form of standardization for debriefing and debriefers, but this seems unlikely at present. There is nothing to stop anyone from conducting a session or doing research and, whatever method or model they might or might not use, calling it 'debriefing'. Perhaps the best we can hope for is that debriefing will be recognized for what it is and not for what people imagine it to be. It would be a beginning if the criteria of Mitchell and Dyregrov were used as standards. If you want to do debriefing, do it properly!

References

Dyregrov, A. (1989) 'Caring for helpers in disaster situations: psychological debriefing', *Disaster Management Journal*, 2: 25–30.
Dyregrov, A. (1998) 'Psychological debriefing – an effective method?', *ESTSS Bulletin*, 6 (4).
Parkinson, F. (1995) *Critical Incident Debriefing*, London: Sheldon Press.

Recommended reading

van der Kolk, B.A., McFarlane, A.C. and Weisaeth, L. (eds) (1996) *Traumatic Stress: The Effects of Overwhelming Experience on Mind, Body and Society*, New York and London: Guilford Press.

Discussion issues

1 What are the main reactions of people following traumatic experiences and what do they need:

   immediately and in the early stages;
   at a later stage?

2 What might the reactions be to the offer of counselling soon after an incident and what would or should a counsellor do if asked to help?
3 How might organizations help their staff to cope with traumatic experiences, what strategies can they develop and what should they offer in the way of support and help?
4 Some psychologists, psychiatrists and other professionals have said, 'We should leave people alone after traumatic experiences, give them time to come to terms with it and only then, if appropriate or asked for, offer help. Most will recover in time anyway.' Discuss.

35

Psychological Trauma

A historical perspective

Suzanna Rose

This chapter was written in the last years of the twentieth century but inevitably investigation into aspects of psychological trauma cannot be viewed in isolation. Such investigation encompasses its contemporary form but also has a historical perspective. One potent view is that, above all, this century has been one of war and bloodshed. Eric Hobsbawm (1994) estimates that the population of the world has been decimated directly by war or indirectly by malevolent human hands since 1900. Given the volume and impact of wars and atrocities this century, it would be surprising if a brief history of psychological trauma did not encompass an explanation of human avoidance as a defensive measure in failing to deal with the intolerable issues of human malevolence. And in some ways the history of trauma, with its times of periodic amnesia (Herman 1992), avoidance and intrusions, reflects, tangentially, the oscillating symptoms of chronic post-traumatic stress disorder itself. But avoidance during this century has largely been impossible. Much of our knowledge and work about psychological trauma comes from the arena of war. However, evidence comes from other sources too, such as civilian disasters and from early work on hysteria by Breuer and Freud (1955/1893–5). The chapter offers a brief historical perspective.

Early accounts

Although there are very early accounts of traumatic reactions as far back as Homer (Alford 1992), a particularly graphic description is given by Daly (1983) recounting the diarist Samuel Pepys' recall of the effects of the Great Fire of London. Pepys' diary entry for 2 September 1666 describes the gradual progression of the fire towards his home, the terror he sees in other people who lost their property and his own preparations to save his valuables. He subsequently developed 'dreams of fire and falling down of houses'. Six months later he was writing that he was still unable to sleep 'without great terrors of fire' and in his diary he refers to the after-effects of the catastrophe for others, which included some attempting suicide. Charles Dickens also left an account of his own traumatic reaction. He was involved in a railway accident at Staplehurst on 9 June 1865 and subsequently wrote a letter in which he described the horrifying scene of 'two or three hours work ... amongst the dead and dying surrounded by terrific sights'. Although that in itself

This chapter was first published in *Counselling*, Journal of the British Association for Counselling, vol. 10, no. 2, pp. 139–42 (1999).

was enough to render his 'hand unsteady', it was some time after the accident that he wrote, 'I am not quite right within, but believe it to be the effect of the railway shaking.' But Forster (1969) tells us there is no doubt that, after the Staplehurst incident, Dickens' diary tells us more and more about 'railway shaking' and not less as one might expect. Dickens also developed a phobia of railway travel but summed up the sequelae as 'I am curiously weak – weak as if I were recovering from a long illness' (Trimble 1981).

A psychodynamic historical perspective

Van der Kolk et al. (1996) state: 'In retrospect, the issue of the traumatic origins of hysteria is probably the most important legacy of psychiatry in the last decades of the 19th century.' This legacy appears to have had its origins in the work of the neurologist Jean Martin Charcot (1887) (quoted in van der Kolk et al. 1996: 49) who, we are told, described how trauma induced 'choc nerveux' could put patients in a mental state similar to that induced by hypnosis. Charcot went on to describe these hysterical attacks as 'dissociative problems – the result of endured unbearable experiences'. Freud visited Charcot at the end of 1885 and subsequently absorbed and adopted much of Charcot's work on hysteria. Indeed, arguably one of the most influential investigations into the psychological responses to trauma was advanced by Breuer and Freud's 'Studies on Hysteria' (1955/1893–5). They noted the importance of trauma precipitating the diverse symptoms of hysteria including dissociation, which Breuer and Freud termed 'double consciousness.' They also went on to discover that hysterical symptoms could be alleviated when the traumatic memories, as well as the intense feelings that accompanied them, were recovered and put into words (Breuer and Freud 1955/1893–5, cited by Herman 1992). Freud, in discovering psychoanalysis or 'the talking cure', had to listen intently to the intimate lives of nineteenth-century women and, in doing so, he found that major traumatic events of childhood were concealed behind the more recent, arguably more trivial, adult traumatic experiences which appeared to have set off the hysterical symptoms. In 1896 Freud published 18 case studies entitled 'The Aetiology of Hysteria' and made the claim:

> I therefore put forward the thesis that at the bottom of every case of hysteria there are one or more occurrences of premature sexual experience, occurrences which belong to the earliest years of childhood, but which can be reproduced through the work of psycho-analysis in spite of the intervening decades. I believe that this is an important finding, of a 'caput Nili' of neuropathology. (Freud 1962/1896)

In the well-known later repudiation of his early descriptive work surrounding the origins of hysteria, Freud abandoned the concept of the actual traumatic stressor as the causation of hysteria and began to formulate the theory that the repression of instinctual wishes formed the foundation of presenting neurosis.

In 'An Autobiographical Study' (1959/1925), Freud wrote:

> I believed these stories (of childhood sexual trauma) and consequently supposed that I had discovered the roots of subsequent neurosis in these experiences of sexual seduction in childhood. If the reader feels inclined to shake his head at my credulity, I cannot altogether blame him … I was at last obliged to recognize that these scenes of seduction had never taken place, and that they were only fantasies which my patients had made up. (p. 34)

Following this original repudiation Freud formed much of his later theory on concepts such as repressed infantile sexuality, formation of the Oedipus complex, conscious and unconscious fantasy and by the sole concentration of interest in the internal psychic world and the exclusion of external reality (Freud 1991/1917). Freud's original repudiation and its consequences have been viewed by some as scandalous (Masson 1984).

Combat neurosis

However, the traumatic aetiology of neurosis was not given up entirely by Freud and was resurrected in his later work 'Beyond the Pleasure Principle' (1955/1920). Notably, this was written in response to the Great War (1914–18). The catastrophe of this war cannot be overestimated. Over 8 million men died in four years, and, perhaps not surprisingly, men facing battle in the trenches began to 'break down' in large numbers. Their symptoms were similar to those seen in hysterical women (Herman 1992). Initially, this 'hysterical' response was seen as having a physical cause. Mott (1919) coined the term 'shell shock' and suggested that the condition was due to a physical lesion of the brain, brought about in some manner by carbon monoxide and changes in atmospheric pressure. Eventually it became clear, however, that soldiers who had not experienced physical trauma were developing 'shell shock'. Sufferers were described as 'moral invalids' (Leri 1919). Treatment for 'shell shock' ranged from the brutal traditional views of Lewis Yealland who advocated treatment which involved threats of court martial for cowardice, punishment and even the application of electric shocks to the throat to 'cure' the mutism exhibited by some patients (Herman 1992). To counter this there were progressive psycho- therapists who claimed that 'shell shock' was a combat neurosis which was a justifiable psychiatric complaint. Perhaps the most famous of these therapists was W.H.R. Rivers who undertook the psychoanalysis and treatment of the poet Siegfried Sassoon. It would appear unlikely that many sufferers from 'shell shock' would have had access to such enlightened treatment.

Quite apart from the mortality, five years after the First World War the International Labour Organization estimated the number of 'invalid soldiers who were receiving state pensions at over ten million' (Orner 1992). In 1938 the British government was still paying out almost half a million disability pensions to men wholly or partly disabled as a result of war service. Of these 25,000 received pensions for 'the after effects of shell shock'. At the time 3,200 patients were confined to 48 mental hospitals established specifically to provide psychiatric care for servicemen (Orner 1992). Europe was, of course, plunged into war once more in 1939.

Although the Second World War (1939–45) caused fewer casualties than the First it none the less involved considerable numbers. In 1948, 413,000 Second World War veterans were receiving pensions or other financial assistance from the British Government (Orner 1992). This war was different too in that it involved millions of civilians who were displaced, deported, bombed or who tried to resist the occupying forces. Additionally, attempted genocide of the Jews was carried out in Nazi concentration camps.

During this war, it was recognized for the first time that any man could break down during combat, and that treatment should be provided in a systematic and planned way. In 1946 two American psychiatrists, J.W. Appel and G.W. Beebe, concluded that 200–240 days in combat would suffice to break even the strongest soldier:

There is no such thing as 'getting used to combat'. Each moment of combat imposes a strain so great that men will break down in direct relation to the intensity and duration of their exposure. Thus psychiatric casualties are as inevitable as gunshot and shrapnel wounds in warfare. (Appel and Beebe 1946)

It was noted the reliance that soldiers placed on their comrades in combat and the subsequent distress that was caused to individual soldiers when separation occurred. Grinker and Spiegel (1945) stated that the strongest protection against psychological breakdown was the morale and leadership of a small fighting unit (cited in Herman 1992). So, acute treatment was therefore aimed at returning the soldier to his fighting unit as quickly as possible (Grinker and Spiegel 1945). Kardiner (1941) suggested that war created only one syndrome and that the varying labels of shell shock, battle fatigue, battle neurosis, combat fatigue were, in fact, all different labels for the same phenomenon and that the symptoms were identical to the traumatic neurosis of peace.

The development of a contemporary diagnosis

The adjustment problems of many of the Vietnam veterans returning to the USA fuelled further interest in the subject and a large five-volume study (Egendorf et al. 1981, quoted in Herman 1992) 'delineated the syndrome of post-traumatic stress disorder and demonstrated beyond any reasonable doubt its direct relationship to combat exposure'. Undoubtedly the psychological sequelae resulting from this war had an enormous political and medical impact in the USA and one result would appear to be the inclusion of the diagnosis of post-traumatic stress disorder in the third edition of the *Diagnostic and Statistical Manual of Mental Disorders* published in 1980 (*DSM-III*, APA 1980). Previous editions of the *DSM* had mentioned 'gross stress reactions' and 'transient situational disturbance' but the precise diagnosis of post-traumatic stress disorder (PTSD) with its twelve symptoms provided, for the first time, diagnostic criteria which covered acute, chronic and delayed manifestations of this psychopathological response to an extreme stressor. It was further refined in the *DSM-IIIR* (1987) when PTSD in children was acknowledged, and again amended in the *DSM-IV* (1994) when the criteria for the stressor (A) was changed to 'exposure to traumatic event that involved experiencing or witnessing event/events which threatened death or serious injury and that this stressor caused a response of intense fear, helplessness or horror'. Prior to 1994, criteria A was described as an event 'outside the range of normal human experience'.

During the 1970s and 1980s it was becoming clearer that the 'battle neurosis' of war had its not uncommon parallels in civilian life which were, for many, part of their normal human experience. Among other things, the emergence of contemporary feminism was the setting which allowed, perhaps for the first time, the violent reality of many women's lives to become public and 'sayable'. Prior to this, Betty Friedan's classic (1963) treatise *The Feminine Mystique* had described the issue as the 'problem without a name'. In 1962 Kempe and his colleagues described 'the battered child syndrome', and in 1974 'the rape response syndrome' was described by Burgess and Holmstrom. Increasingly during the 1980s it became clear that what was being observed was a constellation of symptoms which were a pathological sequela following violence to either child or adult. It was the notion of the range of possible traumatic stressors that could produce similar symptoms that was new. Combat was originally seen as a legitimate stressor in the causation of PTSD, but only after 1980 'did it become clear that the psychological syndrome seen in survivors of rape, domestic battery and incest was essentially the same as the syndrome seen in survivors of war' (Herman 1992). But interest was increasing in the psychological after-effects of all types of violent crime (Davis and Friedman 1985).

Conclusion

This brief history has outlined the course of a bloody century, and noted the ebb and flow of interest in traumatic stress reactions. The paradox is, of course, that we have come full circle following Charcot's and Freud's original work. Hysteria, combat neurosis, rape response syndrome, post-traumatic stress disorder are one. In public health terms the emotional and economic cost of trauma this century is so great it is almost beyond analysis. Currently, there appears to be a resurgence of interest and the formation of an international academic forum, the International Society for Traumatic Stress Studies, has helped to legitimize the subject.

References

Alford, C.F. (1992) *The Psychoanalytic Theory of Greek Tragedy*, New Haven, CT: Yale University Press.

APA (1980) *Diagnostic and Statistical Manual of Mental Disorders* (3rd edn) (*DSM-III*) Washington, DC: American Psychiatric Association.

APA (1987) *Diagnostic and Statistical Manual of Mental Disorders* (3rd edn, revised) (*DSM-IIIR*), Washington, DC: American Psychiatric Association.

APA (1994) *Diagnostic and Statistical Manual of Mental Disorders* (4th edn) (*DSM-IV*), Washington, DC: American Psychiatric Association.

Appel, J. and Beebe, G. (1946) 'Preventive psychiatry: an epidemiological approach', *Journal of American Medical Association*, 131: 1468–71.

Breuer, J. and Freud, S. (1955; original work published 1893–5) 'Studies on Hysteria', in J. Strachey (ed. and tr.), *The Standard Edition of the Complete Works of Sigmund Freud*, London: Hogarth Press, vol. 2, pp. 1–305.

Burgess, A.W. and Holmstrom, L.L. (1974) 'Rape Trauma Syndrome', *American Journal of Psychiatry*, 131: 981–6.

Charcot, J.M. (1887) *Leçons sur Les Maladies du Système Nerveux faites à la Salpêtrière* (*Lessons of the Illnesses of the Nervous System held at the Salpêtrière*), vol. 3, Paris: Progrès Medical en A. Delahaye and E. Lecrosnie.

Daly, R.J. (1983) 'Samuel Pepys and post-traumatic disorder', *British Journal of Psychiatry*, 143: 64–8.

Davis, R.C. and Friedman, L.N. (1985) 'The emotional aftermath of crime and terrorism', in C. Figley (ed.), *Trauma and its Wake*, vol. I, New York: Brunner Mazel.

Egendorf, A. et al. (1981) *Legacies of Vietnam*, vols 1–5, Washington, DC: US Government Printing Office.

Forster, J. (1969) *The Life of Charles Dickens*, vol. II, London: J.M. Dent.

Freud, S. (1955; original work published 1920) 'Beyond the Pleasure Principle', in J. Strachey (ed. and tr.), *Complete Works*, vol. 18, pp. 3–64.

Freud, S. (1959; original work published 1925) 'An Autobiographical Study', in J. Strachey (ed. and tr.), *Complete Works*, vol. 20, pp. 3–74.

Freud, S. (1962; original work published 1896) 'The Aetiology of Hysteria', in J. Strachey (ed. and tr.), *Complete Works*, vol. 3, p. 203.

Freud, S. (1991; Original work published 1917) 'General Theory of the Neuroses', in J. Strachey (ed. and tr.), *The Penguin Freud Library*, Harmondsworth: Penguin, vol. 1, pp. 281–482.

Friedan, B. (1963) *The Feminine Mystique*, New York: Dell.

Grinker, R.R. and Spiegel, J.P. (1945) *Men Under Stress*, Philadelphia: Blakeston.

Herman, J.L. (1992) *Trauma and Recovery*, New York: Basic Books.

Hobsbawm, E. (1994) *Age of Extremes: The Short Twentieth Century 1914–1991*, London: Michael Joseph.

Kardiner, A. (1941) *The Traumatic Neurosis of War*, Psychosomatic Medicine Monographs 2–3, New York: Paul Hoeber.

Kempe, C.H., Silverman, F.N., Steele, B.F., Droegmuller, W. and Silver, H.K. (1962) 'The Battered Child Syndrome', *Journal of the American Medical Association*, 181: 17–24.

Leri, A. (1919) *Shell Shock: Commotional and Emotional Aspects*, London: University of London Press.

Masson, J.M. (1984) *The Assault on Truth: Freud's Suppression of the Seduction Theory*, New York: Farrar, Straus & Giroux.

Mott, F.W. (1919) *War Neurosis and Shell Shock*, London: Oxford University Press.

Orner, R. (1992) 'Post-traumatic stress disorders and European war veterans', *British Journal of Clinical Psychology*, 31: 387–403.

Trimble, M.J. (1981) *Post-Traumatic Neurosis*, New York: Wiley.

van der Kolk, B.A., Weisaeth, L. and Van der Hart, O. (1996) 'History of trauma in psychiatry', in B.A. van der Kolk, A.C. McFarlane and L. Weisaeth (eds), *Traumatic Stress: The Effects of Overwhelming Experience on Mind, Body and Society*, New York and London: Guilford Press.

Discussion issues

1 Why do you think there is a current resurgence of interest in psychological trauma?

2 Do you think Freud's repudiation of his original theory surrounding the origins of hysteria should be regarded as 'scandalous'?

3 'Hysteria, combat neurosis, rape response syndrome, post-traumatic stress disorder are one.' What do you think?

4 How does a knowledge of literature inform our understanding of psychological trauma?

36

Stress Management and Counselling

Michael Neenan and Stephen Palmer

Stress has been defined as 'a demand [environmental and/or internal] made upon the adaptive capacities of the mind and body' (Fontana 1989: 3). If the individual's adaptive capacities can meet the demand, then the situation may be perceived as a challenge with the prospect of successful problem-solving. This may be called emotional excitement or emotional prostress (D'Zurilla and Nezu 1989). However, if the demand cannot be met, then the individual may well buckle under the strain of trying to meet it with inadequate coping resources. When demand has exceeded or overwhelmed capacity, the individual can suffer from physical and mental debilitation that results in burnout, that is, he or she is emotionally spent and deprived of productive energy; stress has turned into *distress* (Neenan and Palmer 1996).

Of course, a problem can be viewed simultaneously as both a challenge and a threat, thereby evoking both positive and negative emotions in the same situation. As D'Zurilla (1990: 337) observes: 'the emotions that dominate in the situation may depend to a great extent on the amount of attention given to the two potential outcomes (harm/loss vs. benefit/gain)'. So if the individual focuses on the gains to be derived from successful problem-solving, 'instead of concentrating on the harm or loss that might result from *failing* to solve it successfully, then emotional *distress* during problem solving might be minimized' (D'Zurilla 1990: 337).

The costs of detrimental stress are enormous. For example, some estimates suggest 180 million working days are lost annually at a cost of £4 billion to industry through workplace stress (Cooper and Williams 1994). Stress is now the most common cause of workplace absence lasting more than 21 days after back pain ('More staff staying off through stress', *Daily Telegraph*, 28 September 1995). Below are listed some of the immediate and longer-term effects of stress (Palmer and Strickland 1996).

- *Psychological:* anxious, angry, depressed, helpless, guilty, obsessive, no enthusiasm, cynical, lack of concentration, mood swings, intrusive thoughts or images, reduced self-esteem, retreat into day-dreams.
- *Physiological:* palpitations, indigestion, muscle twitches, vague aches and pains, skin irritation or rashes, frequent colds, flu or other infections, breathlessness, tiredness, tendency to clench fists or jaw.
- *Behavioural:* accident-proneness, poor work, aggressive or passive behaviour, irritability, increased absence from work, poor time management, increased substance

This chapter was first published as 'A cognitive-behavioural approach to tackling stress', in *Counselling*, Journal of the British Association for Counselling, vol. 9, no. 4, pp. 315–19 (1998).

use, change in sleep pattern, impaired speech, withdrawal from supportive relationships.

Cooper (1996) identifies three stages of negative stress. The first stage is behavioural: the individual has difficulty in concentrating and making decisions; becomes irritable and aggressive, begins to lose their sense of humour. In the second stage, this disturbed behaviour is translated into physical symptoms such as irritable bowel syndrome, stomach upsets, flatulence, constant colds, muscle pains. The third phase in chronic and severe stress can be serious physical illness as stress can trigger genetic predispositions to, for example, heart disease or cancer.

Some stress-management approaches

1 *Anxiety management.* According to D'Zurilla (1990), this has been the most popular form of stress management for many years (Benson 1975; White and Tursky 1982). The focus is on reducing or controlling levels of anxiety through such methods as progressive muscle relaxation, meditation and biofeedback (that is, autonomic arousal can be monitored to show how individuals react under stress).

2 *Cognitive restructuring.* This approach examines how an individual's thoughts, attitudes and beliefs play an instrumental role in creating maladaptive behaviour and unpleasant affect in stressful situations (Beck 1984; Abrams and Ellis 1994; Ellis et al. 1997). By identifying, challenging and changing these stress-inducing ideas, a more adaptive response to such situations can be developed. This approach would include relapse prevention.

3 *Stress inoculation training.* This method 'combines elements of didactic teaching, Socratic discussion, cognitive restructuring, problem solving and relaxation training, behavioral and imaginal rehearsal, self-monitoring, self-instruction and self-reinforcement, and efforts at environmental change' (Meichenbaum 1985). Stress inoculation training helps individuals to develop coping skills for tackling present and future problems.

4 *Problem-solving training.* This provides individuals with a sequential model of problem-solving (e.g., problem definition and formulation, generation of alternative solutions; decision-making, evaluation of outcome) to increase their coping skills in problematic situations and interpersonal conflicts (D'Zurilla and Nezu 1982; D'Zurilla 1990). This model of stress management helps individuals, among other things, to increase their problem-solving ability, self-esteem and satisfaction with life.

5 *Multimodal stress counselling.* The acronym BASIC ID (Behaviour, Affect, Sensory, Imagery, Cognition, Interpersonal, Drugs/Biology) describes the seven discrete but interactive modalities which Lazarus (1989) believes encompasses the entire range of personality. Problems pin-pointed across the modalities (e.g., traumatic imagery, autonomic arousal, catastrophic thinking) would be tackled with appropriate techniques for those modalities (e.g., respectively, imaginal desensitization, relaxation, rational coping statements). This model is described as 'transactional' because it provides 'a realistic explanation of the complicated nature of stress as it addresses the inter-relationship between the internal and external world of individuals' (Palmer and Dryden 1995: 4).

Stress research

Pretzer et al. (1989: 164) suggest that 'stress researchers have gradually approached a consensus on the view that stress is cognitively mediated', that is, an individual's appraisal of the stressor (external or internal stimuli) and his/her coping responses to deal with it will largely determine his/her emotional and behavioural reactions to the stressor. Two levels of appraisal have been identified: first, assessing the significance of an event (primary appraisal); second, determining the effectiveness of one's coping responses to meet the demands of the event (secondary appraisal) (Lazarus 1966; Lazarus and Folkman 1984). For example, a teacher fears an increase in her class size as this will mean greater unruliness from the pupils (primary appraisal); such behaviour from the pupils will push her to breaking point as she is already struggling to impose discipline in her classroom (secondary appraisal). This view of stress reflects the general theoretical model of cognitive-behaviour therapy (CBT) which examines idiosyncratic interpretations of and reactions to events (Beck 1984).

Fontana (1989: 63) states that 'grasping the full significance of the power of our cognitive appraisals over our emotions means realising that we *can* use our thoughts to influence how we feel. This isn't the same as saying it's easy to do so, but it's a vital statement we must understand if we are to develop our power to withstand stress'. Woods (1987a) uses research on the psychophysiology of stress to support the CBT perception that it is our view of events which disturbs us, not the events themselves.

What can be done about stress?

Dr Valerie Sutherland, an occupational psychologist, suggests that making the workplace a more mentally healthy environment could ensure 'that while stress is inevitable, distress is not' (reported in *The Times*, 1997; see Cooper and Williams (1994) for what companies can do to reduce workplace stress). Abrams and Ellis (1994: 39) make the same point about stress and distress but suggest that the answer to why a stressor becomes oppressive 'is largely found within the stressed individual, not in the events'. So one person's response to stress is enhanced performance while another's is potential collapse. Therefore the therapist's task, according to Abrams and Ellis, is to help the stressed individual to identify, challenge and change those patterns of thinking that produce emotional disturbance and problem-solving interference in the face of environmental stressors; this process of cognitive change enables the individual to develop an enduring emotional and practical problem-solving outlook.

CBT stress interventions have been shown to be effective in: decreasing occupational stress levels in working women (Higgins 1986); providing cost-effective employee assistance programmes for work-based stress (Klarreich 1987); preventing and coping with stress among safety officers (Kushnir and Malkinson 1993); treating burnout (Richman and Nardi 1985); improving occupational mental health (Weinrach 1980); reducing Type A behaviour, anxiety, anger and physical illness in corporate employees (Woods 1987b).

Tackling stress: a case study

Bernard (1993: section 3, p. 1) states that 'in order for you to think clearly and thus effectively handle stressful situations and solve practical problems, you first have to develop emotional control. *Emotional self-management is a vital key to stress management'* (authors' emphasis). The first step in emotional self-management is for the individual to become more aware of his/her emotional stress reactions and to understand their self-defeating nature. Counsellors are in an ideal position to help clients with this process:

Client: Since the workforce was reduced, there's been more work for me to do.

Therapist: How do you feel about that?

Client: Pissed off. Every day is pressure, pressure, pressure. I have to work long hours to cope with it.

Therapist: What would a typical day look like to you?

Client: I start about 8.30 a.m. and finish between 6.30 to 7 p.m. Sometimes I have to work through my lunch. I never seem to get ahead. That's why I'm pissed off.

Therapist: You've twice referred to being 'pissed off'. Which emotion do you think is linked to being pissed off?

Client: I'm not sure.

Therapist: How do you behave when you're pissed off?

Client: Tense, can't relax, get headaches, irritable with colleagues, my sense of humour has gone right out of the window, my jaw aches – it always seems to be clenched …

Therapist: Like it is now…

Client: Yes, I know. I feel ready to explode sometimes. I can't get a grip on things.

Therapist: Can you hear any thoughts going through your mind when you're like this?

Client: Apart from the bad language, things like 'I shouldn't have so much work', 'I should be able to cope like most of my colleagues do', 'I can't take much more of this.'

Therapist: Would you say that you're angry?

Client: Yes, very.

Therapist: Does your anger add quality and speed to your work?

Client: I wish it did. No, just the opposite.

Therapist: Does your anger affect your home life?

Client: Absolutely. I'm like a bear with a sore head when I get home and my wife and children suffer because of my moods. I feel angry with myself for being like this and then guilty for my behaviour towards them. Then when I've apologized to them, I start to worry about doing it again. I can't seem to control my moods.

Therapist: So you take your work home in the form of anger, so to speak.

Client: I never seem to get away from work!

Therapist: Does being angry have any benefits?

Client: Well, I suppose that my anger is justified because of the workload and therefore I'm entitled to feel like this. Not much of a benefit though. It doesn't help me work any better or reduce the workload. I'm angry at the company for getting rid of staff and at my boss for dumping this extra work on me. They're responsible for my anger, the way I feel.

Therapist: I'd like to come back to this responsibility issue at a later date if I may, but can I ask you: have you ever thought of leaving your job?

Client: Often, but I want to stay and conquer this problem. Leaving would be running away. That's not an option for me.

Therapist: So, you want to stay and learn a constructive way of handling your workload. Do you think your boss is going to reduce it in the foreseeable future?

Client: No, even though I blame her for my problems.

Therapist: So we need to find another way forward. I would suggest the first thing to do is to keep an anger diary at work for the next seven days so we can get a good idea of the intensity, frequency and duration of your anger.

Client: What's the point of that?

Therapist: Well, that will inform us how much of your time is consumed by anger and how much is actually spent on your workload.

Client: Sounds sensible. What then?

Therapist: On the basis of that information, we'll develop an action plan to tackle your anger and find a healthier way of managing your workload.

Client: Okay. That sounds promising.

Clients usually enter therapy unwilling to give up their anger because they perceive it as justified and believe it is up to others to change in order to make their situation more tolerable. Terjesen et al. (1997: 159) suggest that challenging these ideas early in therapy can lead to premature termination; therefore 'successful anger treatment usually entails exploration of the consequences of the client's emotions, and the generation of new alternative reactions. These maneuvers motivate the client to change.'

The course of therapy

The client's anger diary was a revelation to him: he counted over ten hours a week being angry (and that did not include his home life). Such a loss of productive energy and the sheer embarrassment of the discovery prompted him to start getting his anger under control. Also, detailed discussions were engaged in on the physical, mental and interpersonal effects of prolonged anger – these effects the client termed 'corrosive'. An imagery exercise that the client found particularly useful was inaction v. action: he was encouraged to visualize as graphically as possible the consequences of not tackling his anger (e.g., a heart attack, family break-up), and then contrast it with doing something about it (e.g., greater efficiency at work, happier family life). The client did this imagery exercise several times a day and over the next few weeks was asked to fade out the inaction imagery.

As the client was making progress in reducing the frequency, duration and intensity of his anger episodes, the therapist began to address the thorny issue of who was ultimately responsible for his anger:

Therapist: You said in the first session that your boss is responsible for your angry reaction.

Client: That's right … and the company as well.

Therapist: Now you've made some progress in reducing your anger, so who is responsible for that?

Client: I am of course, with your help.

Therapist: If you can reduce your anger, does it follow that you play some part in creating and maintaining it?

Client: I don't see that connection.

Therapist: Why do you think some of your colleagues cope better with the increased workloads?

Client: Because they accepted the changes and kept their noses to the grindstone. They also leave the office earlier than I do.

Therapist: Another incentive to give up your anger. Now I'm not trying to let your company or boss off the hook, but given the grim reality of the increased workload, what was your attitude to it?

Client: Well, I suppose I refused to accept it, it wasn't fair, those bastards … as if I haven't got enough work to do … are they trying to drive me into the ground? Those sorts of ideas were banging away in my head.

Therapist: And did this 'banging away' create a pressure-cooker atmosphere in your head?

Client: Most definitely.

Therapist: Now, how do you think you would have responded if you had adopted the 'let's get on with it' approach of some of your colleagues?

Client: I know where this conversation is going – you're trying to blame me for my anger.

Therapist: There is an important distinction between blame and responsibility in this kind of therapy: blame involves finger-pointing and fault-finding whereas responsibility acknowledges without censure the significant contribution an individual makes to his/her own emotional problems. So it is the anger-producing ideas we need to examine and not to take you to task in any way for holding those ideas. Does that make any sense?

Client: The way you've put it does. So blaming my boss for my anger is looking at the situation in the wrong way – she gives me the work but it is my choice how I tackle or respond to it.

Therapist: That's right. Some of your colleagues react to the increased workload, which is the same for all of you in the office, in very different ways.

Client: I know they do. Most of them cope better with it than I do.

Therapist: How about conducting a survey among your colleagues to find out their attitudes to work and coping with it and also if they blame the boss like you do?

Client: Okay, That might prove to be very valuable.

The survey method (Burns 1989) enables clients to test out their ideas in discussions with others as well as gain a variety of problem-solving suggestions. In addition, by subjecting his anger-producing beliefs to the sustained scrutiny of realism and pragmatism the client was able to modify them: realism – 'I keep on demanding every day that my workload should not be this heavy yet it remains the same. This is the way that it is, so I'd better adapt to it and get on with it if I want to keep my job. My anger makes the work harder than it actually is'; pragmatism – 'Where's it going to get me holding on to my anger? I can think of dozens of disadvantages yet struggle to think of one advantage. Even that one, my anger is somehow justified, no longer seems compelling.' On his desk at work he placed the following message, 'Stress does not have to turn into distress unless I let it', to remind him continually of his largely self-induced disturbance.

Reading Paul Hauck's (1980) book on anger control, *Calm Down*, provided more techniques for challenging his stress-creating thinking, as well as reinforcing the principle of emotional responsibility as discussed in the above dialogue. The client was also encouraged to select an activity that would help him to 'unwind' before he got home as well as increase his fitness: the client chose to go swimming twice a week. He also started walking to the railway station every day instead of driving to it and taking the stairs at work rather than the lift. At home, the client decided to take his wife out to dinner every week, and once a month he took his family on a weekend break. Therapy lasted a total of ten sessions, the last four being fortnightly instead of weekly.

Therapist: Would you like to sum up what you've learnt in therapy?

Client: The great revelation for me was looking in the wrong direction for the source of my anger – it was her fault, or their fault, but I believed it had nothing to do with me. How wrong I was. Now I see that my boss has got her job to do. It's nothing personal, as most of my colleagues would say. I haven't been singled out in any way.

Therapist: What about the anger itself?

Client: It seems to have vanished. I get irritable sometimes but that's to be expected. It's still a tough place to work in. However, giving up the anger has given me all these extra hours in which to get the work done. Now I'm managing the workload and no longer fear being buried by it. I make sure that I take a lunch break away from my desk and I leave the office every day no later than 5.30 p.m.

Therapist: What about at home?

Client: All that moodiness has gone – my wife says that I'm now more approachable. Her and the kids were always on edge when I got home in case I exploded. I realize now how lopsided my life was: I was either at work or brooding about it at home. My wife kept pointing this out to me but, of course, I didn't pay any attention to her.

Therapist: Well, I hope you won't make that mistake again.

Client: I hope so too. One concern I've still got is I know we've looked at relapse prevention strategies, but I still wonder if my progress will suddenly fall apart and I'll go back to square one.

Therapist: Well, let's schedule a series of follow-up appointments to see if your progress is still holding. The future won't be all plain sailing but it probably won't revert to square one either if you keep putting into daily practice what you've learnt.

Client: Okay, I look forward to giving you a progress report.

Conclusion

We have tried to show in this article that we are largely in control of our responses to stress in our lives. Cognitive-behavioural therapy emphasizes the power of our cognitive appraisals to determine how we feel and behave in the face of stress. We believe that tackling stress successfully is more than just re-evaluating our response to a specific situation; it often calls for a rethinking of our life-style and values in order to create a more balanced, healthier and harmonious existence. As Cooper (1996) remarks, 'Nobody on his deathbed has ever been heard to say: "I wish I'd spent more time at the office."'

References

Abrams, M. and Ellis, A. (1994) 'Rational emotive behaviour therapy in the treatment of stress', *British Journal of Guidance and Counselling*, 22 (1): 39–50.

Beck, A.T. (1984) 'Cognitive approaches to stress', in R.L. Woolfolk and P.M. Lehrer (eds), *Principles and Practice of Stress Management*, New York: Guilford.

Benson, H. (1975) *The Relaxation Response*, New York: Morrow.

Bernard, M.E. (1993) 'Are your emotions and behaviors helping you or hurting you?', in M.E. Bernard and J.L. Wolfe (eds), *The RET Resource Book for Practitioners*, New York: The Albert Ellis Institute for Rational Emotive Behaviour Therapy.

Burns, D.D. (1989) *The Feeling Good Handbook*, New York: William Morrow.

Cooper, C.L. (1996) 'Overwork could send you to an early grave' (interview), *The Times*, 5 January.

Cooper, C.L. and Williams, S. (eds) (1994) *Creating Healthy Work Organizations*, Chichester: John Wiley & Sons.

D'Zurilla, T.J. (1990) 'Problem-solving training for effective stress management and prevention', *Journal of Cognitive Psychotherapy*, 4 (4): 327–54.

D'Zurilla, T.J. and Nezu, A.M. (1982) 'Social problem solving in adults', in P.C. Kendall (ed.), *Advances in Cognitive-Behavioral Research and Therapy*, vol. 1, New York: Academic Press.

D'Zurilla, T.J. and Nezu, A.M. (1989) 'Clinical stress management', in A.M. Nezu and C.M. Nezu (eds), *Clinical Decision Making in Behavior Therapy: A Problem-Solving Perspective*, Champaign, IL: Research Press.

Ellis, A., Gordon, J., Neenan, M. and Palmer, S. (1997) *Stress Counselling: A Rational Emotive Behaviour Approach*, London: Cassell.

Fontana, D. (1989) *Managing Stress*, London: Routledge.

Hauck, P. (1980) *Calm Down*, London: Sheldon Press.

Higgins, N.C. (1986) 'Occupational stress and working women: the effectiveness of two stress reduction programs', *Journal of Vocational Behavior*, 29 (1): 66–78.

Klarreich, S.H. (1987) 'Cost effectiveness of an employee assistance program with rational-emotive therapy', *Professional Psychology: Research and Practice*, 18 (2): 140–4.

Kushnir, T. and Malkinson, R. (1993) 'A rational-emotive group intervention for preventing and coping with stress among safety officers', *Journal of Rational-Emotive and Cognitive-Behaviour Therapy*, 11 (4): 195–206.

Lazarus, A.A. (1989) *The Practice of Multimodal Therapy*, Baltimore, MD: Johns Hopkins University Press.

Lazarus, R.S. (1966) *Psychological Stress and the Coping Process*, New York: McGraw-Hill.

Lazarus, R.S. and Folkman, S. (1984) *Stress, Appraisal, and Coping*, New York: Springer.

Meichenbaum, D. (1985) *Stress Inoculation Training*, New York: Pergamon Press.

Neenan, M. and Palmer, S. (1996) 'Stress counselling: a cognitive-behavioural perspective', *Stress News*, Journal of the International Stress Management Association (UK Branch), 8 (4): 5–8.

Palmer, S. and Dryden, W. (1995) *Counselling for Stress Problems*, London: Sage Publications.

Palmer, S. and Strickland, L. (1996) *Stress Management: A Quick Guide*, Doncaster: Folens Publishers.

Pretzer, J.L., Beck, A.T. and Newman, C.F. (1989) 'Stress and stress management: a cognitive view', *Journal of Cognitive Psychotherapy*, 3 (3): 163–79.

Richman, D.R. and Nardi, T.J. (1985) 'A rational-emotive approach to understanding and treating burnout', *Journal of Rational-Emotive Therapy*, 3 (1): 55–64.

Sutherland, V. (1997) 'Office bullies "make their colleagues sick"', *The Times*, 14 May.

Terjesen, M.D., DiGiuseppe, R. and Naidich, J. (1997) 'REBT for anger and hostility', in J. Yankura and W. Dryden (eds), *Using REBT with Common Psychological Problems*, New York: Springer.

Weinrach, S.G. (1980) 'A rational-emotive approach to occupational mental health', *Vocational Guidance Quarterly*, 28 (3): 208–18.

White, L. and Tursky, B. (1982) *Clinical Biofeedback: Efficacy and Mechanisms*, New York: Guilford Press.

Woods, P.J. (1987a) 'Do you really want to maintain that a flat tire can upset your stomach? Using the findings of the psychophysiology of stress to bolster the argument that people are not directly disturbed by events', *Journal of Rational-Emotive Therapy*, 5 (3): 149–61.

Woods, P.J. (1987b) 'Reductions in type A behavior, anxiety, anger, and physical illness as related to changes in irrational beliefs: results of a demonstration project in industry', *Journal of Rational-Emotive Therapy*, 5 (4): 213–37.

Discussion issues

1 How would you define stress and how do you tackle it in your own life?
2 Stress appears to have reached epidemic levels in our society. Why should this occur now if stress has always been a part of our daily lives?
3 Is stress reduction the responsibility of government, organizations or individuals or a combination of all three?
4 Is attitude change the most effective way to tackle stress successfully?

37

The Aftermath of Abuse

The effects of counselling on the client and the counsellor

Moira Walker

To sit and hear stories of human suffering, pain and betrayal is an inevitable part of a counsellor's working day. But the effects should not be underestimated. There are twin dangers: if the impact is denied, compassion and care can become blunted. If the material invades too deeply and painfully, the counsellor can become overwhelmed and burn out or despair can result. It is a demanding and powerful process for the counsellor and for the client; difficult feelings and dynamics are triggered as the abuse and its effects are worked with. If the client is to be helped and not further abused or damaged, and the counsellor is to facilitate this process without the demands becoming intolerable, it is essential to understand the dynamics and to put in place sufficient support for the counsellor. A crucial question is what do both need to help them. Case examples will illustrate some difficulties and dilemmas.

Cara's story

When Cara was 13 she was sexually abused by her father, on one occasion only. Prior to this she had adored her father, and experienced him as protective, supportive and highly caring. He was her special person. His assault on her took place in a dark room, in silence, and he never referred to it again. He became distant and cold. The loving father had disappeared for ever. She told her mother, who reacted very passively. Her only response was that this must never be mentioned, and that Cara should lock her door at night. When Cara tried, in enormous distress, to talk again to her mother, her mother was angry. Cara was not to fuss; it was all over, and it had only happened once anyway. Cara was told that her father was a good man and a good father, and that surely she could forgive him. The event was not denied but its impact was.

She felt her world had fallen apart. She became the psychological orphan that so frequently characterizes abused children. Her school work suffered; she alternated between being withdrawn and very difficult, and alienated both teachers and friends. She was bullied and her exam results were poor. She left school early, to avoid further bullying

---

This chapter is an edited version of a paper presented at the 21st Association for Student Counselling (now AUCC) Conference, 1992, and subsequently published in *Counselling*, Journal of the British Association for Counselling, vol. 4, no. 1, pp. 40–4 (1993).

and because she was labelled as an educational failure. The cycle of the effects of abuse was in full swing.

Thirty years later Cara was still under-achieving. Following the death of her father a crisis erupted. She became seriously suicidal. Her job – the mainstay in her life – became impossible for her. She finally agreed to see a therapist. This was a huge step for her. She was assessed by a male therapist, another difficulty for her, but in this unit there was no choice. But she was able to say hesitantly that she had been abused, that talking to a man was difficult and that she would like a woman therapist. She was not very assertive: she was unused to being heard, she was totally unfamiliar with making demands and she found herself in the unknown world of psychotherapy.

Eighteen months after her assessment she received an appointment with a male therapist. Again, she felt unheard and not taken seriously. She attended three sessions but could not continue. In her first session she was overcome with terror. She could not speak. For half an hour she said nothing. And neither did the therapist. Her fear grew. His presence became threatening and she experienced a flashback to the abuse, which itself had taken place in silence. After half an hour he commented on the silence. It was interpreted as resistance. She attempted to explain what was happening and could not. The silence continued and the session ended. Session two was similar. After session three, in which she had tried both to challenge her therapist, and to explain her difficulty, both unsuccessfully, she gave up. She wrote to the therapist who had assessed her, explaining and asking for an appointment with a woman. He replied that she must work on her difficulties with the therapist, and she could not be offered another. She did not go back. The events which followed were horribly similar to earlier childhood events. Cara became alternately withdrawn and explosively angry. She felt once again that she had been damaged and betrayed, not listened to, not taken seriously, in another situation in which she had no power and no real voice.

To the world around it seemed ultimately that nothing very dramatic happened. She gradually resumed her old way of life. The angry storming stopped, and obvious withdrawal gave way to a quiet, rather distant sadness, as if she were in a far-away place. She was no trouble to anyone else, but greatly troubled inside herself. Nothing was resolved. Another layer of pain was added, only to be repressed. Cara would not risk seeing other counsellors or therapists: the chance of further hurt was just too great.

Elaine's story

Elaine grew up surrounded by abuse. She witnessed her mother beaten by her father, and in turn experienced the same. Violence was part of life. Father's word was law, and he enforced it with no compassion or consideration. He was powerful outside the home too: he held a very responsible position, was highly paid, highly regarded and the abuse was successfully hidden. As she became older the violence from her father lessened but a teacher she turned to for help began sexually abusing her. She told her mother, who was sympathetic but could not help. She told Elaine that she was sorry, but it was just how men were; neither of them could do anything about it.

Elaine came to counselling in her twenties, was assessed by a woman and was offered the choice of a male or female counsellor. She asked for a woman, although she was anxious not to be thought a nuisance. She was reassured that the choice was hers to make as of right. During her assessment she was able to express her anxieties about counselling and what a big decision this had been for her. She waited six weeks for ongoing appointments. Not long to a counsellor perhaps, but a long time if you are distressed. Elaine's first session was a very different experience from that of Cara, although it too could have had an extremely negative outcome. It was the counsellor's last appointment of the day. Her previous three clients had also been abused. She was tired and distracted by remembering a meeting immediately after the session and her need to leave promptly.

The session progressed well enough. Elaine seemed relieved to be there, and talked freely although with much pain. She was encouraged to take her time and to proceed at her own pace. The themes that emerged were exploitation, lack of power and control in her life, and the hurt and damage caused by the abuse. The theme of abandonment when in greatest need was ever-present. As a teenager she would frequently beg her abuser not to leave her. He would respond that she had no rights, should not fuss, should keep quiet and that her feelings were her own problem. He always disclaimed any responsibility for any of his actions. Elaine also told her counsellor that when she became very upset she would 'fade away', so nothing could touch her. Although Elaine was initially controlled and somewhat distant she became very upset as she was retelling this.

Her counsellor later recognized that she had not handled the ending of the session well. It felt too abrupt and she was concerned that Elaine looked tense on leaving. At the beginning of the next session Elaine was very silent. The counsellor was again weary but also uneasy and asked Elaine how she had felt after the previous session, commenting that it seemed hard for her to begin. Another very long silence ensued. The counsellor did not feel it was a silence that could be safely left and asked Elaine if she could describe what was happening to her. After another silence, Elaine replied that she had not wanted to come and with encouragement explained why. The previous week she had felt pushed out, that the session had ended abruptly without explanation, or acknowledgement of how she might feel. She became frightened and distressed; she dissociated, not fully returning to herself for several days.

Counselling could have become as abusive as it had been for Cara. A transference interpretation could neatly have been offered linking Elaine's feelings towards the counsellor to her earlier experiences. Indeed, later in the work such interpretations were offered appropriately and were therapeutically valuable. As the work progressed Elaine did rage at the counsellor and many negative feelings and experiences were projected on to her. However, at this point the counsellor recognized the reality base to Elaine's feelings and took this seriously. Mistakes had been made and needed owning and acknowledging. The counsellor was genuinely sorry and said so. She realized that she had lacked sensitivity to process issues in the earlier session, and failed to see that she was really repeating in counselling patterns from Elaine's life. Acknowledging this enabled Elaine to talk more about the abuse, enabling a fuller understanding of the significance of that first session, and a greater awareness of the issues that might arise in counselling. An anti-therapeutic beginning was used therapeutically. The counsellor demonstrated that, unlike others, she would listen and take what she heard seriously; she would acknowledge her own responsibilities, and did believe that Elaine had rights. She also began to acknowledge to herself and her supervisor that tiredness increased the likelihood of making just these sorts of errors, and that her workload was too high.

It is crucial to recognize that counselling can be abusive if practised insensitively, arrogantly or over-rigidly. I have written elsewhere (Walker 1992) that working with abuse survivors requires a flexibility in therapeutic approach. A core model is informative, containing and in many ways essential, but is not helpful if it creates therapeutic tunnel vision. The two examples given illustrate how counselling can become abusive, although the latter demonstrates how mistakes can be rectified if they are honestly acknowledged and then worked with. Abuse of survivors can extend to counsellors and therapists breaking sexual boundaries with clients, and, as with perpetrators, then projecting responsibility on to the client (Stean 1993). Hetherington states that when therapists abuse their positions 'therapeutic considerations are overridden by the therapist's own drives and needs, although usually theoretically justified' (2000: 277). It may be too easy for us all as practitioners, whatever our theoretical framework, to see bad practice as elsewhere, and safely distant from our own. Similarly, society prefers to see abuse as not too close to home. In the same way that society needs to recognize the proximity and extent of abuse, so we need to recognize that poor and destructive practices may exist in our own work and that of colleagues.

Seeing clients for counselling or therapy inevitably becomes routine for practitioners, who understand the parameters of their work and what is involved and expected. However much care is taken to explore this with clients it can still be a mystifying, frightening and confusing process, as well as being life-changing and hope-giving as the examples below illustrate.

Effects of counselling on Amy, Jill and Peter

Amy was sexually abused by an uncle and physically abused by her mother and explains that:

> You see I have had some counselling, but I didn't know the words. I didn't make use of it as I could have done. She asked me what happened, and I froze, and I'd chat about anything other than that. I desperately need it now. I now know it won't go away quickly, and that I need two or three years' help. That acceptance is a step forward. I really need that. Hospital was quite useless. Counselling would be my own special time. I need continuity with one person. I need to know they'll stay there, that they won't go away, that they can take it, and won't stick me on drugs.

Amy's words remind us that offering counselling at the right time, and then introducing the correct pace into the work are both essential. Her words also suggest that help may need to be offered on more than one occasion.

Jill, sexually and physically abused by her father, had one bad experience of counselling, but found her subsequent experience very different:

> I saw her for over a year. It was helpful. It was at the right time. I found out some of the things I could expect. And that made me accept more easily what I was going through. I found out what was normal for my circumstances. The recognition was important. I needed someone to know what had happened to me, and since the people in white coats had been so useless – I'm afraid their track record for me was absolutely appalling – that was very good. It was like being given time, time out, and that time was very important; the attention and her ability just to sit and take it. She wasn't astonished, which was useful, and she said some very crucial things to me. That was very helpful. I could find my own answers and direction, but the prompt was essential. She suggested strategies but didn't tell me what to do. Counselling took me right back. All the hurt

and the pain and the sore. It brought it all back. Part of me didn't want to know, but the things that were said made sense.

The combination of the counsellor's ability to contain the client's revelations, to give information appropriately that could reassure, and to offer strategies without demanding they were followed all seem crucial in this account.

And Peter, sexually and physically abused by his father:

> I saw the first counsellor for three months. What helped most was that I believed myself, and he believed me. I needed his acceptance and it was important that he was a man. I was frightened of him – he's a powerful man, and I'm frightened of powerful men – although he was helpful.
>
> I've seen another counsellor since, for longer. It's enabled me to help myself, and recognize myself. I knew psychiatry wouldn't help, especially those who adhere rigidly to certain ways of thinking. It wouldn't have enabled me to move myself. This has allowed me to be me. I was very introverted and frightened, and could be frightening to others. I'm much more free now to look at myself and to be happy with what I see. Before I had this incredible guilt at being happy, as if I wasn't allowed to, didn't deserve to be; and didn't deserve help. Guilt is a huge legacy. Dumping that guilt has been so useful. It's been important to acknowledge that I do need help. It has been so good. My counsellor is a woman and because of my fear of men that was good. Now it wouldn't make much difference, but then it did.

Peter felt helped by both experiences although the two counsellors were of different orientations: the first was psychodynamic, the second was humanistic. It was very apparent that although they worked from different perspectives they had in common a very clear adherence to boundaries. He experienced neither as rigid (and this was a man with therapeutic knowledge) – a key factor for him, as is indicated by his remarks relating to psychiatry. The gender of the counsellor was significant to him, in different ways and at different times, although much less so when he had worked through many of his difficulties.

Impact on counsellors

These accounts give some indication of the impact on clients of counselling and their needs. What, on the other hand, is the impact on counsellors and therapists, and what do they need to manage the work? They regularly encounter a world of agony and despair. They hear details that the majority would prefer to avoid, and they face horrifying realities. Personal and sexual relationships can be affected. Continually hearing details of abuse can make the most trustworthy relationship open to question and doubt: the counsellor begins to feel that nothing is ever what it seems. Sometimes working with such material is more distressing than the counsellor is able to acknowledge even to him or herself, let alone to partner, friends and family. The painful secrets of the client can become the distressing secrets of the counsellors.

Counsellors' relationships with their own children can also be affected. Counsellors know that the world can be a dangerous place, that children are hurt and damaged, that abuse is widespread and that there are abusers throughout society. Achieving the balance between reasonable precaution and appropriate protectiveness is not straightforward, and becoming over-anxious and unfairly restrictive of a child is sometimes difficult to avoid. Working with abuse survivors can be draining and exhausting. Feelings of inadequacy, hopelessness or even despair are commonly experienced by counsellors, who then have to walk the tightrope of their own emotions, while still needing to contain equally difficult emotions in their clients.

Counsellors have to be self-protective, while remaining accessible, available and empathic. They have to try to find a position that represents the ideal interface between objective distance and personal involvement, if they are on the one hand to convince the client that they will be with them, will believe in them, and will fight for them; and, on the other, they are not to collapse with them. Recognizing that experiencing despair and inadequacy often reflects the client's abusive experiences is helpful. Such feelings can then become therapeutically informative rather than simply overwhelming. Some effects of working with abuse survivors can be gender-specific, just as childhood abuse has some gender-specific patterns in adulthood (Bolton et al. 1989).

Abuse invades personal boundaries so totally that it is not surprising if counsellors encounter difficulties with boundaries. Yet boundaries need to be maintained and limits established in order that both client and counsellor are safely contained. Therapeutic grandiosity is dangerous and can lead to the exploitation described by Hetherington (2000). No one can take away all the client's pain and no one can fulfil all their needs.

Abuse survivors frequently feel alone, alienated and different and counsellors similarly experience this. Previous perceptions of how the world is organized, and how people behave, are deeply and starkly challenged. A counsellor new to working with abuse survivors described this:

> We went out to dinner in the evening with friends. They're quite interested in my job, but you can hardly say, 'I spent this afternoon with a woman who was multiply abused. And what you're talking about seems utterly unimportant.' I started to feel as if I was on a different planet; and very angry, quite unreasonably. I remember thinking that if anyone mentions mortgages again, I'll scream. It gives you a different perspective, a different understanding, a different view of the world. It changes you. And it's lonely.

The sense of alienation can be further intensified each time the counsellor is faced with new or different levels of abuse. As Casement suggests:

> [I]t can be a very lonely business when a therapist is prepared to believe that a patient's account of satanic abuse may actually be true. Colleagues are more likely to criticize than be willing to believe what they themselves have not yet encountered. (1994: 25)

Entering the world of abuse can also create feelings of guilt in the counsellor, as if they have no right to enjoyment, to pleasure, or to an easier life. This is further compounded by the sense of alienation described above.

Difficulties and anxieties are inevitably aroused in counsellors and therapists who work with abuse survivors and acknowledgement of these difficulties and appropriate support is essential. Adequate time for reflection, consultation and skilled supervision are crucial. Commitment to survivors and those who work with them must be demonstrated actively through the provision of adequate support, training and supervision. The validation of the counsellor's work and the recognition of its value by employing institutions is ultimately of crucial importance to the client. Counsellors also need to be aware of their own limits. Exhaustion and disillusion created through overload are counterproductive: worn-out counsellors are not actually helpful.

In order to undertake this therapeutic work, a combination of knowledge, skill and energy is required. Underpinning all this a counsellor has to have the ability, with necessary compassion and care, to make contact at a deep level with people in great pain, who themselves have little reason to trust the motives of those who offer help. As I have already suggested, to be effective counsellors give of themselves, while essentially retaining the core of an inner self.

References

Bolton, F., Morris, L. and MacEachron, A. (1989) *Males at Risk, the Other Side of Child Sexual Abuse*, London: Sage.

Casement, P. (1994) 'The wish not to know', in V. Sinason (ed.), *Treating Survivors of Satanic Abuse*, London: Routledge.

Hetherington, A. (2000) 'A psychodynamic profile of therapists who sexually exploit their clients', *British Journal of Psychotherapy*, 16 (3): 274.

Stean, H.S. (1993) *Therapists Who Have Sex with Their Patients: Treatment and Recovery*, New York: Brunner Mazel.

Walker, M. (1992) *Surviving Secrets: The Experience of Abuse for the Child, the Adult and the Helper*, Buckingham: Open University Press.

Discussion issues

1 If worn-out counsellors are not actually helpful, might they be harmful? What do you suggest they do about it?
2 What is the legacy of guilt? How may your understanding help you to work with those clients who feel that they do not deserve help?
3 What have you learned about recovering the counselling relationship and repairing damage to clients after anti-therapeutic mistakes by counsellors?
4 Can you apply this learning to a mistake you have made in counselling?

38

Child Sexual Abuse

The wider context

Colin Crawford and Billy McCullough

In this chapter we are attempting to contextualize, rather than emphasize, the impact of child sexual abuse. We now understand child sexual abuse to be so pervasive as to be normal in many family contexts, yet the media and some professional responses to it continue to be hysterical, obsessive and lurid (which in itself merits empirical investigation). Understandably, perhaps, child sexual abuse tends to be presented as a terrible, unthinkable, obscene occurrence, with crippling psychological consequences. However, there is a real danger that individuals who have been victims of child sexual abuse internalize the media's (and often the professionals') view of the abuse and of the consequences, extending to expectations of psychological disturbance and emotional instability, centrally derived from that source. In this sense the abuse may not be the problem *per se*; the actual problem may be located in social, societal, and indeed professional responses to it.

We were motivated to put pen to paper when a patient inquired, following media reports of a sexually abused male committing suicide, 'Does this mean I might kill myself?' Such is the power of the media, and such is the power of suggestion. This evokes consideration of the 'social construction of reality thesis' (Jarvine 1972; Blumea 1985; Becker 1988), with patients making associations between abuse and suicide, developing them into concrete connections, and then contemplating the implications for self. One can only speculate, however. We would suggest that the reasons behind the young man's suicide were infinitely more complex, but would have detracted from a shock headline which sells newspapers and air time.

The case discussion which follows served to exemplify the problem. In so doing, it draws upon an existentialist perspective (Languilli 1995), with its concern about the relationships between the individual and the social and socially structured environment, which influences or determines perceptions of 'reality'. This approach is closely associated with symbolic interactionist theory (Goffman 1971), with its emphasis upon how the attitudes and dispositions of 'others' (or the social audience) inform and pervade the individual's concept of self. Both these perspectives share the psychotherapeutic concern with the inter-relationship between the internal world (and psychical 'reality') and the external world (and social 'reality'), and as such are central to the case analysis (Bowlby 1969a: vol. 3).

Social and media attitudes toward child sexual abuse in the UK are symptomatic of a society deeply uncomfortable with sex and sexuality, while simultaneously fascinated and

This chapter was first published in *Counselling*, Journal of the British Association for Counselling, vol. 7, no. 1, pp. 16–17 (1996).

obsessed by it. The treatment of sexual deviation and child sexual abuse reflects this discomfort in assuming a consequence of serious psychological disturbance, and reflects the obsession in assuming that this must be the most significant life event for the individual. The problem is that, given exposure to such social attitudes, particularly when the abuse is disclosed and informs the perceptions and evaluations of the 'abused person', these attitudes tend to become internalized and incorporated, profoundly influencing that person's view of his or her abuse. A form of 'status passage' then becomes possible, from a 'normal' person who has suffered child sexual abuse, to an 'abused' person whose disturbance and level of disturbance may be directly influenced, determined or amplified by the attitudes and expectations of others (the social audience who categorize, label and stigmatize the abused person, which can be seen as constituting a form of 'secondary abuse'). Significantly, social workers, counsellors and psychotherapists may, unwittingly, occupy positions of some centrality in amplifying and consolidating, in a client's mind, the 'significance' of the abuse and the extent of its 'disabling consequence'. In so doing, they may actually contribute to and actually amplify the level of disturbance experienced by the client. If one is persuaded by the argument that therapeutic interventions based upon prevailing assumptions can be dysfunctional, this merits careful consideration in terms of group therapy in particular (Foulkes 1965), where a group member may face collective assumptions which may become further consolidated through group encounters and process. (That is, they may internalize the external world view of their abuse, which may lead to an actually harmful re-evaluation of the abuse as subjectively experienced.)

'Robert' had been referred, initially, for group therapy, prior to undertaking individual psychotherapy. While the reader must decide, upon the basis of the case analysis, it could be argued that an over-emphasis on the impact of child sexual abuse, in *group* therapy in particular, may have served only in deflecting him from locating and making connections with the real source of his disturbance.

Case discussion

'Robert' is a 27-year-old who came with the presenting problem of having been sexually abused as a child. This had apparently taken place over a nine-year period, from the age of 7 until he was 16. This was clearly a source of great distress for him, and he became very emotional and angry when discussing this experience of abuse.

However, there were other factors in Robert's background which were clearly significant. His natural father had been an ineffectual man with tendencies towards alcoholism and violence, who left the family home when Robert was 6. His son, Robert, had no sense of a relationship with, or affection for, him. Robert's mother was an ambitious and driven businesswoman determined to rise from the material deprivation which characterized her own family background. Robert and his sister were left virtually to fend for themselves, often going hungry, due to their mother's long working hours (suggesting earlier failed attachment: Bowlby 1969a, vols 1–3; and impeded 'developmental line' progression: Freud 1946). He recalled how, on one occasion when he was sick, his mother was kind to him and slept with him, how he 'felt like a king, and that all was right with the world'. This pointed to the sense of internal desolation arising from affective deprivation which was his more normal psychical reality. When his mother was away, which was virtually all the time, he experienced great 'insecurity and anxiety' – the separation anxiety deriving from an unbonded and unsatisfactory maternal relationship (Bowlby 1969a, vol. 2). He could not even remember being held, hugged, cuddled or kissed as a child.

When Robert was 7 an adult male 'friend of the family' demonstrated an interest in him, and befriended him. He was affectionate, took an interest in him, eventually giving him money. Robert was completely vulnerable; he was rendered completely vulnerable. Any of us in similar circumstances would have been similarly vulnerable. It also appeared that the male abuser was genuinely fond of Robert, opening a bank account for him, and making regular contributions over a ten-year period.

In the course of therapy it transpired that Robert's experience of abuse consisted of being 'handled', not to the point of erection, twice over a ten-year period. He became retrospectively enraged in recounting this, and talked of 'killing the bastard'. However, Robert also experienced great guilt, feeling that he had acted as a 'prostitute' in that he had accepted money, gifts and clothes, which he 'wore to impress the girls'.

It became clear that Robert's obsession with his abuse, and his perception of the psychological distress that derived from it, was a displacement of affect. His real rage was with his mother and her 'abandonment' of him (Bowlby 1969b). She was the one who, in the absence of her love and affection, had left him alone and vulnerable, needing to seek affection and a relationship from whatever source (Bowlby 1969a, vol. 2). Unconsciously there is little doubt that Robert was extracting his revenge on the rejecting mother, adding enormously to the guilt potential of this scenario. A further factor contributing to Robert's conflict was the fact that he derived a sense of acceptance, worth and value from the abuser whom 'he hated', and not from the mother whom 'he loved'. Such was the position that she had placed him in. The reality was that there was a great deal of secondary gain in Robert's relationship with the 'abusive' adult and that he had consciously 'bought into' this relationship, creating enormous ego–superego conflict with the associated need to punish the self. In Robert's case this was managed through his thinking himself into the role of victim (the victim of his own superego responses), as sexually abused, 'soiled', 'unclean' and 'unworthy'. This view is confirmed by what might be viewed as Robert's own indiscretion in often disclosing his abuse to other people, matter-of-factly, at the point of initial social contact.

He wanted and needed to become a victim in his, and in others', perception, as a means of punishing the self, setting the self apart and in discrediting the self. For the sin of acting against and hating (subconsciously) the mother 'he loved' he would have to atone and seek out his own punishment, driven by unconscious superego forces directing his disturbance. (These thoughts and feelings were dealt with subconsciously as their realization into consciousness would have been too threatening and psychically destructive.) Predictably, perhaps, this theme was reflected in Robert's difficult relationship with his girlfriend, which was very sexual but totally void of emotional attachment and intimacy. She did not 'permit' him to accompany her socially in the company of 'her' friends, allowing only public contact where they would not be recognized. In what appeared to be a 'compulsion to repeat' the circumstance of the 'non-relationship' with his mother, Robert contended with his girlfriends' psychological and emotional abuse 'because he loved her'. Furthermore this relationship was sexually exploitative, with the girlfriend making frequent and spontaneous demands for sex and leaving him almost immediately after the act. While Robert did not confide the circumstances of his sexual abuse to her, she demonstrated a lurid interest in the fact that he was 'sexually abused'. It would appear that this knowledge of him was a source of arousal for her (which poses other sets of questions).

There is no doubt that Robert was a victim of child sexual abuse. However, in terms of helping him gain insight and resolve his conflict and distress the real factors which needed to be addressed are:

- failed maternal attachment;
- maternal rejection and 'abandonment' (and 'ego weakness');
- his actual feelings of anger and hatred toward her (currently displaced);
- his subsequent vulnerability to exploitation and abuse (repetition compulsion);
- to explore the reasons why he was left vulnerable and susceptible to an 'abusive' relationship with an adult;
- to also explore the reasons underlying his 'voluntary' participation in the current abusive relationship.

In this context the sexual abuse which Robert was subjected to, while symbolically important, is actually insignificant – that is, when one attempts to understand the experience of sexual abuse within his total psychopathology. Regrettably this approach is not characteristic or typical of counselling or therapeutic approaches toward sexually abused people, given what can be viewed as a professional preoccupation with sexual abuse and a conviction surrounding its 'absolute' importance.

References

Becker, H.S. (1988) 'The labelling perspective', in J.C. Jarvine (ed.), *Deviance and Labelling* (2nd edn), London: Nelson.

Blumea, H. (1985) 'Social construction and human interaction', in P. Worsley (ed.), *Society as Symbolic Interaction*, London: Penguin Books.

Bowlby, J. (1969a) *Attachment and Loss*, vols. 1–3, New York and London: Basic Books.

Bowlby, J. (1969b) 'The influence of the early environment in the development of neurosis and the neurotic character', *International Journal of Psycho-Analysis*, 21: 1–25.

Foulkes, S.H. (1965) *Group Psychotherapy*, London: Penguin Books.

Freud, A. (1946) *The Ego and the Mechanism of Defence*, New York: International University Press.

Goffman, E. (1971) 'Stigma and social identity', in L. Radzinowicz and M. Wolfgang (eds), *The Criminal in Society*, London: Basic Books.

Jarvine, J.C. (1972) *Concept of Society: Society as Subjective Reality*, International Library of Sociology, London and Boston: Routledge & Kegan Paul.

Languilli, N. (1995) *The Existentialist Tradition*, New York: Doubleday.

Discussion issues

1 'Social and media attitudes toward child sexual abuse in the UK are symptomatic of a society deeply uncomfortable with sex and sexuality, while simultaneously fascinated and obsessed by it.' What is your reaction to this suggestion?

2 Is the distinction between a 'normal' person who has suffered child sexual abuse and an 'abused person' helpful in counselling work?

3 Does the psychoanalytic interpretation of this client's distress help you to understand him? How might you describe and understand that distress?

4 How is it possible that some of the responses of people in the helping professions to child sexual abuse may create problems for clients?

39

Attitudes to Ageing

Its social construction, deconstruction and reconstruction

Yvonne Craig

Over a quarter of century ago I interviewed for the Standing Conference for the Advancement of Counselling (SCAC), which became our British Association of Counselling (BAC), the charismatic Ivan Illich who had just written one of the earliest critiques of the caregiving industry, *Disabling Professions* (1977).

He was a forerunner of social construction theory, its links to therapy (McNamee and Gergen 1992), and its application to older people (Estes 1981), which also reviewed the positive as well as negative effects of problematizing special populations, for empowering as well as empire-building purposes.

Social construction theory, further discussed later, has a link with counselling, however tenuous it may be, as it is concerned with the analysis, causes and social contexts of human behaviour, although more focused on group and process formation. Counsellors may see it as a variant of our own basic knowledge, which teaches us to recognize and understand the many different past and present aspects of life which have influenced our service users, and ourselves.

However, social construction theory additionally maintains that people in need of help, and related issues, become problems manufactured for professional groups by powerful political interests which wish to detract responsibility from governments for preventing the infrastructural deficits and discrimination which contribute to their causes. Some professional groups, who benefit from referred clients, can collude with this construction of social problems, although the counselling concern to empower our service-users can strengthen them in the struggle for social justice, which we ethically share.

Ivan caused me considerable personal pain and residual distress when he reviled my work in bereavement counselling, saying that it was obscene that professional people were trying to replace the role of rituals and families in giving comfort and help in mourning. I responded by saying that it was partly *because* these traditions were now breaking down, at least in the West (and Ivan had worked principally in peasant communities), that bereaved persons were now desperately searching for befriending, counselling and sometimes psychotherapy, when loss and grief became unbearable (Parkes 1975; Pincus 1976; Speck 1978).

It has been largely due to the fragmentation of family life, failures of religious sensitivities and changing community structures that counselling has developed to provide

This chapter was first published in *Counselling*, Journal of the British Association for Counselling, vol. 9, no. 1, pp. 49–53 (1998).

needed public and private services to people overwhelmed by isolation, loss of identity, stress and lack of confidence in dealing with their problems, especially new ones. The emerging immune deficiency diseases, such as ME or CFS, and AIDS, are threatening, as for the old are the ambivalent uncertainties of the technological prolongation of life beyond past social expectations (Bouma and Graafmann 1992).

As old and very old people will be increasing service-users of counselling (Terry 1997), this article has been written to raise awareness of the significance of the social construction, deconstruction and reconstruction of ageing, and to suggest enlarged frameworks within which to view, accept, change or resist culturally conditioning processes about it. Conceptual stretching can expand our expertise in counselling, empowering ourselves and our service-users in the never-ending quest for a fulfilled personhood, even in later-life dementia (Kitwood and Breden 1992; Goldsmith 1996).

The introduction to this article concludes with a brief case study showing the value of counselling in the closing stages of life.

James, 84, was an emeritus professor of mathematics, being nursed at home by his wife, Jill, 70, a former neighbourhood law centre worker. James developed Alzheimer's Disease, gradually losing control of his mental, physical and emotional functions, as he began to hit Jill. She was wise enough to seek counselling, in addition to the hospital help and community care they were receiving. The counsellor worked with James at times when his fluctuating mental capacity was at peak, enabling him to feel assured that Jill still loved him as a person, and respected him greatly for his struggle to maintain dignity. Counselling led to punchball exercises to use when he felt furious; it empowered Jill to feel that she was engaged in the most important campaign of her life; and supported her through the coming trials of James's dying.

This case shows the importance of counselling in later-life crises, but it is also relevant to broader social issues with which social construction theory is concerned.

The social construction of ageing

James and Jill were wealthy and influential, receiving prompt teaching hospital treatment, the best community care, and were able to pay for private counselling. The majority of old people are poor and if they come from diverse communities they suffer from 'triple jeopardy' (Norman 1985), and receive few, and seldom culturally appropriate, services (Blakemore and Boneham 1993).

As far as older people are concerned, social construction theory (Walker 1981; Minkler and Estes 1991) points, among other concerns, to the inequitable division of social resources and how these are unfairly distributed by paid professionals to the rich, respectable needy, or provided on a second-class justice basis by voluntary workers to the poor, unrespectable needy. How many poor people would receive the sustained professional care for which James and Jill paid considerable sums of money?

It is argued that an 'ageing' enterprise (Estes 1981) or industry has been developed by powerful national organizations and international coalitions that serve the interests of the middle class in providing activities for later-life leisure, and involvement in any eventual residential care. These organizations are also said to create extensive employment for care-givers, on whose administration and capital expenditure public funding is spent, rather than on service-users. It is further argued that the state utilizes and increasingly tries to manipulate these organizations to provide services which were formerly the responsibility of central or local government.

The social critique of these services, counselling among them, involves accusations of contributing to the social adjustment technology by which the problems of old age caused by poverty, bad nutrition or inadequate housing are viewed as due to personal rather than government failings.

Another aspect of social construction theory, discussed by Lynch (1997) is that the way in which we think about and develop our work is determined by our biographies and social contexts, a view which is compatible with psychoanalytic and other theories. He suggests that Carl Rogers' theories were determined by his personal history. Thus the relevance of social construction theory for us all is consistent with self-reflexive good practice, in that we need to review how far our economic, political, social backgrounds, and counselling tutors, influence our attitudes, work aims and styles. How is our feeling, thinking and counselling work with older people culturally conditioned and socially constructed?

Social construction theory carries further warnings. It is linked to post-modern thinking which is critical of all theories which purport to offer total explanations of human behaviour, and which are reductionist in that collective generalizations introduce stereotypical archetypes which influence our casework. 'Post-modernism involves a reversal of determinacy' (Parton 1994: 102), and social construction theory helps us to understand, change or resist what determines our own lives, and those with whom we work.

A related issue is how our moral attitudes and values are socially constructed, and how our feelings and views about families, AIDS/HIV, religion and sex influence our lives and work, especially the language we use and the knowledge on which it is based, to which Foucault (1980) has attributed such crucial power. It also supports service-user control of data and research, as well as user-led or user-centred projects to encourage self-determinancy and self-direction, which are values Bond (1993) discusses, notably in relation to BAC's standards and ethics, and which influenced the development of the Elder Mediation Project (EMP for empowerment) noted below.

This organizational response to the social construction critique has been to indicate the empowering effect of their work with old people, many of whom are enabled to provide services for their peer group (Craig 1995), as well as pointing to the development of powerful advocacy groups such as the National Pensioners Convention, which also provides resistance to social manipulation. Power is being met by counter-power, and towards this BAC can claim to be socially productive through the valuable work of its counsellors in promoting personal growth (Feltham 1995; Woolfe and Dryden 1996; Palmer and Varma 1997).

However, the social constructionist view of ageing has many positive attributes, especially in showing us how our ideas of later life are shaped by our life experiences, as well as by political policies, economic planning and social strategies (Minichiello et al. 1997).

> I moved sideways from active bereavement counselling as my family felt that my own ageing was being sadly shadowed by 'disengagement' (Cumming and Henry 1961) from the real world. They hoped I would repoliticize my old CND activism and further my involvement with mediation, its domestic and community peacemaking equivalent. Its radical concern for grassroots empowerment through enabling people to participate in decision-making processes and conflict management reenergized me, and I saw its value in the struggle against ageism. So with older multicultural members of Mediation UK we started EMP with a special concern to prevent

rising problems of elder abuse. After five years casework mediating over 50 cases, I increasingly recognized the need for networking with counsellors experienced in the deeper emotional problems of ageing. (Craig 1998)

This self-reflective example shows how my attitude towards ageing had been shaped by theories of ageing as a disengaging preparation for the end of life, even affecting my own family relationships, yet was then transformed through my association with the youthful mediation movement into an empowering activism with my peer group. EMP's focus on working with poorer old people in diverse communities has been an attempt at developing learned resistance, rather than 'learned helplessness' (Seligman 1975) to social injustice as well as to elder abuse (Craig 1997). Our work was being shaped by growing social theories of positive ageing.

The social deconstruction of ageing

Positive ageing (Eweka 1994), made possible by lifespan prolongation, was first viewed as a happier alternative to ideas of disengagement, although more recently both have been seen as complementary, the former preceding the second, as we all eventually face death and need to prepare for it (Coleman 1997).

Gerontologists also increasingly pointed to heterogeneity among old people, and suggested that ageing should not be stereotypically conceptualized in unitary terms. Not only are there unique individual differences in the way people age, and between cohorts, but there are many variables between stages from the old to the very old. The social processes of ageing are being taken apart so that each can be considered for what it is, and given appropriate social responses (Walker 1996).

From this perspective, old-age counselling, as a term, gives an inappropriate social message. Counsellors work with individual persons who may be 50, 70 or 90 years old, and each may have a different problem of emotional, mental, physical, environmental or sexual health. Having said that, it is recognized that ageing has some general features for most people (Knight 1992), with its depressing increase of relatives and friends lost by dying (Scrutton 1995), as well as sensory losses through disabilities, role losses of employment, and financial uncertainties about future care. Yet these experiences may also affect young people with HIV or AIDS.

This deconstruction of ageing as a unitary phenomenon (and, indeed, of any special counselling generational or subject focus), of which only a few elements have been briefly noted here, is salutary in that it encourages us to give people more accurately focused attention, empathy and appropriate counselling responses based on their individual personal needs. It helps us to avoid polarizing people, and being influenced ideologically by current social attitudes to those of us in later life, whether we are considered as nice old dears, or as selfish and senile consumers of the social and health services. We may be neither, or both, and we may be capable of some changes, although not of others, as the following case shows.

Paul, aged 55, had always been a womanizer, but did not leave his wife, Pat, five years younger, until after 35 years of marriage, when he formed a passionate alliance with a student, aged 20. Pat felt ashamed of her ageing body and it was only sexual counselling which restored her self-esteem and made her realize that her passive endurance of Paul's earlier infidelities for the sake of their children had weakened him, herself and the family. She was enabled to work through her feelings of rejection, and reactivated with distinction her old professional life which had been dormant through the marriage. Paul's alliance ended, and he refused counselling, but his sexual needs remained unchanged in his 70s, and he enjoyed serial relationships living apart from the family, but continuing to support them with financial regularity.

Unfortunately, the couple's children followed the parental pattern with broken marriages, the daughter inheriting her father's charms, and the son being hurt by an unfaithful wife. This inter-generational transmission of family patterns (Gelles and Strauss 1988) is relevant to changing ideas about the role of families in promoting social solidarity, and also to the way in which ageing is being socially reconstructed. We need to take apart, or deconstruct, all the various conscious elements that condition us, and this analysis will contribute to the development of our unconscious feelings.

The social reconstruction of ageing

From different perspectives, whether from the widening views of the new genetic sciences, or from the closer look of counselling in seeing each individual as a precious person rather than a social category, there is increasing recognition that we are all linked in our humanity and development. The life-cycle work of Erikson (1982) has re-emerged among gerontologists as life-span theory connected with developmental theory, which encompasses us all, from birth to the grave, as we age from the moment we are born.

This can also be seen as a trend towards the normalization of ageing, reducing the anxieties which it has typically incurred. Although Erikson (1982) pointed to general characteristics of life stages, he stressed that generativity was as much a task of later life as it was in child-bearing years. These ideas were further developed by Gutman (1987), who showed that the human capacity for personal growth and achievement did not need to be diminished by age, even though it would be affected by disabilities and dementias.

The young, and people of all ages, are similarly affected by mental illness and disability, as well as by the poverty in which too many old people, especially from ethnic minorities, find themselves. This is where inter-generational conflicts about different life-styles and competing entitlements to public resources could be more constructively transformed into inter-generational coalitions against poverty, poor housing and inadequate health and social services, as the next case suggests.

> Jim, aged 17, just out of care, was given his first one-roomed tenement flat above Jeannie, aged 80, a childless widow. Both were very depressed. He stomped up and down on his bare-boarded floor. She was frightened of callers, and kept slamming her door shut. Both disturbed and distressed each other. Jim's worker involved community mediators who brought the couple together. Jim liked Jeannie who resembled his dead Grannie, and he awoke her maternal feelings. The mediation empowered them both to go to the council and ask for a better lock for Jeannie's door and carpeting for Jim's floor. The couple got on so well that Jim's worker suggested that they might like to try co-counselling for their depression.

This encouraging story is not atypical of the work that is now being done by Age Concern and other organizations who are sponsoring inter-generational exchanges, such as mentoring by old people on the one hand, and visiting by young people on the other. This can be viewed as a contribution to the social reconstruction of ageing, and also to the maintenance and invigoration of social solidarity through the new forms of family relationships that are developing, with foster grannies as well as foster and step-children.

Another factor which is collapsing some of the earlier constructions of ageing is the fact that life experiences can be as extensive among younger people as traditionally has been the case with elders. Worldwide travel, volunteering in previously unvisited countries with unknown social groups, as well as the cyberspace revolution and crises-marked life histories of serial sexual relationships, substance abuse and deviance, can make youthful reminiscence as rich, or as distressing, as that of the old. The health of some young people may also be more problematic than that of their elders, who, at the moment, make a much smaller demand for counselling. However, this demand is likely to increase from the cohorts of very old people whose great prolongation of life accompanied by chronic physical and mental disabilities will present them and their carers with problems never before met in human history (Craig 1997). Yet here again, many old people are learning to manage this developmental decline in the life-span.

Peter Coleman, our first professor of psychogerontology, cites Brandtstadter and Greve (1994) and their work on the self-stabilizing, protective and reconstructive processes of ageing (Coleman 1997). Three functionally interdependent processes are designated as 'immunizing', 'assimilative' and 'accommodative'.

The first involves the way in which we deny some negative evidence of ageing, and focus on positive effects, as does the woman who dyes her grey hair and goes on cruises. The second aims to develop compensatory activities which prevent or alleviate loss of self-esteem, as does the redundant ticket-collector who becomes a treasurer of a Caribbean club. The third enables people to readjust their personal goals so as to neutralize negative self-evaluation, as did the old couple who sold their house and moved into sheltered accommodation, while renewing church membership.

The aspect of these three processes which is most relevant to one of the themes of this present article concerns the fact that they are *universal*, and are used consciously, or unconsciously, by people at any stage of development, whether in the transitions of youth or age. One of the tasks of counselling may be to enable these processes to become transparent, so that they can be used constructively, or relinquished if they are destructive.

> Ali found it increasingly difficult to get paid work as he grew older so he went to a Community College and did a social care course with young people, which immunized him against his fear of ageing. This enabled him to get expenses-paid voluntary work in a charity that wanted Muslim representation, which affirmed his religious self-esteem. He then failed to get professional social work because of the higher qualifications needed, but a friend with a background in counselling enabled him to rediscover another ability he had, and to focus on this as a more accommodative way of planning more successful future activities.

The processes which underlie the dynamics of this case are well recognized by transpersonal and other counsellors who focus on transitions and transformations in personal growth and development, whatever the age of the individual.

Review

This attempt to provide an ongoing analysis of ageing from the perspective of social construction, deconstruction and reconstruction theory is not meant to detract from primary essential tasks in counselling older people. These include understanding the general physical and psychological effects of ageing and its special problems, and developing appropriate sensitivity and communication skills, as discussed in the books noted above. Also, this effort at social analysis of developing trends is only a limited contribution to continuing evaluations by major authorities in the area of social and psychogerontology.

Nevertheless, as an older person, always on a learning curve, I have shared these reflections in the hope that they will contribute to the critique of the reductionism and determinism which can diminish our value as elders, and as individuals.

References

Blakemore, K. and Boneham, M. (1993) *Age, Race and Ethnicity*, Milton Keynes: Open University Press.

Bond, T. (1993) *Standards and Ethics for Counselling in Action*, London: Sage.

Bouma, H. and Graafmann, J. (1992) *Gerontechnology*, Amsterdam: IOS Press.

Brandtstadter, J. and Greve, W. (1994) 'The aging, self-stabilizing and protective process', *Developmental Review*, 14: 52–80.

Coleman, P. (1997) 'Last scene of all', *Generations Review*, 7 (1): 2–5.

Craig, Y. (1995) 'EMPowerment: not EMPire-building', *Generations Review*, 5 (1): 7–8.

Craig, Y. (1997) *Elder Abuse and Mediation*, Aldershot: Avebury.

Craig, Y. (ed.) (1998) *Advocacy, Counselling and Mediation in Casework*, London: Jessica Kingsley.

Cumming, E, and Henry, W. (1961) *Growing Old*, New York: Basic Books.

Erikson, E. (1982) *The Life Cycle Completed*, London: Norton.

Estes, C. (1981) *The Aging Enterprise*, San Francisco: Jossey-Bass.

Eweka, I. (1994) 'Counselling for old and elderly people', *Counselling*, 5 (4): 296–8.

Feltham, C. (1995) *What is Counselling?*, London: Sage.

Foucault, M. (1980) *Power/Knowledge*, New York: Pantheon.

Gelles, R. and Strauss, M. (1988) *Intimate Violence*, New York: Simon & Schuster.

Goldsmith, M. (1996) *Hearing the Voice of People with Dementia*, London: Jessica Kingsley.

Gutman, D. (1987) *Reclaimed Powers: Towards a New Psychology of Men and Women in Later Life*, New York Basic Books.

Illich, I. (1977) *Disabling Professions*, London: HarperCollins.

Kitwood, T. and Breden, K. (1992) 'Towards a theory of dementia care', *Ageing and Society*, 12 (3): 269–87.

Knight, B. (1992) *Psychotherapy with Older Adults*, London: Sage.

Lynch, G. (1997) 'Therapeutic theory and social context', *British Journal of Guidance and Counselling*, 25 (1): 5–15.

McNamee, S. and Gergen, K. (1992) *Therapy as Social Construction*, London: Sage.

Minichiello, V., Chappell, N., Kendig, H. and Walker, A. (eds) (1997) *Sociology of Aging*, Melbourne: International Sociological Association.

Minkler, M. and Estes, C. (eds) (1991) *Critical Perspectives on Aging*, Baywood: New York.

Norman, A. (1985) *Triple Jeopardy*, London: Centre for Policy on Ageing.

Palmer, S. and Varma, V. (eds) (1997) *The Future of Counselling and Psychotherapy*, London: Sage.

Parkes, C. (1975) *Bereavement*, Harmondsworth: Penguin.

Parton, N. (1994) 'The nature of social work under conditions of (post) modernity', *Social Work and Social Science Review*, 5 (2): 93–112.

Pincus, L. (1976) *Death and the Family*, London: Faber.

Scrutton, S. (1995) *Bereavement and Grief*, London: Arnold.

Seligman, M. (1975) *Helplessness*, San Francisco: W.H. Freeman.

Speck, P. (1978) *Loss and Grief in Medicine*, London: Bailliere Tindall.

Terry, P. (1997) *Counselling the Elderly and their Carers*, Basingstoke: Macmillan.
Walker, A. (1981) 'Social policy, social administration and the social construction of welfare', *Sociology*, 15 (2): 225–50.
Walker, A. (ed.). (1996) *The New Generational Contract*, London: University College London.
Woolfe, A. and Dryden, W. (ed.) (1996) *Handbook of Counselling Psychology*, London: Sage.

Discussion issues

1 Although the human capacity for personal growth and achievement is affected by disabilities and dementia it is not necessarily diminished by age. Do you agree and what evidence do you have?

2 Do you anticipate a need for any adaptations to your counselling style and approach in working with old or very old people as they seek to benefit from counselling in the future?

3 Social construction theory suggests that social resources are unfairly distributed by paid professionals to the rich, respectable needy or provided on a second-class basis by volunteers to the poor, unrespectable needy. Is this theory or practice in the UK?

4 Describe your favourite 'older person'. Are your thoughts and feelings culturally conditioned or socially constructed?

40

Partnership

Some effects of childhood scripts on intimate relationships

Jane Robins

This writing arose out of my counselling work with both individuals and couples experiencing relationship difficulties. It felt important to consolidate the emerging themes from my practice and many couples have found this brief exposition helpful in clarifying destructive patterns in their partnerships. It has relevance to both heterosexual and gay relationships and the underpinning contributory factors are common to both types of partnership. My practical experience is supported by the work of the authors referenced, but this writing stems from the awareness of repeated patterns and issues as couples have worked through their individual and joint concerns in the counselling room.

It is difficult!

Relating to another human being in a permanent intimate way is one of the most challenging aspects of human living. We spend our adolescent years awaiting the 'arrival' of this highly sought-after relationship. Career and educational issues jostle with this emotional and sexual focus, to find within one person, the ideal blend of friend, companion, soul mate and sexual partner.

An effective, creative partnership involves friendship, companionship, sexual intimacy, household and financial management and frequently parenting issues. It also involves many aspects of the individual – their values, beliefs and personal philosophy of life, and their thoughts and feelings on a multitude of diverse subjects. Two human beings, with different histories and unique experiences of life join together because they love each other and hope to live together for life! During the initial stages of meeting, falling in love and deciding this is the 'one', these individual differences are a source of interest, exploration and excitement — time is spent listening to each other and the differences are often acknowledged and seen as stimulating and to be enjoyed. As the partnership moves into a more permanent stage, frequently the listening stops and each partner begins to view the other in a particular and static way. Each begins to make restricting assumptions of the other and responses and reactions are 'expected' and become blurred. Stereotypical interactions become more inflexible, partners move gradually away from real listening and interest in the other, to a feeling of disinterest and boredom which often provokes feelings

This chapter was first published in *Counselling*, Journal of the British Association for Counselling, vol. 6, no. 1, pp. 41–3 (1995).

of anger, resentment and blame of the other who 'doesn't care any more'! Similarly any changes in beliefs, thoughts and feelings that occur in either partner, are often viewed as threatening and destructive, as negative thinking and a feeling of hopelessness overwhelm the positive aspects. There is a swing from idealization to disillusionment, anger and resentment become easily provoked feelings which act to reaffirm the mutual distancing and feeling of partnership malaise and despair.

Two contributory factors

Inherent hopes and expectations

One inherent contributory factor is that everyone comes to such partnerships with inbuilt sets of expectations and hopes. These involve both culturally and socially related norms and expectations and more personally unique beliefs, hopes and fears from their own childhood experiences of partnership and family life. Every man and woman has a powerful set of unconscious but highly motivating oughts and shoulds, for themselves and their partners regarding sex, money, task distribution, power, gender issues and child care. Absorbed during childhood and early educational and social experiences these become as much an accepted implicit part of themselves as having brown or blue eyes.

It can be a creative, if slow and difficult process to bring these aspects of a life 'script' into more conscious awareness and to understand which codes of partnership rooted in past parental influences may now be outmoded and working destructively within a present relationship. In counselling I facilitate this new awareness by a gradual exploration and understanding of the complicated conflict and confusion surrounding past partnership scripts and present here-and-now partnership demands, needs and feelings. The emerging new insights can provide each partner with more understanding and clarity and room to compromise within their relationship. They can begin to talk about their own needs and feelings without the power of the unconscious script distortion.

The parental distortion

A second underlying seed of partnership destruction is 'parental distortion', which describes the unconscious response to, and expectation of, the partner as parent. The needy child lies dormant in the adult and is often powerfully activated within the next significant relationship or partnership (Desteian 1989). This distortion is inevitable, and will be more or less destructive in proportion to the parental deficit in childhood. A child, in its early years, learns ways of reducing conflict with parents, thus lessening the risk of losing love and approval. Children adopt particular ways to win attention and maintain love from their parents — they discover their script, which is unconsciously taken on board as a prerequisite of love and parental acceptance (Bradshaw 1988).

This unconscious script, of how they have to act, and react with their parents, in order to create and maintain value and safety is brought into the adult partnership relationship. The process of falling in love, is a temporary breakdown of these scripted responses and protective behaviours. He/she loves me as I am! There is a euphoria of feeling understood and accepted for themselves — each partner feels safe and comfortable in the presence of the other — a total unity and mutual honesty is felt and, in fact, an ideal mother/child, father/child oneness is experienced.

This in-love, ideal state, is a temporary, if pleasant, stage but soon the inevitable significant moment occurs, when each partner responds to ensure the continuation of the love and value, by enacting the old necessary behaviour, that was a childhood prerequisite of personal value and harmony. They move away from an immediate response to the real here-and-now situation to a distorted response motivated by their past history. It could be such inner messages as:

I mustn't be angry, cry, be sad, be difficult, argumentative.

The other must have what *they want* from colour of paint to sexual frequency.

I must please, I can't be honest. I must always support — I can't be needy.

Similarly, it could be a powerfully triggered response to anger or tears in the other, evoking an unbalanced reaction to the here-and-now partnership issue. A partner reacts with great emotion to a minor irritation or criticism. They defend themselves by attacking, hiding deepest areas of vulnerability and hurt which are not about the today issue, but about hurt caused by being constantly criticized by parents years ago. This reactive drama is acted out in the present setting and relationship, without awareness of what is really happening and what childhood hurts are being responded to and acted upon (Miller 1991).

Again, as with the hidden agenda of hopes and expectations, this parental distortion is a hidden underground agenda, which causes much blurring and inevitable confusion. There is often a feeling of deep inner resentment and futility, that the partner will never understand or hear, and each partner feels they *have to* respond in a certain way, despite the inner belief that 'nothing will change'. Such inner negative thoughts and patterns of behaviour are a sure sign that the partners are responding to an inner set script and not responding creatively to the needs of the specific present situation. There is also often a powerfully driven fear of honesty — this again is a fear established in childhood when honesty in terms of expressing inner feelings has felt dangerous.

The counselling process

It can be a very creative, illuminating exercise, for each partner to become more aware of their own scripted messages from the past. As this script becomes clearer, it is possible to see one's partner more as they really are — to begin to distinguish what past emotions are being triggered, providing a powerful destructive amplification of present difficulties. Both partners can see reality more clearly and begin to explore and discuss issues, and become aware of habitual, outdated modes of response. They can begin to practise honesty with each other, without the shadowed fear of parental reprisal or dismissal.

In terms of the counselling process a broad framework has emerged from my work with both individuals and couples. Experience has shown that when working with couples it is important to work with both partners separately and then together. Both partners bring their underpinning script and parental distortion to their relationship and time is needed for each person to explore and begin to understand how their present and their past are connected. Unless this individual groundwork is done, I have found that the exploration of two inter-reacting parental distortions and scripts can prove too complex and unwieldy to work effectively with a couple.

In the preparation work with individual partners, I use whatever way into awareness of childhood that feels appropriate for the client. This may be a script questionnaire, a feelings life route, journal writing, painting or poetry. We then begin to explore and understand their picture of childhood and how he/she learned 'how to be' to gain love and value. This learned behaviour is then looked at in terms of how it is distorting the present intimate relationship. To what extent each partner feels they have to be a certain version of themselves to be acceptable and if they are in fact acting out sadness, anger and hurt rooted in early years.

At this stage we begin to use a 'parallel dialogue'. The client is encouraged to voice aloud powerful feelings towards their partner in the present and then move to voice similar feelings towards the relevant parent (Stettbacher 1991). A sense of those feelings within the partnership which are powered from elsewhere comes from an awareness that some feelings seem inappropriately powerful within the present situation. The energy is coming from a painful childhood source and getting locked into a present issue or difficulty. Through this process, individual partners begin to distinguish what is from the past, distorting the present and the source of the power of the feelings. They begin to be aware to what extent they are living out or acting out childhood scripts or pain in their adult relationship. This begins to clarify relationship problems and improve real communication.

The healing process also includes taking time to facilitate each partner's expression of other painful feelings towards their parents and childhood situations (Janov 1990). Unless this expression is promoted these feelings will be echoed in the relationship. Partnership situations will trigger a powered response despite a head understanding unless the child's hurt or angry feelings find release towards their true source. The couple then come together within the counselling situation to share their new understanding of themselves and begin to explore and understand how the inevitable difficulties, problems and crises of relationship life have been accompanied by these additional childhood issues. The couple can then begin to make decisions with a new realness and clarity. They slowly begin to see each other more as they actually are and respond to each other and various situations with a developing freedom.

I believe it is impossible to change the learned relating habits of a lifetime in a few months of therapy. In fact, the work with the separate partners and then the couple together often takes over a year. But what the couples who come for counselling gain is an effective extra tool to use, a way of reducing confusion around apparently intransigent communication difficulties and a way of understanding better their own and their partner's emotional responses, bringing hope of clearer communication about all the various aspects of partnership life without so much destructive influence from their past.

Perhaps the most important value I try to promote within couple counselling, is that each partner can only begin to understand, accept and value the other if they begin to understand, accept and value themselves and this involves their own often painful personal childhood history.

References

Bradshaw, J. (1988) *Bradshaw on The Family*, Florida: Health Communications Inc.
Desteian, J. (1989) *Coming Together — Coming Apart*, Boston: Sigo Press.
Janov, A. (1990) *The New Primal Scream*, London: Abacus.
Miller, A. (1991) *Breaking Down the Wall of Silence to Join the Waiting Child*, London: Virago.
Stettbacher, J.K. (1991) *Making Sense of Suffering*, London: Dutton Press.

Discussion issues

1 Do modern children necessarily learn ways of reducing conflict with parents in their early years? How does your experience illustrate this?

2 What do you regard as the strengths of analysing childhood patterns and learning, in working to help couples address the confusions of their intimate realtionships?

3 To what do you attribute the increase in the number of young adults in the UK choosing to live alone?

4 What is your response to the views expressed in this chapter?

Introduction to Practical Approaches

Practical Approaches is an innovative series of chapters initiated by Gladeana McMahon, news editor of the BAC Journal, in August 1994, continuing until 1999, and currently published as Managing Your Practice.

The contributors share their wide experience by offering guidance on practical aspects of counselling itself and activities supporting the work of counsellors, such as note-taking or writing letters of referral, which training courses do not necessarily address.

41

Reflective Practice

Gladeana McMahon

Counsellors have the choice of focusing on a variety of work and personal aspects when undertaking reflective practice and self-evaluation: reflecting on work with clients directly after a session has ended, on practitioner strengths/weaknesses, on personal motives for engaging in counselling (McMahon 1994) on gender and sexuality (Davies and Neal 1996) and on personal counselling philosophy and theoretical approaches. The relevance of research and how it can inform practice and skill efficacy (Legg 1998) also plays a part. Equally, reflective practice allows consideration of the social, cultural and organizational context which may affect the therapeutic relationship (Lago and Thompson 1996; Megranahan 1997). The process of reflective practice provides scope for a considered and systematic analysis of the work of counselling in the round.

Personal and professional experience combine with reflective practice to provide useful information to aid the therapeutic process. While some counsellors accept that a proportion of clients fail to return after the first session without questioning the motives behind such behaviour, others, using reflective practice, explore the meaning non-attendance might have and what contribution their personal style or choice of therapeutic interventions may have made (McMahon 1998). Another group argue that clients are unlikely to discontinue counselling unless outside factors such as lack of money and child-care arrangements or internal factors such as lack of motivation or despair intervene, believing that if the counselling offered meets the client's needs and the relationship with the counsellor is seen as helpful then clients are automatically more likely to return. Examining the possible reasons for client non-attendance in a systematically reflective way may lead to changes in procedures or approach which enable clients to engage more fully in the therapeutic process.

Continued professional development, counselling reviews, supervision and client feedback benefit particularly from the deeper understanding arising from use of reflective practice.

Continued professional development

The willingness of counsellors to engage in reflective practice is influenced by training, personal awareness, individual motivation and personality (Dale 1997). The fact that continued professional development (CPD) is now recommended by the major professional bodies within the helping professions can be seen as another way of encouraging counsellors to enhance their reflective ability in order to deepen therapeutic understanding. Clearly, counsellors' own personal therapy may also be a source of greater understanding

This chapter was first published in *Counselling*, Journal of the British Association for Counselling, vol. 10, no. 2, pp. 105–6 (1999) *and* vol. 10, no. 3, pp. 193–4 (1999).

of those personal motivating factors which affect work with clients (Padesky 1996). Indeed for some, professional and personal development cannot be seen as separate.

Counselling reviews

A professional development log (as used in counsellor training) encourages counsellors to focus on individual practitioner experiences, if it is continued as a reflective tool following basic training (Wilkins 1997). Some counsellors use audio- or video-tape recordings of sessions adapting the principles of Interpersonal Process Recall (IPR) (Dryden and Thorne 1991), valuing the fact that they can stop the tape at significant points to process the thoughts and feelings of that moment. Counsellors undertaking regular therapeutic reviews with clients to monitor progress and therapeutic effectiveness, see a double advantage: reviews can provide clients with a greater say in designing and amending their own counselling programme (Sutton 1997), while for the counsellor they offer an opportunity to consider the positive and negative aspect of their approach.

It is usual for cognitive-behavioural counsellors to undertake mini-reviews at the end of each session to encourage the client to take greater control over therapeutic interaction (Lazarus 1989; Padesky and Greenberger 1995; Scott et al. 1995). Counsellors from certain therapeutic persuasions regard reviews as damaging to the essence of the therapeutic relationship and therefore choose to avoid such a process, some seeing this approach as being more about 'performance than quality of being' (House 1998). A review can be verbal, with questions posed to the client about progress to date (McMahon 1998), though other counsellors prefer to deal with reviews in a more formal way by asking the client to evaluate progress in writing. This approach is based on an adaptation of the termination letter used in cognitive analytic therapy (CAT) in which client and counsellor write a goodbye letter to each other. Evaluating the scores of questionnaires and their associated meaning offers material for counsellor reflection – completing the Beck Depresssion Inventory at frequent intervals may help client and counsellor monitor progress (Hanmen 1997).

Counselling supervision

Counselling supervision is an important part of reflective practice, and aside from it being a professional requirement it is an invaluable source of support, learning and understanding (Carroll 1996). Good preparation ensures that counsellors make effective use of counselling supervision so that their exploration of work with clients enables them to identify the strengths, weaknesses and impact of their practice while considering personal blocks and skills deficits (Feltham and Dryden 1994). Supervisors help supervisees to reflect upon their work in various ways: using tapes of client work to consider the choice and use of skills, adaptations of the IPR method, and encouraging the supervisee to 'role-play' difficult client situations.

In supervision counsellors are sometimes encouraged to write a case study as part of their commitment to their CPD (Parker 1995), in the belief that a case study offers an opportunity to consider their work in a more formal way, and may highlight those aspects the counsellor finds difficult, or the impact their own internal world may be having on their work. Case-series studies may also help in supervision through their focus on

---

CLIENT FEEDBACK FORM

Your views are very important as they help me monitor the quality of the counselling work I offer. Any information you provide will be treated as confidential

Using a scale of 0–8 (0 = very poor and 8 = excellent) please rate the following.

Pre-Counselling Contact

1 How well was your initial enquiry dealt with?
   (e.g. efficiency, helpfulness etc.)
   0 1 2 3 4 5 6 7 8

2 How useful did you find the Client Information Sheet sent to you?
   0 1 2 3 4 5 6 7 8

The Counselling Environment

1 How would you rate the counselling facilities offered?
   (e.g. counselling room, parking facilities etc.)
   0 1 2 3 4 5 6 7 8

The Counsellor

1 How helpful did you find the counsellor?
   (e.g. understanding, approachable, skilled etc.)
   0 1 2 3 4 5 6 7 8

2 What did you like most about your counsellor?

3 Was there anything your counsellor could have done differently that would have been helpful?

Your Progress

Using the rating scale 0–8 (0 = 'feeling awful', 8 = 'feeling good') please rate the following.

1 At the beginning of counselling how would you have rated the way you felt about your problem(s)
   0 1 2 3 4 5 6 7 8

2 Following your counselling how would you rate the way that you feel?
   0 1 2 3 4 5 6 7 8

3 What did you find most helpful about the counselling offered to you?

Any Other Comments

Thank you for taking the time to complete this questionnaire
Please return it in the s.a.e. provided to: Amy Helper, 1 Anywhere Street, Somewhere, YZ1 23
Tel: 01112 234567

Figure 41.1   *Client feedback form*
Source: *Adapted from Bayne et al. 1999.*

clients with similar clinical features, perhaps enabling a counsellor to explore their approach to working with clients who share the characteristics of anxiety, depression or anger. (See Chapter 44.)

Client feedback

Client feedback or satisfaction questionnaires are a way of collecting information to monitor effectiveness (McMahon 1998). Researchers place great emphasis on the need to design questionnaires which are both valid and reliable so that the questionnaire measures what it claims to measure (validity) and consistent results would be obtained if the questionnaire was administered to a range of individuals in similar circumstances (reliability) (Sanders and Liptrot 1993). Although it would be helpful if all client feedback forms were valid and reliable, a lack of understanding or ability to design such questionnaires need not necessarily be deemed a problem. Figure 41.1 provides an example of a client feedback form, which, although not tested for reliability or validity, nevertheless provides the counsellor with an opportunity to collect information in a systematic way. Feedback forms such as those in Figure 41.1 need to be treated with care, for it would be misleading if a counsellor believed the information gathered from such a questionnaire could do more than 'highlight' areas for consideration. Perhaps the most useful way to see such questionnaires is to consider them as an informal rather than scientific method of collecting information. Satisfaction ratings have their limitations – clients may have such low expectations of counselling itself that a high rating may not reflect the real benefits of the counselling received, or, if a client likes his or her counsellor, it may prove difficult to provide a negative rating of the counselling.

Reflective practice has many possible avenues, from those that are based on monitoring the counsellor's internal world to the use of external evaluation and feedback. Whatever the methods used, reflective processes can help counsellors to become better practitioners, clients to receive better counselling and the counselling world to learn more about the needs of individuals.

References

Bayne, R., Horton, I., Merry, T., Noyes, E. and McMahon, G. (1999) *The Counsellor's Handbook – A Practical A-Z Guide to Professional and Clinical Practice* (2nd edn), London: Chapman & Hall.

Carroll, M. (1996) *Counselling Supervision – Theory, Skills and Practice*, London: Cassell.

Dale, F. (1997) 'Stress and the personality of the psychotherapist', in V. Varma (ed.), *Stress in Psychotherapists*, London: Routledge.

Davies, D. and Neal, C. (1996) *Pink Therapy*, Milton Keynes: Open University Press.

Dryden, W. and Thorne, B. (1991) *Training and Supervision for Counselling in Action*, London: Sage.

Feltham, C. and Dryden, W. (1994) *Developing Counsellor Supervision*, London: Sage.

Hanmen, C. (1997) 'Depression', in C.R. Brewin (ed.), *Clinical Psychology: A Modular Course*, Hove: Psychology Press Ltd.

House, R. (1998) 'Counselling: performance or quality of being', *Counselling*, 9 (3): 175, Rugby: British Association for Counselling.

Lago, C. and Thompson, J. (1996) *Race, Culture and Counselling*, Buckingham: Open University Press.

Lazarus, A.A. (1989) *The Practice of Multimodal Therapy*, Baltimore, MD: Johns Hopkins University Press.

Legg, C. (1998) *Psychology and the Reflective Counsellor*, Leicester: BPS Books.

McMahon, G. (1994) *Setting up Your Own Private Practice*, Cambridge: National Extension College.

McMahon, G. (1998) 'News Editorial', in *Counselling*, 9 (2): 89, Rugby: British Association for Counselling.

Megranahan, M. (1997) 'Counselling in the workplace', in S. Palmer and G. McMahon (eds), *Handbook of Counselling*, London: Routledge.

Padesky, C.A. (1996) 'Training and supervision', in P. Salkovskis (ed.) *Frontiers of Cognitive Therapy*, London: Guilford Press.

Padesky, C.A. and Greenberger, D. (1995) *Clinician's Guide to Mind over Mood*, New York: Guilford Press.

Parker, M. (1995) 'Practical approaches: case study writing', in *Counselling*, 6 (1): 19–21, Rugby: British Association for Counselling. (See Chapter 44.)

Sanders, P. and Liptrot, D. (1993) *Research Methods and Data Collection for Counsellors*, An Incomplete Guide Series, Manchester: PCCS Books.

Scott, M.J., Stradling, S.G. and Dryden, W. (1995) *Developing Cognitive-Behavioural Counselling*, London: Sage.

Sutton, C. (1997) 'Reviewing and evaluating therapeutic progress', in S. Palmer and G. McMahon (eds), *Client Assessment*, London: Sage.

Wilkins, P. (1997) *Personal and Professional Development for Counsellors*, London: Sage.

Discussion issues

1 What might be the benefits to clients and to counsellors of engaging in reflective practice?

2 Why might it be helpful to engage in more than one area of reflective practice?

3 How important is it to use reflective practice methods in counselling supervision?

4 What might be the benefits of asking clients to complete a formal feedback form at the end of counselling?

42

Assessment and Contracting

Gabrielle Syme

The initial meeting between counsellor and client is critical for both parties as it will be the first time they meet face-to-face. The very first contact will have been by telephone or letter and will have evoked thoughts, feelings and fantasies for both parties. This is one of the reasons why a lot of thought needs to be given to any pre-counselling information sent out and the first responses whether by telephone or letter.

What happens in these very first contacts will govern both the decision to come to the initial session and what the client may expect from their first face-to-face meeting. Potential clients need to be clear before they arrive about whether there is a charge for this first session or not. Practice on this issue varies within the independent sector.

Safety

Both counsellor and client take a considerable risk the first time they meet. Either party could harass or attack the other physically and/or sexually. To safeguard both parties the first session should never be held without at least a reliable personal alarm at hand in case of an emergency, and having someone else in the building. Some counsellors try to protect themselves by never seeing a client unless they have been referred by another professional, a counselling colleague or a voluntary agency. In fact this is no protection against sudden and uncharacteristic violence and counsellors still need to take every precaution to protect themselves.

Timing

One function of the initial or assessment session is for potential clients to meet the counsellor and to discover whether they are comfortable with each other. They may also need to explore what counselling is and whether it is likely to be the most appropriate form of help.

In most regions of the British Isles, there are likely to be a number of counsellors and a range of approaches available. Therefore clients may well have several assessment sessions with different counsellors before they are able to make comparisons and decide with whom they wish to work. For this reason the timing of the assessment session is critical. This can result in a considerable dilemma for established counsellors with full case-loads. Do they have a waiting list or close their books and suggest the clients look elsewhere? In addition, if they do the former, should the assessment session be shortly after the initial inquiry or only once there is a vacancy?

This chapter was first published in *Counselling*, Journal of the British Association for Counselling, vol. 6, no. 2, pp. 107–8 (1995).

Holding the assessment session close to the initial inquiry allows clients to shop around near the time when their motivation to seek counselling is uppermost. This avoids clients waiting several months only to find that they did not want to work with the counsellor, or to discover that the counsellor felt unable to work with them. There may be a long wait – anything up to six months for some counsellors and this may cause difficulties if the client and counsellor wish to work together. This is an instance where it is good practice to discuss with potential clients the pros and cons of the decision they have to make, to enable them to make as informed a decision as possible. In my own practice the majority opt for an assessment close to the initial inquiry.

For employed counsellors and those working for employee assistance programmes or for voluntary agencies the question of timing may be quite different. There may be a policy that stipulates a maximum waiting time before the initial session and a maximum number of sessions. In this case the problem may be how to continue working with someone having seen them once and being unable to offer them regular sessions immediately; or how to work within a very limited number of sessions when there is evidence of a need for long-term work. Again an open discussion with clients about the situation and the ways they can get support is good practice.

Aims for the counsellor

The broad aim of the initial session is to discover what a potential client is looking for and to match this with what counselling with you will offer. Counsellors vary enormously in what information they require in such a session; in how structured the session is; and in whether they make a diagnosis based on the perceived psychopathology or not. Some counsellors would not choose to use the word 'assessment'. None the less by the end of the session, or sometimes sessions, both client and counsellor need information to decide whether to commit themselves to a counselling relationship for a period of time or not.

The assessment has a similar structure regardless of the context of the setting. First, counsellors have to discover what has led the client to look for counselling now and why. This is often discovered by hearing the client's life-story, asking them to focus particularly on significant life events. This may prove to be a very unusual experience for potential clients. It may help if they are encouraged to start at their birth and then present their life chronologically. Information will then be accumulated on early life events, which might indicate the need for long-term rather than short-term work. Examples are: absence of a parent through illness or death; a period of hospitalization without parental accompaniment particularly under the age of two; a parent having suffered a serious disability or illness, or bouts of mental illness. The client's life-story may give information on whether there have been long periods of psychiatric treatment, which may prove a contra-indication to counselling. If there is no mention of psychiatric treatment in the life-story it is essential to ask directly about this – in particular whether the client is currently being treated by a GP or a psychiatrist.

If counselling seems appropriate, some counsellors think it is important to inform any medical practitioners of the intention to work with someone who is also their patient and currently being treated, and check whether they have reasons to believe it would be unhelpful or ill-advised. Clients need to give permission for a counsellor to inform medical practitioners. They also need to know what will happen if the medical practitioner considers counselling ill-advised. In contacting a medical practitioner the counsellor must be clear why this is being done and whether the advice will be followed.

Even if there has been no history of mental illness it is important to establish the client's emotional strength (ego strength). Supportive work will be more appropriate than in-depth work if someone lacks emotional strength. This is often deduced from such information as an individual's ability to make friends in school and at work; the school and work history; whether there is a tendency to idealize and vilify; the capacity to observe him/herself.

The assessment session is also a trial counselling session, because it is essential to see if a potential client can work with you. This is often done by offering a psychological explanation and seeing how it is understood and what connections are made. The inability to work 'psychologically' is not necessarily a contra-indication, but it would indicate that you would be introducing the client to a completely different way of thinking. My experience is that this is a very exciting voyage of discovery for people and therefore well worth offering.

No assessment session is complete without establishing what outcome is being sought by the client and whether counselling and in particular your theoretical approach will meet this aim. There is some evidence that specific approaches are more effective with certain problems (for example, cognitive-behavioural therapy is effective with panic attacks – Roth and Fonagy 1996; and psychodynamic psychotherapy for anxious, neurotic patients – Siassi 1979). Clearly it is unethical practice if clients are not made aware of the suitability of a particular approach for their problems. A counsellor needs to be just as willing to help someone decide that counselling is not for them as in encouraging them to proceed.

Finally, counsellors have to assess whether they have the appropriate training and experience to work with a particular client. With all this information the counsellor is then ready to decide with the client whether working together is a possibility or not.

The decision is of course a joint one, so what does a client need to know?

Aims for the client(s)

First and foremost clients need to be taken seriously and helped to discover whether counselling is going to be the most suitable approach to their problems. Second, they need to find out whether they are comfortable with the counsellor and could work with and trust him/her with some of their most intimate thoughts and feelings. They will also want to know how long the counselling work will take and how frequent the sessions will be. There is often a worry about how they will know when it is time to stop. It is often helpful to elicit this fear and give guidance about endings.

It is in the best interest of clients to work with a suitably qualified counsellor who works professionally and ethically and belongs to an association with a Code of Ethics and Practice and a complaints procedure. It is rare for clients to ask such questions and therefore important for counsellors to offer this information and also to discuss the issue of confidentiality and whether notes are kept and a client's right to access these. If the counsellor is in the independent sector clients need to be clear about the fees charged and what happens if sessions are missed or cancelled.

At this point both parties are in the position to decide whether they wish to work together. If the counsellor thinks s/he is unable to work with someone, or thinks that counselling is inappropriate, it is important to be honest and to respect the individual sufficiently to explain the reasons why. If clients are shopping around they will not want to make a decision there and then, and it is important to encourage clients to take time over their decision.

Once the decision has been made it is important to make a contract with the client.

Contracting

Making a clear contract with a client 'enhances and shows respect for the client's autonomy' (BAC, *Code of Ethics and Practice for Counsellors*, 1993). It also offers the client containment by giving the relationship clear boundaries. At present the majority of contracts are informal and verbal.

Where the counsellor is given money by the client for a service, the contract is legally binding, however made. This is one reason why it is sensible to make a written contract or at least give clients a leaflet containing all the relevant information (Syme 1994). Another reason is that it is all too easy to omit a piece of information and thus retain power over clients by knowing something that they do not.

If a client refuses to pay for a missed session and insists that this was not agreed upon with the counsellor then both can refer back to the copy of the contract leaflet. If the counsellor was doubtful about the original verbal agreement then it would not be safe to make an interpretation, and the assumption that the client is deliberately forgetting could and would be punitive.

The contract must contain the following information:

a) The frequency and length of sessions;
b) A minimum number or in some cases a maximum number of sessions;
c) A guarantee that the counsellor will be present for the whole of an appointment whether or not the client appears;
d) Use of telephones and letters;
e) Financial arrangements for sessions, telephone and letters (if relevant);
f) Arrangements for the notification of change in fees (if relevant);
g) Arrangements about cancellation for both parties, including the financial arrangements if a client misses a session (if relevant);
h) Arrangements if a client arrives late (e.g. session ends at agreed time regardless of lateness);
i) The boundaries of confidentiality, with special mention (where necessary) of arrangements with the client's GP, psychiatrist or employer;
j) Information on whether notes are made or not and confirmation that if they are made, they are securely stored and separated from any identifiable names;
k) Information on Code of Ethics and Practice and existence of a complaints procedure. (Syme 1994)

In addition counsellors may want to add information about specific situations that could arise and these will have already been discussed in the assessment session. Examples are: the use of audio- or video-tapes to record a session; termination by the counsellor if the client harms the counsellor or the counsellor's belongings (Kopp 1977); a request that the client should not terminate suddenly but always negotiate an ending; the counsellor's approach if s/he has to change the time of a session owing to changed circumstances.

It is unreasonable to expect a client to be clear about the content of such a lengthy agreement. It is therefore wise to let clients read it at their leisure and raise any points they are unclear about at the next session. When it has been agreed (and possibly signed) the client can then keep a copy.

Security and containment are created by a well-structured assessment session and contract, which provides a firm base for future counselling work.

References

BAC (1993) *Code of Ethics and Practice for Counsellors*, Rugby: British Association for Counselling.

Kopp, S. (1977) *Back to One*, Palo Alto, CA: Science and Behaviour Books Inc.

Roth, A. and Fonagy, P. (1996) *What Works for Whom?*, New York: Guilford Press.

Siassi, I. (1979) 'A Comparison of open-ended psychoanalytically-orientated psychotherapy and other therapies', *Journal of Clinical Psychiatry*, 40: 25–32.

Syme, G. (1994) *Counselling in Independent Practice*, Buckingham: Open University Press.

Discussion issues

1 What are some of the risks taken by clients and counsellors the first time they meet?

2 How can counsellors facilitate assessment so that it both establishes the outcome a client seeks and clarifies whether counselling, and that particular counsellor's approach, will meet this aim?

3 For whose benefit might counsellors tell medical practitioners of their intention to work with someone who is in current treatment as their patient, and to check whether the doctor thinks counselling would be helpful or ill-advised?

4 The majority of counselling contracts are informal and verbal rather than formal and written. Which do you favour and why?

43

Referral Letters

Sue Warren-Holland

Referral letters are a professional tool. They are the means by which one professional communicates confidential information, about a third person, to another. Apart from being a tool, referral letters are also a professional courtesy. But – beware! – referral letters can say as much about the referer as the referee. So it helps to get it right.

Counsellors find themselves called on to write letters on behalf of clients in a variety of situations. These may range from supportive letters to Housing Departments for transfers; to lawyers in cases of marital breakdown or accident claims; or to GPs where a client's mental or physical health is causing concern.

On occasion a counsellor may find him/herself dealing with a client whose presenting problem masks a deeper trauma of, for instance, sexual abuse or rape. If the counsellor feels that this area is beyond his/her competence, it is important that a referral is made to a specialist agency. The referral letter in these cases should be much fuller than the specimen provided, covering all the work that the client and counsellor have done together thus far.

Far from feeling inadequate in these situations, it is a mark of professionalism that counsellors recognize the limits of their competence. Fools rushing in where angels fear to tread cause all sorts of problems.

Listed below are a few simple rules to follow when writing referral letters:

1 *Include all relevant information.*
   What would you want to know about a referred client?

   - Name, address and date of birth. (See specimen letter for layout.)
   - What precipitated the client to seek counselling?
   - If referred by another agency, was the client willing?
   - How does the client define his/her problem?
   - How often has counsellor seen the client?
   - What is the reason for referral to another professional?
   - Is the counsellor's view of the problem the same as the client's?
   - If appropriate, what areas of work have been covered, and what methods used?

2 *Tailor the letter to the requirements of the agency.*
   If, for instance, a referral letter is required to the Housing Department you do not need to provide the whole of your client's history. Simply stating that you have seen your client for ten weeks, and that in your view, your client's situation would benefit from better housing is sufficient.

This chapter was first published in *Counselling*, Journal of the British Association for Counselling, vol. 9, no. 2, pp. 96–7 (1998).

Ms A. Listener
Landsend View
London Z2 0PG

20 January 1997

Dr A. Other
The Surgery
Freedom Road
London Z2 1AM

Dear Dr Other,

Re: Ms Irene Forsaken D.O.B.: 2.9.1954
    1 Blinkered View Road, London Z1 3AM

This 43-year-old woman was referred to me for counselling by the Housing Department of Onefield Local Authority on 20 November 1996.

Ms Forsaken's job entailed visits to tenants who are in persistent rent arrears. On 20 October, during the course of her duties, she was attacked by a tenant, sustaining three cracked ribs and a broken left arm. Her injuries were treated in the casualty department of Onefield Hospital, and she returned to work a fortnight later.

Over the next two weeks her supervisor noted that Ms Forsaken was exceedingly quiet and frequently in tears. The quality of her work deteriorated, and she was incapable of resuming her duty visits to tenants, exhibiting behaviour which her supervisor described as 'frozen terror'.

Ms Forsaken was willing to have counselling and I have now seen her for a total of six sessions.

She presented as a well-built woman but I had the impression that all her energies were directed towards maintaining control over herself. Her speech was slow with long pauses between words, and her posture hunched. Eye contact has been minimal. These attributes have remained unchanged.

During her initial assessment she informed me that she used to enjoy a full social life with her partner, with whom she has had a stable relationship of five years' duration. She was in her second year of a part-time sociology degree at Dimlight University, and the couple were enthusiastic amateur mountain climbers.

There has been little change in her demeanour over the past six weeks. Ms Forsaken complains of difficulty in sleeping, waking regularly at 2 a.m. with nightmares. She appears to have lost her appetite, and has little interest or energy in undertaking her normal routine at work or at home. She has abandoned her degree course, is now afraid to go out, and, when pressed, admits to crying a great deal.

Although she is reticent about the support she receives from her partner, from some of her comments I suspect her current state may be a cause of friction between them, for which she blames herself. Indeed, Ms Forsaken considers she is solely to blame for the attack on her, although her supervisor is clear that she followed procedure and is the victim of the tenant's angst.

From the information she has given me, there does not appear to be a history of any psychiatric illness in her family, and Ms Forsaken herself says she is suffering from 'nerves'.

However, in view of her demonstrated flatness of emotional response, together with the early morning waking, loss of appetite and diminished interest in life, I am concerned about her mental state. I have therefore asked Ms Forsaken to make an urgent appointment to see you.

She is aware of my referral to you, and I would value communication with you. I will, of course, continue to see Ms Forsaken until she is able to face and deal with her emotional response to the trauma she suffered.

Thank you for your help with this lady.

Yours sincerely,

Figure 43.1 *Specimen referral letter*

3 *Differentiate between fact and opinion.*
   Generally a referral letter should contain information based on the client's history. The concluding paragraph(s) can contain the counsellor's opinion which is clearly

stated as such: for example, 'Having worked with Mr Blank for six months I consider …', or 'In my opinion he …'.

4 *Use simple words. Keep sentences and paragraphs short.*

5 *Don't teach your grandmother to suck eggs.*

Don't tell the doctor or lawyer how to do their jobs unless you are qualified to do so. It is not helpful to tell the doctor that your client is manic depressive and in urgent need of Lithium. You may be right, but this is more likely to put the doctor's back up, and do your client a disservice.

It is better to describe the behaviour you have noticed and express concern about your client's physical or mental state. For instance, sentences such as 'Mr Blank appears to sweat excessively, even in winter, and drinks up to ten glasses of water during a session', or, 'Ms Blank has, over the past six months, been very lethargic and morose. This has been interspersed with periods when she speaks very fast, is very excitable, and unable to sit still …', give the recipient a better picture and are an aid to diagnosis.

If you do feel a label is necessary, a sentence such as 'It would appear that Mr Blank has many of the symptoms associated with Post-Traumatic Stress Disorder, these being …', gives your opinion clearly, without causing offence. However, it is very important to be careful of your use of words. Other disciplines might view words like 'depression' or 'Post-Traumatic Stress Disorder' in a very different way from you or your client.

For the sake of the client, counsellors need to be aware that labels have power. Labels can go on affecting an individual, in ways which cannot always be foreseen, long after the original incident has been integrated into a client's life.

6 *Confidentiality.*

Ensure that you have your client's permission to write the referral letter. Good practice dictates that if appropriate, you and your client discuss the form the referral letter will take, and you can provide the client with a copy for his/her records.

Mark the envelope 'Confidential', and remember to keep a copy in the client's file.

Discussion issues

1 Why might some counsellors not consider it part of their role to write letters on behalf of clients to Housing Departments, solicitors or GPs? Would you?

2 Labels have power and can go on affecting a person long after the original incident has been integrated into their lives. What do you think?

3 How can counsellors build a list of responsible practitioners to whom referrals may be made with confidence?

4 It is a mark of professionalism that counsellors are willing to refer clients whose difficulties are beyond the limits of their competence. What are some of the personal dilemmas which may arise for client and counsellor?

44

Case-Study Writing

Mary Parker

Throughout our counselling careers we are asked to write case studies for varying purposes, the most common of which is an examination of our professional competence, for training or accreditation purposes. There are even people who write case studies for their own pleasure! As a supervisor I ask supervisees to write one case study a year as part of their professional development and find that many counsellors and counselling students find writing a case study a challenging task.

The principal purpose of writing a case study is to demonstrate how we integrate theoretical understanding into our counselling practice. We aim to convince assessors that we know what we are doing in our counselling work. If a case study is to be effective it needs to reflect the application of core theory and philosophy of counselling, although some assessors require that the 'theory and philosophy of counselling' is submitted as a separate piece of writing.

It is a good idea to begin with this particular task, since once you have done it you can move on to evaluate how your counselling method, interventions and client responses, match with your theory and philosophy.

One way to get started is to think of your 'philosophy and method of counselling' as your personal 'theory of change'. Useful questions to ask are: What is my idea of a healthy person? What causes a person to become distressed/disturbed? Why have I chosen a particular theoretical model above others? How does my model help people to change and what is my part in the process?

By completing your 'theory and philosophy of counselling' you have a foundation from which to understand the counselling process. You are then ready to move on to thinking about writing a case study.

It may help to divide the task into three main stages:

- preparation
- writing up the case study
- checking, correcting and improving your work

Preparation

Good preparation is the key to success. First, you need to establish exactly what is required of you. You do this by:

This chapter was first published in *Counselling*, Journal of the British Association for Counselling, vol. 6, no. 1, pp. 19–21 (1995).

- Studying the criteria and deciding how best to meet the requirements;
- identifying a suitable case;
- planning and structuring your work.

Studying the criteria

Most courses or professional organizations have criteria by which they evaluate case studies. In the absence of these, establish with your tutor or supervisor what is required. Criteria need to be studied carefully, as they provide the key to assessors' thinking.

In summary, for BAC accreditation, candidates are required:

to demonstrate congruence and consistency between current counselling practice, philosophy and theoretical orientation. Case Study 1 should give an account of the counselling process and Case Study 2 should illustrate the way supervision is integrated in the counsellor's practice. BAC (1992)

A fuller description of criteria is available in BAC (2000).

Most criteria specify a word limit which you need to observe. A case study is normally between 1,000 and 3,000 words – not of thesis length. Remember, the smaller the word limit the less space you have to convince assessors of your competence. This means you need to consider carefully what to include and what to leave out. There is no room for padding or repetition, and therefore your material needs to address the *specified* criteria.

Identifying a suitable case

Choose a case which will enable you to demonstrate clearly what is required. It may not always be useful to choose your most successful case. For instance, if you are asked to illustrate your use of supervision, a client whom you have found difficult may demonstrate your work better than one where very little input from your supervisor was needed.

In a short study it is sometimes easier to choose someone whom you have only seen for 8–10 sessions. You will not then be overwhelmed with material. Obviously in time-limited work you have to do this. Include how you think the counselling will evolve and state your prognosis, or comment on work still to be done. Assessors are not looking for 'dramatic cures' or exceptional cases. They want to see your normal ongoing work. It is advisable to discuss the case study with your supervisor before you begin, since they will have been through the same process and can offer emotional as well as practical support.

Planning and structuring your work

Decide on a structure before you start writing. Stick to the structure you have been given unless you have good reason not to.

A *covering sheet* comprising a single side of A4 giving outline information about the client in list form may prove useful as this can quickly guide the reader into the study. Useful data to include:

- client's first name or pseudonym (never give the full name as this would break confidentiality)
- gender, age, nationality/ethnic origin

- number of sessions to date
- presenting problem
- related difficulties such as health, family, or environmental problems
- client's stated goals
- details regarding the counselling contract
- whether counselling is continuing or completed
- how often the client has been 'taken to' supervision.

I usually divide the case study into four sections:

I First Interview
II History and Development of Problem
III Assessment
IV Counselling Process

Section I: First Interview

This may include:

- physical characteristics
- speech
- dress
- body language
- capacity for insight
- motivation for change
- environmental factors/work situation
- present relationships (family of origin, immediate family/partner, friends, work colleagues)
- presenting problem
- present conflicts
- other information that you consider relevant to the study

(If you decide you are not going to attach a covering sheet to your case study you will need to include all that information in this section instead).

Example

Jane was 27. She was slim and her shoulders were bent forward. She had a flat, whining voice. She was dressed in a shirt and blouse which looked rather like school uniform. Jane slumped in the chair. She looked at me with longing, tearful eyes. She had some insight into her problem and seemed determined to change her life. She lived in a shared house but kept to herself. She worked as a librarian and had one friend at work, Susan, who Jane described as 'domineering'. Jane complained of being lonely and depressed. She does not like herself. Her goals were to find a man to love her, to be a good person, and not be depressed. I felt warm to her as she exposed the rawness of her pain. We agreed to meet for six sessions and to review our progress at the sixth session.

Section II: History and Development of Problem

This could include, where relevant:

- family history
- previous counselling history
- psychiatric history

- hospitalizations
- current medications
- substance misuse (drugs, illegal/prescribed, alcohol, nicotine)
- early developmental influences
- key relationships
- significant losses, life changes

Example

Jane described her father as distant and her mother as critical. She is an only child. She went into hospital several times between the ages of 2 and 7 with asthma. She did well at school but was often 'lonely'. Her parents divorced when Jane was 11. She had no psychiatric history. Jane refused anti-depressants for the depression which followed the break-up of a 6-month relationship with her boyfriend. She complained of headaches and was waking early.

Section III: Assessment

There are two sets of points to consider. The first relates to the client and needs to be discussed briefly as the points are relevant to the case study. The second set of points relates to your assessment and the need to show understanding of the process of change in terms of your theory and philosophy of counselling.

Set One
- how the client views their world
- the client's understanding of their problem
- how long the client has had the problem and when it was thought to have arisen
- existential fears
- how the client relates to you
- why the client is seeking help now

Set Two
- how you understand the problem
- how you relate to the client
- your hypothesis of how the problem was acquired
- ideas about how the problem is being maintained
- your hypothesis of counselling process, what the client needs and how you plan to help (this is related to theory and counsellor's goals)

Example

Although Jane thinks her depression started after the break-up with her boyfriend, I think it started in childhood. Her parents' cold and critical attitude and her early hospital separations made it difficult to form emotional bonds. The result is her problem in making intimate relationships. I think Jane unconsciously saw an opportunity with her boyfriend, to get the love that she did not get from her parents. When this symbiotic relationship broke down, Jane was again left isolated and lonely. Her low self-esteem plummeted and confirmed that she was unworthy of love. It also confirmed her personal constructs: 'I must be bad'; 'if I were a better person people would like me'; and 'it's my fault'.

I thought her construct 'it's my fault', stemmed from her parents' divorce. I guessed Jane may have blamed herself for it and thought she had done something wrong. Another of Jane's constructs is 'I must not be angry.' She seems to feel she cannot afford to be angry as she has to defer to others to get approval. This, plus the construct 'if I find the right man I will be happy' keeps her identity weak. She has much unresolved grief. Jane is unable to withstand rejection so cannot take risks in relating to others. This keeps her stuck and unable to move towards her potential.

It is my aim to provide a 'corrective emotional experience' within the counselling relationship so that she can get some of her emotional needs met. A warm and accepting relationship will help her to improve her self-esteem. Hopefully she will then be able to bear the grief of not being loved in childhood and of not having her love received. I would also hope that her fears of separation can be faced and transcended so that she can feel secure in 'aloneness' and enjoy a good ending.

Section IV: Counselling Process

This part carries the main thrust of the case study. It is your space to show your knowledge, skills and sensitivity. A common error is to use most of the word space to write about the client or to record a 'chronicle of events'. This does not amount to a case study.

The skill is to conceptualize clearly and reflect upon the counselling process. The case study needs to show how the counselling process fits into your theory and philosophy by showing *your* attitude, feelings, thoughts, skills, interventions and *your* relationship and responses to the client. It should illustrate self-reflection, give a flavour of the dialogue, and show your main techniques. The reader needs to get a genuine feel for, and sense of, you with your client. Using a personal style may help.

Items for consideration in this section include:

- how you and your client moved through the counselling stages your counselling model identifies – e.g. Egan
- how the counselling relationship evolved and developed – be realistic, not idealistic
- two or three pivotal events where change occurred – points where your use of a technique, intervention, or sudden insight (by self or client) moved the process to a different level
- your theoretical orientation and what you need to be demonstrating, e.g. using a psychodynamic approach would mean considering transference and countertransference
- staying totally congruent with your theoretical orientation
- any mistakes you made, what you learnt, and what you could have done differently
- changes in the person, their attitude to you and others by describing 'in session' and 'out of session' changes
- any alterations in the symptoms of the presenting problem
- if counselling has ended, your reflections about this including your feelings and insights and those of your client

Example (part case study)

As Jane was so emotionally deprived of affection I expected she would quickly form a working alliance. I supported her with empathic understanding whilst she allowed her pain to unfold. She cried throughout several sessions as she remembered the loneliness of her childhood. I felt warm towards her. I could sense the 'little girl' as she began to talk about her life and her needs. Her dependency soon became obvious as she began to ask my advice. I did not confront her strongly about this at first, as her sense of identity was fragile. Instead I gently helped her to find her own solutions thereby reinforcing her capabilities and her 'sense of self'.

During the fifth session Jane said that the senior librarian had taken her aside and told her she was getting divorced. Jane was upset because she had been unable to respond to the woman's distress. I asked what she was feeling and she did not know. I imagined that this was a restimulation both of her parents' divorce, and of the recent break with her boyfriend. I said 'What does this remind you of?' This intervention triggered a flood of deep sobbing as Jane remembered how frightened and upset she had been by the divorce and how she had felt unable to express this because she needed to protect her mother.

In the following session, Jane remained silent for several minutes. She said she could not speak. I asked what would happen if she did. She said 'I would kill someone.' I asked 'Which someone?' to which Jane replied 'My mother because she drove my father away with her criticism.' I wondered if she was strong enough to tolerate the rage inside her. Because of the symbiotic relationship with her mother, Jane needed to preserve mother as good. Therefore Jane introjected her bad feelings – 'I am bad.'

In the following sessions we unpacked Jane's feelings and personal constructs. We went through some of the traditional stages of grief. First her shock – disbelief, then anger and guilt, and sadness about her childhood and the ending of her recent relationship. As we proceed I anticipate that Jane will need to mourn her lost childhood and find a new identity.

Writing up the case study

Give yourself sufficient good quality time and be prepared to write and rewrite your case study before it is finally ready for submission. If your writing skills are rusty it is worth buying a book on writing such as *Vigorous, Lucid, Brief* by Peter Fryer.

Keep to a simple style. Use short sentences. Aim to be clear, not clever. In short studies academic quotations are best used sparingly, if at all. In case-study writing the reader wants to know *your* view and *your* understanding of theory and process. If you do use quotes, enclose them with quotation marks and supply a reference and page number.

Those assessing case studies vary in their preference for verbatim material; if you use it make sure it is relevant and strictly to the point. Satisfy yourself that a word-by-word account is the best way to illustrate what happened in the counselling process.

Checking, correcting, improving your work

Having completed the case study check that it is within the word limit. If not, shorten the first three sections, leaving out details which do not relate to what you have conceptualized in the counselling process. Also check for repetition, spelling and grammar. Make sure every sentence or idea is in the right place and that the study unfolds smoothly. Avoid lurching from one idea to another. Check that it is logically structured and that you are satisfied that you have been clear, concise and informative. See that you have been accurate in your descriptive words, and robust in addressing the criteria.

When you have completed the task, ask your supervisor or colleague to read your work and give you feedback. Do remember to keep within your confidentiality contract and take care that the study is kept in a safe place. You may need to consider a 'secure file' of your computer.

Hang on to the old maxim of 10 per cent inspiration and 90 per cent perspiration. Most people feel nervous when their work is evaluated. However, as Susan Jeffreys (1991) says, 'Feel the fear and do it anyway.'

Note

The sample case-study material used in this article is of a totally fictitious client.

References

BAC (1992) *Guidelines for Completing Application Forms* (Acc.1B Ind/Acc/1/94–95), Rugby: British Association for Counselling.

BAC (2000) *Guidelines for Completing Application Forms* (Ind/Acc/2/99), Rugby: British Association for Counselling.

Fryer, P. *Vigorous, Lucid, Brief*, Index Books.

Jeffreys, S. (1991) *Feel the Fear and Do it Anyway*, Arrow Books.

Discussion issues

1 How might writing one case study a year as part of supervision contribute to a counsellor's professional development?
2 What is your idea of a 'healthy person'? What causes someone to become distressed or disturbed?
3 Have you chosen a particular theoretical model of counselling above others? What influenced your choice?
4 How does your chosen model of counselling help people to change and what is your part in that process?

45

Note-Taking and Administration for Counselling Supervisors

Gladeana McMahon

Many counselling supervisors keep notes of supervision sessions and formulate administrative systems to support the work they do, often creating their own methods, in the absence of any formal training. Some supervisors copy the example of their own counselling supervisor, but since they too are just as unlikely to have received training in structured note-taking, this can prove a rather *ad hoc* approach to a key supportive element of our work.

Key reasons for note-taking

Structured notes can prove an aid to accuracy in:

- memory
- monitoring and recording
- administration and organization
- training and accreditation
- legal or complaints issues

To aid memory

Notes remind supervisors of the content of sessions including:

- client work
- general areas of concern
- ethical issues
- practical problems
- developmental issues
- action to be taken by the supervisor or supervisee between sessions
- outcome of reviews and evaluation sessions

An increasing number of supervisors tape supervision, sometimes offering the recording to supervisees to listen to between sessions. Supervisees who are currently in training, or those who are developing additional skills can find this particularly useful; perhaps a person-centred counsellor wishing to integrate another approach into their

---

This chapter was first published in three parts in *Counselling*, Journal of the British Association for Counselling, vol. 8, no. 1, pp. 18–19; vol. 8, no. 2, pp. 101–2; vol. 8, no. 3, pp. 178–82 (1997).

work may find going over the content of supervision between meetings a bonus, offering a second opportunity to absorb new material. Supervisors use recorded sessions to help them develop their supervisory skills, to monitor their quality of work with a counselling consultant, or for accreditation (respecting confidentiality). Visually impaired counsellors and supervisors use audio-tapes to make oral notes (McMahon 1994).

For monitoring and recording purposes

Notes help in monitoring and recording:

- the actions and reactions of the supervisee
- the actions and reactions of the supervisor
- ideas and models relating to what is happening in the supervision session (e.g. parallel process)
- issues to be taken to the counselling supervisor's own supervisor

To monitor progress

Monitoring progress is linked with the counselling supervisor's own competence and methodology for objectively evaluating work with supervisees, and item B.2.4 of the BAC *Code of Ethics and Practice for Supervisors of Counsellors* (1996) makes it a requirement. The renegotiation of contracts in supervision is greatly clarified through access to monitored progress. Perhaps the supervisee is a person-centred counsellor working long term with a maximum case-load of 15 clients. Nine months later the counsellor takes a new job seeing 20 clients a week for short-term therapy (maximum six sessions) in a GP surgery. Concurrently the counsellor is attending a training programme on solution-focused therapy and seeking to develop a more integrative approach. The original supervision contract could require some renegotiation to accommodate the issues raised by the supervisee's work and counselling approach. The supervisor's experience of short-term or integrative work may be an issue in any such renegotiation, if the two are to continue to work effectively together.

For administrative reasons

Notes remind the supervisor of:

- the number of supervision sessions to date
- review arrangements and dates
- monies paid or outstanding
- materials (books, tapes, manuals) lent to the supervisee

Personal references or reports

A supervisee may request a reference for a new job, training course or a report for accreditation purposes. A number of organizations require quite detailed information which might prove difficult to recall from memory alone.

Organizational requirements

Supervisors employed by, or seeing people externally on behalf of, an organization often find that not only is keeping notes an organizational requirement, but that they are also expected to provide annual reports on the clinical competency of supervisees. Similarly they might be expected to help the organization undertake a therapeutic audit as a way of monitoring and evaluating the quality of the services offered. A consistent note-taking and administrative system is integral to all these procedures.

Personal training or accreditation

Notes are a useful way of providing the background information required for training or accreditation purposes. For example, full details of the range, type, amount and frequency of the counselling supervision sessions are required for the British Association for Counselling's Supervisor Accreditation Scheme. It may prove difficult to provide the relevant information without some form of note-taking and recording procedures.

Legal reasons

Occasionally a supervisee, their client, or the family of one of their clients may decide to take legal action against a supervisor or supervisee. Anyone who has given evidence in a court of law will appreciate how emotionally taxing and stressful the experience can be. Poor record-keeping may make it even more so, particularly if the prosecution decides to use the lack of notes and recording systems as a sign of professional incompetence. Once an idea is planted in the mind of a jury it can be difficult to counter, particularly when the majority of jurors are unlikely to understand the counselling process.

If notes are ever legally demanded from a supervisor, it would be important to demonstrate that no amendments or alterations had taken place. The following guidelines (McMahon 1994) are one way of avoiding such accusations:

- Use lined paper.
- Write in pen.
- Avoid gaps in text (even between paragraphs).
- Draw a line or cross through unused space.
- Date and initial deletions.

Complaints procedure

If a complaint is brought to a professional body, clear and consistent notes and adequate recording procedures help the supervisor demonstrate that they have worked with due care and attention, thereby demonstrating professional competence. A counselling supervisor once said that notes could be used against them and that this was a good reason to record as little information as possible. It is true that even clear and structured notes cannot hide mistakes or errors of judgement on the part of a supervisor, nor should they. However, is the rather defensive idea of avoiding recording our work as supervisors ethical?

Additional administrative issues

Three further administrative points attached to structured note-taking are the arrangements supervisors make for storage and security of notes; the length of time they retain supervision notes, and the requirements of the Data Protection Act

Storage and security arrangements

Supervisors perhaps do not realize how their approach to information and its storage acts as a model for supervisees, demonstrating the degree of thought, care and attention given to the process. Similarly, a lack of such attention may not only leave supervisors and supervisees vulnerable to muddled thinking but also waste their time. Good systems are there to help by freeing time for more creative and rewarding activities, such as the consideration of client work and supervisee learning. Supervisors would be wise to give careful thought to how and where to store supervision notes and the associated security arrangements, within their own available means.

Retaining notes

As with client case notes (McMahon 1994), there appears to be no legal requirement for supervisors to keep notes, but it would seem sensible to devise an effective system and work to it. The British Association for Counselling (1997) instructs counsellors to keep records for a minimum period of six years, in line with the amount of time available to clients wishing to use their internal complaints procedure. Clients, however, have the right to seek legal redress outside a six-year period. A supervisor who can demonstrate a systematic and responsible approach to information-keeping goes a long way towards showing that they have taken 'due care and attention' in this aspect of their work.

Supervisors working for organizations may be required to retain notes according to an existing administrative structure; those in private practice need to think about their own procedures, and may find the following guidelines (adapted from McMahon 1994) helpful:

- Keep all counselling supervision notes/relevant information for six years after the termination of work with the supervisee.
- After six years destroy all material except the Supervisee Details Form (SDF, see Box 6, p. 301–4) by shredding or burning.
- The Supervisee Details Form (SDF) which has basic information about the supervisee can be kept for a further four years and then destroyed by shredding or burning.

The Supervisee Details Form is kept in case the supervisee re-contacts the supervisor for a reference or for some other reason after the termination of the supervision contract.

Data Protection Acts 1984, 1998

The Data Protection Act 1984 applies to anyone who keeps details of people on computer, and individuals have the right to see any information stored in this way. The 1998 Act also includes written records, some of which will be covered from 2001. BAC Information Sheet 15 (Jenkins and Palmer 2000) summarizes the effect of the 1998 act's provisions on counsellors. For further information see Data Protection Commissioners website at www.dataprotection@gov.uk, or telephone 01625 545700. They provide a useful booklet. (See also Chapter 59.)

Note-taking structure

Having clarified the value of note-taking, an important next step is consideration of a method which suits the individual supervisor and meets the maxim that the art of effective note-taking is the ability to capture the key points in as few words as possible. (An example of a note-taking structure for supervision is shown in Box 1.)

Supervision notes form

Some standard information is repeated at each session:

- supervisee's name
- date
- session number
- fee paid/outstanding balance
- action

Supervision Notes

Supervisee Name: _____J.A._____   Date: __15 January 1998__

Session No.: 15____ Fee Paid: £30____   Balance: £ -_____

Action: Review of supervision arrangements for next session_____

_____

_____

_____

_____

Box 1   *Supervision notes form*

A C T

The outline note-taking structure below is an adaptation of a formula used in compiling case notes for clients, and is based on the acronym **A C T**, covering **A**ctual content of session; **C**omments of supervisor; **T**herapist or counsellor development (McMahon 1994).

Actual content of session (Box 2)

- client work discussed during the session
- other factual information or issues raised during the session (e.g. changes in workplace practices, reviews, ethical issues)
- record of missed or cancelled appointments

The supervisor records what was actually discussed during the session.

A: Client work_____

DW (session 3)_____

D appears ambivalent about counselling, J explored. Explored J's_____

> countertransference issues, her desire to mother, his helplessness.
> Organizational issues
> New co-ordinator appointment, J asked to undertake more assessment
> sessions – discussed implications regarding existing workload. In addition, J
> has also been asked to run a course on working with offenders based on her
> experiences of working for the centre. J is not sure whether she wishes to
> expand her expertise into the field of training.

Box 2   *Actual content of session*

comments of supervisor (Box 3)

- supervisor and supervisee responses
- supervisor and supervisee actions and reactions
  (e.g. supervisee's body language, ability to use interventions, transference/counter-transference, parallel processes), ideas or models of supervision
- issues to be taken to the supervisor's external consultant
- issues requiring specialist advice (e.g. input on sexual abuse)
- any matter causing concern to the supervisor

> **C:**   J appeared uncomfortable and defensive when we talked about her work. As
> we explored J's behaviour she became aware that this attitude reflected her
> clients own behaviour – parallel process.

Box 3   *Comments of supervisor*

Therapist or counsellor development (Box 4)

- supervisor's thoughts regarding the supervisee's strengths and weaknesses
- supervisee's concerns regarding ongoing development
- details of current training being undertaken by the supervisee
- supervisor's own developmental needs brought about through work with the supervisee

> **T:**   J mentioned that she had started her own personal psychodynamic therapy as
> part of her requirement to meet the minimum 40 hours required for BAC accred-
> itation purposes. Like many supervisors I have learnt the craft of supervision by
> doing. The BAC *Code of Ethics and Practice for Supervisors* is asking for more
> and more clarity about supervision practices and I now feel I need some formal
> training. Contact BAC regarding training courses in supervision.

Box 4   *Therapist or counsellor development*

Additional record keeping

Note-taking is only one part of record keeping. Other items include:

- all correspondence (e.g. letters, reports, references)
- any information on clients (e.g. photocopies of questionnaires used by the supervisee)

Supervision Services Information Sheet (SSIS: see Box 5)

Prior to their initial meeting some supervisors give prospective supervisees written background information about themselves and their work, other supervisors prefer to give such details either in written form or verbally during the first session, or as the work progresses. Printed information has the advantage of ensuring that the supervisor is relieved of the responsibility of having to remember the details each time, while the supervisee is relieved of the responsibility of remembering to ask for certain details. Such an information sheet outlines the terms and conditions under which supervision is offered, the responsibilities of each party and the approach used by the supervisor. In effect such information forms the basis for the contracting process between both people, including, as it does:

- a definition of counselling supervision
- details about an individual's approach
- comments regarding anti-discriminatory practice (in line with the BAC *Code of Ethics and Practice*)
- general information about frequency of meetings, reviews of work and other associated issues
- fees, including cancellation policy
- confidentiality
- legal responsibilities
- contact between sessions
- professional details relating to the supervisor, including training, accreditation, codes of ethics, experience, relevant memberships and committee activities
- relevant publications and media work
- travelling instructions

AMY HELPER
10 Anywhere Street, Somewhere, YZ1 23
Tel: 01112 234567 Fax: 01112 234568
Email: helper@internet.com

Supervision Services Information Sheet

Supervision is a confidential working relationship in which the personal resources of the supervisor and supervisee are directed, in regular sessions, towards maximizing the competence of the supervisee in helping clients.

The aim of supervision is to provide an attentive and supportive climate within which the individual can develop new options for managing themselves and their work with greater satisfaction and effectiveness.

Supervision aims to achieve this by:

(a) considering responsibility for standards and ethics
(b) sharing the responsibility for the professional development of the supervisee's skills, knowledge and understanding
(c) providing opportunities for discharge and recharging of batteries.

(Inskipp and Proctor 1995)

My approach

The counselling supervision I offer is based upon my regard for an individual's own training and philosophy. My integrative framework is influenced by the work of Gerard Egan – I believe in the importance of exploration, understanding and action in all areas of a person's professional and personal development.

I welcome the opportunity for a preliminary discussion regarding individual needs for which no charge is made. Any subsequent meeting for the purpose of a more detailed briefing may attract a fee.

Anti-discriminatory practice

I seek to provide a service which is anti-discriminatory in nature and endeavour to ensure this commitment is reflected in the supervisory process.

Further information on the practicalities of the supervision I offer, together with details regarding my training and experience follow:

Background information

General
Supervisees normally contract for weekly, fortnightly or monthly sessions of one to two hours' duration. The frequency of supervision will vary according to the volume of counselling, experience of the supervisee, the work setting and current professional requirements.

I ask supervisees (depending on job function) to adhere to either the BAC *Code of Ethics and Practice for Counsellors* or the BAC *Code of Ethics and Practice for the Use of Counselling Skills*.

As part of good practice I encourage regular reviews regarding the effectiveness of supervision which enable changes to be made to the supervision process where appropriate. Methods of self-assessment and the self-evaluation of a supervisee's work are also considered.

The terms and conditions outlined in this Information Sheet are liable to annual review. In line with the BAC *Code of Ethics and Practice for Supervisors* I receive consultative support.

continued

Fees

My fees are £30 per hour, more if special rooms need to be booked or travelling is involved.

If a session is to be cancelled, I require **A FULL 24 HOURS NOTICE**, otherwise the supervisee or sponsoring organization is liable for the full cost of the session. Individuals pay by cheque or cash at the end of each session while organizations are invoiced on a monthly basis.

Confidentiality

As a non-managerial (or consultative) supervisor I treat all information disclosed to me as confidential. Where a professional disagreement about client care cannot be resolved I consult with a fellow professional. I reserve the right to make contact with the relevant organization (e.g. employer, college, external agency or professional body) if I believe a supervisee's work with a client causes serious concern and where a mutual course of action cannot be agreed. Issues of client safety and the safety of those surrounding the client are given primary importance.

Legal responsibilities

Issues for consideration include our respective legal liabilities to each other, any employing organization and to clients. This includes the action to be taken if I have serious concerns about a supervisee's practice – particularly in the area of client safety as outlined above.

Contact

I do not break into sessions to answer the telephone and there are times when I am not contactable. To allow messages to get through I have a telephone answering machine. I am also available between sessions should a supervisee experience difficulties with a client that cannot wait until the next session.

Professional details

Training

1988–1990 Certificate in Counselling, Anywhere College
1990–1992 Diploma in Integrative Counselling, Anywhere College
1994–1996 MA in Counselling, Somewhere University

Accreditation

1998 British Association for Counselling (BAC) Accredited Counsellor

Codes of Ethics

I abide by the BAC Codes of Ethics for Counsellors and Counselling Supervisors

Experience

1990–1997 Work in voluntary, local authority and medical counselling settings
1995   Began supervision and training work
1997   Became self-employed counsellor and since 1998 have worked as a freelance supervisor and trainer

---

Travelling Instructions

Rail: Somewhere Station (quarter-mile walk)
Buses: 101, 96 to Somewhere End (half-mile walk)
Parking: On-street parking

Box 5   *Supervision Service Information Sheet (SSIS)*

Supervisee Details Form (Box 6)

If the supervisor and supervisee are to work together the latter can be asked to complete a Supervisee Details Form (SDF) to ensure that relevant areas of responsibility as outlined, for example, in the BAC *Code of Ethics and Practice for Supervisors of Counsellors*, have been covered. Although most of this information will have been covered during the initial meeting, having it written down by the supervisee provides a means of collecting relevant details in one place and acts as a fail-safe device for picking up areas which may have been innocently overlooked at the first meeting. The supervisee can be asked to take the SDF away to complete and given the opportunity to raise any questions arising from it for discussion at the next session.

Clear contracting between supervisor and supervisee reduces the likelihood of misunderstandings and means that both are clear about what is expected of them in their work together. The SDF and the SSIS together can form the basis of a working supervision contract if they are signed by both parties. No more administration needs to take place unless the circumstances of the supervisee, the supervisor or their external professional requirements change.

SUPERVISEE DETAILS FORM

Personal details

Surname: ....
First name: ....
Address: ....
....
....
Postcode: ....
Tel. no: (Home) .... Fax: ....
          (code)
Email: ....

Employment details

Job Title(s):   1: ....
               2: ....

continued

(e.g. freelance counsellor, volunteer counsellor, youth worker, welfare officer)

Details of work/practice address if different to the above:

Organization/
practice: ....

Address: ....

Postcode: ....

Tel no: (Work)   .... Ext: ....
       (code)

Other relevant information not included above:

Training/qualifications related to counselling

Dates		Training	Course title and qualification
From	To	body	awarded

Counselling experience

Dates		Organization	Job	Duties
From	To		title	performed

Type of work to be supervised

(e.g. individual, counselling supervision, training work)

....

....

....

....

(1) How often do you see clients?: ....
    (e.g. once/twice a week)

(2) For how long?:   ....
    (50/60 min)

(3) Over what time period?: ....
   (*e.g. 6 sessions, 6 mths/1 yr/longer, varied etc.*)

(4) What type of theoretical approach(es) do you use in your work?:
   (*e.g. TA, person-centred, Egan, cognitive-behavioural, etc.*)
   ....

(5) What overall term do you use to describe your counselling style?
   (*e.g. integrative, psychodynamic, humanistic*)
   ....

(6) Maximum client contact hours per week:...

(7) If your counselling had to be terminated unexpectedly for any reason what arrangements are in place to meet the needs of your clients? (*e.g. agency would deal with, arrangement with a colleague locally*)

(8) Who is accountable for the management of your work with clients?
   (*e.g. myself, my co-ordinator, etc.*)

   (8a) Is this the person I should contact if concerns about the quality of your work with clients cannot be resolved?

   YES/NO

   (8b) If NO who is the person who should be contacted?
   ....

(9) Does your organization require any form of formal feedback regarding your work with clients? (*e.g. annual review, report, etc.*)

   YES/NO

Details (if applicable)
....
....

Professional issues

(1) Are you a member of the British Association for Counselling?   YES/NO
   If YES what class of membership do you hold?...
   (1a) If NO are you a member of any other professional organization?
   YES/NO
   Name:...
   (1b) Does the organization have its own Code of Ethics and Practice and do you abide by this?   YES/NO
   (1c) Does the organization have its own complaints procedure?   YES/NO

(2) Do you have Professional Indemnity and Public Liability Insurance?

   YES/NO

continued

(2a) If YES to what level of cover?..

(2b) If NO are you prepared to take this out?   YES/NO

(2c) Not relevant as I am covered by my employer   YES/NO

(3) If you do not already work to a Code of Ethics and Practice would you be prepared to adhere to:

(a) BAC *Code of Ethics and Practice for Counsellors*   YES/NO

(b) BAC *Code of Ethics and Practice for Counselling Skills*   YES/NO

(4) What type of personal therapy/counselling have you undertaken, for how long and in what ways do you feel this has influenced your counselling style (*if at all*)?

(5) What type of supervision, if any, have you previously experienced and for how long?

(6) Do you have any additional supervision arrangements and, if so, what are they?

(7) How do you ensure the secure and confidential storage of client notes and their safe destruction?

(8) How do you evaluate your client work?
(*e.g. evaluation sheets, reviews, use of supervision*)

(9) In what ways do you work towards operating an anti-discriminatory practice?
(*e.g. use counselling supervision to monitor work, relevant training*)

(10) How do you access medical cover for your work with clients?
(*e.g. contact client's GP when appropriate, access to psychiatrist*)

1. My signature below indicates that I have read, understood and am in agreement with the terms and conditions as detailed in the Supervision Services Information Sheet supplied to me.

2. I give my permission for Amy Helper to make contact with the relevant organization (e.g. my employer, college, appropriate external agency or professional body) if she believes my work with a client causes her serious concern and where a mutual course of action cannot be agreed, issues of client safety and the safety of those surrounding the client being given primary importance.

Signed: ....

Date: ....

Box 6   *Supervisee Details Form (SDF)*

References

BAC (1996) *Code of Ethics and Practice for Supervisors of Counsellors*, Rugby: British Association for Counselling.

BAC (1997) *Code of Ethics and Practice for Counsellors*, Rugby: British Association for Counselling.

Inskipp, F. and Proctor, B. (1995) *Becoming a Supervisor*, Twickenham: Cascade.

Jenkins, P. and Palmer, I. (2000) *Record Keeping and the Data Protection Act BAC Information Sheet* 15, Rugby: British Association for Counselling.

McMahon, G. (1994) *Starting your own Private Practice*, Cambridge: National Extension College.

Discussion issues

1 How essential is it to keep notes on supervision sessions?
2 How important is it for a supervisor to have an administrative system?
3 What advantages might there be for both the supervisee and supervisor in having supervisees complete the Supervisee Details Form?
4 Is there ever a case for recording as little information as possible? Can we record too much information?

PART THREE

COUNSELLING ISSUES

Introduction to Part Three

The fundamental issue introducing Part Three is centred in a group of four chapters which question, in different ways, whether or not counselling is necessarily a 'good thing'. Psychiatrist Raj Persaud succinctly and sharply expresses his unease about the growth of counselling, in a chapter remarkable for its idealization of the amount and quality of support available in the general population, from families and friends. Pittu Laungani takes a longer, humorous and historical journey through counselling development, offering a brief questionnaire which, if used with prospective counsellors, might well produce some less than satisfactory answers for clients. Do clients tend to choose a therapist by instinct, recommendation or pot luck? Judicious use of a therapy checklist from Stephen Palmer and Kasia Szymanska (with a delayed action warning for those in distress) will help clients to make the most of therapy. In contrast, Sheila Dainow completes the consumer advice section with a letter to prospective clients preparing them for the new experience of counselling and offering ideas to enable them not just to get the best out of their counsellor, but also to become 'good clients'.

Ernesto Spinelli is interviewed on the related issue of counselling and the abuse of power by Judith Longman, former editor of the BAC journal. He offers an enlightened perspective on the potential 'abuse' in counsellor training occurring when trainers are reluctant to address the power abuse of clients by counsellors. In counselling, he cites allowing our important theoretical knowledge, personal therapy and supervision to blind us to reality for clients who then live their unsupported struggle with life in a world of which we have little knowledge and no experience.

Administrative and ancillary staff who support counsellors would not wish to be bound by a BAC Code of Ethics for Counsellors, nor would this be fitting, but Petruska Clarkson gives helpful suggestions for guiding them in the area of ethics.

A series of chapters illustrate the critical role of the BAC journal as a forum for differences of opinion. Support for National Vocational Qualifications (NVQs) with an emphasis on skills in counselling and accreditation comes from Janice Russell and Graham Dexter, while John Foskett looks robustly at accreditation in his analysis of their chapter. Group work in counsellor training is dissected by Judi Irving and David Williams and trenchantly supported by Amelia Lyons.

Education and counselling have had an uneasy union since the first counsellors began their work in schools in the mid-1960s. Student counselling fared better because colleges had more autonomy, and perhaps maturity. In 1993 there was a move from some inspectors to extend their role of sitting in on lessons or lectures to the privacy and confidentiality of the counselling room. Tim Bond describes the process and outcome of the difference of opinion between student counsellors and Her Majesty's Inspectors (HMIs).

A different cultural context characterizes Stephen Palmer's interview on student counselling and training with Ms Ling Gui Rui and Ms Hou Zhijin of the Capital Normal University Student Counselling Centre, Beijing, China.

The transatlantic migration of litigation has spread its compensatory but debatable benefits into the world of therapy, a change represented by three very different chapters. Pemma Littlehailes portrays how counsellors may feel when faced with a court appearance. Roger Litton updates in detail the dilemma of a clash between counselling, confidentiality and the law first described by himself, Stephen Palmer and Mark Scoggins in 1997, and Peter Jenkins provides a diligently informative account of counsellor liability.

In the BAC *Counselling Reader*, Volume 1, David Williams suggested a competition to find an alternative word to describe 'supervision', with the prize being a place in posterity. No BAC millennium contest has been announced so we revisit supervision in solution-focused form, first with Bill O'Connell and Caroline Jones, then in tandem with short-term psychodynamic work, a colourful hybrid, with Gertrud Mander.

The moving poignancy in counsellors' rare disclosures of pain and distress arising from their work has graced the BAC journal from its very beginning. Maureen Murphy touchingly relates the sudden death of her client, Sandra from a heart attack. In a separate chapter Jackie de Smith pays tribute to Sonia in the last months of her life with leukaemia. Both counsellors ponder the extension of counselling confidentiality after the end of a client's life.

Empathy is a cornerstone of person-centred therapy and an integral aspect of other approaches, which makes the challenge to its 'as if' experience by Susan Ridge, David Martin and William Campbell worth a second look. Similarly the consideration of congruence, probably *the* foundation of person-centredness, and the psychodynamic concept of countertransference offered by Paul Wilkins benefits from another careful perusal.

One of the millennium pieces in the *Reader* is Marie Adams' recent chapter on humour in psychotherapeutic relationships, published in April 2000. This is a seminal subject about which we hope to learn more.

Like Part Two of the *Reader*, Part Three also concludes with an innovative selection of chapters under the title Counselling and Practice Dilemmas. These illustrate ways of approaching potentially problematic issues, in contributions from counsellors, therapists and trainers, whose experience merits revisiting. The first three counselling dilemmas originally edited by Lesley Murdin, offer opinions on clients ending counselling, displays of affection, and suicide threats. The four practice dilemmas, originally edited by Caroline Jones, look at clients as potential counsellors; student appeals in training; counsellors ending counselling; and supervision of bereaved counsellors.

Many of the concepts and practices of counselling raise issues for debate and the BAC journal has a reputation as one medium through which these may be conducted. We have used this opportunity to reproduce some of those issues for renewed consideration in the *Reader*.

46

The Wisest Counsel?

Raj Persaud

Counselling as health care?

As distinct from the counselling which might occur between friends or relatives, counselling as a professional service is developing as a separate, often marketable commodity. Those within a profession should be expert in a sense that members outside a profession are not (Holmes and Lindley 1991). While it may not be possible for the public to detect or assess this expertise, at least the profession's regulatory bodies ought to. Yet drawing a boundary around what constitute the basic recognized skill of professional counselling has proved extremely difficult and there still appears little consensus (Pedder 1989)

Furthermore, exploitation of clients is usually countered in any responsible profession by an organizational attempt to rectify imbalances in power – hence the need for liaison with regulatory bodies, watchdog groups and consumer rights associations. Within counselling, while there are attempts to introduce safeguards for clients, the consumers, for a variety of reasons, have difficulty opposing poor service from counsellors.

For example, according to past legal decisions, clients' complaints about therapist activities are not always regarded as credible because the individual's condition as a patient, or client, is often seen as *prima facie* evidence of mental instability (Lakin 1988). Clients also fear public humiliation due to stigma surrounding emotional problems; hence it is difficult to get abused or exploited clients to present their claims publicly (Lakin 1988).

While trust mediates the encounter with many professionals, such as doctors, it does not constitute it, whereas in counselling this quality of relationship is more fundamental – counselling has been described as *hingeing* on the provision of a 'safe environment' in which 'relationships between self and the world can be explored' (Robins and Hayes 1993).

Despite the importance to counselling of the provision of this safety (and that it is supposed to demarcate the counselling relationship from others available to a client) are there definite reliable differences in terms of safety between the relationships available to clients in counselling, as opposed to outside counselling? Or is one taking pot luck in contacting someone calling themselves a counsellor, in much the same way one does in contacting a friend: in fact, friends we at least know something about! While professional counsellors might be aware of many good fellow practitioners, their perspective remains that of insiders – what happens if instead one looks at the industry as a consumer beginning

This chapter was first published in *Counselling*, Journal of the British Association for Counselling, vol. 7, no. 3, pp. 199–201 (1996).

to try and find a counsellor with no background information, perhaps starting with small ads in the back of a magazine? Are the relationships on offer here really safer on average than those available through friendship? Have the industry's advocates investigated what it might be like to make contact with a counsellor as an outsider, for the few investigations available do not portray a positive picture of the experience for clients (e.g. France 1988)?

Furthermore, the provision of a safe environment as a relationship between two people is deeply problematic, not only because of the difficulty of either member being able objectively to assess safety, but also for this to be guaranteed without recourse to regulation and supervision of the relationship by third parties. While therapist supervision by other therapists is a significant feature of the counselling industry, it is by no means universal, and there is usually little or no attempt by supervisors directly to obtain the client's perspective of the relationship. Therefore regulation goes on with only one perspective of that safety being taken into account. Hence perhaps there is an unresolvable tension between the need for privacy and the requirement for regulation – allowing third parties access to sessions or case material violates privacy. When clients go to clinics for counselling they may be resigned to their case material being accessible to other professionals at the clinic; however, the tension between regulation and privacy becomes particularly acute in private practice counselling.

This complacency about guaranteeing and regulating the provision of a safe relationship may derive from the assumption that most counsellors are ethically motivated, which may be true. Yet the whole question of why people want to become counsellors has been largely neglected, despite the impact of such motivations on clients. Templer (1971) argued the vocation of counsellor was an avenue of fulfilment for eight personality types: (a) those with an uncertain sense of their own identity; (b) the socially inhibited or withdrawn; (c) the dependent; (d) those with rigid defences against dependency needs; (e) the rigidly intellectualistic; (f) the sadistic; (g) those with rigid defences against hostility; and (h) the masochistic.

Another important motivation which requires questioning is that of the client – after all seeking help is not morally neutral behaviour. There are distinctions between illness and mere personal distress, and these differences govern the appropriateness of seeking help from professionals (Parsons 1978). Yet, textbooks on counselling and counsellors do not appear to discern when unpleasant mental states end, and definable psychological problems or medical illnesses begin (e.g. Dryden 1984).

For example, it appears that counselling is frequently sought by those who are not formally medically or psychiatrically ill, but who are unhappy – sometimes described as the 'worried well' (Wood 1983; Green and Davey 1992). But should unhappiness be treated? Attempting to do away with unpleasant mental states regardless of their medical status involves extending the ethics of health. If we ought to be healthy and have rights to health, then professionals have certain obligations to restore us to health (Parsons 1978). However, ought we always to be happy, and do professionals have obligations to restore happiness on demand?

In many situations it is appropriate to be unhappy; it would be questionable to be happy after committing immoral or antisocial behaviour. Rights to happiness appear different from rights to health, and yet those who seek counselling may be equating these two different goals.

Furthermore, the question of moral responsibility for our own mental life seems evaded by the counselling model, with no explicit criteria detailed of which problems of living we are responsible for, and when we might abrogate responsibility to a counsellor for help (London 1964). Existentialists argue that it is characteristic of our society that we seek to provide a professional response to personal and intimate issues – the professionalization of personal problems (London 1964). For the moral philosopher, all attempts to alter behaviour raise ethical questions – how ought people to behave, how ought they to feel, what ought they to want? These are questions of value, and hence enter the remit of ethics. In an attempt to avoid being too interventionist, the counselling model frequently avoids prescriptive practice, yet the decisions over who needs counselling when, and from whom it can be withheld, inevitably involve implicit judgements of what is acceptable or desirable behaviour and emotions.

Those experiencing distress but who have no access to professional help are not usually bereft of alternatives, and a variety of other choices is likely to be pursued, including introspection, speaking to friends or relatives, self-help techniques, distraction and other activities. An issues which then develops is whether the availability of counselling prevents people developing their own solutions to their problems by preventing them from struggling with these issues for long enough and finding the incentive to discover solutions by themselves.

The duty to relieve suffering depends on the perception of the cause, so if a doctor who can cure blindness fails to provide such treatment, the professional will be held partly responsible for the continued disability, yet if no such cure is available the cause of continued blindness will be located elsewhere. Similarly for counselling, if this is perceived as able to relieve a particular form of suffering, then the cause of that suffering will gradually come to be seen as a lack of counselling. If there was no other way an individual could prevent or alleviate their suffering then this would be unproblematic, but is this really the case with counselling? While counselling may even be efficacious, given possible negative side-effects on society at large, has it been demonstrated that counselling is the *only* effective remedy for those ills for which it is recommended?

Since a large part of counselling's success is attributed to the provision of a relationship, it may be that the accessibility of such a relationship from professionals acts as a barrier to people negotiating and developing relationships in their own lives, which would then be therapeutic. It may even be that the availability of counselling is beginning to alter the structure of personal relationships; serious discussion of one's emotional troubles may become increasingly seen as inappropriate for discussion among non-professionals. The recommendation to 'see a professional' may only be a convenient way of pre-empting any entanglement with another's emotions when such help is perceived as readily available.

Since it is undoubtedly true that some people derive some benefit from counselling, the issue perhaps becomes whether this is sufficient to outweigh the problems which inevitably accompany counselling. At first glance this may appear a mathematical problem where benefits and risk need to be added up and subtracted from each other, and the solution will largely depend on what weight is given to these benefits and risks.

An alternative non-empirical approach to this problem is to ask whether counselling benefits clients because it alleviates suffering or enhances happiness (Griffin 1979). Ethicists have argued there is an important difference between the two, and, furthermore, that there is a different moral obligation on us to alleviate another's suffering as opposed to enhancing another's happiness. Human suffering makes a direct moral appeal, the appeal to help, while there is no similar call to increase the happiness of those who are not suffering. Distinguishing whether one is alleviating suffering or enhancing happiness is undoubtedly difficult, and a reliable method has yet to be proposed, but such a method would decide whether one's actions are returning a human being to a notion of a 'par state' or taking him or her from a 'par state' and helping them go beyond (Griffin 1979).

The idea of 'par' is the level at which a recognizably human life is possible, where one is free from great pain and insecurity and where one has the materials available to improve one's life (Griffin 1979). The notion of a par state is important because it reminds us that suffering is perhaps an ineradicable part of human life (James 1982); in a deeper sense it is part of the defining characteristic of life. A life without any suffering would begin to appear unlike any kind of life we could recognize or relate to, but at some point counselling activity may bar the client from normal life experiences.

People will obviously vary widely on where they place 'par', but the crucial issue is that this depends on expectations of what life ought to be like, and in particular how much of life's problems we should be expected to take responsibility for facing and dealing with ourselves. One important point emerges: no conception of a life could reasonably be expected to be free from suffering – upsetting things inevitably happen to people. The issue is whether people are facing difficulties which are out of the ordinary, or whether ordinary difficulties have elicited personal reactions which are too extreme for the individual to cope with.

In this context it is worth reminding ourselves of the British Association for Counselling's (1979) declaration: '*The task of counselling is to give the client an opportunity to explore, discover and clarify ways of living more resourcefully and towards greater well being.*' This statement appears less concerned with relieving suffering and more with enhancing happiness, which appears less morally important.

It is also worth reminding ourselves of page iii of the British Association for Counselling's *Directory of Training Courses* (1988), where those who might need counselling are described as:

> suffering the death of a loved one, or not getting on with their partner, they may have lost a job or be worrying about coping with a new one, they may be finding the strain of work or exams too much, they may be at the end of their tether, anxious about the kids, their parents, or themselves, or simply down in the dumps.

But are not all of these issues part of everyday life? While it is undoubtedly true that those experiencing any of the above problems may benefit in some way from seeing a counsellor, is this benefit in the form of relieving extraordinary suffering or are counsellors instead enhancing the happiness of people who have been made miserable by events which it would be extraordinary *not* to encounter during any lifetime?

The issue of whether counselling enhances happiness or relieves suffering may appear a rather semantic or abstract issue, but it actually goes to the heart of unease over the growth of counselling's availability to all. An analogy might be alcohol. Most people feel better after a drink following a stressful day, but does that render alcohol a health-care enterprise, or is it in fact closer to a leisure industry? These conceptions are crucial in determining the way alcohol is regarded and regulated. Much disquiet might disappear if counselling was similarly classified as a leisure pursuit – something which did indeed enhance the enjoyment of many people's lives rather than relieving suffering. Hence rights of access should not invoke human or health-care rights, but this need not deny the important contribution of counselling to many people's happiness.

If people want to purchase counselling because it might enhance their quality of life, they should be free to do so, but the state should not be under an obligation to provide counselling on demand, and no one should be encouraged to expect to be counselled if they could not arrange such provision themselves. Hence rights to counselling should not be equated with rights to health.

References

BAC (1979) *Counselling: Definition of Terms in Use with Expansion and Rationale*, Rugby: British Association for Counselling.

BAC (1988) *The Directory of Training Courses in Counselling and Psychotherapy*, Rugby: British Association for Counselling.

Dryden, W. (1984) *Individual Therapy in Britain*, London: Harper & Row.

France, A. (1988) *Consuming Psychotherapy*, London: Free Association Books.

Green, J. and Davey, T. (1992) 'Counselling with the worried well', *Counselling Psychology Quarterly*, 5 (2): 213–20.

Griffin, J. (1979) 'Is unhappiness morally more important than happiness?', *Philosophical Quarterly*, 29: 47–55.

Holmes, J. and Lindley, R. (1991) *The Values of Psychotherapy*, Oxford/New York: Oxford University Press.

James, S. (1982) 'The duty to relieve suffering', *Ethics*, 93: 4–21.

Lakin, M. (1988) *Ethical Issues in the Psychotherapies*, New York: Oxford University Press.

London, P. (1964) *The Modes and Morals of Psychotherapy*, New York: Holt, Rhinehart & Winston Inc.

Parsons, T. (1978) 'Health and disease: a sociological and action perspective', in W.T. Reich (ed.), *Encyclopedia of Bioethics*, New York: Free Press, pp. 590–99.

Pedder, J. (1989) 'Courses in psychotherapy: evolution and recent trends', *British Journal of Psychotherapy*, 6 (2): 203–21.

Robins, C.J. and Hayes, A.M. (1993) 'An appraisal of cognitive therapy', *Journal of Consulting and Clinical Psychology*, 48: 205–14.

Templer, D.I. (1971) 'Analyzing the Psychotherapist', *Mental-Hygiene*, 55 (2) (April): 234–6.

Wood, G. (1983) *The Myth of Neurosis*, London: Macmillan.

Discussion issues

1 Are there always alternatives to counselling?
2 Are there clear guidelines for when counselling is helpful or harmful?
3 Is this a criticism of counselling in general or just bad counselling?
4 What are the differences between unhappiness and problems that require counselling?

47

Can Psychotherapies Seriously Damage your Health?

Pittu Laungani

Let us assume there is something the matter with you. You don't quite know what it is, you have tried to understand it, locate its cause, and do something about it. Hot or cold baths, sleeping early or late, jogging, resting, yogic *asanas*, strange diets, aspirins, 'pep' pills, anti-depressants, vitamin tablets, alcohol – you have tried everything you could think of, have read about in the health columns of popular magazines, or that has been recommended by your friends. You feel no better, even worse, as though something were slipping away from you and you were unable to control it. Sometimes you feel haunted by an existential dilemma, a 'human condition' from which intelligent, sensitive persons such as you have no immunity. But in your heart you know that the 'human condition', although it sounds grand, is nothing but sophisticated clap-trap: no one has died of the 'human condition', not even Albert Camus, who made a career out of it. Your general practitioner, seeing your dreadful state, suggests that you consult a psychiatrist.

The search for therapy

The word psychiatrist arouses a sense of unease. Outdated stories force their way to your consciousness and you see yourself as a helpless patient in faded dressing-gown, shuffling aimlessly through the cold, soulless corridors of a large 'mental institution', surrounded by confusion and bedlam. You swallow mind-bending drugs, feel the pain of electric shocks, hear the screams, and avoid looking at the brutal nurses and unfeeling doctors – your fantasies fanned by the film *One Flew over the Cuckoo's Nest*, which you saw several years ago. There is hardly a grain of truth in your ghoulish fantasies, but you are unwilling to accept that psychiatric techniques over the last 30 years have become more refined and humane. Your heart shrinks at the thought of going to a shrink! Their remedies might be more desperate than your illness.

How about a psychoanalyst? They don't mess about with electric shocks and drugs, they sit and talk, or rather listen. Sometimes. They let you look at some strange pictures – you might see a boy gazing at a violin, or people gathered in a cemetery – and ask you to make up dramatic stories around them. They may let you examine some ink-blots, and narrate what these mean to you and what they remind you of. It makes the psychoanalyst happy if you perceive sexual symbols in the ink-blots! It seems innocuous fun, but psychoanalysts take it very seriously. They are extremely concerned about your relationships with your family, and persuade you to talk about your mother, father and siblings;

This chapter was first published in *Counselling*, Journal of the British Association for Counselling, vol. 6, no. 2, pp. 110–15 (1995).

they dig into forgotten and buried episodes of your childhood, and often succeed in finding out the naughty things you got up to – or rather didn't get up to! Nothing is sacred to a psychoanalyst, no subject a taboo. If you're a man they'll even persuade you to talk about your 'willie' and they love probing into your nightly dreams. They elaborate upon them and condense them, attributing all sorts of sexual symbols to them: it's a hidden language.

Psychoanalysis, you learn, is no laughing matter and your spirits drop when you learn the cost. You would be expected to attend three or four hourly sessions a week for at least two or three years! You would either need to dip into your life-savings or to be quite rich, but suspect that if you had *that* kind of money you wouldn't have had any problems in the first place!

Your knowledgeable GP assures you that you could get it free through the NHS but the snag is you might have to wait a while. How long, you ask. It could be months, even a couple of years. Assuming that you were able to undergo analysis for three years, what is the guarantee that you would be cured of your problems? To your alarm you realize that there are no guarantees, and statistics related to cure rates make gloomy reading, varying from 66 per cent (Eysenck 1985) to 80 per cent (Bergin and Garfield 1971). Would you wish to take a two out of three chance of getting better?

How about cut-price therapy, you inquire, lowering your sights rapidly, that doesn't last two or three years? Something short, swift and secure, as recommended by Kutash and Wolf (1986) or Winston (1985).

An exciting world opens before your disbelieving eyes! Every conceivable type of therapy, treatment, counselling is on offer. Bespoke therapies, exclusive therapies, individual or group therapies, elaborate residential therapies, transcendental or yogic therapies. You feel like Ali Baba, dazzled by all the undreamed-of treasures on display. You can shout, be shouted at, abuse, be abused, get massaged, sing and dance, watch others do the same, work yourself into a frenzy, throw tantrums, rest, sleep, dream, have nightmares – all is permitted. The vast storehouse of treasures is bound to confuse and bewilder. How do you decide which is right for you?

Some questions to ask

That, however, is not the right question to ask. Such a question is virtually impossible to answer with any degree of certainty. Your concern instead should centre on the following interrelated issues.

Understanding the problem (diagnosis)

Find out, as far as possible, what your problem is. Not all clients have deep insight into their own problems, nor do the therapists. The person you consult, should, after a careful interview, a detailed case history and sometimes by your performance on a battery of standardized psychological tests, be able to offer a tentative diagnosis of your problem. (Do not let therapists fool you into believing that you are … ah … such a complex, deep, and sensitive soul that it would be impossible for them to arrive at an understanding of your deep-rooted existential and psychological problems in a few interviews. That is often a cover-up for ignorance and a crude attempt at flattery, which may be aimed at keeping the psychotherapist's cash register ringing.) The therapist should be able to arrive at a reasonably firm diagnosis with a minimum of fuss and should also be able to explain all this to you in a language free from obfuscating jargon.

Second, you need to be assured that had you gone to another therapist instead of the one you have consulted the diagnosis would have been the same. If the diagnosis changes from therapist to therapist, how can you be sure which was accurate? A consensus among therapists would be heartening, but a *high degree of consensus is nothing more than a statement of reliability*. If a thousand million people tell you the earth is flat, it doesn't make it so! But consensus in diagnosis is the obvious first step.

Nature of help (therapeutic procedures)

It is important to understand the kind of therapeutic procedures which will be adopted by your therapist. You want them explained, to know if they are going to be painful and, if so, what kind of pain you are likely to suffer (physical, emotional), and you need to be convinced that the recommended therapeutic procedure is the least painful and the most effective one. Also you need to consider whether the therapist you have contacted is suitably qualified to deal with your problem. A therapist may be highly recommended but may lack the expertise which you and your problem merit. Do not consult an orthopaedic surgeon for a gastroenteric complaint!

Probability of success (prognosis)

Should you decide to undergo a recommended therapy, you want to know in general terms (a) the likely duration of the therapy, and (b) its probability of success. Some therapists would be affronted by your reasonable demands. If pressed, they may resort to well-known, well-tried and seemingly convincing clichés such as, 'Counselling or therapy is such a mysterious process that one can never make futuristic statements with any degree of certainty.' Do not be fobbed off by your therapists' sugary clichés. You have a *right* to know and *should insist upon it being recognized and respected*.

You would also wish to be certain what was meant by *effective therapy*. Is there an objective way of judging this, or would other therapists quibble over the meaning in academic journals! How far would you go along with the suggestion that you *were cured only when you felt you were cured*?

Cost of therapy

You would wish to know the cost of your therapy and if you could have the same (or a similar) kind of therapy elsewhere, cheaper. What would happen in financial terms if your therapy were found not to be successful?

These are the issues with which most clients seeking therapeutic help are likely to be concerned. They are less likely to worry about subsidiary problems such as the sex, age, ethnicity, mannerisms, attitudes and values of the therapist. Some might. It may be wonderful to relate to a warm, empathic, understanding, humorous, articulate, good-looking and well-dressed therapist, who shared our values and social concerns! So would having breakfast in a secluded rose garden! But the absence of one or two of these attributes is unlikely to upset a client to an extent where s/he feels impelled to terminate the therapy.

How far do the general expectations of clients match what is actually provided by therapists? Is there a close fit? Is there congruence between expectation and actuality? Or a chasm? Do clients on the whole get their money's worth? Or become dissatisfied customers?

Psychotherapy is one of those rare areas of commercial enterprise where a therapist does rather well out of a dissatisfied customer. The poor client is unable to get his or her money back and there is an expectation that they will return for yet another 'course' of treatment (Laungani 1992).

The historical perspective

The last 50 years have witnessed a dramatic change in the pattern and practice of psychotherapy and in the training of psychotherapists. Until the early 1950s the custody of mental patients (as they were then called) and the treatment of their disorders were largely in the hands of psychiatrists and psychoanalysts who, without exception, were medically qualified, with a conceptual framework based on the medical model. Yet each had irreconcilably different approaches to the definition, aetiology and treatment of mental disorders. Psychiatrists in general preferred physical methods of treatment, including drugs, electric shocks and, in exceptional cases, psychosurgery. Psychoanalysts adhered to verbal methods of treatment, and generally confined themselves to the treatment of non-psychotic disorders.

The usefulness of the medical model – and by implication, traditional psychiatry – began to be questioned. The diagnostic methods used by psychiatrists based on the Diagnostic and Statistical Methods of the American Psychiatric Association (DSMs) came under sustained attack; they were seen as lacking in objectivity, often reflecting the preoccupations of the psychiatrist rather than the mental condition of the patient, and their methods were seen as being crude and injurious to the interests of the patients. Concerns were expressed at the ease with which patients were admitted to psychiatric institutions – particularly on the basis of involuntary commitment orders. The psychiatrist had only to spend on average 10.2 minutes screening the patient! Suddenly the patient had no rights! No civil liberties! No freedom! The patient could be incarcerated for an indefinite period (Ennis and Emery 1978). Appeals were seen – and still are, in many psychiatric circles – as symptoms of paranoia or other disorders (Scheff 1975). Heads I win. Tails you lose! But surely, involuntary commitment is a rare phenomenon. Figures have dropped significantly over the years, on both sides of the Atlantic, but the problem of involuntary commitment is still a serious one which raises fundamental moral questions. Szasz (1970, 1973) asked whether society has the right to detain individuals against their will, how those rights are granted, and by what sets of objectively demonstrable criteria, if any. When can an individual be freed? Szasz argued that the very act of incarcerating an individual in an institution is an offence to the client's dignity – such a process stigmatizes and invalidates the client. He was convinced that psychiatry has never achieved the corpus of knowledge which would distinguish it as a scientific discipline.

Psychoanalytical therapies were challenged and were seen as mechanical, expensive, time-consuming, and as portraying people in unjustifiably pessimistic and negative terms; their effectiveness had not been clearly demonstrated, and the selectivity exercised by the analysts in the choice of clients restricted access to many who needed help.

New brooms for old

In the 1960s California saw an astonishing rise in new methods of helping others to achieve their full potential and realize their personality. The new wave movement swept away past terms and concepts – mental illness, patient diagnosis, disorder, treatment and care. Terms such as realization of personality, self-actualization, authenticity, peak experiences, letting suppressions come to the surface, coming to terms with one's feelings, acquiring holistic changes, acquiring empathy, trust, and being oneself, came into popular usage.

The new psychotherapists recognized no allegiance either to Freudian theory and its variants or to traditional psychiatry, and much of their 'progress' challenged – and rejected – older theories. Therapists of all persuasions from humanistic to cognitive and those in between grew in number to meet the growing demands of their customers. Like fast food, group psychotherapy had at last arrived on the streets to cater instantly to the needs of the masses and it had such a refreshing approach. Gone was the secrecy, stuffiness and artificiality surrounding the psychoanalytical therapies of the past. Gone the stringent selection procedures to 'vet' potential clients, to be replaced by an almost breathtaking openness! Clients could come for as many (or as few) sessions as they desired, drop out of treatment for a few weeks, join another group meanwhile, and return to the fold without loss of face or residual guilt. They were not subjected to the harsh rules of the past, but were liberated and free.

The therapeutic atmosphere and the therapists were relaxed. Group members were referred to by their first names, as were therapists, sometimes called leaders, facilitators or change agents. The group at times was persuaded, inveigled, bullied into doing exercises suggested by the leader(s), or asked to share one person's emotional experience, thereby 'helping' that member to come to terms with his or her own crises. Members were encouraged to explore their feelings and interact with one another freely – not just with words but also with their bodies. More 'radical' psychotherapists tried to help people to resolve their psychosexual problems by encouraging clients to have sex with them – all part of the therapeutic package! For a therapist to volunteer to have sex with his/her client raises very serious moral and professional issues. Your own moral upbringing may provide the best solution to dealing with such a situation. You may be appalled by the very idea and terminate therapy forthwith. You may wish to report the therapist for professional misconduct (to which official authority or organization would you turn?) (see Chapter 48). Alternatively, you may be intrigued by the idea of being involved with what is euphemistically referred to in the trade as a 'surrogate' sexual partner.

In the USA each approach acquired its own mould and ethos. Driven by a buoyant consumer-market economy, offers of therapies became freely available. Since there were vast pecuniary gains to be made, they were advertised in glossy magazines, journals and popular newspapers. The consumer was pampered, but there was a dark and sinister side to this. The smell of easy money attracted its share of grubby, avaricious 'cowboys' who 'set up shop', acquired a prestigious address, covered the office wall with a string of worthless diplomas and certificates, and preyed upon unsuspecting clients, who had no way of telling the genuine from the fake. Clients needed to be protected from such dangerous abuses and malpractices, and if the profession was not to lose its credibility such obnoxious, greasy peddlers in human weakness and vulnerabilities needed weeding out ruthlessly.

The development of safeguards in the UK

How were the rights of clients to be safeguarded and how was the profession to prevent its own image from becoming besmirched on this side of the Atlantic?

There was a felt urgent need for compiling a National Register of counsellors and psychotherapists (Dryden 1994). Serious consideration was given to this problem, and two steps were taken in the right direction. The United Kingdom Council for Psychotherapy (UKCP) was set up in 1993, and BAC (British Association for Counselling), at the request of various counselling organizations, agreed to set up a United Kingdom Register of Counsellors (UKRC), from 1996. These would ensure that people registered as counsellors and/or psychotherapists were duly qualified and were bona fide, accredited members of their profession. The merits of such a move are undeniable, yet there is a loophole for the 'malpractitioners' of the profession. Unless the UKCP and UKRC are awarded statutory powers to impose legal sanctions, the malpractitioners of the profession could still 'muscle in' on unsuspecting clients. That is an unresolved issue.

However, professionally qualified therapists and counsellors are faced with another problem endemic to the very nature of counselling and psychotherapy. If therapists are not to lose their credibility, it is incumbent upon them to state clearly and unambiguously the nature and type of services offered. The client has a right to more than vague, platitudinous assurances. At the very least, psychotherapists need to define and articulate their conceptual framework and be able to offer assurance on the four points (see pp. 315–17) with which clients are most likely to be concerned.

The main questions about the practice of present-day psychotherapies concern their validity, effectiveness and commensurability. Without informed, objective answers to such questions, the present-day psychotherapies will be subjected to the same kind of attack that has been launched on the traditional therapies.

Validity, effectiveness and commensurability of psychotherapies

All psychotherapeutic practices explicitly or implicitly spring from their respective theoretical frameworks. Of this fundamental fact some psychotherapists are sadly ignorant. The theoretical underpinnings of the present-day psychotherapies are in a state of 'epistemological anarchy' aptly summed up by Feyerabend (1975) as 'anything goes'. *If it works, use it* appears to be the guiding policy of too many psychotherapeutic practices. Such a refreshingly pragmatic approach would be welcomed if it could explain and demonstrate what it is that actually works in a given therapy and what are its theoretical links. On this vital point there does not appear to be a clear answer and, in some cases, there is not even a faint resemblance between theory and practice.

When theories from which the practices are supposedly derived are not clearly formulated and are not open to testing, their validity remains a questionable issue. They may be valid, but there is no exact way of telling, nor can one know why they are valid. The decision to help a client by resorting to a particular kind of therapy whose *unintended consequences* may have far-reaching effects on their mental and moral well-being must be made on more than just a caveat of good intentions. Such decisions must be made, as far as possible, on the state of available objective knowledge.

Yet, strangely enough, the evidence – such as there is – seems to suggest that persons who undergo therapy have a better chance of recovering than those who do not. Figures vary, as do the statistics and research methods used for evaluating therapeutic outcomes. Evidence based on the studies done in the 1970s and 1980s (Bergin and Lambert 1978; Luborsky et al. 1975; Rachman and Wilson 1980; Sloane et al. 1975) suggests that therapies do in general tend to work. How they work, the specific identifiable features that bring about the reported positive changes in the well-being of the client, have not been clearly articulated. Nor is it always clear what investigators mean by the word *work* in describing the effectiveness of psychotherapy. Some rely on client's subjective reports, some on the disappearance of symptoms, some on changes in test scores and behavioural measures in the predicted direction; others refer to the holistic changes manifested in the client's attitudes and values concerning his or her mental health, work and interpersonal relationships. It appears that the personality characteristics of the therapists – in particular, warmth, trust and acceptance – play a crucial role in determining the positive outcome of therapy (Luborsky et al. 1986; Omer and London 1988; Patterson 1989; Talley et al. l990). In a sense it is essential to choose one's therapist far more carefully than the therapy which is on offer, and there are specific factors for a client to consider seriously when choosing an appropriate therapist. Avoid:

- therapists who are rude, intimidating and hostile, who humiliate and belittle the client – notwithstanding their disclaimers that such behaviours on their part are an integral part of the therapeutic process. There is no excuse for rudeness;
- therapists who continually talk about *their own* problems instead of concerning themselves with the problems of their clients;
- therapists who resort to sexual innuendoes and even offer themselves as sexual surrogates to the client;
- therapists who skilfully manipulate a prolonged state of dependence on themselves.

Although the personality characteristics of the therapist are known to have a positive influence on the outcome of therapy, we do not appear to have precise knowledge of how different therapies actually work. Some work more efficiently (or less efficiently) than others. Some tend to help more persons than others. But which of the many therapies work 'best' under which conditions, how, with what kind of clients, on what time-scale, with what kind of results, are questions which are not easy to answer with a high degree of certainty because most therapies are not easily commensurable. Legitimate comparisons require a clear delineation of a large set of common parameters, such as the random assignment of cases into control (no treatment) groups and experimental groups, severity of life problems or neuroses, specification of procedures to be followed, agreed definition of effectiveness, period of treatment, the professional expertise of therapists, and their willingness to allow their work to be examined objectively by others. Such conditions are hard to meet and the studies (mentioned earlier) have not produced unequivocal findings. The practical methodological difficulties are so daunting that many therapists, weary of the tedium of commensurability, have questioned its legitimacy, suggesting that there may be an economic, or even an empirical justification. Is there a rational reason for comparing therapies or is this short-sighted and mistaken? This is surely not the issue. The most compelling justification is a *moral* one. It is the moral responsibility of the therapist to ensure that the client who seeks succour is given it. The second consideration is that any therapeutic procedures used must not be *assumed* but must be *seen* to be beneficial to the client. This can be achieved only when therapies are put to crucial tests concerning their effectiveness. Otherwise, sadly, one is back into a state of epistemological anarchy.

Conclusion

Can psychotherapies seriously damage your health? It is suggested that some psychotherapies can have adverse effects on your health. So can some psychotherapists .

Although the few unqualified 'counsellors' and 'psychotherapists' have more than a nuisance value, the majority of the trained, professionally qualified psychotherapists do not get the kind of recognition which is their due. The good they do remains unsung, and instead such dramatically tragic cases as the the fatal stabbing by Christopher Clunis at a London Underground station give rise to many alarmist speculations concerning the work done by psychiatrists, psychotherapists and counsellors.

The number of clients seeking some form of psychotherapy has increased significantly and shows every sign of increasing further. Perhaps clients have come to expect and consequently demand far more than can conceivably be provided by society in general and psychotherapists in particular. The present hedonistic, push-button, instant-gratification, technological Western society has perhaps beguiled potential clients into believing that happiness too can be obtained instantly. A simple prick of a drug needle opens the gates to an ephemeral and unreal Paradise! When the effects wear off, one plunges, like the fallen angels, into the inner layers of the inferno.

My own feelings as an Easterner living in the West, is that the Westerner in search of happiness has concentrated on the right to happiness rather than on the right to pursue happiness (Laungani 1993). Happiness does not, as is mistakenly publicized, come through taking Prozac (Kramer 1994). It leads, perhaps, to *an absence of unhappiness* – which is not the same thing. Happiness, to my mind, does not come instantly. One has to work at it.

Update

See Roth and Fonagy (1996) for a good introduction to evidence-based practice in counselling and psychotherapy.

References

Bergin, A.E. and Garfield, S.L. (eds) (1971) *Handbook of Psychotherapy and Change*, New York: Wiley.

Bergin, A.E. and Lambert, M.J. (1978) 'The evaluation of therapeutic outcomes, in S.L. Garfield and A.E. Bergin (eds), *Handbook of Psychotherapy and Change: An Empirical Analysis* (2nd edn), New York: Wiley, 139–90.

Dryden, W. (1994) 'Possible future trends in counselling and counsellor training: a personal view', *Counselling*, 5 (3) (August): 194–7.

Ennis, B.J. and Emery, R.D. (1978) *The Rights of Mental Patients*, New York: Avon Books.

Eysenck, H.J. (1985) *Decline and Fall of the Freudian Empire*, Penguin Books.

Feyerabend, P. (1975) *Against Method*, London: NLB.

Kramer, P.J. (1994) *Listening to Prozac*, London: Fourth Estate.

Kutash, I.L. and Wolf, A. (eds) (1986) *Psychotherapist's Casebook*, San Francisco: Jossey-Bass.

Laungani, P. (1992) *It Shouldn't Happen to a Patient*, London: Whiting & Birch Ltd.

Laungani, P. (1993) 'Cultural variations in the understanding and treatment of psychiatric disorders: India and England', *Counselling Psychology Quarterly*, 5 (3): 231–44.

Luborsky, L., Singer, B. and Luborsky, L. (1975) 'Comparative studies of psychotherapies: is it true that "Everyone has won and all must have prizes"?', *Archives of General Psychiatry*, 32: 995–1008.

Luborsky, L., Crits-Christoph, P. and McLellan, A.T., et al. (1986) 'Do therapists vary much in their success?', *American Journal of Orthopsychiatry*, 56 (4): 501–12.

Omer, H. and London, P. (1988) 'Metamorphosis in psychotherapy: end of the systems era', *Psychotherapy*, 25 (2): 171–80.

Patterson, C.H. (1989) 'Foundations for a systematic eclectic psychotherapy', *Psychotherapy*, 26 (4): 427–35.

Rachman, S.J. and Wilson, G.T. (1980) *The Effects of Psychological Therapy* (2nd enlarged edn), New York, NY: Pergamon Press.

Roth, A. and Fonagy, P. (1996) *What Works for Whom? – A Critical Review of Psychotherapy Research*, New York: Guilford Press.

Scheff, T.J. (ed.) (1975) *Labelling Madness*, New Jersey: Prentice-Hall.

Sloane, R.B., Staples, F.R., Cristol, A.H., Yorkston, N.J. and Whipple, K. (1975) *Psychotherapy Versus Behaviour Therapy*, Cambridge, Mass.: Harvard University Press.

Szasz, T.S. (1970) *The Manufacture of Madness*, New York: Harper & Row.

Szasz, T.S. (ed.) (1973) *The Age of Madness: A History of Involuntary Hospitalization*, Doubleday.

Talley, P.F., Strupp, H.H. and Morey, L.C. (1990) 'Matchmaking in psychotherapy: patient–therapist dimensions and their impact on outcome', *Journal of Consulting and Clinical Psychology*, 58 (2): 182–8.

Winston, A. (ed.) (1985) 'Short-term dynamic psychotherapy', *American Psychiatric Press*. Washington, DC.

Discussion issues

1 Do you agree that psychotherapies have the potential to damage health? Which of the author's arguments lead you to this view?

2 In your experience is the diagnosis of a client's problem(s) an essential part of counselling and psychotherapy? What leads you to this conclusion?

3 What do you consider are effective ways of helping clients whose behaviour may cause danger to other people, or themselves?

4 In what ways does a knowledge of research findings inform your own work? What might you do to become more informed about research into therapeutic effectiveness?

48

Therapy Checklist for Potential Clients and Those Already in Therapy

Stephen Palmer and Kasia Szymanska

During the early 1990s we developed a checklist to help both potential clients and those already in therapy to avoid being exploited in therapy (Palmer and Szymanska 1994a). The checklist provides clients with essential information about what they could ask the therapist in the first session and about different aspects of the therapeutic relationship. This was in response to a number of cases that had been reported in professional journals and the media.

Response to checklist

Since 1994 the article and checklist has received a great deal of positive attention. Many counsellors and psychotherapists wrote in to commend us on its publication, specifically mentioning the checklist's clarity, brevity and ease of use. The checklist is a single-sided sheet that makes it easy to photocopy. It has been republished in many journals (for example, Palmer and Szymanska 1994b), books (Szymanska and Palmer 1997) and magazines, used by GP practices and published on the Internet (see note, p. 325). The checklist has also been used widely across the world, as far afield as New Zealand.

On the negative side, we received correspondence from therapists who believed our checklist was unnecessary because it states the obvious and 'exploitation does not occur'. We argue that it may state the obvious to experienced therapists but not to inexperienced clients, at whom it is aimed. In one case, a registrar of a hypnotherapy register wrote a letter to a journal that had published our article, complaining that our checklist recommended that therapists should receive supervision. Apparently, this was not mandatory for the therapists on his particular register and was unnecessary!

The research to date has found unequivocally that exploitation does occur and mandatory codes of ethics do not necessarily protect clients sufficiently from exploitation. A British survey of clinical psychologists' attitudes towards sexual contact with clients highlighted the fact that 3.4 per cent of psychologists had sexual contact with current or former clients (Garrett and Davis 1994). This percentage represents 20 psychologists of the 581 who returned their questionnaires. While on average sexual contact occurred with just one client, one psychologist admitted to sexual contact with five current clients and one discharged client. These findings support the data published in North America (see Szymanska and Palmer 1997 for a review of these studies). In addition the Prevention of

---

This chapter was first published as 'How to avoid being exploited in counselling and psychotherapy', in *Counselling*, Journal of the British Association for Counselling, vol. 5, no. 1, p. 24 (1994).

Professional Abuse Network (POPAN), an organization developed to help clients who have been abused by professionals, found that, after doctors, the second and third highest professions of abusers reported to them were psychotherapists and counsellors. This information only serves to verify the persistence of abuse and the need to protect clients through public education, statutory registration and further research.

Issues for the client to consider in counselling, psychotherapy or hypnotherapy

1. Below is a list of topics or questions you may wish to raise when speaking to a therapist (1) on the phone or when attending your first/assessment session:

   a. Check your therapist has relevant qualifications and experience in the field of counselling, psychotherapy or hypnotherapy (2).

   b. Ask about the type of approach the therapist uses, and how it relates to your problem (3).

   c. Ask if the therapist is in supervision (most professional bodies consider supervision to be mandatory (4).

   d. Ask whether the therapist or the therapeutic agency is a member of a professional body and abides by a code of ethics. Where possible obtain a copy of the code.

   e. Discuss your goals/expectations of therapy.

   f. Ask about the fees if any (if your income is low check if the therapist operates a sliding scale) and discuss the frequency and estimated duration of the therapy.

   g. Arrange regular review sessions with your therapist to evaluate your progress.

   h. Do not be coerced into a long-term therapeutic contract unless you are satisfied this is necessary and beneficial to you.

If you do not have a chance to discuss the above points during your first session discuss them at the next possible opportunity.

General issues

2. Therapist self-disclosure can sometimes be therapeutically useful. However, if the therapist discussing his/her own problems at length dominates the sessions, raise this issue in the therapy session.

3. If at any time you feel uncomfortable, undermined or manipulated within the session, discuss this with your counsellor. It is easier to resolve issues as and when they arise.

4. Do not accept gifts from your therapist. This does not apply to relevant therapeutic material.

---

5. Do not accept social invitations from your therapist. For example, going for a meal or drink together. However, this does not apply to relevant therapeutic assignments such as being accompanied by your therapist into a situation to help you overcome your phobia.

6. If your therapist proposes a change in venue for the therapy sessions without a valid reason, do not agree. For example from the centre to the therapist's own home.

7. Research has shown that it is not beneficial for clients to have sexual contact with their counsellor. Professional bodies in the fields of counselling, psychotherapy and hypnotherapy consider it unethical and detrimental to the therapeutic relationship.

8. If you have any doubts about the therapy you are receiving discuss these doubts with your therapist. If you are still uncertain, either talk to a friend, your doctor, the Citizens Advice Bureau, the professional body your therapist belongs to or the agency your therapist works for.

9. You have the right to terminate therapy when you wish.

Footnotes

(1) *In this checklist, the term 'therapist' has been used to denote counsellors, psychotherapists and hypnotherapists.*

(2) *For example: counsellors may be accredited by professional bodies such as The British Association for Counselling and Psychotherapy; psychotherapists and hypnotherapists may be registered with The United Kingdom Council for Psychotherapy, and psychologists may be chartered by the British Psychological Society.*

(3) *Common approaches include, person-centred, psychodynamic, gestalt, transactional analysis and cognitive-behaviour therapy.*

(4) *Counselling supervision is a formal arrangement by which therapists discuss their work in a confidential setting on a regular basis with one or more professional therapists.*

For information on this topic see http://www.geocities.com/clientchecklist/
© 2001, Palmer and Szymanska

Checklist for clients

Conclusion

In recent years, professional therapeutic bodies have received an increasing number of complaints against their members. Even though codes of ethics have been revised, it is likely that this trend will continue. Although many professional bodies are keen to have State Registration of their members, the research has not shown that this will reduce the exploitation of clients. However, State Registration may prevent those therapists struck off from legally practising, which may be a step in the right direction. This checklist helps to prepare the client for the very small minority of therapists who are exploitative.

References

Garrett, T. and Davis, J. (1994) 'Epidemiology in the UK', in D. Jehu (ed.), *Patients as Victims: Sexual Abuse in Psychotherapy and Counselling*, Chichester: Wiley.

Palmer, S. and Szymanska, K. (1994a) 'How to avoid being exploited in counselling and psychotherapy', *Counselling*, 5 (1): 24.

Palmer, S. and Szymanska, K. (1994b) 'A checklist for clients interested in receiving counselling, psychotherapy and hypnosis', *The Rational Emotive Behaviour Therapist*, 2 (1): 25–7.

Prevention of Professional Abuse Network (1997–8) *Annual Report*, 1 Wyvil Court, Wyvil Road, London, SW8 2TG.

Szymanska, K. and Palmer, S. (1997) 'Therapist–client exploitation', in S. Palmer and G. McMahon (eds), *The Handbook of Counselling*, London: Routledge.

Discussion issues

1 A client checklist is unnecessary.
2 Therapist exploitation of clients is increasing.
3 A client checklist will encourage clients to make complaints unnecessarily to professional bodies about their therapists.
4 State registration will prevent client exploitation.

49

Making the Most of Therapy

How to help clients get the best from you

Sheila Dainow

I have spent a great chunk of my working life training people to be counsellors – and another chunk helping them to be counsellors through supervision. From time to time, perhaps when discussing a particularly 'difficult' client (which usually means a client who doesn't behave in the way we expect) with students or practitioners, it has occurred to me that I might be spending my time more profitably by running courses for clients. Possible titles might be: 'How to work with difficult counsellors' or 'How to get the best out of your counsellor'.

On the other hand, sometimes a client will describe prior experiences of counselling which they feel has been less than successful. 'He/she never really discussed anything with me'; 'I don't know why all the focus was on how I felt – I wanted to talk about what the other people were doing to me'; 'I felt awkward all the time – I had to start the conversation and sometimes I just didn't have anything to talk about'; 'He/she never gave me any advice. It was such a waste of time.'

What strikes me about these statements from clients is that the counsellor was probably being a 'good counsellor' but the client had no idea how to be a 'good client', unprepared for the difference between ordinary conversation and a counselling session.

So here is a letter I might send to my next client to prepare him or her for our meeting:

Dear future client,

You are soon coming to see me for your first session, so I thought I would write to you to explain a few things about this whole business of counselling.

To understand better how counselling works, it's worth thinking about what it's not. It's not the same as going to a doctor or other 'expert' where you can expect to be advised, instructed, interpreted or directed. Our relationship will be somewhat different from this. Between us the power will be more equally shared. You will be in charge of the 'agenda', I will do my best to understand what you want to achieve and help you achieve it.

We will spend most of our time together talking but it won't be like the conversations you are used to. Because my job is to understand you as much as possible, I will spend most of my time listening while you talk. It won't matter how long it takes you; you will find that there are times when you don't really know what to say or you might want to

This piece first appeared in *Herm College News* and is reproduced by kind permission of the principal. The chapter was next published in *Counselling*, Journal of the British Association for Counselling, vol. 10, no. 2, pp. 97–8 (1999).

think about something before you say the words. You can take as long as you like; you might even feel like saying nothing for a while, which is fine by me. I'm happy to wait until you want to talk. When you do, what I will be doing is trying to understand how you are experiencing your world and what is happening to you. So when I do join in the conversation it will often be to reflect back what I have understood you to be saying and how you might be feeling. Sometimes I will be right and sometimes wrong, so you will have the opportunity to check on how well I am understanding you.

Another important element in our relationship is that I have no interest in judging what kind of person you are. My interest is in helping you understand yourself and to explore how your life can be as satisfying and happy as possible. If you change anything at all about yourself it will be because you want to, not because I think you ought to. For instance, supposing you are feeling very unhappy about something. It won't be my job to make you feel happier – my job will be to help you fully experience and understand your feelings. The reason for this is that a distressing feeling does not disappear if it is ignored – it may fade for a while but it can come up again and again. Counsellors believe that expressing emotions can be a healing process, so that you don't have to use a lot of energy in keeping old hurts and pain buried. We could explore the options you might have and you might go on to decide to do something to change things – but this part of it will be in *your* hands.

My next big aim is to encourage you to recognize and take responsibility for your own thoughts, feelings and behaviour. It is so easy to avoid this by finding out who is to blame for what is happening to us. If you have ever said (or thought) things like, 'If you hadn't done that, I wouldn't be so unhappy'; 'You make me so angry'; 'I wouldn't do this if you didn't provoke me' you will know what I mean. The problem here is that each of these responses implies that the other person has got inside you and is controlling how you think and feel and what you do. But this is not really how it happens. What is more likely is that the other person has put you in touch with thoughts and feelings that were already there. Your reactions happen in your mind and body and are a result of your particular perception of the event. It would probably be truer to say, 'I was able to hide how unhappy I was until you uncovered it'; 'When I think about you, I feel angry'; 'I lose control over my anger when I think you are provoking me.'

I know this probably sounds a bit picky – but there is an important point to it. Presumably you are coming to counselling because you want something about yourself or your life-style to change. If the truth was that other people were responsible for what was happening inside you – we would have to wait for these people to change before you could get a result. We could be waiting for a long time. If, however, it becomes clear that *you* are responsible – you can change anytime you like – and I will do all I can to help you.

You might find it strange sometimes how I might focus on the words you are using and suggest you change certain words or phrases. For instance, you might say, 'So-and-so is insensitive and thoughtless. I hate him/her. He/she never takes any notice of what I say.' I might suggest you change this to 'I'm feeling irritated with so-and-so. He/she didn't acknowledge what I said at the meeting.' As we discuss this you might realize that the feeling is a familiar one and that your anger is directed at other people in your life who never seemed to take you seriously. We can begin to explore how things that have happened to you in the past might still be influencing how you are now. You might decide that you don't want to continue to react to present situations in the same way – and so begin to change. On the other hand, you might decide that changing carries too much risk and decide to stay the same. I will help you to be clear about what decisions you are making and support you whatever you decide (unless you are contemplating something illegal, immoral or anti-social!).

One other thing that might surprise you is that I will be interested in how you communicate in other ways than speaking. We live in a society which tends to value minds above bodies. From an early age we are taught how to behave reasonably and keep ourselves under control. Our bodies are programmed to prepare us for fight or flight whenever we perceive a threat, but most of the time we can't beat someone up or rush screaming from the room when our safety is jeopardized. We subdue our natural response and face the situation. I'm not saying this is a bad thing – after all, we couldn't really have a society in which everyone reacted as if every threat was a matter of life and death. The problem is that we can take things to the other extreme and hide our natural emotional responses altogether. Some kinds of therapy are almost totally focused on the way the body has responded to various life experiences and how these responses have become our physical presentation to the world. Although I don't follow that practice absolutely, I am interested in how it is sometimes possible to access what is happening in our minds and souls through concentrating on what is happening in our bodies.

So when we are together, I will encourage you to pay attention to the messages you get from your body. For instance, how do you breathe? I know you do – otherwise you wouldn't be reading this, but are you aware of how you do it. Do you, for instance, breathe shallowly – as we tend to do when we unconsciously desire to cut ourselves off from how we are feeling. When we were small children, our bodies responded naturally to the situations in which we found ourselves. If we were frightened, our shoulders moved round to protect our vulnerable inner self, our head dropped as if we couldn't allow ourselves to look the world in the eye. If we were angry, our muscles tensed; sadness might have given us a permanently turned down mouth. You might find it interesting to stand in front of a full-length mirror and examine yourself as if you were a stranger to see what messages your body might be giving.

Another particular interest of mine is how our response to ordinary everyday events usually mirrors how we respond (or responded in the past) to more important matters – and how our responses tend to follow a coherent theme almost as if we were following some life script which resulted from decisions we make in our very early years. So you might be mystified by my attention to what may seem to you a very trivial happening.

Lastly, just in case you were feeling this is all a bit airy-fairy, some practical matters. I will expect you to be on time for our appointments and to keep to whatever arrangements we make regarding payment. If you cancel without reasonable notice or don't turn up, I will expect you to pay for that appointment. Although I will encourage you to express your feelings freely, I don't expect you to act out any violence either towards me or my furniture and I won't condone violence towards any other person. Drinking alcohol or taking mind-altering drugs is not a good idea before coming to a counselling session and I won't permit smoking during a session. This is not because I have any moral objection to these things but because these substances tend to mask our true thoughts and feelings – that's probably why we reach for them in the first place. You will be wasting your time (and money) if you come to a counselling session out of touch with your 'true' self.

In return for these expectations I have of you, I will offer you a contract of confidentiality – that is, I won't talk about you to anyone else in such a way that you could be identified. When we meet, I will make myself as wholly available to you as possible and you will have my entire attention.

I look forward to meeting you.

Discussion issues

1 How essential do you think it is that the client understands your counselling philosophy?
2 How might you prepare a new client to make the most of counselling?
3 Is it true that anyone could benefit from counselling?
4 What factors might prevent a client from benefiting from counselling?

50

In the Counsellor's Chair

Counselling and the abuse of power

Judith Longman interviews Professor Ernesto Spinelli

Professor Spinelli is the Academic Dean of the School of Psychotherapy and Counselling at Regent's College, London. A UKCP registered existential psychotherapist, he maintains a private practice in south-east London. He is Past Chair of the Society for Existential Analysis and Past-Chair of the British Psychological Society's Division of Counselling Psychology, and a Fellow of the BACP. Author of many articles, his most recent book is The Mirror and the Hammer: Challenging Therapeutic Orthodoxies *(Continuum 2001). A more detailed account of the issue of power is discussed in his book* Demystifying Therapy *(Constable 1994).*

ES: The issue of power and the potential for its misuse and abuse in therapy has been one that has become of increasing concern in the last ten years or so. Most of the texts that have addressed this have looked at actual *instances* of misuse or abuse of power, either financial or sexual or physical or whatever. While these are very important, it seems to me that in some ways what has been missed out by these studies is an examination of how our varying theories provide us with assumptions, with values, with attitudes, that may in *themselves* make it more likely for issues of misuse and abuse of power to occur. And I would urge practitioners to explore that, because in that act of exploration, they may be confronted with perhaps previously unconsidered questions of their use and potential misuse of power in the relationship.

JL: Can you give one or two examples of where some misuse of power might occur in, say, an ordinary counselling or psychotherapy setting?

ES: Well. I'll give you an example from my own experience. I was training at one of the better known psychoanalytic institutes in this country and as part of our training we engaged in a group-therapy procedure, which was facilitated by two therapists, one female, one male. After a few weeks of this process, the therapists began to insist that we refer to them as 'mummy' and 'daddy' and I spoke up and said, 'This is nonsense. You're not my mother. You're not my father. And I don't see why you insist that we call you that.' At which point the male therapist interjected and said, 'Look! It's obvious to me why you're saying this. It's to do with the fact that you're an orphan.' I was taken aback by this interpretation, maybe because both my parents were, happily, both alive at the time, and I threw this back at him and said, 'Look, you know, I'm not an orphan. My parents are alive and kicking.' To which

This chapter was first published in *Counselling*, Journal of the British Association for Counselling, vol. 9, no. 3, pp. 181–4 (1998).

331

he replied, 'Ah, but that doesn't matter. What I'm referring to is the fact that you're a *psychic* orphan.' I think in doing that he proved how some therapists at least can reassure themselves that they're always right. But I think, more importantly, what it provoked was a sense of disenchantment and loss of respect for him as a therapist and ultimately a tension between us that was never resolved. I think it reveals very clearly how a therapist's reliance upon an interpretation derived from a theoretical assumption can be in itself misplaced, so that it becomes more abusive than anything else. Even if it were to be found that there was *something* being said that would have actually been worth my attending to, maybe about the way my relations with my parents actually were, even so, the manner in which it was presented was one that promoted the view, 'I as therapist know what I'm talking about, in spite of what you may think or in spite of your own responses to this, and you must listen to me because *I am right*, because I have this whole body of theory behind me to back me up.' I think that while the intention may be good, in that we're trying supposedly to help the person, it seems to me that what we're also doing is helping ourselves: that it's more for us as therapists than it might be for the client.

JL: I suppose the danger is that many clients and patients seeking counselling or psychotherapy are only too happy to be told what to do or what's 'wrong with them' and it can be an abusive collusion, can't it, between counsellors and clients?

ES: Absolutely. The people who come to us, if they come to us willingly, are searching for something from us, whether it's the truth or whether it's relief from anxieties or resolution of problems or a better way of living. And while I would imagine that most models of therapy take some kind of cautious position towards that, I think it's also important for each model to look at how it deals with that need. Does it transform it? Does it say, 'Well, this is what you *think* you want, but through examination we'll discover what you *really* want'; or maybe, 'I know already what you really want, and we're going to manipulate you in some way into agreeing with me'? Does it try to interject and say, 'Well, I don't know if I could offer you *that*, but this is what I *can* offer you'? How does each of us deal with the reality of clients' expectations?

JL: So what might be the best thing for the client is actually the therapist in the end saying, 'I don't know.'

ES: I think one of the fantasies that we have as therapists is that we have somehow accumulated sufficient knowledge about therapy that we can act with some degree of justified knowledge as to what to do with clients. I call it a fantasy because it seems to me that out of all the research that has emerged over the last 20, 30, 40 years there is no hard evidence about what might be the valuable effects of therapy; so we have assumptions about how long somebody has trained as being an important variable – no evidence for that at all; we have assumptions about the type of training, whether it's psychoanalytic or cognitive-behavioural or humanistic; there's no evidence for any one model of therapy being more likely to provoke positive results than any other. We have assumptions about whether the therapist was himself or herself in therapy; no basis for that at all. Then you have research that asks *clients* what they consider to be the most essential factors of effective therapy. In that research you find that there are a number of things that emerge: clients reply that what was most significant to them was that they had a specific time in which they could talk; the second one is that they felt that while they were talking they were being listened to at least some of the time; and the third thing was that the person who was there, the therapist, seemed to be a fairly human, humane kind of person, who was attentive to them, who wasn't some kind of robotic creature who worked by theoretical rules. So there's a lack of evidence for the things we consider to be most important as therapists, and there's evidence that suggests that what clients find to be important are not those things that we consider to be important, but are more basic things about relationship, about talking and listening. 'Can I call myself a professional if all that I'm doing that seems to be of value is listening to somebody else talk and not being machine-like?' So it seems that the obstacles that we're likely to have with regard to shedding the kind of tricks of our trade are not because of the losses the clients might experience but the losses *we* experience. I do think that perhaps there are, for instance, styles of listening or ways of listening that some therapists are more likely to be skilled in, if you can call it a skill, than might be the case in ordinary circumstances. So I think there may be particular things that therapists are able to offer, but until we as therapists are prepared to set aside some of the authority with which we invest ourselves I don't think we're going to get very far. At the same time, if we insist on doing that, then I think increasingly and quite rightly we're going to come up against resistance from the wider world, whether it's the media, or whether it's scientific research or whether it's our clients, saying to us, 'What kind of professional are you? You keep insisting that you're a professional, but what is it that you are, what is it that you do, that is so special, that is so different?' I think that for us to regain whatever authority we might deserve (which is still an open question) the first step is to be willing to set aside the false authority with which we've bequeathed ourselves.

JL: So being a therapist is quite a subversive activity or practice; it sounds as if that way of being is almost going against a sort of common Western assumption of what a professional is.

ES: Even though we've become as a society more open to the idea of counselling and therapy, nevertheless I think there's a great deal of frightened concern regarding what therapy is. It's still not unusual if somebody asks us what we do and we say, 'Oh, I'm a counsellor' or 'I'm a therapist', that the first response will be one of protection: 'I'd better be careful about what I say, then.' I think it's also something that as counsellors and therapists we have tended to promote, again because I think when you are relatively uncertain of what professional authority you might have, one of the best means of dealing with it is to evoke mystery. Maybe you convince yourself that you must have some kind of great authority because you're able to utilize all these words and concepts and so forth that the rest of the world finds incomprehensible. It may be that we as counsellors and therapists have added to this sense of suspicion because it's been advantageous to us to do so. Now, I think the situation has changed. Whether we've earned it or whether we've been manipulated into it, I don't know, but for one reason or another, because public awareness of counselling and therapy has increased substantially over the last few years, this mystique has started to break down and if we can't protect ourselves through mystery, how do we present ourselves now in a more public face?

JL: Do you see attempts by counselling organizations to increase professionalism and to introduce new standards in professionalization as questionable?

ES: Absolutely.

JL: And do you think that we need to stop for a minute and say, 'Hang on, what are we really trying to do here in inventing all these guidelines and working parties and standards and ethics committees?'

ES: Absolutely – all of these things give an illusion of professional bodies. We say: 'Look, if we go to all of these meetings, if we have all these standards, if we have these codes of ethics, we must be professionals.' And we can hide our questions about what we are professionals *of*, or *in*, or *about*, by having all these bodies to protect us. While I suppose most of us, myself included, have, by and large, a positive view towards some of these developments, where I remain sceptical personally is the question of the *basis* for them, because many of the assumptions we take for granted don't really have any basis to them. They're just biases that we might hold because at the very least they keep us employed, or they provide employment for our trainees. You know, sometimes I jokingly say to my students and trainees that we'll eventually reach a point where we'll no longer need clients, because we can just close the circle, we can counsel each other, supervise each other, and train each other … ad infinitum.

JL: Could we ever know what it is that makes a professional counsellor?

ES: It may be that what we need to do, as some people have already suggested, is to look at the very question of research, particularly in the areas of process and outcome research. Maybe we need to devise ways of exploring and examining what occurs in a therapeutic encounter, we need a methodology that is relevant to what we do and maybe that methodology hasn't emerged yet and there needs to be a way of allowing it to emerge. But I think the obstacle to all of that resides in the protective assumptions that we have about ourselves. It's going to expose us as having cloaked ourselves in something that is actually invisible and non-existent, and that's frightening. It's frightening to any one of us as a human being, it's frightening to us as counsellors and therapists. But on the other hand, if this is meant to be a profession that encourages people to look at things that concern and frighten them then surely we should turn that on ourselves and ask ourselves to do what we ask of our clients.

JL: It seems to me that perhaps one of the most important qualities or skills for a therapist is to be able to listen to what's happening at the moment and also to be able to say, 'I don't know what's going on and I must just listen some more and I must just accept that I don't know.'

ES: When I first start working with new trainees, one of the first exercises that we do is one that gets them to examine, much more carefully and much more honestly, what they think being a therapist is about – what they think they're meant to be doing and what their assumptions about counselling and therapy are in general. And, not surprisingly, the most typical answers are things like, 'I want to change people for the better', 'I want to heal people, or cure them', 'I want to make them stronger.' And, on one hand, while those are desirable intentions, faced with the fact that we have no idea as to how help or cure happens, it then becomes questionable for us to act as though we knew. That seems to me to be at the heart of the potential abuse that arises through our theories, because our theories suggest to us a sense of knowledge: this is, how we understand human beings or disturbed individuals or children or whoever, so we *know* something. If we adhere to those models and theories and, in having that filter, we listen out for those things that fit and we put aside and maybe even dismiss those things that a client will say that don't fit the pattern of theoretical beliefs, so that when a client eventually reaches a point that criticizes our position and says, 'You haven't been listening to me' or 'I disagree with what you've said', then we typically have yet another set of theoretical filters that come along and transform even those statements into statements that verify our belief system and dismiss what the client is saying. It would be nice if we could acknowledge our openness in the relationship, but what's going to make it difficult for us to do so? Well, once again, our assumptions about who we are and what we're supposed to be doing. And, you know, if you apply it to everyday situations, I think the absurdity of this point becomes highlighted. If you think of those conversations, those discussions that you've had, not in therapy, when you've come away and said, 'That was really great. It was really important, what was said. I got so much out of that. It's changed me in some ways', was there ever a point where either or both of the participants said, 'Right, we're going to direct our discussion in this way, then we're going to go that way, then we're going to stop here …'? It's the openness that is at the heart of any rewarding human encounter. And you'd think that therapists would connect to that and say, 'Wait a minute, there must be something there', because how do you kill a conversation dead right away? You start to say, 'Right, well, we're here now, we're going to go there in the next few minutes.' And everybody stops talking. You don't know what to do any more. And that's what we do as therapists if we start to direct the conversation or the dialogue or the monologue in a certain way because it fits. I think at the very least we end up with very stilted situations and at worst we end up with a position where the client feels, 'I haven't been heard. I've had words put into my mouth. I've had ideas put on me that I have to somehow accept, but which don't make sense.'

JL: Which for certain clients or patients could be terrifying.

ES: Yes, you're right. Far worse than that is the sense of, 'God, you know, maybe I am like this, and I never knew that and rather than having resolved anything or started to resolve anything, I've now got another issue, an even more serious one …'

JL: 'Who am I?' …

ES: '… about who I am.'

JL: The press, the media or individuals criticize counsellors and therapists because of this potential to abuse power, but I wonder whether, even if counselling and psychotherapy were 'clean' and it never happened, there would still be an assumption that any helping relationship is bound to be abusive? It's almost as if people assume that it *would* happen. So is there something inbuilt into our assumptions of a helping relationship, that somehow we can't bear that there should be such a thing? It's almost as if envy or something gets in the way of actually being able to say 'That's good.'

ES: I do think to some extent that the views you've just expressed may be part of our current age. We're not allowed to have heroes any more; you know, our heroes all need to have clay feet, and if there's something heroic about them, then there's also something that must be fundamentally flawed about them. So I think that part of it is the current *Zeitgeist*, but I think the other side of it is that we present ourselves as mysterious, possibly because we are so scared of our own shaky professional ground that we need to act like Wizards of Oz, and while it's very attractive and you acknowledge that the magic works, some of the time, it's also frightening. And we tend to make fun of frightening things. I think that's the way the media tends to handle it: we're either dangerous or we're charlatans, we're jesters, we're jokers; or we're both. While that's unfair, I think to some extent therapists have a responsibility for it by their unwillingness to talk openly about what it is that we do and the limitations of what we can offer people. We need to be ordinary and admit the lack of knowledge which is at the heart of any deep human encounter.

Discussion issues

1 What are your key assumptions regarding your 'being a counsellor' and 'providing counselling'? What challenges could be made to these assumptions?
2 What might there be within the theory and practice of the model/approach which you espouse that would reveal the potential for the misuse and abuse of power by the counsellor?
3 In considering your own personal experiences as a client, what instances of theoretically and/or interpersonally derived misuse or abuse of power by your psychotherapist/counsellor do you recall? How might these be avoided or minimized within your own practice as a counsellor?
4 'We're not allowed to have heroes any more ... [they] all need to have clay feet, and if there's something heroic about them, then there's also something that must be fundamentally flawed.' A realistic view?

51

Ethics for the Counselling Office

Petruska Clarkson

As far as I know there are few, if any, codes of ethics for administrative and ancillary staff who work in a variety of counselling and training settings even though the professional staff are very thoroughly bound to their code. I would like to offer the following suggestions as an example to other bodies and thus share my experience in this area, perhaps with a view to putting forward a statement to BAC on the basis of such a document. Some points are covered but not all; I would welcome others' feedback and comments and see this as the beginning of a dialogue on the subject of ethical guidelines for administrative and ancillary staff of counselling and psychotherapy practices, training institutes and colleges.

Suggested area for code

Confidentiality

Working as an administrator or other support staff person at a large training institute which runs an assessment and referral service means that many clients and trainees, supervisors and other professional staff may discuss matters which are confidential or within their strict code of ethics, usually outside of your hearing. Sometimes, however, through your presence at meetings or recordings of workshops or written communications between patients, clients, staff trainees or ethics committees you will be exposed to and handling confidential material which is governed by professionally strict rules of non-disclosure.

In this sense you are most similar to legal or medical secretaries and will be expected to adhere scrupulously to the same code of ethics as the professional staff in so far as it affects your functioning alongside and in support of them and the people they serve.

Security of written information

Confidentiality of name, address and other significant details of all clients and trainess must be protected under all circumstances. This includes whether or not a particular person has contacted any of the institute staff, and whether or not they are in counselling or psychotherapy. The appointments book must be kept safe under lock and key and the cover name of the book should be coded.

This chapter was first published in *Counselling*, Journal of the British Association for Counselling, vol. 5, no. 4, pp. 282–3 (1994).

337

All client or trainee information must be kept secure in locked files and specific members of staff should be named as being responsible for ensuring that security procedures are maintained and that access to such files is limited to people bound by the BAC, UKCP, BCP, ITAA, GPTI or BPS codes of ethics, in addition to the institute code.

A coding or password system will protect all confidential letters, etc., which are on computer or disc, and appropriate security – including lodging duplicate keys at the bank or solicitors – may be required for sensitive material. Administrative support staff may go off sick or be non-available in emergencies and access to information at all times for professional staff is *equally important* as keeping it secure. Please ensure that the institute is at no time in breach of the data protection act and take all necessary steps and advice wherever you are unsure.

Security of spoken information

All information about the institute/centre/college, its staff, clients and meetings is to be kept confidential to the institute and not used without permission in outside conversations or communications. The privacy of the clients and staff, the decision-making processes and business plans are the mutual concern of everyone and need to be protected. Where there may be exceptions, please check this first with your Head of Department or the Principal beforehand.

Conversations about people

Conversations about people should be restricted to only necessary confidential discussions and in appropriate spaces – i.e., within closed doors. This also applies to telephone conversations or arguments which may need to be conducted in privacy. Your co-operation in helping everyone to keep to such boundaries will be appreciated.

Sometimes trainees and others may need to be reminded that all discussions of clients must be conducted in a non-trivializing way within supervision/training/meetings and not as part of social conversation – even in break times. Kitchen or caretaking staff are sometimes unnoticed during enthusiastic discussions and they too need protection from the burden of undue information.

Clients or trainees may also be in eating or socializing areas or passages and due care and respect for all is usually preserved when an awareness of the delicacy of our work and the open nature of a learning institute is maintained. It is in the nature of working outside of a padded cell that people in a training and psychotherapy organization may sometimes accidentally overhear things which are private. Such unusual occurrences are of course also to be treated with the utmost respect and privacy, and never to be referred to or discussed by outside parties.

Conversation about counselling and training

It is unprofessional to engage in conversations about the nature of psychotherapy or counselling, its related training or entry requirements, to read references, or select or confirm people on courses without the explicit, preferably written, instruction of the trainers and/or Head of Department concerned or Head of School (as appropriate), or to discuss details of accreditation and validation procedures, etc., which are not within your limits of competency. These are the province of the professional staff who both have the information (or resources) and the skills to deal with such questions, decision or discussions.

Always encourage inquirers or trainees and supervisees to write directly to the Heads of Department and/or the Head of School on professional matters or to make appointments with them for such discussions, rather than attempt to be helpful outside your legitimate brief.

Codes of ethics of professional bodies

It is important that anyone who teaches or supervises at the institute is a member and/or agrees in a written contract or letter of employment (whether short- or long-term) to adhere to the code of ethics and professional practice of their appropriate professional body and of the organization itself.

Code of ethics and grievance procedures of the organization

All staff should familiarize themselves with the Code of Ethics of the organization and the BAC codes of ethics and practices for counsellors, trainers and supervisors. There are also grievance procedures for dealing with ethics, and professional guidelines and appeals procedures for dealing with trainees' concerns about examinations or assessment which administrative support staff need to be aware of in their work.

Handling complaints

Whenever you become aware of concerns about professional staff in terms of these guidelines, it is your duty to speak to them directly in the first instance, to seek clarification of a matter which you may have misunderstood or which may have been an oversight on their part. If you feel that your concern has not been responded to appropriately, approach the Administration Manager and the relevant Head of Department to follow the matter through. A written record of this meeting should be lodged with the Principal, conserving the rules of confidentiality as far as the professional and administrative or ancillary staff members are concerned.

When people make complaints about the management, facilities, training, trainers or supervisors, please direct them to discuss problems directly with the people concerned rather than secretly in your presence. Offer help if they are unsure how to proceed. There is usually an under-used suggestion box which is eagerly opened and frequently contains suggestions which can be successfully implemented where feasible and realistic. If there are complaints about the administration or yourself, please ask the person who is complaining to be specific, and if possible to put it in writing with suggestions for improvement. In consultation with the Administrative Manager, the Head of the Department concerned and the Principal, make the necessary adjustments as soon as possible, apologize where appropriate and solicit the help of the professional staff concerned in preventing recurrences or adapting procedures in more efficient ways in future.

Many errors of system and procedure can be prevented by a review of existing ways and creative problem-solving between all the parties affected by the problem. There is an old saying, 'Those who are not part of the solution are part of the problem.' That applies to everyone. Refer people to the solution team structures as well when there are concerns which need revision, improvements or changes. Welcome appreciation and encouragement and give it so that more of these nourishing elements can circulate throughout the system.

Relationships with colleagues

It is part of most professional codes of conduct to treat colleagues with respect and courtesy. Even when disagreeing with them it is vital that you use the management structures, each other and/or facilitators to resolve differences openly and cleanly. It is equally important that you respect yourselves and do not accept disrespectful treatment from professional colleagues toward you or your colleagues. Please ask for help in communicating clearly when you cannot or should not disclose confidential information or when you need to refuse something to someone, and also in learning how to be assertive in ensuring that your work is smooth, efficient and well supported by the professional staff.

It is important to demonstrate that everyone values and respects each other, clients, trainers and other staff and colleagues whatever their race, gender, religious beliefs or sexual orientation may be.

Dealing with emergencies

All staff, including caretaking and housekeeping personnel, should have special training in first aid, fire prevention and the management of physical, psychological and other emergencies of the kind which can occur within a counselling establishment. If someone is distressed or in need of help in a public part of the building, please help them to a private room (you will know which are free) and call the help of a professional staff member.

It is your duty to ensure that you are adequately equipped for supporting this kind of professional work and to help others who are new to it. In the rare cases where you are exposed to painful or disturbing material through your work (e.g., case notes or ethics enquiries), you should contact the Director of Clinical Services or the Principal who will arrange suitable counselling.

Feedback

It is good professional practice constantly to review and improve systems, procedures and habits, and in this spirit also additions and improvements to this document will be welcomed.

Discussion issues

1 Is a curiosity about details of the lives of other people a help or a hindrance to counsellors and support staff?

2 Have you experience as a student, client or counsellor of difficulties arising from a misunderstanding of the need for confidentiality by non-counselling staff?

3 How might non-counselling staff be helped to understand, appreciate and conform to the ethical issues relating to their work?

4 Are there any circumstances under which support staff may responsibly choose not to observe certain of the ethical areas raised in the chapter?

52

'Ménage à Trois'

Accreditation, NVQs and BAC

Janice Russell and Graham Dexter

The subject of accreditation has been well debated: should we, shouldn't we, what does it all mean, who does it? It would at least be helpful to give it some clarity of purpose and meaning. Currently, both are uncertain and rather vague, as Grant (1992: 89) points out: 'If it is considered appropriate to continue to have BAC accreditation the present scheme must be modified to acquire more value to the accredited counsellors and to have more meaning to the public.'

Moreover, in an increasingly global perspective which is emerging as our counselling world meets with that of Europe, as members of other trained professions take up counselling (e.g. psychiatric nurses), and where standard-setting is an issue for many professions, it would seem ludicrous to let the debate be endless. At some point or another, BAC will have to come off the fence over the whole issue and decide whether it wants to remain a watchdog with no teeth or whether it really wants to set some recognizable standards.

The point of this chapter, then, is to review what we think is the purpose of accreditation; to examine how the current process fails to reach its mark: and to suggest how it might be made a clearer and more worthwhile process within a professional and a public context. We intend to explore how the implementation of National Vocational Qualification (NVQ) standards might enable this outcome.

Getting the client back in the centre

BAC is increasingly seen as a medium for the professionalization of counselling. By tradition and nature, professional bodies adopt codes of ethics and practice in order to work towards autonomy and standardization. This inevitably entails the creation of professional identity which excludes some and includes others. Such identity is not merely altruistic but brings pecuniary rewards as well as those of status and satisfaction. One of the aims of the accreditation process may be seen as elevating counselling to professional status. Unlike other professions, however, BAC has as yet failed to standardize its practice, so that some competent practitioners are excluded, while others who are less competent may have access to the market which the profession seeks to serve indeed to corner.

This chapter was first published in *Counselling*, Journal of the British Association for Counselling, vol. 4, no. 4, pp. 266–9 (1993).

Within this context, one of the stated aims of BAC is to 'maintain and raise standards of counselling training and practice'. It is presumably also to this end that the accreditation process of individuals and recognition of courses has been instigated. How does this currently work?

Martin et al. use the special accreditation issue of *Counselling* (May 1992), to enthuse about the worth of the current system while capturing a flavour of the fuzziness which surrounds it:

> Accreditation in counselling is a benchmark and a burden: a benchmark as it offers public recognition to good practice and protects the client from the charlatan; a burden because it asbsorbs skill, time and effort in an attempt to monitor qualities that many feel to be elusive and unquantifiable. (Martin et al. 1992: 86)

In examining this statement, we can see that the assertions it makes are possibly assumptive and certainly misleading. They seem to typify some of the current discrepancies, which bear closer analysis and we use the quote as an exemplar to elucidate some central points.

(1) '... it offers public recognition to good practice ...'

During our joint experience as counselling practitioners (total 27 years), neither of us has ever been asked if we are accredited. When we discuss the term in public, and even in sensitized groups such as counselling training groups, there is little knowledge of the process or agreement of the necessity for it in professional practice. We maintain that the public are not aware of any difference between unaccredited and accredited practitioners. Currently, we go further and say that there is no identifiable difference in terms of competence.

Perhaps more importantly, since it may well be argued that there are moves to heighten public awareness, the crux seems to be that the public is neither interested nor significantly impressed by their counsellor's possession of accreditation. One of us displayed a framed BAC accreditation certificate in the consulting room from 1985 until its expiry and can point to no more than one client's passing curiosity in its existence, let alone its authenticity or meaningfulness.

The other of us has never been accredited, and is open about this to clients and students alike. So far, it seems that working agreements have not been affected by this but rather by reputation, recommendation or perhaps by 'seeming credible'. Further, the fact that such a small percentage of active counsellors actually seek accreditation may suggest that they themselves perceive the process as either irrelevant or as having little value.

(2) '... protects the client from the charlatan ...'

This case remains unproved. There is no evidence to support the proposition that possession of accreditation prevents exploitation, abuse, or incompetence by the practitioner. Indeed, available research into unethical behaviour suggests that accreditation makes no difference to client safety (Russell 1993). Thus far, then, it would be quite unethical to suggest to the public that this was the case.

We might also argue that it may be easier for the charlatan to become accredited than the honest practitioner. After all, the accreditee does not have to sit an examination either written or oral. As charlatans have the added advantage of being able and willing to lie on their application forms, it is likely that they will fulfill the criteria set. As far as we are aware the only check on the validity of information forwarded by the applicant is the reference from the supervisor. Those familiar with the form required of the supervisor know that this is by no means exhaustive. As an additional aid to the charlatan, the criteria for accreditation are helpfully sent to the applicant as a blueprint. Therefore, we would argue that the current accreditation system offers no protection from the charlatan, but possibly the converse.

(3) '... in an attempt to monitor qualities that many feel to be elusive and unquantifiable ...'

Surely after all the years of debate and research; the advent of governing bodies with tightly constructed definitions of what counselling is and should be; a distinct ethical code, and code of practice; disciplinary and ethical committees; the massive growth in training courses – it is no longer plausible to say that the measurement of competent practice is elusive and unquantifiable. A central point is that if counselling is teachable, it is identifiable and its competent use observable. If it is not, then we must query the validity of counselling courses.

All three purposes so far, then, are questionable. A fourth purpose is identified as that of the counsellor securing employment. 'It seems that some people leave the thought of accreditation until they see a job advertised that they want and which requires an applicant to be of accredited status' (Martin 1992: 88). Although the point is well made, it is ironic that the employer requiring accreditation may not be so keen to demand it if they were conversant with how little faith the association itself had in the process being a measure of competence.

If these are commonly held purposes of accreditation and can all be challenged, what does the current process of accreditation achieve? We see its value as largely for the counsellor, in terms of being educational, challenging, and engendering a sense of professional pride. We imply no criticism of this value to the practitioner. However, we are left with the question of how this safeguards or guarantees a better service to the client. In other words, we question whether this process has anything at all to do with standard-setting which might give some consistency and inform the public, employers and clients alike.

No doubt the debate will continue as to the purpose and usefulness of accreditation. Our own perspective is that it must relate to *standards* of practice which would be used in order to ultimately ensure the best service for clients, and to maximize client safety. Then, and only then, can it be seen to offer a springboard for both internal and external monitoring and for accountability (Rowan 1992). Thus the process becomes client-centred.

Thus far, BAC has omitted to set any recognizable standard for would-be accredited counsellors to achieve. 'Standard' has become one of those rather ubiquitous words which is in danger of carrying all the clout of a wet lettuce, and which is currently open to confusion with the concept of subjective appraisal. Within the current procedure, for example, training hours can be counted from a whole range of disciplines at different standards (Howard 1992).

Further, there is no way for supervisors to know whether the standards which inform their comments on supervisee's performance compare with those of other supervisees. Questions such as 'Have you and your supervisee discussed the code of ethics?' 'Please comment on how the supervisee uses supervision', are open to tremendously subjective response. This cannot claim to be a standard-setting exercise. Individuals have been refused accreditation because of dispute over whether training is recognized as 'core', or on insufficient supervisee hours, neither condition reflecting directly on that individual's competence in the consulting room.

Such vagueness may also be seen as unhelpful in the continuing search for clarification on the similarities and differences between counselling and psychotherapy. A whole range of activities and theoretical perspectives is allowed to come under the current subjective criteria for counselling accreditation. Whether this turns out to be positive or not in the great scheme of things is not the issue here, but it must be recognized that at present we are perhaps accrediting some widely differing activities, delivered more or less skilfully.

In summary, no matter how sympathetic one is to the idea of accreditation by one's peers for a sense of professional verification it is not thus far a very functional or valuable process for the potential client. If it aims to enshrine such value, it must make some attempt to reflect a measure of competence. To do this, the process necessitates a far more consistent framework than is presently in place, and a much clearer measure of competencies. And if this is the case, then it would seem that it would make sense to link it to counselling's other hot potato, the implementation of NVQs.

NVQs – what they are and how they might inform accreditation

Now that the Lead Body for the implementation of National Vocational Qualifications (NVQs) in Advice, Guidance and Counselling is established, and the BAC has become prominent within it, it would seem appropriate to take advantage of what knowledge is being gained in this area to inform accreditation. By becoming so involved in the NVQ process, the organization is giving the nod to the principle of setting up standards and competencies in counselling (Russell et al. 1992).

An NVQ might be seen as a measure of the ability to perform specific activities within an occupation or function to the standards of the relevant employer. As such, it necessitates much more clarity than we have at present. To achieve an NVQ workers must demonstrate that they meet the set standards, and thus the qualification becomes a statement of competence of the range of tasks that the worker is able to perform to those agreed standards.

To reach this standard, the competence of the worker is evaluated in terms of outcomes to the client. One immediate spin-off of this process is that it reminds workers of what it is that they are supposed to be doing, and to what end. In other words, it reminds counsellors to know the *key purpose* of their work, and to be able to explain it to potential clients.

This specificity cannot help but be beneficial to the client. Within our wider practice, we have been struck by the difficulty experienced practitioners have in stating in one or two simple sentences the key purpose of their activity. If this is more generally the case, how is the client to know what they might or might not expect, and how can a clear contract be set? A contract can act as a measure of appropriate or inappropriate behaviour, as well as a referent to evaluation of the counselling process, an excellent perspective of which is provided in Harris (1992).

Having set the key purpose, a series of elements of practice may be set in place to evaluate how that purpose is being met; such elements might be the practice of the counsellor to desirable ethical standards, the demonstration of respect to the client or empowerment of the client. All of these are outcomes which may be observed in the counsellor's practice in relation to the client.

Each element may be further broken down into performance criteria of the micro activities which show how the element is being achieved. Thus, empowerment of the client may be achieved through a series of performance criteria such as accurate reflection, appropriate information-giving and effective challenge. This specific breakdown of tasks is not new to the counselling world and to incorporate this process into accreditation immediately begins to offer a consistency of standards.

With such standard-setting in place, the whole process would become more amenable to equal opportunities practice. Currently, one of the moans or fears of counsellors is that the accreditation process may, at worst, be influenced by who you know, and that it creates an elite within the counselling profession which carries a disproportionate amount of power. At its best, the NVQ process potentiates more equality of opportunity through recognizing standardized practice and leaving less room for subjective preferences.

There is also work being carried out on integrating equality of opportunity within the standard-setting process. This will hopefully take place through a corporate element, that is, candidates would need to demonstrate awareness of issues, skills and knowledge appropriate to equal opportunities practice. Integration will also be recommended through ensuring that the process is made as anti-oppressive as possible, by trying to ensure a range of assessors who reflect the population they serve, offering a choice of assessor to meet gender or racial preference, or through appropriate use of language and assessment media (Bond and Russell 1993).

We also argue that such a process ensures more equality of opportunity through enabling a broader range of individuals to perform counselling services for clients. More practitioners would have access to a system that rewarded their skills and expertise without their having to invest in lengthy academic courses if this was not seen as an appropriate route for them. Many people employ counselling skills, or use counselling, who are unable to attend courses for want of time or money. The cost of achieving a diploma in counselling may be around £2,000, without consideration of time taken out of work, payment for child care, or any other costs which may be incurred. The present system of counselling training supported by the accreditation system is in danger of becoming exclusive if it does not recognize work-based performance. We believe that standard-setting and evaluation provide a fairer and more accessible method of ensuring competence and safeguarding clients.

Concluding remarks

It would be a considerable advantage for the public to know that recognized counsellors could be expected to perform competently. A credible service should be a client's right, especially at a time of need when they may be at their most vulnerable. Safe competent practice, therefore, has to be the single most important aspect for BAC or any truly interested party in counselling practice today.

If accreditation is to be the tool through which competence is governed and quality is monitored, it has to take some more creative and active steps. Recognition of courses has perhaps gone some way to pave the way for a more probable link between training/education and competent practice. This is only one pathway, however, serving the interests of only some potential counsellors, and therefore only some clients. We strongly support the view taken by Rowan (1992) that counselling needs strategies that are 'both and' and not 'either or' in relationship to the monitoring and promotion of competent, safe and high-quality practitioners. Incorporating some of the knowledge gained through research into NVQs strikes us as a way of integrating 'both and'.

Our suggestion is that if BAC is to change from being just a watchdog without teeth it must shake itself now an commit itself to a much more thorough and vigorous policing of standards, by taking an active part in the certification of competent practitioners, rather than the passive recognition and accreditation approach. We believe it should support the NVQ programmes and require its accredited members to demonstrate that they can fulfil the key purpose of counselling. This might be through formal written examinations, oral examination of skills, stimulated counselling sessions, or workplace assessment as used in the NVQ process. This would provide a medium for them to register competent practitioners, and to grow teeth by removing practitioners from the register following upheld complaints or re-accreditation failure.

We recognize that this may be a contentious view, and anticipate the kind of reservations made by Carney (1992) in regard to NVQs, that such measurement cannot capture the essence of counselling, but reduces it to a 'painting by numbers' approach. We believe that his points are both worthy and pertinent but perhaps slightly miss the point of the current argument.

To take the painting analogy further, it could be said that, however unique, the brilliance of an artist's work is still valued as an outcome. The skills, knowledge, and even values and attitudes which fund a masterpiece are better understood when specified as valued outcomes. The artist needs some vision of the purpose of the construction, or some micro-goals that enable a purposeful process to the artistic creation. For example the artist needs to understand that the hue, the perspective and the construction will need to mean something to the viewer. Her/his understanding of this will not detract from the uniqueness of each artist's work. Furthermore, the ingredients of a masterpiece are identified more easily if broken down into units, and much more clearly measured when defined through performance criteria. Identifying these ingredients does not of course instantly enable others to reproduce them, because it is true that the artistic master has something special and unique. However, most of us mortals will perhaps have to settle for mere competence and most of the time both the counsellor's client and the artist's patron will be thankful for it.

This is how counselling should be. At its best, it is not a mysterious process which is inaccessible to the client or the student. It is educational, empowering, and yet each individual counsellor will bring to their work the nuances of their own enthusiasm and personality. If the counsellor knows basically what it is that makes their work worthwhile and productive, this will inevitably aid the enabling process. In other words, if they are not only skilled, but understand the value of a skill, how it operates contextually and relationally, then this must enhance the counselling process for the client. The strength of the NVQ system is in ever relating the activity under review to the outcome, that is the *valued* outcome, for the client. It does not have to detract from the subtle differences which we all have.

We offer this viewpoint in a spirit of inquiry and development within the counselling profession. It is not intended as either exhaustive or definitive, and the hope is that it will help to take the accreditation debate one step further.

References

Bond, T. and Russell, J. (1993) *Report on Ethical Standards and Equality of Opportunity in Advice, Guidance and Counselling*, London: Department of Education.

Carney, P. (1992) 'Deconstructing competencies in counselling', *Counselling*, 3 (4) (November).

Grant, J. (1992) 'BAC accreditation – What value?', *Counselling*, 3 (2) (May).

Harris, J. (1992) 'Questions from a counselling therapist', *Counselling*, 3 (4) (November).

Howard, A. (1992) 'What, and why, are we accrediting?', *Counselling*, 3 (2) (May).

Martin, T. (1992) 'Accreditation – the candidate's perspective', *Counselling*, 3 (2) (May).

Martin, T., Foskett, J., Russell, G. and Potter, J. (1992) 'Angels, fools and lovers', *Counselling*, 3 (2) (May).

Rowan, J. (1992) 'The ins and outs of accreditation', *Counselling*, 3 (2) (May).

Russell, J. (1993) *Out of Bounds: Sexual Exploitation in Counselling and Therapy*, London: Sage.

Russell, J., Dexter, G. and Bond, T. (1992) *Differentiation Project: A Report to the Lead Body on Similarities and Differences between Advice, Guidance, Counselling, Counselling Skills, and Befriending*, London: Department of Education.

Discussion issues

1 How useful is accreditation?

2 What differences may the integration of NVQs and accreditation make for clients, for counsellors and for trainers?

3 How important are work-based performance and the demonstration of skills in the training and accreditation of counsellors?

4 What is your reaction to the arguments put forward in this chapter?

53

Whither Are we Led and by Whom?

A reaction to 'Ménage à trois'
John Foskett

A parable

Once upon a time there were people living around the shores of the Mediterranean, who believed that a Jew called Jesus was the Son of God. As time passed their leaders began to rationalize their faith in order to make it relevant to a world in need of love and wisdom. Many shared in standardizing the faith. There were disputes and disagreements and compromises over the different interpretations of their experience. However, 300 years' work bore fruit, and their faith was enshrined in a creed at the Council of Chalcedon in AD 451, and is repeated in their assemblies to this day. The unity and strength of Christianity has attracted the attention of political leaders from Constantine to Tony Blair, so much so that they have appropriated that strength and unity to serve their own political interests. Similar stories could be told of what has happened to the good things of all the world religions. What chance then has the *Faith of the Counsellors* to protect itself from the political interests of the powerful today?

Accreditation

In their article 'Ménage à trois', Janice Russell and Graham Dexter (1993) (see Chapter 52) expose the inadequacies of BAC's current accreditation procedures, which they claim are irrelevant to their clients. I imagine that accreditation is abused, and that it does contribute to the earning power of a few, and is unjust to others. Nevertheless, the regular and critical letters to *Counselling* have left their mark on the procedure's developments. The personnel of accreditation committees have changed too, so the accusation of exclusivity requires more thorough investigation. Furthermore, the complaints procedures have protected some clients and brought recompense to others. More worrying to me is the time and energy which the procedures consume. How long will it be before a Secretary of State notices that, as in the NHS, more people are adding up our qualifications and hunting charlatans than are actually counselling! That apart, I was enjoying the article's criticisms for unworthy reasons associated with my own current application for re-accreditation. But then, to my horror, the authors proceeded to argue the case for new and better instruments of torture.

This chapter was first published in *Counselling*, Journal of the British Association for Counselling, vol. 5, no. 2, pp. 137–9 (1994).

Unto us a child is born

Their contempt gave way to enthusiasm, hope and faith in the new kid on the block called National Vocational Qualification (NVQ). BAC, which I imagine means the current leadership, has taken a shine to this upstart. According to the authors, 'By becoming so involved in the NVQ process the organization is giving the nod to the principle of setting up standards and competencies in counselling.' They proceed to explain the logic of this development. If we have standards and definable competencies, and apparently counselling does have both, then it makes sense that the workers are measured by them. We would start with the 'key purpose' of counselling. The authors are surprised that some experienced practitioners cannot 'state in one or two simple sentences' what their key purpose is. But provided counsellors have a key purpose they are well on the way to the kingdom of NVQs.

> Having set the key purpose, a series of elements of practice may be set in place to evaluate how that purpose is being met; … such elements might be the practice of the counsellor to desirable ethical standards, the demonstration of respect to the client, or empowerment of the client.… Each element may be further broken down into performance criteria of the micro activities which show how the element is being achieved. (Russell and Dexter 1993)

They go on to say that such specific breakdown of skills is not new to counselling and would immediately offer a consistency of standards. I wonder how familiar this would be. It is my fantasy that counsellors could produce so many different key purposes that the micro activities would be legion, the standards infinite and the consistency only in heaven. These ruminations set me thinking about the parentage of young NVQ, was s/he of the miraculous kind, or were both parents still paying maintenance.

> The Manpower Services Commission in 1981, identified the need in Britain to develop a flexible and adaptable work force for the future. A review group was set up by the Government in 1985 to look at existing vocational education and training and make recommendations for improvement. (BAC 1992)

These recommendations were reinforced by industry's requirements which led to the birth of the 'child' NVQ. S/he was then fostered out with the Employment Department. Once counselling had become an industry too, the time was ripe for NVQ's expansion along with Advice and Guidance. The Lead Body was officially launched in October 1992 with the task of developing five levels of national standards in two years flat. Liberation theologians are much occupied by the hermeneutics of suspicion. My reading of the documents from BAC made me suspicious. It was the governments of the Thatcher years which fed this insatiable child. They of the get-on-your-bike brigade who wanted 'a flexible and adaptable workforce' including counsellors.

An adaptable workforce

NVQs are part of a reaction against the progressive humanism and the person-centredness of the 1960s. The new vocationalism of the 1970s and 1980s represents a swing away from a liberalism which encouraged students to look beyond skills appropriate to occupations, to the broader issues of society and its beliefs and values. The vocationalism of

NVQs narrows the focus of learning to the jobs people do, and the flexible and adaptable workforce society needs. Throughout these developments analysts have noticed the contradictions between words and deeds (Avis 1991; Edwards 1991; Field 1991). It was Field who observed that although education was at the centre of this development, the framework was

> designed to exclude interests; thus education providers are not even represented on the Lead Body for Training and Development. The most plausible explanation is that ... the NVQ system ... is a state-driven creature, in large part designed to effect and secure change in the public education and training system. (Field 1991: 46)

These revelations led educationalists to examine more closely the motivation of the politicians who fostered them. Their critique is disturbing. Whatever the system, its fruits will depend upon the political force behind it. We must know what the mandarins of the Employment Department want in order to decide what we really think about the value of NVQs. They could be, as Russell and Dexter advocate, 'the single most important aspect for BAC, or any truly interested party in counselling practice today', or they could be the new opium for the people. It will all depend upon what *big sister* and *brother* want them to be.

NVQs advice, guidance and counselling

The Lead Body for Advice, Guidance and Counselling (1993) answers the question 'Why a specific set of qualifications?' for these activities, by reference to the present muddle, overlap and inconsistencies between them. Although a feasibility study 'highlighted the unlikeliness of getting a coherent set of qualifications from "such uncoordinated work"', 90 per cent of the organizations and individuals consulted remained unquestioningly 'in favour of establishing a coherent set of vocational qualifications'. However, the paper does not say who was consulted, nor what their personal, professional or political interests in a coherent system might be. This is a very significant omission. I looked to see if the paper gave any clues as to the identity of the individuals consulted and their interests, and discovered that they are the *acknowledged* experts in the fields of advice, guidance and counselling. Furthermore, a task force was created 'representing the interests of employers, staff, professional bodies, and the Employment Department'.

I looked in vain for some references to the contribution of clients or consumers. Does that mean that they have not been consulted, and that the interests of government and practitioners have alone shaped the Lead Body and its work? The evidence of the paper suggests that this is the case, as consumers and users of services are conspicuously absent from the groups established to take the work further. NVQs in advice, guidance and counselling are being shaped according to the views of the *acknowledged* experts – those who, as well as serving the interests of their clients, cannot be entirely disinterested in their own livelihoods, or in the seductions of governments who exert such an influence on all our livelihoods. Our own BAC chair and deputy chair are prominent in this work as are Janice Russell and Graham Dexter. If anyone is going to be my *big sister* or *big brother*, I would not wish for better ones than Elsa Bell and Tim Bond, but I am worried about the use or abuse to which they are being put.

Ambivalence

When I first read about NVQs I was struck by the contradictoriness of my response. I was attracted by valuing people for the competencies they already have, as it reflects what is best in counselling's *faith*. I have witnessed the effectiveness of behavioural and cognitive approaches to therapy, especially with the most vulnerable. But also I have seen how complex communication by behaviour is. Interactions which appear to have achieved certain goals in one case are useless in another. The therapist is often the last to recognize this, not through lack of skill but because he or she is involved in a relationship which is more than any of the abstractions used to define it. The chaos and incoherence the Lead Body encountered is not because of the ineffectiveness of advisors, guides and counsellors, but because their work involves them in a lot of chaos and incoherence. Counselling can only be standardized if we want to produce statues, and people won't stand still.

The politics of counselling

We need to know as much about politics, values and beliefs, as we do about behaviour to assess the usefulness of any advice, guidance or counselling. In their research Truax and Carkhuff (1965) identified certain qualities of relationship, such as empathy and respect, as universally helpful. These were not only skills which practitioners learnt to deliver, but qualities of relationship they had to foster. It was the therapists who continued to develop these qualities who helped their clients most, and the therapists who were stuck at a par-ticular professional standard who put a break upon their clients' development. Hierarchies of standards are meant to move people on from NVQs level one to level five, but there is evidence to suggest they encourage a preoccupation with the standard rather than the movement (Field 1991: 50), and protect professionals rather than help their clients.

I know my empathy and respect for clients is more dynamic than it is static. I try my best to make it available, but it is the clients who do the real work. They have to locate my empathy, draw out my respect and make what they can of my abilities and my short-comings. It is their belief in me that makes me of use to them. If anyone is to be assessed on the skills suitable for counselling, surely it is *clients* who take the tests and reach the standards. Clients can harness our latent and learnt abilities. Our own therapy, training and supervision can help us be more transparent about what we have to offer, and what we need to keep for ourselves. But it is the clients alone who can make something of the raw material which is us.

I favour a system of accreditation which is not fixed or final, embraces politics, beliefs and values as well as behaviour, trusts a degree of overlap, incoherence and chaos, and is suspicious of a surfeit of consistencies. APCC's (Association for Pastoral Care and Counselling) original work on accreditation in the 1970s encouraged an ambivalence about the whole procedure. Applicants had to demonstrate a congruence between their beliefs and their practice. They were also expected to shape the accreditation procedure itself, especially by involving their clients in it. I wondered why Russell and Dexter accepted their clients' lack of interest in their qualifications. Is not a client's scrutiny of our competence the beginning of his or her empowerment in the relationship?

Whither BAC?

Perhaps we could advance our current accreditation procedure by forming a new Division of BAC made up entirely of clients counselled by accredited BAC counsellors, who are not counsellors themselves. They could have representation by right on the Accreditation Committee and the Lead Body for Advice, Guidance and Counselling. Students on courses recognized by BAC might have similar representation on the Courses' Recognition Group. At accreditation, clients could be asked to contribute in some way to the process, and instead of a certificate on our consulting room walls, we could provide written, audio or video examples of our work, and contacts with former clients prepared to give a client's view of what we do. At the point of seeking re-accreditation I am, of course, grateful that I don't have to submit myself to such requirements, but I am even more grateful not to have to repeat an NVQ counselling *creed* at BAC assemblies!

References

Advice, Guidance and Counselling Lead Body (1993) Networks No. 1.

Avis, J. (1991) 'The strange fate of progessive education', in *Education Limited*, London: Unwin Hyman.

BAC (1992) *NVQ News*, No. 1, Rugby: British Association for Counselling.

Edwards, R. (1991) 'The politics of meeting learner needs: power, subject, subjection', in *Studies in the Education of Adults*, 23 (1): 85–97.

Field, J. (1991) 'Competency and the pedagogy of labour', in *Studies in the Education of Adults*, 23 (1): 41–52.

Russell, J. and Dexter, G. (1993) 'Ménage à trois: accreditation, NVQs and BAC', in *Counselling*, 4 (4): 266–9.

Russell, J., Dexter, G. and Bond, T. (1992) *Differentiation Project: A Report to the Lead Body on Similarities and Differences between Advice, Guidance, Counselling, Counselling Skills, and Befriending*, London: Department of Education.

Truax, C.B. and Carkhuff, R.R. (1965) *Towards Affective Counselling and Psychotherapy*, Chicago: Aldine.

Discussion issues

1 Are NVQs a reaction against the progressive humanism and the person-centredness of the 1960s?

2 Does a focus on skills tend to downplay the personal development element of courses essential to constructive relationships with clients?

3 Most professionals seek a special well-paid identity by cornering a sector of the market for themselves via standards, boundaries and qualifications. Does this apply to counselling accreditation?

4 How would you suggest a client choose a counsellor – by reputation, recommendation, accreditation, instinct, or by using a pin? Or by some other criteria?

54

The Role of Group Work in Counsellor Training

Judi Irving and David I. Williams

Group work is usually seen as an integral and essential part of counsellor training. It is our contention that trainers are often not clear as to the the aims and objectives of this work, or, if they are, do not make them explicit. The result may be ineffective training and individual harm to trainees. Making group work mandatory also raises dilemmas.

With the rapid increase in demand for the provision of counselling services over the past ten years, there has been a concurrent increase in the number and variety of counsellor training courses available in the UK. This in turn has raised the issue of professionalization of counselling as a major concern. Both the British Association for Counselling (BAC) and, more recently, the Division of Counselling Psychology of the British Psychological Society (BPS) have provided criteria and guidelines for the training of counsellors. Each of these bodies requires that trainees engage in personal development work. For the BAC (1986) this involves 'regular and systematic approaches to self-awareness work' and 'a balance between individual growth work, group interpersonal experience and "community meeting" interaction'. The syllabus for the BPS Diploma in Counselling Psychology (BPS 1992) includes a requirement for 'experiential workshop training' which 'should encourage and provide trainees with the opportunity to reflect on their own experience and be personally involved in experiential learning'.

In both sets of regulations the requirement for personal development group work is implicit and it is evident that most training courses do include such an experience. (The term group work is used here as a convenient, albeit rather vague, label for the type of group experience often referred to as T-groups, sensitivity training, encounter groups, personal development groups, experiential groups, and so on.) It would appear that this type of work is assumed to be just as essential for counsellor training as are skills training and knowledge of counselling theory. While such work can undoubtedly provide a useful learning experience for trainees, the rationale for group work in counsellor training is somewhat less clear than that for skills training or for theory.

The overall aims of group work have to do with personal growth and development, encouraging inquiry into personal behavioural style and providing participants with an opportunity to gain insights and awareness of the impact of their own behaviours and how they are viewed by others, together with an increasing sensitivity to what others are feeling (Taylor 1981). The assumption within counsellor training appears to be that all trainees can and should experience personal growth and development as a result of

This chapter was first published in *Counselling*, Journal of the British Association for Counselling, vol. 7, no. 2, pp. 137–9 (1996).

participating in group work; if they do not, it is considered to be a failing on the part of the trainee to make use effectively of this opportunity for learning. However, different kinds of groups offer different kinds of learning experiences, and even within a particular kind of group the learning experiences of individuals will vary considerably. It is somewhat naive of trainers to assume that the simple provision of the experience of group work is both a necessary and sufficient condition for personal development. At the very least, facilitators need to be clear about the kind of group work offered and the needs and characteristics of the participants.

There are many, many types of groups, Lieberman et al. (1973) looked at ten basic types and found that each had its own merits in enabling particular aspects of personal development. Taylor (1981) classified groups not by technique but by focus and approach, for example whether the focus was the self or the group and whether the approach was personal growth or structured training. Our impression from talking with trainers and examining course prospectuses is that few courses appear to categorize their group work in either of these schemes. Often the vague expression 'doing group' covers whatever unstructured activity is going on. It is evident that this is no basis for an adequate training programme in terms of both training requirements and safety.

All too often trainees are offered some kind of general group work which draws upon assumptions and techniques from a variety of approaches. In these circumstances it is not surprising that individuals may be unclear about what they are doing and why they are doing it. This not only leads to confusion; for some participants, it can also produce very negative experiences. Also, without a clear statement of the aims and purposes of the work, it is not possible to ascertain whether these have been met. The first task of any trainer is then to be very clear about the type of group and method being utilized, what are the appropriate structures and what are the aims. It is only by such analysis that the opportunity for learning in a group can both be maximized and made safe. There is empirical evidence that some trainees have negative experiences of group work (Back 1972, 1988; Smith 1987; Irving 1993) and handbooks alert trainers to these dangers (e.g., Reichard et al. 1992).

Trainers also need to be aware of the impact that the uniqueness of each participant has on the functioning of the group as a whole. We all develop our own ways of resolving the conflict in achieving a balance between needs for intimacy and needs for autonomy. For some individuals, the group situation may be perceived as an opportunity to experience and work with their own needs for intimacy without feeling that their autonomy is being threatened. For others, this situation may be perceived not as an opportunity but as an environment in which they feel they are 'between a rock and a hard place'. They feel they must either conform to group norms in terms of openness and intimacy or risk rejection by the group. Intimacy and openness are perceived as being required of them and not a matter of autonomous choice. As a result, some will appear to conform without really getting involved, that is, they learn to 'play the game' and so lose hope of learning from this experience. Yet others, who do not get involved, who do not play the game, are candidates for becoming victims of the group. Thus trainers need to be alert to the necessity to intervene, to support and protect those who may be damaged by the experience.

Research is needed to provide guidelines as to who may be 'at risk' in group work. There are two categories of those who are vulnerable. The first includes those who cannot take the emotional experience and for whom the prognosis for being a competent counsellor is poor. The second consists of emotionally robust people whose preferred learning style (i.e., Activist, Reflector, Theorist and Pragmatist as suggested by Honey and Mumford 1986) leaves them exposed to being victimized and set upon by the group. Both groups are in need of protection. The second is the focus of our concern, but trainers need to be aware of the first. Such people should have been weeded out at the selection stage; we believe it is unethical to use group work as a way of selecting out counsellors on a survival of the fittest basis.

Ethical issues

There is an important ethical dilemma in including personal development group work as a component of counsellor training programmes. This is related to the concept of informed consent, in that prospective trainees need to be aware not only of the fact that personal development group work is a component of the course for which they are applying but also of all that this entails. The problem lies in the fact that once a commitment has been made to undertake a course, to defect from the group work part of it is not a realistic option. From the course perspective, such an individual would not have completed the requirements of the training programme. From the personal perspective, a student is likely to experience pressure from staff and other students to persevere. Whatever the extent of pre-course information provided, and however applicants are screened, there is a sense in which participation in group work is forced. There is a general consensus among counsellors that clients ought to come voluntarily and be committed to the counselling process. Students forced to engage in group work are in a similar position to coerced clients, and this lack of freedom of choice contravenes the general ethos of counselling. McLeod (1993) makes a similar point in respect to courses requiring students to undertake individual therapy, which nevertheless is a situation in which the student receives much more personal support.

Within personal development group work, as well as counselling in general, the issue of privacy is paramount. It is suggested here that no matter how much is provided in the way of pre-course information, it is only the experience of participation in group work that will tell the individual what it is about. Within the context of counsellor training, the participant, in theory, has a responsibility to determine both the extent to which he/she is willing to participate or the levels of self-disclosure he/she is willing to attempt. But because of the norms of group work, this sense of choice may be reduced or even experienced as non-existent. A group may be visualized as a tiny society separated from the surrounding culture. It both violates many of the norms of the surrounding culture and creates counter-norms (Lieberman et al. 1973). Group norms include the encouragement of behaviours which create an intense, high-contact group and individual experiences such as openness, honesty, involvement, immediacy, interpersonal confrontation, self-disclosure and strong emotional expression. Group norms are considered to have been violated if a participant engages in intellectualization, avoids confrontation, talks about something outside the 'here and now', maintains a high level of emotional control, or behaves in a remote, non-participative manner. A group is not then a 'free society'. It is a special forum with its own structures, not all of which may be acceptable to all participants. Therefore, not all can be assumed to gain from it.

There is no easy answer to these problems, but it is suggested that course planners ought to (a) identify and make explicit their underlying assumptions about group work, and (b) clarify its aims and purposes within the parameters of their training programme. Information on both should then be made explicit in publicity materials and at interview. It would also be desirable if the course organization were flexible enough to allow students to undertake group work when they feel they know enough about it, and are ready to deal with it – this would include the possibility of students opting out in the early stages of a group and undertaking this requirement at a later date in order to fulfil all course requirements.

We do not believe that a case has been made that group work is an essential component of counsellor training. Nowhere is it made clear what are the transferable skills from the group to the client. The usual argument is that groups are learning laboratories for finding out about relationships, particularly those occurring at an emotional level (Egan 1973). This we would accept, but it does not follow that they are the only way. There are other person-to-person training situations that are very effective in allowing expression of genuineness, confrontation, conflict and emotional exploration.

Conclusion

Some people get good things out of groups and some are hurt by them. There is no solution that would work in the best interests of all participants. However, if a commitment is made to explore and examine assumptions and beliefs underlying counsellor training, it may be possible to move towards creating an optimum learning environment for trainees, to maximize positive effects and minimize negative ones. Trainers need to be more explicit about their methods, their aims and objectives, and the purpose of the programme needs to be adequately explained to trainees.

There is, we believe, not just one kind of person – the one who has positive experiences in groups – who makes a good counsellor. Different people bring different attributes to the counselling relationship. Not everyone will be comfortable in every counselling situation; individuals develop their own ways of working and concentrate on particular client groups which suit their personal values and personal style.

References

BAC (1986) *Recognition of Counsellor Training Courses*, Rugby: British Association for Counselling.

Back, K.W. (1972) *Beyond Words: The Story of Sensitivity Training and the Encounter Movement*, New York: Russell Sage Foundation.

Back, K.W. (1988) 'Encounter groups revisited', *Society*, 26: 50–3.

BPS (1992) *Regulations for the Diploma in Counselling Psychology*, Leicester: British Psychological Society.

Egan, G. (1973) *Face to Face: The Small Group Experience and Interpersonal Growth*, Monterey, CA: Brookes/Cole.

Honey, P. and Mumford, A. (1986) *The Manual of Learning Styles*, Maidenhead: Honey & Mumford.

Irving, J.A. (1993) 'Personal development group work in counselling training and learning style preferences', unpublished M.Sc. dissertation, University of Hull.

Lieberman, M.A., Yalom, I.B. and Miles, M.B. (1973) *Encounter Groups: First Facts*, New York: Basic Books.

McLeod, J. (1993) *Introduction to Counselling*, Milton Keynes: Open University Press.

Reichard, B.D., Siewers, C.M.F. and Rodenhauser, P. (1992) *The Small Group Trainer's Survival Guide*, London: Sage.

Smith, R. (1987) 'Laboratory design and group process as determinants of the outcome of sensitivity training', *Small Group Behavior*, 18: 291–308.

Taylor, B. (1981) *Experiential Learning: A Framework for Group Skills*, Leeds: Oasis Communication.

Discussion issues

1 Group work is considered to be one of the main opportunities for personal development work in counsellor training. What is meant by 'personal development'?

2 What are the explicit links between the experience of group work and effective counselling?

3 What ethical issues does compulsory group work raise?

4 If you were designing the group work component of a counsellor training programme, what would your plan look like?

55

The Case for Group Work in Counsellor Training

A response

Amelia Lyons

In response to Irving and Williams (1996) (see Chapter 54), I explore further some of their points and argue a strong case for group work in counsellor training.

Irving and Williams (1996) argued that:

- A case had not been made for group work as an essential component of counsellor training.
- It was not clear which skills could be transferred from the group work to the client work.
- There was a need for more clarity about the type of group and method adopted so that students were clear about how it fitted into their training.
- Group work does not 'work' for some types of individuals.

Although they discuss what can happen when trainers are not properly equipped to facilitate groups either theoretically or experientially, or perhaps both, this is not the same as proving that there is no role for group work in counsellor training.

The case for an intentional group-work approach in counsellor training includes:

- **purpose**: why do it and how it may be beneficial for trainees;
- **transferable skills and attitudes**: identifying some of the skills transferable from the arena of the group, to work with clients;
- **facilitator skills**: what sort of training and back-up a counsellor trainer may require in order to facilitate groups successfully;
- **observations and feedback** from my work in this area.

My on-going experience consists of working with 18 groups over a six-year period during which, each year and each term, I regularly inquire about trainee experience of the course qualitatively and quantitatively with groups, plus consulting widely and co-operatively with colleagues. We review experience with the groups and within the group of tutors at the end of each year and plan the following year in relation to the outcomes of this 'research'. Thus the experience of each year is cycled into the next and modifies/ refines/changes my approach. (You could call this 'action learning' and I believe most tutors conduct this naturally.) My discussion reflects this accumulated learning and includes questions that I still have. I invite readers to consider and compare their experiences with mine.

This chapter was first published in *Counselling*, Journal of the British Association for Counselling, vol. 8, no. 3, pp. 211–15 (1997).

The case for an intentional group-work approach in counsellor training

The development of the trainee counsellor covers three main areas: skills, awareness and theory which ideally should combine fruitfully towards forming the beginnings of a reflective and intentional practitioner on emergence from a course at diploma level. Group work may be used to develop any of these areas and, in particular, the group-work element is a primary vehicle for the development of the self-awareness of course trainees.

Purpose

Intentional practice

Irving and Williams point out that more clarity is needed on the part of the trainers to explain the purpose and model/method of group work so that its rationale is clearly understood and it is seen to be pertinent. This also models intentional practice (Ivey 1987), such practice being the basis of any well-designed counselling course. Dryden and Feltham (1994) argue for a purposeful personal development programme within the course while BAC (1990) requires that approaches to self-awareness work should be regular, systematic and congruent with course rationale (not a variety of interesting but unrelated self-awareness workshops!).

Bringing theory alive

Group work has the advantage of being systematic and regular by definition as long as it follows a coherent model, and also has the advantage of building on the core model of the course and bringing it alive in an experiential forum – for example the core model (at University of Wales College, Newport in the first year) is Egan and the group-work element is also based on Egan's Interpersonal Group Model (1973 and 1976).

Egan (1976) suggests a range of exercises which enable the group to practise basic and further counselling skills and learn to self-disclose appropriately and within a structured format. The arena of the group combines to bring together skills and theory of counselling in a way which makes sense to individuals, through giving and receiving feedback and experimenting with new behaviours, and which also begins to expand participants' self-awareness.

In our second year Egan is compared with other models from 'purer' humanistic ones such as person-centered and Gestalt to cognitive and psychodynamic approaches. As the group work progresses, it may also be 'made sense of' from some of these other perspectives and members can reflect on their own group's movement from a less directed to a more autonomous/democratic approach.

In terms of Kolb's (1984) experiential cycle of learning the group has a chance to experience, reflect critically on that experience, go back to the theory and experiment once more. This contributes much to trainees' learning of skills and theory in the here-and-now, facilitating both their growth and learning about themselves and their understanding of how others experience them and their interventions. The group work is not assessed formally but is evaluated through methods of inquiry, and of qualitative and quantitative research which also serve to check what has been learned, as well as how trainees evaluate it. The trainees' journals provide a more personal view of what has actually been learned. All of this provides the evidential basis for what I believe and understand to be the usefulness of this work.

Self-awareness and developing emotional competence

Heron (1990: 12) points out that 'One of the primary aspects of character needed for effective helping is emotional competence ... for helpers this means that their own anxiety and distress accumulated from past experience does not drive and distort their attempts to help.' Personal therapy may help to explore this, but the medium of the group offers a rich arena in which to be open to learning about how we are being experienced by others (and ourselves) and to discover through feedback when our helping is 'clean and clear' and when it may have an 'inappropriate quality'. It is precisely through being ourselves in a 'held' and supportive group that such information surfaces, we become more aware of our impact on others and its consequences, and are thus able to make more responsible and life-giving choices both for ourselves and others. The group can form a bridge between the sense we make of our intrapsychic selves (through personal therapy) and how we perform interpersonally with others. Although the group is an experiential learning community and its primary purpose is learning, it is possible that there may also be therapeutic outcomes as part of this process. This differs from a therapeutic group in which therapy is the focus, with learning as a secondary consequence. Thus, in experiential learning groups it is assumed that individuals seek their own therapeutic support outside the group, but their learning about themselves is put into practice in the group in their interactions with others. Provision of such a group provides a unique learning opportunity to test and check out interventions, and their purpose and influence with other group members. Put bluntly, it provides members with a opportunity to 'clean up their act' before prolonged exposure with clients, in an environment which supports their intention to learn even when the intervention itself may be 'contaminated' (Heron 1990) in some relatively unaware way.

How to 'walk the tightrope' between facilitating a useful learning experience that has emotional as well as intellectual meaning, yet avoiding it turning into a 'therapy' group, is an important balance to hold; and when not achieved adequately it becomes a ripe target for criticism, with some justification.

A space for the group to relate

Awareness and expansion of knowledge and skills are not the only reasons for having a group-work component; while the course is ongoing the group is a community and thus requires a space to 'relate'. Dryden and Feltham consider it important to have a built-in system of community meetings 'to allow group issues to surface and receive open attention' (1994: 118). In my experience periodic community meetings do not meet these needs adequately, no matter how well structured. These tend to focus on content issues, and process areas are left largely untouched. This may be due to the periodic and time-limited nature of such meetings. A *regular* group-work component offers the group a chance to grapple with their (sibling?) relationships with one another and those with their tutor at a much more fundamental level.

Dryden and Feltham (1994) has made the point that there is a boundary issue if the group facilitator also has an assessment role and this is a valid argument. It is a dilemma that we, as a team, struggle to resolve and I have no perfect answers. The dual role may inhibit members' contributions. In addition, we are working in an environment that is operating under financial constraints which limit greatly our ability to employ visiting tutors. I have received scant evidence from our feedback trawls that it actually *does* constrain trainees but I am open to hearing that it may.

Victimizing, scapegoating, rescuing and so on go on incessantly in groups, whether a space is allocated for group work or not. All groups have destructive as well as constructive elements. It is better that a space is available in which these elements can emerge in a facilitated environment which is open and will hold, and which to a degree, can control these elements, rather than not deal with them at all. In this way, through appropriate modelling and use of resources in the group, members learn about what is happening, how they buy into and out of it, and then learn to catch themselves in the process and rebalance themselves.

Thus the argument that groups can damage individuals and scapegoat them on a regular basis is, I believe, either about the group being poorly managed or about the lack of a regular space in which these issues can be properly dealt with and used as opportunities to learn. A well-facilitated group offers a chance to vent these issues, articulate them and gain awareness and insight into the part each individual plays in the patterns and norms of group behaviour which are operating, thus giving members a chance to change such patterns.

Administration and business issues need to be handled separately, perhaps in community meetings.

Transferable skills

Relationship skills and process awareness

What kind of modelling would be offered if the facilitator paid little or no attention (through, for example, giving no space ...) to dealing with group issues. If paralleled with the counselling process, it could show that it is acceptable for the counsellor to ignore disturbing issues between him/herself and the client. If the core model of the course is a relationship-oriented therapy (humanistic or psychodynamic), then the group provides not only a focus in which to explore our here-and-now relationships as they emerge, but also a chance for the trainee to practise tackling difficult and challenging issues in the context of a learning environment where mistakes are not treated as catastrophies but as opportunities to learn.

Provision of a regular group space is the optimum way of keeping on top of emerging issues and learning from them. Periodic community meetings can but remain at the level of social interaction (Barber 1993), do not afford the same attention to process, and could easily be swallowed up by administrative and business issues.

The cost of not providing a regular group-work slot (that is, when little or no attention is paid to group process) is that the task of learning to be a useful helper becomes sabotaged. It is rather like a task-focused team that is so taken up with destructive relationships (which remain convert and not directly tackled) that the goal they are working towards is not achieved, or is poorly achieved. I wonder what kind of helpers emerge from such groups?

Questions emerging

My colleagues and I have discussed the timing and pacing of the course group-work element. Some think that group work should be introduced *after* trainees have had time to grasp the theory behind the group experience, so that they can make more sense of the experience (and are less likely to be damaged by it). Conversely, a cognitive therapist colleague questions whether there is a need for group work if the group is sufficiently 'mature'. Might this also reflect a difference in the theories or models of approach? If the therapy is less 'relationship-orientated' (or more 'task-focused') then the need for a group component might be less.

Other transferable skills and attitudes of tolerance

Looking back through the feedback from groups that I have trained reveals further evidence of how group learning may be transferred to work with clients. Comments on learning to tolerate silence, conflict, extreme emotion, uncertainty and unknowing abound, as does enabling members to learn more about immediacy, the here-and-now, relationship skills and our tendencies to play out particular roles which may inevitably deprive clients of their own resources or ability to express themselves fully. The intensity of the group and the fact that there are more people to offer feedback and support accelerates participants' learning over and above the small group (triad) skills work. The group is not about forcing people to conform to group norms, though initially groups will try to do exactly that. A well-facilitated group is about learning to tolerate difference, not trying to 'overcome' it. At its best the group experience provides the opportunity openly to explore and grapple with diversity in such areas as race, religion, sexual orientation and so forth.

It may be useful to assume that the trainees emerging from our courses will not only be working with individuals; many will work with couples, children, families and groups such as support or themed groups, bereavement, or eating disorders groups. Some of course will eventually follow in our footsteps as trainers. Group-work experience equips trainees with many of the skills which will enable them to hold and listen to groups at a more than superficial level, and hopefully in a facilitative way. Running a group, however, is not an easy task for any facilitator, even one who is a well-qualified counsellor, and additional skills are required.

Facilitator skills

Training and preparing to run groups

Aveline and Dryden (1989: 325) argue that the triad of the experience of being in a group oneself, plus supervised practice and theoretical learning (i.e. training) are 'essential and inseparable' in training to be a group leader. I wholeheartedly agree. Thorough and systematic training and experience also enable trainers to offer a degree of clarity and intentionality about their approach which can be clearly communicated to groups. The latter may not still cries of 'I don't know what we're doing here', for these are part of the unknowingness which characterizes most forms of group work and are particularly frequent in the initial stages of it. However, this should not be used as an excuse for facilitators not to familiarize themselves thoroughly with a preferred approach congruent with themselves and what they are imparting to others. It is this *trainer inexperience/lack of relevant training* that I believe lies at the heart of Irving's and Williams' critical reflection of the role of group work in counselling courses.

Aveline (Aveline and Dryden 1989: 321) cites Dies' (1980) point that two of the most frequent problems of inexperienced group leaders are 'insensitivity to group process and inappropriately attempting to do individual therapy in a group setting'. As a consequence, leaders may fly into action (to avoid anxious feelings) or become excessively powerful. I confess to strong tendencies of wanting to 'teach' when I hear a comment like 'I don't know what this is all about.' Tolerance of uncertainty and unknowingness are endemic to this work and are essential qualities to be modelled by the facilitator (and taken forward by the group). Another essential is trusting oneself, the process and the group and never doing for the group what they can do for themselves. None of these seems to get any easier but experience proves how important these attitudes are. I have found supervision specifically for the group aspect of my work most beneficial in supporting and extending my development as a facilitator of experiential groups.

Not everyone is a group animal

I agree with Irving and Williams that not everyone takes naturally to group work. Gaie Houston (1984: 11) remarked:

> People are cussed. Tell them that spinach is good for them, and that what is more you have cooked them some and they are to sit right down and eat it. The chances are that few will comply and fewer yet will enjoy the spinach than if you had left them to work out the whole spinach question for themselves.

Recognizing that comments such as 'I don't know what we're doing here', 'What is this all about?' are part of the whole issue of the uncertainty and unknowingness of the group has enabled me to become clearer about my purpose, and to conduct regular group theory sessions at the beginning, middle and end of the course to articulate clearly the models of approach being used and to explore with the group how they operate and what their aims are. I can also negotiate with the group and compare my vision of it with those of trainees. While we may approach this whole question with a degree of clarity and intentionality about the forthcoming process, we must also remain open and available to the needs of the group. Ownership of the whole process may then be encouraged and accepted by all. Parallels with the counselling process abound, also reflecting a person/student-centred focus to learning.

Concluding summary

Feedback

What proves the usefulness of the group process repeatedly is the experience of the groups throughout the course who find the work invaluable. This is shown not only in the feedback they offer but also in the changes in their degree of tolerance of the more extreme ends of emotion, their process awareness skills, self-awareness and ability to give meaningful and useful feedback to others, and finally in the way in which community members relate to one another overall.

Of course it may be difficult to distinguish how much is due to the group or other course contents, or to external issues such as therapy.

Valid alternatives

While not all individuals will obviously benefit from the group process, this is true for any area of training and I think a systematic group should be in place to tackle any of the issues discussed. It is hard to think of equally valid alternatives, though I am open to hearing about them.

Clarity and intentional practice

Overall I agree with the contentions of Irving and Williams about lack of clarity about the purposes and aims of group work and would concede that at least some of this is due to lack of clarity in the facilitators themselves. I confess to this myself, and while further and continuous training has added to my clarity I have certainly abandoned all thoughts of one day 'arriving'. However, I would argue that some of the lack of clarity is also a parallel of the uncertainty and unknowing which characterizes the here-and-now of any well-facilitated group.

Benefits

Group work is beneficial in a variety of ways which are invaluable for the learning of the trainee. I have:

- clarified the assumptions, beliefs and intentions underlying my practice;
- demonstrated that there are numerous and significant parallels and transferable skills and attitudes from the group experience to the counselling experience;
- been explicit about what is required of the facilitator in order to run groups successfully.

I do not believe that all counselling trainers need to be effective group facilitators – it is possible to invite someone else to do this work while considering parallel alternative routes and other arguably valid ways of providing a rounded counselling training course.

Finally to get the best out of it ...

The group-work component needs to reflect the core theory of the course in a clear and intentional way. Experiential groups are, I believe, invaluable components of any course which has a relational approach to counselling at its core, since groups lend themselves ideally to the here-and-now experience of such a relationship in action. If trainees can learn and assimilate these skills and attitudes during the course I can feel more confident about how they will operate with clients 'out there' on successful completion of it. As a former colleague once said to me on the telephone, 'I'm in a "live" situation – what do I do now?'

Update 2000

Although I wrote the article four years ago and have re-read it on many occasions, my views have remained fairly consistent. There are one or two points that I wish to under-line, however.

Congruence

I have become clearer about the importance of the congruence of the tutor especially when involved with the development of the self-awareness of the student. I have noticed that tutors who feel most strongly about the significance of developing the self-awareness of the students tend to be more supportive of experiential groups. Tutors less focused on this element of counsellor training tend to be less inclined towards, and less enthusiastic about, the use of experiential groups in training. This tends to support the notion that such tutors should not be pressured to run experiential groups against their will.

The *Being* first …

Each tutor has his or her unique style of facilitation even when operating from the same model, and while it is important for tutors to be clear about the purpose of the group and how it links with the core training approach, they should not try to run the groups in *exactly the same way*. What is most important is that tutors are congruent, that they do not try to do what they cannot, or be what they are not. Blind adherence to some kind of model is never healthy; it is the person first and the model second, and not the other way around. *Be* first and then *do*. If there is some incongruence manifesting consistently between the two, a re-examination of both the relevance of the model and how the tutor has drawn from it is called for. It also underlines the importance of training in this area and of tutors having access to (and *using*) ongoing external supervision and support for this element of their work.

When involved in developing the self-awareness of others, there is nothing more powerful that you can do than to be yourself. Tutors and students would do well to remember this.

References

Aveline, M. and Dryden, W. (1989) *Group Therapy in Britain*, Buckingham, Open University Press.

BAC (1990) *The Recognition of Counsellor Training Courses*, Rugby: British Association for Counselling.

Barber, P. (1993) 'An exploration of levels of awareness and change processes in group encounter', in J. Mulligan and C. Griffin (eds), *The Personal Development Handbook*, London: Heinemann.

Dies, R.R. (1980) 'Group psychotherapy: training and supervision', in A.K. Hess (ed.), *Psychotherapy Supervision: Theory, Research and Practice*, New York: Wiley, pp. 337–66.

Dryden, W. and Feltham, C. (1994) *Developing Counsellor Training*, London: Sage.

Egan, G. (1973) *Face to Face*, Pacific Grove, CA: Brooks/Cole.

Egan, G. (1976) *Interpersonal Living*, Pacific Grove, CA: Brooks/Cole.

Heron, J. (1990) *Helping the Client*, London: Sage.

Houston, G. (1984) *The Red Book of Groups*, London: Rochester Foundation.

Irving, J. and Williams, D. (1996) 'The role of group work in counsellor training', *Counselling*, 7 (2) (May): 137–9 (see Chapter 54).

Ivey, A.E. (1987) *Counselling and Psychotherapy: Integrating Skills, Theory and Practice*, Englewood Cliffs, NJ: Prentice-Hall.

Kolb, D. (1984) *Experiential Learning*, Englewood Cliffs, NJ: Prentice-Hall.

Bibliography

Corey, G. (1982) *Group Techniques* (2nd edn), Pacific Grove, CA: Brooks/Cole.

Foulkes, S.H. (1948) *Introduction to Group Analytic Therapy*, London: Maresfield Reprints.

Mumford, A. (1995) *Effective Learning*, London: IPD Booklet.

Yalom, I. (1970) *The Theory and Practice of Group Psychotherapy*, New York: Basic Books.

Discussion issues

For trainers

1 To what extent is your training team in agreement that experiential/ personal development/self-awareness groups are useful as methods of developing self-awareness on your counselling programme?

2 What group-work model do you draw from and to what extent does this reflect the core counselling model of your programme? How often do you discuss the relevance of what you are engaged in on a group-work level with your colleagues? If you have not done this very much, consider why.

For students

3 'There are many paths to the centre of the forest.' Compare group work with another method of developing self-awareness, exploring the benefits and drawbacks of both. Commit yourself to a position. Consider the extent to which this position is congruent with your espoused model of counselling practice.

4 How important is/was the *facilitator's style* in relation to how well you think individuals in your group developed on the counselling programme? Can you articulate more precisely what it was about that style that helped or hindered your own development.

56

HMI's Powers to Inspect Student Counsellors

Tim Bond

Introduction, 2000

Privacy and confidentiality continue to be as important to counsellors and their clients as they were in the events described in this article. The threats to privacy and confidentiality vary according to context and circumstances. In this scenario, student counsellors were encountering the sort of challenge to their clients' rights that can arise for counsellors working in any organization. I have the strong impression that challenges to privacy and confidentiality are probably arising more frequently than when the article was written. Many of these attempts to intrude inappropriately on the counselling relationship are simply based on ignorance of how counsellors work. They can be successfully countered by a combination of educating the would-be inspectors or auditors about the professional ethics of counsellors and suggesting alternative ways of achieving their aims that are less intrusive. The presentation of anonymized but representative case studies and discussions with the counsellor's supervisor are obvious alternatives. Sometimes it is considered less intrusive to permit the inspection of the appointment book or case notes if these can be anonymized and/or adequately protected by confidentiality. More controversially some have experimented with audio-taping and video recordings in ways that protect client identity provided that the counsellor considered that it was appropriate to seek consent and client consent was freely given.

If the disagreement becomes intractable, it is often worth exploring the underlying reasons. Frequently the dispute revolves around whether the organization or the individual is paramount, which was the situation in the instance (Bond 1992). This can seem like a very unequal struggle in which the counsellor needs to find allies and strengthen her side of the argument. As in this instance, the combination of law and professional ethics represent a powerful counter-argument and one which organizations are inclined to take seriously. The ethical principles still stand, though it is wisest to use the latest version of any code or professional guidelines. The legal opinion remains a good summary of the way that English and Welsh law approaches the task of balancing the rights of the individual and the organization in these circumstances. It is worth remembering that only powers granted by statute can override common law. Contractual terms that contradict common law rights are unenforceable in the courts. Government policy cannot be enforced unless converted into law by creating legislation. Going to court in order to enforce a legal right is a last resort but can often be avoided by seeking appropriate professional and legal advice at an early enough phase in any dispute when everyone is still

This chapter was first published in *Counselling*, Journal of the British Association for Counselling, vol. 4, no. 3, pp. 176–8 (1993).

open to alternative courses of action. In organizational settings, it is extremely helpful to be able to combine relevant knowledge with skills in negotiating and conflict resolution. It is worth recording that in this instance the Association for Student Counselling (now the Association for University and College Counselling) was successful without having to go to court.

Since the mid-1980s, the Association for Student Counselling (ASC) has been in discussion with Her Majesty's Inspectors (HMI) of education and ultimately in disagreement about the methods to be used during the inspection of counsellors in educational settings. In England and Wales, the inspectorate have maintained that they should be able to sit in and observe the counsellor at work with a client, subject to the client's consent. (In Scotland, HMIs have considered this an inappropriate method and have used alternatives.) ASC has regarded direct observation as unacceptable and after many attempts at negotiation, eventually an impasse was reached when a senior HMI is reported to have claimed that they have the power to enforce what they thought fit and cited a passage from the *Code of Ethics and Practice for Counsellors* (1990) as evidence of their right to observe counselling directly, subject to the client's consent. This passage states,

> *B.2.2.7 Clients should be offered privacy for counselling sessions. The client should not be observed by anyone other than their counsellor(s) without having given his/her informed consent. This also applies to audio/visual taping of counselling sessions.*[1]

The negotiators on behalf of ASC were understandably dismayed at having all their hard work seemingly undermined by a section in BAC's code. This resulted in a formal motion at BAC's AGM in 1991 asking that the Standards and Ethics Sub-committee review the wording of this section of the code with a view to clarifying and strengthening the powers of counsellors when an inspector insists on a right to observe a live counselling session.

The first task of the Standards and Ethics Sub-committee was to establish what legal entitlements and constraints operate in this kind of situation. Legal advice had been consistently clear about the importance of the client's consent to someone sitting in to observe. If someone observed the counselling without the client's consent this would constitute a breach of confidence and the client could seek a court order to prevent it or sue for damages. It was much less clear how far the counsellor's professional judgement about whether to ask a client to consent could be taken into account. There was a view expressed by experienced senior managers in education that counsellors could be ordered to seek a client's consent under the terms of the counsellor's contract of employment. Failure to comply could result in disciplinary procedures and perhaps dismissal. It was also said that this could apply to counsellors working in other settings. In the negotiations with HMIs, an additional factor had to be taken into account. There are specific statutory powers given to HMIs conducting inspections. S.77 of the Education Act 1944 states that a person who wilfully obstructs any person authorized to inspect an educational institution shall be guilty of an offence which could result in a fine or up to three months imprisonment or a combination of both.

On the other hand, it was succinctly argued by Roger Casemore, a senior manager in an educational authority and former chairperson of BAC, and by others, that under administrative law the inspectorate were required to exercise their powers subject to the constraints and the test of 'reasonableness'. It was argued that it was manifestly unreasonable to insist on direct observation with all the difficulties this raises about confidentiality and consent when there are reasonable alternative methods of inspection which would produce more accurate results and without compromising confidentiality. Unfortunately, 'reasonableness' in a legal context carries a meaning which is not the same as its everyday meaning and therefore this highly rational argument may not be legally enforceable. None the less, it is worth summarizing the concerns about the usefulness of direct observation as a means of assessing the quality of a counselling service because they would apply wherever this method of assessment is proposed. The objections to direct observation are:

1　The presence of an observer changes the way the client interacts with the counsellor and therefore invalidates what is observed.
2　The act of observation undermines the counsellor's ethic and practice of offering the client privacy and confidentiality.
3　There are real difficulties in determining whether clients are in a position to give or refuse consent due to their dependence on the counsellor or the institution through which the counselling is provided, e.g. a young person at school, a redundant worker on an out-placement counselling service.
4　The observer may not be suitably qualified or experienced to assess what is observed.
5　There are better alternative methods of conducting assessments of quality which are more reliable.

The Standards and Ethics Sub-committee was unable to find any way of resolving the conflict of views between the inspectorate and the counsellors. Therefore, BAC sought legal opinion from John Friel, Barrister, which was given in January 1993. The main points made in the legal opinion are:

1　Inspection of schools is now based on section 55 of the Further and Higher Education Act 1993 which makes it the responsibility of HMIs and local education authorities. Section 70 of the new Act creates a new system for further and higher education which requires that each Council of Further and Higher Education sets in place a system for assessing the quality of education provided.
2　The confidentiality of the counsellor/client relationship is as strong as that between doctor and patient.
3　Subject to exceptions which this opinion was not asked to address (e.g. in respect of the confidentiality of confessions in crime), there is no right to override such confidentiality without the client's consent unless there is an express statutory power to do so. The Act does not contain such a power.
4　Inspectors, whether HMIs, or appointed by a local education authority or a Council of Further Education, have no legal basis to insist on observing counselling sessions without the client's consent, and any attempt to do so could be prevented by applying to the courts for judicial review. Counsellors who permitted such observation would be in breach of the BAC's rules.
5　The inspectorate have no right to insist that a request for the client's consent be made against the counsellor's professional judgement. It is a misunderstanding of paragraph

B.2.2.7 of the Code of Ethics and Practice for Counsellors (1992) – which is quoted in full at the beginning of this section – that it gives the inspectorate any such right. At most, this section allows a counsellor who agrees that such an observation is appropriate, to request a client to give consent to observation of a session by an HMI.

What does this legal opinion mean to counsellors? First, it is important to realize that it is a legal opinion and is therefore less authoritative than if it was a judgement given in court. Nevertheless, it is an unequivocal legal opinion and is therefore a reasonable basis for further decisions unless or until it is qualified or contradicted by a decision of the courts. More specifically, counsellors in education subject to inspections under the system first established by the Education Act 1944 or the new systems established under the Further and Higher Education Act 1992, have much better grounds for defending their entitlement to use their judgement about whether or not to ask a client whether he or she consents to being observed.

Note

1 BAC *Code of Ethics and Practice for Counsellors* (1997) states,

B.1.3.3. Counsellors must provide privacy for counselling sessions. The sessions should not be overheard, recorded or observed by anyone other than the counsellor without informed consent from the client. Normally any recording would be discussed as part of the contract. Care must be taken that sessions are not interrupted.

Update

This article was one of my first ventures into the complexity of the law concerning confidentiality and privacy. I have subsequently expanded my consideration of these topics elsewhere (Bond 1998 and 2000). Peter Jenkins has also made important contributions to this topic in general (Jenkins 1997), in health settings (Jenkins 1999) and, with Debbie Daniels, concerning children and young people (Jenkins and Daniels 2000).

References

Bond, T. (1992) 'Ethical issues in counselling in education', *British Journal of Guidance and Counselling*, 20 (1): 51–63.

Bond, T. (1998) *Confidentiality, Counselling and the Law*, Rugby: British Association for Counselling.

Bond, T. (2000) *Standards and Ethics for Counselling in Action*, London: Sage.

Jenkins, P. (1997) *Counselling, Psychotherapy and the Law*, London: Sage.

Jenkins, P. (1999) 'Client or patient? Contrasts between medical and counselling models of confidentiality', *Counselling Psychology Quarterly*, 12 (2): 169–81.

Jenkins, P. and Daniels, D. (2000) *Therapy with Children: Children's Rights, Confidentiality and the Law*, London: Sage.

Discussion issues

1 How important do you consider the protection of confidentiality and privacy in counselling?
2 In what ways are confidentiality and privacy threatened or compromised in counselling settings that are familiar to you?
3 What strategies would you adopt if someone insists on observing the counsellor and client?
4 In what circumstances would you consider it to be appropriate for counselling to be observed directly?

57

In the Counsellor's Chair

Student counselling and counsellor training in China

Stephen Palmer interviews Ms Gui Rui Ling and Ms Zhijin Hou

On my last visit to Beijing during March 1998, I was invited to Capital Normal University to lecture to the undergraduates about suicide and also run a workshop for the Beijing Counsellors Supervision Group. While at the University I had time to drop in at the students' counselling centre which is located on the campus. I had the pleasure of meeting some of the counselling staff and later being treated to dinner at the university campus. An interesting and enjoyable experience.

Due to the packed agenda I ran out of time to interview the staff and this interview was completed by using the internet. The two interviewees are Ling Gui Rui, Director of the Student Counselling Centre, and Hou Zhijin, a university lecturer and counsellor.

Stephen Palmer: In this interview I will be focusing on the development of your Student Counselling Centre. In addition I want to discover more about the training of counsellors at your centre and elsewhere in China. How long has the University's counselling service been established?

Gui Rui Ling: It has been established for five years. It was set up in 1993.

SP: Why was it set up?

GRL: There were a number of reasons for establishing the counselling centre. First, we wanted it to meet the training goals of the University. Students in our university are similar to those elsewhere in China. The educational goal is to foster healthy adolescents both mentally and physically. Students in our university are trainee teachers; therefore they need to have healthy personalities. These qualities are not only for their own benefit but to help the next generation too.

Second, it would meet the needs of social reform. The change from a traditional society to a market economy brings a lot of stresses that people must face. This is also reflected in our university students. Unfortunately, some have psychological problems and need to see a counsellor.

Third, as most students will become teachers in either a middle or high school, they will need to learn a range of skills and techniques to deal with their own students' problems.

This chapter was first published in *Counselling*, Journal of the British Association for Counselling, vol. 9, no. 4, pp. 268–9 (1998).

SP: Just to clarify, what is your middle or high school?

GRL: When students graduate from primary school they go to middle school which equates to grades seven to nine in the United States. High school is similar to grades ten to twelve.

SP: Who funds the centre?

GRL: There is a department of student affairs. It is both responsible for it and funds it.

SP: How many counsellors work at the centre?

GRL: There are ten counsellors in total. Two of them are full-time counsellors. The others include two professors from the Department of Education, a doctor from the university hospital and five teachers who have specialized in student management.

SP: What do you mean by student management?

Zhijin Hou: In my opinion, the student management department is unique. It is similar but not the same as the administration office in the US. In China, there is a teacher in overall charge of a class in each grade in every department, and there is an administration department in charge of all student affairs. The teacher takes on almost total responsibility for the students which includes the freshmen's registration, the organization of activities and the assigning of jobs to the students, etc.

SP: Are the counsellors volunteers or on the payroll?

GRL: The full-time staff are employed while the others are volunteers who may receive a small fee once a year.

SP: What counselling training have they received?

GRL: Almost all of them have attended short courses provided by foreign experts or Chinese professional institutions. Some may have a Master's Degree in Psychology.

SP: What approaches to counselling are used by the counsellors?

GRL: There are three main approaches used: cognitive-behaviour, client-centred and psychoanalytical therapy. Generally, the counsellors tend to be eclectic.

SP: How well used is the counselling service?

GRL: The counselling centre is open Monday to Friday, 8.00 a.m. until 5.00 p.m. with a two-hour break. In all there are about 400 sessions per term. The centre provides an optional course on mental health education for the students. In addition, we sometimes offer a counselling facility for middle schools. We also undertake some research.

SP: What research do you undertake?

GRL: We do a mental health survey of the freshmen. We are interested in the types of mental health problems people have in the university. We undertake research into mental health education.

SP: What types of problems do the students bring to counselling?

GRL: There are a range of problems such as freshmen's adaptation to university life; problems related to studies including exam anxiety, failing exams, lack of motivation; interpersonal relationship problems including those related to love and sex; career issues related to profession and job choice; and disorders related to depression, trauma, neurosis and personality disorders.

SP: The range of problems is very similar to universities in Britain. Do you have any suicides?

GRL: There are very few suicides.

SP: What types of group therapy do you offer?

GRL: In 1996 we offered a developmental counselling group focusing on self-assertiveness and social skills training. This year we ran a self-awareness group. This term we will be running a self-acceptance group.

SP: How do you evaluate the effectiveness of the service you provide?

GRL: We do not employ any specific methods to evaluate the effectiveness of the service. However, sometimes we receive feedback from the teachers and clients.

SP: What professional groups are attracted to work as counsellors in China?

ZH: The three main groups are psychologists, doctors, especially psychiatrists, and, as previously mentioned, teachers who manage students in universities and high school. On some of the telephone counselling 'hotlines' other professional groups are involved.

SP: I want to return to the topic of training. In China, what training is available to people interested in becoming a counsellor or psychotherapist?

ZH: As there is no systematic training available in China, they are interested in receiving almost any kind of training. The training offered has included Morita therapy, cognitive-behaviour therapy, hypnosis, psychoanalysis and systemic family therapy. The short courses offered by the mental health institutions include a basic introduction to the counselling approach, general theory and techniques.

The German–Chinese three-year advanced continuous training psychotherapy programme is the best course available. It provides training in three main approaches: behaviour, psychoanalytic and systemic family therapy. There are two periods of 'face-to-face' training each year. All entrants were assessed for suitability by a panel of experts. After each training period students have to undertake homework assignments, translate them into English and forward them to the German teachers. During the training each student attends at least two supervision sessions.

SP: Describe the type of training you receive.

ZH: The training run by the foreign experts is a combination of both theory and practice. The Chinese professional training only usually provides counselling theory with less case discussion.

SP: Do counsellors receive regular supervision of their counselling?

ZH: At the university, counsellors do not have regular supervision. If they are enrolled on the German–Chinese training programme then they receive supervision from the German teachers.

Some counsellors have established a support group. They have regular monthly meetings and hold case discussions as well as talk about themselves. The group participants also learn techniques.

SP: Finally, are there any national organizations that represent counsellors or allied professions?

ZH: Yes. The national organization is the Chinese Mental Health Association. There are some divisions such as the National Professional Association of Counselling and Psychotherapy and the Professional Committee for University Counselling in Beijing.

SP: Thank you for the interview and for showing me over your counselling centre.

Discussion issues

1 What are the similarities and differences between student counselling centres in the UK and China?
2 There is little difference between the problems students bring to counselling in China and the UK.
3 Will the lack of systematic counselling training and supervision in China affect the effectiveness of the counselling offered?
4 What could we learn from the experience of counsellors practising in China?

58

Counsellor in Court

Pemma Littlehailes

In April 1996 I was contacted by the Child Protection Unit to give a statement, with the consent of my client, in support of her complaint to them of serious sexual abuse starting when she was 7 and lasting until her periods began when she was 13, which was 20 years ago. I had been seeing J., the client, for just over two years at that point, and will continue as long as she needs.

The accused, her half-brother, was arrested and charged with seven offences including actual bodily harm because he had blacked her eye when she confronted him with what he had done to her. He has been held on remand since then. He was also accused of two sexual offences against a child who is 11 now. These two cases were to be heard together but the defence managed to get them split, thus weakening both, and the case against the child was heard last autumn. He was found guilty on both counts but sentencing was delayed until the second would be heard in March 1997.

I was very apprehensive of being a witness and not at all sure it was right that I should. J. had first disclosed the abuse to her GP three years before counselling began, when her handicapped son was six months old, but had not felt able to take up his suggestion of counselling then as she was too busy dealing with the many needs of this only child, and she a single parent. I was told by the GP that J. had been abused by the half-brother, so she had no further disclosure to make to me. I did see the black eye and grazed cheek two years later. I was worried about confidentiality and about what impression the 'spectators' (prosecution, defence, judge, jury, press and people in the public gallery) would gain of counsellors and counselling if this one was prepared to talk about the content of those confidential sessions.

I asked everyone for help and advice on what to say and what I could expect this, my first and (I hope) last, experience would be like. Alan Jamieson gave me the BAC recommendations (and suggested I write it up for the Newsletter so other courtroom virgins could benefit). He said I was to say that 'X came to see me for counselling to help her with her feelings following the abuse by Y' and to be specific about significant dates and the number of sessions to date. A solicitor friend said to ask if I was the expert witness (I wasn't – there wasn't one) but I was the *only* witness apart from J., which was even more frightening, as I felt a great pressure to get it very right for J. who had no support from her parents or her four remaining siblings. Other helpful advice was that the court is the judge's and to speak to him, watch his pencil and speak slowly, and to ask for clarification of tricky questions or if a question must be answered at all. A warning was to beware the 'slippery slope' type of questions that could lead me into a pit I had dug for myself. (See Chapter 59.)

This chapter was first published in *Counselling*, Journal of the British Association for Counselling, vol. 9, no. 1, p. 16 (1998).

Came the day and J. and I had prepared for it, reviewed possible outcomes, recognized that the case was really her word against his, anticipated questions, planned answers and discussed how she would dress – certainly not the skirt her mother wanted, as she never feels safe in a skirt and always plays down her femininity, dressing and hairstyle being decidedly masculine.

The pre-hearing matters were swiftly dealt with and the prosecution opened his case. We were told this, but of course J., the Child Protection Officer and I were not allowed in court until we would be called to the witness box, from which point we would not be allowed to speak to each other until we had each given our evidence. J. was called first and was on the stand for almost four hours, emerging for a break of one hour at lunchtime, which she spent with the day-care centre worker who had come to support her, while I wandered off to find a sandwich and sit in my car with the radio for company.

About 3.15 p.m. 'they' decided not to call me to the stand after all but my statement was read out and I was allowed into the public gallery – relief and disappointment! All that preparation and angst for nothing, apart from the 'learning experience'!

In his summing up for the jury the judge asked them to consider if False Recovered Memory Syndrome could have been occasioned by the counselling. I was very angry, feeling this was a slur on my profession and professionalism – and it was impossible, given the fact that J. spoke first to her GP.

The case lasted a day and a half. And the outcome? He was found not guilty on all six abuse charges, the bodily harm charge was dropped, despite it being the reason for remand, and the sentencing for the two abuse charges of the 11-year-old were two years each, concurrent, amounting to only two more months. He was released in May/June, and J. is terrified he will come looking for her. Her reply when I told her '"Not Guilty" is not the same as "innocent"' was 'No chance my family will believe that'!

I will live to fight another day – I hope J. will too, but I'm not confident she will.

Postscript

Since this article was published I have wished it had been possible, from the public gallery, to interrupt the judge in his summing up to the jury to point out his factual error. Had I done so would I have been liable for prosecution for contempt of court?

Discussion issues

1 Does being a witness provide a risk to the confidentiality, or of damage to the belief in the confidentiality, of counselling?
2 How is your work as a counsellor affected by suggestions about the unreliability of memory?
3 How can you keep up to date with new developments and prepare for new challenges such as that of the possibility of being a 'courtroom virgin'?
4 Is there a need for a particular kind of legally informed supervisor to help counsellors in the future?

59

Confidentiality and the Law

Roger Litton, Mark Scoggins and Stephen Palmer

When a BAC member was obliged to reveal his client notes and audio-tapes in court SMG Professional Risks, who administer the BAC members' Professional Liability Insurance Scheme, were one of the parties involved in advising him. SMG therefore thought that it would be helpful to promote a wider discussion and understanding of the issues involved, so commissioned a review of the law relating to confidentiality from the Scheme Insurer's appointed solicitors who have many years experience in the counselling and therapy fields. Also included in the article are a first-hand account of Dr Palmer's experiences and SMG's comments on the insurance position.

Introduction

Of all the ethical issues worrying psychotherapists and psychologists, the one which caused the most concern was confidentiality. This was the finding from surveys of 1,000 British psychotherapists, 1,000 British psychologists and an earlier one of American psychologists. Thirty-one per cent of the members of the United Kingdom Council for Psychotherapy, 17 per cent of the British Psychological Society members and 18 per cent of the American psychologists said that this was the ethical issue which concerned them most. The authors of the UK study (Lindsay and Clarkson 1999) suggest that the higher figure for psychotherapists may be because all of the psychotherapists were practitioners whereas a proportion of the psychologists will have been academics and other non-practising groups. While there does not appear to be a similar recent survey of counsellors it seems likely that confidentiality issues would similarly come very high up their list of ethical concerns.

As Lindsay and Clarkson (1999) suggest, the dilemmas concern the need to reconcile the benefits of maintaining confidentiality to ensure the trust necessary to the counselling relationship with the need to protect the client or others from harm. The ethically troubling incidents were grouped into these areas:

- risk to third parties – sexual abuse, other child abuse and neglect, threatened violence, HIV;
- risk to the client – threatened suicide;
- disclosure of information to others – particularly to medical agencies, other colleagues, close friends, relatives;
- pressure to disclose – particularly when working in an organizational setting where there may be pressure from those who hold the purse strings to know what happened

This chapter is a revised, expanded version by Roger Litton of the article by Litton, Scoggins and Palmer first published in *Counselling*, Journal of the British Association for Counselling, vol. 8, no. 4, pp. 258–62 (1997). © Litton, Scoggins and Palmer, 2001.

in the therapy room. While strictly a sub-set of the previous dilemma this is worth making explicit as a particular concern of counsellors;

- careless/inappropriate disclosure – by the psychotherapist or others.

A case study – a counsellor's view by Stephen Palmer

Confidentiality is a means of providing the client with safety and privacy. For this reason any limitation on the degree of confidentiality offered is likely to diminish the usefulness of counselling.

(BAC 1997: B.3.1)

Stephen Palmer's measured tones in the description which follows do not convey the feelings of outrage and betrayal which both he and his client felt at what they both saw as an enforced breach of trust. All counsellors regard confidentiality as paramount and to have to break a confidence is anathema to them. In Dr Palmer's case the situation was so much worse because as well as being ordered to read out his client notes he was compelled to produce his audio-tapes of his client sessions. Not only did he have no control over their interpretation by lay people but he was powerless to prevent the almost inevitable harm to his client's well-being if they were used. Despite being able to access advice from his two professional bodies, his liability insurance brokers and from the legal helpline, he still must have felt alone and powerless to resist a process which all his training had led him to view as wrong – although it was, of course, legally right and even, to a degree, necessary to the course of justice in this case.

This case study is published with the permission of the client.

At my initial meeting with my client, we agreed that it would be helpful if we recorded the counselling sessions both to enhance my supervision and to aid her understanding of topics covered. Unfortunately, after a number of sessions, she had to cease counselling temporarily. As her problems with her ex-partner were escalating, and she considered herself at some personal risk, it was agreed that it would probably be useful not to destroy her notes and the audio-tapes of our sessions. We thought that they would be good reminders at some time in the future of the events that she had described. This decision was recorded in her client notes.

Some months later she returned to counselling; at the same time, the police decided to prosecute her ex-partner. With her permission, I provided a written statement regarding the extent to which a number of incidents had affected her. I was concerned that if the Crown decided to prosecute then my client notes would be subpoenaed by the defence. My records included a range of typical personal issues that are often discussed in counselling which were not directly related to her ex-partner but could be misinterpreted by lay people. She was led to believe by the investigating officer that only my statement would be referred to in court. Her ex-partner was subsequently arrested for grievous bodily harm and burglary.

Prior to my appearing in court, I spoke to BAC, the British Psychological Society and SMG regarding my legal position with special reference to the issue of confidentiality. It was suggested that I should raise this issue in court with the judge; all were unanimous in advising that an order of the court must be obeyed.

Both the defence and prosecution barristers wanted me to refer to my original clinical notes in court. When I raised the issue of confidentiality, the prosecuting barrister told the judge that this was not an issue. After some debate between the three of us the judge told me to continue. As far as I was concerned this was an important part of the proceedings. The implications would be that the court could, technically speaking, photocopy my notes as evidence. At this point, I wanted to confirm that I had been formally instructed by the judge to refer to my clinical notes. I turned directly towards the judge and asked him the following question. 'Your Honour, are you instructing me to refer to my notes?' He replied, 'Yes.'

During the lunch break, my notes were photocopied for both the prosecution and the defence and I again tried to contact both of my professional associations and my insurance brokers and succeeded in getting hold of BPS and SMG. They both reiterated that I *must* comply with any instruction given to me by the judge. I then showed the prosecution barrister the type of topics that a client might raise during counselling sessions. She then understood my resistance in referring to my notes and later in court asked the judge if Crown Immunity could be applied to a number of them. The judge decided that he'd have to read the notes first and adjourned the court to enable him to do so.

It is worth noting that I was advised not to contact my client as this could prejudice the case. Over the weekend, as I was re-reading my client's notes, I became aware of the frequent reference to our audio-tapes of the sessions. I decided to take further advice from BAC and the insurance scheme's legal helpline. The legal helpline said that, even though I was only asked for my notes, my audio-tapes were also relevant material, especially as they were referred to in the client's notes. If I did not mention the tapes then the court could consider that I was deliberately withholding evidence. They suggested that I should tell the prosecution barrister about them and also state my view that their use in court might cause my client psychological harm. It was also made clear to me how wrong is the belief held by some counsellors that they can just destroy records and pretend that they did not exist. This is not allowed and may lead to a charge of perverting the course of justice or to contempt of court.

In court the judge ruled that, if the client gave her permission for their use, then they would be used. The Crown implied that they would drop the case against her ex-partner if the tapes were not used. The client was left with Hobson's choice and, after a great deal of anguish, she finally gave her permission for their use. Even though we were both sitting outside the courtroom, I was not supposed to talk to her about this particular issue. I arranged for a BAC accredited counsellor to support her through this difficult period.

The court support services had to arrange for two sets of copies to be made for the defence and prosecution barristers. I ensured that I received a receipt for the tapes from the court and reminded the relevant staff of the confidential nature of the tapes.

The court was adjourned again to allow the barristers to listen to the tapes. Some days later in court, the Crown dropped their prosecution. As soon as the case was discharged, I immediately followed the barristers back to their rooms and obtained their copies of both the notes and the tapes. I also secured my tapes back from the court. Again, I kept my insurers informed of the outcome.

The main lesson this taught me was that my confidential notes and tapes can be heard by anyone the court directs – including reading/playing in open court – and the counsellor has no opportunity to influence how the material should be interpreted. This can include all records – even tapes of interviews which are normally used only for supervision purposes. I reiterate that, once a case has started, we cannot just destroy records or pretend that they do not exist, as doing so can be a criminal offence.

Confidence in the law – a solicitor's view by Mark Scoggins

Counsellors owe clients clear duties to keep confidences and maintain the privacy of dealings, but clients can release the obligation and courts can order confidences broken. This section reviews the main instances where disclosure will be allowed or compelled, and offers some guidance for counsellors facing requests to reveal what has passed between them and their clients.

No guarantee of secrecy

Confidence and confidentiality are the core of counselling. Clients will open their minds in the expectation that what passes will not be revealed without their consent. But no guarantee of secrecy can properly be given.

In 1776 the Duke of Kingston sought a court order declaring him judicially separated from his wife. The Duchess had given details of her private life in strictest confidence to her physician and to a close friend. Both were called as witnesses at the trial and both asked the judge whether they were obliged to reveal what they had been told. Lord Chief Justice Mansfield gave them a blunt answer:

> [v]oluntarily to reveal these secrets ... would be ... a breach of honour and a great indiscretion; but to give that information in a court of justice, when by the law of the land ... bound to do, will never be imputed ... as any indiscretion whatever.

The witnesses spilled the beans, the Duke got his court order, and English law continued down a path from which it has never since strayed.

With very limited exceptions and privileges, almost all of them belonging to the domain of dealings with lawyers and none applying with any significance to the counselling profession, things said or written in confidence *must* be revealed – even though the confider refuses to agree to disclosure – if a court so orders or some other legal requirement triggers a duty to disclose.

Occasions of disclosure

For the purposes of this review there are six principal occasions on which disclosure of confidential material by a counsellor will be justified or required:

(i)   with the client's consent;
(ii) by order of a court trying a civil dispute;
(iii) by order of a court in criminal proceedings;
(iv) by order of a tribunal (outside the conventional court system) holding power to compel the giving of evidence;
(v)   under statutory powers compelling disclosure in the course of investigations by official agencies;
(vi) where the public interest justifies the counsellor volunteering disclosure even though the client refuses consent and there is no court order or statutory compulsion to disclose the particular information.

Save perhaps in a very few exceptional cases falling within the public interest category (vi), there is no duty of disclosure unless and until it is ordered by someone who has power to make such an order. It is not uncommon, in the preliminary stages of litigation, for a solicitor to write to a counsellor and ask for disclosure of confidential information in terms which imply that the counsellor has no choice but to comply. While there is nothing to prevent the solicitor making such a request, the counsellor is under no duty to disclose the information and, indeed, would probably be in breach of duty to the client if the request were complied with in the absence of the client's consent to disclosure. Such requests should be politely but firmly declined unless the client has given permission for the particular disclosure in question.

The client's consent to disclosure

The obligation of confidence is owed to the client, so the client can agree to waive it in normal circumstances; but the client should be told precisely what and why he or she is being asked to agree.

It is good practice to ensure that, whenever an approach is made to or by a client on the question of consent to disclosure, both client and counsellor agree at least the following details before disclosure takes place:

(i) the identity of the person to whom disclosure is to be made;

(ii) the extent of disclosure and the particular materials, matters, opinions and information to be disclosed and (in the case of documents) whether originals or copies are to be revealed;

(iii) the purpose for which the disclosure is to be made;

(iv) the means by which matters are to be disclosed: whether by personal delivery of papers, post, fax, e-mail, telephone or otherwise;

(v) any necessary safeguards to prevent disclosure extending beyond the agreed scope.

It is prudent also to have a formal written record of these points and for both client and counsellor to sign at the time consent is given.

Consent to disclosure can be inferred in some instances from a client's conduct or actions short of express and clear agreement but, wherever practicable, no assumptions should be made about the client's state of knowledge and intent: confirmation and clarity are important.

Disclosure in the civil courts

A counsellor with relevant evidence to give as a witness in a civil dispute can be compelled to testify and, if the court so orders, to disclose what passed and arose in the course of counselling. None the less, and on the assumption that the client refuses consent to disclosure, the counsellor is released from the professional duty of confidentiality in regard to particular information only once the court has formally ordered that information given.

The fact that a counsellor will in due time be called as a witness does not provide a safeguard for disclosure of confidences in advance of attendance at court. Only once the counsellor is in the witness box (whether voluntarily or under a court summons) can the protection usually be triggered. Even then it is good practice for the counsellor to raise and describe – before inviting the judge to rule on whether disclosure of confidences be ordered – the circumstances in which the information sought came to his or her knowledge.

Whether the court in fact orders a counsellor to reveal and testify to what passed in confidence with a client is a question for the judge hearing the case. Though the contents of counselling sessions and the counsellor's views and opinions on the client are not immune from disclosure, judges will in practice order confidence breached only if they think it necessary in the interests of justice in the particular case.

That question involves a careful balance of competing interests. It is no part of the counsellor's role as a witness to argue the one side or the other. The counsellor is there to assist the court, not to take a position on disclosure. That said, there can be no objection to emphasizing to the judge the existence and importance of the obligation of confidentiality normally owed to clients and airing any views the counsellor may have on the implications for the client of the confidence being ordered broken in the particular case.

A counsellor should not, then, go meekly to the witness box and straight away volunteer to break a confidence; but if instructed by the judge to answer then the counsellor must do so, however mistaken he or she considers the judge to be in compelling disclosure. If a judge's ruling is wrong then appeal courts can correct it, but the counsellor is protected whatever the outcome of an appeal.

Disclosure in criminal cases

The counsellor's position as a witness in criminal proceedings, whether for prosecution or defence, is for present purposes identical to that which holds in civil litigation. The question of disclosure is one for the judge or magistrate. The counsellor must disclose information and produce documents if ordered to do so by the court.

Tribunals and other adjudications

Outside the conventional court system there is a range of statutory and other tribunals which take evidence and have powers to compel attendance of witnesses and disclosure of confidential material and in which a counsellor may be required to give evidence. Principal among them are industrial tribunals hearing, for example, claims of unfair dismissal or sex discrimination; and public inquiries into catastrophes such as Hillsborough and Dunblane or (two in which Mark Scoggins has been involved personally) the Southall and Paddington rail disasters.

The principles on which counsellors can be compelled to disclose information and opinions in such tribunal proceedings do not differ materially from those applied in the civil and criminal courts.

Official inquiries and investigations

An often overlooked source of inquiries to counsellors and others holding confidential material is many statutory agencies which have powers to compel the giving of information in the course of their investigations.

A full list of those agencies and their various powers is beyond the scope of this review but there is one in particular which might come knocking on a counsellor's door and ask to know what has passed between counsellor and client: the Health and Safety Executive (HSE), investigating for example a workplace accident in which emotional stresses may have played a part. The HSE has extremely wide powers of investigation. Among them is the right of an HSE inspector under section 20 of the Health and Safety at Work Act 1974:

> to require any person whom he has reasonable cause to believe to be able to give any information relevant to any ... investigation [into health and safety matters] to answer ... such questions as the inspector thinks fit and to sign a declaration of the truth of his answers ... [and] to require the production of ... any ... documents which it is necessary for him to see for the purposes of any [such] investigation.

The power is couched in terms which appear to give to HSE inspectors the same powers to order disclosure as are held by a judge in a civil or criminal trial. Must a counsellor comply with an HSE inspector's demand to know what passed in confidential counselling?

There seem to be no reported cases on the point, but it is very difficult to see how the counsellor's response to a demand from the HSE should differ in any way from that which is appropriate in the formal atmosphere of a courtroom.

Counsellors should pay particular regard to ensuring that, if disclosure is to be made to the HSE without the client's express consent, there is a clear written confirmation from the HSE that the powers to require information under section 20 of the 1974 Act are being exercised in the particular case and a written declaration by the counsellor that he or she makes disclosure only because those compulsory powers have been invoked to obtain the information in question.

Disclosure in the public interest

In highly extraordinary circumstances, a counsellor will be justified in disclosing his or her confidential views and concerns about a client, and what passed in sessions with that client, even though the client refuses consent and even though no order has been made by a court, tribunal or statutory agency to compel disclosure and otherwise protect the counsellor from a charge of breach of confidence and a lawsuit from the client.

These justified occasions of 'voluntary disclosure' will be rare indeed. They involve very difficult decisions on the part of counsellors. A client may, in the course of counselling, have threatened harm to himself or others. Or the counsellor may take the view that there is a serious risk of such harm's occurring.

In most such cases the client's consent to disclosure will first have been sought but refused. In some instances the counsellor may come to the opinion that the client should not know that disclosure to third parties is even being contemplated.

Codes of professional ethics assist little with the problem, since they are necessarily couched in general terms and each case will depend on its own particular circumstances. Furthermore, views within the profession as to the rectitude and appropriate extent of unconsented disclosure in any particular case are unlikely to be unanimous.

A brief review of the leading English case on the point shows just how exceptional the facts may need to be to excuse an unconsented and voluntary disclosure. In the late 1970s five people were shot dead and two seriously wounded by a gunman suffering paranoid delusions of persecution. He was committed to Broadmoor without limit of time. He asked to be considered for transfer to a less secure hospital and to a programme which could eventually have led to his release. He was examined and assessed at his own request by Henry Edgell, a distinguished psychiatrist.

Dr Edgell concluded that the patient was very far from ready for transfer away from the secure confines of Broadmoor: there were no signs of remorse for the killings and strong indications that the patient continued to pose a serious danger to the public. The patient confessed to him a long-standing and continuing interest in explosives. Dr Edgell recommended strongly against transfer.

The patient's lawyers did not send Dr Edgell's report to the Home Office. Instead, they withdrew the transfer application. When Dr Edgell discovered that his views had been withheld from the authorities he asked the patient's solicitors to release him from the duty of confidentiality. They refused. Dr Edgell felt so strongly that his opinion should be known to those responsible for the patient's future that he none the less sent a copy of his report to the assistant medical director at Broadmoor, who forwarded it to the Home Office.

The patient sued Dr Edgell for breach of confidence, but in November 1989 the Court of Appeal threw out his claim. Holding that the public interest in safeguarding society from the patient justified the authorities' having the highly relevant information and opinion which Dr Edgell had provided, Lord Justice (now Lord Chief Justice) Bingham concluded:

> Where a man has committed multiple killings under the disability of serious mental illness, decisions which may lead directly or indirectly to his release ... should not be made unless a responsible authority is able to make an informed judgement that the risk of repetition is so small as to be acceptable. A consultant psychiatrist who becomes aware, even in the course of a confidential relationship, of information which leads him, in the exercise of what the court considers a sound professional judgement, to fear that such decisions may be made on the basis of inadequate information and with a real risk of consequent danger to the public is entitled to take such steps as are reasonable in all the circumstances to communicate the grounds of his concern to the responsible authorities.

The future

There is no sensible prospect that dealings between a client and counsellor will be afforded any greater protection from disclosure than currently applies under English law. The courts will not reverse the practice of 200 years and legislation is most unlikely.

The United States long ago passed laws creating a special privilege for communications between a client and those caring for that client's physical or mental health. But those laws have been subject to so much abuse by clients, and hedged by the courts with so many exceptions and reservations, that they have lost their way. There is no enthusiasm for English law to follow the American lead.

The insurance position – Roger Litton

If a client threatens legal action for a breach of confidentiality, does the counsellor's professional liability insurance policy provide protection? The BAC members' policy does. Cover for breach of confidentiality is only a small part of the wide cover which is designed to protect the counsellor against legal liabilities across the whole range of problems they could face in the course of their counselling activities. The following comments are based on the BAC policy; other covers may not be as wide.

The BAC scheme policy covers the insured member against legal liability in the event of a claim for damages being made by another person – usually, but not necessarily, the client. The cover is against 'any civil liability' so clearly would include claims arising from an alleged breach of confidentiality. Most – but not all – other professional indemnity policies also cover breach of confidentiality. The cover is not only for any award of damages made against the counsellor but also, almost more importantly, pays for the legal costs involved.

How, therefore, do insurers expect their clients to act when faced with issues of confidentiality? All that they expect is that the counsellor will act reasonably. If you photocopy your client notes and hand out sets of them to passers-by then insurers would probably regard that as being within the policy's exclusion of 'deliberate acts'. At the other end of the scale, our advice to Dr Palmer was that the details were revealed in obedience to an order of the court (with which, in any event, he had no choice but to comply) which should be an absolute defence to a claim from a client for breach of confidentiality – although, if such a claim was to be made, the policy would defend him.

SMG have dealt with a number of claims for breach of confidentiality, including claims against counsellors, although none has led to a payment being made to the claimant. However, each was defended by insurers and the often fairly substantial legal costs were paid by them. Two examples of claims involving confidentiality are:

- A psychologist agreed to record a relaxation tape for a client. Unfortunately, he made the recording on the reverse of a tape which already contained a conversation the psychologist had with the client's psychiatrist; the conversation included several derogatory comments by the psychiatrist about the client's believability and trustworthiness.
- Another client was asked to compile a report on a child for Social Services. The report included an interview with the child's mother who alleged that her parents had abused her as a child. By some unknown route, a copy of the report found its way into the possession of the child's mother who used its contents – including details of the abuse allegations – in an argument with her parents. The parents sued the therapist for defamation and the child's mother sued for breach of confidentiality.

The message to those BAC members who have purchased the SMG cover is that, if a claim is made against you in this area – or indeed any other area of liability – your policy stands ready to defend you. All that insurers ask in return is that you notify us promptly of any incident which you think may give rise to a claim against you. The same advice holds good if you hold cover elsewhere. Notify your insurers promptly and keep them fully informed. We or they will require from you full details of the incident, including copies of complaints or claims being made. They will also need a summary of your version of events – and, the sooner you prepare that, the better the chance of its being complete and of not missing important details. As the claim progresses, be sure to keep notes of important telephone conversations – especially any contact from the claimant.

Members of the team at SMG will talk through the implications with you and advise on the next step. We are all fully aware of how traumatic it is for a counsellor to have a claim made against them. Such an event challenges your professionalism and can leave you feeling very vulnerable and, particularly, let down by someone whom you have been trying to help. We shall try to let you know that you are not alone and that we are here for you at the end of the phone. The fact that we have seen other claims against other professionals can often be a help by letting the counsellor know that they are not the only one to whom this has ever happened and that there are people out there who not only can help but are willing to do so.

If and when a claim is made against you, insurers will take over the handling of the case on your behalf and will, as appropriate, instruct solicitors. As mentioned earlier, the policy not only provides cover for any award made against the counsellor but also, most importantly, covers legal and other fees incurred in the defence of the claim.

As can be seen from Dr Palmer's report, the BAC insurance scheme includes access to a legal helpline on a 24-hours-a-day, 365-days-a-year basis. The helpline is available for advice on any personal or business legal matter and has proved invaluable, as a source of immediate and very professional legal advice, to many counsellors and other clients. However, we must insert a word of caution. If the matter on which you are seeking advice from the helpline could be a potential claim, you should also notify us at SMG – there's no cross-referral because of the total confidentiality of advice from the helpline.

The message is a simple one. Counsellors buy professional indemnity insurance in the expectation that they will never need it. It is a 'well-known fact' that claims for negligence are only ever made against other people. It is unthinkable that someone as professional as you could ever be on the receiving end of a claim. However, if the unthinkable *should* happen – do not panic. Your insurance policy stands ready to respond and there is a good, knowledgeable, professional team of people there waiting to help.

Data Protection Act 1998

This new act brings certain categories of paper records within the ambit of data protection regulation for the first time – the 1984 Act referred only to computer records. Certain manual records will be covered by the Act from 2001 and others will be subject to its provisions from 2007. Counsellors are referred to the BAC Information Sheet 15 (Jenkins and Palmer 2000), published in the March 2000 issue of Counselling, *which gives an excellent summary of the Act's provisions, together with guidance of how they affect counsellors; this section briefly summarizes some of its salient points. Further advice on the implications of the Act is available on the Data Protection Commissioner's website at www.dataprotection@gov.uk.*

The new Act widens access

The crucial point about the 1998 Act is its firm commitment to widening the rights of individuals to obtain access to information held on them. The degree to which this objective may conflict with established practices regarding the making and holding of counselling records is, as yet, not known. However, it appears certain that clients will, in most cases, have a right of access to the counsellor's notes about them. It is apparent, though, that counselling records will present particularly complex issues for the Data Protection Commissioner to resolve, given that they frequently contain much personal, reflective material which relates primarily to the counsellor.

The law is currently uncertain

In terms of ensuring compliance with the law, limited guidance is currently available. Some key definitions are uncertain and the precise application of the law will depend upon future decisions of the courts. However, some key points – the guiding principles behind the Act, its operative dates and the client's right of access – are set out in the BAC Information Sheet 15 (BAC 2000: Jenkins and Palmer).

Sensitive data

Counselling records will fall within the new category of 'sensitive personal data' introduced by the Act. The rules relating to the processing of sensitive personal data are stricter than those relating solely to personal data; while recording of such data will be explicitly permitted the advice which follows about obtaining consent from the client is particularly relevant.

Counsellors and organizations must comply

Counsellors and counselling organizations are expected to comply with the new Data Protection principles in a proactive manner and to develop best practice. Counsellors will need to address the question of what records should be kept and, most importantly, for how long they should be retained, particularly in the light of BAC guidelines.

Obtain consent to keep notes

It is now, more than ever, advisable, in making the contract with the client, to obtain specific consent to keep notes. It might be prudent to agree on the form of the notes, the purposes (including supervision) for which they may be used and the length of time for which they will be retained (see Chapter 45).

Technology and confidentiality

There has been an undoubted increase in the availability of technology to counsellors as in every other walk of life to the extent that most of us now take such modern devices entirely for granted and without necessarily considering whether there are confidentiality issues involved in their use. Following questions from clients, this section addresses some of these issues.

Until recently, client confidentiality could be more or less guaranteed by physical security of written records. However, in this age of electronic data transmission, new risks – both technological and human – may appear.

- *Deleting information from computers* – we need to be aware that information deleted from a hard disk or floppy disk can be recovered relatively easily using readily available software. Always re-format used floppy disks that have contained client information and make sure that the hard disk is either properly wiped or removed before you dispose of your computer.[1]
- *Security of computer files* – encrypt or password protect all of your client files and consider retaining them only on floppy disks (which you can physically lock away) rather than on the hard drive, particularly if other people can use your computer or if it is networked.
- *Audio dictation tapes* – when client notes are dictated, it is good practice to ensure that your cassette is wiped after typing.
- *Mobile phone conversations* – if your discussion is confidential, remember that conversations on certain types of mobile phone can be overheard by anyone with a scanner. Might a landline be safer? And how many irritating mobile telephone conversations have you overheard – whether you've wanted to or not – on the train? If you can overhear other people's conversations, remember that it is entirely possible that they can overhear yours.
- *Discussions* – it is appreciated that talking to people is nothing to do with technology but do we always take enough care to ensure that our discussions about confidential matters are not overheard by staff, colleagues or even members of the public? Also, make sure that staff in your own offices are aware of the crucial importance of confidentiality. If they do read or overhear something, it must not be treated as just another item of juicy gossip (see Chapter 51).
- *Faxes* – faxes are quick and convenient and we all, no doubt, take care to ensure that we either send confidential faxes ourselves or that someone we trust sends them. However, they can so easily be sent to a wrong number. If the information is confidential, it might be advisable to telephone the recipient first so that they can stand over the fax machine until the message is received. Make sure you have a policy for safe faxing including ensuring that you are not breaching confidentiality by sending the fax without the client's permission in the first place!

The ethical dilemma

Dilemmas about confidentiality are part and parcel of the counsellor's role and guidance on how such issues should be resolved is not easy to acquire. The usual first port of call is BAC itself but we, at SMG, are frequently approached for guidance because counsellors correctly appreciate that decisions on confidentiality issues can have insurance implications. It is also flattering that counsellors view us as part of their support network although the practical help that we, or indeed, BAC can give may be more limited than the counsellor would wish.

If you have a dilemma about confidentiality, what should you do? The bad news is that only you can resolve that dilemma and decide what to do. No one else can decide for you. SMG frequently receives calls from clients explaining that they have a problem about a confidentiality issue and asking for guidance. We have to explain that all we can do is reassure them that, as long as they have given the matter proper consideration, their insurance policy will protect them if there is a subsequent claim.

Usually, this is not what they want to hear. 'Yes, yes, I understand about the insurance position but what should I *do*? Should I break confidence – for these very good reasons – or must I remain silent to protect confidentiality?' The reality of the situation, unpalatable though it might be, is that, having sought guidance on the ethical, insurance and legal implications, the only person who can resolve a confidentiality issue is the counsellor themselves.

However, within that constraint, we at SMG can, and do, try to give them positive guidance along the following lines:

- *Consult your professional body* – they will not be able to tell you what you should do, either, but they will be able to refer you to published sources for guidance, including codes of ethics and practice, and may be able to tell you what other counsellors have done in similar circumstances – and the results of those decisions. They may be able to refer you to other counsellors with whom you can discuss your dilemma but, if you do that, remember your duty of confidentiality and do not compound the problem.
- *Consult colleagues* – if you have a supervisor, consult them. Consult other professional colleagues but, again, remember that you can only seek guidance – do not expect to be told what to do and then do it unthinkingly. Again, make sure that any colleagues you consult will respect confidentiality.
- *Consult books/articles* – there is published literature which can help. Use it!
- *Consult codes of ethics and practice* – but be aware that these are, of necessity, written in general terms so may not provide the detailed guidance about what you should do in *this* particular dilemma.
- And finally – *keep notes of all these things*. Probably the most important thing you can do is to makes notes of everything you have done to try to resolve the dilemma. It has to be a reasonable start to a defence to be able to demonstrate that, when you either did or did not break confidence, you took the decision only after a lot of careful thought, research and, perhaps, agonizing. It is probably not negligent merely to take a wrong decision – but it probably is negligent to take a wrong decision where you have not taken at least some steps to make sure that you are taking the best decision which *you* can take in all the circumstances.

We then repeat our reassurance. Taking these steps gives the counsellor the maximum possible protection against an action for breach of confidentiality but, if the worst does happen, their policy stands ready to respond and they will have us and the insurer backing them up.

Summary

Major points are:

- You may disclose information if the client gives informed consent – and that consent should preferably be in writing.
- Disclose confidential information only in response to a valid order or for a valid reason. This is either an order of court or written confirmation from a statutory agency

or, of course, on your own judgement that disclosure is necessary in the public interest. Do not think that you have to disclose information just because a solicitor or the police – or, for that matter, a doctor or other professional – asks for it.

• Take guidance and keep a record of the various steps you take in the process of deciding whether or not to breach confidentiality – and do not panic. You can only be expected to do your best – but it will help your case if you can demonstrate that the decision was not taken lightly or on the spur of the moment but only after a lot of heart-searching and consultation.

• Carry insurance – in case the worst comes to the worst.

Notes

1. In the context of the technology issues raised, SMG have just been notified of settlement details of a claim. An SMG client's computer broke down. He returned it to a major retailer who replaced it. The retailer promised that, if they repaired the computer and resold it, they would erase the hard disk first. They did not do that and the computer, with full details of several high profile clients on it, ended up in the hands of a journalist. Insurers incurred substantial fees to recover the disk, to erase the data and to prevent publication of the information.

The authors are happy for this chapter to be used for training purposes.

References

BAC (1997) *Code of Ethics and Practice for Counsellors*. Rugby: British Association for Counselling.

BAC (2000) 'Record keeping and the Data Protection Act, 1998', (Jenkins, P. and Palmer, I.) Information sheet 15. Rugby: British Association for Counselling.

Lindsay, G. and Clarkson, P. (1999) 'Ethical dilemmas of psychotherapists', *The Psychologist*, 12 (4).

Discussion issues

1 What are your thoughts and feelings about the disclosure of client material in court?

2 Why did Stephen Palmer ask the judge whether he was instructing him to refer to his client notes?

3 In your opinion, did Dr Edgell take the right action when he sent a copy of the psychiatric report to the assistant medical director at Broadmoor?

4 Are you sure what you would do if an issue of confidentiality arose regarding one of your clients?

60

From Transference to False Memory

Counsellor liability in an age of litigation

Peter Jenkins

The use of the law to resolve conflicts and disputes between opposing parties seems to be increasingly a feature of modern society, with disturbing implications for those engaged in counselling practice. There has been an enormous increase in civil litigation, doubling to almost 3 million cases per year over the last 15 years (*Guardian*, 20 May 1995). Recent reforms of the civil justice system under Lord Woolf have included the introduction of conditional fee arrangements. Under this scheme, solicitors will take on a case for a predetermined higher fee if successful in winning the case. In addition, there is scope for 'fast-track' litigation for claims such as defamation and negligence up to £10,000, together with expansion of the existing small claims procedures for claims of up to £3,000 via the County Court.

Moreover, the boundaries of successful civil action seem to be expanding to include areas such as sport, where personal risk was previously seen to be an unavoidable part of the activity, rather than as a potential source of legal action for compensation (Greenfield and Osborn 1996, 1997). Elsewhere, out-of-court settlements have been made following legal action in the cases of children bullied or subject to racial harassment at school, to the families of child victims killed by a nurse while undergoing hospital treatment, to a social worker experiencing severe anxiety as a result of pressure of work, and to the mother of a baby with Downs Syndrome inadequately diagnosed by a hospital. Public services have increasingly faced legal action which seeks to challenge the decisions made and action taken, and parameters of professional liability are further widened (Cragg and Harrison 1997; Hartshorne 1997).

In medicine, the costs of meeting negligence actions increased from an estimated £125 million in 1994–5 (BMA, 1996: 320) to £200 million in 1998 (*Guardian*, 27 February 1998). In the counselling field, professional indemnity insurance is increasingly accepted as a necessary protective measure for practitioners (Litton 1996). This measure has arisen partly in response to the changing background of civil litigation described above, and to the rapid growth of counselling as a professional activity during the last decade. In addition, there has been concern amongst counsellors over the rising numbers of legal cases against therapists in the US, including action for failure to report child abuse, and for implanting allegedly false memories of abuse in clients. While rates of litigation in the US are traditionally higher than the UK, there is evident apprehension that the UK will follow the US down the road of increased legal action against counsellors.

This chapter was first published in *Counselling*, Journal of the British Association for Counselling, vol. 9, no. 1, pp. 40–44 (1998).

However, the increasing trend towards the use of the law to settle disputes is not a uniform development. The growth of legal action may be slowed or displaced by the existing responses of the counselling community to client dissatisfactions. These responses include the development of formal complaints systems, and of voluntary systems of registration for accredited counsellors and therapists. Therapists' organizations, such as the British Association for Counselling, United Kingdom Council for Psychotherapy and British Psychological Society, each have well-established complaints procedures, although operating to somewhat different criteria. One complicating factor here is that the relationship of complaints systems to litigation is not always clear-cut. In some cases, pursuing a complaint precludes legal action, as in the case of the BAC complaints scheme. Providing a credible and responsive complaints system may in fact reduce the likelihood of client dissatisfaction being pursued through the courts. At the initial level, BAC, for example, records dealing with some 400 inquiries relating to complaints during 1995–6 (BAC 1996: 16). Inquiries may be taken up as formal complaints, or referred to the small claims court if relating to disputes over contracts. (This article explores the wider issue of professional negligence related to counselling, rather than the more circumscribed focus of legal action over contracts.)

An important additional factor has been the move to set up voluntary registers of competent practitioners, such as the UKCP, BPS, British Confederation of Psychotherapists and, more recently, the BAC. Registers are intended to indicate to clients and to the general public that practitioners have met relevant professional standards of training and practice, and that they are bound by codes of ethics and complaints procedures.

Litigation against counsellors

However, despite the overall increase in litigation, counsellors are not yet a major target for successful lawsuits brought by dissatisfied clients. The limited number of reported legal cases brought against counsellors under UK law (more precisely, England and Wales) has been noted (Cohen 1992; Bond 1993: 50). This may well change, but would require a prior shift in the law towards the empowerment of clients. The barriers to a significant increase in litigation against counsellors are substantial, and are built into the nature of the legal system itself. This is clear from the operation of the system for medical negligence, arguably the closest relative to a body of case law relevant to counsellors (Conaghan and Mansell 1993: 40).

Apart from criminal action against a counsellor for rape, fraud or assault, legal action is based on the civil law. Such action may take the form of breach of contract, or for a tort. Tort, from the French term for a civil 'wrong', covers a wide area of potential action for redress by a dissatisfied client. The criteria for successful action under tort, such as for damages caused by negligence, require that the plaintiff establish that the defendant owed them a duty of care, which was breached, and that damage to the client was caused as a direct result of this breach.

The barriers to clients winning their case under tort law are substantial. The existence of a 'duty of care' for the relevant practitioner may not be in doubt, nor the damage to well-being or health experienced by the client. It is necessary, however, to prove on the balance of probabilities that an alleged breach actually caused the damage. A client, for example, may argue that a counsellor's incompetent practice caused him or her to develop clinical depression, or an anxiety state. Without an established causal connection, however, it could be successfully claimed by the counsellor or their defending solicitor that the depression would have developed in any case, and that the counselling provided may well have delayed its onset or reduced its severity. Claiming damages solely for psychological distress short of a recognized psychiatric condition, and without a physical injury, is, in any case, yet to be established in the law. Establishing that negligent counselling has caused the client's damage is not an easy task in court.

In the field of medicine, where the dangers of misdiagnosis, and incorrect or delayed treatment, are more evidently harmful to patients, a substantial body of case law has grown up, based on the principles of tort law. However, while litigation against medical practitioners may be increasing, the basic protective function of tort law continues to operate. Under the *Bolam* principle, the standard for deciding if an act or omission was negligent is a failure to act 'in accordance with a practice of competent respected professional opinion' (*Bolam* [1957] at 121). In this situation, the patient had received electroconvulsive therapy (ECT) without a sedative, and had suffered a fractured spine during the treatment. Given that ECT was accepted medical practice at the time, it was not seen to be negligent by the court. Practitioners are therefore protected to the extent that they work within what is accepted to be mainstream practice, as established on the evidence of expert witnesses.

The counter-argument to the defence of following mainstream or established practice may well be that other expert witnesses can be found to argue a contrary point of view. Under the decision in the *Maynard* case, this argument had limited value in proving a case of negligence. In this case, the plaintiff had suffered damage to her vocal cords as a result of an exploratory operation, which one set of expert opinion claimed was both unnecessary and negligently carried out. Yet, according to the judge,

> it was not sufficient for the plaintiff to show there was a body of competent opinion which considered that the decision was wrong if there also existed a body of professional opinion, equally competent, which supported the decision as being reasonable in the circumstances. (at 635)

The client's task, therefore, is to establish that the practitioner acted in a way that was not only damaging to the client, but could not be justified be appealing to established practice within that professional group.

Therapist case law

The parallels between medical case law and potential action against counsellors are suggestive, but limited. Counsellors do not diagnose, prescribe medication, or carry out surgery on their clients. Reliance on primarily psychological means of working with clients removes the hazards related to some of the potentially harmful techniques to be found in medicine. This shifts the issue of counsellor responsibility on to a different terrain, one that has rarely been explored by the courts in the UK. The key case here is that of *Werner* v. *Landau* (1961), significantly one of the few reported cases of therapist negligence to be heard at Appeal Court level. The case illustrates central issues of professional responsibility toward clients, and the ascertainment of an appropriate standard of care directly relevant to counsellors.

This concerns a case brought by Miss Alice Landau against Dr Theodor Werner, concerning 24 sessions of psychotherapy, which took place between March 1949 and August 1949, and during the resumption of treatment in March 1950 up until January 1951. In April 1951 she attempted suicide. During therapy she had developed a strong emotional attachment to Dr Werner, and there was a period of social contact between them after the first part of treatment was ended, including letters, discussion about a weekend away together, and visits by Dr Werner to her flat. She brought a successful case against him for £6,000 damages for personal injuries and pecuniary loss sustained by her as a result of wilful misconduct and/or negligence by him as her medical attendant. This was upheld at Appeal (*Times Law Reports* [*TLR*] 1961).

The judge concentrated his criticism on the second phase, when the doctor had introduced social contact with his client, claiming this was necessary to prevent her relapsing into an 'anxiety neurosis'. The social contact constituted negligence on the doctor's part, based on the views of expert witnesses. According to the judge, 'the evidence of the doctors was all one way in condemning social contacts' (*TLR*, 23 November 1961). The standard of care applied therefore followed the *Bolam* test, in that here 'it was the duty of a doctor to exercise ordinary skill and care according to the ordinary and reasonable standards of those who practised in the same field' (ibid.).

The success of the case did not hinge on doubts about the *adoption* of this psychoanalytic approach, but in the therapist's *departure from accepted wisdom about the safeguards to be observed within this model of working*. In fact, one of the aspects of the case most interesting to counsellors is the court's sympathetic discussion of the concept of transference.

> Describing the system of treatment known as 'transference' his Lordship said that in the course of the process a great deal of past emotion became reactivated. A great deal of past emotion released could be attached or attracted to the doctor who had undertaken the treatment. (*TLR*, 8 March 1961)

Thus, it is not enough to establish negligence by simply finding other practitioners who can express criticism of the therapeutic method under scrutiny, if there is support for the method by an equally competent body of professional opinion as in *Maynard* [1985].

The case, a benchmark in professional negligence case law against therapists, has been discussed in detail by legal analysts. They have noted the barriers to winning similar successful negligence action which would face most clients (Feldman and Ward 1979; Otto and Schmidt 1991). Cohen's conclusion is that 'we are unlikely to see a dramatic increase in such cases' (1992: 11). Clients face significant difficulty in proving that negligent therapy has caused psychiatric illness or financial loss. Supporting evidence, in the form of letters and other documents, may not be easily available to the client. In the *Werner* case, an award of £6,000 was made for personal injuries, approximately £60,000 in current value; Miss Landau had made a suicide attempt, and had been unable to earn a living following her negligently handled therapy.

Vicarious liability

In private practice, the individual is personally liable for negligent harm to clients. Where the practitioner is employed, or working as if employed by an organization, then the employer holds vicarious liability for their employees' actions. A voluntary agency or organization employing a counsellor would arguably, therefore, be liable for the practice of the individual practitioners according to this principle. The implication is that Dr Werner was working in private practice, which determined his personal liability for damages. If he had been working as an employee of the National Health Service, then vicarious liability would presumably have been borne by the relevant Health Authority. In medical case law, this was established in the case of *Cassidy* [1951]. Here treatment of a patient's hand resulted in it becoming paralysed. The subsequent legal action found that the employer of the medical and nursing staff, the NHS, was liable for the damage caused.

Given the wide and increasing range of situations in which counsellors work, establishing the limits of liability can become complex. This is particularly true in the case of counsellors working in primary care. The principle of vicarious liability rests on the *employment relationship* which underpins the provision of counselling (Scott 1994: 64–5). A self-employed counsellor working in primary care is, consequently, personally liable for their own practice. Where the counsellor is employed directly by the practice, perhaps under fundholding arrangements, or is working as if employed, then vicarious liability is held by the employing practice, according to this principle.

The complexity of counselling relationships and practice in primary care is borne out by a report into the care of a man with schizophrenia provided by health and community services. While this did not result in legal action, there are significant issues of potential counsellor liability to be drawn from the inquiry report (Jenkins 1999). In this situation, the client was receiving counselling from a qualified counsellor on placement at a general practice, which also had a second counsellor in post. The report investigated the sequence of events which resulted in the deterioration of the client's mental condition, and his subsequent murder of his mother and step-brother. The client appeared to benefit from the counselling received, but the report expresses concerns about the communication between the counsellor and general practitioner.

In order to maintain client confidentiality, it appears that no report was made to the client's general practitioner on the progress of the counselling. In retrospect, the report refers to the deterioration in the client's mental condition, including fears of being harmed, an interest in collecting weapons, and worsening relationships with his immediate family. The report is careful not to imply criticism of the counsellor concerned, given that the support provided to the client was experienced by the client as beneficial. The failure to liaise with the GP on these specific issue could not be held to be directly responsible for the client's behaviour on discharge from psychiatric hospital. Clinical responsibility for patient care continues to be held by the general practitioner, even if delegated to other practitioners, such as a counsellor (GMC 1998: 12). The practice also holds vicarious liability for the care provided to the client. The report does make important observations, however, on the appropriate limits to client confidentiality in a primary care setting, and the adequacy of training of counsellors regarding symptomatology of psychiatric conditions. It recommends 'the appropriate integration of the work done by the counsellor into the general pattern of medical and social work help available to a patient' (SDHA/DCC 1996: 9).

One of the issues raised by the report concerns arrangements for supervision (SDHA/DCC 1996: 36–7). Concerns have been raised about the potential liability of counsellor supervisors in the UK for the negligence or malpractice of their supervisees. Case law in the US provides a number of instances whereby supervisors have been held liable for their supervisees' actions. However, this has been under very specific circumstances, where registered psychologists and social workers have carried liability for staff working directly under their supervision. This does not seem analogous to the situation obtaining for many counsellors in the UK, where supervision is carried out as a process of professional consultation required by a code of ethics, rather than as a specific condition of state registration. Supervisor liability for their supervisees in the UK would arguably be diminished by the very different degree of direct knowledge and control held here, in contrast to some instances pertaining in the US (Jenkins 2001).

Liability regarding third parties

Liability to third parties such as client's parents and families is a further area of potential concern to counsellors. The immediate point of reference with counsellor's liability to third parties is the contrast with the US. In the well-known *Tarasoff* case (1976), a therapist notified the police concerning the threats made by his client against a former girlfriend. The client acted on his threats two months later, and the victim's parents successfully sued the employing authorities, the University of California. The court determined that the University was liable for failure to warn the intended victim, a judgement later amended to refer to *foreseeable* victims, arguably a much less exacting standard to follow (Mangalmurti 1994: 395).

In the similar case of *Peck* (1985), a counselling agency in the US was found to be liable for failing to prevent a client carrying out a declared threat to a third party's property made during therapy. A young man in counselling acted on his threat to burn down his parents' barn, which the counsellor failed to take appropriate steps to prevent, or to alert those at risk. In contrast, case law relating to counsellors working in the statutory sector in the UK has tended to restrict their vulnerability to being sued, for reasons of public policy.

In the case of an allegedly faulty assessment carried out by a psychiatrist and social worker investigating a report of child abuse (*M* v. *Newham LBC* [1995]), the court ruled that the aggrieved parent could not sue the individuals or their employing authority for negligence. The plaintiff's case was that her daughter had been wrongly taken into care, when the identity of a potential abuser was mistakenly thought to be someone in her current household, rather than someone else of the same name living elsewhere. In the court's view, despite the complexity of the case, the primary responsibility of the professionals working in the delicate area of child protection assessment was to their *employing authority*, rather than to the child/client or to a third party, the child's mother. However, public sector professionals in the police force or social services, for example, no longer enjoy immunity from negligence actions, following key decisions at the European Court of Human Rights.

One of the current testing grounds for this area of professional third-party liability is that concerning discharged psychiatric patients. Where discharged psychiatric patients have killed or harmed members of the public, the courts have been reluctant to permit aggrieved relatives to sue the psychiatrist allegedly responsible for the discharge decision.

In one instance, Jonathon Zito was stabbed to death by Christopher Clunis, a psychiatric patient released from hospital. Jonathon's widow, Jayne Zito, was unable to sue the relevant health authority. However, no doubt there will be other similar cases appearing before the courts, which may challenge this protective principle for mental health professionals and their employing authorities in the future.

False-memory claims

The best known legal case of alleged false memory in the US is that of *Ramona* (1994). Gary Ramona successfully sued his daughter's counsellor and psychiatrist for damages, on the grounds of their inducing false memories of childhood sexual abuse during therapy (Johnston 1997). Significantly, however, he was awarded only $475,000 rather than the $8,000,000 claimed. The actual legal basis for third-party false-memory claims is probably less well known, but is significant in opening up to scrutiny the problematic logic inherent in such cases. *Molien* v. *Kaiser Foundation Hospitals* (1980) provides the case which lays the legal basis for false-memory cases in Californian law. In this instance, the plaintiff sued a hospital for misdiagnosis that his wife had syphilis. This incorrect information not only contributed to the later failure of their marriage, but also involved further, unsuccessful expenditure on counselling in response to their resultant distress. The ever-expanding lines of liability opened up by this ruling have since been qualified and redrawn under Californian law (Bowman and Mertz 1996: 569–74). The problems in using this case as the basis for later false-memory claims are evident. Analogies between the misdiagnosis of a sexually transmitted disease and claims of false memory are clearly limited. In the first place, syphilis is a clinical condition open to objective testing, whereas false memory is described as a 'syndrome' precisely because it lacks objectively verifiable characteristics, and is the subject of continuing professional dispute as to its accurate definition and aetiology (McGuire 1997). Crucially, third-party action against a counsellor for encouraging false memories of abuse ignores the role of the *client* as an active party in this process, by ascribing primary responsibility to the counsellor involved in the recovery of abuse memories. The whole legal basis of third-party claims against US counsellors is thus open to criticism on these counts.

There is, currently, no clear precedent for third-party action of this kind in the UK. False-memory claims in the UK have, to date, manifested themselves primarily via complaints to professional associations such as the British Psychological Society, rather than as successful third-party action against counsellors in the courts. This is distinct from the use of a claim of counsellor-induced false memory as a successful defensive tactic by lawyers in a limited number of cases in the UK. Parties trying to bring a legal case against a counsellor for inducing false memory of abuse would face the usual hurdles of tort law described above, made more complex by the difficulty of establishing proof of harm to a party not directly involved in the therapeutic process itself. UK courts may well be reluctant to push the barriers of liability this far, unlike courts in the US. Even in the US, it should be stated, the fragile principle of third-party liability for false memory is established only at the lower levels of the court hierarchy, and as yet lacks more authoritative endorsement by higher courts.

Conclusion

Current rates of civil litigation in society at large have raised concerns that counsellors may be at increasing risk of legal action from dissatisfied clients. However, action against counsellors for professional negligence faces a number of difficulties inherent in the nature of tort law, illustrated by the *Werner* case. Case law relating to counsellors is limited, but key principles of liability can be drawn from wider case law relating to medical negligence. Supervisors' liability has yet to be established in the UK. While there is pressure to draw the lines of third-party liability ever wider, to permit legal challenge by clients' families and parents, there are well-established legal arguments to counter this. False memory may represent the most publicized form of third-party legal action against counsellors, but the UK legal system has thus far resisted attempts to transplant its problematic logic from the US. While the risk of litigation of US proportions against counsellors may be overstated, counsellors clearly need to be vigilant in maintaining the highest professional standards to prevent this occurring in the future.

References

BAC (1996) *Annual Report 1995/6: Promoting the Value of Counselling in Society*, Rugby: British Association for Counselling.

BMA (1996) 'Medical litigation faces British revolution', *British Medical Journal*, 312: 330.

Bond, T. (1993) *Standards and Ethics for Counselling in Action*, London: Sage.

Bowman, C.G. and Mertz, E. (1996) 'A dangerous direction: legal intervention in sexual abuse survivor therapy', *Harvard Law Review*, 109 (3): 551–639.

Cohen, K. (1992) 'Some legal issues in counselling and psychotherapy', *British Journal of Guidance and Counselling*, 20 (1): 10–26.

Conaghan, J. and Mansell, W. (1993) *The Wrongs of Tort*, London: Pluto.

Cragg, S. and Harrison, J. (1997) 'New guidelines for police misconduct damages', *Legal Action* (May): 22–3.

Feldman, S. and Ward, T. (1979) 'Psychotherapeutic injury: reshaping the implied contract as an alternative to malpractice', *North Caroline Law Review*, 58: 63–96.

GMC (1998) *Duties and Responsibilities of the Doctor – Good Medical Practice*, London: General Medical Council.

Greenfield, S. and Osborn, G. (1996) 'The referee's fear of the penalty', *Professional Negligence*, 12 (2): 63–6.

Greenfield, S. and Osborn, G. (1997) 'Aesthetics, injury and liability in cricket', *Professional Negligence*, 13 (1): 9–13.

Hartshorne, J. (1997) 'The liability in negligence of the fire service – the Court of Appeal decides', *Professional Negligence*, 18 (2): 53–8.

Jenkins, P. (1999) 'Client or patient? Contrasts between medical and counselling models of confidentiality', *Counselling Psychology Quarterly*, 12 (2): 169–81.

Jenkins, P. (2001) 'Supervisory responsibility and the law', in D. King and S. Wheeler (eds), *Supervising Counsellors*, London: Sage.

Johnston, M. (1997) *Spectral Evidence: The Ramona Case*, Colorado: Westview.

Litton, R. (1996) 'Professional indemnity insurance for counsellors', *Counselling*, 7 (1): 19–24.

Mangalmurti, V.S. (1994) 'Psychotherapists' fear of *Tarasoff*: all in the mind?', *Journal of Psychiatry and Law*, 22 (3): 379–409.

McGuire, A. (1997) *False Memory Syndrome: A Statement*, Rugby: British Association for Counselling.

Otto, R. and Schmidt, W. (1991) 'Malpractice in verbal psychotherapy: problems and some solutions', *Forensic Reports*, 4: 309–36.

Scott, W. (1994) *The General Practitioner and the Law of Negligence*, Buckinghamshire: Business and Medical Publishers.
SDHA/DCC (1996) *Report of the Inquiry into the care of Anthony Smith*, South Derbyshire Health Authority/Derbyshire County Council.

Legal references

UK

Bolam v. *Friern HMC* [1957] 2 All ER 118.
Cassidy v. *Ministry of Health* [1951] 2 KB 343.
M (a minor) and another v. *Newham London Borough Council and others* (1994) 2 WLR 554 (1995) 3 All ER 353 (HL).
Maynard v. *West Midlands Regional Health Authority* [1984] 1 WLR 634 [1985] 1 All ER 635.
Werner v. *Landau* (1961) Law Reports, *The Times*, 8 March 1961: 23 November 1961: *Solicitor's Journal* (1961) 105: 1008.

US

Molien v. *Kaiser Foundation Hospitals* (1980) 616 P.2d 813 (Cal. 1980).
Peck v. *Counselling Service of Addison County Inc.* (1985) No 83–062 (Vt. Sup. Ct.).
Ramona v. *Isabella, Rose M.D. and Western Medical Centre, Anahelm* (1994) C61898 Calif. Sup. Crt Napa County.
Tarasoff v. *Regents of the University of California* 118 Cal. Rptr. 129, 135 (Sup. Ct. Cal. 1974): 113 Cal. Rptr. 14, 551 P.2d 334 (Sup. Ct. Cal. 1976).

Discussion issues

1 Is the tort system of 'peer defence' one that favours counsellors at the expense of clients, or a necessary protection of professional standards?
2 Should third-party legal action (for example for inducing false memories of abuse) be introduced into the legal system of this country?
3 Should all counsellors be required to take out professional indemnity insurance, or does this step simply encourage the drift towards a culture of litigation?
4 How should counsellors and supervisors keep up to date on developments in the law affecting their practice? Is the process of the 'legalization of therapy' a threat or an opportunity for the counselling profession?

61

Solution-Focused Supervision

Bill O'Connell and Caroline Jones

In this article we would like to describe how solution-focused skills and ideas can be used in counselling supervision. Each of the authors supervises and practises using solution-focused (SF) methods, while drawing from other sources, as and when their clients or supervisees might benefit from such inclusion. One of the writers uses the model in group supervision of a team of SF therapists. Our experience suggests that elements of the SF model can be valuable in supervision whichever therapy model the counsellor uses. The key ideas of solution-focused therapy have been clearly described elsewhere (Wilgosh 1993; Saunders 1996; O'Connell 1998). We believe that the solution-focused approach is most clearly understood and applied by counsellors who have undergone counselling training previously and who understand the values of the therapeutic alliance. We also believe that good supervision from any tradition will tend to have similar positive qualities. It is not our intention therefore to claim that SF supervision has a monopoly on the practices described in this article.

What is SF supervision?

SF supervision validates the competence and resources of the supervisee, emphasizes the importance of clear incremental goals and identifies pre-existing solutions and exceptions to problems in supervisee's work. It focuses more on what the supervisee is doing, rather than on client issues directly. It attends to process from an interactional perspective rather than from an intrapsychic one. Wetchler (1990) describes the role of the supervisor as concentrating on what the supervisee is doing effectively, and assisting him or her to continue to do those things. By affirming and extending competence, the supervisor is helping to lay the foundations for professional identity and continuing professional development. In SF supervision there is a clear contract which identifies learning goals for the supervisee based on his or her current level of professional development (Selekman and Todd 1995).

Respect and curiosity

A solution-focused approach tends to emphasize the more collegial aspects of the supervisory relationship. The supervisor fosters an atmosphere of mutual respect in which

This chapter was first published in *Counselling*, Journal of the British Association for Counselling, vol. 8, no. 4, pp. 289–92 (1997).

both parties celebrate skills, creative ideas, personal qualities and therapeutic successes. Thomas (1994) describes supervision as an 'inventive art'. Curiosity, an attitude encouraged in SFT, prompts the supervisor to find out how best to co-operate uniquely with this supervisee. This exploration may cover the supervisee's own preferred learning styles, use of language, prior experience of effective supervision, stage of professional development and personal qualities and circumstances.

SF supervision is essentially a collaborative partnership in which both sides take responsibility for negotiating the goals and options available. In practice, the balance of collaboration will vary according to the level of expertise and experience of the supervisee. As in SF therapy itself, 'resistance' is viewed, not so much as a defence mechanism used by the client/supervisee, but rather as evidence for the supervisor to improve co-operation by renegotiating the relationship. This may demand that the supervisor does something different or something differently, such as facilitate further problem-talk or increase empathy.

One-down position

The supervisor, while conscious of the ethical and professional responsibilities of the role, adopts a 'one-down' position in order to learn from the supervisee how to act as supervisor. The supervisor, in Cantwell's (Cantwell and Holmes 1995) phrase 'leads from one step behind'. In practice, this means that the supervisor does not assume the role of expert in all matters, but seeks to validate expertise in the supervisee. Contrary to some opinion, solution-focused methods do not pressurize the client or the supervisee, but instead employ creative, reflective silences in which both parties can explore possible ways forward. Such encounters develop a respectful partnership in which the central role of the counsellor receives full recognition. The 'one-down position' also helps to reduce the chances of unintentional oppressive practice which is always possible, given the range of differences which may potentially be present between supervisor and supervisee: age, gender, class, race, beliefs, sexual preference or disability. This egalitarianism does not, of course, remove from the supervisor the obligation to confront an incompetent counsellor or one whose personal issues are interfering with therapeutic processes.

Try something different

If supervision, in the opinion of either party, is not working, a pragmatic, non-defensive attitude towards change is taken, based on the solution-focused principle that 'if something is not working try something different'. This requires flexibility, a willingness to experiment and a constant discipline in evaluation. The supervisor aims to create a climate in which change is the norm and the supervisory relationship itself is reviewable. Given human nature and professional sensitivities, such an ideal is not always met! Although the effectiveness of the relationship is open to review, transference and counter-transference issues are not normally addressed as fully as may be the case in other models. No problem remains constant, but is always evolving. Supervisors regard supervisees as capable of changing. This expectation tends to increase the possibility that change will happen.

Language and social construction

From a SF standpoint, supervision is a mutual social construction in which the meaning of language is negotiated within a specific context (Anderson and Swim 1995). There is an understanding that there is no 'one truth' about either the counselling or the supervision. There are multiple realities, voices to be heard, contexts to be respected. The supervisor will draw the worker's attention to the way he or she uses language to describe realities 'out there' as if they had independent objectivity. This sensitivity towards language can help to make the supervisee think carefully about the ways in which he or she shapes the client's problem and deals with it. It can also open up rich possibilities for understanding the many meanings which clients attach to events in their lives.

Supervision can be seen as a 'parallel process' to therapy itself, though not to be confused with it. If, for example, a counsellor is having a problem in moving a client forward, the supervisor might use a number of interventions which are also used in therapy, such as the miracle question, to help the supervisee move on. Supervision then becomes a form of reflective experiential learning for the supervisee. The supervisor models good practice.

This solution-focused template will include values, attitudes, expectations and techniques. The techniques will include exception-seeking, the miracle question and scaling.

Exception-seeking

In this example, the supervisee had succeeded in gaining the confidence of an initially suspicious and cautious client.

> *Supervisee:* It was very hard going for the first few weeks. There were long silences which didn't feel very productive. I felt as if she was testing me out. When I started to offer suggestions, she always had some reason why she couldn't do anything.
> *Supervisor:* You mean things got a bit easier after the first few sessions? How did that come about?
> *Supervisee:* I stopped making suggestions, so I felt less frustrated. I told her that many people would not have coped as well as she had done. I began to compliment her on the way she was thinking about the problem and said that she would know when to do something about it.
> *Supervisor:* It sounds as if once you made less demands on her and took a more positive view, you began to get on better with her.
> *Supervisee:* It was really strange how the less I tried to push, the more she seemed to come out of her shell. I think she was amazed at me complimenting her.
> *Supervisor:* Your approach seems to have opened a few doors for her. Some counsellors might have been tempted to batter the door down, but you seemed to sense it was better to back off and give her some space. Is that something you intend to continue with or even do more of?

The supervisor invites the supervisee to recall those times when, as the counsellor, he or she managed, if only temporarily, to do something different with the client which worked. Exception-seeking follows the SF principle of finding solutions more in solution- than in problem-talk. Rather than analyse *why* things may have felt stuck (which could lead into a long speculative exploration), the supervisor helps the supervisee to reflect on those exceptions when the stuckness was not there, or not there to the same degree. What was happening on those occasions? Who said what? How? What made the difference? How did it make a difference? Could this be developed? In the above example, the coun-sellor had learnt to give the client space and genuine positive feedback. This was the key which opened the door for the client. Counsellors need to have their own therapeutic skills validated and due credit given for good practice, just as they in turn give clients credit for their successes. They need to know what they did well and how they did it, in order to be able to reproduce it. SF supervision sessions are likely to begin with the ques-tion. 'What did you feel you succeeded in doing with this particular client?' (Merl 1995). Identifying competence is more likely to increase professional confidence than is a pre-occupation with deficits and mistakes. If supervisees can come to believe that they are basically competent they are more likely to be receptive to new learning and more will-ing to experiment in their practice. They may also accept that mistakes are permissible and present opportunities for valuable learning. Counsellors who are clear about their strengths and their limitations are more likely to work within their competence as stated in the Code of Ethics and Practice.

Miracle question

The supervisor may use the miracle question. 'If you were working better with this client and your current difficulties had been overcome, what would be the first signs for you that a miracle had happened?'

Supervisee: My heart wouldn't sink when I saw him in the waiting room.

Supervisor: After the miracle how would you be feeling and what would you be thinking when you saw him there?

Supervisee: I would smile at him the way I do with most clients and sound a bit more enthusiastic in asking him to come in.

Supervisor: What else?

Supervisee: When he starts talking he would let me get a word in edgeways, rather than just launch into the verbal attack he usually does.

Supervisor: What difference would that make to you?

Supervisee: I'd feel I had something to offer rather than just be a dumping ground for all his complaints, without him being willing to let me help him change.

Supervisor: What else would be happening once the miracle has happened?

Supervisee: I wouldn't be feeling so weary and hopeless after seeing him.

Supervisor: How would you be feeling at the end of a session?

Supervisee: I would feel that he had worked harder than me and that it was worth while trying to help him.

Supervisor: If we were talking about this client three months from now and you were telling me things were much better, just the way you've described, how would it have come about? What would have happened to make it happen?

Supervisee: I would have found ways of keeping him on the subject and listening to what I have to say for a change.

Supervisor: I wonder how you will have managed to do that?

Supervisee: I would have an agreed agenda for a session and interrupt him once he goes off on a tangent. I also think I would give him things to do between sessions and start off a ses-sion by asking him whether he'd done them or not. I think if I could get him to keep to the point most of the time I wouldn't mind if occasionally he went off on a tangent.

Supervisor: So you would have more of a structure to the session than you have at the moment?
Supervisee: I think I would have limited the sessions to less than an hour as well. Then I wouldn't feel so drained at the end of them. I think I could do a better job with him in half an hour rather than an hour.
Supervisor: That sounds as if you are thinking of ways which will help you to be more effective and to look after yourself at the same time. How will you have done this without your client feeling you are rejecting him or can't handle him?

The miracle question encourages supervisees to talk about improving their practice without feeling that they have to defend or justify themselves. The future orientation reduces the possibility of them feeling discouraged or de-skilled by past failures. As long as the supervisor moves at the right pace, the miracle question should not raise unrealistic expectations, but should relate closely to the supervisee's current level of expertise.

Scaling questions

Scaling is often used in solution-focused supervision to develop answers to the miracle question, but it can also be used at other points.

Supervisor: On a scale of 0 to 10, 10 being your effectiveness with this client after the miracle and 0 the lowest it's ever been, where would you say you are today?
Where would you like to get to?
What would it look like when you got there?
What would be happening that's not happening at the moment?
What would have stopped happening?
What would need to happen for that to happen?
What would be the first thing you would do?
What would the client notice was different?
What would you need to remind yourself about?
If there were setbacks how would you get back on track?

The supervisor might ask scaling questions in relation to the supervisee's confidence or motivation to work more effectively with this client.

Supervisor: On a scale of 0 to 10, 0 being the lowest you can get and 10 being the highest, how confident are you that you can improve your work with this client?
Is that good enough for you to make a start?
If not, where would you need to get to for that to happen?
What would be the first step for you to build up your confidence?
What would your client notice was different about you?

In terms of motivation to change, the supervisor uses the same scale and follows it up with supplementary questions:

Is that motivation high enough for you to make a start?
If not, where do you need to get to?
How could you move one point on the motivation scale?
How would the client experience your new motivation?
If things were to improve with this client how would it affect your work with other clients?
How would it affect your level of job satisfaction?

Compliments

There is a legitimate place for the supervisor to encourage and compliment the counsellor on what he or she is doing well. The restorative function of supervision is very important (Inskipp and Proctor 1989). Supervision should recharge the batteries, stimulate the brain cells and empower the worker.

Goals

Solution-focused work stresses the importance of negotiating a clear picture of specific outcomes to result from counselling. Both parties monitor whether clear and realistic goals are being set with the client and whether progress is being made towards achieving them. Counselling is a purposeful activity to be pursued in such a way that it does not last any longer than is necessary for the client to move significantly towards the agreed goals. Perhaps one of the most useful ways an SF approach can help supervisees is in the focus on endings. As a model of brief therapy, it aims to have a clear sight of the ending from the very beginning. This decreases the chances of the work finishing abruptly or drifting. Using a scaling question, for example, might reveal that the client expects the counselling to finish when he or she moves from two to five. In supervision the counsellor can focus on how they are progressing towards these goals, how they will recognize the signs they are getting there and how to stop when they have been reached.

Conclusion

The solution-focused approach with its emphasis on building a respectful, collaborative relationship, its affirmation of the supervisee's competence and its attention to the goals of counselling, is a useful addition to the repertoire of any counsellor or supervisor.

References

Anderson, H. and Swim, S. (1995) 'Supervision as collaborative conversation: connecting the voices of supervisor and supervisee', *Journal of Systemic Therapies*, 14 (2): 1–13.
Cantwell, P. and Holmes, S. (1995) *Journal of Systemic Therapies*, 14 (2): 35–45.
Inskipp, F. and Proctor, B. (1989) *Being Supervised: Audio tape 1, Principles of Counselling*, St Leonard's-on-Sea: Alexia Publications.
Merl, H. (1995) 'Reflecting supervision', *Journal of Systemic Therapies*, 14 (2): 47–56.
O'Connell, B. (1998) *Solution Focused Therapy*, London: Sage.
Saunders, C. (1996) 'Solution focused therapy in practice', *Counselling*, 7 (4): 312–17.
Selekman, M. and Todd, T. (1995) 'Co-creating a context for change in the supervisory system: the solution focused supervision model', *Journal of Systemic Therapies*, 14 (3): 21–33.
Thomas, F. (1994) 'Solution-oriented supervision: the coaxing of expertise', *Family Journal*, 2 (1): 11–17.
Wetchler, J.L. (1990) 'Solution focused supervision', *Family Therapy*, 17 (2): 129–38.
Wilgosh, R. (1993) 'How can we see where we're going if we're always looking backwards?', *Counselling*, 4 (2): 98–101 and *BAC Counselling Reader*, Volume 1, Chapter 49, London: Sage.

Further Reading

Amundson, J. (1995) 'Supervision as an exercise of mythic proportions: the healer, the magician, the warrior, the seer and the sage', *Journal of Systemic Therapies*, 14 (2): 26–33.

Discussion issues

1 As a supervisee, which elements of this approach to supervision do you think you would find helpful?
2 As a supervisor, does this model offer you additional skills and opportunities to work differently?
3 This model is clearly helpful for counsellors working briefly or within time limits. Do you think these skills would also be helpful for counsellors working long term?
4 What would need to happen for you to integrate some of these solution-focused ideas into your practice either as a counsellor/supervisee or as a supervisor?

62

Supervising Short-Term Psychodynamic Work

Gertrud Mander

Nothing in my dozen years of supervising long-term psychodynamic work, in groups and individually, prepared me for the task of supervising counsellors doing brief and time-limited work. This was virgin territory and I had to invent a method that allowed me to cope with the particular issues confronting me – issues of assessment, structuring, focusing, ending, loss, and, also, that of a quick turnover of people.

The first task was to overcome a prejudice against the new fashion for short-term counselling contracts being offered to employees, in the context of Employment Assistance Programmes (EAPs). Then I had to familiarize myself with a growing tendency in institutions and health authorities that aimed for modest goals and a module model for the counselling of the multitudes at the workplace, in colleges and in GP surgeries. This new development in the counselling world goes hand in hand with greater awareness of the value of therapeutic interventions and promises a much wider distribution of our wares than has been possible in the past, at the expense of orthodoxies and cherished beliefs about giving people what they need or are supposed to need. To work as a supervisor in this sector was quite a challenge, promising a learning experience and a distinct possibility of helping to break down barriers of prejudice and privilege.

My previous short training in the brief focal psychotherapy model developed by Balint et al. (1972) and Malan (1963) had trained me to work psychodynamically with contracts of up to six months or 25 sessions, and I had become familiar with formulating a psychodynamic focus and working with the ending from the beginning. I had also looked at the time-limited model of Mann (1973) and attended workshops given by Davanloo (1978) and Molnos (1995), all of whom focused on concepts of time and favoured time-limited contracts. Further reading, of de Shazer (1985), and Haley (1973) on Milton Erickson, proved most intriguing, and when the invitation came to supervise a counsellor working with time-limited contracts in a GP practice and a group of counsellors for Counselling in Companies (CiC) at Westminster Pastoral Foundation (WPF), who were working with a five-session solution-focused brief therapy model, I took my chance.

CiC is one of many employment assistance programmes (EAPs) which enable employees of large firms to receive free counselling support through their workplace. It calls on a large body of professional counsellors to whom it refers clients from the many

This chapter was first published in *Counselling*, Journal of the British Association for Counselling, vol. 9, no. 4, pp. 301–5 (1998).

commercial companies who use it as a service provider. The counsellors see their clients in private practice and much of supervision also happens in the private practice setting. Supervision is compulsory and free, and the supervisor is chosen for the counsellor by a clinical manager. This is a three-cornered employment relationship in which the supervisor follows the guidelines set up by the service provider who pays for their supervision work. It creates an interesting dynamic situation in which the clients can be held firmly, the counsellors feel supported and the supervisor is entrusted with the responsibility to implement the contract. However, as nobody is guaranteed ongoing work (including the supervisor), there is an uncertainty about supply and demand that may mirror the clients' employment situation while emphasizing all the difficulties the self-employed counsellor in private practice experiences at a time when the profession is unable to balance supply and demand for all its members. As a CiC (EAP) supervisor I never know from one week to the next whether my services will be called upon.

Five years of work for CiC have made me realize that this is a completely different ball-game, both for the supervisor and for the counsellor. Time is of the essence and the supervision space quickly fills up with people jostling each other. This kind of supervision is like watching people travel up an escalator; they are on and off in a flash and you catch no more than a glimpse of them, while they are achieving the task of moving from one level to the next.

By now, I have seen dozens of them do it. I briefly make their acquaintance, see them in close-up sharply lit, then have to let them go and turn my attention to the next person. Even the counsellors are short term. They come when they have a case, for the space of the five sessions they have with the client, and are off again, until such time as they have been allocated another client. And, as *they* do with the client, we always work flexi-time in supervision – not with regard to the hour and the analytic frame, but with regard to frequency, gaps between sessions and appointment times.

There is none of the continuity and regularity of the analytic setting, where we have months or years to look at cases and develop relationships and hypotheses with leisure. It is now or never, one week on, the next week off, fitting in with the counsellors' time as they fit in with their clients', and supporting them in the task, from the beginning to the end of their particular contracts. Scheduling hence becomes an art, or a headache, whichever way you look at it. As with everything to do with brief work, there is an urgency that makes one inventive: the clock is ticking, one thinks on one's toes, responds fast, finds quick solutions, does not look back and always has to hold many things in mind simultaneously, because, in the words of the poet Andrew Marvell, 'at my back I always hear/Time's wingèd chariot hurrying near'. The end is always close in sight, awesomely pressing in on the meetings as it gets closer. This is why some people compare the brief therapy experience with a death experience.

In supervising short-term work I need to observe the frame carefully. I insist on hearing about all clients immediately after their first session, and carefully go over the assessment session in order to help the counsellor focus on the problem brought by the client, to understand its psychodynamic implications and to hypothesize about the goal and possible solution that can be reached in the short time allocated. We also look at first impressions and countertransference in order to learn as much as possible about the client and to identify early on what might be difficult for the counsellor with every particular case.

Assessment

Even more than in long-term therapy, assessment in brief work establishes quickly the future course of the treatment and of the working alliance, while its powerful impact on the client will determine their motivation, their willingness or their defensiveness. It will open doors for them to understanding and experience of a kind they have not known before – 'In my beginning is my end' (T.S. Eliot, *East Coker*). Everything will be there in a nutshell in that first session: the client's problem and the client's expectations for its solution; their belief and disbelief in the possibility of being helped; their willingness to engage in the task and their anxiety about the difficulties and suffering this might entail, together with their fear about the unknown events likely to happen, and their uncertainty of being with a stranger, whose motives and methods are unfamiliar. All this is there and needs to be harnessed, mobilized and transformed into curiosity and trust, and into a functioning working alliance that allows the work to be done and completed in a short space of time.

Assessment is like anatomy where careful dissection of the body, the search for the probable cause of the illness, leads to the making of a diagnosis on the basis of the symptoms and morbidity discovered. Scanning the client's story systematically to find the cause for the psychic turbulence and discomfort that has made them seek help, the counsellor becomes the anatomist/investigator, who tracks down a core problem, tries to read its symptoms in the light of professional knowledge and experience of pathology, and makes a quick decision about how to contain and tackle the disturbance, and how to involve the client in the task for the short period of time at their disposal. The counsellor will also test the client's suitability for counselling, their ego-strength, ability to relate, to cope with strong feelings, to sustain the intense experience of exploring a dilemma that has seemed insoluble and to separate at the end of this endeavour without harm to either participant.

In supervision, after the initial assessment, the task is to deepen the findings and to examine the decisions reached, confirming or adjusting the focus envisaged, and preparing carefully for the next and the following sessions. The counsellor may be uncertain about the client's suitability, ego-strength and disturbance levels, overwhelmed by a wealth of material and therapeutic possibilities, longing to offer long-term work and daunted by lack of time. This requires a supervisory experience that is both challenging and supportive, firming up the knowledge that *making a difference* (de Shazer 1991) is all that can be done in the short time available. The supervisor helps the counsellor set something in motion that can cause a ripple effect in the client's life, which may turn into a process of self-examination (as the psychodynamic counsellor believes) or into solution behaviour (as the cognitive behaviourist calls it). A limited goal needs to be found and clear strategies discussed of how to implement this in the few sessions to come.

Sometimes the counselling may not go further than the assessment, and the counsellor will have to be helped to accept this and make the experience as meaningful and therapeutic as possible. At other times it may be necessary to consider a different option, a referral on or a change of direction which had not occurred to the counsellor. An example could be a situation in which the counsellor's anxiety or defence against anxiety has produced a blind spot, as with a supervisee who ignored a client's recent traumatic bereavement and focused on her inability to enjoy life, when the counsellor herself had just been diagnosed with a severe illness. Another example is the frequent lament, 'this client needs long-term work', which can be unhelpful at the beginning of a short-term contract, when the client has not yet had the chance to prove their ability for change. Such a comment often demonstrates high anxiety levels which may abate as the work proceeds and may reflect the counsellor's own guilt feelings about not giving a client as much as they have had themselves.

At this point in the therapy anything is possible, and the participants' *belief* in the method can work small wonders, if the iron is struck while it is hot. The supervisor will need to defuse or take over the counsellor's anxiety by communicating their own belief that something can be done that can be enough, for the time being, and that on the whole a process is set in motion that will lead to change. If nothing at all happens, which in my experience is rare, then nothing will be lost – except an opportunity for the client to use an offer of help. If the work done leads to the realization in the counsellor that the client is ready for much more counselling and the client agrees to be referred on, supervision is used to explore the possibilities and to enable the counsellor to initiate a referral (with the help of procedures developed at CiC), while managing the difficult task of letting go themselves and of persuading the client that they will need to work with someone else without feeling deprived or aggrieved.[1]

Thorough assessment needs to be followed up by disciplined batting and fielding of the ball. The supervisor becomes the guardian of the focus, once this is firmly set, and reminds counsellors when they wander off it, or when their attention strays from the imperative need to keep the ending in mind. Supervisors monitor and contain the psycho-dynamics of the interaction, identifying the transference and countertransference situation so that the therapeutic relationship can function effectively without becoming so difficult to end that both partners wish for a continuation of the therapy.

Supervision and the three-stage model

The five-session model practised by CiC counsellors works best with one-on-one supervision, as this ensures maximum concentration and monitoring, but with more experience the minimum requirement seems to be three supervision sessions, whether the contract is for 5, 10, 12 or 15 client sessions. Mann (1973) divides brief therapy work into three parts and others compare it to a game of chess: beginning, middle and end. While opening games, middle and end games can be marked as in any relationship, the three stages require somewhat different supervisory input.

In the middle stage the view forward and backward allows review, prediction and limitation, an interim assessment of what has been achieved and of what is still needed and can be done. At this point it is apparent whether the client is benefiting and it can legitimately be asked whether they have been helped to work towards solving their problem, whether more therapy might be useful, and whether they have been initiated sufficiently into clienthood for this to be possible.

My belief in the efficacy of brief therapy modes rests on the experience that in many cases it can be an initiation into a psychological way of thinking, and hence a priming for further therapy. In my supervisory endeavour I always stress this aspect of the work, partly to lessen the counsellor's anxiety that they are not giving their clients enough, partly to remind them of the general rule that nothing is ever enough, and that all through life there are moments when even the best-analysed person might contemplate further bouts of short- or long-term work.

Ongoing supervisory tasks in brief work are:

- concentrating on the intense countertransference experience, the counsellor's and one's own, for diagnostic clues, ethical dangers and emotional containment;
- modelling in a relationship the model's active style of intervening, questioning, decision-making, requiring an alertness, quickfootedness, preparedness, and a firm resistance to seduction, elation, dejection. Last but not least, abstinence in the Freudian sense, no acting out or acting in and a stance of remaining realistic in one's goals all through;
- assisting in the necessary brief mourning, grief work and any other finishing business after the end of each contract, clearing the ground and the memory for the next beginning, attending to issues of referral, follow-up and feedback.

CiC (EAP) clients come from an organizational context, where work issues and relationships can easily become a focus of psychic turbulence and hence the focus for the therapeutic work. Their particular way of object-seeking and object-relating is reflected in relationships with bosses, colleagues and employees, and their core problems can be tackled in this arena as well as in their personal situation. Helping them to withdraw projections and transferences, to see themselves as others do, to assert their rights, to plan and reduce their workload, and to manage the anxieties arising from restructuring, redundancy threat, or impending retirement are tasks that can be achieved or at least started in brief work, with a view to the clients learning new ways of looking after their own needs. In supervision these tasks can be planned, discussed and conceptualized in relation to each individual client.

In my supervisory experience of counselling at work I find again and again that the client new to counselling and perhaps rather wary of it can best find a way into their blocked internal world by becoming aware of their unconscious contribution to blockages in the difficult work relationships they blame on others. It would be grandiose to claim that a few sessions can move them permanently from the paranoid/schizoid to the depressive position, but steps in that direction undoubtedly occur and the new experience of being able to affect and shift a seemingly hopeless work situation can be one of those momentous steps. In other words, they may be helped to start on their journey of individuation, which involves being more self-aware and less in need of projecting their own unwanted bits on to others.

Reinforcing such experiences of potency both for the counsellor and for the client can be done in supervision, but the opportunity for a repeated working through of a stuck position is, of course, what the model lacks and what the prophets of brief work may underestimate in its importance. It may be too early to expect conclusive research and outcome studies concerning relapse or referral-on rates, and in my opinion not enough work is done on providing follow-ups or repeated contracts. However, the success of the Malan model, which includes follow-ups over extended periods of time, and of Ryle's (1990) CAT model which allows repeats, may be a pointer to the future, when short-term work may become a form of successive contracting.

Supervising counsellors in GP practices and student counsellors

Here I experience some interesting differences to the CiC/EAP supervision due to client populations and organizational contexts which demand a different supervisory style. Both student counselling and GP practice work offer clients an environment in which they are held and develop transferences to a number of people, in particular doctors and tutors. The counsellor receives self-referrals or referrals from colleagues and sees the clients on the premises, while CiC/EAP counsellors operate from home. This means both more and less containment, depending on whether it is a GP practice or an educational setting, on organizational size, atmosphere and trust, and on the split or shared transferences which can support or undermine the counselling work. Also, clients tend to be more transitory and often attend no more than one session, disappearing after an assessment that established crisis and pathology levels beyond the powers of the counsellor to contain. Or they come and go, as they please, as long as they are attached to the setting. If they are practice patients this may be over many years; if they are students, over the duration of their course, yet mostly not in the holidays, which rules out long-term work.

Supervising this kind of short-term work is different and difficult, because most of it consists in one-off consulting, focusing on assessment, diagnosis, suitability, or frame issues. GP clients tend to be somatizers, worried well, or chronic patients of some kind or another; student clients suffer from specific stresses such as leaving home, exam or social phobias, crises and breakdowns triggered off by isolation and separation issues characteristic of adolescence. They seem to be the most difficult clients to engage and induct into the regular, once-weekly rhythm, and hence provoke particular anxieties in their counsellors to do with uncertainty, feeling let down or rejected, disappointed or frustrated. Often the counsellor's supervisory needs are not met because of lack of funding and generally they feel undervalued and marginalized by their employers, which becomes a regular subject for complaint in supervision where organizational issues can take over and swamp the session, to the detriment, but also as a reflection, of the clinical work. The supervisor needs to resist the pull of getting sidetracked and drawn into the counsellor's personal authority issues, and will have to watch for and monitor the extent to which the organization dwarfs everything else, as this can reflect imbalances and resistances in client, counsellor and supervisor sometimes counter-productive to creative work. But it can also be very helpful to analyse the organizational dynamics which get taken on by the counsellor.

A multicultural dimension

An area that requires special attention in these two contexts is the multicultural dimension, which is more often encountered there as clients from different ethnic groups are less likely to find the private practice way into counselling, but avail themselves of the free counselling service offered by both settings. In addition, they are likely to be referred by authority figures such as doctors and college staff, and hence present the 'sent' syndrome, a combination of compliance and reluctance that is difficult to work with, particularly for inexperienced counsellors of whom there are quite a few, as these settings are used for placements required by many counselling courses.

What concerns the supervisor in relation to the multi-ethnicity of these client populations is their sensitivity to issues of prejudice and discrimination, and the counsellors' denial or apprehensiveness of these. I maintain that these issues are still rarely tackled firmly enough and that they need to be put into words as soon as possible, as they belong to the first impression both participants have of the other, and will always influence the client's decision whether to enter into the counselling relationship or not, and affect their resistance and the counsellor's counter-resistance. They can also become the main creative focus of the work, but generally require the sensitive handling that any problem of difference demands.

Some pitfalls of short-term work

There is a decisive difference between the short-term work of the counsellor whose inexperience considers the work finished at the first indication of a client's feeling better or expressing a desire to stop, and the short-term counsellor who uses the honeymoon period at the beginning of therapy to maximum effect, structuring the contract around this and defining the therapeutic space in advance. Beginners invariably mistake flight into health for change and mishandle the onset of ambivalence. Everybody is aware that doing short-term work requires skill and experience of assessment and a well-developed technique and knowledge of the potential of what can be done (and not done). The supervisor has to supply this experience when it is lacking in the counsellor and teach the rudiments of technique by constantly reiterating the basics and rigorously holding the counsellor to the task. There is a constant need to assess the counsellor, too, and if necessary counsellors have to be told in supervision that they have not got it in them to do short-term work. This can be due to an inability to let go, to contain the transference, to curb the client's desire to become dependent, or simply to make quick decisions, to think on their feet and to work fast which is necessary for this sort of work. This is not surprising. Not every client benefits from brief therapy, and, equally, not every counsellor wants to or is able to work in this mode. It may follow that not every supervisor can or wants to supervise it. There are pack horses and race horses …

Whether it is done in a group or individually, this kind of supervision demands that often more than one client is discussed in a session, and this means a supervisory style that is flexible and focused. To call it 'bite-sized' might be accurate, but this does not mean hurried or superficial – rather more active and concentrated than supervision of long-term casework or of training cases. I guess the secret is to focus on the counsellor and on the countertransference, and to trust that the unconscious process of reflections and parallels will guide and activate one's intuition and thinking. Of course, much is left out and once an avenue of thought is chosen, one has to follow where it leads. The maxim in short-term work is that there is only one chance.

Supervising a student counsellor

As a clinical example I have chosen a fairly typical session with a student counsellor who comes fortnightly to supervision and this may illustrate what the work is like. She comes first thing in the morning before going to work and we both have to make an effort to get up early. She starts out with her own rather difficult domestic situation in order to clear her mind for the task. It is a marital problem and may require her to set a condition. Having established that, we move on to a past case from her small private practice where there is an issue of unsettled fees, which requires her to write a firm letter. Then she talks briefly about a colleague at work who has 'absolutely no boundaries' and who has asked her for an appointment to discuss some work and personal problems. After talking about this for a while the counsellor understands that this is inappropriate and itself a boundary problem and that the colleague needs to be helped to find a counsellor external to the college. Next, she says she has many clients at the moment. Who to start with? There is the man who came to talk about his relationship problems and whom she finds sexually exciting. He missed the last session and she feels that he wants her to ask him to come back. What does this tell her about his problems and his seductive ploys? Pondering this, she says, 'Now I know what to do', and moves on to another student who is German, but has excellent English and talks so fast that she has to 'get on her bicycle' to follow her. The client is an ex-drug addict doing a course in nursery nursing. She talks in a mechanical sort of way like a textbook, as if vomiting over the counsellor, who struggles to keep up with the flow of words, trying to follow a complex and chaotic story, but she can neither think nor focus on anything. It reminds me of how she feels about her domestic situation, and I realize that this is a reflection process. I try to help her identify a problem in the client's material that could be solved and hence could become the focus of the work.

When I mention solution talk the supervisee brightens up and can now attend to the material in a creative way, focusing on the client's entanglement with her mother and with the parents of her boyfriend who was killed in a fatal accident. She realizes that the client's problem is that she needs to disentangle herself and suddenly understands that she herself needs to do the same thing. 'I have to set a condition,' she says hopefully as she gathers up her things. It feels as if she has understood one of the fundamentals of brief work which applies to all the different situations she has brought to this session.

Note

1 EAPs often include a contractual clause preventing counsellors from seeing their EAP clients privately at the end of the specified number of 'free' sessions. Hence the need for referral (Ed.).

References

Balint, M., Ornstein, P. and Balint, E. (1972) *Focal Psychotherapy: An Example of Applied Psychoanalysis*, London: Tavistock Publications.
Davanloo, H. (ed.) (1978) *Basic Principles and Techniques in Short-Term Dynamic Therapy*, New York: Spectrum.
de Shazer, S. (1985) *Keys to Solution in Brief Therapy*, New York: Norton.
de Shazer, S. (1991) *Putting Difference to Work*, New York: Norton.
Haley, J. (1973) *Uncommon Therapy: The Psychiatric Techniques of Milton H. Erickson*, New York: Norton.
Malan, D.H. (1963) *A Study of Brief Psychotherapy*, London: Tavistock Publications.
Mann, J. (1973), *Time-Limited Psychotherapy*, Cambridge, MA and London: Harvard University Press.
Molnos, A. (1995) *A Question of Time*, London: Karnac Books.
Ryle, A.J. (1990) *Cognitive Analytic Therapy: Active Participation in Change*, Chichester: Wiley.

Discussion issues

1 Does the new fashion for time-limited counselling go hand in hand with a wider distribution of our counselling wares than has been possible in the past? What is the likely effect for clients?
2 Are there any particular supervision difficulties for counsellors engaging in short-term work?
3 Not all counsellors are able to manage short-term work with clients and not all supervisors can supervise such work. How do you decide if you are one of these?
4 Can all clients benefit from short-term work? What are the potential draw-backs and/or advantages of referral at the end of a short-term contract?

63

On the Death of a Client

Maureen Murphy

I had been seeing Sandra since July 1992 when she had rung me in a desperate state – eager to put to rest finally some of the memories that haunted her. Over the course of almost five years we worked extremely hard – she working much the harder. We shared the highs and the lows of an intense counselling relationship. I witnessed Sandra's bravery and courage as she faced each memory and worked with it and through it. During the course of our work together she made such progress that she felt able to enrol on, and complete, a counselling course. Her intention, eventually, was to offer her counselling skills to other survivors of child sexual abuse.

We were nearing the end of our work together, and, although she felt that there were some events from her past still hidden from her, we were looking ahead to how she would deal with these events were they to surface. At her last appointment we discussed whether she wanted to do more work or whether she would take a break – maybe returning or maybe not. However, before Sandra could keep her next appointment her daughter rang to tell me that she had died very suddenly from a heart attack on her way to keep a doctor's appointment. She was 52. The news stunned me and I found it difficult to take it in. I had such a small place in Sandra's life – once a week for one hour – we had never met outside of the counselling room and her death did not seem real. The unreality remained even when her daughter came to see me to thank me for all I had done for her mother – I just could not believe it. It seemed to me that we were just between appointments.

I was invited to attend Sandra's funeral and saw this as a way of acknowledging the reality of Sandra's death and helping me have some kind of ending with her. It had been my plan to honour her commitment to our work by keeping our last appointment, spending it quietly in the counselling room. However, ironically, the funeral was planned for that time so our last appointment would be kept at the church where she was to be buried.

I went alone – I knew one or two people there but could not take part in any of the reminiscing that often accompanies the passing of a loved one. What we had shared was confidential and would remain so. I stood in the church watching her family and friends grieving, hearing the vicar's words and feeling so completely alone. I was neither friend nor family – my relationship with Sandra was unique. As her counsellor I was grieving at the loss of all that she had been and all that she could have been and had no one to share that with. I did not attend the gathering after the funeral. It did not seem appropriate – I did not know how many of Sandra's family and friends knew that she had been receiving counselling and did not want to compromise confidentiality for either of us. It seemed safer to stay away from that part of the ritual.

This chapter was first published in *Counselling*, Journal of the British Association for Counselling, vol. 8, no. 3, p. 176 (1997).

During supervision I was able to explore my feelings at Sandra's death and about feeling lost and alone at the funeral. I have become aware of a need to work on these feelings at some depth. I am aware also of wanting to reminisce about her and talk about her life as my client and do not know what to do with that.

I am still trying to make sense of Sandra's death and my reaction to it and have wondered how other counsellors have coped with the sudden death of a client. Have they too felt uncertain about how to grieve, the 'appropriate' level of grief, how the family should be dealt with, whether we should see members of the family – and, if so, whether we should attend the funeral. So many questions and so few answers at the moment.

What is absolutely clear to me is that Sandra's death has symbolized the unique place in a client's life that we have. We are important in their life's journey and their growth towards wholeness but remain put away in a compartment – brought out once or twice a week. Their daily life remains hidden from our view – we hear of it, and the people in it, once removed. What do we do when that life has ended? How do we grieve? How do we celebrate the work done?

Update

Three years have elapsed since Sandra's death and she is often in my thoughts. I think of her with a great deal of affection and gratitude for all that she taught me about being able to be with someone in their pain and to witness the supreme struggle to attain wholeness and health. In supervision I was able to talk about her and the shock of her death and to weep for the loss of a very brave and courageous woman who would not be beaten by her past.

Discussion issues

1 Would you agree to see member(s) of the family and why?
2 Would you attend the funeral and how would you introduce yourself?
3 How would you grieve and honour the work you and your client have done together?
4 Would you accept a close family member, such as husband, daughter, son, as a client?

64

Farewell Sonia

Jackie de Smith

Sonia came to me for counselling in October 1995, aged 31. She was physically fit and always busy but she wanted to find time, once a week, to explore her inner world of emotions, relationships and self. She had a bright smile and her eyes would penetrate mine as though searching for meaning. We explored many issues together and developed a comfortable rapport, often experiencing and sharing our similar sense of humour. There seemed to be an urgency about her and she wanted to learn and move quickly.

Five months into our counselling relationship I had every reason to feel satisfied with the way things were going. I had only just qualified and felt proud of my first, paying, regular client. Life as a qualified counsellor was beginning.

Then came the shocking news from Sonia after our Easter break. She told me that she had an acute form of leukaemia. The prognosis did not look good. I felt totally inadequate and ill-equipped to deal with this nightmare of Sonia's. But without hesitation I knew that the only way forward for both of us was for me to be there for her in whatever way she needed me. This was by no means straightforward. How would I hold those sacred 'professional boundaries'? How would I contain my own anxieties and grief? In what way could I 'be there' for her, when she could no longer attend regular sessions? These and many other questions flooded through my mind. After all, I felt untrained for this. There were no clear answers, just a sense of being open to listening and learning my way through.

Our relationship took on a new and regular pattern. While Sonia was in hospital receiving treatment for her cancer, I would phone her once a week and she would talk if she wanted to and if she didn't, that was fine too. My regular calls were always welcomed as though Sonia knew this was my way of saying 'Our relationship is still here for you and I'm holding it open.' When Sonia was allowed home, I never called. She would be inundated with calls and inquiries and this was always difficult for her. She would have to explain her position over and over again to worried callers. I always felt it was right to do the opposite of what would cause her pressure and I learnt how to do this by listening to what she didn't like. Sonia always called me when she got home and I was always delighted to hear from her. She would then either ask to see me for a counselling session or tell me she wanted to use her time in a different way. She always had a choice. But when she did come, we always kept to the time arranged and she paid for her session. She wanted it that way, as it felt good for her to be treated like a 'normal' person and not a 'sick' person. She didn't want special concessions, pity, or life being made different for her. She would experience this as patronizing when she felt people's pity. 'You poor thing' was what she most hated to hear.

This chapter was first published in *Counselling*, Journal of the British Association for Counselling, vol. 8, no. 3, pp. 176–7 (1997).

During the months of Sonia's illness, we were able to explore her relationships, feelings, loss, anger, pain and suffering. I was able to give her something that perhaps others found difficult. I could withhold my anxiety, curiosity, grief and questions because my training taught me how to hold on to my own feelings and keep them separate. My supervision and personal therapy were crucial during this time. Sonia could experience herself with me, without experiencing my agenda, which was different from how she experienced herself with others.

However, it is vital that I don't overstate my role. She needed me but she also needed all her family and friends, who gave her constant support and love. It was important not to see myself as a parent substitute but as an additional, impartial, consistent support system in her world of fear and pain.

Today was Sonia's funeral. She died, aged 32, eight months after she told me of her cruel illness. Holding on to professional boundaries of confidentiality at her funeral, when surrounded by her family and friends was difficult, but at least I could share my grief with others who actually knew her. However good my own support system, the fact that neither my supervisor nor my therapist actually knew Sonia had made me feel disconnected in my grief. Today was the opportunity for me to connect my grief with others and to say my own 'good-bye'.

Sonia's courage and shining spirit will always be remembered. I learnt so much from her along the way. Sonia said to me at the beginning of our counselling relationship, 'I'll probably come here forever.' I don't know if she realized how prophetic those words were but I just want to say to Sonia, 'God bless you. I learnt so much from you. You brought light, a spiritual vision and added another dimension to my world and I thank you for that; my love goes with you.'

Discussion issues

1   How would you know whether to continue your relationship with a client who suddenly developed a life-threatening illness, or whether to refer them to a more experienced counsellor?
2   What would be the role of a supervisor working with a counsellor facing such a situation?
3   Consider the possible impact and feelings of a client in these circumstances, on being told by their counsellor that they thought it best to refer them to someone more experienced.
4   How significant is a counsellor's need for therapy, whatever the decision about referring their client? What are the implications of the counsellor's feelings affecting their client if they do have therapy or if they do not?

65

Empathy and the 'As If' Condition

Any room for conscious identification?

Susan Ridge, David Martin and William Campbell

There are occasions during a counselling session when a counsellor experiences strong feelings and thoughts within him/herself as a direct response to life events described by a client. These feelings and thoughts could be triggered by specific identifiable issues, problems or situations that are 'shared'. As such, the counsellor may begin to dwell, however reluctantly or indeed painfully, on past, present or future personal experiences that may either now be resolved, or may continue to feel raw. It is quite likely within this experience that the counsellor may become distracted from the client, with potentially damaging consequences. We present a view of such occasions, which we describe as the process of Conscious Identification (CI). This is defined as a process of differing levels of cognitive and emotional recognition and identification within the counsellor (ranging from a brief cognitive recognition of a similarity through to an overwhelming feeling of emotional over-identification, or cognitive distraction), the precise level of which is dependent upon intra-, inter- and extra-personal factors.

In exploring the relationship between CI, the 'as if' condition of Empathy and the counsellor's ability to maintain separateness, we pay particular attention to the extent to which the presence of CI impinges upon the counsellor's ability to maintain the 'as if' condition required for empathic understanding. Although not assuming that when experiencing CI the consequences are necessarily problematic for either counsellor or client, at the very least we suspect that an awareness of the experience of Conscious Identification is crucial if the essence of the counselling relationship is to be protected. We question what the potential effects of CI may be on the counsellor's ability to be truly empathic within practice. This question deserves further examination, as CI could potentially either enhance or obstruct a counsellor's ability to be empathic, which is such an integral and crucial element within the person-centred approach. If issues remain unresolved (and not examined within supervision or personal therapy), they could surface within a counselling session, which might affect both the counsellor and the client.

> [I]f the therapist's intent is totally (as much as humanly possible) dedicated to acceptant understanding of the perceptions and experiences of the client then nearly everything the therapist does is meant to achieve this goal and/or to prepare him or herself to be in the relationship in that way. (Bozarth 1999: 66)

The experiencing of the process of CI within a counsellor may in fact distract the counsellor from achieving that goal and therefore may affect the client.

This chapter was first published as 'Conscious identification: a challenge to the "as if" condition of empathy', in *Counselling*, Journal of the British Association for Counselling, vol. 10, no. 2, pp. 131–4 (1999).

Conscious identification: a challenge to the as if condition of empathy?

Rogers (1959: 210) defined empathy as the ability

> to perceive the internal frame of references of another with accuracy, and with the emotional components and meanings which pertain thereto, as if one were the other person, but without ever losing the 'as if' condition. Thus it means to sense the hurt or the pleasure of another as he senses it, and to perceive the causes thereof as he perceives them, but without ever losing the recognition that it is as if I were hurt or pleased etc. If this 'as if' quality is lost, then the state is one of identification.

Clearly, there is a substantive difference between this idea of identification and empathy. Rogers' definition captures the fundamental nature of empathy as being concerned with the sensing of the other's world, 'as if' the counsellor were the other, while being aware of this *separateness* between the feelings and thoughts of counsellor and client. According to Bozarth (1999: 55), Rogers was insistent that this 'as if' should be maintained and not lost. However, we suggest that this 'as if' characteristic (which plays such a crucial part in the empathic experience) is threatened by the presence both of Rogers' 'identification' and by our concept of conscious identification, as we argue that this necessary 'as if' quality may be lost if CI is experienced.

Counsellors may not sense and understand the other's world 'as if' they were the client but as themselves, as they get in touch with their own similar experience. The recollection of this 'similar' situation may mean that a counsellor becomes unable to separate experiences and risks merging with the client; or becomes increasingly distracted in this remembrance as s/he withdraws into these personal memories; or, indeed, is able to continue to retain a sense of self and still be with the client.

Is the critical issue relevant to the 'as if' quality a fine distinction between either the counsellor merging with the client, or maintaining separateness; forgetting self or retaining a sense of self? Crossing this line could lead to possible over-involvement with the client or, paradoxically, to detachment and separateness from them, if the counsellor were to become too self-involved by the remembering of personal experience. The counsellor could either enter the world of the client and lose a sense of self (which could be helpful if the counsellor is still able to understand 'as if', or potentially damaging if merging occurs), or re-enter his/her world and 'be in' self, which may lead to distraction and distance. The crucial issue, Rogers notes, is that a counsellor strives to be a strong enough person to remain separate from the client (Rogers 1961). However, counsellors who experience certain levels of CI may not be able to maintain this separateness and therefore may lose this 'as if' quality.

This issue of maintaining a degree of separateness is also an essential aspect of empathy (termed empathic attunement) within the process-experiential approach to psychotherapy (Greenberg et al. 1993). The therapist 'takes in and tastes' (p. 104) the client's intentions, feelings and perceptions, developing a sense of what the client is at that moment. At the same time, the therapist keeps a sense of self, as opposed to being swamped by, or 'fusing' with the client's experience (ibid.). Kottler and Brown (1992) also describe the 'as if' quality of empathy as being an ability to sense and feel what it would be like to be in, and walk around in, the client's shoes. These definitions highlight the important distinction between the counsellor being in and sensing the world of the other, and remaining or returning to his/her own.

It follows that the 'as if' quality of empathy requires that the counsellor is aware of a necessary distinction, or separateness in feelings or thoughts, between those feelings which originate in the counsellor him/herself, and those which originate in the client. Barrett-Lennard (1965) suggests that within a counselling session the client's experience does become more real and alive in the counsellor, but the counsellor should not confuse the origin of these feelings. He believes this experience of maintaining a distinction between feelings originating in self (counsellor) and feelings originating in the client to be 'very challenging, and often difficult.' (Barrett-Lennard 1965: 2). If separateness is not maintained, the counsellor's feelings or thoughts may become merged or fused with those of the client.

Thus Barrett-Lennard (1965) proposes that when the counsellor is being empathic s/he understands how the client feels inwardly, how things are to him or her, but doing so does not imply that these thoughts and feelings of the client, originating in the client, also become the counsellor's thoughts and feelings. Empathy does not include the process of identification, whereby feelings originating from the counsellor's own experience, similar to the experiences of the client, 'take over' (p. 2) and unconsciously serve as a reference point for the understanding of the other. Our definition suggests that certain levels of conscious identification may be characterized by the inner retreating of the counsellor into the dwelling of his/her own personal past, present or future experiences. But within this, we stress that the counsellor may experience something very different from the client and may also feel differently about their similar issue.

Conscious identification and empathy – are they mutually exclusive?

Barrett-Lennard's definition of the process of identification echoes certain aspects of CI, implying that if, during the experience of identification with a client, the 'as if' condition is lost, then a counsellor is not being truly empathic, according to this specific characteristic. There is a distinction within the counsellor between a process of feeling into and feeling with. Feeling into occurs when the counsellor allows him/herself to be fully with the client's feelings and experiences, but without ever losing the knowledge that the client is a separate self. Feeling with, which he calls 'sympathetic identification', involves the counsellor responding and reacting from his/her own experience, set in motion by the client's experience, as could occur within certain levels of the process of CI (Barrett-Lennard 1981: 92).

Mearns and Thorne (1988) tentatively describe the process of experiencing identification as 'false empathy'. They suggest that if identification is experienced instead of empathy, this may lead to a wrong assumption, namely that how the counsellor felt in a similar situation is how the client is feeling in the here-and-now of the session.

Findings from an extensive research study concerned with conscious identification undertaken by the writers, suggest that the continued ability of the counsellor to be empathic, and understand 'as if' the client during the process of conscious identification, depends upon the level and type of CI experienced. If the issue which had triggered an experience of CI had taken place in the past and had been resolved for the counsellor, then his/her ability to understand the client could be enhanced, likeness and similarity creating a base for understanding, and s/he could continue to understand 'as if'. If, however, the issue remained unresolved, was current, or was feared in the future, then the experiencing of CI might lead to distraction and a returning to the counsellor's own world, and consequently to the loss of the 'as if' condition.

Conscious identification – its place in the counselling relationship: theoretical and practical implications

Bordin cited in Truax and Carkhuff (1967) suggests that some personal involvement by the counsellor is a necessary prerequisite for understanding the client. To understand how the client feels, the counsellor should draw upon his/her own personal experience. Real understanding can take place, according to Bordin, when the counsellor is involved in a way that makes full use of his/her own personal experience, but at the same time remains sufficiently detached to be able to distinguish this experience from that of the other (as such a balance is required).

Vanaerschot (1990) expands on this issue of remaining separate while maintaining the essential closeness and understanding that empathy requires. In 'The process of empathy, holding and letting go', she questions her ability to refrain from referring to her own phenomenological world, the world of her own experience when striving to understand the client. She suggests that it is not possible for the counsellor to have a direct knowledge of the client's phenomenological world; a counsellor's knowledge of the client's experiences are based upon the counsellor's perception of the client, but she states:

> 'As if' does not refer to the subjective feeling of keeping distance, but to the continuous awareness of the client being the source of experiences and to the therapist maintaining openness towards the client's frame of reference. (Vanaerschot 1990: 289)

Importantly, she feels it would be an error to view empathic moments in which the 'as if' condition was lost as getting empathy wrong. She argues that 'deep' empathy inevitably implies that the counsellor's thoughts and feelings increasingly resemble the client's and that the gap between the counsellor's personal and subjective feelings and those of the client becomes minimal or 'even completely fades away for an instant' (pp. 289–90). Thus she implies that this synchronization of feelings is helpful to the process of empathy. Perhaps, similarly, the experience of CI can promote understanding.

We believe, however, that if the experience of CI is sufficiently powerful, either the counsellor may feel so like the client at that particular moment, in terms of similarity of experience, that separateness may no longer be viable, or the counsellor may retreat so far into self that the sense of the client is temporarily lost. A crucial issue remains, namely the degree to which this experiencing affects the counsellor's sense of self in terms of separateness or merging, this in turn depending on the level or type of CI experienced. This is also likely to influence the ability of the counsellor to remain aware that the client is the source of the described experience and associated feelings.

Vanaerschot (1990) asks whether Rogers means by the 'as if' condition that the counsellor can only be empathic up until the moment when the line of distinction between self (the counsellor) and the other (the client) begins to disappear. In a later work, she refers to Buie's (1981) notion of 'inner referents', including similarities between the counsellor's own experience and the client's (which could represent thoughts and feelings as experienced during CI). She emphasizes that these can be assimilated through life experiences, to help the counsellor to 'tune in' to the client (1993: 48), and believes that when Rogers describes the 'as if' condition it refers to 'the vicarious or substitutive aspect' of empathy. While the counsellor can use these personal inner referents to understand the client,

> [e]mpathy is not emotional identification: the therapist himself as a person does not experience these feelings for he is only experiencing this pain and sorrow temporarily, that is, restricted to the contact with the client, and the therapist is continuously aware of the fact that these feelings belong to the client and are not originating from himself. (Vanaerschot 1993: 49)

We suggest, however, that when experiencing Conscious Identification the counsellor may indeed feel his/her own pain or sorrow, which may be in direct response to the client but which evokes genuine feelings originating within the counsellor. Therefore, in order for inner referents to be used constructively to aid understanding, the counsellor should try to disconnect the cognitive structures and contexts which these referents hold, as suggested by Vanaerschot. However, we question the difficulties of achieving this when experiencing certain levels of conscious identification.

The counsellor strives to keep distance and not merge with the client. Vanaerschot provides us with an important way in which we can utilize our conscious identification. She suggests that the 'as if' condition can be understood in terms of the counsellor having *continuous awareness* that the experiences and feelings that they are trying to empathize with, always originate in the client. It remains important that the counsellor is aware of this distinction and as part of the empathic process is able to 'let go'. It is possible for the counsellor to be able to shift between 'touching' and 'letting go' as a process. 'Touching' refers here to empathizing and is the first part of the process; 'letting go' refers to the 'capacity of the mind to relax fixation' (Harman cited in Vanaerschot 1990: 291). If 'letting go' does not take place, the 'as if' condition may be lost and the counsellor may become 'fused' with the client. The practice of 'letting go' appears to have great potential in the utilization of conscious identification experiences. If 'letting go' of personal thoughts and feelings does not occur as part of the process of CI, then merging with, or distraction from, the client may be unavoidable and may lead to undesirable consequences.

'Letting go' may not occur if the counsellor becomes bound up in similar personal issues. If feelings and thoughts become overwhelming, it may mean that the counsellor has yet to cope or deal with the issue, which in relation to the understanding of the process of empathy, would not allow for a better understanding of the client. On the other hand, if a counsellor experienced CI and was able to be touched by the client's story on a personal level in terms of remembering his/her experience and *not* be overwhelmed by this, then this experiencing might help the counsellor to understand the client's world accurately (Vanaerschot 1990). We have suggested that this depends upon the nature and degree of the experience of CI.

Conclusion

If the 'as if' condition of empathy is to be achieved and maintained by the counsellor when s/he experiences conscious identification, several issues must be addressed: the degree of separateness between the counsellor and client and whether this is maintained or lost; the continuous distinction in feelings between those originating in the client and those originating in the counsellor, and the constant awareness of this origin; and, finally, the ability of the counsellor to 'let go' of the experience of CI. The maintenance of these factors may depend upon the degree, strength and nature of the experience of the process of CI.

We believe in the importance and necessity of the counsellor continuously questioning and bringing into awareness all personal issues – past, present and future – with which CI may occur, which can then be examined and worked through. This personal awareness and examination should be undertaken within supervision and continued personal therapy.

References

Barrett-Lennard, G.T. (1965) 'Significant aspects of a helping relationship', *Canada's Mental Health*, Supplement 47, vol. 13: 1–5.

Barrett-Lennard, G.T. (1981) 'The empathy cycle: refinement of a nuclear concept', *Journal of Counselling Psychology*, 28 (2): 91–100.

Bozarth, J. (1999) *Person-Centered Therapy: A Revolutionary Paradigm*, Ross-on-Wye: PCCS Books.

Buie, D.H. (1981) 'Empathy: its nature and limitations', *Journal of American Psychoanalytic Association*, 29: 281–307.

Greenberg, L.S., Rice, L.N. and Elliott, R. (1993) *Facilitating Emotional Change The Moment-by-Moment Process*, New York: Guilford Press.

Kottler, J.A. and Brown, R.W. (1992) *Introduction to Therapeutic Counselling* (2nd edn), Pacific Grove, CA: Brooks/Cole.

Mearns, D. and Thorne, B. (1988) *Person-Centred Counselling in Action*, London: Sage.

Rogers, C.R. (1959) 'A theory of therapy, personality and interpersonal relationships, as developed in the client-centered framework', in S. Koch (ed.), *Psychology: A Study of a Science*, vol. 3: *Formulations of the Person and the Social Context*, New York: McGraw-Hill, pp. 184–256.

Rogers, C.R. (1961) *On Becoming a Person*, London: Constable.

Truax, C.B. and Carkhuff, R.R. (1967) *Toward Effective Counseling and Psychotherapy*, Chicago: Aldine.

Vanaerschot, G. (1990) 'The process of empathy: holding and letting go', in G. Lietaer, J. Rombauts and R. Van Balen (eds), *Client-Centered and Experiential Psychotherapy in the Nineties*, Leuven: Leuven University Press, pp. 269–93.

Vanaerschot, G. (1993) 'Empathy as releasing several micro-processes in the client', in D. Brazier (ed.), *Beyond Carl Rogers: Towards a Psychotherapy for the 21st Century*, London: Constable, pp. 47–71.

Discussion issues

1 How important do you think the presence of the 'as if' condition is to both the theoretical and practical aspects of empathy?

2 How does conscious identification manifest itself within you? How does it occur, with which issues, when and how often?

3 What effect does this experiencing of conscious identification have on your ability to understand 'as if' you were your client?

4 In what ways has this chapter been helpful and/or problematic in your understanding of the empathic element of counselling?

66

Congruence and Countertransference

Similarities and Differences

Paul Wilkins

In my work as a therapist and trainer I have heard colleagues and students speculate on the differences and similarities in the concepts of different therapeutic orientations. There has often been particular confusion between congruence and countertransference, perhaps because each is understood to be about the counsellor-in-relation-to-the-client, but this does justice to neither and is at best only part of the truth. Therapists of different orientations do use different words to describe the same processes, but to confuse congruence with countertransference indicates a profound misunderstanding of each, for they are not only different concepts but have very different implications for the practice of therapy. It may be helpful to both person-centred and psychodynamic practitioners to try to be clear about these differences, as they relate to the concepts, their similarities and their practical applications.

Definitions

Congruence is seen by Mearns and Thorne (1988: 75) as a *state of being*, a description which many person-centred therapists find unambiguous. Spinelli (1989: 151–2) defines congruence as:

> the therapist's ability to be present and without façade, that is, to be a living embodiment of integration. The congruent therapist acts as a role model for authentic being.... It is not so much what the therapist does as the therapist's willingness to be as real, as transparent, as free of defences as possible that, Rogers argues, provides clients with the necessary strength and willingness to engage in honest and accurate self-exploration and revelation.

Laplanche and Pontalis (1988: 92) describe countertransference thus:

> The whole of the analyst's unconscious reactions to the individual analysand – especially to the analysand's own transference.

They suggest that, since the time of Freud, countertransference has 'received increasing attention', and mention that 'a large measure of disagreement exists regarding the extension of the concept'. The principal division seems to be between therapists for whom countertransference includes everything in the personality of the therapist which is likely to impinge upon the therapeutic process and those for whom countertransference is only those unconscious processes which are brought about in the therapist by the transference of the client. Sandler et al. (1992: 81–98) discuss this difference in usage and origins: 'a

---

This chapter was first published in *Counselling*, Journal of the British Association for Counselling, vol. 8, no. 1, pp. 36–41 (1997).

major development in psychoanalytic writing on countertransference occurred when it began to be seen as a phenomenon of importance in helping the analyst to understand the hidden meaning of the patients' material'.

That the therapist's reaction to the client (and actions and reactions while with the client) may be helpful in the therapeutic relationship is a notion shared with adherents of the person-centred approach and may contribute to questions about the similarities and differences between the theoretical concepts underpinning person-centred and psycho-dynamic practices.

For Smith (1990: 32) countertransference is *'any disruption of the analytic attitude of neutrality'*. The concept of analytic neutrality is alien to the person-centred approach where the therapist's effectiveness is seen to rely on the ability to be really and fully present (to be congruent).

A further difficulty in attempting to compare these two concepts lies in the notion that there may be more than one form of countertransference. Hawkins and Shohet (1989: 57–9) describe four different kinds:

- The transference feelings of the therapist aroused by a particular client.
- The feelings and thoughts resulting from playing the role projected on to the therapist by the client.
- The thoughts and feelings of the therapist which *counter* the transference of the client (that is the thoughts and feelings which resist the projection).
- The somatic, emotional or mental adoption by the therapist of material projected by the client.

None of these forms of countertransference is the same as congruence (although each may have an implication for the congruence of the therapist).

Definitions of congruence make no reference to the unconscious. Rogers (in Kirschenbaum and Henderson 1990: 224) makes explicit reference to the *awareness* of the therapist in stating that being congruent in the therapeutic relationship means that therapists are deeply themselves and that their actual experiences are accurately repre-sented by self-awareness. I know of no definition of countertransference which makes reference to it as a state of being.

The debate about the nature of countertransference

Psychoanalytic and psychodynamic literature contains many considerations of counter-transference which centre on its complexity and/or its use in clinical practice. Racker (1957: 310) offered 'total countertransference' as a way of coping with this complex-ity. Embracing the whole of the therapist's reactions to the client, 'total countertrans-ference' has two aspects, 'concordant identification' and 'complementary identification'. Complementary identification is countertransference as it was originally understood (that is, as the therapist's response to the client's transference). Concordant identification is 'those psychological contents that arise in the analyst by reason of the empathy achieved with the patient and that really reflect and reproduce the latter's psychological contents'.

Sandler et al. (1992: 95–6) (extending the work of Little 1951: 32–40) discern the following elements of countertransference in 'current usage':

1 'Resistances' in the analyst due to the activation of inner conflicts within him – these disturb his understanding and conduct of the analysis, producing 'blind spots'.

2 The 'transferences' of the analyst to his patient – here the patient becomes a present-day substitute for an important figure in the childhood of the analyst; the projections of the analyst on to his patient should also be included.

3 The consequence of externalization or projective identification on the part of the patient, in which the analyst comes to experience a response to the patient in which the analyst is then the vehicle either for an aspect of the patient's own self or for an aspect of the object.

4 The reaction of the analyst to the patient's transferences and to his own counter-transference responses.

5 Countertransference as an interactional product of the 'communicative field' in which both the analyst and patient are involved.

6 The analyst's dependency on the patient for 'validation'.

7 The disturbance of communication between the analyst and the patient due to anxiety aroused in the analyst and by the patient–analyst relationship.

8 Personality characteristics of the analyst or events in the analyst's life (e.g. illness) which are reflected in his work and which may or may not lead to difficulties in the patient's therapy.

9 The whole of the analyst's conscious and unconscious attitudes to his patients.

10 Specific limitations in the psychoanalysis brought out by particular patients.

11 The 'appropriate' or 'normal' emotional responses of the analyst to his patient – this can be an important therapeutic tool and a basis for empathy and understanding.

The broadening of the concept to include all the analyst's conscious or unconscious attitudes, and even all his personality traits, renders the term practically meaningless; and it can most usefully be considered as referring to 'the specifically emotionally based responses aroused in the analyst by the specific qualities of his patient' (Sandler et al. 1992: 96).

Each of the aspects of countertransference listed may have implications for the congruence of the therapist. Although none of them is the same as congruence, that is not to say that there is no equivalence with person-centred concepts.

Countertransference and empathy

Whereas congruence is a *personal state* (it is possible to be congruent alone), counter-transference takes place in the context of a relationship, which sets it apart from congruence. A closer correspondence is with the person-centred concept of empathy which also describes a process. Jacobs (1992: 83) states that countertransference includes the monitoring of thoughts and feelings aroused in the therapist by the client, thus enabling the therapist to better understand the experience of the client. Similarly, in the experience of empathy the feeling state of the person in the client role might manifest as physical or emotional sensations in the therapist. Such empathic experience, when recognized by the person-centred therapist as 'not mine' (that is, as a product of the process and not a personal feeling or reaction), is assumed to be an accurate sensing of the subjective experience of the other, somewhat similar to Racker's (1957: 311) concordant identification.

If these physical or emotional sensations are indeed accurate products of empathy clients will often recognize and own them. A client describing a recent experience was calm and smiling. I became aware of the flesh of my back beginning to creep, a strange discomfort in my shoulders and an increasing sense of panic, as though I wanted to fly from the room. I had no reason to feel like this, and knew this sense of panic was 'not mine'. Despite her apparent calm and collected appearance, my assumption was that these feelings were somehow a reflection of my client's true feeling. I named and described my sense of panic and the wish to run from the room. My client burst into tears (rarely has that metaphor been more appropriate) saying that was exactly how she felt *all the time*. In person-centred terms, I communicated my empathic sensing of her experience. Sandra Garfield (personal communication, 1996), a colleague whose practice is informed by object-relations theory, recognized this as an example of countertransference and said that she uses similar experiences to inform interpretations she offers a client. She would not report her experience to the client directly.

Another therapist whose practice is informed by psychodynamic principles responded to a recent illustration of empathy (Wilkins 1994: 43) in a broadly supportive way but insisted that my example was of *somatic countertransferene*. This understanding appears to fit the fourth category of Hawkins and Shohet and to agree with Jacobs' (1988: 107) description.

Most practitioners informed by psychodynamic theory would use their experience of 'concordant identification' or 'somatic countertransference' in the therapeutic relationship, but it seems an implicit tenet of psychodynamic practice that *any* internal process of the therapist is actually a product of the therapeutic encounter and therefore (by definition) countertransference. Practitioners of the person-centred approach, emphasizing therapist 'genuineness', hold that some experiences of the therapist may *not* be a response to the client but to something else. This difference exemplifies the difference between an attitude of 'therapeutic neutrality' and the intention of a person-centred practitioner to be 'real' within the therapeutic relationship. Whereas countertransference is used to increase the therapist's interpretations and understanding of the client, the purpose of congruence and responses from congruence is to offer the client the chance to make use of the experience of the therapist *if it is meaningful and useful*. As a person-centred therapist this difference in emphasis and the locus of power are crucial. My understanding of clients is far less important than their understanding of themselves – my job is to facilitate that self-awareness.

Incongruence

Lietaer (1993: 23) stresses that the importance of congruence is most clear when it is lacking. In the person-centred approach any *incongruence* in the helper is seen as detrimental to the therapeutic process. Whereas congruence may not be directly perceived by the client, incongruence often is and may reduce the trust placed in the therapist and the effectiveness of the therapeutic encounter. A client who had previously been in therapy with another therapist came for our fourth encounter and our relationship was progressing well. I seemed well able to be fully present with my client and to be aware of my feelings, his feelings and the differences between us. In the middle of the session, as I made a response to the material being presented, my client stopped me and said, 'Don't give me that "active listening" stuff. I don't need it and I don't want it!' This brought me up short and I replayed my recent responses. To my chagrin I realized I had been responding mechanically and had slipped into my own thoughts. An observer might have thought that my responses were accurate and facilitative. In many ways they were no different from those made when I am paying attention and genuinely tracking my client's experience. My client knew the difference and detected my incongruence. Because we had a good enough relationship for him to bring this to my attention I was able to acknowledge the legitimacy of his reaction, and our relationship moved on. With a less assured client, a greater inhibition of the process might have occurred.

It may be that countertransference led to my inattentive state (perhaps my own material was touched upon in some way) and I am sure that a psychodynamic response to my client's challenge would have been possible, but what matters is that my client was aware of the difference between my outward behaviour and my inner state. If clients do perceive their therapists saying or doing something in disharmony with the therapist's inner state, is this counter-therapeutic? Person-centred theory concludes that it is and (by implication at least) that the attitude of 'therapeutic neutrality' interferes with the processes of therapy and prolongs it. Rogers (in Kirschenbaum and Henderson 1990: 130) acknowledges that people do have transference feelings but sees them as something to be transcended, which happens automatically when 'the therapist's understanding is accurate and his acceptance is genuine, when there are no interpretations given and no evaluations made' (ibid.: 133).

> To deal with transference feelings as a very special part of therapy, making their handling the very core of therapy, is to my mind a grave mistake. Such an approach fosters dependency and lengthens therapy. It creates a whole new problem, the only purpose of which appears to be the intellectual satisfaction of the therapist. (ibid.: 134)

This would be equally true of countertransference in so far as it is seen as a reaction *to* the client rather than *of* the therapist. For therapists to attribute to their client, disguise or deny their *personal* somatic, emotional, cognitive or intuitive experience (whether the product of countertransference or not) leads to incongruence.

> When I am experiencing an attitude of annoyance toward another person but am unaware of it, then my communication contains contradictory messages.... This confuses the other person and makes him distrustful, though he may be unaware of what is causing the difficulty. (Rogers 1961: 51)

Is it possible to understand incongruence in terms of countertransference? Incongruence can arise from the personal difficulties of the therapist which may result in an inability to follow the experience of the client. This process may be an 'unconscious' reaction to the client's material and thus could be seen as countertransference. Equally, incongruence may have more immediate and 'real' causes. Not all incongruence results directly from the client's material. If therapists are tired, ill or unable to distance themselves from their own material then incongruence is a likely state.

Whatever it causes, incongruence has an importance in the person-centred approach which finds no equivalent in the notion of countertransference. Rogers was quite clear that congruence was the most important of his core conditions. 'Empathy is extremely important in making contact with another person but if you have other feelings then congruence takes precedence over anything else' (Hobbs 1989: 21). 'The therapist daring to be real assumes a new potency which can dissolve barriers at a stroke and establish a new level of intimacy' (Thorne 1991: 187).

My experience shows that clients appreciate my acceptance and feel understood when I am empathic yet it is my congruence which is most facilitative in the building and sustaining of a therapeutic relationship. When I am true to myself, inwardly and outwardly consistent and hiding no feelings from myself or my client then an atmosphere of trust develops and movement towards mutuality and a sharing of power within the relationship becomes not only possible but likely. This empowerment of the client is a desirable outcome of therapy. The experience I describe and to which Rogers refers does not seem to be the same as countertransference. My understanding of some of the processes that are included in the concept of countertransference inform my ability to be congruent, to make therapeutic use of my congruence, but I am sure that countertransference is not congruence.

Implications for practice

A shared implication of the two concepts is that the effectiveness of therapists depends upon their acceptance and knowledge of themselves. To be able to recognize countertransference, therapists must be aware of their own issues and have addressed them. Similarly, the person-centred therapist's ability to be congruent resides in self-awareness and self-acceptance. Both approaches require their practitioners to engage in personal exploration, personal growth and (or) therapy. The purpose of such exploration by a person-centred therapist is to reduce conditions of worth (that is, to overcome the need to win approval or to avoid disapproval from others (Mearns and Thorne 1988: 26) and more closely align the organismic (or real) self with the self-perception (and thus become more congruent). The situation with respect to countertransference seems less clear.

Crown (1986: 45) refers to countertransference as something with which the therapist must *cope*. A key to this is that the therapist be aware of the countertransference, neither denying it nor acting on it. However, countertransference may enhance the therapeutic process because it 'suggest[s] possibilities which might not be obvious from the client's verbal and non-verbal communication' (Jacobs 1988: 108). Because countertransference applies to more than one process (or is perhaps a process that manifests in more than one form), there is disagreement about whether it is to be coped with or to be welcomed and used. It is important that the therapist be able to recognize internal processes that are the result of the therapeutic encounter and those which arise from their personal experiences; this is vital to the well-being of the client.

Lietaer (1993: 18) usefully distinguishes between congruence and transparency. Congruence is the inner side of genuineness and is 'the unity of total experience and awareness'. Transparency is the outer side of genuineness which involves the 'explicit communication by the therapist of his conscious perceptions, attitudes and feelings'. Tudor and Worrall (1994: 198) extend this re-examination and identify four elements in congruence:

- self-awareness
- self-awareness in action
- communication
- appropriateness

They argue that congruent communication involves more than transparency and offer the term *apparency* (ibid.: 200), the quality of being actively apparent 'which has a more active, relational, transitive quality'. They also give criteria for *appropriate* communication and write of the importance of communicating personal experiencing rather than disclosing personal experience (ibid.: 201–2).

It is transparency (or apparency) which is most easily confused with countertransference, a confusion exacerbated by the notion of appropriateness. However, transparency is different from countertransference because the former is to do with the awareness of the therapist and a communicating of that awareness to the person in the client role. Countertransference is usually closely connected with unconscious processes and is a product of a relationship. It is the recognition of the importance of the relationship between therapist and client that draws person-centred therapists and those informed by the analytic tradition closest together. The relationship between analyst and analysand is important because

> [w]hat distinguishes this relationship from others, is not the presence of feelings in one partner, the patient, and their absence in the other, the analyst, but above all the degree of the feelings experience and the use made of them. (Heimann 1950: 81–2)

Heimann suggests that analysts who work without consulting their feelings can offer only poor interpretations. Barring differences of terminology, it is easily possible to imagine a person-centred practitioner saying much the same.

Conclusion

Congruence is defined in a different way from countertransference and the implications of each for the practice of therapy are equally different. Countertransference, which Freud mentioned twice 'and then only in passing' (Jacobs 1992: 83), has expanded as psychodynamic practitioners became more interested in the process *between* therapist and client. It now includes the process of empathy (in the sense of the use of the therapist's self to understand the experience of the person in the client's role). Congruence is defined simply as a state of being – it is not something to be used – it is somehow to be, and it is acknowledged to have an active component (which may usefully be viewed as transparency or apparency). In practice, consideration is given to *appropriateness* in the communication to the client of either countertransference or transparency/apparency but this does not imply an equivalence. However it is defined, countertransference always has something to do with the relationship between the therapist and the client and is a product of it (that is, it is a process). Congruence and its more active aspects are products of a therapist's inner state.

As the interest of psychodynamic practitioners in the relationship between the therapist and the client has increased, so has an awareness of a number of different processes within this relationship. The Freudian concept which seemed to address these processes is countertransference, and thus all of them acquired that label. This appears confusing within the approach and leads to confusion in making valid comparisons with other approaches. Just as person-centred thinkers are re-interpreting the notion of congruence and seeing that perhaps it is a complex phenomenon involving more than one process (which therefore acquires separate identities) so it would be helpful if a similar re-examination and re-naming happened in the psychodynamic field. This would make true comparisons more obvious and also make differences clearer.

While the various processes described as countertransference may help me to understand myself in relation to my client, it remains an unnecessarily complex and (occasionally) overemphasized element of the therapeutic relationship. This may sound like the 'anti-theoretical' stand that person-centred practitioners are often accused of, but a theory that is simply stated is not necessarily an inconsequential theory.

My reactions to clients or to material are as much (or probably more) to do with me as with them, but in the therapeutic encounter I also have many thoughts and feelings which stem even more directly from my own experience. While this is potentially useful to me either directly with my client, in supervision or in my own therapy (and I suspect that psychodynamic therapists would agree), what is important is that I am open to my experience, whatever it is. This experience need not be communicated directly to my client although I believe that any denial of it to myself or to others is recognized and is counter-therapeutic.

References

Crown, S. (1986) 'Individual long-term psychotherapy', in S. Bloch (ed.), *An Introduction to the Psychotherapies*, Oxford: Oxford University Press.

Hawkins, P. and Shohet, R. (1989) *Supervision in the Helping Professions*, Milton Keynes: Open University Press.

Heimann, P. (1950) 'On countertransference', *International Journal of Psycho-analysis*, 31: 81–4.

Hobbs, T. (1989) 'The Rogers interview', *Counselling Psychology Review*, 4 (4): 12.

Jacobs, M. (1988) *Psychodynamic Counselling in Action*, London: Sage.

Jacobs, M. (1992) *Sigmund Freud*, London: Sage.

Kirschenbaum, H. and Henderson, V.L. (1990) *The Carl Rogers Reader*, London: Constable.

Laplanche, J. and Pontalis, J.B. (1988) *The Language of Psychoanalysis*, London: Karnac.

Lietaer, G. (1993) 'Authenticity, congruence and transparency', in D. Brazier (ed.), *Beyond Carl Rogers*, London: Constable.

Little, M. (1951) 'Countertransference and the patient's response to it', *International Journal of Psycho-analysis*, 32: 32–40.

Mearns, D. and Thorne, B. (1988) *Person-Centred Counselling in Action* (2nd edn, 1999) London: Sage.

Racker, H. (1957) 'The meanings and uses of counter transference', *Psychoanalytic Quarterly*, 26: 303–57.

Rogers, C.R. (1961) *On Becoming a Person*, London: Constable.

Sandler, J., Dare, C. and Holder, A. (1992) *The Patient and the Analyst*, London: Karnac.

Smith, D.L. (1990) 'Psychodynamic therapy: the Freudian approach', in W. Dryden (ed.), *Individual Therapy: A Handbook*, Milton Keynes: Open University Press.

Spinelli, E. (1989) *The Interpreted World*, London: Sage.

Thorne, B. (1991) *Person-Centred Counselling: Therapeutic and Spiritual Dimensions*, London: Whurr.

Tudor, K. and Worrall, M. (1994) 'Congruence reconsidered', *British Journal of Guidance and Counselling*, 22 (2): 197–205.

Wilkins, P. (1994) 'The person-centred approach to psychodrama', *British Journal of Psychodrama and Sociodrama*, 9 (2): 37, 48.

Discussion issues

1 'Congruence takes precedence over anything else' in the person-centred approach. Why do you think Rogers made this the most significant of his core conditions?
2 In your view how much do the language styles which characterize the person-centred and the psychodynamic approaches, respectively, contribute to the perceived differences in the two?
3 What is a 'state of being' in the person-centred sense?
4 What is your understanding of the similarities between congruence and countertransference?

67

Humour in the Psychotherapeutic Relationship – Not to be Trifled With

Marie Adams

Several years ago I attended a Billy Connoly performance. For two and a half hours I laughed. I laughed until I cried, my sides ached and the next morning my face hurt from so much stretching of unfamiliar muscles. During the performance Connolly actually warned us that the next day we would try to tell people how much we had laughed and try to recount some of the jokes, and we just would not know how to do it. He was right.

When I told a friend I was going to write an article about humour in the psycho-therapeutic relationship he groaned and said, 'Oh no! Whenever people try to talk about humour seriously they're dry as a bone! Terrible subject, humour.'

Humour, however, is very important to me. I like, even need, my therapist to be warm and have a sense of humour. In turn, I often share laughter with my clients. I find humour life-enhancing. I feel good when I have laughed, and I feel closer to people when I have shared a joke.

I am surprised that there is remarkably little written on the subject of humour in the counselling process. This is despite the fact that I cannot think of a single colleague who does not admit to humour as an important aspect of the therapeutic relationship with at least some of their clients. Interestingly, the majority of articles and books have been written from an analytical perspective, the first being Freud, initially in his *Jokes and their Relation to the Unconsciouus* (1905) and later in his paper *Humour* (1927). While humanistic writers, Erving Polster and Miriam Polster for instance in *Gestalt Therapy Integrated* (1974), refer to the quality of a client's laughter to reveal their inner state, specific and extended focus on humour and laughter in the counselling setting is decidedly absent.

The subject of humour has many facets, encompassing laughter, jokes, irony, wit and mockery – not all of them pleasant. For the purposes of this article I am defining humour in its broadest sense as: 'A mental quality which apprehends and delights in the ludicrous and mirthful; that which causes mirth and amusement; the quality of being funny' (Chambers Dictionary 1992).

Tapping the unconscious through humour

Freud (1905) claimed that along with dreams and parapraxis (Freudian slips) jokes are a route to the unconscious. We can say through jokes and laughter perhaps what we

This chapter was first published in *Counselling*, Journal of the British Association for Counselling, vol. 11, no. 3, pp. 159–61 (2000).

cannot bear to say otherwise. Rather than laughter in a clinical setting being considered a defence against feeling, Poland (1994) and Birner (1994) both argue that laughter can offer a momentary haven of safety in which the painful can be absorbed into the client's experience rather than be denied.

> Humour is the emotionally healthy way of dealing with the problems and dilemmas of life, as opposed to unhealthy ways such as drug addiction, depression, neurosis, and psychosis. The ability to use humour easily is a wonderful psychological aid to both staying in reality and upholding the use of the pleasure principle. (Birner 1994: 81)

I suggest that, while much of our training cautions against the use of humour in therapy, there are times when a client can come to terms with his own experience only through the protective shield of humour. At the Billy Connolly performance much of the humour focused on the performer's own childhood experience within a violent household where many of his basic needs for affection, warmth and protection were quite blatantly not met. His performance, and his humour, were based largely on his remarkable capacity to survive. In *The Sickening Mind* (1997: 134), Paul Martin asks the question:

> What is the opposite of a stress response? Humour is a strong contender for the title. When we laugh, our psychological and emotional state is about as far removed as it can be from the bowel-churning anxiety and po-faced solemnity of stress. A humorous attitude can often prevent a stressful situation from arising in the first place. ... Scientists have investigated what goes on inside the body when someone is having a good laugh and, lo and behold, have discovered that the biological changes are virtually the reverse of those that occur during a stress response. When American scientists showed volunteers an amusing video and then measured their blood hormone levels they found that cortisol and adrenaline levels had dropped significantly.

The real relationship

On a hot, summer day my client G came for his regular weekly appointment. G's childhood was blighted by his parents' apparent indifference to his loathing of boarding school and the terrible bullying he suffered for years. He cannot believe that someone might care for him unless he does something for them. How else can he explain his mother giving him away to boarding school when he was only seven, and, even after his desperation led him to run away repeatedly, sending him promptly back to school every time?

So, it was hot and G began the session by saying he would have the air conditioners on at work all the time if he could. I remembered that I had a fan in the cupboard of another room and I said, 'I haven't used it yet this year. Would you like me to get the fan?'

'No', he said, 'That's okay ... anyway', he teased, 'you're a fan aren't you?'

I burst out laughing and said, 'Yes, I most certainly am!'

I feel this was an important moment in the therapy. In a life where he has experienced very little belief that he is cared for, G told me quite categorically, through his humour and quick wit, that he knew that I did. And I was able to affirm my caring for him through my spontaneous response. I do not believe that the same measure of affection would, or could have been, expressed in any other way between us. The moment, to use Rogers' core conditions, was empathic and congruent and certainly I expressed unconditional positive regard for my client (Rogers 1990).

The reparative relationship

I believe this occasion was also a reparative moment, echoing a developmental deficit of G's early years when his humour and wit were not appreciated, when his feelings and affections were negated through banishment to boarding school and a litany of parental 'shoulds' limited his repertoire for emotional expression.

> Moments of humour arise during the analytic journey. When they do, they are as multiply determined as are all other associations: their unconscious and instinctually charged aspects demand analytic attention. However, there are times when the humour appears like unexpected clearings in internal conflicts, moments not mainly defensive but rather exposing new understandings and integrations. (Poland 1994: 8)

Both Poland (1994) and Barry (1994) argue that everyone has a sense of humour, though it is often repressed. Poland says further that part of the work of therapy is to draw humour into the open – a sense of humour is a sign of health. A child growing up in a household devoid of humour may grow into an adult apparently unable to access their sense of humour.

S grew up in a family constantly on guard against her father's temper. Over the two years we have worked together she has set up a running gag which she plays out in almost every session. There is a picture in my hallway. It is a large picture depicting a North American farm scene in winter and is entitled 'Peace in the Valley'. As S leaves her sessions she tells me to stay back in the counselling room so she can 'steal' the picture. Sometimes she lifts the frame slightly to see if it might be nailed to the wall. She jokingly asks when I'll be out so she can come back to pinch it. When she returns for sessions after one of my breaks the first thing she checks is the picture, to make sure that it, like me, has not vanished.

In a moment when my own unconscious processes surfaced during our work together S telephoned to tell me she would not be attending her session that week as she 'wanted to prove' she could do without me. This was not the first time I had engaged with her on the subject, and, after several minutes of speaking patiently and gently and suggesting we discuss this face to face, I finally snapped and said, 'Actually, S, what I really want to tell you is to get your ass in here on Saturday morning.'

Not surprisingly there was a rather stunned silence from S before she burst out laughing and said, 'What did you say?'

Still reeling from my own sense of disbelief at what I had just said to a client, I choked out that I was not really willing to repeat myself.

'Okay, I'll come', she said very cheerfully indeed, and turned up promptly for her appointment on Saturday morning. When I suggested that perhaps I owed her an apology she laughed again and said, 'It made you human.'

'I guess I'm just not very good at 'gently gently' a lot of the time.'

'No', she said, 'You're not', and she grinned.

In reflecting on this incident (and because of its extreme features I certainly have reflected) I am increasingly convinced that in my congruent response she was actually able to trust me further, to feel we had shared a moment where my exasperation had actually invited her into the relationship rather than excluded her, as her parental experience so often had done.

Danger of humour in the psychotherapeutic process

I have put forward the view that humour can be a means of accepting the painful, a way of absorbing and acknowledging what otherwise might be too terrible to bear. I have also shown that humour and a shared joke can be an important part of the process of developing trust, and thereby healing. I would like to stress that laughter can also be used to distance ourselves from an experience, to diminish its significance or be used as a displacement tool to distract ourselves from uncomfortable feelings.

Kubie (1994: 102) believes that humour is almost never appropriate in a therapeutic setting. While I certainly find that a bit extreme, I appreciate his caution. I do agree when he says:

> It is never justifiable to make fun of patients or their symptoms, no matter how strange or grotesque these may seem.... This serves only to increase the patient's pain, resentment, and defences.

Pierce (1994: 106) says further:

> Demeaning humor is used frequently by a few therapists and probably some time or another by all of us, but it is without doubt harmful and to be avodied whenever possible.

Reinforcing original psychological damage through the misuse of humour

I will return here to my earlier point: to laugh with the client, but never at the client. I am particularly interested in that dangerous thin line from familiarity into cruelty which I may not even be aware I am crossing.

My client B has been with me for two years. Her family history is violent, with many episodes of sexual, verbal and emotional abuse. During our first months together I cannot remember any laughter during our sessions. But as our work progressed she showed herself to have a delicious sense of mischief, an ability to be spontaneous and enjoy herself, though she often punished herself afterwards, feeling foolish for having exposed herself and believing herself open for ridicule. B was looking through my bookcase towards the end of a session and I suggested she could borrow the book she was holding once she returned the 'pile' she already had at home. I realized immediately that my use of the word 'pile' had stung her. In fact she had two books at home but she had borrowed many more and always returned them as soon as she was finished.

Because the session was drawing to a close I had to wait another week before working this through. In the first instance I needed to apologize. My joke had been unnecessary and thoughtless and had quite obviously tapped into her family history of teasing, 'always looking for the weak spot', she had told me.

The next week we spoke of what had happened. My hunch had been right: I had overstepped the mark. My remark had hurt her, just as her brothers' and sisters' remarks had always been designed to cut through to where she was most vulnerable. She experienced me as wielding the same cruel humour as her family – and I had done just that, mistaking her rich sense of humour as an invitation to make a thoughtless and not very funny remark. Since then we have spoken of her sense of humour further and recently she said, 'My humour has always been based on making fun of someone, of laughing at someone else's expense. I don't know how I can have a sense of humour if I don't do that any more and it frightens me.'

Before I engage in humour with my client I need to ask myself a number of questions: when does humour mask mockery or sarcasm to demean my client? When does my own need to be 'clever' or to be noticed by my client interfere with therapy – after all, my job can be lonely (Pierce 1994: 106). When am I masking my anger under a disingenuous cloak of humour? And when is my humour/laughter actually collusion rather than holding of the therapeutic boundary?

Conclusion

I began this article with the intention of defending the use of humour in therapeutic work. In conclusion I have not swerved from this path, but I am also conscious of the dangers of misusing humour. My over-riding belief is in the power of humour and laughter to heal, to make the unbearable bearable. I also believe that, like every other force for good in the world, it can be used to wield great damage in the guise of laughter. A sharp remark intended to be funny can punch a hole through the tender membrane of a fragile ego. While we are in the business of assisting our clients in their journey of self-discovery, we also have an obligation to monitor our own processes to ensure we are not using humour for our own aggrandizement in the therapy room. Humour is to be appreciated, but never to be trifled with.

> Mature humour offers an opportunity for sustenance and consolation throughout life. Insightful humour not only has its 'given' aspects but is itself a gift, a gift the ego gives to itself. It offers self comfort without denial. Indeed, its mark is precisely its capacity to soothe while at the same time respecting the power of inner conflicts and outer hurts. The facilitating of the development of the patient's capacity for mature humour is one of the happiest and proudest effects of clinical analysis. (Poland 1994: 23).

References

Barry, R.R. (1994) 'Recognizing unconscious humor in psychoanalysis', in H. Strean (ed.), *The Use of Humour in Psychotherapy*, Northvale, NJ: Jason Aronson.

Birner, L. (1994) 'Humor and the joke of psychoanalysis', in H. Strean (ed.), *The Use of Humor in Psychotherapy*, Northvale, NJ: Jason Aronson.

Chambers (1992) *Chambers Maxi Paperback Dictionary*, Edinburgh: W. & R. Chambers.

Freud, S. (1905) *Jokes and their Relation to the Unconscious*, London: Penguin Books.

Freud, S. (1927) *Humour*, Standard Edition 21, London: Hogarth Press.

Kubie, L.S. (1994) 'The destructive potential of humor in psychotherapy', in H. Strean (ed.), *The Use of Humor in Psychotherapy*, Northvale, NJ: Jason Aronson.

Martin, P. (1997) *The Sickening Mind*, London: HarperCollins.

Nathanson, D.L. (1992) *Shame and Pride: Affect, Sex and the Birth of the Self*, New York: W.W. Norton.

Pierce, R.A. (1994) 'Use and abuse of laughter in psychotherapy', in H. Strean (ed.), *The Use of Humor in Psychotherapy*, Northvale, NJ: Jason Aronson.

Poland, W.S. (1994) 'The gift of laughter: on the development of a sense of humor in clinical analysis', in H. Strean (ed.), *The Use of Humor in Psychotherapy*, Northvale, NJ: Jason Aronson.

Polster, E. and Polster, M. (1974) *Gestalt Therapy Integrated*, New York: Vintage Books.

Rogers, C. (1990) *The Carl Rogers Reader*, London: Constable.

Discussion issues

1 What forms of humour were used in your family of origin, and how did these affect you?
2 Are there occasions when you use humour to distance yourself from your own feelings, or to make the unbearable bearable?
3 What do you perceive as both the positive and negative effects of humour in the counselling relationship?
4 When might humour be considered collusion in the counselling relationship?

Introduction to Counselling Dilemmas and Practice Dilemmas

Both these sections of the BAC journal have illustrated ways of approaching a variety of problematic counselling situations.

Counselling dilemmas

The vignettes in this section describe common dilemmas faced by both clients and counsellors. Following each one are the views of various counsellors and therapists of different orientations. We hope that there will be some value in seeing how people approach some of the dilemmas that we all face. There are usually no 'right' answers and we look for a response which may be technical, theoretical or ethical in orientation.

Lesley Murdin, editor, 'Counselling dilemmas', August 1996–May 1997.

Practice dilemmas

In May 1998 the dilemmas column reappeared under the title 'Practice dilemmas', which reflected a wider focus encompassing counselling, counselling training and supervision issues. Dilemmas are suggested directly by BAC members, arise from discussion with colleagues, or provide further exploration of issues raised in previous journal articles or in the letters page.

Contributors responding to both counselling and practice dilemmas include the current chairs of two (then) key BAC committees – Complaints, and Standards and Ethics – (or members of those committees), together with others offering a balance of expertise from differing theoretical approaches and practice, and a variety of settings. The result demonstrates ethical practice as codified by BAC, and a number of ways to consider commonly encountered situations.

Caroline Jones, editor 'Practice dilemmas', May 1998–December 1999. Currently a regular editor, of Counselling challenge', in the relaunched journal, Counselling, *from February 2000.*

Composite list of contributors

May Brun	*Derek Hill*	*Fiona Palmer Barnes*	*Janet Tolan*
Cathy Carroll	*Michael Jacobs*	*Carole Pocknell*	*Janet Watson*
Roger Casemore	*Caroline Jones*	*Val Potter*	*Gill Westland*
Dawn Collins	*Susie Lendrum*	*Fiona Purdie*	*Diana Whitmore*
Stephen Crawford	*Gladeana McMahon*	*Hillary Ratna*	
Anne Garland	*Simon Needs*	*Joy Schaverien*	
Gaye Giles	*Bill O'Connell*	*Gabrielle Syme*	

68

Clients Ending Counselling

I have been having counselling for eight weeks. I wanted to get some help with my relationship.
We have terrible fights because I get angry when he's never home and I wanted to stop that.
I don't think the counselling has been any good. I got a few ideas from the counsellor about how
I could talk to my partner a bit better – tell him what I want from him, but he's still really awful.
So I told the counsellor last week that I wanted to stop the counselling and she said that I should
go on because I feel bad about her and somehow this is supposed to help but she wouldn't say
how. Now, I don't know what to do. My friend says counsellors are well known to exploit people
and never let you stop.

Does this counsellor have an ethical dilemma or a purely technical one?

As this case is presented it would appear to be one of confusion and therefore a technical dilemma, but it could easily become an ethical one and even the basis of a complaint. This could happen if the cause of the confusion was due to not recognizing the client's autonomy and therefore right to end when s/he wished, and/or the lack of accurate pre-contract information, and/or an unclear or inadequate contract. In making the contract the counsellor should have made it clear what psychodynamic counselling involved, the number of sessions being offered, the method of handling endings and the effects of breaching the therapeutic frame by talking to other people about counselling sessions.

If the client could express her/his concerns in the next session then the counsellor would realize that the client did not understand the nature of psychodynamic work, nor the possible links between her/his relationship with the counsellor and the dynamics of the relationship which she/he had come in to counselling to explore.

Other themes which the counsellor would need to address would be the client's fear of exploitation and her/his need to seek other people's opinions. The technical problem would then become the management of these concerns and whether a therapeutic alliance could be established. Possibly psychodynamic counselling was inappropriate for this client.

Fiona Palmer Barnes
Analytical psychologist
Chair, BAC Complaints Committee

Gabrielle Syme
Analytical psychotherapist
Chair, BAC Standards and Ethics Commitee

* * *

The client is clear that she sought counselling in order to get help with her relationship with her partner, but does not say if there was any discussion at the beginning of her sessions

This chapter was first published in *Counselling*, Journal of the British Association for Counselling, vol. 7, no. 3, pp. 204–5 (1996).

about how long she might need to attend. Now, after eight weeks, of once-weekly sessions presumably, the client wants to stop, feeling that the counselling has not been any good.

Endings often evoke strong feelings for both participants in the counselling relationship. The client in this case does now seem angry, or at least dissatisfied, with her counsellor; perhaps the counsellor feels unfairly judged, that the work has not been given enough of a chance and, if so, she is likely to feel rejected.

There are both ethical and technical aspects to the position the counsellor is now in. The ethical aspect is to do with the client's right to be able to decide when s/he wants to end the sessions. However, it is important that the counsellor tries to explore the client's reasons for wanting to stop, and in some cases, where, for example, the counsellor feels that the proposed ending is being put forward by a self-destructive aspect of the client's personality, I think it is appropriate for the counsellor to try and show the client how the ending could be self-destructive. In other words, it could be seen as poor practice for a counsellor to comply with a client's plan to end without exploring, or at least trying to explore, the plan, and its motivations, in depth. The ideal case is one where the outcome of such an exploration is that both client and counsellor come to an agreement, either for the work to continue or for it to stop, and, if it is the latter, that there might also be an agreed plan about when to end, for example after an agreed number of further sessions.

The ethical position, that the client has the right to decide when to end, does need to inform the counsellor's technique. An important technical problem for the counsellor is how to explore the client's wanting to end, without this exploration being interfered with by whatever has been evoked inside herself by the client's wanting to end. For example, if the counsellor feels hurt or rejected, and is not able to process these feelings sufficiently, there is the danger that she may retaliate against the client. The counsellor therefore needs to try to be aware of the feelings that have been evoked inside herself, and try to contain these feelings, partly through thinking about what is happening in the relationship with the client, in the context of what she knows about the client, to see if she can arrive at some understanding of why the client is thinking of ending now.

It seems that in this particular case, the counsellor has tried to make a link between what is happening in her relationship with the client and the client's wanting to end, but that the client does not understand why this link may be significant and, as a result, is left wondering if the counsellor is simply trying to hold on to her. It looks as if the counsellor might be thinking that what is happening in the counselling relationship could throw some light on the dynamics of the client's relationship with her partner and, if so, it could seem that she needs to try to find a way of saying this to the client, drawing attention to what she sees as the similarities of the client's experience in the two situations and presenting the counselling as a forum in which the client's experience could be explored and understood.

The technical problem is then to do with how much to say, how to say it, and when to stop and accept the client's decision to end, if indeed it seems that the client is remaining firm in the position of wanting to stop. All of these can be difficult to judge, and the risk for the counsellor is of getting caught up in a power struggle with the client if the exploration is pushed too far or too hard.

Stephen Crawford
Psychoanalytical psychotherapist and psychodynamic counsellor

*   *   *

There is both an ethical question and a technical question here. Or, to put it another way, there are reality issues in what the client says – that is, there are counsellors and therapists who appear to exploit the needs of the client by prolonging therapy, whether for financial gain or for the difficulty of admitting that their therapy may not be the treatment of choice. One certainly hears examples of clients who have expressed the wish to terminate, even on the grounds of what they have already achieved in therapy, and to whom it is suggested (or is heard as being suggested) that they are 'acting out' by leaving, and not facing issues that remain to be worked with.

I cannot rule out that this may be the case: that this client is feeling that she (I assume this is a heterosexual partnership) is being pressurized into staying. But I suspect that this counsellor has difficulty explaining what counselling can and cannot offer, and that this client has, at the very least, not understood that counselling may involve a period of time exploring issues before any clarity can begin to be achieved. Furthermore, if we were to explore the links between the relationship at home and the relationship with the counsellor, it is possible that there are parallels, and that transference is involved in this situation: that is, the counsellor appears to be unresponsive because she cannot tell the client what to do, just as the partner is also actually or perceived to be unresponsive; that this client wishes she could talk to the counsellor more fully, as she wishes she could talk with her partner more fully, but finds that difficult to do.

Of course it may be that in the course of expressing her discontent with the counselling, this client is also on the way to learning that it is okay to voice discontent, and to get angry with others when there appears to be no response from them. Perhaps that is what this counsellor is clumsily saying when she indicates that the client may feel bad about her. And leaving the counsellor for such reasons might be seen as acting out; but it could also be seen as an act of assertive following through of discontent, something that she may also feel it is appropriate to consider in relation to a frustrating relationship at home.

Michael Jacobs
Psychodynamic psychotherapist

* * *

The main problem is technical but I consider that there is an underlying ethical dilemma. There is a potential for abuse of the power imbalance of the therapeutic relationship. This client (the gender is not specified but I shall assume it to be a woman) indicates that she started counselling because she wanted help with her relationship. She gets angry with her partner because he is 'really awful' and is never home. She seems to present the main problem as her partner. The counsellor has only the client's inner world view, as she has not met the partner. It seems that the counsellor is recognizing, in a negative transference, that she, like the partner, may be experienced as 'never home', and this makes the client angry. Thus she seems to be using the transference to understand how it might be between the couple and so suggests the client should continue the counselling just because she 'feels bad about her'. The client appears to be confused and fears being trapped and exploited. This anxiety, which is quite appropriate for this stage in the work, may be increased if the counsellor is using her understanding of the transference without explaining it. In order to interpret the transference a therapeutic alliance needs to be established. The adult part of the client needs to be engaged and respected in order to observe, and so understand, the symbolic nature of the transference. It is part of the educative function of therapy in certain cases for the counsellor to explain this in quite simple terms. Without some explanation of the technique there is a potential for abuse of the power imbalance of the situation. A respectful acknowledgement of the anxiety and an explanation of procedures which confuse or mystify is appropriate. This is primarily a technical problem but I think it has ethical implications.

Joy Schaverien
Analytical psychologist (SAP)
Associate Professor of Art Psychotherapy (University of Sheffield)

Discussion issues

1 How do the comments affect your thinking about counselling contracts?
2 What is your view on this counsellor's dilemma?
3 Which of the comments do you most agree with?
4 Which views challenge your current thinking and practice?

69

To Hug a Client – or Not?

Client: *What would really make me feel better would be a hug. No one will just love me for myself and let me feel they want to be near me. Nobody seems to understand what I really feel. John is always too busy and rushing off to do something important. He makes me feel as though I'm not important enough just for him to put his arms around me. I'm sick and tired of it.*

Counsellor: *Maybe if you let people know what you want, if you put it into words, you would find that they would give you what you are asking for.*

Client: *So if I let you know, will you hug me?*

What comment would you make on the dilemma facing the counsellor?

The vignette raises a number of technical and ethical issues.

Let us look at what seems to be happening. The client is quite obviously distressed and feels uncared for, unwanted and even unnoticed at times. The counsellor encourages the client to make these needs known, to be noticed, and from the language the counsellor uses we must assume that the counsellor believes that a positive response would be forthcoming. The client remains in a powerless position and asks if a hug can be asked for from the counsellor, attempting to draw the therapist in to respond to the client's perceived need.

This situation needs to be reflected back, worked with and interpreted; because it portrays the background that will have brought the client to counselling and demonstrates the client's needs for care and comfort. For the counsellor to act out with the client would not be helpful at all.

To look at the matter from the point of view of a potential complaint, it is situations like this that can lead to a complaint about inappropriate behaviour on the part of the counsellor. The client may perceive the hug from the counsellor in any way that fulfils their conscious or unconscious need. It might be perceived as merely comforting, as the vignette suggests. However, it could be perceived as a real expression of love, feeding confusion and ambivalence in the transference. The client is obviously very needy, and should the counsellor refuse repeated requests for hugs a sense of rejection, negative reaction and fury may follow. As with all requests for the counsellor to break normal boundaries, counsellors need to think very carefully what is happening if they consider doing so or actually find themselves doing so. These are the clients with whom the work needs close supervision and where the work needs to be supervised more often. Issues may also be raised for the counsellor that belong in their own therapy, particularly if they feel themselves drawn into colluding with the client's request.

Fiona Palmer Barnes
Analytical psychologist
Chair, BAC Complaints Committee

* * *

This chapter was first published in *Counselling*, Journal of the British Association for Counselling, vol. 8, no. 1, pp. 15–17 (1997).

Within a humanistic, process-oriented body psychotherapy, touch may be an integral part of the psychotherapy. Touch is discussed at the contractual stage, and subsequently, if it might be used during the therapeutic process. So, the use of appropriate touch is not unethical in itself, and the vignette does not pose a particular dilemma with regard to the client's question about hugging.

However, the counsellor has not explored the client's opening statements, and has attempted to solve the client's problem as s/he sees it. It is not clear what the client is expressing; more information is needed to determine whether a hug would be suitable or not as a therapeutic intervention. Although information about the client's history and the current stage of the process, including the transferential relationship, would suggest a partial answer. Further information would come from attending to the unconscious bodily movements of the client to 'see' what the deeper emerging dynamic might be. Additionally, the psychotherapist could ask questions to deepen the experienced meaning of the statements, and to connect the client with an organic, bodily sense of him/herself. Out of this, to hug or not may become irrelevant.

If a hug became a possible intervention it should be made slowly and with due regard to the client's reaction to it. A hug is a strong intervention and should not come at the end of a session, when there is insufficient time for exploration and resolution. This sort of intervention requires skill and training. A counsellor using touch is advised to have training in the use of touch and a highly developed body awareness. These are best discovered from experiencing body psychotherapy. Touch is not advisable with clients who have difficulty experiencing reality, those who have been sexually abused, those who give indications that touch would be eroticized (unless there is therapeutic space to unravel the process), and those with a fragile therapeutic alliance with the psychotherapist.

Gill Westland
UKCP Registered Body and Humanistic Psychotherapist

* * *

Views on the counsellor physically touching or hugging the client are as many and as varied as are forms of counselling – from political correctness (which I find tedious), through body-orientated counsellors who believe that touch is essential, to the 'no not ever' (it would be a violation of professional boundaries) camp. Personally I do not feel there is one 'right' answer to this counselling dilemma, but several possible responses the counsellor could make based upon his or her assessment of the client.

Unless you are of the 'no not ever' school, this dilemma cannot appropriately be answered without knowing this particular client. The intervention which the counsellor *could* make will depend on two factors.

The first can be called the counsellor's countertransference response to the client asking this question, 'Will you hug me?' The counsellor would be wise to pay close attention to the emotional response evoked by the question. Is the countertransference illusory, in the sense of evoking historical responses to demands for affection from significant people in his or her past? *Or* would a positive response be fulfilling some unconscious and unrecognized need of the counsellor? Alternatively, is the countertransference complementary in the sense of the client's transference ('I want you to be the mother I never had') and for the counsellor to fulfil this need would amount to a repetition of the transference? If the answer to any or all of the above is *yes*, giving the client a hug could be inadvisable.

Although not unrelated to the first, the second factor for the counsellor to consider is the whole area of 'boundaries' with this particular client. Are the boundaries between counsellor and client clear and established? Are they secure or are they frequently threatened? What is the overall subjective reality here? If boundaries are not or have not been an issue in the therapeutic relationship, giving the client a hug poses no threat to them. However, if this particular client is always challenging the boundaries, caution is called for.

Having said the above, alternative interventions could be:

1   Give the hug. This may be what, strangely, is sometimes called concordant counter-transference – when the counsellor responds in an empathic way which the client really needs. (Whatever happened to good old authentic human relating? Why must we label an authentic human response?) I dare to believe that with some clients a sincere hug can go a long way towards their experience of lovableness and their basic humanity.

2   Explore further before making a decision: What do you feel when you ask me this? Have you done so before in your life? What has been the outcome? Have you asked John for a hug before? How would it serve or support you if I did give you a hug? What need would be fulfilled if we hugged? What would you feel if I did not give you a hug? When was the last time you did receive a hug? From whom?

I am slightly suspicious of the client's 'no one' and 'nobody' statement. I imagine a person who is victimizing themselves and is reluctant to take responsibility for the part they play in this experience.

3   Refuse the hug. If the counsellor feels either unable to give the client a hug or that it is inappropriate to, a boundary needs to be asserted and the client deserves a sincere response and explanation. It would be important to respond and attend to any negative feelings this rejection might evoke from the client.

Diana Whitmore
Chairperson, Psychosynthesis and Education Trust

*   *   *

Counsellors need to have already considered their own views about the appropriateness of giving hugs to clients, taking into account their theoretical approach(es), the client group, the setting, issues brought to counselling, their own personality, the effect of the differences between themselves and the client in terms of age, gender, race, culture, etc., the counselling contract, including boundaries that have already been made explicit, and any other significant matters.

This will help the counsellor to respond with integrity and respect to the client's question in the context of all the circumstances of that particular counselling relationship.

The vignette perhaps illustrates that the counsellor has not yet fully heard the client. The client may be tentatively voicing concern of not feeling important within the counselling relationship.

Further exploration of how the client experiences him/herself, inside and outside the counselling room, would be my way forward, with, in addition, more effort to convey to the client genuine acceptance, understanding and empathy through counselling.

Caroline Jones
Acting Chair, BAC Standards and Ethics Committee

*   *   *

This is a self-created dilemma – one that arose because the counsellor did not heed the basic training offered about not giving advice! (It hardly rates as a dilemma – more like a pitfall waiting for the unwary/unaware.)

Having fallen in, the counsellor has to climb out and make it possible for the client to go on. Therefore, the counsellor can hardly admit to having made a mistake, because that would create anxiety about their reliability/skills which would not further the client's ability to work successfully. There is the possibility of giving the hug because the counsellor does not know how to get out of it. We will not consider that one because we are going to assume that this counsellor wants to work usefully and ethically.

The refusal will hurt. Will it damage irreparably? Counsellors can only do their best in the light of their personal model. That is where ethics come in. There has to be an ethical reason for refusing (or not!) which is based on the counsellor's understanding of doing the best for the client as part of a contracted relationship. The counsellor's understanding of the dilemma has to be based on what is useful for the client as part of an overall understanding and theory of therapeutic method, and not how to satisfy the immediate circumstance of the consequences of inattention.

Assuming the answer is 'no', the counsellor needs to say it in such a way that it does not hook the client into unfruitful projections. S/he has to be prepared to be 'bad' and use this insightfully, rather than dealing out a back-hander and expecting the client to cope with the mistake alone.

If the client does not run out of the room in a turmoil of feeling, they will probably be in a turmoil anyway. The counsellor may want to use any possibility of the client understanding what is going on by looking at that rather than focusing entirely on getting out of their own difficulties.

May Brun
Counsellor, trainer

Discussion issues

1 How do the comments affect your thinking about the place of touch in therapy?
2 If a client posed this question, how might you respond?
3 Which comments are you most in agreement with?
4 Which contributors challenge your current thinking and practice?

70

Suicide Threat

The client is a young man aged 25. He came to counselling with problems over relationships with women in which he would always lose interest as soon as the woman became interested in him. His mother died of heart disease when he was 3 and he had been brought up by a series of aunts. After a few sessions, he began to arrive smelling of alcohol, and, when the counsellor challenged him, acknowledged that he had been drinking. He has no apparent desire to work with the counsellor and says that he does not know why he comes. Counselling is not helping. In the sixth session of a twelve-session contract, he says that he is thinking of ending it all. He has a large supply of drugs of all sorts and is thinking about what would be most easy.

The counsellor is anxious that the client should be referred to his GP and to specialized help for drug and alcohol problems. After speaking to her supervisor, she raises the need for the client to see his GP, but the client says that there is no way that he will have anything to do with doctors. They did no good to his mother.

The counsellor is very anxious that she is not helping him, and is very worried that he will try to kill himself. Should she go on seeing him, and what help can she hope to be?

The counsellor needs to consider what has happened so far in the counselling relationship. The client came originally with problems over relationships with women, where he finds he loses interest as soon as the woman shows interest in him. He is now in a counselling realtionship with a female counsellor whose interest and concern has to be affecting him.

The counsellor is feeling anxious about whether she is helping this client and needs to consider whether these are typical feelings of hers or how much these feelings are picked up by her from him. There is a need to reconsider the effect of any referral on, in the light of the client's history of being passed on in childhood through a series of aunts.

There are many areas of exploration possible in this counselling relationship, such as bereavement, loss and attachment, as well as feelings of despair to contain. Most importantly, the counsellor needs to be sure of the quality of her counselling supervision, so that her anxieties and the client's fears can be contained appropriately if these continue. Any decision to continue or to end should, ideally, be a joint one between the counsellor and the client. Factors to consider include:

- the question of whether the client wants to continue and, if so, what he hopes to achieve in the remaining sessions. Is the counsellor competent enough to work to that contract?;
- that the client understands that arriving not smelling of alcohol or under the influence of non-prescribed drugs is necessary for effective counselling and that sessions cannot go ahead otherwise (this is also a sensible precaution for counsellor safety);
- that the counsellor explains to the client what her normal approach is when a client discloses suicidal thoughts and feelings.

Caroline Jones
Chair, BAC Standards and Ethics Committee

* * *

This chapter was first published in *Counselling*, Journal of the British Association for Counselling, vol. 8, no. 2, pp. 98–9 (1997).

The first question I would want to ask the counsellor is how the original therapeutic contract was made. If the counsellor is working in private practice, what kind of psychiatric support does she have? Does she consult a psychiatrist from time to time? Or does she ask clients for their doctor's name at the beginning of the work, at the time that the contract is made? The counsellor also needs to say to the client that, if she has a grave concern for his safety or for others, she should speak to his doctor; this would be discussed in a session with the client before any action is taken, if at all possible.

We know from the case history of the client that he had lost his mother when he was 3 and had had a series of carers who passed him on. This might suggest that he may have difficulties about holding on to hope or that anyone could look after him or contain him. The fact that he seemingly loses interest in the therapeutic work would strengthen the view that issues around whether he is likeable enough to be cared for would be important to him.

Boundaries and contract-setting are particularly important in the case of a client who may act out as well as be compulsive. The drinking before the sessions and the threat of taking drugs certainly feels to me like a desperate plea to be held and contained. If the client does not feel contained by the contract or in the work with the counsellor, he is far more likely to threaten to act out or to act out in fact. It is up to the counsellor and supervisor between them to contain this situation and if, and only if, the counsellor and supervisor feel that he really could act out and take his life should they consider breaching confidentiality. By breaching confidentiality they would probably also destroy the possibility of continuing any counselling work.

Fiona Palmer Barnes
Analytical psychologist
Chair, BAC Complaints Committee

*   *   *

The counsellor has taken on a young man who has told her that he has problems with women: we do not know if she has taken up the question of the fact that she is also a woman and that he may act out his patterns with her. In fact, he has given her a valuable clue when he tells her that when women show an interest in him, he withdraws. He has acted this out, once their relationship has been established, by telling her that counselling is doing him no good (although he still comes). If she did not pick this up, then we hope her supervisor would have done.

There is also the issue, in time-limited counselling, of the ending looming right from the start. This client is also talking of ending (leaving counselling, killing himself) before the counsellor can leave him, bringing up his feelings of abandonment at his mother's death. This is probably why he has established a pattern of being the one to end relationships with women.

Where the drinking is concerned, it should become part of their contract that he will not drink when coming to counselling and that if he turns up drunk, she will not see him. This sort of behaviour is a testing of boundaries and it is important for the counsellor to hold them. The suicide threats may or may not be genuine, but the counsellor is entitled to tell her client that confidentiality ends where she feels concerned that he might harm himself or another person. If she is really worried, she should inform the GP herself, telling the client that she feels this to be necessary.

Ultimately, no counsellor can stop a client who seriously wants to die, but if he wants to live, she may be able to help him work out how to do that well. She should confront the client about what is going on between them and ask him to make a choice about proceeding.

Hillary Ratna
Counsellor, supervisor and trainer with a special interest in working with deaf people

* * *

A cognitive-behavioural psychotherapist would implement a systematic and proactive intervention across three stages:

(a) assessing suicidal risk
(b) managing suicidal behaviour
(c) dealing with suicidal thoughts

(a) *Assessing suicidal risk*
Initially, this would take the form of a mental state examination focused on ascertaining:

- the frequency of suicidal thoughts (e.g. hourly, daily, weekly, persistent);
- intensity of these thoughts, that is the strength of the urge to act on the thoughts as rated on a 0–8 scale;
- duration of the thoughts, that is how long they last (e.g. one minute, several hours, persistent);
- triggers to the suicidal thoughts.

What the therapist is seeking to define is a measure of variablity across these factors.

This would be informed by current research data that suggest the client, a young man living alone and using alcohol to regulate affect, is in a high-risk group.

Assessment would also utilize the Beck Depression Inventory, as a measure of his current level of depression, and the Hopelessness Scale. Again, research demonstrates that low depression scores on the BDI combined with high hopelessness scores on the Hopelessness Scale, increases suicidal risk. A high level of hopelessness (not depression) is a predictor of suicidality. The therapist would also aim to ascertain any suicide plans the client may have, what medication specifically he has at home and whether there are any factors which currently act as deterrents to suicide.

(b) *Managing suicidal behaviour*
Most (95 per cent) CBT psychotherapists currently work in the NHS. All are bound by a professional and legal obligation to inform what is termed the Responsible Medical Officer under certain circumstances, of which suicidality in the client would be one. Thus, ultimately, the therapist would inform the GP as a matter of course as well as a psychiatrist or CPN (if involved in overall care) in order that all professionals responsible for the client's care and treatment can respond to any crisis that may arise. In addition, most therapists would be aware that admission to hospital is sometimes the most appropriate way of managing suicidality and would be aware of their responsibilities under the Mental Health Act (1985).

A crucial aspect for the therapist would be access to their supervisor after each contact with the client. This will involve ongoing assessment of the client's ability to deal with suicidal thoughts as well as helping the therapist to deal with their own thoughts and feelings about the client's current problems and behaviour.

(c) *Dealing with suicidal thoughts*

In CBT there is a theoretical assumption that the cognitive construct underpinning suicidality is hopelessness regarding the future. In someone who is actively suicidal it is considered a short-lived phenomenon and specific strategies implemented by a well-trained and skilled therapist with access to frequent skilled supervision can have a powerful impact on suicidal thinking and behaviour.

Therefore, sessions would be increased to three times weekly for a discrete time period (one–two weeks) or alternatively twice weekly with 'phone contact between sessions. There is a specific aim of helping the client limit their future-orientated thinking toward the next hour only. A variety of strategies can then be implemented:

- plan activities throughout the day;
- plan activities with others at high-risk times;
- challenge hopeless/suicidal thoughts;
- develop a written hierarchical crisis plan for use at high-risk times;
- problem-solve difficulties.

Anne Garland
Behavioural Cognitive Therapist working in the NHS

Discussion issues

1 How do the comments affect your attitudes to the working relationships between counsellors and medical practitioners?
2 How might you proceed in such a situation?
3 Which comments do you most agree with?
4 Which comments most challenge your current thinking and practice?

Practice Dilemmas

71

Clients Becoming Counsellors

You are in a long-term counselling relationship with a client who has presented a range of difficulties including childhood abuse, trust issues and alcohol abuse. The client started counselling after a serious alcohol-related conviction which also resulted in the loss of employment. The client has recently talked about plans to apply for a counselling course. At the most recent session, the client arrived very angry because an application to a local college has been turned down on the grounds of non-suitability. At the end of the session the client asks you to write a letter of support for an appeal against non-selection. There is insufficient time for any discussion and you have until the next session to consider the request.

Assuming that an initial assessment had engaged the client in exploratory work and that the alcoholic symptoms had been understood and were no longer relevant to the counselling work, I would want to be thinking about three main ideas before continuing the work with this client.

In the first instance, the client's reasons for telling me about wanting to join a counselling course might indicate a wish to identify with me and to get something which I also have (training in counselling). This could be the beginning of a wish to share something. However, the non-selection (depriving the client of something that could have been shared) might have turned the potentially growthful envy, and the wish to share or be included, into something more destructive, leaving the client angry and upset. I would want to explore these feelings and hope to make some sense of them in the present.

As I am a psychodynamic counsellor and therefore interested in how the past influences the present and in how patterns from the past get re-enacted, I would then want to wonder about situations the client might be remembering from the past, or might myself be reminded of situations I had been told about, when the client had experienced exclusion or rejection and perhaps had to hide feelings of pain, envy or intense anger. These feelings re-evoked by the current situation might then be open to exploration.

Depending somewhat on the client's awareness of such feelings and also on the relative 'reasonableness' of the client's chances of success on application to a counselling course, the third strand I might want to explore would be that of 'repetition': the possibility that the client was setting up yet another experience of rejection, both in relation to the application and in the request for a letter of support. A counsellor would not normally give a letter of support or a reference (BAC 1997: B.1.3.5) as they in principle break confidentiality and affect the power balance of the relationship, turning it more towards judgement and away from reflection, thus creating a kind of 'dual relationship'.

This chapter was first published in *Counselling*, Journal of the British Association for Counselling, vol. 9, no. 3, pp. 191–2 (1998).

I think that clients usually 'know' this at some level, and I imagine that an 'expectation of rejection' would not be too far from the surface.

However, if the client is able to understand the reason for being drawn towards situations of exclusion or rejection, it may then be possible to work through the associated feelings of hurt and anger, and get the repetition to work out differently this time. Instead of being excluded, the client could be included back into the counselling relationship where the question of the appeal about non-selection to the counselling course could be more rationally explored. That at least would be my hope!

Susie Lendrum
Co-Chair, BAC Standards and Ethics Committee

* * *

I would not see this as a particular dilemma for me as a person-centred therapist. I am very clear that it is not my role to act on behalf of my clients even when they wish me to do so. It is important that clients take responsibility for taking their own actions and dealing with their own feelings. I would not see it as appropriate for me to write in support of their appeal against non-selection. I would see this as taking me beyond the boundaries of the role of therapist in my relationship with this client, and I would state this gently but clearly and firmly to the client.

My role in this situation would be to enable the client to explore the feelings about not being selected and to work towards resolving or coming to terms with those feelings and the situation which has given rise to them. Second, I may wish to work with my client to explore why it is they want me to write a letter of support and what this is reflecting in our relationship. It might be appropriate to enable the client to explore the reasons for wanting to train in counselling, to further consider their commitment to getting that training and to help them to consider how they might wish to pursue that goal. I am also quite clear that it is not my place to make judgements about my client's suitability or otherwise to undertake a counselling course. That is the responsibility first of all of the course staff and their selection criteria and processes, and, second, of the client.

Roger Casemore
Chair, BAC Complaints Committee
Fellow of BAC

* * *

This dilemma involves the counsellor in consideration of the client's past difficulties and current situation, as well as the dynamics of the relationship between counsellor and client. There are also issues concerned with confidentiality, boundaries and contracts.

We have no information about the state of the counselling relationship, how long ago the serious alcohol-related conviction was or whether alcohol abuse is still occurring. It could be that the wish of this client to do a counselling course reflects attachment to the counsellor. This would suggest, along with the length of the counselling relationship, that the relationship is positive and trusting. Thus, if the counsellor refuses to write a letter of support for the appeal, feelings of anger would arise, and feelings of being abused might possibly resurface and need to be worked through. Also the client would be disappointed that the counsellor has failed to be the desired, perfect parent. However, there would also be an opportunity for exploration of these painful issues and for the counselling work to move on.

Most psychodynamic counsellors would, I think, see this request as a boundary issue and that acceding to it might lead to others, such as for a job reference or the loan of money, which could pull the counsellor out of role. Any contract made would have been clear that counselling is a professional relationship with agreed boundaries and a commitment to confidentiality. This situation does not seem to be one of 'exceptional circumstances' as discussed in B.3.4 of the *Code of Ethics and Practice for Counsellors* (BAC 1997) but B.1.3.5 states that although counsellors do not normally act on behalf of their clients, such a course may be followed at the client's express request.

Janet Watson
Member of BAC Standards and Ethics Committee and Convenor of the Working Group on the Code of Ethics and Practice for Counsellors; recently retired university counsellor

* * *

For me there is no real dilemma here. I would not be prepared to write this 'reference'. I would want to communicate this information clearly and sensitively. I would be prepared, upon written request from the client, to write a letter of confirmation that I was this client's counsellor to the college, and nothing more.

My reasons for declining the request are mainly due to the irrevocable change to our counselling relationship that would ensue were I to comply. I also believe that it would require a degree of breach of confidentiality. This client has shared a lot of difficult issues and, as it would appear our relationship is not over, the safe space needed to address his/her problems needs to be maintained. If I had written the letter it is possible that the client would then feel uneasy about disclosing negative thoughts, feelings, behaviour in the future. These are the reasons I would tell the client I was declining the request.

Clearly there would probably be many issues raised as a result of my decision, such as a power imbalance where I was perceived to hold the ability to decide the client's future, possible anger, the client's 'trust issues' may be reactivated, and feelings of rejection. Maybe I have been requested to do this to test my trustworthiness, confidentiality, congruence in dealing with negative feedback to this client.

Perhaps this client needs to look at the issue of responsibility, external locus of evaluation, and, on a practical note, to find out the real reasons for the college rejection.

I suspect this would be a testing time for our relationship, and my ability to maintain unconditional positive regard, empathy and congruence would be crucial for the client's well-being. I also think that this incident could prove fertile ground for positive work with this client.

Simon Needs
BAC accredited counsellor working full-time for the NHS and the Royal Academy of Dramatic Art

Reference

BAC (1997) *Code of Ethics and Practice for Counsellors*, Rugby: British Association for Counselling.

Discussion issues

1 Although counsellors do not normally act on behalf of their clients, under what circumstances might you consider doing so?
2 What is the significance of requests (or disclosures) made at the end of a session?
3 How do the comments affect the way you think about boundaries, contracts and confidentiality?
4 How do you see this counsellor's dilemma?

72

Student Appeals

You are a personal tutor for several trainees who are in the final year of their counselling training. One of them books an individual tutorial with you half-way through the year to discuss her progress. The trainee expresses worries about the supervisor's assessment of her work. She feels that the supervisor has favourite supervisees whose work she praises and that those who are not favoured are constantly criticized, until their confidence is diminished and their work suffers.

The tutee wants your support in preparing her appeal for what she is sure will be a disappointing half-year assessment report from the supervisor. She wants you to say that she has been unfairly assessed. You have two problems with doing this: you are not convinced that the tutee's work with her clients is good enough (she just scraped through the previous year) and her supervisor is a senior and highly respected member of the course team. At the same time you have heard this supervisor talk about her supervisees in the staffroom and you suspect that she is not entirely even-handed in her assessments of their work. There may be some truth in your tutee's complaint.

What should you do?

I have always believed that the various Codes of Ethics and Practice should not be seen as immutable 'tablets of stone' but rather as enabling guidelines. One of the important processes that the Codes of Ethics and Practice should encourage us to undertake, is to ask the 'What if?' questions about any practice situation we find ourselves in. Clearly in this situation as a personal tutor, I should be asking a number of 'What if?' questions to identify possible breaches of ethics and good practice, by myself or by the student. The following are just some of the questions I might ask myself.

What if I take this student at face value and listen to her concerns? Is that in itself unethical?

What if I refuse to listen and insist that she takes it up with the supervisor? Is that good practice?

What if I decide that my first loyalty should be to my colleague, the supervisor, and the course team? Is that good practice?

What if I decide that my first responsibility must be to support the student? Is that ethical?

What if I say nothing to the supervisor? Is that unethical or bad practice?

What if I do as the student asks? Is that unethical or bad practice?

What if I refuse to do as the student asks? Is that good practice?

What if I take the matter up with the course team? Is that ethical?

What if I take it up directly with the supervisor? Is that good practice?

What if I arrange to see the student and the supervisor together? Can I do that in an ethical way?

I do not know that there are any intrinsically 'right' answers to any of these questions. However, it does seem to me that any of the actions resulting from them are likely to lead

---

This chapter was first published in *Counselling*, Journal of the British Association for Counselling, vol. 10, no. 1, pp. 21–4 (1999).

to the student or my colleague or the course team, or even all three, being dissatisfied with me and leaving me open to complaint as a trainer. Clearly, on the facts as they are presented, the student may have a cause for complaint against the supervisor and, in the first instance, she should be encouraged to use the internal procedures to raise this face to face with the supervisor, or to use the internal complaints procedure in the college.

In responding to this student, I suspect that I would want to do a number of things, recognizing that all of them carry a degree of risk for the student, for me, for the supervisor, for the course team and for other students. However, whatever the truth or otherwise about the ways in which the student alleges she has been treated, I must first of all concern myself with responding to her as a trainer, in an ethical and appropriate way. I must also take account of the procedures within the college and be sure to behave in a way that is ethical and appropriate in relation to my colleagues in the course team and to other students on the course. In thinking through my actions, I must also avoid reacting precipitously or being frozen into inaction by the dilemma!

To begin with, I need to act ethically as a good personal tutor, so would want the student to feel listened to and understood. I would also immediately make it clear that I would not be prepared to treat a complaint against a colleague as a confidential matter and also that I expect her to take responsibility for taking action about her concerns. Thirdly, I would be clear that I would neither be prepared to help her to prepare an appeal against an assessment which she has not yet received, nor to state that I believe that she has been unfairly assessed when I have no direct evidence of that.

I would make it clear that I would be prepared to help her think through what she is feeling and experiencing at this time in order for her to decide what action she wishes to take. I would want to help her to consider what she is experiencing of the ways in which she perceives that she is being treated differently from other students and to encourage her to think about what she might do to challenge or change this. I would also want to enable her to think through why she is preparing to appeal before the assessment has been carried out, rather than putting her energy into improving her performance and ensuring a reasonable assessment.

I would want to check if she has in fact raised the issue directly with her supervisor and, if she has not, to encourage her to do so at the first opportunity. I would help her to think through how she might do that, how she might prepare for and make best use of the time with the supervisor and whether she should see the supervisor on her own or be accompanied by a friend.

I would also want to ask her if she would find it helpful for me to give her some feedback on how I perceive her progress, to enable me to be open with her about my concerns about the standard of her work and how I think she might improve. I would try to give her some balanced feedback and then ask if there was any particular help or support that she required that would enable her to be more effective.

On considering the issue of informing my colleague and/or other members of the course team, I suspect that initially I would want to talk to the supervisor on my own and check out how they felt about their relationship with this student and their view of the student's performance. I would want the supervisor to know that the student was feeling anxious about the relationship and the effect that this might have on the forthcoming assessment by the supervisor. I would feed back to the supervisor my perceptions of the student's progress and ask if there were ways in which we could work together to get her to the required standard. I would also want to check out with the supervisor if they had any particular difficulties in relating to this student and say that I felt the need to discuss this student's progress and current anxiety at a course meeting. In telling the supervisor about the way in which I had tried to help the student and that I had insisted that the student take the matter up directly with the supervisor, I would also offer to be available to facilitate that meeting if both parties were in agreement, or arrange for someone else to do that.

Finally, I would want to raise the issue at a course team meeting: first of all, to consider how each member of the team could contribute best to enabling this student to reach the required standard and support each other in doing that; second, to enable the team to consider how we could each ensure that we are perceived as treating all students equally and fairly and to reiterate our commitment to that principle.

Roger Casemore
Chair, BAC Complaints Committee
Fellow of BAC

*   *   *

I am responding particularly from the perspective of the BAC *Codes of Ethics and Practice for Trainers* (1996), the *Code of Ethics and Practice for Supervisors of Counsellors* (1995a) and the *Guidelines for Client Work, Training Placements and Supervision in Counsellor Training Courses* (1995b). This scenario touches on substantial areas of various codes, so I have, necessarily, been selective.

Two vital issues exist, namely to ensure a fair assessment for the trainee and to establish whether or not the supervisor is prejudiced. However, my first concern is to support the trainee: after acknowledging her anxiety I would reassure her that there are effective and fair assessment and appeals procedures in place (BAC 1996: B.4.1 (c) (h) (i)). Although supportive of the trainee in the correct procedure, I would seek not to be prejudiced against her or the supervisor (BAC 1996: B.1.3).

The trainee is assuming she will receive a poor assessment so I would encourage her to ask the supervisor for an informal review to check out her fears and I would offer to help her rehearse what she needs to say in the review. In addition, I would suggest that the trainee reflect on personal feedback from other trainees, clients and tutors (BAC 1996: B.4.3). I would discuss these concerns with my line manager in keeping with the 1995 BAC course guidelines (1995: 2.2 and 2.2.5) and 1996 Trainers' code (BAC 1996: B.3.3 (d)).

If the informal review proves unfavourable, the next step is to ask for a formal assessment report according to the laid-down procedure for the training agency. If this too is unfavourable the trainee may, under the appeals procedure, submit a taped recording of her client work to the course external examiner for objective assessment (BAC 1996: B.4.7).

If the collaboration required for effective supervision has broken down, the trainee needs a new supervisor to ensure her development and the well-being of clients (BAC 1995a: 3). Training courses need to ensure supervisors of trainees are aware of their responsibilities, particularly around assessment procedures (BAC 1995a: B.3.1.5 and B.3.1.8). If the supervisor had concerns about the trainee's practice she needed to discuss these with her.

If the supervisor gives evidence of prejudice, this is a breach not only of the supervisors' code (1995a: 4) but also of the ethos of all the codes which uphold the need for impartiality and valuing of the individual, and as such it needs to be addressed. Initially this is through informal discussion with the supervisor. If this fails to resolve matters I would discuss this with my line manager and my supervisor and after careful consideration may, sadly, need to institute an internal complaints procedure (BAC 1995a: B.1.14 and BAC 1996: B.3.6). These steps are necessary for the safety of other supervisees, clients and the profession.

This situation highlights two important issues: the need to ensure fair and objective assessment of trainees by clear internal procedures, and how to address potentially anti-discriminatory practice. Integrity, impartiality and respect are at the heart of counselling, supervision and training and we each have a responsibility to uphold them even when this may be difficult.

Cathy Carroll
Member of BAC Standards and Ethics Committee
Tutor, Diploma in Counselling at Work: University of Bristol

*   *   *

As a person-centred trainer, I believe the core conditions to be as important in my work with students as with clients, with the difference that I would place more emphasis on congruence and on voicing my own perceptions of the trainee and her work. So the first question which occurs to me as I read this vignette is: 'Have I been sufficiently clear with this person about how I perceive her and her work? Have I, in my wish to be supportive and encouraging, over-emphasized her strengths and failed to communicate to her the work she needs to do?' If, upon reflection, I believe that I *have* been clear with this student, it might be that she has been unable to 'hear' my perceptions. At some point in our tutorial, I must check this out.

But my other task is to listen to and understand the student's distress and anger about the supervisory relationship – without making any judgements about 'right' and 'wrong'. Has she been able to voice any of this to her supervisor? If not, what are her fears? Empathic understanding might help her to acknowledge how scared she is of 'failure' and to become more aware of how she is responding to this perceived threat. Can she express to her supervisor how criticized and unsupported she feels? If she has not been able to be open with her supervisor about her struggles in working with clients, this of itself will have prevented her from getting the help she needs to develop as a counsellor.

None of this is to deny the supervisor's part in the relationship. The supervisor may indeed have become critical, or even punitive, towards the student. Irrespective of whether this is or is not the case, it seems unlikely that an appeal will be helpful to the student. She has only half a year to complete the course, and my focus is on her learning.

What practical help *am* I prepared to give? Whatever the ins and outs, this supervisory relationship has not, in the student's eyes, been helpful in her development as a counsellor. I would be entirely supportive if she felt she could take the risk of saying that to her supervisor. I might also be prepared to help her make a case with the course leader for a change of supervisor and an extension of her deadlines for submission of her work. In my mind would be the hope that she can learn from this, and there is much potential learning for her about the way she handles difficult relationships.

And what of my responsibility in relation to the supervisor? This is a more difficult one. I do not see it as appropriate for me to tell a colleague how someone else has experienced her. But perhaps I do have a responsibility to say how I have experienced her, which means taking a deep breath the next time she disparages students in the staffroom and telling her about my own discomfort.

Janet Tolan
Principal Lecturer in Counselling at Liverpool John Moores University

*   *   *

As a trainer working from a person-centred approach, I would want to respect the trainee's feelings of persecution and low self-confidence and to offer her my support. However, appeals and complaints procedures are very much a last resort and should be avoided if it is possible to resolve the problem by other means.

I would ask if she had raised her concerns with her supervisor. If not, I would offer to help her prepare herself to do so. I would make it clear to her that the overall assessment of her competence as a counsellor would be based on all aspects of her work and not solely on the opinion of one supervisor. I would then ask her about her own assessment of her client work and the feedback from tutors and peers on the course. If there was an overall pattern of criticism, I would want to address the areas of concern with her and help her to accept and use feedback in a positive way.

At the same time I would want to discuss it with the supervisor. It is clear that a trusting, collaborative relationship has failed to develop between the supervisor and trainee. The fact that the supervisor is discussing trainees in the staffroom may be contributing to this failure and the staff team may be colluding with her. Therefore confidentiality is being eroded and students' work is being trivialized and two codes are relevant here (BAC 1995a: B.3.2.7 and BAC 1996: B.3.5). If the disagreement between the supervisor and the trainee cannot be resolved between them within the supervision relationship, and a collaborative relationship cannot be established, then the trainee should have the option of being referred to an alternative supervisor as a guard against bias (and/or accusations of partiality).

Gaye Giles
Person-centred counsellor and trainer

*   *   *

As a personal tutor I am very ready to assist trainees who are facing difficulties which hinder their professional development. My reaction to this particular request was to arrange a time when we could discuss it further. I needed time to think.

The trainee talked of constant criticism from her supervisor and of being unfairly assessed. Has she raised the matter with the supervisor? I am also struck by the fact that she appears to have no sense of the complexity and the dilemmas to be faced in responding to her request.

I have my own doubts about the standard of this trainee's casework. What bearing do those perceptions have on my response to her request? I have heard the supervisor talk in a way that suggests she is less than totally even-handed with her trainees. I have not done anything about that and must think why that is. Lastly, I find it odd to be asked to help shape an appeal about something that has yet to happen.

First, I must put my own house in order. I will take the next opportunity to challenge any bias in the supervisor's comment about her supervisees.

I am going to frame my response to my tutee in terms of the ethics which underpin her working relationships and hope that she will see the need to address any unfair criticism directly with her supervisor. She may need some help in thinking through how to do that. My own view about the tutee's competence is not relevant and it may be that, if she has challenged her supervisor appropriately and still receives an assessment that appears unfair, I will help her assemble the facts for an appeal. After all, my *primary* responsibility is for the welfare and professional development of my tutees.

Derek Hill
Member of BAC Complaints Committee
Fellow of BAC and Former Head of Practitioner Training, Relate

References

BAC (1995a) *Code of Ethics and Practice for Supervisors of Counsellors*, Rugby: British Association for Counselling.

BAC (1995b) *Guidelines for Client Work, Training Placements and Supervision in Counsellor Training Courses*, Rugby: British Association for Counselling.

BAC (1996) *Code of Ethics and Practice for Trainers*, Rugby: British Association for Counselling.

Discussion issues

1 How easy do you find it to challenge other practitioners when you have concerns about their attitudes or actions?
2 Effective work with clients is one of the criteria on a counsellor training course. How can this be assessed given the ethical and practice issues around recording sessions?
3 How do the comments affect your thinking about the roles of tutors, supervisors and students in counselling training?
4 What have you learned from your understanding and discussion of this dilemma?

73

Counsellors Ending Counselling

What, if any, fundamental right does a counsellor have to end a counselling relationship if the client disagrees and refuses to end?

In your opinion, what are some of the legitimate therapeutic reasons for ending and who has the ultimate right to determine that the counsellor is no longer helping the client?

What steps are recommended to manage an ending in these circumstances in order to do so according to BAC's Codes?

My view is that a counsellor does have a fundamental right to end a counselling relationship, in exceptional circumstances. I would hope to pre-empt such a situation by taking responsibility for contracting the number of sessions with the client at the first meeting (BAC 1997: 3.2, A.4, B.4.3.1). Usually I contract for an initial six-week period and review the state of play at the penultimate session. Then I will contract a further number of weeks at the sixth session. Towards the end of the *mutually agreed* time I will signal the ending several weeks beforehand to enable any unexpressed feelings or thoughts to be processed during our 'ending period'.

Many reasons spring to mind for the counsellor to initiate an ending; unexpected 'life events' for the counsellor, such as major traumas. (BAC 1997: B.1.1 states: 'The ... relationship ... does not exist in social isolation'; B.1.3.9: 'External circumstances may lead to endings for other reasons which are not therapeutic.') If the counsellor feels the counselling has moved beyond their area of competence it would be irresponsible to continue (BAC 1997: A.6 and B.6.1.2). If the client's issues closely resembled the counsellor's, and the counsellor was unable to separate the two, possibly leading to collusion, or the counsellor's feelings for the client were so overwhelming that the professional relationship was jeopardized, it might be time to refer on (BAC 1998: B.6.1.4). These are some of the issues where the counsellor has the right to decide that they are no longer helping the client.

The reasons for ending should be clearly and sensitively communicated to the client. Sufficient time must be given to facilitate a satisfactory ending, allowing the client an unconditional 'space' to voice previously unexpressed feelings about the ending (BAC 1997: B.1.3.8). The counsellor is responsible for addressing the issue in supervision and monitoring the situation regularly with the supervisor (BAC 1997: B.6.3.1). An appropriate onward referral must be offered if the client wishes to continue in counselling with another counsellor.

Simon Needs
BAC accredited counsellor working full-time for the NHS and the Royal Academy of Dramatic Art

* * *

This chapter was first published in *Counselling*, Journal of the British Association for Counselling, vol. 10, no. 2, pp. 107–9 (1999).

The fundamental rights of counsellors are the same as those of everybody else. 'Every reasonable effort' to act ethically does not *oblige* a counsellor to sacrifice those rights. That said, it is most unlikely that a counsellor will face that kind of dilemma. It is much more common to find that work with a client has reached a point at which the therapeutic benefits are outweighed by its negative consequences, and at which compliance with the client's wishes would rob the counsellor of integrity and offend a sense of justice. Such situations are inevitably charged with emotion and should not be handled without close counselling supervision. In many cases specialist advice is also needed if decisions are to be made on the basis of comprehensive assessments. Impasse, substance abuse, erotic transference and violent behaviour could each be major factors in a decision to end a counselling relationship. Whatever the complexities of a particular situation, and however many the sources of advice used, the right and responsibility for a decision to end counselling unilaterally lies with the counsellor. And if those decisions are to be safe they must result from the use of thorough clinical assessments to inform a scrupulous balancing of the ethical principles that are in tension. The *ultimate* right to end such a relationship will rest with the society's ultimate authority. In practical terms such decisions may be taken by the counsellor's employer and by the courts. For the time being the counselling profession may express views, but has no power to enforce compliance with them. It is important to acknowledge that such decisions may not be agreed with by other members of their profession. However, if care is taken they may none the less be respected as genuine attempts to resolve intractable therapeutic and ethical dilemmas.

There are three processes that will assist in achieving that outcome. First, judgements should be made with the assistance of supervision and, if necessary, expert advice. Second, informing the client and enacting a decision to end counselling unilaterally should be an integral part of the counselling undertaken with consideration given to its therapeutic implications. Third, as a critical event, it should be the subject of detailed records – the writing of them is itself a valuable professional discipline and their availability will witness to the care and attention given to the matter.

Derek Hill
Fellow of BAC
Member of the Complaints Committee and former Head of Practitioner Training, Relate

*   *   *

The BAC *Code of Ethics and Practice for Counsellors* (1997: 3.1) states the following: 'The overall aim of counselling is to provide an opportunity for the client to work towards living in a way he or she experiences as more satisfying and resourceful.' The counsellor has an absolute and fundamental right to end the counselling relationship, even where the client disagrees and wishes for it to continue. The counsellor needs to have good grounds for taking this drastic move and should, wherever possible, attempt to negotiate this ending within the context of the ongoing therapeutic relationship.

The continuation of a therapeutic relationship beyond its period of usefulness for the client is unethical and, at its most extreme, could constitute professional abuse (especially if you are earning money by seeing them). It is the counsellor, and not necessarily the client, who understands the significance of endings and their relevance to the counselling process, and it is the counsellor who must take responsibility for working with this material and not ignoring it. Failing to do so may well take away from the positive gains of counselling.

Counsellors need to inform their clients about the limits of the counselling relationship and to place ending dates firmly on the agenda. Confusion and lack of clarity about boundaries in counselling are not helpful or professional. In a situation where the client does not wish to end, it becomes the role of the counsellor to help the client to face this ending as well as possible and, in the most extreme situation, to end it for them.

In terms of what is legitimate (or not) in counselling, this decision must rest with the individual counsellor, with guidance from their supervisor. Counselling is not for everyone and it is not (in my view) a lifelong undertaking. At all stages, the counsellor must try to convey clearly, and with the least amount of jargon, why they think that counselling is no longer appropriate or useful, and to work with the material the client brings in response to this. But for a client who steadfastly refuses to acknowledge the reasons or the need for ending and is unable to explore this further, we may have to accept that, in some situations, therapeutic endings are far from ideal.

Dawn Collins
Counselling supervisor and tutor

* * *

The dilemma about responsibility for ending counselling clearly raises many issues. These are not always clear cut, and situations may arise when clauses in the current code are apparently in conflict. Consider the following example. A counsellor has been working (ethically) with a client over a number of months. After a recent crisis in the client's family situation, the client has been displaying increasingly aggressive behaviour towards the counsellor. All attempts made by the counsellor to address this with the client have not resolved the situation. The client has become more aggressive and is accusing the counsellor of incompetence. The counsellor now feels harassed and unsafe, even after discussion with the counselling supervisor.

Several ethical principles are called into question by this situation, and relevant clauses from the *Code of Ethics and Practice for Counsellors* (BAC 1997) are cited below.

- The counsellor–client relationship is the foremost ethical concern (B.1.1).
- Counsellors take responsibility for clinical/therapeutic decisions in their work with clients (B.1.2).
- Counsellors must take all reasonable steps to ensure that the client suffers neither physical nor psychological harm during counselling sessions (B.1.3.1).
- Counsellors work with clients to reach a recognised ending when clients have received the help they sought or when it is apparent that counselling is no longer helping or when clients wish to end (B.1.3.8).
- Counsellors should take all reasonable steps to ensure their own physical safety (B.6.2.1).

While the above statements may not guarantee that the counsellor can reach a decision about the way forward, there is nevertheless solace to be found in the following clause: 'Even after conscientious consideration of the salient issues, some ethical dilemmas cannot be resolved easily or wholly satisfactorily' (B.1.6.3).

As a counsellor in private practice, I find the following steps helpful in establishing a clear working agreement:

- being clear about the agreements and its boundaries;

- discussing the endings of counselling at the beginning;
- asking the client for the name of their GP and explaining procedures for referral on if necessary;
- reviewing the work at intervals.

Within the inherent asymmetry of the counselling relationship, I endeavour to provide a forum for openness so that the issues can be explored together.

Carole Pocknell
Independent counsellor, trainer and counselling supervisor in private practice

* * *

A counsellor must be able to end a client's counselling if they believe that it is inappropriate to continue. If this were not so, any counsellor could be forced to work in situations which have become unprofessional and unethical. This may be for reasons to do with the scope and limits of the counsellor's practice. The counsellor may decide, for example, that it would be unprofessional to continue working with a client because he or she can no longer provide the necessary therapeutic skills to deal with the client's needs which may require specialized or advanced skills which are not in the counsellor's repertoire. In this situation it is an ethical requirement to refer the client on to someone who can best help them (see section B.6.1 of the *Code of Ethics and Practice for Counsellors* (BAC 1997)). A similar situation may arise if the counsellor becomes unfit to practice, perhaps through illness or a life crisis such as bereavement.

Other legitimate reasons for ending counselling without the client's agreement have to do with the client. One of the difficulties of these situations is that it is often the most vulnerable clients who find it hard to accept that it may not be possible to continue as they would wish. If a client persists in behaviour which threatens the counsellor's safety and is unable to work within the limits of the therapeutic contract, the counsellor may feel that to continue to accept the situation would be to collude with destructive acting out. Sometimes a client finds it difficult to let go of the safety offered by the counselling and may need fairly firm encouragement to move on and rely on their own resources. This can be a bit like the situation of the grown child who finds it difficult to leave home and needs to be helped, protesting, over the doorstep.

It is important to deal with all therapeutic endings with care, but especially so in these circumstances. The preparation should begin at the start of counselling when the contract is agreed. This should include statements about the possibility of referral on, about the importance of sticking to the agreed conditions for the work (for example regular attendance, payment, etc.) and about the fact that the ending is a matter for the client and the counsellor to negotiate. It is always important to leave time to prepare to end, wherever possible. This gives a client the opportunity to express some of their regret, anger, fear and so on. It is important to prepare for the possibility of having to stop working suddenly by having an arrangement for a professional colleague to support clients and to keep them informed.

Above all, it is vital to be clear about the arrangements for ending and to stick to them. If it is your policy to do so, inform referrers that counselling is ending. Set a clear end date and stick to it. Make sure that you fully discuss the situation with your supervisor, so that you are supported. We become counsellors because we believe that counselling can help. It is difficult to acknowledge when it has ceased to help, and when we are not the best person to help, but if we are to be clear about what we can do we must also be clear about what we cannot do. Ultimately this may be one of the most important factors in enabling a client to accept themselves – abilities, limitations and all.

Val Potter
Former Co-Chair, Standards and Ethics Committee, currently Deputy Chair, BAC and Chair of BAC Professional Standards Committee

Reference

British Association for Counselling (1997) *Code of Ethics and Practice for Counsellors*, Rugby: British Association for Counselling.

Discussion issues

1 In what circumstances would *you* bring a counselling relationship to an end?
2 How might your theoretical approach and setting of the counselling influence the decision?
3 Counselling sessions also have a beginning and ending – what skills are required to end sessions at the agreed time and what issues arise when working with a client who is reluctant to leave the counselling room?
4 How does this dilemma affect your thinking about the occupational hazards of being a counsellor?

74

A Bereaved Counsellor and Supervision

> *You supervise a counsellor who works in several settings: a hospice, a counselling agency for women (issues of childhood sexual abuse, poverty, domestic violence and addiction) and in her own independent practice with five private clients, some recently new, some long term.*
>
> *The counsellor's partner has recently suffered a third and fatal heart attack.*
>
> *How do you and the counsellor determine when she is functioning well enough to resume counselling and how much might her theoretical approach(es), the needs of individual clients and the settings of her work influence the decision(s)?*

As part of the supervisory process discussion would have already taken place regarding the functioning of the supervisee throughout the illness of her partner. This discussion would have considered the way in which the supervisee deals with stressful situations, her coping mechanisms, their impact on client work and the actions required to ensure a baseline of counselling effectiveness is maintained while taking into account the counsellor's own emotional and physical needs and limitations. For example, the supervisee may well have cut back on client numbers or even ceased counselling during her partner's previous hospitalizations. Discussion would have therefore taken place regarding the most professional/ethical way of managing a sudden break from counselling, for example, if, when and how reallocation of cases at the hospice and counselling agency should take place; the impact of a break on her private clients and how this should be managed. In addition, the need for personal therapy during this particularly difficult period would also have been explored, as would the need for additional counselling supervision. As a counsellor paid for sessional work and running a small private practice the need for a 'fallback' fund of six months' salary to act as a financial buffer for times when the supervisee could not work would also have been discussed.

During this time discussion would have taken place regarding the possibility of her partner's death and what implications she imagined this might have on her work and what course of action she might take. During supervision hypothetical questions such as the following would have been explored:

- Given your work at the hospice, how might you feel working with the terminally ill and their grieving relatives?
- What type of emotions or client situations might you find hard to deal with?
- Given that you work in a variety of settings, do you imagine there would be a difference in your feelings about the type of clients and client problems being presented?
- When thinking about client x whom you found hard to work with, what would happen if you were faced with a similar client situation?

In addition, consideration would need to be given to the supervisee's theoretical model and its impact. For example, the demands placed on an integrative counsellor with a bias

This chapter was first published in *Counselling*, Journal of the British Association for Counselling, vol. 10, no. 3, pp. 195–7 (1999).

towards a psychodynamic way of working might be different from those of an integrative counsellor working more cognitive-behaviourally.

It would also be important to consider the supervisee's ethnic, cultural and religious origins and beliefs and the impact these might have on how the supervisee views death. Although the supervisee may feel very sad at the death of her partner the impact of this bereavement could be affected by a variety of factors. For example, if the supervisee was a lesbian and her partner female she might face additional pressures from negative societal attitudes which could impede her grieving process. If the supervisee had strong religious beliefs which celebrated death as a transition to a better life or if she belonged to a culture which saw death as a natural part of living she might be affected quite differently.

When we did meet to discuss her current position this meeting would build on previous discussions. For example, we would consider whether the supervisee was feeling the way she thought she would, how she was feeling about returning to work, whether she should return in a staged manner and, if so, what discussions needed to take place with her employing organizations, how much counselling supervision was required and whether any changes in emphasis either in client type or theoretical bias were required during this period.

Gladeana McMahon
BAC Fellow, accredited counsellor and counselling supervisor, BABCP accredited cognitive-behavioural psychotherapist.

*   *   *

I have used a solution-focused approach in answering the question. I don't think there can be a set rule which states that all counsellors must stop work for a certain length of time after a bereavement. I would be more interested in how this unique individual has coped with previous losses or difficulties in her life and whether these past experiences hold lessons for the present situation. This ongoing conversation would pay attention to how well supported she is at the moment, how her current needs are being met and how she is able to express her grief.

The key question is obviously how far the person has begun to adjust to the loss *in relation to the demands of her work as a counsellor*. This is not to be confused with her adjustment in other areas of her life. I am aware that grieving is an intensely personal experience and that I would not want the supervisee to conform to any pre-conceived formula. Much would depend on the circumstances of the bereavement and whether the grief was complicated or pathological.

I would explore how she herself would know when she was ready to begin counselling again – what would be the signs for her that she was able to cope? How can I as her supervisor help her to look out for these signs? I would invest a lot of trust in my supervisee's judgement.

I would want to join with the supervisee in constructing a plan which fits her best. She may, for example, want to reintroduce herself gradually and gently with a much reduced caseload. She may prefer to resume work in one setting rather than another. I would not see myself as the expert who knows best what she should do, but a respectful partner who can help her to make a balanced decision. I would draw upon my knowledge of the person to decide how much or how little I should challenge her reading of the situation.

At times of personal disequilibrium it can be helpful to have an outsider to guide one temporarily through the darkness.

On the one hand, I would not want to collude with an excessive preciousness which claims that counsellors need a longer break from their work following a bereavement than other caring professionals, such as doctors or social workers. We do not live in an ideal world in which people can take as much time out as they want. Sometimes we have to grit our teeth and just carry on despite personal feelings of sadness and loss. Good and supportive supervision and possibly personal therapy may enable the counsellor to work ethically and effectively as they 'work through' their grief. On the other hand, we live in a society which tends to rush people through major life transitions so that they 'have the experience but miss the meaning'. Lacking the rituals and structures with which previous generations protected a time for mourning from the demands of daily living, organizations now often pressurize people to return to work prematurely with destructive results in the long term.

Work at some stage can be therapeutic for the bereaved person but not at the cost of client safety or the long-term interest of the worker. I would want to ensure that the counsellor took the time and space she needed and that she had a sense of what she needed to do during that time.

I would be influenced by my prior knowledge of the supervisee's ability to take care of herself, to ask for what she needs and to distinguish her own issues from those of her clients. The supervisor also needs to be aware of how he or she deals with loss and change as this is likely to affect his or her attitude to the supervisee.

There could be a serious practical aspect of the dilemma if the counsellor was dependent upon counselling for her livelihood. The supervisor would need to take this into account in advising the counsellor when to return. The safety of the client and the counsellor are the key values, but they need to be evaluated in a real world in which counsellors inevitably experience personal crises in their lives. For some counsellors the loss of a job or the break-up of a relationship could have a greater impact on their effectiveness than a bereavement. Experiencing a personal loss need not be a disabling event but could lead to a deepening of empathy and understanding.

Bill O'Connell
Fellow of BAC, BAC accredited counsellor, lecturer and trainer in counselling, counselling supervisor and writer on solution-focused therapy

*   *   *

Rather than a dilemma where I am faced with a choice between right and wrong solutions, this seems more like a paradox in which I am faced with the existence of two 'truths', where whatever I do will be both right and wrong!

First of all it will be important for me to maintain the boundaries and the nature of the supervision relationship, remembering that we are meeting together to enable my supervisee to maintain the ethical standards of her counselling practice. While I need to take account of her recent bereavement and to be compassionate and supportive, I must not enter into a counselling relationship with her. It will be important to encourage her to get the therapeutic help she needs, that will enable her to return to counselling when she is ready. I will also need to feel that I am enabling her to make that decision and taking my responsibility for checking that decision out so that I feel I can support it.

I would spend some time checking out her current case-load and making sure that her clients are being properly informed and taken care of in her absence. I might need to help her to find apppropriate 'locum support' and to work out a process for taking her clients back later on. We would need to agree how much time she thinks she needs to take off and a process for reviewing that and reaching agreement about when and how she should recommence counselling. We would also need to explore her feelings about stopping seeing her clients and it may be that I might have to encourage her to take some of that work to her therapist.

We would need to discuss the different kinds of client work which she is involved in and to identify different issues arising in each situation. For example, she may well be much more supported in her agency work and able to return to that work sooner than her private practice. However, her agency work in the hospice may involve a considerable involvement with death and other forms of loss and it may be quite some time before she can return to that work.

The paradox is contained, in that it may well be beneficial to her and her clients to return to work, to take her mind off her loss and develop a new normality for herself. At the same time it will be equally true that this may well be quite harmful for her and for her clients, to return before she has dealt fully with her bereavement. The 'right' time will be one that she has to decide for herself, for each of her groups of clients. My responsibility to her and to her clients will be to help her to try to stay with the existential nature of the paradox and try to make a wise decision which she and I can both live with.

Roger Casemore
Chair, BAC Complaints Committee, Fellow of BAC

* * *

This practice dilemma throws up more questions than answers. The BAC *Code of Ethics and Practice for Counsellors* (1997: B.6.1.3) states that counsellors must monitor their functioning and take action when they are no longer competent to practise in situations of personal or emotional difficulty. There was a short debate in this journal last year about the client, not the counsellor, determining the end of their counselling (BAC 1997: B.1.3.8). Carol Shillito-Clarke (1998), in a letter to the editor talks about the rights of the counsellor to end and whether, if the client disagrees, we could be 'held hostage' to the codes. Looking at this pessimistically, we could have potential difficulties if the counsellor wanted to stop work and the client did not, or if there was dissension between the supervisor and counsellor regarding her readiness to return.

Working in the best interest of the client may mean that this counsellor should not work in the hospice for some considerable time, given that the issues for both are going to overlap. This does not, however, take into account the individual client's needs. What may be seen as best practice may not be the most beneficial action for the counsellor; both need to be considered and a balance struck between the two, at times, opposing needs. Working in the women's counselling agency it may be difficult for the counsellor to empathize with women 'complaining' about their partners when she is grieving hers. Her private clients must also be viewed individually, and ideally more supervision offered while she finds her way back into the work.

The environmental practical issues will affect this woman. What are her cultural and religious beliefs in terms of how she deals with death and bereavement? What are her support systems like? Has she done enough personal work to give her an emotional maturity to help her cope with what can be an excruciating period of her life? Was her partner male or female? If the latter, was it a closet relationship which means she would not be able to express her grief publicly? Has her financial situation changed? Is she in a position where she may become homeless or has to generate more income to survive?

Fiona Purdie
Counsellor, supervisor, trainer

References

BAC (1997) *Code of Ethics and Practice for Counsellors*, Rugby: British Association for Counselling.
Shillito-Clarke, C. (1998) Letter to the Editor, *Counselling*, 9 (3) (August): 189.

Suggested reading

BAC (1998) 'How much supervision should you have?' Rugby: British Association for Counselling.

Discussion issues

1 How comprehensive are your contingency plans for sudden breaks and endings?
2 How does a supervisor maintain the distinction between offering support to a supervisee during personal difficulties and taking a therapeutic role?
3 What are the responsibilities and options for the supervisor and the counsellor in the event they disagree about the counsellor's functioning?
4 Do you have help available in times of personal pain and distress?

PART FOUR

COUNSELLING AND RESEARCH

Introduction to Part Four

In Britain, there are now many counselling courses at Masters level for which the participants have normally to carry out a research project. We raise this issue, since currently much counselling research is being undertaken which, as yet, does not appear in the published literature. As editors, trainers and supervisors, we have personally encouraged counsellors to publish their studies but have been disappointed in the poor response. We have so much to learn from these unpublished studies – we wish that they were not just destined for a dusty shelf or folder somewhere! Perhaps courses should devote more time to supporting the publication of these works and helping participants to overcome any fears they may hold about their articles being rejected by journals or the daunting possibility of editors seeking adaptation of thesis material to a journal format.

Part Four contains nine chapters on counselling research. Gordon Lynch introduces us to a brief exploration of the philosophical issues that are relevant to this important area. He focuses on the nature of reality and knowledge, advocating that we become reflective researchers, aware of the assumptions that we bring to our work. William West considers two qualitative approaches to counselling research: the human inquiry and the heuristic method. He asserts that neither are easy options, both demanding good research supervision. The use of the self in counselling research can become all-consuming and can take the researcher over if care is not taken.

The next three chapters relate to research regarding some aspect of the National Health Service (NHS). Judith Brech and Peter Agulnik investigate whether brief interventions reduce waiting times for counselling in the Isis Centre, which is an open NHS facility. Even with extra resources, the Centre had not been able to keep up with the growing demand for its services. Over time, this had led to a growing waiting list, with some clients having to wait for more than six months. This is a common problem shared by many other NHS facilities. The Centre decided to offer session-limited therapy in addition to its usual service, and the outcome and implications are discussed in this chapter. Mary Burton, Penny Henderson and Graham Curtis Jenkins used an in-depth eight-page questionnaire to investigate the experiences of supervision by primary care counsellors. Many interesting issues were found. For example, in one case the preferred therapeutic approach of the supervisors was different from that of the counsellors, a situation which could not only create ongoing difficulties within supervision, but also raise ethical issues, especially with inexperienced counsellors. One concern worth noting is that 11 per cent of counsellors were expected to offer counselling to all patients referred regardless of the severity of the presenting problem. This is an extreme pressure to put on counsellors, especially when counselling could be inappropriate for the particular client. Not surprisingly, the study also found differences in the level of qualifications between the counsellors and their supervisors. Interestingly, more counsellors had a first degree whereas more supervisors held Masters or Doctoral degrees. In an examination of differential client referral patterns either to practice counsellors or to community psychiatric nurses in GP settings, Margaret Ward and Del Loewenthal found that the referral criteria were not systematically consistent among GPs and the reasons for the referral choice were not consciously articulated in the majority of cases.

David King and Sue Wheeler discuss the limits of responsibility of supervisors working with counsellors in private practice. Semi-structured one-hour interviews were undertaken with 'experts' or experienced professional counsellors and supervisors, who had published relevant material or held positions within BAC. Tensions were found between the limits of the role and function of counselling supervision and the professional expectation that supervision should be the linchpin of quality control. In addition, it was found that supervisors were very selective in their choice of supervisees. Are less experienced supervisors supervising the inexperienced counsellors? Surely this impacts upon quality control.

Andrew Grayson, David Clarke and Hugh Miller describe a systematic qualitative analysis method. They examined students' everyday problems using hierarchical cluster analysis in conjunction with multi-dimensional scaling to provide a systematic representation of the data. The chapter demonstrates the power of this method. In the next chapter, Roy Moodley and Shukla Dhingra look at an area of counselling that has received minimal attention in the literature: the characteristics and effectiveness of the black counsellor/white client dyad. Although they found in their study that such relationships could develop a rich environment for effective and creative therapeutic outcomes, they suggest that more research is necessary using clearly defined and systematic methodologies. In considering the nature of therapeutic issues for sexually abused adult males, Kim Etherington undertook in-depth interviews with a non-clinical sample of 25 men. In her summary, she concludes that few men present initially as sexually abused, although more recently the disclosure of male abuse has increased. The last chapter in this section, by Patricia Hunt, surveys counselling course prospectuses and brochures. Surprising items were missing from some brochures, such as student and staff numbers. Even less information was provided about the qualifications, orientation and experience of the staff. This suggests that choosing a course can be problematic for many potential students.

75

What is Truth? A Philosophical Introduction to Counselling Research

Gordon Lynch

The aim of this chapter is to give a brief exploration of some philosophical issues that are relevant to the conduct of counselling research. The particular issues that I want to focus on are ontological (that is, issues concerning the nature of reality) and epistemological (that is, issues concerning the nature of knowledge). I will set out below three different perspectives on reality and knowledge, and identify the kind of research that is most consistent with each of these perspectives. This chapter is not intended to be a thorough survey of this area of philosophical thought, but rather its aim is to promote further discussion and reflection by identifying certain key ideas and questions.

But what's the point of this?

Already, at this point, you may be questioning the relevance of what I am setting out to do here. A question may be emerging for you along the lines of, 'Isn't this kind of philosophical speculation too abstract to be of any practical use for counselling research?' Certainly it seems that this view is shared, at least to some extent, by key writers in the field of research methodology. Robson (1993) dispenses with any philosophical reflection about research, adopting a more 'pragmatic' approach. Similarly Strauss and Corbin (1990) launch into a discussion of qualitative research without giving any philosophical consideration of what kind of knowledge such research provides us with. It is also reasonable to acknowledge that agencies commissioning research (such as Health Authorities, voluntary agencies) are unlikely to want to read extensive discussions of the philosophical basis of the research in the final report. It can be tempting, then, for those involved in counselling research to neglect philosophical issues and simply to get stuck in with the 'practical' work of getting the research done.

I think it is important that these philosophical issues are not neglected, however. All of what we understand about life is based on certain assumptions about reality and the nature of knowledge. For us to be truly reflective researchers therefore requires us not only to be critically aware of the focus of our study, or of the research methods we are using, but also to be aware of the assumptions about reality and knowledge that we bring to our work. It may well be that, for some research reports, it is not appropriate to make these assumptions explicit. The reflective researcher will be aware of their assumptions, however, whether they choose to identify these in a particular research report or not.

This chapter was first published in *Counselling*, Journal of the British Association for Counselling, vol. 7, no. 2, pp. 144–8 (1996).

This philosophical awareness has become increasingly important as the range of methods used by counselling researchers expands. Earlier in this century, research into counselling was largely based on established quantitative methods, which sought to test predictions (or *hypotheses*) by subjecting numerical data to statistical analysis. With the quantitative approach to research, it has been possible to assess the validity of particular studies on the basis of agreed criteria such as internal and external validity, reliability and objectivity (McLeod 1994: 97ff.).

The past 30 years, however, have seen the growth of 'new' paradigm research using qualitative methods which use verbal data to build up descriptions or explanations of particular phenomena. The development of these new research methodologies has raised important questions about whether there are any criteria against which all forms of research can be assessed, or whether there should be different criteria for assessing quantitative and qualitative studies. My own view is that, while different criteria need to be established to assess quantitative and qualitative studies, there is one criterion against which all research can be assessed. This criterion is that a piece of research should possess *internal consistency*.

A research study demonstrates internal consistency when there is a consistent logic *from* the philosophical basis of the research *to* the way in which the focus of the research is approached and research questions phrased, *to* the research methods that are selected and *to* the conclusions that are drawn from the research. In other words, a particular philosophical perspective on the nature of reality and knowledge will lead logically to certain approaches to research rather than others. A piece of research achieves internal consistency when the approach taken in the research is consistent with the philosophical perspective on which the research is based.

What I intend to do now is to identify three different philosophical perspectives on the nature of reality and knowledge, and to point to the approaches to research that are most consistent with each perspective. In doing this, I hope to enable those coming to do counselling research to clarify their own philosophical perspectives, and to give some indication of what it may mean for them to do research in a way that is consistent with their own philosophical views.

Perspective 1: There is an objective reality and we are able to have an objective knowledge of this reality through the use of reason

The idea that we are able to gain an objective knowledge of reality through the use of our reason has a long history and dates back to classical Greek philosophers such as Plato and Socrates. In Western thought this perspective has been particularly dominant over the past 200 years. The strong emergence of this perspective in the eighteenth century was due in part to the work of the philosopher René Descartes.

Central to Descartes' thought was the notion that we are only able to gain a truly objective knowledge of reality through the use of reason. His emphasis on human reason as the most sure method for true knowledge of the world is captured in his most famous dictum: *cogito ergo sum*, 'I think therefore I am.' In Descartes' view, then, we could be confident that there was such a thing as objective reality and our knowledge of this reality was obtained through the use of human reason. This understanding of reality and knowledge has been called a *modern* epistemology.

This view of reality and knowledge has certainly been influential since the time of Descartes. Scientific research in this period has been on the assumption that there is an objective reality and that we are able to understand it through the use of scientific methods based on reason. The traditional model of the scientific experiment as a controlled test of a hypothesis using established methods reflects this philosophical view. Scientific research, in this form, has sought to identify links of cause and effect between different phenomena (for example, burning coal produces carbon dioxide) and to develop logical theories that explain these links (for example, a theory explaining the molecular changes in coal when it reaches a certain temperature). This approach to scientific research has been called the 'positivist' model. The aim of the 'positivist' approach to science is to formulate general laws of nature which help us to predict what will happen under certain circumstances (Harre 1981). This approach to research has also been referred to as being the 'old paradigm' of scientific research.

For those engaged in counselling research who wish to adopt a modern epistemological perspective (Perspective 1), it is most consistent to adopt a positivist approach to counselling research. In practice this means that counselling research based on a modern epistemological view should seek to achieve scientific rigour as this has been defined over the past two centuries. Such counselling research should therefore conform to the pattern of the 'well-designed' experiment. It should begin with a clear hypothsis which relates to previous research conducted in that area of study. It should then test this hypothesis on a sample representative of a wider population which further split into test and control (or 'no-test') groups. Statistical data should then be gathered from this test, and this data subjected to accepted procedures of statistical analysis in which results from the test and control groups are compared. From this analysis conclusions are drawn in relation to the original hypothesis.

An example of a counselling research study following this approach would be a quantitative study into the outcomes of counselling. A simple form of such a study would begin with a hypothesis, for example, 'Clients receiving cognitive-behavioural counselling experience a significant reduction in their level of anxiety.' It would then divide its participants into those who would receive cognitive-behavioural counselling and those who would not. A test measuring levels of anxiety would then be administered to both groups on two or more occasions over a period of time. Results from these tests would then be compared to see if changes in anxiety levels for those who received counselling were significantly different from those who did not. Depending on what these results were, a conclusion could then be formed in relation to the original hypothesis.

Perspective 2: There is no objective meaning to reality; all meaning is a human creation influenced by social and cultural factors

In the 20th century, modern epistemology, as defined in Perspective 1, faced strong challenges. As groups which have previously struggled to find a voice (such as women, black persons, lesbians and gay men) have found expression through various liberation movements there has been an increasing recognition that what has often been taken for objective reality is in fact only the perception of reality of a minority of white, European, ruling-class men. The recognition of the diversity of possible perspectives on reality has tied in with other important intellectual trends. For example, there is increasing academic support for the view that our understanding of reality is shaped by the particular language, symbols and culture of our social context (see, e.g., Mannhelm 1936; Berger and Luckmann 1966; Gergen and McNamee 1992). This also connects with Wittgenstein's (1963) powerful assertion that language is a public, social phenomenon rather than an individual, private one. The implication of Wittgenstein's view is that our ability to speak about reality is therefore shaped and limited by the particular forms of language that we have learnt from our particular linguistic community.

The result of these (and other) social and intellectual trends is that there is now a widespread questioning of the modern epistemological view that it is possible to have an objective view of reality. Rather, many writers now take the view that our knowledge is *socially constructed*, that is to say, our knowledge is fundamentally made up and influenced by the language, symbols, concepts and culture of the particular social context in which we live. In this view, no knowledge is truly objective – indeed, we only see knowledge as objective because our particular social group *believes* that a particular piece of knowledge is objectively true. This social constructionist view of knowledge therefore challenges the modern epistemological belief in the possibility of an objective knowledge of reality. Social constructionist perspectives may therefore be said to lead to *postmodern* views of knowledge.

Postmodern views of knowledge (or epistemologies) can be divided into two important camps. First, there is the postmodern view that there is no inherent meaning in reality and that any meaning in life is a human creation (what I have called Perspective 2). Then there is another brand of postmodern epistemology which believes that there is an objective meaning to life, but that our knowledge of it is always constrained by our social context. I shall discuss this latter view below as Perspective 3.

It is important to recognize that the first of these views does not take the ontological view that there is no such thing as reality. So a person holding this view would not deny the existence of the thing that I am currently sitting on, that I call a 'chair'. They would, however, deny that there is a single, objective meaning or order to reality. In that case, then, it is possible to have many different explanations or accounts of reality, all of which are human creations and all of which are equally valid.

This view has had a number of supporters in this century. Sartre wrote that there is no inherent meaning in life, and that human persons face the challenge of choosing their own meaning. Derrida has developed the 'deconstructionist' critical approach which emphasizes that there is no objective meaning in life and that all attempts to create meaning are simply fragile linguistic conventions (see Widdershoven 1993). Novels by Umberto Eco (1984, 1990) have also challenged the idea of an objective truth about reality, and have criticized those who would pursue this 'truth' with brutality and fanaticism.

Rather than attempting to pursue objective truth, this particular postmodern perspective logically gives rise to research which offers explanations or accounts of reality which seem plausible or pleasing at some experiential or aesthetic level. Such research seeks to compel, to entertain, to draw the reader into a world of meanings that seem useful and interesting (see Gergen 1985: 14). Although this perspective would be open to the use of qualitative research methods, it would not exclude the use of quantitative approaches. Quantitative research methods would be seen, however, not as a means to objective truth but as another socially constructed way, of doing research which can add useful perspectives to our knowledge.

Research arising out of what I have called philosophical Perspective 2 should always be conscious that it is shaped and constrained by the social context of the researcher and the researched. Such research does not therefore seek to generate conclusions that may be generalized across all cases and cultures, but seeks to establish pleasing and plausible descriptions and explanations of specific phenomena. The purpose of such research is not to enable us to know the objective truth about reality (as there is none), but is to give us descriptions and explanations of reality that 'help us to go on', that help us to live in ways that we find meaningful and purposeful.

An example of counselling research in this vein would be a phenomenological study examining clients' experiences of counselling relationships. This would use methods such as in-depth interviews to build up a picture of how the client experienced their counselling. The aim of this research would not be to ascertain the 'truth' of what happened during the counselling, but to render a faithful description of the client's experience. While not claiming to produce objective knowledge, such research is still valuable in helping counsellors to reflect upon their relationships with clients.

Research based on the view of reality and knowledge held by Perspective 2 is not therefore bound to the conventions of positivist scientific research. Rather it is an approach to research that seeks to establish descriptions and explanations that help us to live with a sense of meaning and purpose.

Perspective 3: There is an objective order and meaning in reality, but our knowledge of this is always constrained by our social context

This postmodern perspective shares the epistemological view of Perspective 2 that it is not possible to have a truly objective knowledge of the meaning and order of reality because all knowledge is socially constructed. Because our knowledge is shaped and limited by the linguistic and conceptual resources of our particular social context, our knowledge can be said to be *contextual* and *local* rather than *universal*.

Perspective 3, however, does not share the ontological view of Perspective 2, namely that there is no objective order or meaning to reality. Rather it holds that there is an objective order and meaning to reality, but that our knowledge of it is always partial (contextual and local, rather than universal). In other words, there is an ultimate order and meaning in life, but rather than seeing the whole picture, we can only see as much as the linguistic and conceptual resources of our social context will allow us to see.

John Heron (1988) has acknowledged that we are unable to obtain an objective knowledge of reality – we are always co-creators of meaning, he writes – but he nevertheless accepts that there is an objective order and meaning that our research should seek. The distinction between the *existence* of an objective order and meaning in life, and our inability to *comprehend* objectively the nature of this truth, is also a feature of the work of the contemporary theologians Oliver O'Donovan (1986) and George Lindbeck (1984).

Research arising out of Perspective 3 will share certain characteristics with research emerging from Perspective 2. It will reject any notion of being able to obtain objective truth through scientific research. It will therefore see qualitative research methods as no less useful than quantitative methods; indeed, given the experiential nature of the material often examined within counselling research, qualitative methods may be seen from this perspective as a more preferable route to knowledge about the human person.

What distinguishes research based on Perspective 3 from research based on Perspective 2 is the notion that the description and explanations that emerge from the research have, in some way, to be measured against the objective truth of existence. Whereas research based on Perspective 2 seeks simply to provide material that may help us to live with a sense of meaning and purpose research based on Perspective 3 has to seek truth. The problem here, though, is how we assess to what extent a piece of research provides us with objective truth when we only have at best a partial and perspectival understanding of what that truth is. In other words, if we do not have a pure, objective knowledge of the truth about reality, then how can we recognize truth when we see it?

This problem is almost as old as philosophy itself. In my view there is no clear, objective solution. I am attracted to John Heron's (1988) idea that a piece of research possesses a greater measure of truthfulness if it is able to make coherent and consistent connections between our concepts about existence, our pre-linguistic experience of existence and our ability to act effectively in the world. I recognize, however, that this is simply my preference, and that someone schooled more in traditional approaches to research would see criteria such as reliability and objectivity as more effective measures of truth. It seems to me that ultimately we can have no objective, intellectual certainty about the truthfulness of a piece of research. Rather we are left with the moral responsibility to make judgements about what is truthful as best we can.

An example of a research study conducted on the basis of this third philosophical perspective could be a qualitative case study of a specific counsellor–client relationship. Such research would seek to collect a range of verbal information about the counselling relationship, for example transcripts of sessions, and/or interviews with the counsellor, client and someone close to the client. This data would then be examined to see if any common threads began to emerge. If, for example, there was a convergence of opinion between the counsellor, client and another observer that the counselling process had helped the client to resolve their key concern, then the conclusion that the counselling had been effective would seem to possess a reasonable degree of truthfulness. This study would therefore seek to build conclusions about the counselling relationship on the basis of points of convergence between different perspectives on it (a process referred to by researchers as 'triangulation').

To summarize: if we adopt the philosophical view of Perspective 3, then we are compelled to consider how truthful our research findings are, but we can have no intellectual certainty, about how to do this. Instead of certainty, we bear a moral responsibility to judge what is Good and True in the hope that we will judge wisely. We find ourselves at an existential point where certainty ends, and faith and hope begin.

Wider implications

In the same way that counselling research is based on certain assumptions about reality and truth, the theory and practice of counselling itself rests on particular beliefs about existence. Thus behaviour therapy shares the view of Perspective 1, that there is realilty that we are able to know objectively through the use of reason. The focus of behaviour therapy is therefore upon diagnosing and treating what can be observed objectively about people, that is, their behaviour. Other models of counselling place greater emphasis on the way in which people create meaning through the way in which they interpret their world, and do not make any claims about the existence of any objective truth (see Perspective 2). Examples of such models would be personal-construct counselling, possibly cognitive-behavioural counselling, and person-centred counselling as set out by Carl Rogers. The notion of Perspective 3, that there is objective truth but that our knowledge of it is always constrained, might find expression in some forms of existential counselling or of person-centred counselling as set out by Brian Thorne.

Even from this brief survey, it is evident that the work of counsellors is underpinned by a range of different beliefs about our existence, with different views even being taken by adherents of the same model. It is clear from our earlier discussion that counselling research can also be grounded in a range of different philosophical views. As counselling becomes an increasingly sophisticated and professional discipline, a key part of this process must be the development of a critical awareness of the values and beliefs that underpin our work. Initially this must involve a process of identifying the core beliefs for ourselves as theorists, practitioners and researchers. Then follows the task of exploring the adequacy of these beliefs in accounting for our existence.

References

Berger, P. and Luckmann, T. (1966) *The Social Construction of Reality: A Treatise in the Sociology of Knowledge*, London: Penguin.

Eco, U. (1984) *The Name of the Rose*, London: Picador.

Eco, U. (1990) *Foucault's Pendulum*, London: Picador.

Gergen, K. (1985) 'Social constructionist inquiry: context and implications', in K. Gergen and S. Davis (eds), *The Social Construction of the Person*, New York: Springer Verlag, pp. 3–18.

Gergen, K. and McNamee, S. (eds) (1992) *Therapy as Social Construction*, London: Sage.

Harre, R. (1981) 'The positivist-empiricist approach and its alternative', in P. Reason and J. Rowan (eds), *Human Inquiry*, Chichester: Wiley, pp. 3–17.

Heron, J. (1998) 'Validity in co-operative inquiry', in P. Reason (ed.), *Human Inquiry in Action*, Chichester: Wiley, pp. 40–59.

Lindbeck, G. (1984) *The Nature of Doctrine*, London: SPCK.

Mannheim, K. (1936) *Ideology and Utopia: An Introduction to the Sociology of Knowledge*, London: Routledge & Kegan Paul.

McLeod, J. (1994) *Doing Counselling Research,* London: Sage.

O'Donovan, O. (1986) *Resurrection and Moral Order*, Leicester: IVP.

Robson, C. (1993) *Real World Research*, Oxford: Blackwell.

Strauss, A. and Corbin, J. (1990) *Basics in Qualitative Research*, London: Sage.

Widdershoven, G. (1993) 'The story of life: hermeneutic perspectives on the relationship between narrative and life history', R. Josselson and A. Lieblich (eds), *The Narrative Study of Lives*, London: Sage, 1–20.

Wittgenstein, L. (1963) *Philosophical Investigations*, Oxford: Blackwell.

Discussion issues

1 What is truth? Is it always tainted by the observer's perception and beliefs, which are embedded within the cultural and social milieu?
2 Which perspective provided by Lynch do you favour and why?
3 Is there a reality that we are able to know through reason?
4 The philosophical aspects of counselling research are unimportant to most counsellors. True or false?

76

Critical Subjectivity

Use of Self in Counselling Research

William West

> Most therapy is based on the pre-supposition that both client and counsellor are able to reflect on their personal experience. In the past, research has been conducted in a way that denies reflexivity. (McLeod 1994: 189)

Whenever we decide to undertake any form of research we are faced with the decision of what methodology to use. Our choice can be an ideological one based on how we see the world, or it can be pragmatic, based on what research questions we are wanting to explore or answer, or on what type of research we think funding bodies are likely to support, or even on what is the pet methodology of our research supervisor.

What I want to consider here are two approaches to research that feel close to the practice of counselling and hence more readily accessible to counsellors undertaking research. These are: the human inquiry approach whose key exponent is Peter Reason (Reason and Rowan 1981; Reason and Heron 1986; Reason 1988, 1994); and the heuristic approach of Clark Moustakes (Douglass and Moustakas 1985; Moustakas 1990, 1994; West 1998). Both approaches are intrinsically qualitative but neither is necessarily incompatible with a quantitative approach. For example, a human inquiry group might well consider undertaking a quantitative survey, and a heuristic inquiry might choose to test out its findings via a quantitative questionnaire.

These two approaches share a common feature which puts them clearly in the qualitative camp: they both make use of the researcher's involvement with the research, as a source of data and as a way of making sense of the research. Reason (1994) argues for what he calls critical subjectivity, that is, an acceptance of our involvement with those we research, but an involvement that is 'critical, self-aware, discriminating and informed' (Reason 1994: 11). This may seem both challenging and daunting to the novice researcher. However, counsellors working within the psychodynamic or person-centred traditions are familiar with the use of self in their work. Person-centred counsellors use empathy and congruence to guide their work, while psychodynamic counsellors put trust in working with their countertransference, that is, the way they are affected by being with their client. Counsellors, then, are used to monitoring the way their clients affect them and in using this data to guide their work. Increasingly this process is seen as an holistic one involving body, mind, emotions and spirit.

This chapter was first published in *Counselling*, Journal of the British Association for Counselling, vol. 9, no. 3, pp. 228–30 (1998), and based on a paper presented at the second BAC Research Conference in Birmingham University in March 1996.

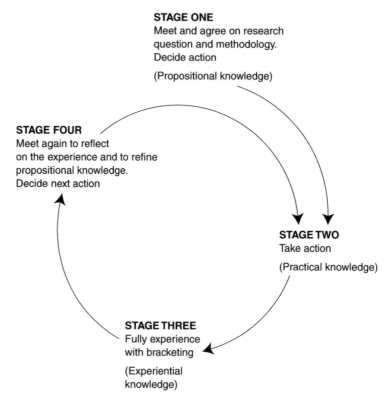

Figure 76.1   *The human inquiry cycle*

Human inquiry

> The essence of a co-operative experiential inquiry is an aware and self-critical movement
> between experience and reflection which goes through several cycles as ideas, practice, and
> experience are systematically honed and refined. (Reason 1988: 6)

Figure 76.1 illustrates the cyclical nature of human inquiry. As an example of this, consider my doctoral research into counselling, psychotherapy and healing (West 1995,
1996, 1997). Part of this research involved a human inquiry group meeting for four
weekends over the course of a year. When such a group meets to consider doing human
inquiry research it may find that there is not sufficient agreement or commitment by
group members to the process to make the research possible. In the case of my doctoral
study there was. This still left the question of how.

One way chosen to explore more fully what we meant by therapy and healing was to
use a Gestalt therapy exercise in which we stuck labels on to chairs describing different
types of practitioner: e.g., 'humanistic', 'transpersonal', 'laying on of hands', 'healing that
just happens', 'talk counselling'. Group members were then invited to choose the label
which most clearly defined their work and to speak in turn from that label. This
represents stage two of the human inquiry cycle. (In later inquiry cycles we chose which

label most attracted us that day and also dialogued between labels.) Group members strove to experience fully the action taken (stage three). On reflecting on this experience (stage four) a deep debate ensued about the use of labels, about the difference between 'the map and the territory' and about what became a shared desire not to be labelled. For a fuller discussion of the use of human inquiry groups in counselling research, see West (1996).

Demands on the human inquiry researcher

The demands on a human inquiry researcher include:

1 Having to share the research with the group, including the managing of role conflicts. For instance, the group may well want the initiator to stay in a leading role, tell people what to do, etc. Having a co-initiator of such a group would help.
2 Allowing the group to define what is explored and how. This involves the researcher letting go of what s/he wants to know, to discover what the group wants to know and explore.
3 Data collection, analysis and presentation, which is a key issue for all qualitative research. Most qualitative research projects gather more data than can be analysed. Human inquiry research, with its emphasis on the whole person, on experiential knowing, raises its own issues about representation of research data (Reason 1994). Heron (1992) argues for the use of non-orthodox forms of presentation, including the use of poetry, artwork and movement to capture this whole person form of knowing. It is important that the group members have some input into the final report. They should at least comment on drafts of the report, but preferably have a more central role in its writing. An academic report is only one version of various possible reports that could be produced by a human inquiry group.
4 Keeping the group focused on the research question represents a challenge as the group can become lost in either activism or theorizing, stuck in chaos or avoidance of conflict, in collusion or in not supporting group members. It is important that the group is not afraid to experience chaos (Reason and Heron 1986). Time spent on movement work, yoga, Tai Chi, time for group members to raise niggles, all help to enable the group to function effectively as a human inquiry group (Reason and Heron 1986).
5 Closure is a key issue. How to know when the group is finished? Does it close when enough data is collected, when nothing new is happening, or is there a natural end? Should it end at all? My group decided to continue to meet as a kind of peer supervision group around these issues of therapy and healing, and has since offered consultative support to people outside the group.
6 The role of the research supervisor is crucial with human inquiry research, and s/he will need knowledge of group processes and preferably a familiarity with human inquiry research.

Heuristic research

The power of heuristic inquiry lies in its potential for disclosing truth. Through exhaustive self-search, dialogues with others, and creative depictions of experience, a comprehensive knowledge is generated .... Passionate yet disciplined commitment is vital. (Douglass and Moustakas 1985: 40)

Heuristic research is a way of exploring deeply some phenomenon which we wish to know more about. We start by acknowledging and exploring our own understanding of the phenomenon before engaging with other people's understanding. Finally, having gathered data from a variety of sources, we come to a new realization of the phenomenon which we then write up. Heuristic research is crucially different from many other forms of research in its insistence on not only including the researcher in the research, but in allowing the data analysis to occur via tacit processes within the researcher. The test of the success of an heuristic inquiry, indeed its whole validity, rests on how the report produced by the researcher is received by those who shared in the research and the wider community of people interested.

According to Moustakas (1990) there are six phases to heuristic research:

1 *Initial engagement*. This begins with inner dialogue, an exploring of possible research questions, and it must include a passionate need to know. Without this passion there will not be sufficient energy committed to complete the research.

2 *Immersion* – a deep engagement with the research, awake, asleep, in dreams, fully living the research. In my doctoral study mentioned above I several times dreamt I received supervision on my research. I was also shown a diagram in a dream that made a lot of sense to me but when I woke up I could not understand it. Six months later I was writing an interim report on my research and was stuck for a rounding-off paragraph. Suddenly the diagram sprang to mind and at last I understood it consciously.

3 *Incubation* – a retreat to allow tacit and unconscious processes to occur. This is a time to stand back from the research and put it on the 'back burner' for a while, and to get on with some other task. This should then lead on to the next stage.

4 *Illumination* – in which new awareness, new insights, emerge leading to a synthesis. This is a natural process if one is open to tacit and intuitive knowledge. Qualities and themes relating to the question emerge into consciousness. However, this cannot be forced or striven for. Illumination can be helped by putting the research aside for a while, perhaps engaging in some other task.

I remember, after the first meeting of my human inquiry group, how I sat in the library at Keele with the transcript of that first weekend in front of me. It was just prior to an academic supervision session and I wanted to present something of it to my supervisor. The more I read, the less it made sense to me; I felt leaden and uncreative. I began to daydream; suddenly a sentence used by one of the group members came to mind about there being a bridge between healing and therapy. In my mind's eye I saw three interlocking circles consisting of the words therapy, healing and spirituality, and there were various bridges between the circles. I had been given a vision of a map of my research. I had something to offer my supervisor. I was re-energized about the research.

5 *Explication* – fully examining what has emerged, really teasing out that new understanding. In the above case, labelling the bridges, trying out different versions of the circle map, with them not overlapping, overlapping a bit, a lot, containing each other and so on.

6 *Creative synthesis* – telling the story, producing the final report, maybe using diagrams, artwork, poetry, movement, with perhaps several reports according to who the audience is. Moustakas advocates sending a draft version of this final report to all those who have contributed to the research to check how complete the report is.

It is important to appreciate that these phases are not completed in a linear fashion, that there is movement between the different stages, backwards and forwards towards the final synthesis.

Demands on the heuristic researcher

1   A passionate need to know about the research question or themes, otherwise the research will not happen or be completed.
2   The need to allow the research to take one over, to live it fully.
3   The need for patience and trust, especially during the incubation phase awaiting illumination.
4   Facing the challenge of synthesis can be tough. It is important to check with and include comments and feedback from those one has researched with. The final report may resemble what Denzin and Lincoln called a '*bricolage*': 'a complex, dense, reflexive, collagelike creation that represents the researcher's images, understandings, and interpretations of the world or phenomena under analysis' (Denzin and Lincoln 1994: 2–3).
5   The role of the research supervisor is critical in supporting the researcher through these testing phases of heuristic research.

Conclusion

I hope that I have made it clear that both human inquiry and heuristics are suitable for at least some forms of counselling research. However, neither is an easy option, and both demand good research supervision. Both are exciting, engaging, frustrating and life changing. Both are able to capture something of the real meaning and experience of counselling, are very close to the practice of counselling, and therefore represent valuable forms of qualitative counselling research.

References

Denzin, N.K. and Lincoln, Y.S. (eds) (1994) *Handbook of Qualitative Research*, Thousand Oaks, CA: Sage.
Douglass, B.G. and Moustakas, C. (1985) 'Heuristic inquiry: the internal search to know', *Journal of Humanistic Psychology*, 25 (3): 39–55.
Heron, J. (1992) *Feeling and Personhood*, London: Sage.
McLeod, J. (1994) *Doing Counselling Research*, London: Sage.
Moustakas, C. (1990) *Heuristic Research, Design, Methodology, and Applications*, London: Sage.
Moustakas, C. (1994) *Phenomenological Research Methods*, London: Sage.
Reason, P. (ed.) (1988) *Human Inquiry in Action*, London: Sage.
Reason, P. (ed.) (1994) *Participation in Human Inquiry*, London: Sage.
Reason, P. and Heron, J. (1986) 'Research with people: the paradigm of co-operative experiential inquiry', *Person Centred Review*, 1 (4): 456–76.
Reason, P. and Rowan, J. (eds) (1981) *Human Inquiry: A Sourcebook of New Paradigm Research*, Chichester: John Wiley & Sons.

West, W. (1995) 'Integrating psychotherapy and healing: an inquiry into the experiences of counsellors and psychotherapists whose work includes healing' (doctoral thesis), Department of Applied Social Studies, Keele University.

West, W. (1996) 'Using human inquiry groups in counselling research', *British Journal of Guidance and Counselling*, 24 (3): 347–55.

West, W. (1997) 'Integrating counselling, psychotherapy and healing: an inquiry into counsellors and psychotherapists whose work includes healing', *British Journal of Guidance and Counselling*, 25 (3): 291–310.

West, W. (1998) 'Passionate research: heuristics and the use of self in counselling research', *Changes*, 16 (1): 60–1.

Discussion issues

1 What are the overlaps and differences between counselling and qualitative research interviews?
2 What difficulties arise in obtaining informed consent for exploratory research and how may they be dealt with?
3 What are the key research supervision needs in qualitative counselling research?
4 The heuristic researcher should allow the research to take him or her over, to live it fully.

77

Do Brief Interventions Reduce Waiting Times for Counselling?

Judith M. Brech and Peter L. Agulnik

Over the last years, there has been a steady growth in demand for counselling and psychotherapy services. New services have sprung up throughout the country under the auspices of both professional and voluntary agencies. The NHS has responded through increased availability of psychotherapy from hospital bases and the development of new counselling services in the community, particulary those within the primary care setting.

Despite this growth, demand may exceed supply, and within the NHS resources are inevitably limited. The issue arises of how best to deploy these resources in the face of ever-growing demand. This is a particular problem within open-access services, where there are no intermediaries to filter referrals. High demand is one of the consequences of easy accessibility to the service provided. Where supply of the service cannot keep up with this demand, accessibility is in turn reduced by virtue of the length of the waiting list that develops. Within the health services, long waiting times for first appointments appear to be associated with high drop-out rates before patients are even seen and treatment eventually started (Orme and Boswell 1991; Dockerty 1992).

The Isis Centre, which is an open-access NHS facility, was set up in 1970 to provide a responsive community mental health service, to which people could refer themselves directly, as an alternative to referral to specialist services through the primary care system. The rationale for setting up such an open-access service has been set out elsewhere (Agulnik et al. 1976) and the issues have been further developed in a full description and evaluation of the service undertaken in 1980 (Oldfield 1983).

The Centre is in a small street close to central Oxford, and looks, from the outside, like one of the shops which surround it. It only has a small core counselling staff, consisting of two whole-time equivalent posts held by a co-ordinator/counsellor and two part-time senior counsellors. This small team is enchanced by some additional hours provided by professionals otherwise employed by the Oxfordshire Mental Health Care Trust, and work contributed by up to twelve honorary staff, some of whom are members of the Centre's diploma course in counselling practice.

Despite having created these extra resources, the Isis Centre has still not been able to keep up with the growing demand for its services. In the early days people were seen promptly but, as demand for the service grew, it was inevitable that a waiting list should develop. In 1990, the average waiting time for on appointment was five months and some clients had to wait for more than six months. This was a cause for concern as it clearly reduced the accessibility and responsiveness of the service, these being key features in its

This chapter was first published in *Counselling*, Journal of the British Association for Counselling, vol. 7, no. 4, pp. 322–6 (1996).

original conception. It also seemed likely that it resulted in a less efficient use of resources. People were no longer being seen close to the time when help was requested. Evidence available suggests that this is when clients are most motivated and most accessible to change (Caplan 1964). Additional costs were also incurred, as a proportion of these were likely to have appointments booked for them which they failed to keep.

Of the 100 first clients joining the Isis Centre waiting list in 1990, only 49 eventually attended an appointment at the Centre. Some would consider this as failing over 50 per cent of those in need; others would suggest that this is an appropriate mechanism for selecting out those clients for whom counselling is really necessary. In a system that relies on self-referral, there is, however, additional cause for concern in relying on such a crude rationing instrument as a waiting list. It may be that those who are most in need are those who are least likely to have the resources to cope with a long delay or be able to find alternative sources of help. The Centre has also had anecdotal evidence from GPs, who become reluctant to recommend the Centre's services because of the long waiting time.

Strategies that have been attempted in managing a waiting list include an initial assessment procedure, requiring clients to complete and return questionnaires and offering reduced numbers of sessions (Baggately 1993; Eynon and Gladwell 1993). The Centre chose the latter strategy, offering brief, time-limited counselling and targeting clients who had recently joined the waiting list. It was felt that this strategy was most in keeping with the normal functioning of the Isis Centre, both with respect to treatment philosophy and the fact that a significant percentage of all clients only attend for up to four sessions. If such clients could be targeted, would this make a significant impact on the waiting times without detriment to the clinical quality of the service offered?

The study

In January 1991, due to a change in personnel, some short-term funding became available and it was decided to use this temporary funding to try and reduce the length of the waiting list.

It has been a key aspect of the counselling service provided at the Centre that clients should first meet directly with their counsellor, rather than have a separate initial assessment interview, and that client and counsellor should then plan together the length of their contract. Appointments are usually on a weekly basis. Under this arrangement it has been shown over time that approximately 40 per cent of clients have between one and four counselling sessions, a further 40 per cent between five and twenty sessions, leaving 20 per cent with counselling contracts extending beyond six months.

The new strategy involved five experienced counsellors being employed to provide brief, time-limited counselling. Clients who had newly joined the waiting list were offered the option of being seen promptly for up to four sessions, with the understanding that it would be possible to return to the waiting list for longer-term counselling, if this were considered appropriate. The period for which counsellors were specifically employed to provide brief counselling extended from the beginning of January to the end of July 1991.

The purpose of this audit is to examine the impact of this strategy on the Centre's waiting list. Clinical evaluation of the process and outcome of the four-session counselling, including a survey of clients' views, is considered elsewhere (Brech and Agulnik 1996).

Implementation of the brief intervention strategy

In January 1991, letters were sent to people who had recently joined the waiting list offering them an immediate contract of up to four counselling sessions at weekly intervals as an alternative to remaining on the waiting list. Letters were sent to all clients, except those where there was a specific contra-indication from information given at the point of first contact to such a short-term intervention.

The four-session option continued to be offered both to people newly joining the waiting list and to those already on the waiting list – the list was gradually worked through backwards, eventually to include clients who joined the waiting list from the beginning of October 1990.

In total, from the beginning of January 1991 to the end of July 1991 the four-session option was offered to 154 people. Of these, 88 clients (57 per cent) accepted and attended at least the first session. They form the study group for this paper. Twenty-five clients (16 per cent) refused the four-session option and took their names off the waiting list. Thirty-four (22 per cent) refused the four-session option but chose to remain on the waiting list for longer-term counselling. Eight clients (5 per cent) did not reply at all.

Of the 88 clients who accepted:

14 per cent used 1 session
20 per cent used 2 sessions
19 per cent used 3 sessions
48 per cent used all 4 sessions

Looking at a year-on view, an initial effect of the strategy appears to have increased the overall proportion of all Isis Centre clients using up to four sessions from approximately 40 per cent to 58 per cent.

Effect on the waiting list numbers

The impact of the brief intervention strategy on the waiting list appears to have been favourable. More clients were seen without there being any increase in counselling resources available. In the period January to the end of July 1991, 183 new clients were seen. This compares with 102 new clients seen in the same period in 1990 and 125 new clients seen in the same period in 1992.

Locum counsellors were specifically employed during this time to provide the four-session counselling, using the salary of the member of the counselling staff who had recently left. There was, however, no significant increase in the total counselling hours available for this period.

Average counselling hours available per month were:

January–July 1989 261
January–July 1990 219
January–July 1991 222

At the beginning of January 1991, there were 194 people on the waiting list; by the end of July 1991, there were 117. This reduction in the size of the waiting list cannot be explained by any decline in the numbers of people approaching the Isis Centre. In the period January to the end of July 1990, 218 people joined the waiting list and 212 during the same period in 1991.

Effect on waiting times for first appointments

Most importantly, the reduction in numbers on the waiting list also resulted in a decrease in the length of waiting times for all Isis Centre clients, that is, both those taking the four-session option and those who elected to remain on the ordinary waiting list.

Eighty per cent of four-session clients who had joined the waiting list before the end of January 1991 waited for more than a month for their first appointment but, for clients referred between February and June 1991, this figure had reduced to 10 per cent and again to 5 per cent for those referred between July and the beginning of October 1991.

Thus there was a progressive reduction in the waiting period for those electing to take four sessions. While this was expected, significantly, waiting times also reduced for non-four-session clients.

For non-four-session clients joining the waiting list between October 1990 and the end of January 1991, 36 per cent had to wait more than six months for their first appointment and a further 34 per cent between four and six months. For the equivalent cohort of clients joining the waiting list between the beginning of February and the beginning of June 1991, only 11 per cent had to wait more than six months; most (38 per cent) waited for five months and a further 20 per cent waited for six months. No clients who referred themselves from the beginning of June to the beginning of October 1991 had to wait more than six months for a first appointment and only 20 per cent waited for more than four months. Just over 50 per cent of those who had referred themselves in this time waited for fours months and approximately 30 per cent waited for three months or less.

Effect on non-attendance rates for first appointments

As anticipated, the implementation of the brief intervention strategy, probably because of the reduced waiting times, also had the effect of increasing the proportion of people on the waiting list who did attend for a first appointment. Out of 113 four-session clients, 25 (i.e., 22 per cent) joining the waiting list between January and July 1991, declined or did not attend their first appointment. This compares with 75 out of 135 non-four-sessions clients (i.e., 56 per cent) joining the waiting list in the same period.

Looking at the original group of 154 people who were offered four-session counselling between January and July 1991, there was an overall non-attendance rate of 32 per cent (see Table 77.1).

The drop-out rate for the first 100 people on the waiting list in 1990 was 51 per cent; for the first 100 on the waiting list in 1991 this figure had reduced to 36 per cent.

Returns to the waiting list

While the initial impact of the brief counselling strategy on the waiting list was undoubtedly favourable, the benefit may have been offset by a relatively high rate of return to the waiting list. Of the 88 four-session clients in the study group, 19 (i.e., 22 per cent) had put their names back on the waiting list for further counselling by the end of 1991.

Table 77.1 *People offered four-session counselling between January and July 1991*

Total number	Number 154	% 100	%
No. who accepted and came to 4 sessions only	61	40	58
No. who accepted 4 sessions and subsequently returned to the waiting list	27	18	
No. who refused 4 sessions, attended for longer-term counselling but had no more than 4 sessions	7	5	11
No. who refused 4 sessions, attended for long term and had more than 4 sessions (average = 17)	9	6	
No. dropped out who were originally offered 4 sessions	25	16	32
No. refused 4 sessions, stayed on long-term waiting list but subsequently dropped out	17	11	
No. who did not reply to letters	8	5	

Sixteen of these clients had done so in discussion with their counsellors immediately after the end of the four sessions. A further eight clients had rejoined the waiting list by the end of 1992, that is, in total a 31 per cent return to the waiting list. Of these 27 people who returned to the waiting list, 22 were subsequently offered and accepted an appointment, one of these being an assessment for group therapy.

This would suggest an overall re-attendance rate for four-session clients of approximately 25 per cent. Although there are not the relevant statistics available to make a true comparison, this would appear to be significantly higher than the normal re-attendance rates at the Isis Centre. Figures over the years indicate that approximately 12 per cent of clients report having previously had counselling at the Isis Centre (Isis Centre Annual Reports).

Comparison of the uptake of longer-term counselling by members of the study group with those who had rejected the four-session counselling option

Of the 88 four-session clients in the study group, 27 had returned to the waiting list by the end of 1992; 25 of these were waiting for longer-term individual counselling. Of these 25 clients, five did not attend an appointment when offered, two had up to four sessions, four had between five and ten counselling sessions, and 14 (56 per cent) had more than ten sessions.

This contrasts with the outcome for those 33 clients who rejected the four-session option in favour of waiting for longer-term counselling. Of these 33 clients, 17 (52 per cent) did not attend a session at all (i.e., broadly comparable with the average drop-out rate from the waiting list); seven had up to four sessions; two had between five and ten sessions and only seven (21 per cent) had more than eleven sessions. Looking at those clients who chose the long-term counselling option and who eventually did attend, only 56 per cent had more than four sessions of counselling, and 44 per cent had more than ten sessions. By contrast, 90 per cent of the ex-four-session clients who re-attended had more than four sessions and 70 per cent had more than ten.

Ex-four-session clients appear to have had a higher rate of take up of longer-term counselling.

Discussion

The effect of the brief intervention strategy over the period in which it was implemented was to reduce the number of people on the Isis Centre waiting list and this resulted in significantly reduced waiting times for *all* Isis Centre clients.

It is, however, possible that, because of the higher rate of return to the waiting list and the higher total proportion of referred clients being seen (i.e., reduced non-attendance rate), this effect could be eroded with time and might eventually lead to longer waiting times for those clients who rejected the four-session option. Against this, however, would still have to be set the benefits of a higher proportion of clients being seen relatively promptly and the consequently reduced non-attendance rate.

The clinical advantages and disadvantages of the brief intervention strategy, both from the counsellors' and the clients' perspectives, are fully described elsewhere (Brech and Agulnik 1996). Of particular note in that study was a high level of agreement between counsellors' and clients' accounts of outcome.

In brief, it seemed that most clients who took up the four-session option gained significant benefit from the experience: for 25 per cent the counselling was useful and sufficient; for a further 50 per cent it was a useful beginning, which also helped people to plan the possibility of further, longer-term work, either at the Isis Centre or elsewhere. (A significant number of people went into private therapy or to Relate.) Interestingly, those four-session clients who returned to the Isis Centre waiting list for longer-term work had significantly higher uptake rates than those who had rejected the four-session option in favour of longer-term counselling in the first place.

There was little evidence that benefit derived from the four sessions was superficial or of temporary effect; rather, the main danger seemed to be that many people did not anticipate how quickly they would become deeply involved in the process, and some were left with painful and unresolved feelings. In the case of a few people, these feelings were very intense, and it could be argued that, for them, the four sessions did more harm than good.

Overall, the brief intervention strategy was popular with clients. While most who accepted the four-session option would have liked more sessions to have been available, the majority considered that, in retrospect, it had been worth accepting the limited number of sessions in return for being seen promptly.

Because of the encouraging result of the audit presented in this paper, it was decided to continue the brief intervention strategy, albeit in a more limited way, subject to the availability of sufficiently experienced counsellors.

Implications for other services

Given that the four sessions were only sufficient for a minority of clients (25 per cent) the main justification for the strategy would seem to be the success in reducing waiting times for the service as a whole. A watch would, however, need to be kept on the waiting list to ensure that this continued to be the case in the longer term. An additional benefit was that the strategy also acted as a successful informal selection filter for longer-term therapy.

A prerequisite for the success of such a brief intervention strategy would seem to be the use of sufficiently experienced counsellors because of the technical practice issues involved. Experience is necessary in understanding and managing the intense transference which can emerge, even within very brief interventions. Counsellors also need to be able to sustain the dynamic tension between aiming at a focused and completed piece of work with each client and being open to looking at future options for those clients who need further help. It seemed to assist many clients, and the Centre's waiting list, when counsellors enabled clients to consider a range of other options available. It was, however, also very valuable to some clients that there remained that of returning to see the same counsellor.

A few clients accepted the four-session option out of a sense of desperation, as they felt unable to wait for the longer-term counselling they really needed. Most of these clients felt needy and disappointed at the end of four sessions. It would seem important to devise a mechanism which might filter out such especially vulnerable clients, ideally before they were offered the four-session option, otherwise afterwards, by offering them appropriate further help.

This study may be of relevance to other counselling services offering open access, or NHS psychotherapy departments with a high demand for services.

References

Agulnik, P.L., Holroyd, P. and Mandelbrote, B. (1976) 'The Isis Centre: a counselling service within the National Health Service', *British Medical Journal*, 2: 355–7.

Baggately, M. (1993) 'Improving the attendance for new psychiatric outpatient referrals', *Psychiatric Bulletin*, 17: 347–9.

Brech, J.M. and Agulnik, P.L. (1996) 'The advantages and disadvantages of a brief intervention strategy in a community counselling service' (submitted for publication).

Caplan, G. (1964) *Principles of Preventative Psychiatry*, New York: Basic Books; London: Tavistock Publications.

Dockerty, J.D. (1992) 'Outpatient clinic nonarrivals and cancellations', *New Zealand Medical Journal*, 22: 147–9.

Eynon, T. and Gladwell, S. (1993) 'Too high a hurdle? The use of pre-assessment questionnaires in psychotherapy', *Psychiatric Bulletin*, 17: 149–51.

Isis Centre Annual Reports (1988–1992).

Oldfield, S. (1983) *The Counselling Relationship*, London: Routledge & Kegan Paul.

Orme, D.R. and Boswell, D. (1991) 'The pre-intake drop-out at a community mental health centre', *Community Mental Health Journal*, 27 (5): 375–9.

Discussion issues

1　What are the advantages and disadvantages of offering potential clients the option of receiving four-session therapy instead of longer-term therapy?

2　Is it sufficient for experienced counsellors to offer brief therapy or do they require specific training in this type of work?

3　What are your views regarding the results of this study?

4　Many counsellors believe that clients are being short-changed when they are offered brief therapy. Do you agree?

78

Primary Care Counsellors' Experiences of Supervision

Mary Burton, Penny Henderson and Graham Curtis Jenkins

Nearly all psychotherapy and counselling trainings require students to be in supervision, and the British Association for Counselling requires continuous ongoing supervision of all their members who work as counsellors. There is much anecdotal but limited empirical evidence of the impact of supervision on clinical practice. Clinicians often say they learn more from their personal therapy and supervision than from other parts of their training, but few studies have examined the impact of supervision in clinical work or supervisees' satisfaction with the supervision they receive.

The literature on clinical supervision is vast and covers a number of disciplines – psychoanalysis, psychotherapy, psychiatry, clinical and counselling psychology, social work and counselling – as well as a variety of theoretical orientations – psychodynamic, cognitive-behavioural, humanistic, systemic, eclectic/integrative, and brief focused therapy, to name but a few. The supervision of group, family and couples psychotherapy was excluded from the literature review for the present study, narrowing the focus to work with individuals. Nevertheless more than 1,500 relevant books, book chapters or journal articles were found in *Psychological Abstracts and Medline*. No attempt will be made to summarize this complex literature here, although a bibliography on clinical supervision is available in Burton (1998) and Carroll (1996).

In his review of the counselling supervision literature in Britain and the USA, Carroll (1996) observed that the American literature has concentrated on theoretical models while UK studies have focused more on the practice of supervision. As counsellors move in greater numbers into the primary care setting in this country, interest in the supervision of counsellors in primary care has moved sharply into focus. Until now little or no empirical data have been available to inform purchasers and providers. We wished to study how the supervision needs of counsellors in primary care were currently being met across the UK. Our research questions included the following:

What is the impact of supervision on the clinical work of counsellors in primary care?
How well does supervision meet counsellors' needs at the moment?
What are counsellors' experienced difficulties with supervision?
How good is the 'match' between supervisors' and counsellors' theoretical orientations
    in the primary care setting?

This chapter was first published in *Counselling*, Journal of the British Association for Counselling, vol. 9, no. 2, pp. 122–33 (1998).

How satisfied are counsellors with their supervision?
How adequate is supervision in addressing problems unique to the primary care setting?

Method

Items for the eight-page postal questionnaire were drawn from published and unpublished sources:

- counsellors' and supervisors' age, years of supervised counselling experience, education, core professional discipline, place(s) of work, and theoretical orientation;
- counsellor/supervisor congruence of theoretical model and personal style (Steinhelber et al. 1984);
- frequency and type of supervision, choice of supervisor, payment for supervision, supervisor's training in supervision, supervision techniques (Hart 1982);
- positive and negative impacts of supervision on clinical work;
- details of the primary care counselling setting and common problems in primary care (Hoag 1992; Jones et al. 1994; Monach and Monro 1995; Papadopoulos and Bor 1995; Watts and Bor 1995; House 1996; see Chapter 22);
- the supervision contract and counsellor satisfaction with aspects of supervision (Doehrman 1976; Nelson 1978; Greben 1979; Wallerstein 1981; Casement 1985, 1993; Allen et al. 1986; Borders and Leddick 1987; Mollon 1989; Crick 1991; Bernard and Goodyear 1992; Shanfield et al. 1993; UCL 1993; Carroll 1996);
- the counsellors' openness to learning from the supervisor (Doehrman 1976);
- learning from negative counselling outcomes and 'impasse' with the supervisor (Ruskin 1994);
- the supervisor's support of the counsellor's personal development (Moriarty 1995);
- the counsellors' personal therapy and the theoretical orientation of their personal therapist(s); the impact of therapy on counselling work (Glass 1986; Burns and Holloway 1989; Gerin and Orlinsky 1991);
- issues at the interface between supervision and personal therapy;
- abusive supervisory relationship (Carroll 1996).

Three UK counselling supervisors contributed items (Ros Draper, Joan Foster and Antonia Murphy). Most questions requested answers on a five-point Likert scale, but some were left open-ended to encourage detailed replies. A copy of the questionnaire is available from the first author on request.

The subjects were 90 counsellors working in primary health care (general practice). Group A consisted of 64 recent graduates of Diploma in Primary Care Counselling programmes in London, Bristol, Manchester and Strathclyde. The total response rate in this group was 49 (77 per cent); questionnaires were fully completed by 43 (67 per cent). In order to ensure that Group A was not idiosyncratic or highly selected, Group B, a one-in-ten random sample comprising 103 non-diplomates working as counsellors in primary care were selected from the mailing list of the Counselling in Primary Care Trust, matched with Group A for age, gender and geographical area. The total response rate in this group was 60 (58 per cent); questionnaires were fully completed by 47 subjects (46 per cent).

Table 78.1 *Counsellors and their supervisors*

Counsellor's age: mean 49 years (range 29–73)
Gender: 92% female
Years of supervised counselling experience: mean 7 years (range 1–18)
Counsellor's educational background:

10%	6%	2%	82%
First degree	Masters degree	Doctoral degree	Other qualifications

Counsellor's
  professional discipline:

Counsellor (BAC accredited)	12%	Counsellor (non-BAC accredited)	59%
Counselling psychologist	2%	Clinical psychologist	0%
Psychotherapist	4%	Social worker	10%
Nurse/CPN	9%	Other	3%

Counsellor's place(s) of work: GP surgery 63% Outside GP surgery 2% Both 36%

Supervisor's age: mean 50 years (range 34–70)
Gender: 72% female
Approx. years of counselling experience: mean 17 years (range 4–32)
Supervisor's educational background:

4%	22%	10%	44%	19%
First degree	Masters degree	Doctoral degree	Other qualifications	Don't know

Supervisor's
  professional discipline:

Counsellor (BAC accredited)	15%	Counsellor (non-BAC accredited)	22%
Counselling psychologist	7%	Clinical psychologist	11%
Psychotherapist	22%	Social worker	8%
Nurse/CPN	7%	Psychiatrist	3%
GP	1%	Other	2%

Supervisor's place(s) of work: GP surgery 8% Outside GP surgery 75% Both 18%

Chaser letters were sent to subjects who had not returned questionnaires within a month of posting. Reasons for not returning questionnaires included no primary care counselling experience (4), not practising as a counsellor (4), ill health (1), address unknown (1), and travelling abroad (1). One respondent who declined to return a questionnaire wondered why the research had been commissioned, why it had been commissioned now, what use the results would be put to, and what 'agenda' lay behind the research. Some questionnaires were returned blank or very partially completed. Two were passed by the addressee to counsellors currently working in primary care. The response rate of recent diplomates was higher than non-diplomates, possibly because they had received bursaries from the Counselling in Primary Care Trust who commissioned this study.

Results

Very few significant differences were found between Groups A and B at the 0.01 level, enhancing confidence in the representativeness of the sample. Counsellor and supervisor characteristics are compared in Table 78.1.

Where more than one discipline was given, the core professional discipline was scored. Most counsellors were non-BAC accredited. Counsellors held a variety of 'other' qualifications: counselling diplomas and certificates, qualifications in nursing, social work, occupational therapy, massage, teaching, transactional analysis, and psychotherapy. Sixty-three per cent counselled only in a GP surgery; 36 per cent worked both in a surgery and elsewhere. Other settings included private practice, employee assistance programmes, community mental health teams, NHS Trust hospitals, clinical psychology departments, and counselling agencies in the private sector. Several counsellors worked in more than one GP surgery.

Supervisors came from a variety of professional disciplines including counselling, clinical and counselling psychology, psychotherapy, social work, nursing and psychiatry. Supervisors' 'other' qualifications included family therapy, analytical psychology, Gestalt, occupational therapy, psychoanalysis and group analysis. There were more male supervisors than male counsellors in the sample. The male supervisors were mostly BAC or non-BAC accredited counsellors and psychotherapists, although clinical and counselling psychologists, social workers, nurses and psychiatrists were also represented. Only 25 per cent of supervisors worked clinically in a GP surgery. Other places of work included private practice, NHS Trust hospitals, universities, counselling agencies in the private sector, and counselling and psychotherapy training organizations.

Counsellors' theoretical orientations were principally psychodynamic, humanistic, brief focused or eclectic. Systemic and cognitive-behavioural models were much less common. Eclectic combinations included Gestalt and TA, cognitive-analytic therapy (CAT), Rogerian, Jungian, person-centred, psychosynthesis and integrative. Supervisors' orientations were predominantly psychodynamic or humanistic. The correlation between counsellors' and supervisors' theoretical orientations was highly significant ($p < 0.003$). Asked whether the match on theoretical orientation between themselves and their supervisors was good, 89 per cent replied in the affirmative; personal style was rated as a good match by 96 per cent of the sample. Where mismatches occurred, some were described as complementary while others were more problematic. Differences mentioned were in attitude toward brief therapy, cognitive-behavioural techniques, directiveness, willingness to see more disturbed patients, and personal style, such as a 'closed' interpersonal manner.

Frequency and type of supervision

The most common form of supervision was individual, once a fortnight; only 15 (17 per cent) received individual supervision once a week. Thirty-five counsellors (39 per cent) participated in more than one form of supervision (individual plus group or peer supervision). The most common combinations of supervision were individual once or twice a fortnight and in a group less than once every three to four weeks. Most counsellors had a choice of supervisor, most chose supervisors by recommendation or personal knowledge, some chose according to personal style, and some interviewed potential supervisors before choosing one. When a choice was not available, problems ensued for some. One counsellor had to argue for a supervisor linked to her integrative psychotherapy training. Two counsellors initially assigned to a clinical psychologist supervisor whose cognitive-behavioural background contrasted strongly with their own were able to persuade their employers to allow them to seek supervision from an external supervisor of their choice.

Only 25 per cent of supervisors were known to at least one of the GPs in the practice. Comments included 'They do not seem to be interested in who is supervising', and 'They don't ever ask', but also 'I prefer it that way', and 'I feel this makes for objectivity.' Payment for supervision differed widely. Forty-seven per cent of counsellors paid for their own supervision. GP practices paid for 20 per cent, and health authorities for 29 per cent. Six per cent of supervision was funded jointly by GP practices and health authorities. There were a few other payers such as a university counselling centre.

Supervision techniques

Most supervision was discussion-based, with or without case notes. Problem formulations or treatment plans and Interpersonal Process Recall (IPR) were uncommonly used. Audio-tape, video-tape and role-play were rarely used, no supervisors observed from behind a one-way mirror, and only one supervisor sat in with the counsellor as co-therapist. Counsellors rated their supervisors' training in supervision more highly than is probably warranted because a great deal of training in clinical supervision is by apprenticeship. Seventy-seven per cent of counsellors said their supervisor had been trained in counselling supervision, 69 per cent said their supervisor was experienced in the supervision of counselling in primary care, and 79 per cent said their supervisors received supervision for their supervisory work. These probably inflated percentages are noteworthy given that 'don't know' was an option taken up by only 14–16 per cent of the sample.

Asked to rate the importance of supervision to their clinical effectiveness on a five-point scale, most rated it 'very' or 'extremely' important. An open-ended question about the greatest positive aspect of supervision elicited thoughtful replies. Common themes were support, containment, feedback, and working through areas of 'stuckness' or difficulty; transference and countertransference, projective identification, premature interpretation, learning from mistakes, and developing confidence in one's own 'internal supervisor'; assessment and formulation of new cases, learning new skills, untangling muddles, and help in maintaining boundaries and staying focused in brief therapy. 'A fresh and objective view of the patient', said one counsellor; 'Surprisingly, the supervisor's focus on the *client*', said another.

One counsellor mentioned the helpfulness of observing parallel process in supervision; another audio-taping and role-play. Several cited the supervisor's ability to identify the counsellor's own material in session material: 'looking at blocks to empathy caused by restimulation of my own emotional traumas', as one counsellor put it. The supervisor's knowledge of the primary care setting was cited as helpful by several counsellors. Some looked for 'constant backup', reassurance, increased self-confidence, confirmation of their assessment, or validation of their approach by the supervisor, while others sought a balance between acceptance and challenge. A very experienced counsellor said supervision was very important in a few difficult cases, but was generally not needed.

Counsellors were also asked to describe any negative impacts of supervision. One counsellor's previous supervisor had been the psychologist working for the same GP surgery, which engendered competition and lack of co-operation. There was some overlap between this question and a later one on abusive supervisory relationships:

Can be dogmatic in approach. I do not let it happen now.

My supervisor was punitive in the first year of our relationship. I challenged her.

I place more emphasis on working with ending than my supervisor.

On occasions I have felt de-skilled when my supervisor has illuminated some aspect of my work (my own stuff, I know!). When I next approach the client, I am perhaps not as confident.

The primary care setting

Most funding for counsellors came from GPs (37 per cent), health authorities (27 per cent) or a combination of the two (11 per cent). Four per cent of counsellors were paid directly by their patients, NHS Trusts paid 12 per cent, and 10 per cent were funded by other sources such as social services, Relate, or a university counselling service. Pay ranged from £5 to £34 an hour with a mean of £14.90 an hour; the modal rate of pay was also £15. Ten counsellors were unpaid volunteers. Half the unpaid volunteers had less than six years' supervised counselling experience, and slightly more than half the volunteers were recent graduates of the Diploma course. Nearly half of all the counsellors considered their hourly rate of pay inadequate and had tried to renegotiate it.

Waiting times varied from 0 to 26 weeks for assessment (mean 5.6 weeks) and counselling (mean 7.1 weeks). The average maximum number of sessions offered per patient was 13 (range 4–100), and the mean number of sessions per patient was 7 (range 3–20), confirming the consensus that most primary care counselling is short-term focused work. However, one-third of the sample said the number of sessions for patients was unlimited. Case-loads varied from 3 to 65 patients with a mean of 15, about 75 per cent of the full-time case-load recommended by the BAC. However, 48 per cent of counsellors in the study worked part-time, carrying 10 or fewer patients at any one time.

Referral matters

Eleven per cent of counsellors were expected to offer counselling to all patients referred regardless of the severity of the presenting problem. Ninety per cent felt sufficiently trained in assessment for the patients being referred to them. The nine counsellors who wanted more training in assessment tended to have fewer years of experience. One singled out a better understanding of borderline patients as an area of particular need. Nearly half the sample (45 per cent) reported problems referring patients to secondary mental health services. The most frequently reported problems were under-resourcing of services and long waiting lists. Other issues included the stigma of a psychiatric referral, patient reluctance to be 'labelled', the poor quality of care offered, and time-limited contracts.

Initially, the GP did not take me seriously. Now I have a waiting list.

They tend to refer back to us saying they only deal with serious mental illness.

Undermining of counselling by psychiatrists.

If they're psychiatrically ill they get help very quickly but if they have major traumas to work through from childhood, then it's very difficult to get them help, e.g. childhood sexual abuse.

No good local service for eating disorders.

Counsellors were only moderately well informed about statutory, voluntary and private resources for onward referral. If a patient should ask to continue working with a primary care counsellor privately beyond the contracted number of sessions at the surgery, 33 per cent of counsellors would agree to see them, although 70 per cent would discuss this with their supervisor before agreeing. Almost one-third reported problems referring patients to private practitioners, citing patients' lack of financial resources and counsellors' lack of knowledge of private practitioners' skills.

Seventy-two per cent of counsellors had refused to work with particular patients referred by GPs. Reasons given included *diagnosis* – dementia, psychosis, learning disability, borderline personality, obsessive-compulsive disorder, drug or alcohol addiction, potential violence, 'long-term problem', too severe a problem for short-term work'; *boundary issues* – close relative of an existing patient; personal knowledge of family and shared social connections; already in couple and/or group work; *motivational deficits* – 'told to come' and does not want counselling, not motivated to work, incapable of developing a therapeutic relationship, unable to recognize that counselling is not about being told what to do, looking only for 'support', or in one case the patient hoped the counsellor would 'collude in labelling his wife'; and *match between therapist skill and patient need* – inappropriate to counsellor's level of competence, for example sexual dysfunction work, 'clash of personality', would be better helped by another form of therapy such as cognitive-behavioural, or requires long-term psychotherapy.

Common problems in primary care counselling (medical vs. biopsychosocial models, confidentiality, and dual transferences)

Surprisingly, the reported incidence of these problems was infrequent. Disagreements with GPs on patient care traceable to the different cultures in which GP and counsellor were trained occurred infrequently, and disagreements concerning psychotropic medication happened rarely. This issue was not often discussed in supervision but comments included:

> It depends on which doctor.
>
> Not openly discussed because it's probably easier that way.

Patients were not always discussed with the referring GP, and breaches in confidentiality seldom occurred around suicide risk or child protection issues. Counsellors who use the traditional model may not discuss patients with GPs, whereas those using the collaborative model would do so. Confidentiality issues were discussed in supervision more often than not. Comments included:

> Nothing to discuss: legal requirements.
>
> I don't regard a child's safety as confidential.
>
> I cover this with the patient at referral assessment and therefore it is not a breach of confidentiality.

Asked whether acceptance of counselling referrals was possible only because of a strong positive transference to the GP, counsellors thought this factor has at best a moderate impact. Counsellors seldom encountered split transference such as 'brusque uncaring GP and kind, caring counsellor' or its converse, and these issues were infrequently discussed

Table 78.2 *Issues in primary care counselling*

	YES Number	(%)
Do you feel a part of the primary health care team?	66	(78)
Do you provide informal support for others in the primary health care team?	64	(75)
Do you know to whom you are accountable for your work?	86	(97)
Do you have an office dedicated exclusively to counselling work?	27	(30)
Do you keep your own diary for counselling appointments?	81	(92)
Does someone else in the surgery make appointments for you?	24	(27)
Do you keep vacant slots for one-off emergency appointments?	38	(43)
Do you have adequate secretarial and administrative support?	52	(58)
Do you have a reasonable case mix of easier and more difficult patients?	88	(99)
Do you have a clear contract with each patient re. number of sessions?	59	(67)
Do you ever extend the agreed length of treatment for a given patient?	83	(95)
Do you vary the frequency of sessions, e.g. some weekly, some fortnightly?	76	(95)
Do you have a waiting list for your counselling work?	68	(85)
Do you keep written records?	86	(98)
Do you have sufficient time during your contracted hours to keep records?	40	(45)
Do you liaise regularly with GPs about your patients' progress?	54	(61)
Do you have an information leaflet for patients about counselling?	59	(66)
Do you use pre- and post-counselling forms to evaluate your treatment effectiveness?	25	(28)
Do you have good links with secondary mental health services, facilitating the referral of patients when needed?	50	(57)
Do you experience difficulties deciding whether or not to refer patients on?	32	(36)
Do you have difficulty when there is no one to refer a given patient on to?	61	(72)

in supervision. One counsellor commented that unsupportive GPs had not referred patients.

Issues in primary care counselling

This section of the questionnaire inquired about issues commonly encountered in primary care. The results are shown in Table 78.2.

Items of note were the small number of counsellors who had an office dedicated exclusively to counselling, lack of secretarial support, insufficient time during contracted hours to keep records, few pre- and post-counselling evaluation forms, the difficulty of making onward referral, and the presence of a waiting list for counselling. Somewhat surprisingly, extending the length of treatment for certain patients tended to occur across orientations, including counsellors of a psychodynamic, humanistic or brief/focused orientation. It was noted that the issues described in Table 78.2 were discussed in supervision infrequently. The issue was discussed *somewhat* in only five of the areas mentioned: (i) feeling part of the primary health care team; (ii) a clear contract for the number of sessions; (iii) extending an agreed length of treatment; (iv) problems with onward referral; and (v) difficulties when there was no one to whom to refer a patient.

Other items were only rarely discussed in supervision. On average, counsellors discussed between two and three cases during each supervision hour, and most thought this

Table 78.3   *Satisfaction with supervision*

There was virtual unanimity on being 'very satisfied' about:
A safe place to do the work.
Empathy toward me and my patients.
Believes in and fosters my potential to become a competent counsellor to my patient.

Slightly less unanimity was expressed around:
Encouraging and sensitive to my needs for reassurance.
Welcomes mistakes as learning experiences.
Gives me the chance to raise personal issues related to my work where appropriate.
Follows my emotional experience of the session and allows the story to unfold.

A wider spread of responses was evident for these items, but still within the 'very satisfied range':
Reliable boundaries, time clearly set aside for the work.
Available in emergencies.
Warm, approachable, sense of humour, good rapport.
Demonstrates expertise, inspires confidence.
Promotes constructive feedback in both directions.
Appropriately challenging.
Helps me overcome my shortcomings.
Respects value differences between us.
Helps me consider my interventions from the patient's point of view – trial identification/'internal supervision'.
Helps with formulation of patients' problems.
Advises on handling problem situations, e.g. suicide risks, child protection issues, 'heartsink' patients.
Tolerates ambiguity, complexity, and not knowing.
Provides support with my own feelings.
Sensitive toward power imbalance, age, race and gender issues in counselling and supervision.
Grasps organizational and contextual issues, e.g. medical model, confidentiality, appointment system, waiting lists, ethical issues, time management.
Committed to developing own skills, presents self as a fellow student of the therapeutic process.

More disagreement was seen around these issues but satisfied overall:
Pinpoints my shortcomings.
Uses an appropriate range of teaching methods.
Specific suggestions rather than abstract ideas.
Supports my moves toward greater autonomy.
Clarifies treatment goals and objectives.
Makes theory–practice links, suggests readings.
Offers clinical advice and support with tricky cases.
Hypothesizes about patient's personality dynamics, interpersonal processes, hidden motives.
Clear supervision contract, including termination.

A wide range of responses including some clear dissatisfaction:
Keeps written record of supervision sessions.
Models alternative approaches from own clinical work.
Acknowledges own areas of weakness or rigidity.
Provides support for me with colleagues.
Explores and clarifies countertransference problems.
Fosters learning from parallels between the patient/counsellor relationship and the counsellor/supervisor relationship ('parallel process').

---

was about right. Most felt they had a clear contract with their supervisor and that they were able to describe what they needed from supervision. Most said they reflected regularly on supervision and feedback was given in both directions, although 12 (13 per cent) said this discussion rarely if ever occurred. Few counsellors said their supervision monitored their ongoing relationship with the primary health care team.

Q: If a collusive relationship should develop between you and your supervisor, who would monitor this?

Many hoped that they and/or their supervisor would notice and address it, others assumed the supervisor's supervisor would pick it up, those who received supervision in a group suggested the group would monitor it, and some said they would raise it in personal therapy. A sizeable minority said 'No one', and several replied 'Good question'. One said, 'I monitor it myself by seeking a new supervisor every three years.'

Satisfaction with supervision was very high across the wide-ranging items in Table 78.3. The few counsellors who reported dissatisfaction mentioned issues such as theory–practice links, a range of teaching methods, suggested readings, supporting counsellors' moves toward greater autonomy, modelling alternative approaches, exploring countertransference problems, fostering learning from 'parallel process', and supervisors' acknowledgement of their own areas of weakness or rigidity. Asked about their openness to learning from their supervisor, counsellors rated themselves as very open to admitting mistakes and to sharing both positive and negative feelings about patients. However, they were somewhat less open to discussing the ups and downs of the supervisory relationship with their supervisor.

Three open-ended questions asked how supervision had helped when counselling hadn't worked: at one end of the continuum, 'minor failures' such as problems in technique or lack of empathy; 'moderate failures' such as malignant regressions, therapeutic impasse, substantial learning blocks ('dumb spots') or countertransference problems ('blind spots'); and 'major failures' such as sexual acting out, violation of boundaries, incompetence or negligence, or suicide of the patient.

Supervisors' responses to 'minor failures' mentioned by counsellors included:

The value of bringing anything and everything [to supervision].'
Often due to countertransference which has been pointed out.

The successful supervision of 'moderate failures' included:

Gives me space to be lost.
Helpful experiences of sticking with the holding/containing situation, without the need to bolt in some other direction.
When a patient dissociated in therapy, regressing to four years old for several hours, I needed the help of a consultant psychotherapist for supervision. It was out of the supervisor's experience.

More than a third said major failures had not yet occurred in their work. Comments included:

I've learned with my supervisor's help to set boundaries around my competence and to return clinical care firmly to GPs where I've felt the client is not robust enough for counselling.
Extremely supportive with a difficult borderline client having problems ending therapy.

Table 78.4   *Supervisors' support of counsellors' personal development*

There was virtual unanimity on 'very much so':
  Recognizes your sources of anxiety and difficulty.
  Recognizes your response to stress.
  Helps you to be appropriately reflective and self-questioning.
  Helps you cope with failure, compromise, anger.
  Helps you grow through experience.

Slightly less unanimity was expressed around:
  Shows awareness of how your personal experiences affect your work.
  Helps you admit your personal limitations as well as strengths.
  Helps you maintain self-esteem, taking care to avoid burnout.

A wider spread of responses was evident for these items:
  Helps you anticipate and face difficulties at work.
  Encourages you to keep a balance with life outside work.

A wide range of responses including some clear lack of attention to the following:
  Helps you to avoid distortions of reality.
  Encourages you to seek your own counselling or therapy where appropriate.
  Encourages you to take responsibility for your own personal development.

Asked how well the supervisor supported their personal development, levels of satisfaction were very high overall, but a number of low scores were recorded in some items which are worthy of note (Table 78.4).

Despite the very high levels of reported satisfaction with supervision, 17 per cent of counsellors reported having been in the equivalent of a treatment impasse with their supervisor:

> One occasion, when I wanted to extend the time-limited work and was advised not to, and that proved OK.

> I tackled it at the next session, using the acute discomfort as a therapeutic tool.

Personal therapy

Ninety-eight per cent of respondents had personal therapy, 43 per cent in the past only and 47 per cent both in the past and currently. Most therapists were of a psychodynamic or humanistic orientation, with few described as cognitive-behavioural, systemic, eclectic or brief/focused.

Counsellors were asked how important personal therapy was to their effectiveness as a primary care counsellor, and to what extent personal therapy should be required of all counsellors (Table 78.5). The answers of the nine counsellors who said personal therapy was 'irrelevant' or 'may be desirable for some' were examined in more detail. Two-thirds of this group had less than six years' supervised counselling experience, two were unpaid volunteers, and those who were paid earned on average £10.50 an hour. Two had personal therapy lasting three months and three had therapy lasting 9–12 months. None had undertaken a second personal therapy, in contrast to 47 (52 per cent) counsellors in the total sample with more than one experience of personal therapy during their career.

Table 78.5   *The impact of personal therapy on counselling effectiveness*

	Number	(%)
How important would you say your personal therapy has been to your effectiveness as a primary care counsellor?		
Not applicable.	2	(2)
Definitely not important.	0	(0)
Of little importance.	4	(4)
Probably not very important.	8	(9)
Very important.	35	(39)
Extremely important.	40	(44)
How important, in your opinion, is it for counsellors to have experience of personal counselling or therapy?		
It is undesirable.	0	(0)
It is irrelevant whether counsellors have personal therapy.	1	(1)
It may be desirable for some counsellors, but not necessarily for all.	8	(9)
It is definitely desirable for most counsellors, but should not be required.	21	(23)
It is essential and should be required for all counsellors.	60	(67)

Benefits of personal therapy to clinical work were described. Common themes included:

- growth, greater self-understanding and self-awareness about one's own material including 'sorting out what belongs to me and what doesn't', exploring personal issues which are likely to be triggered in counselling patients, and 'clearing one's own debris';
- the experience of being a patient, being listened to, knowing what it is like to take the decision to have counselling and to look inwards in depth;
- working through childhood trauma, the effect of early relationships with parents and painful experiences that had been buried, the powerful influence of personal history in shaping who one is and inhibiting change;
- considering the whole person, and seeing bodily symptoms and stresses as 'encoded' information about inner processes;
- respect for boundaries, recognition of transference and countertransference, dependence on the therapist at some stages;
- reducing defensiveness, highlighting areas of particular sensitivity, reduction of blind spots and own projections and assumptions;
- awareness of the process unfolding, the experience of transition from not coping to understanding and moving on, while still learning; importance of applying learning in everyday life;
- awareness of the power held by the counsellor, damaging possibilities, iatrogenic effects of counselling and what *not* to do as a counsellor;
- the proof that therapy works, experiencing great pain and coming through it;
- developing clarity about one's own limitations, feelings of failure and over-concern to be helpful, and enabled to feel freer and more tolerant and kind to oneself.

Nineteen per cent of the sample reported that personal therapy had a negative impact on work with patients:

> I saw a therapist for two or three sessions who was so judgemental and 'damaging' that I withdrew from working with clients for six months until I decided counselling needn't be like that. I still feel it can be very damaging in the wrong hands.

> Not always easy to work with one's own regression when a client is experiencing something similar.

> Very occasionally it's brought up more than I could cope with which has sometimes left me in a place where it was hard to be there for my clients.

Asked who had been the most important models of how to be a counsellor, personal therapists and clinical supervisors headed the list. Teachers, colleagues and authors came second, and counsellors demonstrating in workshops, films or videos ranked third. 'Other' sources of learning included observing oneself on video, feedback from patients, meditation teachers, respecting silence, watching what does and doesn't work in everyday interactions, and 'living with people'.

Ninety-three per cent of counsellors were satisfied with the interface between personal therapy and supervision. Supervisors rarely took on the role of personal therapist, and counsellors rarely brought personal issues to supervision. Supervisors occasionally suggested certain issues be taken to a personal therapist for further exploration. In cases where supervisor and personal therapist knew one another, very few counsellors had concerns about confidentiality. Comments included:

> I really see this as a continuum and expect there to be an overlap.

> My supervisor will work with my personal stuff if it affects my work, but if it requires any length of time will suggest personal therapy.

Eleven per cent of counsellors said they had experienced at least one abusive supervisory relationship, an umbrella term which included use of supervisory material for the supervisor's gratification, a rigid or authoritarian stance, pathologizing the supervisee, giving consistently negative feedback, sexualization of the relationship, breaching boundaries, or persistent lack of clarity about the contract. Comments referred mainly to an authoritarian stance, consistently negative feedback, and breaching boundaries between supervision and personal therapy:

> Some negative feedback received in my last session was very badly timed as there was no place for working through or discussion. The negative feedback related to my supervisor's report to the college.

> In the past it nearly resulted in my leaving counselling. Instead I found a good therapist and began to understand why I had allowed myself to be in such an abusive relationship.

> Rigid authoritarian stance, consistent negative feedback which she admitted to freely when I asked to change supervisor. This problem was due to our both working in the same surgery, she as clinical psychologist and I as counsellor. I was getting more referrals and I was cheaper, and she was feeling threatened.

> As a trainee I was supervised by someone who broke the boundaries between supervision and therapy. At the time I was too inexperienced to know it was inappropriate.

> In this relationship, no, but with a Kleinian supervisor I felt infantilized and afraid (my material) but it disempowered me as a student. I changed supervisor!

At the end of the questionnaire in the space for other comments counsellors identified important issues in the new specialty of primary care counselling supervision:

The FHSA has contracted with a psychodynamic organization for the supervision of *all* counsellors. I have been fortunate as my supervisor is so highly qualified the FHSA have not felt able to refuse my request to continue supervision. However many of my colleagues are *extremely* concerned about their supervision and I urge you to stress the importance of not allowing one therapeutic approach to dominate in a whole health authority.

I think primary care counsellors, well trained and with some basic medical knowledge are a completely new profession, and I think we need quite specialist supervisors. I think supervision for primary care counsellors is becoming a real problem.

I had a lot of difficulty persuading my manager and the steering committee of the project that I required external supervision. Originally they planned for my line manager, a psychologist of strong cognitive-behavioural orientation, to also supervise me clinically. I was not at all happy with this idea.

I feel in a fortunate position of having had my request for an independent supervisor respected. I know of others employed in my area who have been given no choice and where the 'mismatch' of orientations has created great problems.

Discussion

Although response rates were adequate, especially in the diplomate group, the question of self-selection should be taken into account particularly in association with the finding of having had a personal therapy. Only two counsellors in the sample had not had personal therapy. The few negative comments about the questionnaire itself tended to come from those who had not had therapy or only a brief experience of therapy. This raises the question of whether those who had not had personal therapy had decided not to return the questionnaire. It is also possible that those who had experienced an abusive supervisory relationship were more likely to return questionnaires, while those lacking such an experience may not have done so. Some non-BAC-accredited counsellors in the non-diplomate group may not have been receiving regular supervision. Another reason for failure to return a questionnaire was undoubtedly its length and the time required to complete it.

Despite these caveats some interesting trends in primary care counselling were revealed by the study. The mean hourly pay rate of less than £15 continues to be inadequate despite attempts made by counsellors at renegotiation. Ten counsellors were unpaid volunteers and must be a cause for concern. Nearly half the sample had to pay for their own supervision at rates of up to £37 an hour. It is also apparent that primary care counselling services are beginning to experience the same waiting list problems as secondary mental health services. Counsellors report that not all the work is short term, with a third of the sample describing the maximum number of counselling sessions as unlimited. Although 90 per cent felt 'sufficiently' trained in assessment of the patients being referred to them, the literature suggests this is a serious overestimate (Parry and Richardson 1996). The important question of assessment for short-term counselling versus longer-term psychological therapy will be addressed in Burton 1998. Most counsellors surveyed had refused to see some patients and the reasons cited for refusal were sound. Counsellors reported problems with accommodation, secretarial support, time for record-keeping, and service evaluation questionnaires. Secondary mental health services caused significant problems due to under-resourcing which resulted in long waiting lists and inadequate provision for patients with, for instance, eating disorders, personality disorders, or a history of childhood sexual abuse – problems noted elsewhere in the review of NHS psychotherapy services in England (Parry and Richardson 1996).

An important finding was that 63 per cent supervisors came from disciplines other than counselling (counselling or clinical psychology, psychotherapy, social work, nursing or psychiatry), and only 25 per cent of supervisors actually currently worked clinically in primary care. Although satisfaction with supervision was high, a number of practical issues in primary care counselling were infrequently discussed in supervision. These findings highlight the need to ensure that supervisors for this work have had at least some experience of the GP surgery setting and are aware of the unique problems faced by counsellors in primary care. Counsellors expressed concern over being assigned supervision with their line manager (often a clinical psychologist), and of having to argue for an external clinical supervisor from their own theoretical orientation. When counsellors and clinical psychologists are for instance competing for the same contracts, the countertransference problems likely to develop on both sides in supervision can be considerable (Burton 1997). Several counsellors also drew attention to the fact that supervisors were used to working long term and did not adequately appreciate the short-term nature of primary care counselling. Similarly, if short-term therapy is increasingly the treatment of choice in primary care, psychotherapy supervision models need to be adapted accordingly (Watkins 1995).

Curtis Jenkins (1996) has identified four aspects of primary care counselling supervision: management, mentoring, psychological supervision and expert consultation. Supervisors without first-hand knowledge of the setting may fail to address sufficiently the *managerial* issues arising in the GP surgery. This was a finding in the present study. In some cases managerial supervision had become the province of the line manager (who might be a clinical psychologist) while clinical supervision was delegated to an external supervisor of the same theoretical orientation as the counsellor. *Mentoring* allows less experienced counsellors to gain confidence and support from more experienced practitioners. The benefits of mentoring were reflected in counsellors' comments about helpful aspects of supervision. BAC-accredited counsellors (and members too who are working as counsellors) are required to be in *psychological (Clinical) supervision* at least 1.5 hours a month, or receive one hour of supervision for every six 50-minute sessions worked. Counsellors' replies in the present study suggest that clinical issues were universally addressed in supervision. Finally, *expert consultation* is often available for counsellors from NHS psychologists or psychotherapists who advise on managing difficult patients. Those without access to an NHS psychotherapy department commented on the serious implications of the lack of provision for such consultations.

This study raises important issues concerning supervisor training and accreditation for this new counselling specialty. Counsellors' estimates of their supervisors' training in counselling supervision and in primary care counselling supervision were probably an overestimate. Similarly, satisfaction with supervision was every high, prompting speculation on whether there was an unconscious attitude among some respondents that they had to defend themselves and their supervisor. Those aspects of supervision about which there was some clear dissatisfaction included important areas such as using an appropriate range of teaching methods, making theory–practice links, suggesting reading, clarifying treatment goals and objectives, supporting the counsellor's moves toward greater autonomy, clarifying countertransference problems, using insights gained from parallel process, and acknowledging own areas of weakness or rigidity. If these areas of dissatisfaction are representative, there is cause for concern, especially as a related finding was the relative lack of audio, video, role-play or Interpersonal Process Recall in supervision. Only 17 per cent of the sample received individual supervision once a week, but approximately half the counsellors in the study worked part-time.

Very high ratings of the perceived importance of supervision to clinical work were found in this study, but alongside this must be placed negative impacts of supervision, lack of attention to aspects of counsellors' personal development, impasse with the supervisor, lack of confidence in procedures to monitor collusive supervisor–supervisee relationships, and abusive supervisory experiences. Recent work on reason for non-disclosure to supervisors suggests that trainee therapists may not disclose certain events to supervisors if the material is too personal, involves negative feelings, or reflects a poor alliance with the patient (Ladany et al. 1996). Supervisor style was related to non-disclosure in that study. In terms of the variables measured in this study, one might expect that the match between supervisor and supervisee and the quality of their working alliance would affect non-disclosure. The relevance to clinical outcome is that it is precisely with those patients with whom one has a poor alliance that supervision can offer the most important insights.

The richness of learning experienced in personal therapy was reflected in the comments we have summarized. However, as with supervision, negative therapy experiences were also reported, so there is little cause for complacency. Experiences such as these are sometimes used to argue against trainees having therapy: the problem may worsen initially, trainees often lack time and money for therapy, the trainee may be abused in therapy and may experience stigma within and outside the training course (Duff et al. 1996). However, the overall benefits of personal therapy were reviewed by Darongkamas et al. (1994), and the present study lends support to the conclusion that a personal therapy is, in balance, beneficial to counsellors in primary care. Indeed, 67 per cent of the counsellors in this sample believed that a personal therapy should be required of all counsellors.

Steinhelber et al. (1984) noted that few if any studies have directly assessed the impact of clinical supervision on the outcome of counselling or psychotherapy. Thirteen years later, the comment remains justified. The methodological problems inherent in studying this question are considerable, and the present study does not address it empirically with pre- and post-supervision measures of patient change. We have relied on supervisees' self-report and the usual caveats about self-report methodologies apply. Steinhelber et al. discovered that patients showed significantly greater improvement when their trainee therapists had theoretical orientations congruent with those of their supervisors. The present study confirms this finding indirectly, in that primary care counsellors reported major difficulties when the theoretical 'match' between supervisor and supervisee was poor. Further work might study both supervisors' and supervisees' experience of working together more closely than has been possible here.

A number of issues remain for further research: empirically measured in-session impact of supervision on clinical work, supervisor–supervisee agreement on critical events in supervision, supervisor training and accreditation in the specialty of primary care counselling, monitoring collusive and/or abusive supervisory relationships, personal therapy as a requirement for trainee counsellors, and the periodic use of questionnaires such as this one to help supervisors and supervisees review their work and identify areas for improvement.

Acknowledgements

We gratefully acknowledge the financial support of the Counselling in Primary Care Trust, and the valuable comments of counselling supervisors who attended two study days in 1996 to discuss these and other issues. We extend particular thanks to the counsellors who gave so much of themselves to this learning process.

References

Allen, G.J., Szollos, S.J. and Williams, B.E. (1986) 'Doctoral students' comparative evaluations of best and worst psychotherapy supervision', *Professional Psychology: Research and Practice*, 17 (2): 91–9.

Bernard, J.M. and Goodyear, R.K. (1992) *Fundamentals of Clinical Supervision*, Boston: Allyn & Bacon.

Borders, L.D. and Leddick, G.R. (1987) *Handbook of Counselling Supervision*, Alexandria, VA: ACES.

Burns, C.I. and Holloway, E.L. (1989) 'Therapy in supervision: an unresolved issue', *The Clinical Supervisor*, 7 (4): 47–60.

Burton, M. (1997) 'Counsellors in primary care: supervision issues', *Clinical Psychology Forum*, 101: 29–31. Special issue, 'Clinical Psychologists and Counsellors Working Together'.

Burton, M. (1998) *Psychotherapy, Counselling and Primary Mental Health Care*, Chichester: Wiley.

Carroll, M. (1996) *Counselling Supervision: Theory, Skills and Practice*, London: Cassell.

Casement, P. (1985) *On Learning from the Patient*, London: Tavistock.

Casement, P.J. (1993) 'Towards autonomy: some thoughts on psychoanalytic supervision', *Journal of Clinical Psychoanalysis*, 2 (3): 389–403.

Crick, P. (1991) 'Good supervision: on the experience of being supervised', *Psychoanalytic Psychotherapy*, 5 (3): 235–45.

Curtis Jenkins, G. (1996) 'Aspects of supervision in general practice', Counselling in Primary Care Trust. Unpublished manuscript.

Darongkamas, J., Burton, M.V. and Cushway, D. (1994) 'The use of personal therapy by clinical psychologists working in the NHS in the United Kingdom', *Clinical Psychology and Psychotherapy*, 1 (3): 165–73.

Doehrman, M.J.G. (1976) 'Parallel processes in supervision and psychotherapy', *Bulletin of the Menninger Clinic*, 40 (1): 3–104.

Duff, J., Hopper, G. and Redfern, J. (1996) 'Clinician heal thyself: trainees in therapy?', *Clinical Psychology Forum*, 94: 46–7.

Gerin, P. and Orlinsky, D. (1991) 'Common core questionnaire', Collaborative Research Network, International Study of the Development of Psychotherapists. Unpublished manuscript.

Glass, J. (1986) 'Personal therapy and the student therapist', *Canadian Journal of Psychiatry*, 31: 304–11.

Greben, S.E. (1979) 'The influence of the supervision of psychotherapy upon being therapeutic: II. Modes of influence of the supervisory relationship', *Canadian Journal of Psychiatry*, 14 (6): 499–506.

Hart, G.M. (1982) *The Process of Clinical Supervision*, Baltimore: University Park Press.

Hoag, L. (1992) 'Psychotherapy in the general practice surgery: considerations of the frame', *British Journal of Psychotherapy*, 8 (4): 417–29.

House, R. (1996) 'General practice counselling: a plea for ideological engagement', *Counselling*, 7 (1): 40–4.

Jones, H., Murphy, A., Neaman, G., Tollemache, R. and Vasserman, D. (1994) 'Psychotherapy and counselling in a GP practice: making use of the setting', *British Journal of Psychotherapy*, 10 (4): 543–51.

Ladany, N., Hill, C.E., Corbett, M.M. and Nutt, E.Z. (1996) 'Nature, extent, and importance of what psychotherapy trainees do not disclose to their supervisors', *Journal of Counseling Psychology*, 43 (1): 10–24.

Mollon, P. (1989) 'Anxiety, supervision and a space for thinking: some narcissistic perils for clinical psychologists in learning psychotherapy', *British Journal of Medical Psychology*, 62: 113–22.

Monach, J. and Monro, S. (1995) 'Counselling in general practice: issues and opportunities', *British Journal of Guidance and Counselling*, 23 (3): 313–25.

Moriarty, A. (1995) 'Personal issues in supervision and personal development of trainees: guidelines for supervisors', *Clinical Psychology Forum*, 78: 24–5.

Nelson, G.L. (1978) 'Psychotherapy supervision from the trainee's point of view: a survey of preferences', *Professional Psychology*, 9 (4): 539–50.

Papadopoulos, L. and Bor, R. (1995) 'Counselling psychology in primary health care: a review', *Counselling Psychology Quarterly*, 8 (4): 291–303.

Parry, G. and Richardson, A. (1996) *NHS Psychotherapy Services in England: Review of Strategic Policy*, Wetherby: Department of Health.

Ruskin, R. (1994) 'When supervision may fail: difficulties and impasses', in S.E. Greben and R. Ruskin (eds), *Clinical Perspective on Psychotherapy Supervision*, Washington, DC: American Psychiatric Press, 231–61.

Shanfield, S.B., Matthews, K.L. and Hetherly, V. (1993) 'What do excellent psychotherapy supervisors do?', *American Journal of Psychiatry*, 150 (7): 1081–4.

Steinhelber, J., Petterson, V., Cliffe, K. and LeGoullon, M. (1984) 'An investigation of some relationships between psychotherapy supervision and patient change', *Journal of Clinical Psychology*, 40 (6): 1346–53.

UCL (1993) 'Supervisors' Handbook', M.Sc. in Clinical Psychology, University College London. Unpublished manuscript.

Wallerstein, R. (ed.) (1981) *Becoming a Psychoanalyst: A Study of Psychoanalytic Supervision*, New York: International Universities Press.

Watkins, E.D. (1995) 'And then there is psychotherapy supervision, too', *American Journal of Psychotherapy*, 49 (2): 313.

Watts, M. and Bor, R. (1995) 'Standards for training and practice in primary care counselling', *Counselling Psychology Review*, 10 (3): 32–7.

Discussion issues

1　What are your experiences of supervision? Can you relate to any of the findings of this study?

2　Do the level of qualifications, age and gender of the counsellor and their supervisors in this study surprise you?

3　Seventy-two per cent of counsellors had refused to work with particular patients referred by GPs. When would you refuse to see a particular client?

4　What are the advantages and disadvantages of using lengthy questionnaires in studies?

79

On What Basis Do General Practitioners Make Referrals?

Margaret Ward and Del Loewenthal

This pilot study examines on what basis general practitioners make counselling referrals to in-house practice counsellors in contrast to the community mental health team (CMHT).

A CMHT in one locality, serving four primary health care practices, was examined. Ten of the GPs, the three practice counsellors and all three community psychiatric nurses working within the CMHT were invited for interview.

Results suggest referral criteria were not systematically consistent across GPs, and reasons were not consciously articulated in most cases. While a broad range of problems requiring counselling were referred to both groups, differences were found in cases referred to counsellors in contrast to members of the CMHT. Namely, the more obviously mentally disturbed clients were more likely to be referred to CMHT members.

When do GPs refer patients to their in-house practice counsellors and when to community psychiatric nurses and other members of the community mental health team? What is best for the patient? Should there be a clearer divide between patients referred to a counsellor and those referred to the community mental health team?

Comparison was made of the psychological problems seen by CMHT members and in-house practice counsellors. It had been hypothesized, for research purposes, that there would be no systematic or significant differences between referrals made to practice counsellors and referrals made for counselling to the CMHT. This is an important area of investigation as 'counselling is believed to be an important therapeutic tool in the treatment of emotional distress' (Lee 1993); and GPs are probably the largest body of individuals able to recommend counselling to those in the general population who may benefit (Corney 1990a).

Over the last decade, there has been an accelerating growth in community mental health teams (Patmore and Weaver 1991). They have, however, been allowed to evolve differently and have targeted different areas of mental health (ibid.). Most CMHTs, however, devote a considerable proportion of their time to counselling clients with mental health problems (Sayce et al. 1991). Again the type of intervention is not uniform, depending, it would appear, on the training and supervision received by the CMHT member. Thus clients do not always, for example, have counselling sessions with clear boundaries, and CMHT members (as with some counsellors) will often not have been in a similar therapy themselves to that which they are offering.

At the same time as these developments, GP practices have tended to become larger, employing more practice members, and it is these practices that tend to employ their own

---

This chapter was first published as 'Differential client referral patterns in the GP setting', in *Counselling*, Journal of the British Association for Counselling, vol. 8, no. 2, pp. 129–31 (1997).

Table 79.1   *Diagnoses of patients seen*

Community psychiatric nurses (CPNs)	Overlapping problems seen by both CPNs and practice counsellors	Practice counsellors
anxiety schizophrenia (in remission) long-term problems manic depression financial problems post-natal depression	short-term problems anxiety marital problems neurosis bereavement couples therapy panic attacks anorexia other eating disorders sexual abuse	alcohol (if other support) minor anxiety

counsellors (Mowbray et al. 1961; Thomas and Corney 1993). GPs were given financial incentives to expand their range of services and by 1993 nearly one-third of practices were now thought to be actively using counselling (Financial Pulse 1993). However by 1998, Corney, in asking 'A counsellor in every general practice?' questioned whether this was an appropriate use of resources and whether developing the skills of primary care professionals might be more effective for the patient group as a whole. By 2000 the concerns were: 'Against a background of changes in the NHS where funding for counselling is being withdrawn from what were "fund holding practices", there are issues concerning who should provide counselling within the Primary Health Care team. Will general practitioners who have lost their funding for counsellors refer more of their patients to the community psychiatric nursing services?' (Thorpe 2000).

Method

In this small, essentially qualitative pilot study the interviews were semi-structured. A phenomenological approach to analysis was employed, as described by Hycner (1995). A stratified sample of GPs (based on sex, age and size of practice), together with all three of the practice counsellors and all three of the community psychiatric nurses (CPNs) in the CMHT, were interviewed.

Findings

Previous research suggested that GPs do have referral preferences according to diagnosis, but this is not consistent and GP counsellors and CMHTs do have a considerable overlap. Further research (McLeod 1988; Corney 1990a; Sibbald et al. 1993) also confirmed these findings and concluded that counsellors are referred a wide range of problems, ranging from overt psychiatric illness to relationship and family problems. In addition, GPs' age, length of time in practice, size of practice and interest in psychiatry all have a bearing on the number and type of counselling referral made by them (Mowbray et al. 1961).

The research conducted for this study reported here confirmed the diagnosis of patients referred for counselling included a large overlapping group (Table 79.1).

Patient's wish	Patient diagnosis	GP personal interest in counselling
Patient's financial standing	Home visit needed agencies	GP links with other counsellors
Patient's age	Patient insight	Length of counsellor waiting list
Patient involvement with other professionals	Knowledge of patient	GP past experience of counselling
	Geographical location	GP time
		Practice time

Figure 79.1   *Criteria used in GP choice of counsellor*

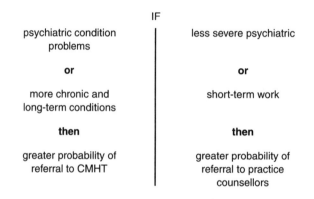

Figure 79.2   *Most frequent criteria involved in GP referral decision*

It will be seen that there is a wide range of problems seen by both teams. The core is similar, but there are differences and it is largely left to individual preferences as to whether a person is taken on. There are no clearly defined boundaries. It is perhaps easier for the CPNs to have some choice of the type of referrals they accept as there are other members of the CMHT whom patients can see.

It does appear, however, that it is very difficult for GPs to decide where the divide should be. The CMHT do have referrals with a very small psychiatric element to them and likewise practice counsellors have patients with a somewhat larger psychiatric component than was anticipated.

The research findings suggest that all the GPs do use multifactorial criteria when deciding on the counselling referral route, although it was found that GPs did not have explicit criteria but considered implicitly the criteria list in Figure 79.1 above. The most frequent criteria involved are shown in Figure 79.2.

To summarize the information collated, it can be seen that:

- The diagnosis of the patient was a usual consideration.
- The type of problem presenting was important.

- The probable length of the 'talking' treatment was alluded to.
- The complexity of the case was commented on.
- The financial benefits to the practice were mentioned by one GP.
- The patient's financial standing was considered in some cases.

Other factors having a bearing on the chosen route of referral included: the patient's age, their insight into the problem, their ability to travel to a counsellor, the GP's links with other counselling agencies, and his/her interest in counselling. A major factor was the length of the practice counsellor's waiting list. Practice counsellors maintained a waiting list, unlike the CMHT.

Conclusions

The results of this small pilot study cannot be generalized, but provide information that offers indications of what GPs say makes them decide if and where to send patients for counselling. This now requires further research. The findings of this study indicate GPs' diverse criteria for referral of patients for counselling. Yet all GPs interviewed recognized a need for counsellors and counselling, and all used this facility. It is further confirmed that there is an abundance of psychological problems seen in general practice (Corney 1990b). From this research there are indications that GPs perceive a need for a type of counselling that the GP practice counsellors cannot meet alone.

It seems that there will remain overlap in types of cases seen and that there is room for both community mental health counsellors, private and practice counsellors. More research on outcomes, costs, etc. is required on what would be the most appropriate basis of different referral routes. More clarity by GPs and all those involved on what is offered and why (with implications for training and supervision) is recommended. The question then of whether a more explicitly targeted referral system across all primary care patients would be more efficient and effective could also be examined.

References

Corney, R. (1990a) 'A survey of professional help sought by patients of psychosocial problems', *British Journal of General Practice*, 40: 365–8.

Corney, R. (1990b) 'Counselling in general practice – does it work? Discussion', *Journal of Royal Society of Medicine*, 83: 25307.

Corney, R. (1998) 'A counsellor in every general practice?', *European Journal of Psychotherapy, Counselling and Health*, 1 (1): 5–20.

Financial Pulse (1993) *Cost to a Practice Counsellor*.

Hycner, R. (1995) 'Some guide-lines for the phenomenological analysis of interview data', *Human Studies*, 8: 279–303.

Lee, F. (1993) 'When analysis is all talk in practice', *Doctor* (22 May), Reid Publications.

McLeod, J. (1988) 'The work of counsellors in general practice' (Occasional Paper 37), Royal College of General Practitioners.

Mowbray, R. et al. (1961) 'The general practitioner's attitude to psychiatry', *Scottish Medical Journal*, 6: 314–21.

Patmore, C. and Weaver, T. (1991) *Good Practice in Mental Health*, London: GPM4.

Sayce, L., Craig, T.K.J. and Boardman, A.P. (1991) 'The development of community mental health centres in the UK', *Social Psychiatry and Psychiatric Epidemiology*, 26: 14–20.

Sibbald. B. et al. (1993) 'Study of counsellors in England and Welsh practices', *British Medical Journal*, 306: 29–33.

Thomas, R. and Corney, R. (1993) 'Working with community mental health professionals: a survey among GPs', *British Journal of General Practitioners*, 43: 417–42.

Thorpe, R. (2000) 'What it means to the community psychiatric nurse to be a provider of counselling and psychotherapy'. Unpublished MA thesis, University of Surrey, School of Education.

Discussion issues

1 Are you surprised that the referral criteria were not systematically consistent across GPs? Would you have been more surprised if they were?
2 If you were a GP, what criteria would you use for referral?
3 Are semi-structured interviews effective when undertaking this type of research?
4 How could GPs improve their referral procedures?

80

Counselling Supervision

To Regulate or Not to Regulate?

David King and Sue Wheeler

This chapter is about the responsibility of supervisors working with counsellors in private practice, written from the experience of researching this topic. The authors are the researcher, David King, who was a student on a Master's degree course at the time, and his research supervisor, Sue Wheeler. Both took a keen and close interest in the development of the research and the analysis of the data collected, but when the dissertation was written up, they came to completely different and opposite conclusions. The work is reported here to bring the debate to the counselling profession. The controversial issues include how much responsibility supervisors have or should have, and how far their behaviour should be regulated by the profession. The research is briefly described and the alternative conclusions are presented and debated. David presents his conclusion and rationale and Sue presents the alternative scenario.

Introduction

During the second year of a Master's degree course in counselling, supervision for counselling work took place in pairs of students. During one of the early sessions my supervision partner asked the supervisor to confirm that she was taking 'clinical responsibility' for her (the student's) clients. The supervisor declined to assume such responsibility and stressed that it was the student herself, and the agency in which she was based, that had to take responsibility for her counselling work. At about the same time the Anthony Smith case (SDHA 1996) hit the headlines. As I live near Derby this case had both a local and a professional interest for me. For those not familiar with the Anthony Smith case, a man suffering from a severe mental illness killed his mother and younger half-brother in a deranged episode of violence in August 1995. Before his diagnosis as suffering from paranoid schizophrenia, the patient's GP had referred him to a counsellor based at the practice and the patient attended counselling regularly for a year, prior to his admission to hospital. The inquiry report raised a number of serious issues about the clinical responsibility of counsellors and the responsibility that supervisors have for the work of their supervisees. The report questioned whether the counsellor 'took' the patient to supervision, criticized the lack of clarity regarding the supervision role and doubted whether the supervision available to the counsellor was adequate. Case notes, neither of supervision sessions, nor of counselling sessions were available.

This chapter was first published in *Counselling*, Journal of the British Association for Counselling, vol. 9, no. 4, pp. 306–10 (1998).

These two occurrences led me to ponder on the nature of clinical responsibility and the extent to which supervisors have responsibility for the clients of supervisees. They also coincided with the time that we were formulating our ideas for research dissertations, and my choice was easily made. What follows discusses aspects of my research study that investigated the extent to which counselling supervisors regard themselves as clinically responsible for the work of their supervisees.

Methodology

'Experts' or experienced professional counsellors and supervisors who had published articles or books on supervision, or who held positions within BAC, were invited to participate in semi-structured, one-hour interviews. My thinking was that high-profile practitioners and supervisors who were at the forefront of the profession would be able to enrich and inform the discussion with the most up-to-date thinking about clinical responsibility. A semi-structured interview schedule was devised and addresses were obtained from various BAC publications. The potential interviewees embraced a range of theoretical counselling orientations. Everyone approached agreed to be interviewed, appointments were made and the interviews, which were conducted in the offices of the subjects and lasted approximately one hour, were tape-recorded. The taped interviews were transcribed in detail and the data was analysed using the constant comparative method of analysis (Strauss and Corbin 1990), following which a number of themes subsequently emerged. The interviews focused on the supervision of counsellors working in private practice.

Clinical responsibility

That the supervision of counsellors is a responsible task is not in doubt; what is debatable is how much responsibility supervisors have for the work of their supervisees and how they are accountable for their work. Despite the frequent use of the term 'clinical responsibility' in BAC publications (BAC 1996a) and others (Dryden et al. 1995), the supervisors in the sample interviewed were unanimous in their rejection of the term. Moreover, there was no clear agreement as to its meaning: 'Clinical responsibility is a term that is currently fashionable yet there is a lack of clarity as to its meaning in counselling.' One supervisor put forward the hypothesis that the more humanistic the counsellor, the more alien would be the concept of clinical responsibility. The psychodynamically oriented supervisors did not concur with this assumption. All agreed that counsellors were responsible for their work with clients. In accordance with Daines et al. (1997) the term 'clinical' was seen as having medical connotations and was regarded by some of those interviewed as being incongruous with counselling. Indeed the use of the term 'clinical responsibility' was seen as an attempt to add a gloss of medical respectability to counselling, 'an attempt to legitimise the profession in the public eye'.

The notion of clinical responsibility did have salience, however, in the context of client safety. The participants readily agreed that there were occasions when a medical intervention was needed, which the counsellor, in consultation with the supervisor, might have to instigate. Some supervisors insisted on their supervisees asking clients for details of their GP, but admitted that they did not always do this with their own clients.

Selection of supervisees

All the supervisors interviewed, without exception, were selective in their choice of supervisees when supervising counsellors working in independent practice: 'I am quite choosy when I have a vacancy' was a view commonly expressed. Moreover, there was a degree to which the participants believed that in supervising particular supervisees there was an assumption that the counsellor's practice was thus being endorsed: 'If the supervisee's work is bad then so am I.'

It was frequently the case that the participants already knew of their potential supervisees, through colleagues or training experiences, and hence had some knowledge of their practice before they took them on. There was definitely the sense that the supervisors were backing a 'sure thing' when choosing their supervisees, in order to minimize risk and uncertainty. There was general agreement that the work of the counsellor reflected on the supervisor and their reputation. The supervisors only wanted to be associated with 'good' work and competent practitioners. The name of the supervisor seemed to be a 'badge worn with pride' by counsellors, and such badges could only be given to those whose practice warranted them. The implication is that experienced supervisors are likely to shy away from inexperienced counsellors and those who need help to improve their practice, unless they are clearly designated as trainees. Another aspect of the rationale for being so choosy was expressed in comments such as 'I enjoy supervision and I want it to be a contrast to client work. I like the counsellor to have the ability to think for themselves, so that we can engage in a lively debate, rather than having to work hard with a counsellor who cannot take things in.'

How much do supervisors know about their supervisees' work?

When asked whether they routinely asked about or worked with all the counsellor's case-load, the answer from all those interviewed was a resounding 'No'. The responsibility for deciding what or who to bring to supervision rested with the supervisee. 'Supervisees tend to bring to supervision those cases that they need most help with.' The supervisors interviewed were frequently unaware of many of the clients in the supervisees' case-load. Even the clients who were discussed in supervision could only be seen through the eyes of the counsellor as discussed by Mearns (1995) in the 'Tale of the Missing Client'. The supervisors interviewed were frequently unaware of the premises in which the counsellor's practice was housed and it was taken on trust that suitable arrangements were made.

This raises a serious issue: if the supervisory relationship is founded on equality between supervisor and supervisee, a checking or policing role is inappropriate. However, if the supervisor bears some responsibility for the counsellor's work through the process of supervision then it is a matter for concern that they are unfamiliar with the counsellor's case-load and that not all cases are discussed. In the Anthony Smith case, for example, it is not clear whether the supervisor was aware of his existence, let alone the severity of his difficulties.

Unethical behaviour

Interviewees were asked how they managed ethical dilemmas that emerged in supervision and to give examples. Generally supervisors allowed themselves a degree of flexibility in working with supervisees who might be deemed to be behaving unethically and/or illegally. For example, when instances of child sexual abuse emerge in counselling, the policy in most statutory or agency settings is to involve Social Services. One supervisor gave an account of the work that a supervisee was doing with the father of a teenager, with whom he had an incestuous relationship. The supervisor and the counsellor concluded that counselling should continue with the father, without disclosure to any other body. This highlights one way in which supervisors have added responsibility and scope for discretion when working with counsellors in private practice. Counsellors working with an agency would usually have a clear code of practice issued by the agency to cover these eventualities. Neither the BAC Code of Ethics for Supervisors (1996a) nor for Counsellors (1997) offer assistance in making these decisions.

Page and Woskett (1994) agree with the Code of Ethics for Supervisors (1996a) that supervisors have an ethical responsibility to monitor counsellors' practice and if necessary to take action to protect the interests of clients. However, what emerged from the research interviews was the reluctance of some of the participants to take action when a supervisee had been practising unethically. One participant described the experience of ceasing to work with a supervisee because she was in breach of the ethical code: 'I felt torn between wanting to offer support and "friendship" without condemning the supervisee's malpractice.' The supervisor described in anguished terms the tension between the responsibility felt towards the client and the need to offer continued support for the supervisee, who was in great distress. It was a case in which a formal complaint could have been made, but there was a fear that, in doing so, the counsellor's career could be ruined.

Several of the participants acknowledged that as they were known figures in the counselling profession, they would be forced to complain about supervisees who behaved unethically, even though they were reluctant to do so. Other interviewees expressed the view that supervisors are sometimes aware of poor or unethical practice on the part of supervisees but rarely take any action. This accords with the work of Gartrell et al. (1987) whose research in the USA revealed how unwilling colleagues were to inform on each other in cases of malpractice. A major reason for this unwillingness was that supervisors would see it as a poor reflection of them and their work.

Impaired supervisees

Evidence emerged from the interviews to suggest that supervisors were equivocal in their attitude to supervisees whose functioning was impaired. In private practice there was a tension between the need for counsellors to look after themselves and the need to make a living. When personal crisis or illness dictated that counselling practice should be suspended, counsellors often continued working because it was the source of their livelihood. The Code of Ethics for Supervisors (BAC 1996a: B.1.12) clearly states the need for a supervisor to confront their supervisee when their functioning as a counsellor is impaired. One interviewee reported an experience of working with a supervisee who was being seriously harassed by an ex-client. The supervisee was very distressed and anxious and the supervisor acknowledged that if they had behaved 'according to the rules' then the counsellor should have been persuaded to stop practising. However, the counsellor was given the benefit of the doubt because, for freelance counsellors, 'who are dependent financially on their practice, to ask them to stop working is a terrible decision to have to make'.

Conclusion (David King)

These interviews with experienced supervisors indicate that there are clear limits to the role and function that counselling supervision can fulfil, yet the profession has an expectation that supervision should be the linchpin of quality control. There are several issues that arise from this research that need urgent attention. These include the monitoring of a counsellor's full case-load, the supervision of inexperienced counsellors, flexibility to interpret ethical codes, and making complaints.

The evidence collected and described here suggests that only selected parts of a counsellor's casework are currently monitored by their supervisor. Most work will inevitably be unsupervised and the notion of the supervisor 'overseeing' the counsellor's case-load is naive. Hence the expectations that the profession has of the supervisory process to safeguard clients and ensure ethical practice are unlikely to be met. The Code of Ethics for Supervisors should be amended to require supervisors to have an overview of all the work that their supervisees are engaged in. It is not sufficient that counsellors choose which cases to take to supervision. As well as consideration for the clients, who may not be receiving the best possible service from their counsellors, supervisors also put themselves at risk, if the counsellor is found to be working incompetently or unethically.

The highly respected practitioners involved in this inquiry gave themselves considerable freedom to interpret the Code of Ethics for Supervisors, which raises a concern about the flexibility with which the Code can be interpreted. Some consideration needs to be given to producing codes of ethics that are both more comprehensive and clear-cut. There need to be more specific guidelines on how sexual abuse disclosures in counselling should be managed. Public confidence in counselling could be seriously undermined if supervisors and counsellors are seen to be in collusion with an abusive client, as discussed by Dryden and Feltham (1992). As long as the codes of ethics are unclear and lacking in prescription, then openness to interpretation is bound to cause conflict.

Supervisors involved in the study were very selective in their choice of supervisees. Hence, the issue of who supervises less experienced practitioners, and the quality of that supervision, is a question that needs to be addressed by the profession. If 'good' supervisors do not want to take the responsibility for supervising 'less able' counsellors, the implication is that those who need the most support are likely to be seen by inexperienced supervisors looking for work.

Supervisors interviewed were reluctant to make complaints about their supervisees if they erred, and also to discourage them from practising when they were ill or distressed. Clearly, if supervisors are to be ethically responsible for the quality of counsellors' work then their role and function needs to be enhanced. The Code of Ethics would need to be more prescriptive, giving the supervisor more power and control and at the same time making them more accountable. If supervisors are held responsible for the counsellor's behaviour, and that is understood by all, there will be less reluctance to take action in uncomfortable circumstances. At the same time, counsellors need to be encouraged to make financial arrangements for themselves to ensure that they receive some remuneration when they are forced to take a break from their work.

At the moment, supervision is compulsory for all practising counsellors, but its effectiveness is open to debate. I recommend that the following changes are made:

- The BAC Code of Ethics for Supervisors needs to take into account the difference between supervising counsellors working in private practice and supervising counsellors in other settings.
- BAC needs to be more prescriptive on the length of training, qualifications and experience needed before counsellors work independently.
- BAC needs to be more prescriptive about the action required of supervisors when a counsellor's functioning is impaired or he/she fails to practise ethically.
- BAC needs to have a policy on the action required of counsellors working privately when issues of child abuse arise.

Conclusion (Sue Wheeler)

Zinkin (1989) describes supervision as 'the impossible profession'. Just as the counselling profession is hampered with the word 'counselling' which has such a multitude of meanings, so is it hampered with the term 'supervision' (Williams 1992). Stoltenberg and Delworth (1987) propose that the nature of supervision varies as counsellors progress through their training, and Hawkins and Shohet (1989) offer a model of supervision that takes counsellors through their working life, using the term 'consultative support' for more experienced counsellors, which I think is the most helpful way of describing a relationship that all counsellors can use.

Counsellors in training both need and benefit from close supervision. The supervisor has to give serious consideration to the responsibility they assume with their supervisees in training. I would want to take account of the agency in which a trainee was working and would only take on a trainee if the placement provided supportive containment for their counselling work. As supervisor, I would then feel free to engage fully with the trainee in an educative and supportive role with the knowledge that I could involve the placement if I was seriously concerned about the trainee's work.

David suggests that the Code of Ethics for Supervisors should be more rigorous. While I agree that more clarity might be useful for work with trainees, I am opposed, for many reasons, to any increase in the responsibility that is assigned to the supervisor for work with more experienced counsellors. Professional counsellors are responsible for their work, particularly when they choose to work in private practice. Individuals are accountable to themselves. This is not to say that they do not need support and vehicles for professional development, of which supervision or consultative support is a part. As responsible practitioners they are expected to take whatever steps are necessary to ensure that their work is both ethical and of the highest possible standard. The supervisor or person providing consultative support is contracted to enable counsellors to think about their work with clients and other aspects of their practice in a climate of non-judgemental acceptance.

David is concerned about supervisors who disregard the Code of Ethics for Supervisors when the practice of the counsellor is unethical or unprofessional. The Code of Ethics provides helpful guidelines for making decisions, but it is important that supervisors are empowered to exercise discretion. It is not possible to legislate in a way that takes account of all the nuances of a situation. Symington (1994), well-respected analyst, tells us that he always follows the rules in therapy, unless exceptional circumstances make him choose not to. I am not convinced that a totally rule-bound profession will have the flexibility to respond to the range of dilemmas that have to be faced.

If the Code of Ethics for Supervisors were more prescriptive and comprehensive as David suggests, the role would be less appealing. If supervisors had more power and control, inscribed in the ethical code, relationships with supervisees would be adversely affected. Ladany et al. (1996) and Webb (1997) have found that supervisees are hesitant to discuss aspects of their work in supervision, with anxiety about being seen as incompetent. If supervisors had more power, reluctance to disclose sensitive thoughts and feelings would be greater.

David makes the specific suggestion that supervisees should take all their casework to supervision over time. While I would concur that the work of trainees needs to be closely monitored, it seems important that professionally trained and qualified counsellors take responsibility for their casework and use the supervisor in a consultative capacity, choosing their own focus for supervision.

This issue is crucial to the development of the counselling profession. Other allied professions – clinical psychology, medicine, psychotherapy, occupational therapy – do not require their practitioners to have supervision for their work when their training is completed, although many may choose to have it. It is a concern that the counselling profession, through BAC, is moving towards over-regulation and infantalization of their practitioners with an implication that counsellors cannot be trusted to graduate and behave as competent professionals. While being a wholehearted supporter of the notion that counsellors should have a rigorous training and make good use of consultative support throughout their career, I suggest that perhaps BAC has already gone too far in making 'supervision for life' mandatory. This could be seen as an insult to professional integrity. House and Totton (1998) marshal many arguments against the professionalism of counselling. In contrast to them, I consider professionalization to be essential, but trust and respect for well-trained and experienced practitioners must underpin ethical codes, rather than suspicion and mistrust, evidenced by strategies that highlight and regulate for the minority who fail their clients. Increased regulation of the work of counsellors with an enhanced role for supervisors will give a message to the public that counsellors cannot be trusted to behave as professionals.

Last words (from David)

After the Bernard Manning fiasco, the publicity given to Fay Weldon's views of 'therapism' in the national press and the Anthony Smith inquiry commenting on the inadequacy of the supervision available to the counsellor in the case, I am led to conclude that what the public really want is for the counselling community to be more accountable, not to themselves but to society.

We hope that our debate will echo some of the concerns of the counselling community and look forward to an interesting dialogue with those moved to respond.

References

BAC (1996a) *Code of Ethics and Practice for Supervisors of Counsellors*, Rugby: British Association for Counselling.

BAC (1996b) *The Recognition of Counsellor Training Courses*, Rugby: British Association for Counselling.

BAC (1997) *Code of Ethics and Practice for Counsellors*, Rugby: British Association for Counselling.

Cohen, K. (1992) 'Some legal issues in counselling and psychotherapy', *British Journal of Guidance and Counselling*, 20 (1): 10–26.

Daines, B., Gask, L. and Usherwood, T. (1997) *Medical Law and Psychiatric Issues for Counsellors*, London: Sage.

Dryden, W. and Feltham, C. (1992) 'Psychotherapy and its discontents: concluding comments', in W. Dryden and C. Feltham (eds), *Psychotherapy and its Discontents*, Buckingham: Open University Press.

Dryden, W., Horton, I. and Mearns, D. (1995) *Issues in Professional Counsellor Training*, London: Cassell.

Gartrell, N., Herman, J.L., Olarte, S., Feldstein, M. and Localio, R. (1987) 'Reporting practices of psychiatrists who knew of sexual misconduct by colleagues', *American Journal of Orthopsychiatry*, 57: 287–95.

Hawkins, P. and Shohet, R. (1989) *Supervision in the Helping Professions*, Buckingham: Open University Press.

House, R. and Totton, N. (1998) *Implausible Professions*, Hay on Wye: PCCS Books.

Ladany, N., Hill, C.E., Corbett, M. and Nutt, E.A. (1996) 'Nature, extent and importance of what psychotherapy trainees do not disclose to their supervisors', *Journal of Consulting Psychology*, 43 (1): 10–24.

Mearns, D. (1995) 'Supervision: a tale of the Missing Client', *British Journal of Guidance and Counselling*, 23 (3): 421–7.

Page, S. and Woskett, V. (1994) *Supervising the Counsellor: A Cyclical Model*, London: Routledge.

SDHA (1996) *Report of the Inquiry into the Care of Anthony Smith*, Southern Derbyshire Health Authority and Derbyshire County Council.

Stoltenberg, C.D. and Delworth, U. (1987) *Supervision of Counselors and Therapists*, London: Jossey-Bass.

Strauss, A.L. and Corbin, J. (1990) *Basics of Qualitative Research: Grounded Theory Procedures*, Newbury Park: Sage.

Strauss, J.H. and Ziegler, L.H. (1975) 'The Delphi Technique and its uses in social science research', *Journal of Creative Behaviour*, 9 (4): 253–9.

Syme, G. (1994) *Counselling in Independent Practice*, Buckingham: Open University Press.

Symington, N. (1994) *The Analytic Experience*, London: Routledge.

Webb, A. (1997) 'What counsellors choose to disclose in supervision: an exploratory study', dissertation submitted in part fulfilment of the M.Ed. Counselling, University of Birmingham.

Williams, D.I. (1992) 'Supervision: a new word is desperately needed', *Counselling*, 3 (1): 96.

Zinkin, L. (1989) 'The impossible profession', *Clinical Supervision: Issues and Techniques*, Jungian Training Committee of the BAP, pp. 19–24.

Discussion issues

1 What does 'clinical responsibility' mean?
2 If the supervisee's work is bad then so is the supervisor.
3 The responsibility for deciding what or who to bring to supervision rests with the supervisee. Is this realistic with trainee counsellors?
4 This study highlighted that some supervisors were reluctant to take action when a supervisee had been practising unethically. If you were a supervisor, what would you do if this situation occurred?

81

Students' Everyday Problems

A systematic qualitative analysis

Andrew Grayson, David Clarke and Hugh Miller

Abstract

The growing acceptance of qualitative research promises to minimize the perceived gap between counselling practitioner and counselling researcher, but brings with it the challenge of finding methods for dealing systematically, yet respectfully, with textual data. This article presents just such a method. Seventy-five students provided brief descriptions of the everyday problems of their university careers. A random sample of these first-hand accounts was then sorted by 30 further students. Hierarchical cluster analysis and multi-dimensional scaling procedures were used to construct a categorical and dimensional framework within which the original first-hand accounts are explored in more detail.

Introduction

This article is an empirically based exploration of the characteristics of everyday problems in a student population. It acts as the basis for further empirical work into students' help-seeking strategies.

Help-seeking among students has been extensively studied in the literature of counselling psychology. A variety of issues have been examined, such as students' attitudes to counselling (Halgin et al. 1987), the sorts of problems students present to counselling services (Heppner et al. 1994), the characteristics of students who use (and who do not use) counselling facilities (McLennan 1991), the help-seeking behaviour and attitudes to counselling of students from minority groups (Nickerson et al. 1994; Solberg et al. 1994), the characteristics of preferred sources of help (Kaczmarek and Jankowicz 1991), and the question of who students prefer to turn to in relation to the variety of problems they may experience (Grayson et al. 1998; Hutchinson and Reagan 1989).

Our research has focused on the last of these issues. In other words, our aim has been to understand student's help-seeking across a variety of problem types. But in order to progress with this work we have found it necessary to take one step back from the direct study of help-seeking itself in order to examine the nature and characteristics of students' everyday problems.

This chapter was first published in *Counselling*, Journal of the British Association for Counselling, vol. 6, no. 3, pp. 197–202 (1995).

In our work on help-seeking we have been struck by the important role that is played by people's own descriptions of their problems (see Grayson et al. 1998), particularly in relation to what, if anything, they do to deal with those problems. Indeed 'description' might not be an appropriate word here, for the way that people talk about a problem that they are experiencing is an intimate part of the identity of the problem itself; perhaps 'characterization' or 'construction' or 'appraisal' (Lazarus and Folkman 1984) might be better terms.

However, it is only very rarely (see Brannen and Collard 1982, for a notable exception) that one comes across people's first-hand accounts of their problems in the literature on help-seeking preferences, because research in this area is dominated by checklists, inventories, and structured questionnaires. We have no argument in principle with these methods of investigation which yield useful information, particularly for policy makers and service providers. But if we are correct in our assertion that people's accounts of their problems really are an important part of those problems, and an important basis for the way they deal with those problems, then the over-reliance on these traditional methods of inquiry may not be providing a good empirical basis for the study of help-seeking, because it forestalls the development of a sufficiently theorized analysis of 'problems'.

Furthermore, we wish to raise the issue of precisely who research studies are done for. Traditional 'quantitative' methods appeal to academic researchers because the data that accrue can be handled systematically with statistical techniques of ever-increasing sophistication. But in areas of applied work, such as in counselling psychology, one consequence of the hegemony of these methods is a 'growing gap between the interests of clinicians and the output of researchers' (McLeod 1994: 42). One reason for this sentiment is the distance which quantitative methods put between the sources of research data (the participants) and the consumers of research data (the readers of published articles). Qualitative methods, in dealing directly with first-hand accounts of subjects' experiences, promise to close this gap.

A key challenge for qualitative research in counselling psychology is finding strategies for dealing systematically, yet respectfully, with people's own accounts of their experiences. We offer this article as an illustration of just such a strategy. Here it has been used to explore the characteristics of students' everyday problems. But the strategy has a general applicability to any research programme which deals in the rich currency of talk.

The study is based on brief, first-hand accounts of problems that students experience while at university. A randomly selected sample of these accounts was employed as a set of items in an 'unconstrained sorting task' (see Weller and Romney 1988) which was undertaken by student volunteers. Hierarchical cluster analysis was used in conjunction with multi-dimensional scaling to provide a systematic representation of the data set. The resulting picture is one that has been generated virtually from start to finish by students themselves.

An important outcome of these methods is an opportunity to present a corpus of first-hand accounts of students' problems to a wider audience. In this way the study is unashamedly descriptive. One of the most constructive things we can do to help people with problems, particularly if they do not seek help, is to increase the whole community's awareness of those problems.

Method

Participants

Seventy-five students from a large university in the UK participated in a problem-elicitation (free-listing) task. The students were from six different degree courses (B.A. Communication Studies, B.A. Humanities, B.A. Modern European Studies, B. Engineering, B.A. Accounting and Finance and B.A. Education), and included first-, second-, third- and fourth-year undergraduates. No formal sampling was undertaken. Resources were allocated instead to producing quality data by ensuring that small groups of volunteers were highly motivated to participate, having been convinced of the importance and relevance of the research. The spread of students across all years of various undergraduate degree courses ensured that no constituency of students was systematically excluded from the study. The data were collected from small groups of students in order that the anonymity of the respondents could be guaranteed. No breakdown of demographic information about the subjects is provided because we wish to move away from statistical notions of 'representativeness', towards more substantive notions of 'meaning', by focusing readers' attention on the actual data that were generated. Furthermore we wish to make no claims about the relative prevalence of the problems that are examined below.

Procedure

Each participant was asked to list any problems which they had experienced during the course of their life as a student. They were encouraged to include problems from all stages of their university careers. Having listed and briefly described the problems in the left-hand column of a pre-prepared form, the participants were asked to describe anything they did in response to each situation in the right-hand column of the page.

The resulting set of data comprised 365 'problems' and 365 related 'strategies'. A random selection of 100 of the listed problems was extracted, and the problems were printed verbatim on separate index cards which were numbered on the back. The listed 'strategies' form the basis for a follow-up study on help-seeking which is not reported in this paper.

Thirty students from a social work degree course undertook an unconstrained sorting task. Each sorter, working individually, arranged the 100 index cards into piles of similar problems. The similarity judgements were the sorters' own, and no restriction was placed on the number of piles to be created. Upon completion of the task each sorter described the categories that they had created. Weller and Romney (1988: 25) suggest that a high level of reliability is achieved in unconstrained sorting tasks when at least 30 informants are used.

Analysis of the sorted problems

A symmetrical 100×100 similarity matrix which cross-tabulated each problem with every other problem was constructed for each sorter. In each sorter's matrix a score of one was assigned to appropriate cells to indicate which problems co-occurred with which other problems in their personal category system. The matrices from the individual sorters were then added to give an overall similarity matrix; the higher the score in any given cell the more frequent the co-occurrence of those two problems in the sorters' own category schemes, and the greater the implied similarity between the two problems (see Table 81.1).

Table 81.1   *Excerpt from similarity matrix*

Problem no.	1	2	3	4	5	6	7	8	.	100
1	30	2	3	0	10	2	0	1	.	0
2	2	30	0	0	0	4	0	9	.	7
3	3	0	30	2	4	3	0	5	.	1
4	0	0	2	30	0	0	1	0	.	0
5	10	0	4	0	30	1	2	1	.	2
6	2	4	3	0	1	30	0	18	.	0
7	0	0	0	1	2	0	30	0	.	16
8	1	9	5	0	1	18	0	30	.	1
.	.	.	.	.	.	.	.	.	30	.
100	0	7	1	0	2	0	16	1	.	30

An excerpt from the 100 x 100 similarity matrix. The cell at column 2 row 3 contains a value of zero, showing that no sorters placed problems 2 and 3 in the same category. On this basis we can assume that these two problems are quite different. In column 6 row 8 the value is 18. This means that 18 of the 30 sorters placed these problems together in a category. On this basis we can assume these problems are 'quite similar'. Very high similarity would be denoted by values approaching 30. Note that the matrix is symmetrical; column 8 row 6 also shows a value of 18.

The similarity matrix was converted into a dissimilarity matrix by subtracting the value of each cell from 30. SPSS for Windows (Version 5.0; 1992) was used to perform hierarchical clustering and multi-dimensional scaling on the dissimilarity matrix.

A 13-cluster solution and a five-dimensional solution were selected from the output of the hierarchical cluster analysis and the multi-dimensional scaling analysis respectively. The solutions were selected on the basis of interpretability and in consultation with 'goodness-of-fit' measures (details of which are available from the first author).

The output of multi-dimensional scaling is a set of coordinates which fix every item in the analysis (in this case the 100 sorted problems) at a given point on each 'dimension'. The meaning of each dimension is interpreted by examining how the problems are ordered on it, paying special attention to those problems which fall at its extremes.

Results

Table 81.2 provides an overview of the complex data set. It lists the 13 main categories of problems produced by the cluster analysis (middle column), and gives extracts of the accounts from each category. A superordinate five-cluster taxonomy is shown in the left-hand column.

Table 81.3 shows our interpretations of the five bipolar dimensions from the multi-dimensional scaling analysis. These dimensions are the basis for our exploration of the first-hand accounts.

The first dimension from the MDS analysis captures a key discriminating feature of student problems: whether or not they are related to the students' courses. When this dimension is considered in relation to each other dimension in turn, some potentially useful insights emerge, particularly where dimensions four and five are concerned.

Figure 81.1 shows the 100 problems plotted in a two-dimensional space defined by dimensions one (the x-axis) and four (the y-axis). Each symbol in this space denotes one

Table 81.2   *Hierarchical clustering solution for unconstrained sorting task*

Five-cluster solution	Thirteen-cluster solution	Exemplary extracts
FINANCIAL	Financial (18)	*financial – making money last*
COURSE	Academic (12)	*trying to get all assignments in on time – and do well in them*
	Relationships with staff (9)	*hard to ask [lecturers] when stuck with work*
	Frustrations, complaints and disappointments (7)	*high expectations of course not always fulfilled*
	Placement-related problems (4)	*worried about placement – no real help given*
DOMESTIC	Conflicts (5)	*clashes – especially with those [I] live with*
	Practical accommodation problems (11)	
INTERPERSONAL AND PERSONAL CRISIS	Leaving home and new-found independence (9)	*difficulty with finding accommodation* *initial fear of being alone ... having to make new friends*
	Personal and social crises (7)	*breakdown ... caused by marriage problems*
	Illness and injury (2)	*end of first term ... ended up in hospital*
MANAGING RESOURCES AND FACILITIES	Univ. resources (3)	*lack of facilities, entertainment*
	Time-management and self-organization (5)	*how to balance a social life with study*
	Travel (3)	*I'm commuting and used to find travel exhausting*

(The number of items in each cluster is shown in rounded brackets)

Table 81.3   *Interpretations of the five-dimensional scaling solution*

1   **Course**
[Problems to do with the person's course]

- **Not course**
[Problems not to do with the person's course]

2   **Individual/private**
[Individual, private and personal problems]

- **Social/public**
[Social, public and interpersonal € problems]

3   **Home life**
[To do with life away from the university city]

- **University life**
[Problems to do with life in the university city]

4   **Expressive**
[Expressive, more serious, one-off problems]

- **Practical**
[Practical, less serious, recurring problems]

5   **'Personal'**
[Problems very much to do with the individual; internal locus]

- **'Structural'**
[Problems to do with wider institutional/ societal structures; external locus]

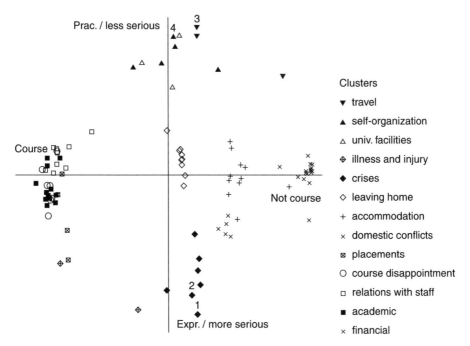

Figure 81.1   *Scatter graph of student problems plotted in a two-dimensional space defined by dimensions one and four (see Table 81.3)*

problem, and category membership (according to the cluster analysis; see the middle column of Table 81.2) is denoted by the different types of symbol. Course-related problems (those on the far left of the figure) cluster either side of the mid-point of the 'expressive-practical' (see Harré 1979) dimension. This suggests that course-related problems are unlikely to be as wholly expressive and serious as bereavements and breakdowns (labelled as 1 and 2, respectively, in Figure 81.1). They are equally unlikely to be as earthily practical as difficulties in travelling and in deciding what to do with one's spare time (labelled as 3 and 4, in Figure 81.1). Indeed academic courses provide the context for problems which have an intriguing mixture of practical and expressive features.

A careful examination of the problems classified as 'Academic' shows that those that align towards the expressive end of dimension four tend to focus on personal and intellectual insecurities:

> *Feeling inadequate … with work piling up and thinking others are much more competent and self-assured than you.*

and:

> *Will the grades for coursework/exams be as high as other students?*

and:

> *Fear of failure. Feeling useless when it comes to handing in assignments …*

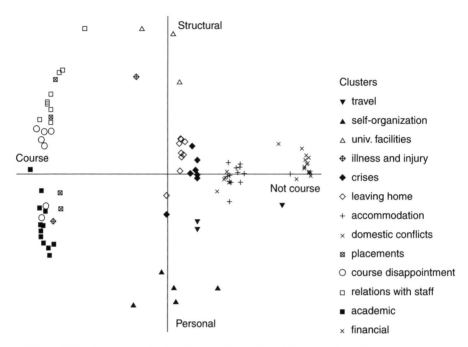

Figure 81.2 *Scatter graph of student problems plotted in a two-dimensional space defined by dimensions one and five (see Table 81.3)*

Intellectual insecurities are a particularly interesting kind of problem. Many students who have participated in our research programme readily admit to these feelings. But the feelings are sustained partly because of a false belief that other people do *not* have the same feelings. Doubts and insecurities about one's own capabilities are grounded in the belief that everyone else is much more secure and confident in their everyday lives than oneself. Many of the students who took part in the sorting task of this study commented on how reassuring it was to read that other people experienced the same kinds of insecurities that they did. Perhaps the biggest single thing we can do to address this particular type of problem, then, is straightforward descriptive research which simply informs people of the existence of the problem.

Dimensions one (the x-axis) and five (the y-axis) form the basis for Figure 81.2. The fifth dimension ('personal-structural') is notable for the way that it spreads the course-related problems from the top to the bottom of the chart. Academic insecurities stretch towards the 'personal' pole of dimension five. More 'structural' are 'course disappointments' (which include complaints about and frustrations with courses), and difficult relationships with lecturers. Examples of these are:

> *High expectations of course not always fulfilled. Some aspects good but a little directionless at times. Worry about whether arts degree will prove valid in employment market (big worry given extent of overdraft). Also … running down facilities (library etc.) for arts courses – we get the impression that we are becoming 2nd class citizens …*

and

> *Sexism of some of the male staff.*

and

> *Proportion of students i.e. staff/student ratios and the lack of personal supervision is extremely evident. Being just another 'face in the crowd' to most lecturers often makes them unapproachable and many academic problems and queries are never solved.*

The last is a challenging kind of problem for help-seeking research. How, and from where, does one get help for the problem of not being able to get help?

The fifth dimension incorporates the theme of perceived levels of control over different types of problem (with problems located at the structural end of the dimension being those which seem least controllable). Financial and domestic problems cluster closely around the mid-point of the dimension, perhaps implying that they are seen as problems which are *somewhat* under the control of the individual; if you do not get on with someone with whom you share (a very typical part of the student experience) you can move ... if you can find somewhere to move to, find someone else to live with, and find enough money for another deposit.

A number of the listed problems describe the difficulties caused by leaving home, and by leaving the support networks that one has lived within for up to an entire lifetime:

> *Adjustment from home life to college life, i.e. having the independence yet being totally responsible for oneself – not having parents to run to if something goes wrong.*

Accounts such as these cluster together at one end of the third dimension, a dimension which highlights that one characteristic feature of life in higher education can be the living of *two* lives: one involving friends and family 'at home', the other involving new friends and colleagues 'at university'. The juggling of priorities and loyalties in this respect can itself be problematic:

> *Alienation from home i.e. having problems with home but being too far away to solve them. Trying not to lose touch with the people who you ultimately will return to.*

When these sorts of problems are plotted in a space defined by dimensions three and four, one account in particular is separated out from the cluster by virtue of being nearer than the others to the 'expressive/more serious' end of the fourth dimension:

> *I am an overseas student and I find myself DIFFICULT to get along with the english students. This maybe due to language barrier and different culture background. My english has deteriorated due to lack of communications between students. ... I am scared and my english is very bad and people don't understand me* [emphasis as in original].

It is particularly distressing to think that this anonymous exercise may have been the only time that the student was able to express such fears, because being unable to talk to people and to get help seems to have been so much part of the problem itself.

Figure 81.3 plots dimension four (x-axis) against dimension five (y-axis). Most of the problems cluster towards the origin of the chart. According to our interpretations this means that most of the problems in the data set are seen as neither very serious nor very trivial, and neither completely individual (and controllable) nor completely structural (and not controllable). It is tempting to suggest that the origin of the chart somehow represents the stuff of everyday, mundane experience; the point at which the feeling, experiencing individual meets the real, concrete world.

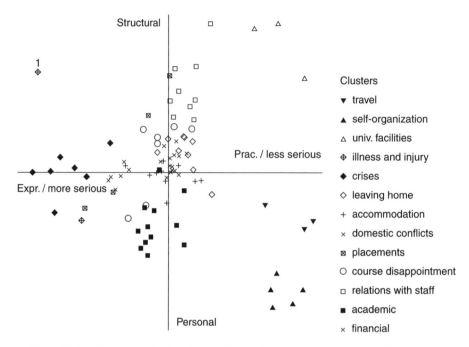

Figure 81.3 *Scatter graph of student problems plotted in a two-dimensional space defined by dimensions four and five (see Table 81.3)*

If this latest point tends to over-interpretation it should not detract from the observation that the 'personal-structural' dimension discriminates progressively less among problems the closer they are to the expressive pole of dimension four. The more expressive and serious a problem becomes, the more it is seen as lying at the very threshold of the personal and the structural. The isolated positioning in this space of the one problem which mentions disability (labelled no. 1) is suggestive and challenging, bearing in mind that the picture has been constructed using a 'social consensus approach' (Forgas 1982).

Discussion

This study has resulted in a picture of a domain of everyday problems in a given population which has been constructed virtually from start to finish by members of that population. The structure of that picture has been given a concrete form by the statistical analyses. We regard this 'concrete form' as an heuristic device (rather than a 'finding') which has been used to examine some core features of the specific accounts of everyday problems.

The analysis we present is not intended to be exhaustive. The picking apart of underlying dimensional and categorical features of first-hand accounts of everyday problems is a major undertaking and is, at this stage, an exploratory process. Yet we believe there is scope for much useful work in this respect; work which can inform both research and practice in the field of counselling psychology, and which may help to narrow the gap between clinician and researcher. An increasingly detailed analysis of first-hand accounts of everyday problems, for example, should lead to a sounder theoretical basis for help-seeking research, while fitting well with the growing trend of doing qualitative research which respects the insights and accounts of research subjects and clients.

In conducting the study in the way that we have done we have laid ourselves open to the criticism that there is no way of knowing how our findings might generalize to other groups in other settings. An additional objection might be that we have not established sufficiently robustly the 'dimensions' that we claim to see in our analyses. We acknowledge these objections, but believe that there needs to be more room in every research field for exploratory work. At some stage, of course, exploratory work must be converted into something more robust, but that stage should sometimes come later rather than sooner in the research process. The drive to pin down 'findings', and assess their general applicability right from the outset is part of a culture that can ultimately stifle research, and one that certainly pushes researchers down the traditional paths of quantification. The more space that is devoted to shoring up interpretations, the less space there is for including excerpts from the first-hand accounts, with the attendant danger that voices like that of the overseas student (cited above) become hidden once again, this time in our raw unreported data.

If researchers in the field of counselling are to capitalize on the growing acceptance of qualitative research methods, then strategies are needed which allow for the systematic handling and analysis of large quantities of texts. But these strategies must respect the texts, and not obscure them from the eventual readership of research reports. In person-centred (or client-centred) research the real knowledge and understanding comes directly from 'people's life stories, freely offered and infinitely precious' (Thomas 1994: 45). We believe that the methods that have been used in this study may be particularly well suited to these ends.

Note

All three authors have an interest in student welfare.

References

Brannen, J. and Collard, J. (1982) *Marriages in Trouble: The Process of Seeking Help*, London: Tavistock Publications.

Forgas, J.P. (1982) 'Episode cognition: internal representations of interaction routines', in L. Berkowitz (ed.), *Advances in Experimental Social Psychology*, vol. 15, London: Academic Press, pp. 59–101.

Grayson, A., Clarke, D.D. and Miller, H. (1998) 'Help-seeking among students: are lecturers seen as potential sources of help?', *Studies in Higher Education*, 23: 143–55.

Grayson, A., Miller, H. and Clarke, D.D. (1998) 'Identifying barriers to help-seeking: a qualitative analysis of students' preparedness to seek help from tutors', *British Journal of Guidance and Counselling*, 26: 237–53.

Halgin, R.P., Weaver, D.D., Edell, W.S. and Spencer, P.G. (1987) 'Relation of depression and help-seeking history to attitudes toward seeking professional psychological help', *Journal of Counseling Psychology*, 34: 177–85.

Harré, R. (1979) *Social Being*, Oxford: Basil Blackwell.

Heppner, P.P., Kivlinghan, D.M. Jr, Good, G.E., Roehlke, H.J., Hills, H.I. and Ashby, J.S. (1994) 'Presenting problems of university counseling center clients: a snapshot and multivariate classification scheme', *Journal of Counseling Psychology*, 41: 315–24.

Hutchinson, R.L. and Reagan, C.A. (1989) 'Problems for which seniors would seek help from school counselors', *The School Counselor*, 36: 271–80.

Kaczmarek, P.G. and Jankowicz, A.D. (1991) 'American college students' perceptions of counselor approachability: professional implications', *International Journal for the Advancement of Counselling*, 14: 313–24.

Lazarus, R. and Folkman, S. (1984) *Stress, Appraisal and Coping*, New York: Springer.

McLennan, J. (1991) 'Formal or informal counselling help: students' experiences', *British Journal of Guidance and Counselling*, 19: 149–59.

McLeod, J. (1994) 'The research agenda for counselling', *Counselling*, 5: 41–3.

Nickerson, K.J., Helms, J.E. and Terrell, F. (1994) 'Cultural mistrust, opinions about mental illness, and black students' attitudes toward seeking psychological help from white counselors', *Journal of Counseling Psychology*, 41: 378–85.

Solberg, V.S., Ritsma, S., Davis, B.J., Tata, S.P. and Jolly, A. (1994) 'Asian-American students' severity of problems and willingness to seek help from university counseling centers: role of previous counseling experience, gender, and ethnicity', *Journal of Counseling Psychology*, 41: 275–9.

Thomas, G. (1994) 'A counsellor first …', *Counselling*, 5: 44–6.

Weller, S.C. and Romney, A.K. (1988) *Systematic Data Collection*, London: Sage.

Discussion issues

1 What are the benefits of qualitative research as opposed to the traditional quantitative methods?

2 What are the key aspects of the procedure used in this study?

3 Can you relate to any of the findings in this study reported by the students?

4 What are your criticisms of this study? Is it sufficiently 'robust'?

82

Cross-Cultural/Racial Matching in Counselling and Therapy

White clients and black counsellors

Roy Moodley and Shukla Dhingra

Preamble

At the Counselling in Education (CIE) Conference in March 1984 at the University of Nottingham, four of the five black participants (Bill Hall, Josna Pankhania, Shukla Dhingra, Roy Moodley), after an inspiring keynote from Gus John, met to discuss ways in which more black people could get involved in counselling. Bill and Josna, who were members of CIE's working group RACE (Race Awareness in Counselling Education), which was set up in 1983, immediately recruited Shukla and Roy into RACE. We met again on 19 May 1984 at Skiddaw, not the 'mountain' in the Lake District but a humble little cottage in Skiddaw Drive in the city of Derby. This drive became the site for further communion between the four of us. It was also the beginning of a new phase in the development of the RACE group and the start of the Association of Black Counsellors (ABC)

The RACE group, which met at the home of Jean Clarke in Leicester, focused on training issues and material development for counsellors in all the sub-divisions in the British Association for Counselling (BAC). Meanwhile ABC, with its headquarters in London and branches in Birmingham and Derby, under the chairpersonship of Bill Hall (who gave up the chair of the RACE group to chair ABC), attempted to engage more black people in training as counsellors and raising black mental health issues generally. By the beginning of the 1990s many of us gave way to 'new blood' in both organizations. RACE went on to become RACE (Race and Cultural Education), a sub-division of BAC under the chairpersonship of Joyce Thompson, and ABC, after actively engaging for a while, seems to be out of the public eye (see Lago and Thompson 1997).

The four of us are still engaging with these issues but in different parts of the world: Bill Hall is practising as a psychotherapist in Philadelphia, USA; Josna Pankhania is a counsellor and researcher in Sydney, Australia; Shukla Dhingra practises as a counsellor at Loughborough University; and Roy Moodley is a freelance consultant in 'race', counselling and psychotherapy.

While our research and professional interest lay primarily with black client issues, we nevertheless felt that our work with white clients (which in many cases are our greatest

This chapter was first published in *Counselling*, Journal of the British Association for Counselling, vol. 9, no. 4, pp. 295–9 (1998).

case-load) also needed analysis and understanding. The paper below is an attempt by Shukla and Roy to discuss the issue of white clients and black counsellors and therapists.

Introduction

Numerous studies in counselling and therapy have explored the issue of cross-cultural/racial matching (Heppner and Dixon 1981; Pomales et al. 1986; Lago and Thompson 1989, 1996; Sue and Sue 1990; Wade and Bernstein 1991; Nickerson et al. 1994; Carter 1995). Many have focused particularly on the white counsellor/back client dyad, and the advantages and disadvantages of such matching. The characteristics and effectiveness of the black counsellor/white client dyad has received minimal attention in the counselling literature. In general, the focus has been on white clients' negative reactions towards black counsellors therapeutically (Carter 1995). The relatively few authors in the field of cross-cultural counselling in Britain, for example d'Ardenne and Mahtani (1989) and Lago and Thompson (1996), have attempted to explore some of the issues of counselling and therapy in a multicultural context, including the black therapist/white client dyad, but not in any great depth.

The paucity of research in 'race', culture and counselling and the lack of substantive literature on black counsellors/therapists in counselling and therapy have led to misconceptions that reinforce a number of stereotype notions about black people in the mental health field. Of particular consequence is that black people are usually seen as clients, thereby fuelling the argument that black counsellors are more apt to be helpees than helpers. This may also account for the small number of trainees and practitioners in this field. Admission policies on some counselling courses and many institutional employment policies may be subtly contributing to these notions (see Lago and Thompson 1996). The way intercultural therapy is presently defined may also create the perception that black people are suited for therapy. For example, in cross-cultural counselling the white counsellor and black client norm excludes white people from the process as clients (Sashidharan 1986). This paradigm reinforces the notion that the black person is 'signified' as 'ill' and can only be helped by the white therapist (see Fernando 1988; Kareem and Littlewood 1992; Littlewood and Lipsedge 1997).

Another perception which problematizes the black counsellor as a professional therapist is the notion that the relatively few ethnic minority counsellors who work in this field are best suited to work chiefly with clients from their own or similar culture background. While in some situations it may be appropriate for same-race therapy to occur (see Mills and Topolski 1996), it does, however, place the back counsellor within a very narrow cultural practice, questioning their skills and competence to work beyond the 'race'/culture, gender and disability dynamic in therapy. Our research although small and not a representative sample of ethnic minority counsellors/therapists in Britain, shows that black counsellors work with just as many white clients as they do with black clients. And, in many cases, black counsellors work with fewer ethnic minority clients than white clients as a result of the demography of the institutions they work in. Some work exclusively with white clients.

In the context of a growing interest in counselling and psychotherapy by ethnic minority groups, both as clients and as practitioners, it seems important that this aspect is researched and evaluated. Using material from a case vignette by one of the authors and from the published literature on cross-cultural counselling, we have attempted to show the strategies that white clients use in accepting black counsellors. We also interviewed a small number of black counsellors/therapists to ascertain their views on working with white clients. This paper, therefore, is an attempt to consider the black counsellor/white client relationship, examining the particular processes and characteristics that lead to effective outcomes.

Client's choice of a counsellor

A client's preference for a therapist of his or her choice is of particular importance in the relationship and to the eventual outcomes in therapy. Engaging a client at the pre-entry process with the issue of choice of counsellor will support the therapeutic alliance. Clients' awareness and understanding of the process of counselling and therapy will also contribute to positive outcomes. Beutler et al. (1986) suggest that patients who are familiar with psychotherapy may benefit from an informed understanding of what to expect in treatment. The same could be said for counselling. Beutler et al. (1996) suggest that the integrity and strength of the therapeutic alliance may be fortified by assigning therapists to patients with similar demographic backgrounds, sex, age and ethnicity. However, matching done purely on the basis of race or colour can imprison both the professional and the client in their own racial and cultural identity (Kareem 1992: 24). Making a choice is often closely tied up with a client's actual presenting problem. By addressing the issue of counsellor choice, even before the counselling process begins, clients confront aspects of themselves which contribute to their disturbances and discomforts. In this way, the processes of considering, inquiring and being interviewed for counselling/therapy become paramount in constructing the parameters which may either confine or liberate the client in the relationship with the counsellor.

The opportunity to choose a counsellor is usually available to many white clients but not to the majority of black clients. McLeod (1993) reminds us that counselling remains a predominantly white occupation with relatively few ethnic minority counsellors. 'Black counsellors, by virtue of their training and background, will have been predominantly geared to working with white people, not black people' (Lago and Thompson 1989: 289). Many white clients who are not offered the opportunity to choose a counsellor may be reluctant to enter into any kind of therapy. Indeed in a postmodern democratic environment, clients may offer resistance to any counsellor irrespective of 'race' or gender if they perceive that their right to choose has been infringed. However, for white clients the appearance of a black counsellor may unconsciously evoke certain prejudices and stereotypes which could lead to the rejection of the counsellor but be interpreted by the client as not having a right to choose. This was reflected by Mary (not her real name), in counselling with one of the authors, who had this to say:

> And I thought maybe she's got different view points, something she's find me really Western and really extrovert and lot weird and stuff and I thought maybe there will be some barrier and that you wouldn't be able to help me as much as the other counsellor would, that was white same as me.

As it happens, Mary did not reject her black counsellor but clearly expressed her fear of the 'other'. These issues may not arise in a white counsellor/white client match since it is the norm, and on the surface presents an agreeable and acceptable pairing, even if the client experiences other types of conflict, such as differences of gender, personality and so on.

Exploring the question of 'race' in therapy

In our research, the black counsellors we interviewed used a variety of strategies to consider 'race' in therapy with white clients. Some (less than 40 per cent) would take a proactive approach to the subject of 'race' earlier on in the therapy but were clear that the timing and readiness of the client would be key in deciding precisely when the subject was explored. Others (more than 60 per cent) adopted a non-directive approach, indicating that they would leave it up to the client and then negotiate the most appropriate way for the 'client to talk about "race" issues'. Almost all the black counsellors we interviewed were sensitive to the complexity and confusions surrounding the issues of 'race', culture and ethnicity. Some black counsellors who used the proactive approach were confronted by some of the answers they received. For example, one counsellor asked the question: 'How do you feel about working with me, a black therapist?' She received the following responses from white clients: 'I'm not prejudiced', 'You seem all right', 'You speak good English', 'I didn't realise you were Asian.'

Another counsellor who confronted a client found herself at the receiving end of a barrage of negative perceptions about 'race'. This was difficult for the counsellor to receive initially but good supervision and being clear about her therapeutic approach offered this counsellor strength to understand her client. Six months into counselling, this same client is now emulating the counsellor in dress and other non-verbal manners as a way of identifying with the therapist. Many of the counsellors interviewed felt that the issue of 'race in the hands of an unskilled counsellor would intimidate and oppress clients. Competent counsellors using positive aspects of themselves offer clients the opportunity to 'risk take', challenge previously held assumptions and transform themselves in counselling. Skilful handling of the therapy will prevent clients from feeling guilty or putting up defences and resistances. This was seen in Mary's therapy, when she said:

> When I first realized that you are a different race to me, I did think she can't be able to help me you know she, eh, especially, I used to live in, eh, a big Asian community around a big Asian community in (…) and they were just so very different to me.

Clearly Mary was able to establish sufficient confidence and trust in the relationship with the black counsellor to share these thoughts knowing that they showed her prejudice about the Asian community. In moving from the first-person to the third-person pronoun – 'I did think she can't be able to help me you know she …', Mary was able to reduce her anxiety and also attempted to protect her counsellor from her 'race'-based remarks.

Carter (1995) offers a case study in which Tina, a white client, reports that her friend who is 'light-skinned' told her that she was lucky to have a black clinician. In the therapy she becomes confused and distressed when 'race' is raised. The excerpt below is a small part of the case study described by Carter:

> *Tina:* Are you very much aware in here that I am White and you are Black? Because I'm not.
>   (Pause)
> *Therapist:* Sometimes. (Silence) I mean, it's hard not to be aware that you're, White.

Tina: Yeah.

Therapist: When I hear you talk about your experiences, then I think some of your experiences can only be understood by seeing you as White. The expectations and perspectives that you hold come about as a result of your racial experiences. So, I'm aware of that. I do have to understand you in the context of your race and gender.

Tina: I don't know what that means exactly.

Therapist: Well, it means there're differences between people from various races, I might interact with you differently, talk to you differently; if you were Asian, for instance, our pattern of communication would be different. Thus, race affects our work. Do you see what I mean?

Tina: Yeah, I do. (1995: 207)

Carter noted that black counsellor/white client dyads like their counterparts are strongly influenced by each participant's racial identity attitude development and advocated an active introjection of these issues with clients. In another case study, Tom, a white client, who clearly thought that his black therapist was 'superior' to him 'by virtue of the age, education and academic experience (i.e. a doctorate) and "down-to-earth"' was 'unable to share himself and his inner struggles in a consistent and productive way…. Tom was emotionally closed and defended' (1995: 202). Clearly there are no rules to follow in exploring the issue of 'race' as a variable in therapy; black counsellors must themselves be 'ready' to enter the complex, confusing, profound and artificial world of 'race'. 'The race of the therapist will inescapably affect the therapy as it does when the therapist is white and the patient black' (Thomas 1992: 139). Both black and white patients use race to express transferences of object relationships and drive derivatives (Holmes 1992).

White clients' strategies in accepting black counsellors

The negative attitude of white clients to black counsellors must be acknowledged and understood in the context of a society which reflects racism in different degrees. In a postmodern multicultural and multiracial society such as Britain, counselling is always set in a political context. Socio-political variables are now part of the terrain that black counsellors and therapists find themselves in. Therefore, researchers who focus on just the negative aspect of the relationship can miss the important strategies which white clients use to develop and maintain the therapeutic relationship with black counsellors. Clients may adopt subtle strategies to ensure that they are being 'short-changed'. For example, the excerpt below shows Mary's way of accepting her counsellor:

Mary: But you have to be professional because you can't be anything else otherwise you get into a big mess, but I do feel you understand me.

Counsellor: Em.

Mary: I feel understood as a woman.

Counsellor: Em.

Mary: When especially a lot of my issues in patriarchal society in and stuff like that and I feel you understand me. I can trust you.

Mary's strategy involved a complex and logical reasoning of the counsellor's commitment to the professional role and an assertive request for good practice. She continues to make sure that she gets her 'money's worth' by recognizing and acknowledging the gender similarity of the relationship. 'Race' then becomes more acceptable because it engages in the discourse of gender and it can also be contextualized professionally, for example Mary's utterance – 'otherwise you get into a big mess' – is at best a friendly threat or, at worst, litigation. But this is a strong scenario that we are alluding to and clearly from Mary's relationship with her counsellor this was not the case. This last excerpt from Mary's therapy demonstrates that trust and honesty between the white client and the black counsellor is the key ingredient for positive outcomes of the process:

> *Mary:* I think one of the biggest things I got out of counselling was being honest.
> *Counsellor:* I found you very honest. Extremely honest and, and open.
> *Mary:* Yea, it was important for me. I was counselled before again by a women. And it didn't, didn't help me like it has now. I wasn't being honest with myself, let alone with the counsellor. But this time around I was just so desperate, I was in such a situation with everyone that I knew. I just felt it was time to be honest, I just wanted to take the step and be honest with you.

Honesty in this instance may also be understood as a metaphor, reflecting the various stages of undoing the suspicion and then building the level of trust that the therapeutic process requires for effective outcomes. Lago and Thompson (1996: 105) remind us that 'it is important to respect the enormous risk faced by the client especially when the therapist is so clearly identifiable as a member of the (complained about) racial group'.

Carter (1995: 205–6) suggests that:

> In the therapeutic setting, a White client may assume that a Black or visible racial/ethnic therapist should act, think, and feel as he or she does. The White client also believes that the non-White clinician will comply with the client's wishes and conform to the client's stereotypes. This results in a power struggle, because the therapist assumes that he or she is responsible for the direction of the psychotherapeutic process.

Not only may the therapist be required to understand the client's projections but he/she has to cope with his/her own fantasies about the client's projections and meanwhile attempt to stay open and receptive to what the client is bringing (Lago and Thompson 1996: 105). The issue of power in counselling is still not clearly understood and perhaps may need further research in all types of therapeutic relationships. Lago and Thompson (1989: 27) remind us that, from the perspective of power, the white counsellor and black client relationship also has a potential danger, namely a perception of the notion of white superiority. In our research a number of black counsellors indicated that this may present a problem if the therapist fails to understand 'where the client is coming from' in terms of socio-economic background, poor self-concept, acceptance of their abilities and disabilities, and so on. Sometimes these issues are the very core of the problem clients face in the first place. Many of the counsellors in the research felt that if the therapeutic outcomes were experienced negatively or perceived as unsatisfactory with the black counsellors it might reinforce the 'white supremacy complex' (see Moodley 1998).

Black counsellors' strategies in managing the relationship

In our study, the black counsellors we interviewed emphasized the complexity of their professional roles as counsellors, while at the same time they were aware that their skin colour was part of their practice. This was understood both in terms of their presence in the institution as well as their relationships with colleagues and clients. Many (more than

80 per cent) were overtly anxious to be seen as a professional first but were aware that in the counselling relationship their ethnicity and colour was an important variable. For many counsellors (more than 70 per cent) the problem was not with 'race' and white clients, but with 'race' and the institutions they work in. Many indicated that they were often made invisible through staff development policies, subtle employment and promotion policies, and so on. While institutional issues were important to discuss, most counsellors felt that their work with clients overshadowed these institutional policies.

In d'Ardenne's and Mahtani's (1989) example of a black counsellor working with a white client, although the analysis of the therapy is very specific to the one client, Fred, a number of conclusions can be drawn for black counsellors in general. In this case, although the black counsellor has experienced racism and hostility in society, she still has to be aware of how the white client can respond to her. To prepare herself she 'uses her white friends and acquaintances to provide her with insights into the prejudices and fears expressed by the major culture' (1989: 35). She is also 'in contact with several discussion and support groups for black counsellors who will help her make sense of all her trans-cultural experiences' (ibid.: 35). Clearly in this way the counsellor has constructed a professional approach to her practice. The client, on the other hand, appears to cope with the 'reversal of power' by literally relating the counsellor to his Asian GP, to whom he has given status. For the client, this kind of coping strategy is vital in forming a favourable relationship with his counsellor and at the same time dealing with the complexity of 'race', culture and ethnicity.

The black counsellor in the above example was able to construct a strategy for maintaining her professional 'health', but many in our research indicated that the limited supervision that they were offered, and often with therapists who were not familiar with the dynamics of 'race', culture and ethnicity, must be a cause for concern by all those who work in this field. We are aware from our interviews that some of the black counsellors were underplaying the 'race' context for a number of reasons. Maintaining an invisibility in the institution may offer rewards and may be a misguided loyalty to the institutional racism which pervades some workplaces. If black counsellors would rather be known as professional counsellors (like architects, lawyers and so on), as this may subvert the negative impact of blackness in their practice, the question we need to ask is, 'Can this stop white clients from seeing them as black?'

We are aware from our interviews that many counsellors (more than 60 per cent) believe that not all white clients come into therapy with a conscious awareness of 'race' as a variable to explore in therapy. 'Some white patients who deny any difference between a black therapist and themselves, do so to preserve politeness and to secure against the seepage of unconscious material' (Thomas 1992: 140). Therefore, it behoves black counsellors to be very sensitive about introducing the concept of 'race', culture or ethnicity, and to do so only at the request of the client. The interpretations of the transference and the countertransference feelings must be clearly understood within the context of the developing relationship with the client. Counsellors and therapists must work at achieving this position. Dupont-Joshua (1997: 284) suggests that 'counsellors must continually work on their attitudes, on their own racial identity and also work with the aspects of race and culture reflected in the relationship', which she, as a black therapist had to work through: 'very painful issues around my racial identity ... because I know that I cannot work with others on their racial identity unless I work on my own' (ibid.: 282).

We talked earlier about counsellors and therapists needing to be aware of 'projecting' on to clients their 'psychological baggage' which is best dealt with in their own therapy.

Conclusion

The process and outcomes of counselling in relation to cross-cultural/racial matching is becoming particularly important as a result of the growth of counselling and the increase in ethnic minority clients and counsellors. In this paper we have attempted to highlight through some of our findings of a small and limited research project that although black counsellors and white clients enter into a complex relationship *vis-à-vis* the socio-political variable, they nevertheless can develop a rich environment for effective and creative therapeutic outcomes. This research has convinced us that more research needs to be done using clearly defined and systematic methodologies to investigate the dynamics of the black counsellor with white clients as well as the other growing practice of black counsellors with black clients.

Acknowledgement

We are grateful to the client Mary (not her real name) for giving us permission to use transcribed material in this study, and to all the black counsellors who took part in the interviews.

References

Beutler, L.E., Crago, M. and Arizmendi, T.G. (1986) 'Therapist variables in psychotherapy process and outcomes', in S.L. Garfield and A.E. Bergin (eds), *Handbook of Psychotherapy and Behavior Change* (3rd edn), New York: Wiley.

Beutler, L.E., Zetzer, H.A. and Williams, R.E. (1996) 'Research applications of prescriptive therapy', in W. Dryden (ed.), *Research in Counselling and Psychotherapy*, London: Sage.

Carter, R.T. (1995) *The Influence of RACE and Racial Identity in Psychotherapy*, New York: John Wiley & Sons.

d'Ardenne, P. and Mahtani, A. (1989) *Transcultural Counselling in Action*, London: Sage.

Dupont-Joshua, A. (1997) 'Working with issues of race in counselling', *Counselling*, 8 (4): 282–4.

Fernando, S. (1988) *Race and Culture in Psychiatry*, London: Croom Helm.

Heppner, P.P. and Dixon, D.N. (1981) 'A review of the interpersonal influence process in counselling', *Personnel and Guidance Journal*, 59: 542–50.

Holmes, D.E. (1992) 'Race and transference in psychoanalysis and psychotherapy', *International Journal of Psycho-analysis*, 73 (1): 1–11.

Kareem, J. (1992) 'The Nafsiyat Intercultural Therapy Centre: ideas and experience in intercultural therapy', in J. Kareem and R. Littlewood (eds), *Intercultural Therapy*, London: Blackwell Scientific Publications.

Kareem, J. and Littlewood, R. (eds) (1992) *Intercultural Therapy Themes, Interpretations and Practice*, London: Blackwell Scientific Publications.

Lago, C. and Thompson, J. (1989) 'Counselling and race', in W. Dryden, D. Charles-Edwards and R. Woolfe (eds), *Handbook of Counselling in Britain*, London: Tavistock/Routledge.

Lago, C. and Thompson, J. (1996) *Race, Culture and Counselling*, Buckingham: Open University Press.

Lago, C. and Thompson, J. (1997) 'The triangle with curved sides: issues of race and culture in counselling supervision', in G. Shipton (ed.), *Supervision of Psychotherapy and Counselling: Making a Place to Think*, Buckingham: Open University Press.

Littlewood, R. and Lipsedge, M. (1997) *Aliens and Alienists: Ethnic Minorities and Psychiatry* (3rd edn), London: Routledge.

McLeod, J. (1993) *An Introduction to Counselling*, Buckingham: Open University Press.

Mills, M. and Topolski, C. (1996) 'SHANTI: a women's therapy centre', *Counselling*, 7 (2): 108–12.

Moodley, R. (1998) '" I say what I like": frank talk(ing) in counselling and psychotherapy', *British Journal of Guidance and Counselling*, 26 (4): 495–508.

Nickerson, K.J., Helms, J.E. and Terrell, F. (1994) 'Cultural mistrust, opinions about mental illness, and Black students' attitudes towards seeking psychological help from White counselors', *Journal of Counseling Psychology*, 41 (3): 378–85.

Pomales, J., Claiborn, C.D. and LaFromboise, T.D. (1986) 'Effects of Black students' racial identity on perceptions of white counselors varying in cultural sensitivity', *Journal of Counseling Psychology*, 33 (1): 57–61.

Pope-Davis, D.B. and Coleman, H.L.K. (eds) (1997) *Multicultural Counseling Competencies. Assessment, Education and Training, and Supervision*, Thousands Oaks, CA: Sage.

Sashidharan, S.P. (1986) 'Ideology and politics in transcultural psychiatry', in J.L. Cox (ed.), *Transcultural Psychiatry*, London: Croom Helm.

Sue, D.W. and Sue, D. (1990) *Counseling the Culturally Different: Theory and Practice* (2nd edn), New York: John Wiley & Sons.

Thomas, L. (1992) 'Racism and psychotherapy: working with racism in the consulting room – an analytical view', in J. Kareem and R. Littlewood (eds), *Intercultural Therapy*, London: Blackwell Scientific Publications.

Wade, P. and Bernstein, B.L. (1991) 'Culture sensitivity training and counselor's race: effects on black female clients' perceptions and attrition', *Journal of Counseling Psychology*, 38: 9–15.

Discussion issues

1 What are the key issues to consider when assessing clients for a similar 'race'/culture therapist?

2 When and how would a counsellor explore 'race' and power with a white client?

3 What strategies do white clients adopt in therapy with black counsellors to ensure a 'safe' environment for psychological exploration?

4 What techniques do black counsellors use when working with white clients?

83

Therapeutic Issues for Sexually Abused Adult Males

Kim Etherington

This article is based on in-depth interviews with a non-clinical sample of 25 men who identified themselves in response to advertising for 'adult male survivors of childhood sexual abuse'. The author approached the work from the assumption that patriarchal socialization creates barriers for males in defining their experience as abuse and this in turn influences the reported prevalence of males who have been abused. She also assumes that sex-role stereotyping creates a barrier for the recognition of females as abusers and this creates problems in definition and reported prevalence. Full findings and many of the men's stories can be found in Adult Male Survivors of Childhood Sexual Abuse *published by Pavilion Pubs. (1995). The author has recently completed* Narrative Approaches to Working with Adult Male Survivors of Child Sexual Abuse: the Client's, the Counsellor's and the Researcher's Story *which is published by Jessica Kingsley (2000b). It provides us with a rare opportunity to discover the therapeutic issues for two adult male survivors from their point of view, using their own words, as well as from the perspective of their counsellor.*

Introduction

Recovery from childhood sexual abuse for males is in many respects the same as that for females although there are some essential differences (Etherington 1995, 2000a). There is much useful literature on female recovery issues (Bass and Davis 1988; Hall and Lloyd 1989; Sanderson 1990; Briere 1992; Elliot 1993) so I will limit myself in this article to issues that have been identified through the research and are particularly pertinent for males.

Difficulties in identification with the victim role

At a very early age males are taught to become responsible; socialization messages such as 'take care of mummy while I'm gone' serve to train boys to believe that being male invests them with power over and responsibility for females. These attitudes are reinforced throughout life, creating a society in which male sexual abuse victims have had to remain invisible if they were to avoid judgement as 'less than a man'.

Socialization messages about the nature of females (sugar and spice and all things nice) perpetuate the myth that females can only be seen as nurturers – thereby negating the reality of females as abusers. Thirteen of the 25 men in my study were abused by females and seven of those by their mothers. The abuse perpetrated by females was more

---

This chapter was first published in *Counselling*, Journal of the British Association for Counselling, vol. 7, no. 3, pp. 224–8 (1996).

frequently coercive and seductive than aggressive and forceful. Language that focuses on violence created difficulties of definition for men abused in non-violent ways. One man said: 'Sexual abuse carries overtones of wickedness and prison; I don't like applying that to my mother.'

Perhaps such phrases as 'the abuse of sexuality' (Bolton et al. 1989) or 'sexual misuse' could more usefully be included at the early stages of therapy to allow the reframing of the experience to develop in a way that allows the client to face up to his victimization.

'Sexual victim' usually conjures up an image of a small, female, powerless creature who is trapped by a dominant male into a role of submission. The word 'victim' has been rejected by most sexually abused females in preference for the word 'survivor', a more powerful image. If this is how women react against 'victim' it is likely that males will have an even stronger reaction. Recovery cannot begin until he is able to acknowledge the word 'victim' as a human condition which has resulted from a traumatic event and one with which he can identify (Hunter and Gerber 1990). Whereas it may be important to encourage a female to change 'victim' to 'survivor' – it is equally important to encourage a man initially to accept his victimization. If there is no 'victim' then there are no adverse effects and no need to engage with what might be overwhelming feelings of powerlessness.

Identification with the aggressor

One of the more gender-specific coping mechanisms used by males (and sometimes by females) is 'identification with the aggressor'. When a boy has been socialized to believe that 'real men are powerful', the degree of dissonance created by a sexual assault may cause him to identify himself as the one in control. A young male who is abused by an older or more powerful female will frequently adopt this belief and his thinking is reinforced by societal attitudes towards sex and gender roles in which the male is always seen as the sexual predator. A man told me of his difficulty in defining his mother as an abuser:

> apart from being my mother, she was a woman. I'd been educated by my father that women were there for the cooking, cleaning and sex. They were put on earth for our benefit and every man should have several. They were not the abusers, they were to be abused upon. So how could she abuse me when I was the man?

A male might acknowledge symptoms but deny their basis in sexual abuse. Paul accepts that his serious medical condition is stress-related but cannot connect the stress with his severe, long-term sexual abuse by both parents. He cannot afford to see his mother as his main abuser and because he was actively involved during penetrating her, he interpreted that as 'behaving like a man should': 'I didn't feel what was happening was abuse; it was very loving and part of giving affection. ... Because it was my mother it was acceptable – if it had been a man then it wouldn't have been.'

The 'you should be so lucky response' often displayed by society when a young boy is sexually abused by an older woman creates confusion and denial for the victim; societal attitudes educate males to experience any sexual activity with a woman, especially an older woman, as a welcome initiation into manhood.

Males who are abused by males might identify with the aggressor who shares their gender. George, a paedophile, says he felt that 'it was almost as if I was in control' when he was molested by a stranger at the age of 10. By this means he defends himself from his unconscious feelings of victimization. George attributed to his victims equal status (and therefore responsibility) to himself; he says of his childhood neighbour, 'I think she has fallen in love with me. I tell her we just cannot have a relationship.'

Robert who was abused by his mother, abused his daughter and her friends. He refers to his victims as 'precocious' and for this reason it was acceptable to touch them sexually. By identifying himself as the aggressor to avoid acknowledging his mother's abusing behaviour, he is unable to perceive the children he abused as victims. He will only be able to take full responsibility for his abusing behaviour when he identifies himself as his mother's victim, thereby undoing the defence mechanism which has helped him survive to adulthood.

When a child has been subjected to an uncontrollable event, he may deal with his anxiety by re-enacting this event; he gains a sense of mastery by becoming the powerful one. Eight men in my study re-enacted their own abuse on other children during childhood/adolescence; two continued to abuse children as adults. Several re-enacted their victim role in their adult relationships; two men who had been anally raped as adolescents were also raped by men as adults.

Men who experience pain or force during their molestation can more easily identify themselves as victims, thereby making it less likely that they go on to abuse others. When the victim becomes aroused or when the abuse is part of a 'loving' relationship, they are less likely to define themselves as abused; arousal can be wrongly interpreted as consent, erection as pleasure and ejaculation as orgasm. A male's response to sexual stimulation is usually immediate and obvious; the feeling of involvement and responsibility may be the greater for that. Men need help to understand that arousal during abuse is the outcome of a healthy body's response to unhealthy circumstances; that a child who enjoys sexual stimulation and seeks it out in his relationships with adults is no more responsible for the abuse than a child who felt no arousal; that it is always the adult's responsibility to hold the taboo.

Males who equate the word 'victim' with 'passive' may reassert their 'maleness' by becoming sexually and physically aggressive or promiscuous. Reaction formation has been identified as a coping mechanism when a person behaves in ways that deny his deep-seated feelings. Robert, who was aggressively abused around the age of 7, describes how at the age of 13 he became a tyrant, and in his twenties he engaged in frequent and promiscuous behaviour: 'I had a little black book of conquests … my wife was the sixty-third woman I had slept with. It was how I measured my manhood; notches on my gun.'

Externalized responses

Externalized responses seem to be more common in males generally, and therefore are more likely among abused men. Men in my study described drug and alcohol abuse, sexual addiction, aggressive, anti-social and sexually abusive behaviour (Etherington 1995). Acting-out behaviour is a way of coping with unexpressed feelings and may be a way of avoiding the feelings that are a necessary part of healing. However, until the client has new coping mechanisms at his disposal it is unhelpful to attempt to dismantle the outdated ones.

Homophobic concerns

Homophobic concerns can be dealt with by exploration of feelings and may involve clarification that arousal is likely to be the same whatever the gender of the abuser and may not be an indicator of sexual orientation. These issues have been dealt with elsewhere (Sgroi 1989; Hunter 1990a, 1990b; Etherington 1995).

Family, personal and societal values need to be explored with the client in order to help them to accept their sexual identity; dissonance may have been created by introjected heterosexist messages about acceptable and unacceptable sexual behaviour. Martin told of his pain at his mother's response to his disclosure of homosexuality: 'My mother screamed repetitively "I wanted a boy". To this day she refers to the make-up of our family being two girls, Martin, and two boys.' He describes how this message was reinforced by his church: 'I was back again into the "Yes, you are a pervert. Yes, the Church is right; you are a sinner and you are dammed." And it was very much in those feelings that I walked in front of a double-decker bus.'

Many men assumed that their male abusers were homosexual rather than paedophiliac; or that they themselves must be homosexual if an adult male wanted to engage sexually with them; or that abuse by a male contributes to their development of homosexuality which they may have introjected societal judgement of as shameful. Men who were abused by females were more likely to identify themselves as heterosexual than men abused by men or by both men and women. This issue has been dealt with in greater detail elsewhere (Etherington 1995).

The recovery process

Once the man has accepted that he has been a victim of childhood sexual abuse, recovery has begun. This realization may initiate a crisis during which there may be flashbacks, intrusive images, thoughts and feelings which need to be 'contained'. The man may fear 'going mad' and may need reassurance that this is part of a normal process of healing. Chronic post-traumatic stress disorder has been described in detail elsewhere (Mezey and King 1992; Etherington 2000b).

Recovery will entail cognitive work which permits the processing of the abusive incident/s, identification and changing unhelpful beliefs and attitudes related to responsibility, trust and self-concept; exploration and discharge of feelings; and identification of useful behavioural changes and the provision of a safe environment in which these changes can be supported and rehearsed.

Client autonomy is central to the counselling process in general (Bond 1993) and is of particular importance in situations where the traumatic experiences of the client and their gender role socialization is concerned with power and control. A safe environment will require clearly negotiated and maintained boundaries. In this way the therapist models for the client how to set personal boundaries in other areas and relationships in their lives.

Controlling behaviour, such as the client coming late or staying away, attempts to bully the therapist as a symbol of authority, can be made conscious and explored within the therapeutic relationship, which can become a 'laboratory' for experimenting with new ways of coping.

Trust needs to be earned by the therapist and develops over time; this relationship can provide the client with a testing ground for future relationships and, at best, will heal some of the damage created by the betrayal of trust in the abusive relationship. If the therapist is the same sex as the abuser, this will usually impact on the process. Andrew described his feelings when a male and a female member of the community psychiatric team were sent to his home following his rape as an adult; he had been raped previously by a peer at the age of fourteen:

> They sent me some chap and a female student with him. I responded very well to her but I loathed the chap. I did not want a man there. She had that natural ability and human warmth; he was very analytical and probing, very good – he probably would have made me tackle things but what I needed was some human kindness. On the last meeting she said to me 'the first time I saw you I thought you were going to cry and I could have hugged you', and I thought 'Oh God, I wish you had – that was what I needed,' because nobody hugged me and let me cry in their arms.

Having been twice raped by males it is understandable that he did not want to expose his vulnerability to a male. Working with a male might be most useful for both male and female survivors at a later stage but there is an argument for using female workers at the initial stage of helping. A man may allow himself to be vulnerable with a female whom he may perceive to be more comfortable with emotions and less likely to criticize him as unmasculine. Blagg (1989) reports in an NSPCC report, a study by Broussard and Wagner (1988) which indicates that male professionals in particular were inclined to hold boy victims responsible for the abuse.

The work with abuse is likely to be long term although some advocates of brief therapy have developed solution-focused ways of working with survivors (Dolan 1991). However, Martin's case highlights how difficult it is to work with a client who has time-limited sessions; a trusting relationship takes time to build.

> I told this person in the first session that I had recently remembered that I had been abused and wanted to deal with it. Although I went for twelve sessions the abuse was never mentioned. The therapy was client-centred in its approach so it was for me to give the agenda for each session. It's fair to say that at the half-way point the therapist said that I hadn't mentioned it and asked if I wanted to; I declined. Four sessions from the end the therapist once again offered me the opportunity and once again I declined. Looking back I realize that I wasn't ready at that point; I wasn't comfortable enough to access such painful memories.

Referral to another therapist might be more appropriate if during the assessment period it becomes clear that long-term work is required. This can arise in situations when sexual abuse is uncovered in another setting, such as during detoxification, attendance at a clinic for sexually transmitted disease or other medical settings, or during marital therapy. The timing of suggestions about referral are crucial. It might be damaging for a therapist to make this suggestion immediately following disclosure when the client might be most vulnerable to feelings of rejection. Martin, a priest, described his feelings when he disclosed that he remembered his childhood abuse during a writing workshop:

> I went to the man in charge of my formation and told him. He panicked; he didn't know what to do; he said he would get me help. This felt quite devasting. It felt like he was saying 'don't bring it to me; I can't cope, take it somewhere else, go away!'

Some therapists have become anxious about the accusations levelled by those who propound the so-called 'False Memory Syndrome' and this may create an atmosphere in which both therapist and client avoid working with dreams and falshbacks for fear of being accused of implanting memories. A therapist who avoids leading questions, interpretation, and remains tentative has little to fear. Staying with the client in a spirit of shared and supportive exploration will enable clients to discover *their* truth. Further discussion of the issues raised by false memory lobbyists can be found elsewhere (Etherington 1995, and Accuracy About Abuse).

It is important that the therapist believes the client's 'truth' which might sometimes change over time as it becomes clearer. James, a young man who clearly remembered his abuse by a stranger when he was 12 years old and had vague feelings of having been abused much earlier, described his experiences of working with a psychoanalyst who interpreted his experiences as fantasy:

> I saw an NHS psychoanalyst; he denied my reality and told me I was imagining things. Psycho-analysis goes wrong because it's based on a theory that things have to fit; that process devalues the survivor's reality and truth; it can be used as a form of denial – used to suppress memories.

He went on to highlight other responses:

> The first person I told was dad; I was 18. He told me to stop making a fuss about nothing. I felt angry with his response but I couldn't tell him.

Some time after the research process was completed James contacted me to say that he · had now connected with earlier memories of abuse by his father.

Clients sometimes fear being disbelieved almost more than the abuse; they think they might be judged as 'going mad' because people around them at the time of abuse told them that everything was fine. William described how, at the age of 11,

> I had 'controlled breakdowns' lasting about an hour during which I would hysterically cry and laugh alternately. At school the teacher asked me if I was OK (obviously aware the I wasn't) and I broke off, looked up and said in a coherent, calm voice that I was fine and then burst out laugh-ing again. She asked me if there was anything wrong at home. I replied (in a coherent pause) that everything was fine at home. I honestly believed what my Dad continually told me – that I was very lucky indeed, very privileged and happy.   ·

Uninformed professionals may invalidate the client's reality. Sam, a man I interviewed in prison, tells how his anger at society was fuelled when he realized that even those he turned to for help were unwilling to believes his story:

> At the age of 14 I tried to tell my social worker and she said 'It doesn't happen; women don't abuse blokes.' That reaction hurt. It made it hard to tell someone else about it. I thought 'If you don't believe me then who is going to?' So I kept it inside myself.

This man was convicted of indecent assault on his under-age girlfriend a year after his attempt at disclosure. He has been convicted of arson and burglary which he committed to finance his drug addiction. He had been sexually abused by three of his sisters from the age of 6, the age at which he first attempted suicide.

Repressed anger causes depression, suicidal feelings and self-destructive behaviours. Twenty-three of the men in my study have acknowledged depression and 18 of them have felt suicidal. They describe self-punitive behaviour arising from guilt, feelings of responsibility and badness. Men have rarely been taught a language to express feelings. Feelings may be expressed through dreams which can be healthily externalized through gestalt work, drawing or clay work in order to gain a sense of mastery over the childhood feelings.

The therapist helps the client to tell the story without interpretation, explores feelings, helps to clarify details and establishes a safe therapeutic relationship. Once this has been established the client can be helped to reframe the experiences, recognizing cognitive distortions and blind spots. Justin may have experienced this happening too soon:

> I have seen people from the NHS for pills and short interviews but I have always felt that I have been interrogated, as if it had been my fault.

At this stage it might be useful for the therapist to use the term 'victim', even if the client is still demonstrating intermittent denial.

At this stage the client may be saying 'It did happen but it didn't have any effect' – or 'I'm over it'. The client may feel affection for the abuser and need to protect them. Positive feelings towards the abuser need to be accepted especially when the abuser has been a close family member. Clients may have coped by idealization of the abuser and internalized all the 'bad'. They can be helped to understand that conflicting feelings can exist within and towards the same person. This might also give them permission to both love and hate their abuser.

As this process develops the client may feel his fear. Validation of fear contributes to the understanding of the event as abuse, even though coercion rather than force was used and he may see himself as a willing participant. Fear is an appropriate response to being violated and, if he has been socialized not to acknowledge fear, it might feel overwhelming. During this phase the client might respond by extreme acting out. The right to confront or challenge this behaviour needs to be earned; inappropriate or untimely confrontation can reflect the original abuse of power.

During this stage the client might prematurely wish to forgive the abuser to avoid the painful feelings or the pressure from family or Church. Andrew describes his need to forgive his rapist:

> To not forgive is to twist yourself up with hate and I don't think it does you any good; it might for a while, but forgiveness is part of having compassion and letting go and forgiveness isn't words, it's doing something.

His need to 'do something' was satisfied when he unexpectedly met up with his rapist one night in a pub:

> I bought him a drink and felt really proud of myself. He didn't notice but I was gripping the bar and my knuckles were white 'cos if I took my hands off the bar they would have been shaking. I didn't accuse him because I don't think he would have understood. To be fair he has got an argument; as an adult you are responsible for your own actions to some extent. It was up to me to make sure that I didn't make myself so vulnerable.

Andrew was still avoiding his fear and anger and was caught up with a sense of having some responsibility for his rape because he had drunk too much.

Anger may create fear and shame. The client may fantasize violent revenge. Jeremy says:

> I would have just got my mates to have battered him to hell, then taken all his money and burnt his house down. I don't care if I go to prison for it. It would give me the satisfaction of really hurting him. Maybe I'll do something really horrible like cutting his knob off and chuck it in his mouth and say 'Suck that! Look what you made me do – you can do it yourself now.'

Such strong feelings might frighten the client who may judge himself to be as bad as the abuser, triggering shame and self-loathing, Most of us have been indoctrinated to believe we have no right to anger; we may have been punished for anger. He might also feel anger towards others who did not protect him from the abuser. He may have been neglected or emotionally abused within the family even if the abuse occurred outside the home. All of the men in my study had been emotionally abused in some way and many of them had been physically abused (Etherington 1995).

The client may grieve for the loss of childhood innocence. 'Big boys don't cry' is a phrase that still echoes in homes and institutions today. Jeremy internalized these messages:

> I never cry in front of anyone. I've felt like committing suicide loads of times. My friend found me once when I'd taken some paracetamol. I have fantasized about killing myself to get rid of the pain. I suffer from a lot of pain about my life, in my mind and in my heart. No one knows the way I feel. I tried to tell a girlfriend once and she said 'pick yourself up and get on with it'. And that's when I started thinking I was damaged goods; I go to sleep crying and I wake up crying.

Eventually the client begins to shift attention from the abuse to ways he can live an enjoyable life; the abuse becomes a memory of an experience that has affected his life but no longer dominates it. Men in the study had found some meaning in the experience and felt strengthened by dealing with the abuse. Almost half were in voluntary or professional healing roles – reflecting the concept of the wounded healer. Martin reflected on his abuse:

> It has given me so much to bring to my life and other people's lives by way of compassion, by way of empathy, by way of energy against any form of abuse or exploitation.

Presenting recovery in the above way may seem to oversimplify what is a complex, lengthy, painful and usually non-linear process of healing. The client may go in and out of stages and return at times to previous ones. I do not wish to underestimate the difficulties but recognizing a process might enable the helper and client to avoid feeling overwhelmed. Knowledge of the process can be shared with the client as a tool for self-empowerment, particularly when the going seems rough and clients are tempted to retreat.

Summary

Few men present initially as sexually abused, but rather with some of the symptoms and life problems which I have highlighted elsewhere (Etherington 1995). Perhaps the best we can offer is an awareness that males are abused, that women can be abusers and that definitions of abuse are incomplete. It is interesting to note that disclosure of male abuse has rapidly accelerated in recent times. None of the men in my study was included in prevalence figures. One man disclosed in the 1960s and two men in the 1970s; nine men disclosed in the 1980s and thirteen in the 1990s. Bearing in mind that the interviews were conducted in 1993 – only three years into the 1990s – there is therefore a rapid increase in the number of men disclosing as the climate changes from the denial of and ignorance about male sexual abuse. My hope is that the contribution I have made by the study and this article will make us better able to help those who come forward in need of understanding and healing.

References

'Accuracy About Abuse'. PO Box 3125, London NW3 5QB. Contact Marjorie Orr.

Bass, E. and Davis, L. (1988) *The Courage to Heal*, New York: Harper & Row.

Blagg, H. (1989) in C. Wattam. J. Hughes and H. Blagg, *Child Sexual Abuse: Listening, Hearing and Validating the Experiences of Children*, NSPCC, Essex: Longman.

Bolton, F.G., Morris, L. and MacEachron, A. (1989) *Males at Risk: The Other Side of Sexual Abuse*, Newbury Park, CA: Sage.

Bond, T. (1993) *Standards and Ethics in Counselling in Action*, London: Sage.

Bradshaw, J. (1988) *Healing the Shame that Binds You*, Deerfield Beach, FL: Health Communications.

Briere, J. (1992) *Child Abuse Trauma*, New York: Sage.

Dolan, Y. (1991) *Resolving Sexual Abuse*, New York: Norton.

Egan, G. (1986) *The Skilled Helper* (3rd edn), Monterey, CA: Brooks/Cole.

Elliot, M. (ed.) (1993) *Female Sexual Abuse of Children: The Ultimate Taboo*, Essex: Longman Group.

Etherington, K. (1995) *Adults Male Survivors of Childhood Sexual Abuse*, London: Pitman.

Etherington, K. (2000a) 'When the victim is male,' in H. Kemshall and J. Pritchard (eds), *Good Practice in Working with Victims of Violence*, London: Jessica Kingsley.

Etherington, K. (2000b) *Narrative Approaches to Working with Adult Male Survivors of Child Sexual Abuse; the Client's, the Counsellor's and the Researcher's Story*, London: Jessica Kingsley.

Hall, L. and Lloyd, S. (1989) *Surviving Child Sexual Abuse*, London: Falmer Press.

Hunter, (1990a) *The Sexually Abused Male*, vol. 1, Lexington, MA: Lexington Books.

Hunter, M. (1990b) *The Sexually Abused Male*, vol. 2, Lexington, MA: Lexington Books.

Hunter, M. and Gerber, P.N. (1990) 'Use of terms "victim" and "survivor" in grief stages commonly seen during recovery from child sexual abuse', ch. 2 in vol. 2 of *The Sexuality Abused Male*.

Mezey, G.C. and King, M.B. (eds) (1992) *Male Victims of Sexual Assault*, Oxford: Oxford Medical Press.

Sanderson, C. (1990) *Counselling Adult Survivors of Child Sexual Abuse*, London: Jessica Kingsley.

Sgroi, S. (1989) *Vulnerable Populations*, vol. 2, Lexington, MA: Lexington Books.

Discussion issues

1 What is your response to seeing the words 'victim' and 'male' in the same sentence?
2 Research findings have shown that male professionals are more inclined than female professionals to hold boy victims responsible for their abuse – discuss.
3 What is the impact of the media portrayal of young males who are 'taught' or 'initiated' about sex by older females, such as the film, *The Graduate*?
4 What would you do if a man disclosed abuse to you and asked for help?

84

Marketing Counselling Courses

Patricia Hunt

During the process of executing a research project on counselling and psychotherapy trainings (Hunt 1995) I had occasion to examine and analyse 69 course brochures and prospectuses, 50 of which were for counselling and counselling skills courses. All the courses were for one or more years' duration.

For the purpose of the survey I needed to obtain from the brochure the kind of information which the average potential student might require when making a decision about whether to pursue a particular course or not – viz: level of course; duration of course and time commitment required; entry qualifications and selection procedure; staff numbers and qualifications; student numbers; aims, objectives and theoretical orientation of the course; syllabus and teaching methods; clinical practice requirements; personal therapy requirements; supervision arrangements; required written work; evaluation procedure; accreditation body and the qualification awarded; whether failure occurs and the procedures for that eventuality; the cost of the course, i.e., the fees plus the 'hidden' costs (personal therapy and supervision).

The quality of the written information on courses

The overall impression gained from the examination of prospectuses and course brochures was that not only were they often deficient in many of the areas listed above but that they were woefully inadequate in a number of other ways. Often they are poorly presented and of unappealing appearance. Some were professionally printed, but some were in leaflet form or just typed sheets of paper. The latter is not really acceptable in these days of word processors, desktop publishing software and superior printers, and is at odds with the drive for courses to be 'marketable' and thus the need for them to be attractively presented. Prospectuses were often difficult to read and sometimes so discursively written it was difficult to extract the 'hard' information. Some information had the potential to mislead (deliberately?) the uninitiated, like 'This course provides in-depth training to enable students to function formally as counsellors within the guidelines laid down by the British Association for Counselling.' Does this mean automatic entry to BAC as an accredited counsellor? Or perhaps the course is accredited by BAC? Neither is the case! Often the courses were described in such a generalized manner as to be meaningless. Phrases like 'personal/interpersonal perspectives', or 'theories of human development' abounded. Which theories I wondered? The aims and objectives of courses were often equally ill-defined or absent and very few referred to the client categories for

This chapter was first published in *Counselling*, Journal of the British Association for Counselling, vol. 7, no. 3, pp. 202–3 (1996).

which the course prepared the students, although there was a generalized assumption they would be adults. Teaching methods were mentioned but not well defined. Again, for the uninitiated, phrases like 'experiential exercises' or 'participatory workshops' could be confusing and perhaps need a brief explanation for potential students who have never experienced anything other than lectures. While it is acknowledged that a detailed description of the syllabus and what the course entails is likely to be offered once the student has enrolled, and that too much detail could be burdensome in a prospectus, it remains debatable as to whether some prospectuses had enough information for the student to make a properly informed choice.

The prospectuses of counselling courses

To be more specific about the 50 counselling courses – of which 26 were Certificate courses and 24 were Diploma/MA courses – it was dismaying to discover, for example, that only 10 per cent of the 50 counselling courses gave any information on student numbers and only a third gave information on staff numbers. Thus it was difficult to gauge the student–staff ratio, something a prospective student might also wish to know. In fact, even fewer course brochures gave any additional information about the staff – their qualifications, experience, orientation and areas of interest – yet this kind of information can be important also to the decision-making process. Dryden (1994) has attacked the high student-to-staff ratios on some courses and opines that the quality of teaching is likely to be adversely affected as a result. He recommends that prospective students check on the staff–student ratio before applying for a course. Course prospectuses should therefore be clearer on this point. Wheeler (1994) is critical of the quality of counselling course staff, some of whom she says have not actually had any counselling experience as practitioners. Hence the need for prospectuses to be more specific about the staff's qualifications, etc.

Most brochures mentioned the duration of the course, the time commitment required and the entry qualifications, but fewer noted the aims of the course, and only 20 per cent mentioned objectives. As mentioned above, aims were often couched in quite vague and generalized terms – for example, 'To provide a training that will enable students to work with clients in the counselling situation'. Perhaps the fact that so few brochures spelled out the objectives – which are normally more concrete and specific – is a reflection on the muddle that currently exists in counsellor training in relation to standards and levels (see Dryden 1994).

Roughly a third of the brochures did not mention the theoretical orientation of the course, the syllabus, the teaching methods or the written requirements, and although more mentioned the accrediting body and the qualification which could be obtained, almost none said anything about the possibility of failure. No brochure mentioned an appeals procedure for that eventuality, but then the impression given in most of the brochures was that students went smoothly through a course and received a qualification at the end of it.

The costs of the course were noted in 76 per cent of brochures, but these were sometimes ambiguous or 'fudged' and it was hard to work out the true cost of pursuing the course. The fee for the course would be noted in one place, while the cost of a compulsory residential event would be noted elsewhere and the fee to the accrediting body and the costs of supervision tossed in somewhere else. Only 2 per cent mentioned sources of funding for the course.

Information specific to Diploma courses

The usual distinguishing feature of a Diploma in Counselling course is that students should have access to and regularly work with clients in the role of a counsellor, and that their practice should be supervised in some way. Increasingly, too, there may be a requirement for the student to have his/her own personal therapy at some time during the course. Of the 24 Diploma course brochures, 46 per cent referred to clinical practice requirements, 46 per cent to personal therapy requirements and 54 per cent to supervision arrangements; i.e., approximately half of the brochures did not refer to these important issues, and some of those that did, confined themselves to laconic statements which were vague and uninformative.

Conclusions

On the whole, brochures for counselling skills courses and counsellor training are unattractive, poorly presented and confusing. In many cases the information provided is limited in some way or another and often not adequate enough for the prospective student to be able to make a properly informed choice or to make comparisons between courses. I would particularly single out the costs of embarking on a course as being an area which is in need of greater clarity and honesty in prospectuses. Course fees should be clearly stated and should include any additional fee required by the training institution or validating body for the qualification. Fees for residential events should also be clear. If the student is required to have regular supervision it should be noted whether this is included in the course fee or not and, if not, the costs of regular supervision and also of personal therapy if this too is required, should be properly estimated and stated unambiguously.

The experience of examining the prospectuses resulted in some guidelines being devised on the minimum information required in a course brochure, which is included in the report (Hunt 1995). Dryden et al. (1995: 57–8) also address the issue of course booklets and have a similar list and a similar exhortation for course booklets to provide a detailed picture of *all* the costs of undertaking the training programme. They also make the pragmatic comment that there is an advantage in making a course booklet fairly comprehensive, because the more questions it answers, the more staff time is saved in handling subsequent enquiries.

References

Dryden, W., Horton, I. and Mearns, D. (1995) *Issues in Professional Counsellor Training*, London: Cassell.

Dryden, W. (1994) 'Possible future trends in counselling and counsellor training: a personal view', *Counselling*, 5 (3): 194–7.

Hunt, P.A. (1995) 'Regional training audit: a survey of counselling, psychotherapy and related trainings within Merseyside and adjacent regions' (unpublished and obtainable from the Administrator, Merseyside Psychotherapy Institute, c/o 26 Barchester Drive, Liverpool L17 5BZ for £7.50).

Wheeler, S. (1994) 'Counselling training – choosing the right course: "All that glitters is not gold"', *Counselling*, 5 (3): 210–12.

Discussion issues

1 What do you think are the most important pieces of information a prospective student might need in deciding which counselling course to select?
2 Do you think the presentation of counselling course brochures has improved since the time this research was undertaken? If the answer is 'yes', are you able to identify the improvements?
3 What are the advantages and disadvantages of course brochures being specific about such areas as the theoretical orientation of the course; staff numbers, names, qualifications and areas of interest; the true costs of undertaking the course, etc.?
4 Are course brochures now a thing of the past? Can other methods be used to market counselling courses and will the type of information provided and its format be affected as a result?

PART FIVE

FUTURE TRENDS

Introduction to Part Five

In the penultimate section of the *Reader*, 'Future trends', we have included current debates and developments that we think are still on-going. Inevitably, we have included on-line counselling – a recent phenomenon which has already provided counsellors and psychotherapists with another exciting, yet challenging medium through which to undertake therapy (Goss et al. 2001).

Brian Thorne opens Part Five by discussing his concerns about the dangers and challenges of brief therapy. He fears that Britain may experience a similar fate to America with insurance companies only underwriting a limited number of counselling sessions, delivered by a therapist practising an approved, empirically validated approach. In looking at a number of brief approaches including Talmon's single-session therapy, he wonders whether short-term therapy is the inevitable dysfunctional response to a sick society and if it will become illegal to practise long-term therapy because it could be considered exploitative?

Sue Wheeler pertinently asks whether counselling is, or can become, a profession. She considers this issue from a number of different perspectives and looks for the evidence that counselling has the characteristics of a profession. She compares counselling to allied professions such as psychotherapy and psychology but suggests that the BAC may have compromised its own standards, by initiating a scheme, the Faculty of Health Care Counsellors, that offers registration without strict evidence of competence. It is her conclusion that unless BAC meets the needs of aspiring professional counsellors, other organizations such as the UKCP or BPS may fill the gap.

John McLeod engages in frank talking in his chapter on counselling as a social process rather than as a psychological process. This approach has been influenced by the social constructionist philosophy of Kenneth Gergen and his associates. McLeod looks at the nature of the social process that occurs when counselling ensues, and considers its implications.

Through reconsidering some of the ideas he holds about multicultural counselling and psychotherapy Roy Moodley attempts to answer many challenging questions. He asks, 'What kind of training would be most appropriate for therapists to counsel a client who is black, working class, deaf and lesbian?' The question can be answered in a number of ways but he suggests that we are just at the beginning and we still have a long way to go in our consideration of multicultural counselling.

The last two chapters focus on on-line counselling. Colin Lago revisits an article he wrote in 1996 about computer therapeutics – not so much an approach, but a medium for therapy to take place. This article was one of the first papers on this topic published in a British counselling journal and it attracted considerable interest at the time. Yet, only a few years later, the BAC has taken up the gauntlet, publishing a document entitled, *Counselling On-Line* (1999), and, during 2000, including a number of articles in *Counselling* on this topic more recently, they have published guidelines (Goss et al. 2001). Student counsellor Steve Page's chapter on hypothetical counselling by e-mail is one of these. Finally, Stephen Goss, Dave Robson, Nadine Pelling and Deborah Renard discuss the challenges of the Internet and conclude that any predictions about the future of the Internet are likely to be outdated rather rapidly. A suitable ending for this section, perhaps.

Reference

Goss, S., Anthony, K., Jamieson, A. and Palmer, S. (2001) *Guidelines for Online Counselling and Psychotherapy*, Rugby: British Association for Counselling.

85

The Move Towards Brief Therapy

Its dangers and its challenges

Brian Thorne

This address was delivered to the BAC/EAC Training Conference at Southampton University in August 1998.

My summer holiday in North Wales was punctuated, as for everyone else, by a series of bizarre and tragic events on the global scene. Bill and Monica seemed to take up a lot of newspaper space only to be followed by the horrific bomb in Omagh. This, with the terrorist outrages in Africa and the American retaliation on targets in Afghanistan and Sudan, made for some pretty dismal reflections on the current state of humankind. And then came the news of the disintegration of the Russian financial markets and the plight of Boris Yeltsin. I decided that the only answer was to be thankful that I was a counsellor and not a politician or a financier, let alone a president, and to seek solace in the Welsh hills and a ride on the Ffestiniog steam railway.

Sadly I had reckoned without Catherine Pepinster who on 23 August managed to get an article in the *Independent on Sunday* sandwiched between Boris, Bill and Osama Bin Laden. Suddenly the therapists were up there among the dubious world leaders and destroyers, for Catherine Pepinster had located us even if she had not quite spotted me lurking in Harlech Castle. In an article entitled 'Grey days for therapy junkies' (1998) she began with this ominous reflection:

> For a significant number this [August] is a tricky time, an angsty month. It's the season when therapists, shrinks and their ilk take off to Tuscany, Cork or Cape Cod. The result? All those fears of abandonment and rejection their clients learnt at their parents' knees come back to haunt them. Angry? They're absolutely livid at being left behind. This is the midsummer madness with a vengeance.

And so on, and although the good Catherine acknowledged that plenty of people emerge from therapy at ease with the world and themselves, she finished her piece with this parting shot: 'Confusion prevails, the unlovable continue to fret through August, and many will go into the coming autumn and winter with the tantalising dream of being free from their past, only to remain chained to their therapist.'

The therapist as gaoler is an engaging if somewhat sinister metaphor. Is this really the nature of the power exerted by the analyst whose patient has been coming three days a week for ten years? Is this really what is going on in a thousand private practices up and down the land where clients or patients (terminology dependent on therapeutic orientation) dutifully report in week by week in their quest for happiness and relief from

This chapter was first published in *Counselling*, Journal of the British Association for Counselling, vol. 10, no. 1, pp. 7–11 (1999).

psychic suffering? I was reminded of the much maligned Jacob Moreno who in the 1920s and 1930s was already fulminating about the scandals of shameless analysts who robbed the neurotic rich of their money and left the suffering poor to their own devices. Moreno was wont to claim that six hours of decent psychodrama would achieve more than six years of supine analysis. People, he maintained with impeccable logic, wanted to be set free to live their lives – they did not wish to spend half their lives discovering the reasons for their unfreedom. I confess to a soft spot for Moreno although I recognize in him the manipulative genius of the charismatic healer who has no doubt about the rightness of his approach and the exercise of his power.

As a person-centred practitioner I have spent much of my professional life trying to ensure that I do not abuse my power. Most of my clients have suffered at the hands of those who had few scruples about the exercise of their power and authority, and I do not wish to join their ranks. On the contrary, I am concerned to help my client find his or her own *personal* power so that autonomous living becomes possible. So great is the abuse of power in our culture that I have no wish to apologize for placing such a high premium on not falling into the same trap. And yet, in recent times, I have come to wonder whether in my deep desire not to impose my power on my client I have not somehow emasculated myself and as a result deprived my client of the richness of a true encounter. After all, I think I am worth knowing and would not wish either deliberately or in deference to theoretical dogma to absent myself from existential meeting.

This worrying thought reminds me that lives can be changed in the twinkling of an eye. Falling in love, religious conversion, near-death experiences, even the reading of a great book can change people for ever. The notion that meaningful change can only come about as the result of long and painstaking processes is clearly untrue. What is more, profound and instant change more often than not comes as the result of a highly charged encounter with another person or with a perception of reality which drives away fear.

This somewhat lengthy preamble is intended to take us out of the psychotherapeutic ghetto and to place us in the bewildering complexity of the world of which we are members. Ours is the world of Bill Clinton, Boris Yeltsin, of Osama Bin Laden, of Princess Diana, of bombs and outrages, of near-death experiences, of passionate love, of astounding works of art, of joys and griefs which lie beyond all words. What in this bewildering, frightening, magnificent and desperate world are we counsellors and therapists supposed to be doing? What is the purpose of all our efforts? What is our *raison d'être*? I challenge every member of this conference solemnly and truthfully to attempt an answer to this existential question.

I hypothesize a variety of answers, many of them overlapping. The person-centred practitioner might well begin with the concept of companionship – to be a faithful companion to the client and to accompany where the client leads. Are we then committed to the task of being companions on an unknown journey? Or are we problem-solvers, or diagnosticians? Perhaps we are insight facilitators or emotional nourishers committed to compensating for bad emotional experiences. Perhaps we are spiritual guides in this age of waning religious faith. Nearly always we are responders to unhappy people, dissatisfied people, anguished people. We confront, on a regular basis, misery, depression, existential angst, questions of life and death. My God – what a profession! Must we be prepared to be all things to all men and women or must we make choices and ensure that our clients know precisely what it is we purport to offer?

However we define ourselves – and it is certainly worth attempting a personal definition – and no matter what choices we make, there can be no doubt that we shall face the insidious allurement of psychological power, for we make ourselves available to those who, by definition, are vulnerable, fearful and sometimes desperate. I would suggest that the way we exercise that power will be crucial to everything that we undertake. If I serve a tyrant I am likely to be tyrannical; if I serve a loving master I am likely to be loving. Who, then, or what are the powers to which we as therapeutic practitioners are subject?

Certainly the *Zeitgeist* exerts its own pervasive influence. We live in the era of management values where the articles of faith are short-term effectiveness, value for money, performance indicators, return on investment, accountability. It is good to remember that this is a modern and upstart faith with few moral roots, with no power to nourish souls and every capacity to destroy them. Then there is the power of the cash-flow. We need as counsellors, most of us, to earn our bread and butter and this power of the availability of money may affect us in different ways. If we work in some counselling agencies – particularly those based in commercial organizations – our money may be dependent on our willingness to offer brief therapy in six sessions, to adhere to strict administrative procedures and to produce structured reports on our clinical work. If, on the other hand, we are in private practice this power of the cash-flow will exert itself in a different way. We need a full appointments book and that aim is unlikely to be well served by a constantly changing clientele with all the concomitant anxieties about finding replacements for terminating clients.

Then, increasingly, there is the power of the professional associations – the BACs and EACs of this world. The emphasis on accreditation, professionalism, ethical guidelines, boundaries and contracts – all this weighty infrastructure exerts tremendous power, a power which in an ironical way we have brought upon ourselves. We tremble at the fear of transgressing: we have nightmares about being struck off. The associated power of the complainant – or worse, the potential litigant – is never far distant. Be careful, we tell ourselves. Watch it. Don't try anything too unusual or unconventional in case it goes wrong.

For our American colleagues a recent insidious power on the scene is the insurance company. Increasingly insurers will only underwrite a limited number of counselling sessions and in many cases these must be delivered by a practitioner of a therapeutic orientation which the insurance company in its wisdom has decreed empirically validated. Such a scenario may not be far away in the UK and other European countries where health care and the insurance companies are striking up inglorious partnerships.

Perhaps for most counsellors, however, the greatest power is exerted by the theoretical orientation to which they subscribe. Conferences of counsellors always remind me of ecumenical gatherings of the Christian churches. The Baptists and the Roman Catholics, the Anglicans and the Pentecostalists can just about sit in the same room together and, indeed, at times recognize that they worship the same God. But when the chips are down and matters of doctrinal conflict occur, there is often a hasty retreat to the terrain occupied by friendly forces. Is it very different, I wonder, when the denominations are labelled psychodynamic, person-centred, cognitive-behavioural or transpersonal? Is a spurious unity between these competing orientations only achieved in the face of the despised eclectics or those who cloak their promiscuity in the guise of something called integrationism?

I have dwelt at some length on these cultural, professional, doctrinal and survival issues which undergird the powers to which we as counsellors are subject because

I believe that they inform both consciously and unconsciously our likely attitudes to the escalating move towards brief therapy at the present time. If we are supportive of the tendency or hostile to it we are likely to defend our position in terms of our concern for clients. 'No client', we may say, 'who has experienced years of abuse is going to benefit from a mere six sessions of therapy'. Or, contrariwise, we may pontificate that every client is entitled to a focused and businesslike approach to his or her concerns and deserves a counsellor who is constantly alert to therapy addiction. What we may be less willing to admit is that our passionate plea on behalf of clients is rooted in our fear of not making both ends meet or in blinkered commitment to our own brand of therapy or in our own enslavement to some other force of which we are only dimly aware. Could it be, for example, that I am devoted to long-term therapeutic contracts because I find them immensely more fascinating, or am I all for short-term therapy because I cannot bear the thought of a dependent client or someone who will expose my own lack of psychological depth and my superficial knowledge of myself?

The facts, if facts they can truly be called, are intriguing and in some ways disturbing. One of the most startling books I have read is that by Moshe Talmon entitled *Single Session Therapy*. Writing in 1990 Talmon records how he discovered that many clients – the vast majority, in fact – who drop out of therapy after one session do so because they felt sufficiently helped by the one encounter and do not feel in need of more. Based on this discovery, Talmon then systematically developed a way of making the most of clients' ability to heal themselves within the context of a single session. The effectiveness of his approach makes exciting reading but he warns that the single session provides therapists with the smallest financial reward, often leaves them with little information or knowledge about their clients and does not permit of a close and intimate therapeutic relationship in most cases. His book concludes with a checklist of attitudes which he deems helpful for the single-session therapist. They make entertaining – and thought-provoking – reading:

1. This is it
2. View each and every session as a whole, complete in itself
3. All you have is now
4. It's all here
5. Therapy starts before the first session and will continue long after it
6. Take it one step at a time
7. You do not have to rush or re-invent the wheel
8. The power is in the client
9. Never underestimate your client's strengths
10. You don't have to know everything to be helpful
11. Life is full of surprises
12. Life, more than therapy, is a great teacher
13. Time, nature and life are great healers
14. Expect change. It's already well under way.

(Talmon 1990)

Talmon's single-session therapy is at the radical end of a whole school of therapies which have developed in the last 20 years and are committed to short-term work – even if short is defined in a variety of ways. When we remember that some of the briefest therapeutic relationships on record are those that Freud had with his early patients it is perhaps not so surprising that there is a school of short-term dynamic therapy. Anthony

Ryle's cognitive-analytic therapy is also now much favoured in the British National Health Service. Cognitive-behaviour therapy, rational emotive behavioural therapy, multimodal therapy, brief solution-focused therapy are all part of this brief therapy family and the 2 + 1 model, where two sessions are designed to produce a strong impact and the third follows three months later allowing for self-change and self-reflection, is another favourite in a National Health Service beset by long waiting lists and an ever-escalating clientele. The fact is that all these approaches exist – and others which I have not mentioned – and they are seemingly in good health and have many satisfied clients. When a few years ago – again in response to ever-increasing waiting lists – I offered focused counselling in the person-centred model for a mere three sessions, I was startled to discover that I could provide effective help for such diverse concerns as delayed grief, the aftermath of rape, performance phobia and physical abuse. What is more, by offering these intensive sessions at 8 o'clock in the morning their effectiveness seemed much enhanced (Thorne 1994).

To use Alex Coren's telling phrase, is brief therapy base metal or pure gold (Coren 1994)? I suspect it is both in different contexts with different clients. For the moment, however, there is no convincing evidence to suggest that it is inappropriate for particular concerns, and Wolberg (1965) suggests it is better to assume that short-term therapy is suitable for everyone until proven otherwise. Certainly a strong case can be made for the validity of defining and working for modest goals even among the most dysfunctional clients.

Colin Feltham (1997) in his excellent book *Time-Limited Counselling* provides a word of caution while not seeking to dampen the ardour of the short-term therapy enthusiasts. He suggests that there are, perhaps, certain kinds of *people* (rather than certain kinds of problems) who may not benefit from time-limited counselling. He cites five categories which I found to be significantly revealing:

1 People who seek immediate gratification and need instant results. Such people, Feltham suggests, are often men who deny dependency needs.
2 People with over-busy lives. For such people time-limited counselling will simply collude with their 'hurry sickness' and exacerbate their neurosis.
3 People who are severely damaged psychologically and who also have no solid support. Such people – usually impoverished – are often those who present themselves to voluntary community counselling services.
4 People who are usually unwilling to collaborate or to accept responsibility for their own lives.
5 People with extensive personal growth agendas.

There is something about this list which sends shivers up my spine and which alerts me to my profound fear about this brave new world of short-term therapy. In the first part of this lecture I have focused on the power of the counsellor and the potential for self-deception because of the many forces to which the counsellor is himself or herself subjected. Money, the ethos of management values, the tyranny of professionalism, therapeutic credos – these are formidable forces which threaten constantly to undermine the counsellor's integrity and to deprive him or her of the ability to be fully present for the encounter with the mysterious other who is the client. Colin Feltham's list of those unlikely to benefit from time-limited work provides a further shaft of light into the same dark landscape. Men who deny dependency needs, people with over-busy lives, people who refuse to collaborate, people severely damaged psychologically, are these not all persons unable to be present to themselves or to others, unable, in short, to find the anchorage which comes from a sense of continuity and security?

Could it be, I ask myself, that short-term therapy is the inevitable dysfunctional response to a sick society and that it seems to work for that very reason. We no longer have time to put down roots, to consolidate our beings, to reflect upon our place in the eternal order of things. We are forever in a rush, we are consumed with busyness, with our lives increasingly ruled by mobile telephones or inane e-mail messages. We are becoming people of no substance, soon to disappear altogether into virtual reality. Could it be that short-term therapy is the ultimate collusion? What *really* happened when I offered the quintessence of my person-centredness in a concentrated form to clients who had opted to be with me at 8 o'clock in the morning for three brief sessions? Certainly I felt powerful, we seemed genuinely to meet, they professed themselves helped. Why can I not simply celebrate the success of our venture and rejoice in having responded so admirably to a new challenge? Why does part of me now look back on that experience with scepticism, even with fear?

Immediately I pose the question, I find myself resisting it and moving over once more to the up-beat, positive point of view. After all, the challenge *was* exhilarating. I remember well the satisfaction of deliberately and consciously setting out on the three-session journey – its compactness, neatness, efficiency. Not that, curiously enough, its length was in any way unusual for clients coming to the University Counselling Service. Many already came for only three sessions, or less, and the average number of sessions throughout the clientele was little more than six. But it was the consciousness, the deliberateness of the enterprise which made all the difference. There was something so disciplined about it which appealed to the ascetic in me. Of course, this was strengthened by the decision to offer these sessions early in the morning. That matinal hour was a real test of motivation for both counsellor and client – and, excitingly, it worked. Clients were often early – on the doorstep at 7.55 a.m. all eager to get started. How different to the missed appointments (there were none during the experiment) and the late arrivals which characterized so much of the daily experience within the Service at that time. Then there was the almost delinquent excitement of doing something which had about it the smell of heresy in the person-centred community of faith. How could three crisp, disciplined sessions really be a true response to the client's process, how could such a take-it-or-leave-it package constitute valid companionship? But I revelled in the heresy. After all these clients had *chosen* the package: it was not forced upon them. Indeed, it could be argued, and I so argued, that it increased the options open to them and respected their capacity to discover an inner wisdom in making the choice. There were other pay-offs. I remember the buzz of being on psychological full alert through every minute of every session. I became the very embodiment of the core conditions and allowed my energy no respite. It was as if the relationship with each client was so precious that not a moment of it could be squandered. We person-centred therapists often talk about being fully present in the here-and-now, and here, it seemed, was a structure which aided this vibrant co-presence of counsellor and client.

I called the experiment *focused* person-centred counselling and the client's desire to focus on specific issues and his or her determination not to be side-tracked were again a liberating experience for me as the counsellor. I did not find myself being in the least bit coercive but was able to marvel at the client's ability to stay single-mindedly with the area of most concern. Again it was as if the limited time ensured that the client quickly established an agenda and did not deviate from it even if deep water flooded in after half an hour. I also became aware of how much preparation clients had undertaken between the booking of a first appointment and their appearance in the counselling room. Person-centred practitioners, unlike therapists of other persuasions, do not prescribe homework for clients but it was clear that nearly all my short-term clients did indeed set their own homework both before the first session and between sessions. Again, there was the sense of an intense experience which had to be utilized to the full throughout its duration and that included the time outside the counselling hours.

Perhaps most surprising of all, I found myself bonding with these short-term clients in a deep but uncomplicated way. It was as if they had taken the decision to trust me and the process and then jumped in with both feet. There was no agonizing testing out the relationship nor was there great pain at its ending. I was reminded of those meetings of yester-year when railway carriages still existed where souls were laid bare between London and York and two people who had shared astonishing intimacies disappeared into the night, never to meet again.

There was the subsequent satisfaction of being able to report on the success of my little experiment to sceptical colleagues. I even wrote a chapter about it for one of Dave Mearns' books and have since been bombarded with requests to talk about brief person-centred therapy – requests which have so far been refused. Being a heretic is one thing but spreading heresy is another, although I suppose writing the chapter in the first place was asking for trouble.

Dare I now return to my fear? Having described the challenge and how both I and my clients rose to it in triumphant fashion, can I now face that part of me which says it was a charade, an abject capitulation to a mad world. What, after all, was the challenge? The challenge was to cut down the appalling waiting list and, at the same time, to demonstrate to the University at large that the Counselling Service could be endlessly inventive in finding new ways of mopping up the psychologically and emotionally wounded. It had little to do with discovering new ways of responding to human distress. Brief therapy in this context was a pragmatic answer to escalating misery in a dysfunctional institution strapped for money. And what, it may be asked, is wrong with pragmatism? We have to do the best we can with what we've got and the British are reputed to be experts at making the best of a bad job. More therapy for more people without more cost. What could be better, and it has about it the ring of equal opportunities and the rejection of the therapeutic elite addicted to their once- or twice-weekly dose of therapy for years on end. What is more, brief therapy works and this must surely be the clinching argument. Clients, it seems, are satisfied and we all know in this age of citizens' charters that the client is always right.

Is my real fear that the day will come when brief therapy will have won so many accolades that it will be enthroned not only as the preferred option but as the *only* option? Do I foresee a time when it might even be illegal to practise long-term therapy because it is deemed exploitative and abusive? Now I am getting near the heart of my terror. I glimpse within myself the powerful allurement of the short-term reward and allied to it the fear of commitment. I see, too, the seductive satisfaction of rapid results and the magical quality of the instantaneous response. I am half way towards willing surrender to the quick-fix world which spins ever faster so that soon we shall know what tomorrow brings before today has ended. Of course, brief therapy will win the day because it suits the freneticism of a world which cannot wait. Of course, it works because it is the therapy for a world which is constantly on the hoof, where individuals are for ever seeking to be a jump ahead of the next person, where instant knowledge is the key to survival, where to stand still or fall by the wayside is to court annihilation.

But did I not say somewhere towards the beginning of this lecture that we can be changed in the twinkling of an eye by a chance encounter? Such an encounter, however, is invariably with a person who embodies in some way an 'at homeness' with the created world, a refusal to be uprooted by passing storms, an in-touchness with an eternal core which is the bulwark against anxiety, selfish ambition and the achievement neurosis. Such a person knows how to wait because time stands still in the light of eternity. 'Learning to wait', said Richard Church, 'consumes my life. Consumes and feeds as well.' If as therapists we have about us the marks of such a person then perhaps we can offer our brief therapy contracts with quiet hearts and clear consciences. If not, we may be courting the insidious satisfaction of being known by clients and employers as efficient, effective, value-for-money practitioners with a sound record of therapeutic throughput.

References

Coren, A. (1996) 'Brief therapy – base metal or pure gold?', *Psychodynamic Counselling*, 2 (1): 22–8.
Feltham, C. (1997) *Time-Limited Counselling*, London: Sage.
Pepinster, C. (1998) 'Grey days for therapy junkies', *Independent on Sunday*, 23 August 1998, p. 26.
Talmon, M. (1990) *Single Session Therapy*, San Francisco: Jossey-Bass.
Thorne, B. (1994) 'Brief companionship', in D. Mearns, *Developing Person-Centred Counselling*, London: Sage.
Wolberg, L.R. (1965) *Short-Term Psychotherapy*, New York: Grune & Stratton.

Discussion issues

1 What does the expression 'client throughput' do to you?
2 What do you understand by 'the quality of presence' of the therapist?
3 How does the 'spiritual dimension' in therapy inform this debate?
4 We tremble at the fear of transgressing: we have nightmares about being struck off.

86

The Professionalization of Counselling

Is it possible?

Sue Wheeler

Since the British Association for Counselling (BAC) was founded 24 years ago, and as counselling took hold in Britain to become a major resource for people experiencing personal difficulties, it has worked rapidly to set standards and to refine codes of ethics for good practice. The organization has grown and now has a large membership of people interested in or practising counselling. The organization is professionally managed, financially sound, has organized countless important initiatives, developed valuable accreditation schemes, contributed to government bodies, initiated a scheme for registering counsellors and has gained international credibility.

However, it faces a major crisis of identity that could bring about its demise in the next few years. BAC is threatened on all sides; from its membership who are split in demands for a professional organization and a learned society; from government seizing the power to regulate professions allied to health (HMSO 1999); from the imminent impact of qualifications related to National/Scottish Vocational Qualifications (NVQ/SVQ) in Counselling; and from other organizations vying to represent the interests of counsellors.

The current threats focus primarily on the question of whether counselling is, or can become a profession. Professions are not created overnight, but evolve as a result of demand for services, the supply of skilled personnel to meet the demand, public opinion, competition with other professional groups, government legislation, the identification of a knowledge base and the provision of training. The emergence of counselling as a potential profession has gathered pace in recent years. The supply of counsellors, membership of counselling associations, and organizations providing counselling and counsellor training have steadily increased during the past 30 years, in parallel with the development of sophisticated ethical codes and national standards, by which counsellors can be judged. However, the professionalization of counselling is entering a new phase, unprecedented in terms of impact, as both external and internal forces demand change. To make sense of some of the issues that confront the counselling fraternity and BAC, as a representative organization of counsellors in Britain, it is necessary to consider the nature of a profession and to examine the historical context in which counselling, one of several professional or occupational groups purporting to offer services to those who suffer from psychological, emotional or personal difficulties (however these might be defined), has developed.

This chapter was first published as 'Can counselling be a profession? A historical perspective for understanding counselling in the new millennium', in *Counselling*, Journal of the British Association for Counselling, vol. 10, no. 5, pp. 381–6 (1999).

Can counselling be described as a profession?

There is no doubt that many counsellors view themselves as professionals. Whether 'counselling' is a profession itself is more questionable. Numerous groups have claimed jurisdiction over work related to 'personal problems' during the last century, some with more success and credibility than others. There are also varying opinions about the definition of a profession. Reference to these definitions and a brief review of the history of the 'helping professionals' may contribute to the understanding of the current situation.

There is a range of perspectives considering what constitutes professions and how they may be analysed, emphasizing traits, process, power or position within a system of professions (Abbott 1988). Carr-Saunders and Wilson (1933) describe a profession as an organized body of experts, who apply esoteric knowledge to particular cases. There are 'elaborate systems of structure and training, entry by examination and other formal requisites, including a code of ethics and behaviour' (in Abbot 1988: 4). Millerson (1964) defines three general traits of professionalism as being organizational structure, education and ethics. Larson (1977) adds to this with the specification that the organization should serve the interests of a particular client group and dominate the market for that group. Johnson (1972) lists six traits that define a profession: skill based on theoretical knowledge; provision of training and education; testing competence of members; organization; code of conduct and altruistic service. He also emphasized the relationship between professions and the state, noting the power of state intervention to confer professional status. Abbott (1988), within his analysis of competition between groups claiming professional jurisdiction, offers an explanation of the difference between an occupational group and a profession. The profession controls abstract knowledge and generates practical techniques that can be delegated to occupational groups. Thus, for example, the medical 'profession' controls the knowledge base and advisory function, but nurses do the work that is abstracted from that knowledge. Engineers are professionals, but delegate work such as automobile mechanics to trained technicians. The word 'jurisdiction' is used by Abbott (1988) to describe the legal, social, political and practical influence that a particular group has to provide a service to the public or a particular section of the public. Professions vie for jurisdiction over work with a client group.

'Counselling' can be seen from different perspectives. It fits into several of the definitions of a profession, although it could also be defined as an occupational group, within the area of psychiatry and psychoanalysis. Many professionals – the clergy, social workers, doctors and psychiatrists – include counselling as part of their overall set of skills and responsibilities, drawing on only part of the knowledge base available to them. Counsellors increasingly work with doctors in general practice, where, like nurses, they see a sub-set of the patients using the practice, when their particular set of skills and expertise are in demand. However, using Johnson's definition of a profession, counselling is clearly a skill based on diverse theoretical knowledge, for which training and education is available, *some* of which is approved by the professional organizations representing counselling. Competencies of *some* members are tested, yet there are *several* organizations to which counsellors can belong. That there are codes of conduct and altruistic service is a principle of practice. The doubts about its claim to be a profession are contained in the clauses, '*some* members are tested,' '*some* training courses are approved' and '*several* organizations represent the interests of the members' (see Table 86.1).

Table 86.1 *The compatibility of counselling with the characteristics of a profession*

Characteristics	Yes/No	Compatibility	Evidence
Specified task/specialist skill	Yes		BAC 1997a
Peer judgement of competence	Yes	Accreditation scheme assessment by peers	BAC 1998a
An organization that represents practitioners	Yes	But not all practitioners are members	House and Totton 1997
Code of ethics	Yes	But only if you are a member	BAC 1997a
Esoteric body of knowledge	No	As a discreet package perhaps?	Thorne 1997
Entry by examination/ regulation of entry	No		Mowbray 1995
Education and training controlled by the professional body	No	It tries to influence training	BAC 1996
Defined area of work	Yes/No	Not a discrete client group	BAC 1997b
Demand from consumer	Yes		BAC 1997b
Legal recognition	No	Health Act, 1999; potential regulation	HMSO 1999
Competition with other occupational groups	Yes	Considerable competition – wins on price	Abbott 1988;
Closed system	No		BAC 1998b
Research base/university training	Some		BAC 1998b; Saunders 1999
Jurisdiction: public, legal, workplace	Yes/No	In some areas	Bayne et al. 1996
Does not encourage volunteers	No	Thousands of them!	Tyndall 1993
Economic monopoly	No		
Altruism/community interest rather than self interest	Yes	Although members need support	Tyndall 1993
A system of rewards (monetary and honorary)	Yes/ No	No national pay scale	BAC 1997b
Homogeneous occupational community/low degree of specialization	No	Many specialists who form specialist groups	Palmer and McMahon 1997
Authority in organization in which they practise	Yes/No	Depends on organization	Carroll and Walton 1997
Do not usually need supervision	Yes/No	Supervision is required, but other health-related professions now expected to have supervision	BAC 1997a; DoH 1998
Delegates lesser tasks to other professional groups	Yes	To advice-giving occupational groups	Sue and Sue 1990

At present there is no legal control over who provides counselling, no specific training requirements are enshrined in a code of practice and counsellors can practise without being a member of any professional organization. There is no jurisdiction over any particular client group, although counselling is beginning to lay claim to work with certain groups. The fact that private health care insurance and employers will often pay for counselling provides some evidence that the aspiring profession is gaining credibility, as Abbott (1988) suggests that third-party payments for services can be an indicator of professional recognition. However, membership of BAC, the organization representing the majority of counsellors, is not restricted to those who have been tested to be competent in their practice as counsellors and the organization has no control over the training that is provided for aspiring practitioners.

If counselling were to be more strictly controlled by a professional body as defined above, it would have a more legitimate claim to be described as a profession. One impediment to this development is the word 'counselling', a term used to describe a skill or set of skills that can be claimed by almost anyone. At its root, the word 'counsel' (meaning *to advise*), is widely owned. Another is that the organization representing counsellors, BAC, is not exclusive, with no rigid requirements for membership. Almost anyone can join, providing they agree to abide by the Code of Ethics. There are more specific categories of membership, but BAC does not prioritize the needs and interests of one group over another. There is an internal hierarchy of esteem, but that is not transparent to the general public.

Competition between professional groups for jurisdiction over work with different client groups

Using Abbott's analysis of competition for jurisdiction over 'professional' work (in this case, counselling), there are numerous 'professional' and non-professional groups that purport to offer help to the public in dealing with their personal problems, however these problems are defined. To identify the client groups that counsellors serve, it is useful to survey the spectrum of 'helping professionals' and the 'rigidity' of access to such professions. When the problems of day-to-day functioning are given a medical definition and considered to be mental health problems or severe behavioural problems, they are likely to be treated in the domain of a psychiatrist, a medically trained professional with expertise in the mechanics of psychological disturbance. Both psychiatrists and clinical psychologists work in hospitals, mental health centres or clinics controlled by the National Health Service, and there is some overlap in their work. Clinical psychologists usually work with children, people with learning difficulties, adults with phobic, obsessional or other disorders, older adults and sometimes with families. They are often involved in assessments, using psychological tests. The clinical psychology profession, unlike counselling, is strictly controlled. The National Health Service is the primary employer, and controls the provision of training through designated universities. There are a limited number of places on training courses each year, trainees receive an NHS bursary and there is stiff competition. The training is always at Masters degree level and, increasingly, at clinical doctorate level. Successful candidates have no difficulty in securing employment and salary scales are both generous and nationally agreed. Abbott (1988) would describe clinical psychology as a 'rigid' profession, difficult to gain entry into, and maintaining strict exclusion barriers. Consequently, clinical psychologists are in great demand, well paid, and with clear career progression paths. However, demand for help with personal problems outstrips the supply of psychiatric or clinical psychology professionals and these services are expensive. Hence there are waiting lists for treatment and therapeutic appointments may be spaced at irregular intervals.

Other professional (or occupational) groups compete to fill the gaps in provision, and may be the chosen source of help for some groups of people. Counselling psychology has produced a relatively new occupational group, often employed in clinical psychology services or general practice surgeries. Counselling psychologists have psychology degrees and are trained through courses affiliated to the British Psychological Society (BPS). Their training is at postgraduate level, and is not dissimilar to that provided by some counsellor training courses and they have their own professional organization within the BPS.

There are also the psychoanalysts and the psychotherapists. Analysts (usually members of the British Confederation of Psychotherapists (BCP)) are a specialized group of psychotherapists and a minority group in terms of numbers, although they are often seen as an elite. Their training is long, arduous and expensive, and the therapeutic work undertaken with clients is intensive, involving several sessions each week. The majority of analysts work in private practice in London and their clientele tend to be the middle and upper middle classes, who can afford the cost of private treatment. Psychotherapists are a mixed group, trained in various therapeutic modalities. Some psychotherapists who are medically trained and some who are not, work in medical settings; others work in voluntary, public or private institutions or in private practice. Psychotherapists are represented by the United Kingdom Council for Psychotherapy (UKCP).

Psychotherapists tend to work with clients over a long (more than one year) period of time, some see clients or patients who are described as borderline or more disturbed, but most will be involved with neurotic clients, psychotherapists in training, or the 'worried well'. Psychotherapists and professional counsellors probably see the same group of people with similar problems, but are often to be found in different institutions with varied aims and objectives. Psychotherapy centres will expect to see clients for long-term treatment. A 'drop-in' counselling centre would not have these expectations.

Counsellors are often employed in educational establishments, general practice surgeries, and increasingly in industry and commerce, providing staff support services. Some counsellors work in specialist agencies providing couple, alcohol, drug or pregnancy counselling. Hence, the 'counselling profession' could be seen to have jurisdiction over work with a particular clientele, such as work with specific client groups, work in particular kinds of organizations, short- to medium-term psychotherapeutic work, and work with clients who are not classified as mentally ill or too disturbed. It is with this group of people that social workers, the clergy, and sometimes nurses also work; these are occupational groups which have been providing support, counselling and guidance services for at least the last century and which, like counsellors, are claiming professional status.

Who has historically had jurisdiction over 'personal problems'?

The demand for help, support and guidance for personal problems dates back to the Industrial Revolution (Abbott 1988). The decline of a rural economy and the development of an industrial society living in towns and cities led to people experiencing social and personal difficulties in a way that had been previously disguised by the containing environment of villages, where horizons were limited and expectations modest. Urbanization demanded that people move from their traditional homes, to seek alternative accommodation in cities, with the loss of extended families and the support of community living. The need for additional help created a demand for personal services. Initially the existing professionals provided the help and support that was familiar to them; lawyers, the clergy, and doctors gave advice relating to their expertise and experience. The clergy were the most involved in the personal lives of families and individuals and concentrated on using their skills as Christians to give holy guidance to sufferers. Social upheaval continued, as men were required to adjust to fit the factories they were employed in. Increasingly nerves and nervous ailments were identified as a distinct category of complaint taken to the medical profession, and by 1910 nervous diseases were identified and various professions claimed their right to treat people with nervous affliction.

The clergy made moves towards developing their skills in a pastoral way, placing less emphasis on their religious beliefs and more on their interpersonal skills, but they were unable to fulfil the needs of the many sufferers. In the mid nineteenth century neurologists such as Charcot began researching the functions of the brain and experimenting with hypnosis. Neurologists saw themselves as having something to offer nerve sufferers and moved into treating these 'diseases' (as they were described). However, neurology 'became as much a hermeneutical act as a natural science' (Abbott 1988: 289) and neurologists were unable to document or indeed demonstrate how their treatment worked. Routine procedures included rest, electro-convulsive therapy, hydrotherapy and a procedure that could be seen as the beginning of psychotherapy. Odd treatments emerged for brief periods such as gynaecological interventions, which were short-lived as the treatment lacked credibility, being only for women. Between 1880 and 1920, neurologists, a small and elite group, with rigid training requirements, were besieged by patients needing treatment.

Meanwhile, the clergy were working in a much less formal way, using a social model, and working in the community. Freud was developing his ideas and his theories, and had gathered a group of followers practising psychoanalysis. From 1900, psychiatrists entered the frame, by providing mental hospital accommodation for those who were mad rather than bad, who had previously been in workhouses or jails. They claimed the work with the untreatable, although at the time there was considerable experimentation with curative treatments. Neurologists continued with their efforts to find clinical cures, while psychiatrists engaged with preventative work and containment of the mentally ill.

Freudian analysis was gaining popularity as an alternative treatment for those with nervous diseases. The system of analysis cut across the medical struggle for supremacy and developed a new jurisdiction centred on problems of everyday life. The analysts in the early twentieth century tended to be psychiatrists and neurologists. However, demand for treatment was greater than the supply of analysts, and social workers started using psychotherapeutic/analytic techniques. From social work evolved the work of psychotherapists (Hooper 1997).

From the mid nineteenth century to the mid twentieth century, the professions involved in servicing the neurotic, mentally ill or anxious members of society have ebbed and flowed. New areas of jurisdiction have been won and lost. Rigidly organized '(ring fenced)' professions have flourished, but when demand has outstripped their ability to deliver, they have been undermined by new professional groups able to offer similar services.

Hence, 'counselling' has carved a path through social work, the clergy, psychiatry, neurology, psychoanalysis, psychotherapy and other professions, providing easily accessible services to the public through voluntary agencies or private practice at reasonable cost. Analysts appear at times to be contemptuous of counsellors. Counsellors are doing much of the work that the analysts once had jurisdiction over. The psychoanalytic community has skill and expertise that is in demand but numbers are low and the intensity of treatment is prohibitive in terms of time and cost.

The current threats to BAC and the development of counselling as a profession

There are several issues within BAC itself, within the counselling community and related to government policy that threaten the development of counselling as a profession. There are two external forces for change, which are directly linked. The first emanates from government legislation and the second from other organizations that have responded to the legislation, ostensibly to protect the interests of counsellors.

The changes in the NHS service provision dictated by the requirements of clinical governance, expect all treatment to be determined by evidence-based practice, which is in itself a threat to counselling as evidence of effectiveness is inconclusive. The other threat is the requirement that all professional groups working within the NHS are self-regulating, imposing their own system of regulation and accountability. While counsellors who are accredited members of BAC can demonstrate that they have achieved a recognized standard of practice and that they are accountable to a professional body, only a minority of counsellors are accredited and some do not belong to BAC. Moreover, the Health Act (HMSO 1999) gives the government the power to insist that professions allied to health become self-regulatory and more accountable. In response to these changes two significant moves have been made to protect the interests of counsellors. A new organization called the Association for Counsellors in and Psychotherapists Primary Care (CPC) has been formed with the stated aim of becoming the professional body for counsellors working in primary care. Part of the rationale for this move stems from the govenment white paper, *The New NHS* (HMSO 1998) which places a substantial emphasis on quality assurance through clinical governance. It makes general practitioners responsible for all health care professionals employed within their practice – hence such employees should be subject to the standards set by the professional body that regulates their profession. BAC sets standards but does not regulate the profession. The Counselling in Primary Care Trust has already been instrumental in setting up courses within universities for counsellors working in primary care. The premise for these courses is that counsellors need specialized training to work within the setting of primary care. The CPC has been a natural development from this initiative and it will set about influencing general practitioners to employ counsellors who have been approved by an organization that has the appropriate expertise. This arrangement could benefit both practitioners and employers. Using Abbott's (1988) schema, what seems to be happening is that CPC is establishing itself as a subordinate professional group to the powerful profession of medi-cine, potentially breaking away from BAC, which has dallied too long in establishing exclusivity for counsellors who seek professional status.

In response to the requirements of the NHS and to the establishment of CPC, BAC announced, in February 2000, the Faculty of Health Care Counsellors. The Faculty invites applications from experienced counsellors in primary care, to become registered members. There is a series of requirements including experience and training, but the Faculty stops short of demanding BAC accreditation, the benchmark of competence that has been established. The intention is to give counsellors in primary care an alternative to CPC that provides them with registration and accountability. The net effect is, however, that BAC has compromised its own standards, by initiating a scheme that offers registration without strict evidence of competence. While at first counsellors in primary care may be pleased to have a route to registration that is less arduous than the accreditation route, they may be sorely disappointed when they realize that the scheme offers false security. A second-class registration scheme brings the credibility of the standards set by BAC into disrepute.

Yet another organization is set to compete with BAC for membership. The Universities Psychotherapy Association (UPA) was set up to provide a route for university psychotherapy courses to gain membership and validation by UKCP. UPA has now recognized that there are many counselling and psychotherapy courses in universities which are not dissimilar, some of which are interested in being associated with a professional body that provides an alternative to BAC. There are many reasons for this, but one relates to the conflict over BAC accreditation. At present, students who complete a counselling qualification at a university or other organization have to apply for individual accreditation with BAC, regardless of whether the course they completed was BAC accredited. The UKCP system is quite different. Institutions and training courses organized within them are accredited by UKCP and students who successfully complete the training courses can be recommended for membership of, and registration by, UKCP. It has been a long-standing source of irritation by counselling course providers and students that successful graduates have to undertake the arduous, expensive and taxing task of applying for BAC accreditation when they have already completed an accredited course. UPA provides a route for students to gain UKCP registration, which respects the authority of colleagues examining therapy students within universities, and the opportunity to gain registration or similar accreditation on completion of a course is attractive. Although it has been a topic under discussion for several years, BAC has yet to announce a scheme that will enable students of accredited courses to gain their individual accreditation without recourse to further bureaucracy.

There is another reason why the UPA might gain considerable momentum in challenging the territory of BAC. While training in counselling and psychotherapy has developed extensively in the private and voluntary sector, many training courses have developed in universities during the past 20 years. Furthermore, there is currently a trend towards courses in private agencies being validated by universities. National organizations such as Relate, or famous independent agencies such as the Tavistock Institute have sought university affiliation through validation. Such moves concur with Abbott's analysis of the process of professionalization, whereby universities take responsibility for training and for developing research associated with the knowledge base of the profession. In recent years universities have recruited psychotherapists such as Andrew Samuels, as professors in their psychotherapy departments. Consumer demand is for training that is legitimized and accompanied by credit ratings recognized by universities and that has credibility in the workplace. As higher education is expanded and no longer the preserve of the elite, so aspiring professions such as nursing, social work and other paramedical professions move towards acquiring graduate status and to becoming more research active. Despite the critics (House and Totton 1997) and resistance to accepting that counselling should be a professional activity, training for counselling or psycho-therapy professional practice is abundant and professional recognition is demanded. Graduate status adds credibility to the credentials of the individual as well as to the image of the claimant profession. The prestige of academic knowledge strengthens a profession's claim for jurisdiction. 'Higher education … [is] the most important element of professionalism' (Ben-David 1963: 256). Hence, membership of an organization that stresses the graduate nature of the occupation is desirable.

Internal threats to BAC

BAC is also facing a period of change, created from within the organization. In 1998 it announced its strategic plan for 1998–2003 and also drafted a proposal for a review of its membership structure, in line with the strategic plan. BAC's overall purpose, as defined by the strategic plan, is as follows: 'BAC to be the professional organization for counsellors; the voice for counselling; the provider of access to counsellors and other counselling activities; and educator of the public about counselling and its uses.' With regard to membership, the plan states: 'Increasing membership to provide access to more counsellors …. Introducing membership categories that voting members can advertise' (BAC 1998b: 1). New membership categories have now been proposed (BAC 1999), including individual membership for those interested in and involved in some way with counselling, and registered membership for accredited members. The individual membership category continues to give BAC an (almost) open membership policy. The registered membership category continues to dilute the potency of the accreditation process with a 'Registered Associate Membership' category for counselling practitioners *en route* for accreditation. These proposed changes perpetuate the problem that hinders BAC in ever becoming the professional association for counsellors, as 'Professions begin with the establishment of professional associations that have explicit membership rules to exclude the unqualified' (Abbott 1988: 11).

Another important and associated issue is raised by the changes BAC proposes under membership: 'increasing membership to provide access to more counsellors' (BAC 1998b). BAC has always straddled the dual role of a 'learned society', promoting and developing the understanding and practice of counselling in Britain, and a 'professional body', representing the interests of its 'professional' members. This was entirely appropriate as the interest in counselling in Britain grew – whether it continues to be appropriate is now much more doubtful, and certainly a mass membership will not be conducive to the activities of a professional body. The tensions between professional (accredited) counsellors and people interested in counselling, using counselling skills or practising as counsellors without accreditation are increasing. Needs of groups within BAC are distinct. The 'professional' (accredited) group urgently needs BAC to work towards making the profession more exclusive. It demands tighter controls over training, clearer definitions of client groups for whom counselling is appropriate and more work on the adoption of a career structure, pay scales and conditions of service for counsellors that can be promoted and eventually adopted nationwide. The rest (the majority of the membership) will not necessarily share these values or aspirations – indeed, many argue along the lines of House and Totton (1997) that counselling is an activity so diverse and prevalent in their community that it cannot possibly be regulated.

Opportunities

The threats that BAC faces are considerable, but there are also opportunities. The framework for clinical governance within the NHS (DoH 1998) includes requirements such as Continuing Professional Development (CPD), evidence-based practice, peer review/ supervision, clinical audit, complaints monitoring and public accountability. Through the work of BAC, the counselling 'profession' has already established the infrastructure and policy to meet many of these demands. Supervision, CPD and complaints procedures are fundamental to ethical practice and research has increased its profile within BAC in recent years, particularly with the appointment of a research officer. The sound financial base of BAC, its strong management team and new streamlined committee structure (BAC 1999) place it in a powerful position to face the threats.

As a result of its sustained involvement in the development of NVQs, BAC is now well placed to influence the direction that is taken as qualifications in counselling through the NVQ route are developed. BAC has gained a voice in the QCA (Qualifications and Curriculum Authority) that regulates the qualifications proposed by awarding bodies. By relinquishing its former claim to awarding body status itself, BAC can claim to be the professional body that represents counsellors, and can participate fully as an independent body in the crucial decision-making process involving NVQ qualifications, that may shape the future of counselling.

Conclusion

Unless the needs of the aspiring professional counsellors within BAC are met, other organizations such as UKCP, BPS, UPA and CPC are likely to fill the gap. Counsellors who see themselves as professionals are less tolerant of being part of an organization that embraces volunteers and others. A look across at the experience of the UKCP and the breakaway group, BCP, illustrates this point. The analysts and some psychoanalytical psychotherapists could not tolerate being in the same organization as other psychotherapists, who subscribe to different therapeutic orientations that have less stringent training and personal therapy requirements, or who have a less developed knowledge base. Professional status can only be claimed if exclusivity is a policy of the professional body representing the occupational group. For counsellors who have engaged in a rigorous, theoretically taxing, expensive and time-consuming education, professional recognition is important.

According to many definitions, 'counselling' cannot claim professional status. In order to make such a claim, much tighter control on training would have to be exercised, which would be difficult to achieve for an unregulated 'profession'. The example of the Association of Counsellors and Psychotherapists in Primary Care is to be watched closely. The conflicting demands made by different parts of its membership, and the threat of statutory regulation, mean that BAC may not be able to continue in its current form if it wishes to support the development of a profession. A new professional body that represents the interest of 'professional' members could be created, possibly under the auspices of BAC. Perhaps BAC should seek alliance with universities and give more consideration to ways in which such organizations, experienced as they are in maintaining standards and exercising quality control, could be licensed to produce accredited counsellors, otherwise other organizations may move into the breach. Challenges, conflicts, opportunities and threats to counselling and the profession loom large, but can be faced. Managing change is painful but ignoring the power of government initiatives and competition from other groups vying for jurisdiction is not an option.

References

Abbott, A. (1988) *The System of Professions. An Essay on the Division of Expert Labour*, Chicago: University of Chicago Press.

BAC (1996) *Recognition of Counsellor Training Courses*, Rugby: British Association for Counselling.

BAC (1997a) *The Code of Ethics and Practice for Counsellors*, Rugby: British Association for Counselling.

BAC (1997b) 'Survey of the membership', unpublished report, Rugby: British Association for Counselling.

BAC (1998a) *The Scheme for the Accreditation of Counsellors*, Rugby: British Association for Counselling.

BAC (1998b) 'Seeing ourselves as we are!', *The Voice of Counselling* (February), pp. 1–2, Rugby: British Association for Counselling.

BAC (1999) *Agenda for the 23rd Annual General Meeting of the BAC*, Warwick, September.

Bayne, R., Horton, I. and Bimrose, J. (1996) *New Directions in Counselling*, London: Routledge.

Ben-David, J. (1963) 'Professions in the class system of present day societies', *Current Sociology*, 12: 247–98.

Carr-Saunders, A.P. and Wilson, P.A. (1933) *The Professions*, Oxford: Oxford University Press.

Carroll, M. and Walton, M. (1997) *Handbook of Counselling in Organizations*, London: Sage.

DoH (1998) *A First Class Service. Quality in the NHS*, London: Department of Health.

HMSO (1998) *The New NHS*, White Paper, London: Her Majesty's Stationery Office.

HMSO (1999) *The Health Act*, London: Her Majesty's Stationery Office.

Hooper, D. (1997) 'Then, now and tomorrow', in S. Palmer and V. Varma (eds), *The Future of Counselling and Psychotherapy*, London: Sage.

House, R. and Totton, N. (1997) *Implausible Professions: Arguments for Pluralism and Autonomy in Psychotherapy and Counselling*, Ross on Wye: PCCS Books.

Johnson, T.J. (1972) *Professions and Power*, London: Macmillan.

Larson, M.S. (1977) *The Rise of Professionalism*, Berkeley: University of California Press.

Millerson, G. (1964) *The Qualifying Associations*, London: Routledge.

Mowbray, R. (1995) *The Case against Psychotherapy Registration*, London: Trans Marginal Press.

Palmer, S. and McMahon, G. (eds) (1997) *Handbook of Counselling* (2nd edn), London: Routledge.

Saunders, S. (1999) 'It has been amply demonstrated that psychotherapy is effective', in C. Feltham (ed.), *Controversies in Psychotherapy and Counselling*, London: Sage.

Sue, D.W. and Sue, D. (1990) *Counselling the Culturally Different* (2nd edn), Chichester: Wiley.

Thorne, B. (1997) 'The accountable therapist: standards, experts and poisoning the well', in R. House and N. Totton (eds), *Implausible Professions: Arguments for Pluralism and Autonomy in Psychotherapy and Counselling*, Ross on Wye: PCCS Books.

Tyndall, N. (1993) *Counselling in the Voluntary Sector*, Milton Keynes: Open University Press.

Discussion issues

1 How important is it that counsellors achieve and maintain accreditation?
2 What are the arguments for not controlling the profession of counselling and opening membership of BAC to all interested parties?
3 What differences might you expect to see in the organization and regulation of counselling in ten years' time?
4 Has BAC compromised its own standards, by initiating a scheme that offers registration without strict evidence of competence?

87

Counselling as a Social Process

John McLeod

For the most part, counselling is generally thought of as comprising a primarily psychological process. A person (client) with some kind of problem is helped by means of their gaining awareness or insight into their cognitions and beliefs, feelings, or patterns of interacting with others. The term 'psychotherapy' embodies this emphasis on the psychological. 'Psychotherapy' is a form of healing, or cure, of the 'psyche' or mind. The majority of theoretical models which inform counselling practice – psychodynamic, humanistic, cognitive, behavioural – are drawn from the discipline of psychology, and have generated substantial bodies of psychological research. Institutionally, counselling is regarded by many people as something like a branch of applied psychology. Counsellors are people who apply psychological models and principles. Some practitioners even choose to call themselves 'counselling psychologists'.

The aim of this paper is to offer an alternative way of seeing counselling, as a social rather than psychological process. This approach is influenced by the social constructionist philosophy of Kenneth Gergen and his colleagues (Gergen 1985, 1994). From a social constructionist perspective, counselling represents one of many ways in which the cultural norms and values of a society are affirmed, and operates as a means of helping individuals to negotiate their own relationship with these cultural norms. To regard counselling as a social process carries with it a number of implications for training and practice. However, before exploring these implications it is necessary to describe in more detail the exact nature of the social process which occurs when counselling takes place.

The aims of counselling from a social perspective

One of the most important aspects of a social constructionist theory of counselling is the realization that counselling reflects society. Counselling is an activity that has emerged during the twentieth century, during a period which sociologists have characterized as 'modernity' (Lyon 1994). To be a 'modern' person is to be an active member and participant in a culture which offers many alternative stories about what it means to be human. Compared to many previous periods in European history, the present time can be understood to be an era in which people have access to many more sources of information and influence around how to live life. In previous historical eras, life was dominated much more by the Bible or other religious texts and by the immediate physical control exerted by family and community authority figures. Now, for most members of contemporary society there exists a diverse range of influences and possibilities. As the sociologist

---

This chapter was first published in *Counselling*, Journal of the British Association for Counselling, vol. 10, no. 3, pp. 217–22 (1999).

Anthony Giddens has observed, one of the tasks or 'projects' of life in a modern society is that of constructing an identity from these component parts (Giddens 1991). Identity is no longer, or not to anything like the same extent, 'given' by reason of gender or social class. Identity is something you keep working at. This process of reflecting on 'who I am' and trying out new identities can be seen in many areas of contemporary culture, for example in television programmes, magazines and advertising.

It can be argued that the key values of modern culture centre on rationality, progress, consumption and safety. Behind the great achievements of modern civilization lies the hand of science, which depends on a rational, detached approach to the world. The actual day-to-day operation of modern society relies on bureaucratic forms of administration which are grounded in rational (or pseudo-rational) procedures. There is therefore great pressure on people in modern cultures to be rational and to control the expression of feeling. This control is necessarily internal and psychological, rather than external and collective, because of the breakdown of communal forms of life and the anonymity of mass society. Modern culture is also built on an assumption of progress – the future will be better than the past because of the advancement of science, technology and general knowledge. The notion of progress is also applied to the person. Each of us can become a better person. The concept of the person as consumer is integral to the advanced capitalist economies of the modern world. The economic system depends (apparently) on a steady expansion in markets and production. One way of achieving this economic growth is to give people choice in the objects they buy and use. At the same time, the exercise of choice reinforces the value of rationality and provides opportunities for identity construction. Finally, as a social system based on rationality, control, progress and consumption expands, it comes to resemble a self-contained perfect world, clean and safe like Disney or McDonalds. Outside of this bubble are unfortunate human realities such as catastrophe, war, famine and disease. Increasing effort is devoted to fending off these risks.

These are some of the issues around which members of modern cultures are required to construct an identity and a life. For most people, this struggle is either largely denied ('getting on with it') or takes place within the various arenas provided by ordinary everyday life – marriage, family, friendship, the workplace, the church. Modern societies have generated vast industries around the question of identity construction. For example, advertising, fashion, consumer magazines, Oprah Winfrey-type shows, heritage exhibitions and novels can all be seen as providing narratives and symbols around which people can create individual identities. Only very occasionally do people have recourse to counsellors or psychotherapists to help them sort out their position on these issues. On the whole, counsellors and psychotherapists know and socialize with other people in the business, and at work respond to a seemingly endless queue of clients. But the role of counsellor creates a disorted picture of the uptake of counselling in society. The majority of people only use a counsellor under the most exceptional of circumstances.

From a social perspective, the decision to seek formal counselling is triggered by the experience of being an outsider, of being excluded from everyday discourse in relation to a problematic issue (Bergner 1987; Bergner and Staggs 1987). Usually, someone who encounters a problematic issue will either work out a solution on their own, ignore it so it goes away, or talk about it to a friend or family member. Very occasionally, all three of these strategies may prove to be ineffective. In such an eventuality, the person is likely to experience a range of feelings that are particularly difficult to manage in modern society. There can be a sense of powerlessness, hopelessness and demoralization ('I am worthless because I cannot sort this out'). There can be a strong sense of not belonging ('I am different'). Then there may also be a feeling of shame ('If I tell anyone, what will they think of me?') and of fear, especially fear of loss of control ('Am I going mad?' 'If I act on these feelings, anything might happen').

The role of the counsellor is to act as a bridge back into participation in the social world. At the moment of seeking counselling, the person is in some respect outside of everyday life. There is some part of their experience, their story, which cannot be shared with others. The task of the counsellor is to help the person to rejoin the human conversation. The social anthropologist Victor Turner, who has studied the role of shamans and healers in other cultures (e.g Turner 1964, 1982), describes such people as liminal figures, on the edge of society. Counsellors, too, are *liminal* figures, who exist on the edge of social groups or institutions for the purpose of enabling individuals to re-enter the social world. For example, a counsellor in a university will not be a tutor to a student, will not meet their counselling clients in a tutorial room or lecture theatre, and will not report on the student to the academic registry. The counsellor does not participate in any of these central activities of the university, but will meet the student away from the public space of the university for the purpose of discussing just those issues that are not part of the 'official' discourse of the institution. Often, an indicator of whether counselling has been successful hinges on the extent to which the student is able to re-enter fully the ordinary everyday world of the university.

From a social perspective, therefore, one of the purpose of counselling is to make it possible for people to belong, to be members of and participants in a social world, to be citizens. Sometimes people fall 'off the edge' of the social. This can often occur when a person is striving to integrate competing stories of what life should be. Counselling is one of the means through which a person can cease to be 'different', and can rejoin everyday life. This is not to argue that counselling promotes conformity to prevailing social norms, rules and values. To some extent it must do this, but every time someone makes the journey out and then back they learn something new, they gain a different vantage point on everyday life. They may re-enter the social in a different place. To return to the example of student counselling introduced earlier, some students who seek counselling use it not to return to the world of university life but to leave that world. The modern world offers a multiplicity of cultural arenas and identities, and counselling can be a vehicle for leaving one social world or identity and entering another.

The role and tasks of the counsellor

If the purpose of counselling is to enable the person to participate in the social, what does this mean for the role of the counsellor? From a social perspective, how can we understand what a counsellor actually *does*? It seems to me that a social approach sheds a different light on familiar counselling concepts and practices. As a liminal figure, a counsellor must be experienced as a person who at the same time presents or embodies the values and beliefs of the culture, but also can be seen as someone who is able to transcend these norms, who is comfortable with the chaos or despair of being at or beyond the edge of the social. A great deal of the time, counselling takes place in settings which signal that the practitioner is a member of the culture who enjoys status and good standing. What is often important is that the counsellor is also able to signify that he or she is personally able to share the suffering which the 'client' is experiencing. Within the person-centred approach to counselling, much emphasis is placed on the expression of congruence or authenticity on the part of the counsellor.

Within psychodynamic practice, Carlberg (1997) has shown the importance for clients of acts of spontaneity. This capacity to diverge from 'normal' behaviour and discourse conveys that the counsellor is capable of bridging the ordinary and the extraordinary. The counsellor is able to enter into the unknown, the irrational, the out-of-control, but without losing his or her grasp on normally accepted ways of being. The counsellor, as a liminal figure, needs to show that he or she is able to enter the unknown. It has always been one of the great strengths of classical psychoanalysis that it so powerfully emphasizes social conformity and weirdness at one and the same time. The psychoanalyst is clearly a representative of middle-class professional norms and standards, and yet behaves in ways that radically contradict these norms, for example by refusing to answer questions, being silent for long periods, being interested in sex and dreams, and so on. Both the social status and liminality of most counsellors is less marked than that enjoyed by psychoanalysts, so they have needed to adopt other strategies for conveying this combination of being at one and the same time a 'member-of-the-culture-in-good-standing' and an outsider. At the same time, as potential users of psychotherapy have become familiar with the way that psychoanalysis is conducted, for some clients the analyst's approach has come to be seen as expected and routine, and less convincing as a demonstration of a capacity to visit the edge.

From a social perspective, another crucial task for a counsellor is to accept and value what the person has to say. If the person is going to develop a sense of belonging within a social world, then he or she needs to believe that who and what they are is acceptable within that world. In this respect, the counsellor acts as a representative of a broader social world. The counsellor's acceptance is a first indication to the person that what they wish to say could be acceptable to other people too. There are at least three aspects of acceptance that come into play. The first is the counsellor's capacity to abstain from moral judgement. In all probability, a major factor in deciding to seek counselling would be, for many people, the anticipation of shame and fear if they were to tell their story to a friend or family member. Any inkling of a critical or judgemental reaction from the counsellor would be likely to stop counselling in its tracks. A second aspect of acceptance lies in the feeling of being an interesting and worthwhile person, being special. Absence of judgementalism can be achieved by counsellors who adopt a neutral stance in relation to whatever the client says, but in the end everyone wants to be *wanted*, to be on the receiving end of liking and warmth. There is a difference between tolerance and welcome.

The third facet of acceptance centres on an experience that I would describe as that of 'being understood'. The work of David Howe on the client's experience of therapy indicates that people expect this from their counsellors (Howe 1993). To be understood is to be accepted ('I am known, I am no longer a stranger who is merely labelled'). Being understood also releases some of the fear of being crazy ('No one could understand me'). It seems to me that a proper sense of being understood can only take place as a result of empathic sensitivity on the part of the counsellor. Some counsellors are good at offering 'standardized' understandings (often in the form of little sermons or lectures), but as a client unless the understanding is an understanding of *me*, capturing all or most of the nuances and contradictions within my personal story, then it will not help me to gain a sense of really belonging.

For the most part, the medium available to the counsellor to facilitate acceptance and inclusion is language. When it is working well, counselling is what Hobson (1985) calls a 'feeling conversation', a dialogue through which painful or confused areas of experience can be discussed. It is important to emphasize the *dialogical* nature of the counselling conversation. In all probability, someone who comes to counselling may have no shortage of words to describe the issues in their life. These are words that form an endless internal monologue in the person's head. At the beginning of counselling these words may spill out, often at great length, as a kind of pre-formed generalized narrative to which the counsellor can only listen as an external observer. This is not a true dialogue. It is when the client begins to tell more specific, concrete stories of events, stories that convey more of the dramatic quality of their lived experience, and leaves spaces for conversational responses, that the counsellor is more able to enter into the story and to be involved in co-creating the narrative. The story of troubles that the person tells in their head is likely to be stuck. If the person had been able to transform this story alone, no doubt they would have done so. Entering counselling is an acknowledgement that there is a need to talk, that personal reflection, physical exercise, prayer, willpower, etc. did not work. Once the counsellor enters into dialogue, the problem story opens out. For example, the person may realize that the story that he or she told to the counsellor was only one version; there are other stories that could be told about the same troubles. Or the counsellor may summarize or reflect back the story in a form that links elements of it together in a new way, or may introduce an image or metaphor that clarifies the storyline. Counsellors may rehearse alternative endings of the stories told by clients, or question the pervasiveness of negative and self-critical evaluations in the way the story is told. All this depends on the counsellor's sensitivity to language, to his or her capacity to be aware of how the story is being told, and consistently to offer back a more dialogical way of using language. As the client's 'troubles' become part of a continuing conversation they become less troubling. An area of experience or a personal story that was previously locked away and which represented the isolation and separation of the person from a social world gradually becomes a source of connection with the social. As the person becomes able to engage in conversation with the counsellor on the topic or issue, they also become able to do so with the people with whom they live their lives, or, if necessary, seek out new people who are willing to participate in such conversations. They also become more able to take advantage of the many different 'solutions' to their problem that already exist within the culture. From a social perspective, the goal of a counselling process through which the person and their counsellor joining together in a dialogical conversation is *not* that this activity will bring about change in the internal mental structures of the person (their self-concept, emotional schema or conflictual relationship themes). The aim is to make it possible for the person to join, or rejoin, everyday social discourse around whatever issues have been bothering them.

A phrase which captures some of the sense of a social approach to counselling is 'frank talking' (Moodley 1998). Counselling offers people an arena for 'frank talking'. To enable this to happen, the counsellor must be someone who is capable of it themselves, but must also be willing to accept how difficult frank talking can be, and be sensitive to the extent to which the person's direct meaning might be embedded in figurative language or lost in silence.

Another image which conveys something of what is meant here is that of the counsellor as *witness*. As we all know, what brings many people to counselling are experiences of violence, humiliation, fear and shame. Many people who turn to counselling have been on the receiving end of cruelty. These people are often silenced, either because of the threats of the perpetrator or because others do not believe or do not want to listen. There is a terrible burden of 'otherness' and exclusion in carrying such a story and not being able to tell it, or tell it to the full. A counsellor does such a person a great service in being able to receive such a story, particularly if they listen openly and humanly and respond personally rather than interpreting.

The cultural positioning of the counsellor

A social perspective on counselling draws attention to the role of the counsellor as an actor in a social world. The counsellor cannot be seen as constituting some kind of socially neutral figure, adopting a stance that is merely 'person-centred' in the sense of reflecting only the beliefs and values of the individual client. Nor is the counsellor's response to the client merely a matter of the intrusion of personal experience and feeling, as would be implied by notions of countertransference. Counsellors stand for something, they are representatives of particular viewpoints or discourses that exist within a culture. To understand the cultural positioning of counselling it is necessary to be able to place counselling within its historical context, and to see the extent to which the 'image of the person' conveyed by theories of counselling represents statements about what it means to be a person at a particular point in history. These statements also express the image of the person espoused by a particular group of middle-class professional men who had access to and control of publication outlets in psychology and medicine.

The work of placing counselling and psychotherapy in a critical historical context has only recently been attempted (Cushman 1995). This is a difficult and complex undertaking, but it has become possible to begin to see some of the ways in which counselling concepts and practices have arisen from social circumstances. In the late nineteenth-century European culture in which Freud operated, there was a strong interest in the biological dimensions of life, and at the same time a cultural movement in which members of the middle classes increasingly were seeking to separate from parental control and develop a more autonomous sense of self. The conditions of mid-twentieth-century USA, according to Cushman (1990), added to the psychoanalytic equation a set of people with an inner 'emptiness' which could be filled through the consumption of psychotherapy. Later, the ideas of the humanistic therapies continued the business of constructing autonomous individuals, but in this instance individuals with more of a potential for enjoyment and a capacity to use their own feelings as a source of values in a world in which externally defined value systems were increasingly being questioned. The notion of temporary intense and intimate relationships implied in the writings of Rogers and Perls seemed also to speak of a world in which people were able to travel more easily and were much more socially mobile. These are just two of the ways in which counselling approaches have acted as channels of expression for changing conceptions of the person within modern Western culture. Similar socio-historical interpretations can be constructed for other counselling models.

What seems to happen is that the counsellor implicitly offers the client a way of telling their story that fits with the cultural ethos of their time and place. The person seeks out a counsellor, according to a social model, because their story is silenced, painful or stuck. Typically, counsellors listen much more than they speak, but when they do speak they are usually very effective at keeping 'on message', by consistently assimilating the client's version of things into the language of their therapeutic metanarrative (story of how people get problems and what they do to resolve them). Gradually, the person develops an ability to give a psychoanalytic, or humanistic, or behavioural account of their lives (Schafer 1992). In fact, I believe that this overstates the power of counsellors to influence their clients, and that most of the time the client will integrate some aspects of the therapeutic metanarrative into their own way of telling their story without taking on board the whole package being offered to them.

Counsellors can therefore be seen as recruiting agents for particular cultural discourses. This fact is most apparent in situations where counsellors attempt to work with people from different cultures from their own, and find that the story of 'what it means to be a person' that they are implicitly offering just does not map on to the other person's experience at all. The cultural discourses that have underpinned mainstream approaches to counselling – psychodynamic, humanistic, cognitive-behavioural – have all been perceived by certain groups of people to be liberatory and empowering, especially when compared with, for example, medical-psychiatric or everyday stories of how to cope with anxiety, stress and depression. These therapeutic discourses have therefore been highly acceptable to clients, and thus have 'worked'. What seems to have happened in recent years, however, is that the language and storylines of psychotherapy have been more and more assimilated into ordinary culture, to the extent that for some people in therapy a psychoanalytic interpretation or use of relaxation for behaviour change no longer represents a new way of telling their story. But, also, there is an increasing appreciation that there are profound limitations to the psychological metanarratives around which counselling and psychotherapy have been built. There are perhaps two main reservations that have been articulated. First, therapeutic narratives omit any reference to spiritual experience, and thus deny what is for many people a primary source of meaning and belonging. Second, in emphasizing a concept of an autonomous, bounded individual self, therapeutic discourse obscures the extent to which the good life depends on relationship, community, tradition and place.

Feminist, narrative and social constructionist counsellors and psychotherapists of the new wave (e.g. White and Epston 1990) have made efforts to position themselves outside the dominant discourse of therapy and to define themselves in terms of their own version of a postmodern image of the person. Postmodernism has sometimes been interpreted as promoting a somewhat bleak concept of the person, in which nothing is fixed and people reshape and redefine themselves almost at random. Postmodern counsellors and therapists have, I believe, not taken this tack but have used an appreciation of the constructed nature of social life, and an awareness of the degree to which modernity has eroded communal and relational values and practices, to create a form of practice that maintains and reinforces community, relatedness and social justice. It is possible to characterize this new approach as *post-psychological* in so far as it recognizes that, in a counselling relationship, a reliance only on psychological concepts and language severely restricts what can be said and the kinds of stories that can be told.

Some implications of a social approach to counselling

The counselling stance being described here draws on several other developments within contemporary counselling and psychotherapy. The emphasis on the person as a participant in a social system is found in family therapy. The awareness of the social, political and cultural dimensions of life are present in multicultural and feminist models of counselling. However, a social approach aims to draw attention to important social processes that occur in *any* type of counselling or psychotherapy. A social perspective does not prescribe any specific techniques or counselling interventions, but offers a set of principles which may be of value both to consumers and practitioners of counselling and psychotherapy (Greenberg 1994). For practitioners, who are the people most likely to read this paper, some of the main implications of a social perspective can be sketched briefly.

- *The image of the person.* People are seen as being human through their membership and participation in a culture and social world. Personal identity is primarily located within a historical and cultural framework. Persons are continuously actively engaged in the co-construction of meaning and identity, and in maintaining relatedness. The extent to which a person understands their personal existence in terms of an inner 'self', and the nature of that 'self', is a matter of cultural convention. The notion of 'self', is not foundational.
- *The goals of counselling.* The aim is to strengthen the culture within which we live, by enabling persons to participate, contribute, give and receive care, and to belong. Counsellors strive to create opportunities for frank talking and witnessing in everyday life as well as in formal counselling settings.
- *The counselling process.* Given that the person is a participant and actively engaged in a social world, counselling is just one among several things they do in their search for meaning and relatedness. The main task of a counsellor is to be available and responsive. The counsellor does not try to modify or cure structures within the person. To attempt to do this is to run the danger of reinforcing a language of deficit (Gergen 1990), in which it is assumed that there is something 'wrong' with the person. Counselling occurs when the person needs it rather than comprising a 'course of treatment' leading to permanent change. The counselling process is built around ways of facilitating the co-construction of meaningful and satisfying dialogue and conversation.
- *Counselling theory.* Theories of counselling are no longer regarded as maps or mirrors of reality, reflecting 'objective' or 'real' facts about human beings, but as language systems which exist to enable dialogue over problematic aspects of experience, and as narrative ' templates' which offer alternative ways of telling the story of a life.
- *The training and preparation of counsellors.* Counsellor education and training is grounded in multiculturalism; it is only from a comparative perspective that the cultural construction of one's own identity can become apparent. It is necessary for counsellors to be able to locate their approach within its social and historical context. The study of the social history of counselling (e.g. Cushman 1995; Danziger 1997) is an important

element of counsellor education. Training needs to include development of the capacity to appreciate the intricacies of language use through the study of topics such as narrative, discourse and conversation. Training and education prepares counsellors to engage in conversations that go beyond the psychological, and to encompass important areas of human experience such as the spiritual, political, environmental and moral.

Finally, a personal note. In writing this paper, I have been aware that I have been engaged in my own version of frank talking, which brings with it all kinds of fears about whether what I have to say is acceptable or will make sense to anyone else. Much of what I feel is important in counselling goes against the grain of the prevailing wisdom. I see counselling, to use Illich's term, as a 'tool for conviviality', as a means of helping people to live a good life together, rather than as a technical intervention that addresses psychological dysfunction. For me, this makes 'counselling' the preferred term, rather than 'psychotherapy', because the latter will always evoke an image of a technical/medical intervention focused on the mind. I believe that the 'good moments' in any form of counselling are those times when both participants are able to share in a conversation that is moving, meaningful and memorable. Such moments are all too rare. My position is that such moments do not function to 'heal the mind' but serve to bring us back together, to take part in a human conversation that goes beyond any of us as individuals.

References

Bergner, R.M. (1987) 'Undoing degradation', *Psychotherapy*, 24: 25–30.

Bergner, R.M. and Staggs. J. (1987) 'The positive therapeutic relationship as accreditation', *Psychotherapy*, 24: 315–20.

Carlberg, G. (1997) 'Laughter opens the door: turning points in child psychotherapy', *Journal of Child Psychotherapy*, 23: 331–49.

Christopher, J.C. (1996) 'Counselling's inescapable moral visions', *Journal of Counselling and Development*, 75: 17–25.

Cushman, P. (1990) 'Why the self is empty: toward a historically-situated psychology', *American Psychologist*, 45: 599–611.

Cushman, P. (1995) *Constructing the Self, Constructing America: A Cultural History of Psychotherapy*, New York: Addison-Wesley.

Danziger, K. (1997) *Naming the Mind: How Psychology Found its Language*, Thousand Oaks, CA: Sage.

Gergen, K.J. (1985) 'The social constructionist movement in modern psychology', *American Psychologist*, 40: 266–75.

Gergen K.J. (1990) 'Therapeutic professions and the diffusion of deficit', *The Journal of Mind and Behavior*, 11: 353–68.

Gergen, K.J. (1994) *Toward Transformation in Social Knowledge* (2nd edn), London: Sage.

Giddens, A. (1991) *Modernity and Self-Identity: Self and Society in the Late Modern Age*, Cambridge: Polity Press.

Greenberg, G. (1994) 'If a self is a narrative: social constructionism in the clinic', *Journal of Narrative and Life History*, 5: 269–83.

Hobson, R. (1985) *Forms of Feeling: The Heart of Psychotherapy*, London: Tavistock.

Howe, D. (1993) *On Being a Client: Understanding the Process of Counselling and Psychotherapy*, London: Sage.

Lyon, D. (1994) *Postmodernity*, Buckingham: Open University Press.

Moodley, R. (1998) '"I say what I like": frank talk(ing) in counselling and psychotherapy', *British Journal of Guidance and Counselling*, 26: 495–508.

Schafer, R. (1992) *Retelling a Life: Narration and Dialogue in Psychoanalysis*, New York: Basic Books.

Turner, V. (1964) 'An Ndembu doctor in practice', in A. Kiev (ed.), *Magic, Faith and Healing: Studies in Primitive Psychiatry Today*, New York: Free Press.

Turner, V. (1982) *From Ritual to Theatre: The Human Seriousness of Play*, New York: Performing Arts Society Publications.

White, M. and Epston, D. (1990) *Narrative Means to Therapeutic Ends*, New York: Norton.

Discussion issues

1 To what extent does the idea that the outcome of counselling is the enhancement of 'social inclusion' match your own experience, either as a counsellor or as a client?

2 What are the implications for counselling agencies of regarding counselling as a *social* process? How might this perspective shift the emphasis of the work of counselling agencies with which you are familiar?

3 The notion that counselling is an activity that transcends a merely psychological way of understanding persons and relationships challenges existing models and practices. In what ways might you see yourself integrating ideas from philosophy or sociology into your own approach to counselling?

4 What 'good moments' have you experienced in counselling?

88

Counselling and Psychotherapy in a Multicultural Context

Some training issues

Roy Moodley

Recently, I was asked a question about transcultural counselling and psychotherapy which challenged me in a way that has not happened before. It led me to confront and reconsider some of the fixed ideas I have held about multicultural counselling and psychotherapy. It also led me to search for new meanings for terms such as transcultural, intercultural, cross-cultural and ethnocultural. The questioner was keen to find out if a transcultural counselling course would qualify someone to be professionally called a transcultural counsellor, in the same way as someone who experiences a person-centred counselling course and is then entitled to be a person-centred counsellor. This question may be relevant also to the providers of counselling and psychotherapy programmes, as well as to prospective students wishing to train and specialize in counselling and psychotherapy with the culturally different client.

The common understanding of 'transcultural'

In exploring this question I discovered that many people in the counselling and psychotherapeutic field are of the understanding that there is 'something out there' called 'transcultural counselling' which has a huge body of conceptual and theoretical knowledge/s and particular methods of clinical practice. A study of this body of knowledge/s together with a modicum of cross-cultural communication skills would lead one to practice as a transcultural counsellor. It seems that this perception is informed by the 'confident' use of multicultural counselling and its associated terms, both anecdotally and in the literature. There is no doubt that multicultural counselling and its numerous, sometimes hyphened descriptors, have not only offered a critique of Western counselling but also emphasized the need for a more culturally based 'world-view' model of practice with ethnic minority clients. However, while the use of a wide variety of nomenclatures for counselling ethnic minority clients is reflective of the growth and development of therapy generally, it has also promoted ambiguities and contradictions in counselling training and in the actual practice. As Sue (1997: 177) notes: '[t]he inability to define multicultural counseling has caused a great deal of confusion in counseling programs'.

A version of this paper appeared in *Counselling*, Journal of the British Association for Counselling, vol. 11, no. 3, pp. 154–7 (2000) and vol. 11, no. 4, pp. 221–4 (2000).

Confusion, conflict, contradiction

Even the writers in this field, while agreeing that variables such as 'race', culture and ethnicity are the chief constructs of therapy with ethnic minority clients, are themselves divided in terms of the status or value and the clinical application of these variables in therapy. For example, Pope-Davis and Liu (1998: 157) state that 'while there is agreement that race, ethnicity and culture are socio-political domains, there is not much discussion about how one would discuss race, ethnicity and culture socio-politically as part of the counselling process'. Where attempts have been made to discuss 'race', culture and ethnicity, some writers have criticized the emphasis of one variable over another. For example, Carter (1995) contends that issues of 'race' are less conspicuous in counselling because practitioners are more comfortable in considering cultural and ethnic issues. On the other hand, Shafi (1998) in a study of four Asian women clients in counselling found that racial similarity is not necessarily a factor that engenders positive and effective counselling outcomes.

These views clearly indicate that the practice of multicultural counselling and psychotherapy is riddled with complexities, confusions and challenges. In part, this is due to the ambiguities, ambivalences and contradictions inherent in multiculturalism itself. For these and other reasons, training therapists in this area is problematized. A study by Bimrose and Bayne which attempted 'to evaluate how counsellor training should prepare practitioners to respond effectively to client difference' (1995: 264), confirmed the need for multicultural training but raised questions regarding the choice of frameworks, methods and length of this type of training. Although a subsequent critique by Morrison (1997) questioned the methodological rigour, the research still demonstrated that a 'thorough re-examination of counselling from a multicultural perspective is "the task of the next decade"' (Bimrose and Bayne 1995: 264). This view is also reflected in 'Possible future trends in counselling and counsellor training' in which Dryden (1994: 195) suggests that 'we will need to consider how to modify our training courses to make the world of counselling more attractive to potential helpers from [ethnic minority] groups'.

An 'examination of counselling and therapy from a multicultural perspective' becomes necessary if counsellors and psychotherapists are to enter the millennium as clinicians ready to encounter the 'psychological distresses' of the future. However, before we undertake an exploration of the 'questions regarding the choice of frameworks, methods and length', there are the 'Other' (dis-ability, gender, class, sexual orientation) questions that need to be considered. It may be (im)possible to find answers to the 'Other' questions, especially those on multi(ple) cultural rights, counselling and psychotherapy.

Major issues to consider

The contemporary therapeutic view seems to suggest that what happens between a client and a therapist is a construction by both parties. Postmodernism suggests that notions such as 'race', culture and ethnicity are not trans-historical or essentialistic but flexible and multiple in the way they influence an individual's identity (see Hall 1992). Therefore in therapy the meaning-making or the (re)construction of therapeutic narratives is dependent on both parties accepting and acknowledging each other's differences, similarities and multi(ple) cultural identities. In terms of the power relations the client can be reassured that therapy is conducted in a human rights framework within which the client's group and individual cultural rights are understood and explained. So that, when a therapist is 'working with' a deaf client who also happens to be black, gay and working-class, multicultural counselling and psychotherapy will need to reflect these various cultural identities and rights.

Multicultural counselling and psychotherapy as it is presently understood may be constrained when we are presented with such a client, requiring us to ask a number of questions:

- Do we see transcultural counselling as meaning ethnic minority counselling?
- Is multicultural counselling an approach that is used exclusively with ethnic minority clients or could it be applied to white clients also?
- What about the mental health needs of the other ethnic minority groups in the UK, who are not from the Commonwealth?
- Has multicultural counselling developed only for people who experience racism – 'colour discrimination'?
- What about people who are seen and experience themselves as white, but are Moslems, like the recent refugees in the UK – the Bosnian Moslems who 'suffered' through 'ethnic cleansing' and the Albanians from Kosovo?
- Can other refugees, asylum-seekers and natural disaster victims benefit from transcultural counselling?

This concern is also expressed by Littlewood (1992: 4) who has this to say:

> The psychological adjustment of European as opposed to non-European migrants and their children has not been the subject of such medical interest and that in itself is perhaps a matter of concern. Racism based on 'colour' may be less evident here, but we are still working with communities which have experienced dislocation, adjustment to a new physical and psychological environment and often to a new language and new values.

Littlewood raises an important issue which has consequences not only for the way we think about multiculturalism generally, but more specifically about counselling and psychotherapy in a multicultural context. Before we engage in the new multicultural counselling and psychotherapy, yet more questions will need answering, for example:

- Are there particular psychological theories (e.g. theory of personality, epistemologies of 'self', Oedipus, infantile sexuality, the unconscious) which constitute the multi(ple)-cultural/racial/ethnic experiences?
- To train as a multicultural therapist, must a person be identified as being black?
- What about those who experience themselves as being 'in-between' white and black?

And many more …

The challenge for multicultural counselling, then, is to transform itself, to embrace all these differences without stereotyping any of the other identities that a client may also present in therapy. But this is just the beginning. Transformation does not end here. In a situation where the therapist is able to accommodate the multi(ple)-identities multiculturally, questions of clinical relevance and application may still need to be asked, even at the training stage. Before we explore this issue, it is necessary to consider counselling and multiculturalism and the multiplicity of multicultural counselling approaches.

Counselling and multiculturalism – are we Eurocentric?
Are we racist?

Under the general rubric of 'multicultural', we seemed to have found an authentic episte-mology that acknowledges similarities but also makes difference more acceptable and meaningful. However, multicultural theory and practice has been neither consistent nor coherent. The critique, especially the post-colonial discourse on multiculturalism in the 1970s and 1980s, raised a number of questions regarding the ideas that were held about the West and the 'Other' (see, for example, Fanon 1967; Said 1978, 1993; Spivak 1988; Bhabha 1994). Ethnic minority communities began to seek changes in many aspects of their lives, especially in school education where anti-racist ideologies and conceptualizations took the place of multiculturalism. Transformation, however small and always under a critical gaze, was being felt in many other areas, for example housing, employment and in health care (see Ahmad 1993). These changes gave rise to a wide variety of nomenclatures such as multira-cial, multi-ethnic, multicultural, cross-cultural, transcultural ... 'race', culture and ethnicity.

However, multiculturalism in one form or another has continued to be part of the theorization of the multitude of cultures, 'races', ethnicities, religions and languages in the UK. As a discursive practice it has embodied a complex, ambiguous, confusing and contradictory framework within which individuals and groups are encouraged to 'self/ group actualize'. At the same time, it has also shaped an individual's 'psychopathology'. Therefore, counsellors or psychotherapists who work with culturally diverse clients will be presented with the complexities of multiculturalism in more challenging ways than the presently theorized multiculturalism. According to Willett (1998: 1):

> Multiculturalism has not yet been fully theorized. In part, the lack of a unifying theory stems from the fact that multiculturalism as a political, social, and cultural movement has aimed to respect a multiplicity of diverging perspectives outside of dominant traditions. The task of theorizing these divergent subject positions does not easily accommodate the traditional genre of the philosophical treatise penned by some single great mind.

In following the psychotherapeutic tradition of a 'single great mind' such as Freud, Jung, Klein, Rogers, Adler, Perls, Ellis, Beck and many others, multiculturalism and multicultural counselling and psychotherapy has yet to find its own single mind to achieve some certainty of practice. But, on the other hand, the desire for certainty in tran-scultural counselling has led to the exclusion of issues of gender, class, dis-ability and sexual orientation.

Since the process of multiculturalism is constantly changing in different times and different practices, its contribution to multicultural counselling and therapy has run in parallel with these changes, both in the UK and the USA. In the latter, a well-developed canon of literature on multicultural counselling theory and practice has contributed to specially designated multicultural therapy programmes. In comparison, multicultural counselling and therapy in the UK is just beginning to develop. One of the most signifi-cant aspects of this process is the establishment of RACE (Race and Counselling Education), a sub-division of BAC (British Association for Counselling) with its own multicultural journal. Some would argue – using the old cliché, too little too late – that, given the history of black communities in the UK and more than a century of psycho-therapy, multicultural therapy development should be at least on a par with the USA or at a more advanced stage. After all Freud as the cultural 'Other' made the UK his home. However, we need to acknowledge that in many ways we have a completely different history and philosophy of multiculturalism than the USA, which is contextualized within particular socio-political experiences. Counselling and psychotherapy developments have been limited for this and other reasons – for example, the relative newness of counselling itself, the lack of popularity of Western counselling and psychotherapy among ethnic minorities, the lack of a representative sample from the various ethnic minority groups in training and practice, and many more.

Being on the periphery has not 'helped' multicultural counselling and psychotherapy development. Its position has resulted in a paucity of critical ideas in relation to theory and practice, lack of researchers, clients, practitioners, research funding, and the list goes on. The relatively few new ideas in this area appear to be struggling against the tide of many of the fixed and (out)dated 'treatment' models which still persist in the practice. While the critique of counselling, psychotherapy and psychiatry has been gaining ground, taking its cue seemingly from feminist theorizing of psychoanalysis, it has, however, been restricted to the now outdated and repetitive attack on aspects of traditional psychoanalytic theory for at best being Eurocentric and at worst for being racist, particularly the writings of Freud and Jung (see, for example, Dalal 1988). The ideas of the early writers in this field, such as Rack (1982), are still regarded as being significant in transcultural counselling, psychotherapy and psychiatry. Some of their ideas may be questioned for the kinds of assumption that were made regarding 'race', culture and ethnicity. An example of this can be found in d'Ardenne and Mahtani (1989: 10):

> Rack (1982) has given us a very clear transcultural approach to psychological problems, stemming from work at the Lynfield Mount Hospital in Bradford, England. He maintains that therapists dealing with an alien culture will encounter difficulties in distinguishing between normal and abnormal behaviour. He argues that cultural differences in behaviour are those that are determined by the beliefs and values of the individual's culture. Any dysfunction, therefore, must be seen in relation to that culture.

Understanding psychological problems through this particular analysis is problematic. Lawrence (1982) refers to 'cultural problematic' as the practice where issues such as 'identity crisis', 'culture conflict' and 'inter-generational conflict' become located in the black family and culture. The emphasis on 'culture' and dysfunction in this kind of way is just one of many examples which have shaped the theoretical and clinical approaches in counselling and psychotherapy with ethnic minority clients/patients. Perhaps, a re-theorizing of multiculturalism may support newer clinical approaches to understanding the culturally different client. It may be that adopting a multiplicity of approaches, a plurality of methodologies, and a flexibility in liberating the multiple identities of a client, will engage multicultural counselling and psychotherapy in a more consistent and clinically oriented way than presently experienced.

Multiplicity of multicultural counselling approaches – is there a common thread?

The critique of Western counselling and psychotherapy has in some way prevented the exploration of psychological or clinically useful ideas in counselling the racially and culturally different client. The continual emphasis on the acquisition of cultural knowledge/s and experiences, or the focus on race-awareness training for counsellors wanting to work with ethnic minorities, still seems to dominate the theory and practice of multicultural counselling and its many other related formulations, namely cross-cultural (Pedersen 1985), transcultural (d'Ardenne and Mahtani 1989), multicultural (Pedersen 1991; Pope-Davis and Coleman, 1997), intercultural (Kareem and Littlewood 1992), transcultural (Eleftheriadou 1994), afrocentric (Hall 1995), black feminist (Pankhania 1996) and ethnic minorities (Ramirez 1991). Other descriptors have also been added to this list, for example race and culture (Lago and Thompson 1996) and counselling the culturally different (Sue and Sue 1990), race and racial identity theories (Cross 1971, 1978; Helms 1986, 1990; Ponterotto 1988; Cross et al. 1991; Sabnani et al. 1991; Atkinson et al. 1993; Carter 1995), black consciousness (Moodley 1998a), and existentialism as a cross-cultural counselling modality (Vontress 1979, 1985). These examples are not the entire composition of multi-cultural descriptors by any means, but the range and diversity of ideas does suggest that practitioners are (re)searching for the most appropriate and relevant approach to addressing the mental health needs of ethnic minority groups. The more recent debate on the inclusion of traditional cultural healing practices (see Lago and Thompson 1996; Moodley 1998b) is yet another addition to the compendium of multicultural counselling and psychotherapy.

As McLeod (1993: 116) suggests, 'All these approaches are essentially exploring the same set of issues regarding the impact of race, culture and ethnic identity on the counselling process'. Also, Ramirez (1991) argues that the common theme running through all cross-cultural counselling is the challenge of living in a multicultural society (cited by McLeod 1993: 117). Although there is a general agreement about what constitutes multicultural counselling/cultural differences, the authors of all of the above-mentioned approaches do set out particular definitions of their approach. For example: Kareem (1992: 14) defines intercultural therapy as a process which 'takes into account the whole being of the patient – not only the individual concepts and constructs presented to the therapist, but also the patient's communal life experience' and adds that 'intercultural therapy was developed from certain core ideas: that there are indeed some intrinsic differences between individual human beings, either in their biology, their personality or both, and that both inter- and intrapsychic events profoundly affect an individual's psyche and develop as part of their unconscious life' (ibid.: 19). D'Ardenne and Mahtani (1989: 5), on the other hand, explain why they have chosen 'the term "trans" as opposed to "cross" or "inter" cultural counselling because we want to emphasize the *active* and *reciprocal* process that is involved. Counsellors in this setting are responsible for working across, through or beyond their cultural differences' (italics in the original).

Kareem's definition of intercultural appears to be inclusive of all clients (black and white). Lago and Thompson (1996) indicate that all counselling should be multicultural but also emphasize the need for training therapists to work with different client groups. Sue (1997: 177) reminds us that '[s]ome argue that all counseling is "multicultural" while others feel that the emphasis should be on the counseling of different ethnic minorities'. Sue refers to Pedersen's and Ivey's (1994) criticism of the narrow 'multi-ethnic' definition of multiculturalism, and also to Helms (1994: 163) who argues that:

> It is by no means clear that the same competencies required to deliver effective services to clients for whom racial-group membership is central are equally appropriate for clients for whom other social identities (e.g. gender, age, or religion) are more central.

In the UK, multicultural counselling and therapy seems to be 'reserved' for black, Asian and some ethnic minority groups, although these groups do not necessarily request it or get access to it. Clearly it is not in the 'power' of these groups to construct therapy in a way that sets limits to its provision. The evidence in terms of interest and attendance suggests that ethnic minority groups do not see multicultural counselling and therapy in its present formulation as a viable form of dealing with its mental health needs. In acknowledging this fact, we began to question the 'obsession' or motivation of writers and practitioners with the 'reservation' orientation.

On the other hand, if counsellors are to work 'beyond their cultural differences', then the training must cover all aspects of 'race', gender, class, dis-ability and sexual orientation. The depth of learning and experience will depend upon individual trainees and the courses they choose. If training covers all the issues of the 'Other', the question of naming courses appropriately becomes pertinent. Do we call such courses 'transcultural' if the definition of culture remains locked in 'race', ethnicity and ethnic minority. D'Ardenne and Mahtani stress that 'transcultural work offers a perspective on counselling rather than a particular school of thought' (1989: 5).

It seems that the multi(ple) cultural descriptors are problematized. Reconstituting and redefining them may be necessary. However, emptying out the (multicultural) crucibles may not be possible since some signify the 'containing objects' (Bion 1963) of 'cultural inheritance' (Winnicott 1971), whilst others provide 'psychic retreats' which Western counselling and psychotherapy fails to do. In attempting such a project we are reminded not to throw the multicultural 'baby out with the white-coloured-bath water'. Although it may be possible in the future for someone to train exclusively to work with ethnic minority clients, it does, however, raise questions as to whether this is the most appropriate or relevant way of training counsellors for a multiracial and multicultural society. One way of beginning this process is to ask the following question.

Do black people want a special course in counsellor training?

Lago and Thompson (1996: 133) suggested that:

> many basic counselling training courses within the United Kingdom ... spend relatively little time and attention on the preparation of counselling trainees to work with culturally and racially different clients. Given the huge amount of material to be learned in terms of knowledge acquisition and skills development in counselling and psychotherapy this situation is understandable, though it becomes less defensible within the reality of the UK as a multiracial society.

Therefore, when we hear of a special course catering for ethnic minority groups, we 'free associate' in terms of 'equal opportunities, affirmative action, accessibility for the disadvantaged, increased participation, equitable provision, empowerment ... and many others'.

However, the setting up of a special course to train someone for a specific group is far more difficult than it seems and far easier to justify if the complexities and contradictions are not fully understood. The issue is not 'if' or 'when' such training should take place, but 'how' and in 'what' form such training should take place. A transcultural counselling course offered alongside other counselling courses will once again fall prey to the 'apartheid' of separate development while espousing equality.

In a recent paper, a colleague and I reported on research we had undertaken with some black counsellors/therapists (see Moodley and Dhingra 1998). Although it was not a representative sample of ethnic-minority counsellors/therapists in Britain, some of the findings do reflect more general views. For example, we found that:

> black counsellors work with just as many white clients as they do with black clients. And in many cases, black counsellors work with fewer ethnic-minority clients than white clients as a result of the demography of the institutions they work in. Some work exclusively with white clients. (1998: 296)

All of these counsellors trained as counsellors and none of them attended any special programme, such as transcultural or multi-ethnic, which prepared them for counselling. All the black counsellors in the research emphasized that they were first and foremost professional counsellors, like the members of any other profession – be it architects, lawyers, medical doctors – and would then like to be seen as people who specialized in multicultural work. Most felt that if they were offered a very specific course or a discrete programme called transcultural counselling, then they might not have got the kinds of jobs they were in (usually in university or college counselling units or in general practice settings). Some of the black counsellors worked in special settings which involved working exclusively with ethnic minority clients/patients (e.g. black mental health projects). But even these counsellors were employed as counsellors first and foremost and seen secondarily as workers familiar with issues of 'race', culture and ethnicity. A 'perception which problematises the black counsellor as a professional therapist is the notion that relatively few ethnic-minority counsellors who work in this field are best suited to work chiefly with clients from their own or similar culture background' (Moodley and Dhingra 1998: 295).

Almost all the counsellors we interviewed had prepared themselves consciously or unconsciously through further study (some before the counselling course) to incorporate issues of 'race', culture and ethnicity knowledge/s and experiences whether they were working with black or white clients. Many saw this process as part of their personal development plan as well as acquiring additional skills as professionals. Since many of the black mental health projects were part of the government's Mental Health Challenge Fund and the Target Fund, it meant that employment was neither permanent nor guaranteed beyond the lifetime of a particular government. Indeed, the black counsellors were reassured by the fact that they were trained as counsellors and could seek work outside the black community, if the funding climate changed. A training in transcultural counselling alone would have rendered them unviable for work with white clients. This is because transcultural counselling excludes white people from the process as clients. Sashidharan (1986) emphasizes that this black–white paradigm has reinforced prevailing notions which exist in our society about 'race', culture and illness.

About psychiatry, Sashidharan writes: 'transculturalism is not just about black clients. Without its white practitioners it would have no reason to survive and no vested interest or political energy to sustain it' (1986: 159–60). And 'the reliance on such exotic explanations about the "alien" nature of clinical problems could no longer be sustained in the light of contemporary developments' (Sashidharan 1990: 8). But some practitioners would argue that counselling and psychotherapy is different, especially multicultural counselling. But how different? Furthermore, Sashidharan (1986: 159) argues that:

there is a more important issue that is obscured by the semantic argument. This has to do with the ethnocentric, and Eurocentric bias that has been built into transcultural psychiatry [counselling, psychotherapy, counselling psychology] and in such a context, words like 'culture' or 'ethnicity' take on a special, politically loaded meaning ... their apparent neutrality of meaning becomes instrumental in signifying ideologies, preferences or norms which are subsequently imposed at all levels of understanding. ... Invested with a new meaning these mere words or concepts suddenly become powerful tools with which the transcultural psychiatrist [counsellor, psychotherapist, counselling psychologist] sets out to particularise social structures which are products of historical and political struggles. As a result, culture or aspects of people's lives and experiences are reduced to mere manageable problems falling within the clinical or professional competence of the culturally informed practitioner. (Inclusions are the present author's.)

Words like 'culture' and 'ethnicity' which have been used in transcultural work do fall prey to ethnocentric, Eurocentric, political, ideological and social influences. Their meanings can sometimes be historicized into an *a priori* construction which justifies a particular 'world-view' approach or a 'culture-fit' method of counselling with ethnic minority clients. As trainers of counsellors and psychotherapists we must seek to understand fully how the dynamics of 'race', culture and ethnicity can be used/misused/abused ... confused in training counsellors. For example, as mentioned earlier, the exclusion of whites as clients from transcultural counselling reinforces the prevailing notions held in society about black people and mental illness. Furthermore, this notion suggests that black clients have 'illness' which are different from those of white clients. Going down this route will eventually lead to the eugenic movement, pseudo-scientific racism or the more recent bell curve debate (see Thomas and Sillen 1972; Gilman 1985).

Another dilemma which is present in counsellor training can be seen in the example below from Sue Wheeler's research:

Daniel is a Black probation officer. He has done well on the course but continually challenges staff about the lack of attention paid to Black issues. He has been on placement with an agency offering counselling to Black clients and insists that he is not prepared to see any white clients. How likely is Daniel to pass the course? (Wheeler 1996: 101)

In her study, responses varied from '[d]epends on whether this is a personal or political issue ... to ... his stipulation about working with one client group would lead to failure to demonstrate core components and hence failure on the course' (ibid.: 101).

So ... perhaps for now, the answer to the question 'Do black people want a special course in counsellor training?' may be an uncompromising 'NO' or a reserved/qualified 'No', which waits in abeyance until further discussion takes place on this matter. A 'YES' answer at this stage, which seems to be the response that some providers of counselling use to argue the case for a transcultural or multi-ethnic counselling course, may pre-empt any of the research that is being done to increase multicultural clinical ideas.

Is there a lack of knowledge of multicultural clinical conceptualizations?

For transcultural counselling to be offered as a fully pledged course there must exist a body of theoretical and clinical knowledge/s that inform the practice. A great part of the literature in this area has been a socio-cultural and political critique of traditional Western European counselling and psychotherapy. While raising some of the same arguments as feminism on psychotherapy and the 'Other', it has also called for training to ensure that counsellors acknowledge, be aware of and be sensitive to, cultural and racial differences (see Pedersen, 1985, 1991; d'Ardenne and Mahtani 1989; Sue and Sue, 1990; Lago and Thompson 1996; and others). Furthermore, counsellors would need to be aware of their own racial identity and possess appropriate communication skills in relation to ethnic minority clients (see also Carter 1995; Dupont-Joshua 1997). Very little, however, has been written on how ethnic minorities represent and present their 'psychological distress' and how these in turn are understood or 'interpreted' by counsellors and psychotherapists. Jones (1984) argues that the acknowledgement of cultural differences has done very little to 'guide the conduct' of counselling and psychotherapy with black patients. He argues that the black client/patient is not a diagnostic or clinical type and knowing that the client/patient is culturally black is not enough. They are individuals too. This latter concept, which counselling and psychotherapy is functionally organized around, often remains hidden, closed and left undisclosed in the actual therapy with ethnic minority clients. The discourse of 'race', culture and ethnicity takes over, overwhelming both client and therapist sometimes at the expense of meaningful change, although at the same time it could be argued that the 'self as individual' or the 'individual self' is constituted of, and constructed by, 'race', culture and ethnicity. Without the exploration of these constructs therapy would be missing an important part of the client's life experience. Indeed, this is the very critique that is levelled against the essentialist and closed view of traditional counselling, psychoanalysis and psychotherapy and its universal applications. The assumption was that transcultural counselling with its contradictions could address these issues. But as Helms and Richardson (1997: 61) point out, this may not be so easy a role to perform, since

> [t]he controversy stems in part from the lack of precise psychological conceptualizations of multiculturalism and related terms as well as the absence of relevant theoretical models for inter- preting the role of such factors in the counselling process as broadly defined.... Consequently the tendency has been to impose the same set of multicultural competencies on clients regard- less of their cultural characteristics. For the most part, 'cultural' in such instances typically means whatever the advocate would like it to mean at the moment.

The (re)search for 'precise psychological conceptualizations' to inform clinical prac- tice with ethic minority clients has been problematized for a number of reasons: research, particularly in the UK is difficult to undertake in a field that is generally conducted 'behind closed doors'. The fact that there are very few ethnic minority clients, counsel- lors and therapists also adds to the problem of uncovering useful clinical concepts in this area. Most researchers will not only need to overcome these hurdles but also to confront some of the entrenched views embedded in the profession, namely, 'Ethnic minorities do not verbalize as white clients and therefore do not need counselling and psychotherapy', 'Asians do not think psychologically and therefore somaticize their distress', 'Blacks transfer aggression and evoke complicated countertransference reactions', ... and many more. Any transformation in this field may need to be understood not as a 'reactionary response' or a 'revolutionary uprising' of black militant thought, but as an organic and ecologically sustained process which emerges from the roots of counselling and psychotherapy.

Conclusion

In a postmodern multiracial and multicultural society there is no argument that all counsellors must be trained to work with all clients irrespective of 'race', culture, ethnicity, class, gender, dis-ability and sexual orientation. If we accept that the constitution of the 'subject' and the evolving epistemologies and ontologies are reflective of a multiracial and multicultural society, then we would have no problems in seeing training as an all-inclusive process. Within this 'general practice' preparation, counsellors may then choose to specialize in different ways which may prepare them to develop their particular practice further. A specialism in issues of 'race', culture and ethnicity, may be one such route. This process may also meet the requirements of individual accreditation by BAC, that

> applicants for Individual Accreditation should be asked to supply evidence that they have addressed the issues of difference and equality in their practice ... [and] ... that clients should be able to expect counsellors to have addressed these issues and that training courses should also take account of such a requirement. (BAC 1998: 2).

This requirement seems to point the way for training providers that an all-inclusive programme would be best suited to prepare trainees for the profession. In developing such a curriculum one should also bear in mind that 'a broad definition of multicultural counseling may dilute attention to issues such as racism faced by ethnic minority groups' (Sue 1997: 178; see also Sue et al. 1992). On the other hand, Draguns (1997: 240–1) concludes that:

> While addressing the needs of underserved and disadvantaged cultural minorities is of paramount importance, the field should venture forth and explore the differences and similarities in counseling techniques with disadvantage removed... [This] would help isolate the effects of culture in the counseling process and thereby eventually contribute to making it more sensitive and effective at all sites of its application.

In a society which is multilingual, multi-religious, multi-sexually oriented, multi-cultural, multi-aged, multiracial, and so on, it may seem that every training course may have to physically incorporate and embody these concepts. This may be neither possible nor desirable to achieve. However, what seems important is that counselling and psychotherapy begin to incorporate the changing ideas of subjectivity and multiple identities in their practice. So that the question, 'What kind of training would be most appropriate for therapists to counsel a client who is black, working-class, deaf and lesbian?' can be answered in a number of ways. For example, Crouan (1996: 36) states that, 'many of the suggestions for making counselling training more relevant and accessible to lesbians could equally be applied to black people, disabled people and other members of oppressed groups'. In 'A deaf counselling trainee: can it work?' Pauline Monks and Linda Martin (1997: 264–5 (and see Chapter 27 in this volume)) have this to say:

> we have, at her [Monks'] suggestion, occasionally used non-verbal exercises to help all of us be more aware of how it might feel to be deaf and to experiment with communicating in different ways, such as gesture and drawing ... I [Martin] have found that my fears were groundless – it can work and work well, the course can benefit rather than suffer ... both students and tutors, have gained from Pauline's joining us.

These and many 'Other' similar examples illustrate that there are different ways of multicultural counselling and therapy. But this is just the beginning and we still have a long way to go.

The point of a comfortable arrival – an understanding of clinical conceptualizations in counselling the culturally, racially and ethnically different, will mean that until then the client who is deaf, black, gay, working-class may be transferred (culturally) from one therapy to another. Or would such a client need to seek support from a state psychiatrist to provide 'treatment of care'? Can anyone be reassured that through such a journey a client will 'self-actualize' and not 'actualize their self' out of existence? (see Littlewood and Lipsedge 1997 for a discussion on suicide and the black community). In the final analysis/paragraph of *Aliens and Alienists*, Littlewood and Lipsedge remind us that:

> Our aim then must be, not just 'therapy', but a self-reflexive practice which examines its own prejudices, ideology and will to power, which is aware of the ironies and contradictions in its own formation, and which is prepared to challenge them. (1997: 310)

One such irony and contradiction may be the interesting fact that all those practitioners, authors, academics who call for the training of transcultural counsellors and psychotherapists, are themselves mainstream trained and prefer to be called a counsellor, or a therapist, or a psychotherapists of a particular orientation – 'person-centred counsellor', 'psychodynamic psychotherapist' – but not a 'transcultural counsellor' or 'transcultural psychotherapist'. Why? Is it about clinical credibility? Is it about employment? Is it about status? Or is it part of the complexities, confusions and contradiction which this paper has attempted to highlight? There are still many more questions that need to be asked.

Acknowledgement

My thanks to Maggie Pettifer for suggesting changes to the draft manuscript.

References

Ahmad, W.I.U. (ed.) (1993) *'Race' and Health in Contemporary Britain*, Buckingham: Open University Press.

Atkinson, D.R., Morten, G. and Sue, D.W. (eds) (1993) *Counseling American Minorities: A Cross-Cultural Perspective* (4th edn), Dubuque, IA: Brown & Benchmark.

BAC (1998) Minutes of Annual General Meeting, British Association for Counselling, 8 September at Southampton University.

Bhabha, H. (1994) *The Location of Culture*, London: Routledge.

Bimrose, J. and Bayne, R. (1995) 'A multicultural framework in counsellor training: a preliminary evaluation', *British Journal of Guidance and Counselling*, 23 (2): 259–65.

Bion, W.R. (1963) *Elements of Psycho-Analysis*, London: Heinemann.

Carter, R.T. (1995) *The Influence of RACE and Racial Identity in Psychotherapy*, New York: John Wiley & Sons.

Cross, W.E., Jr. (1971) 'The Negro-to-Black conversion experience: towards a psychology of Black liberation', *Black World*, 20: 13–27.

Cross, W.E. Jr. (1978) 'The Thomas and Cross models of psychological Nigrescence: a review', *Journal of Black Psychology*, 5 (1): 13–31.

Cross, W.E., Jr., Parham, T.A. and Helms, J.E. (1991) 'The stages of Black identity development: Nigrescence models', in R.C. Jones (ed.), *Black Psychology*, Berkeley: University of California Press.

Crouan, M. (1996) 'Pushing against the wind: the recognition of lesbians in counselling training', *Counselling*, 7 (1): 36–9.

Dalal, F. (1988) 'Jung: a racist', *British Journal of Psychotherapy*, 4 (3): 263–79.

d'Ardenne, P. and Mahtani, A. (1989) *Transcultural Counselling in Action*, London: Sage.

Draguns, J.G. (1997) 'Abnormal behaviour patterns across cultures: implications for counselling and psychotherapy', *International Journal of Intercultural Relations*, 21 (2): 213–48.

Dryden, W. (1994) 'Possible future trends in counselling and counsellor training: a personal view', *Counselling*, 5 (3): 194–7.

Dupont-Joshua, A. (1997) 'Working with issues of race in counselling', *Counselling*, 8 (4): 282–4.

Eleftheriadou, Z. (1994) *Transcultural Counselling*, London: Central Books.

Fanon, F. (1967) *Black Skins, White Masks*, London: Grove Press.

Gilman, S.L. (1985) *Difference and Pathology: Stereotypes of Sexuality, Race, and Madness*, Ithaca, NY: Cornell University Press.

Hall, S. (1992) 'New ethnicities', in J. Donald and A. Rattansi (eds), *'Race', Culture and Difference*, London: Sage/Open University Press.

Hall, W.A. (1995) 'Afrocentric counselling', paper presented to the 2nd Annual Black Access Conference at Sheffield University.

Helms, J.E. (1986) 'Expanding racial identity theory to cover counselling process', *Journal of Counseling Psychology*, 33: 62–4.

Helms, J.E. (1990) *Black and White Racial Identity: Theory, Research and Practice*, Westport, CT: Greenwood.

Helms, J.E. (1994) 'How multiculturalism obscures racial factors in the therapy process: comment on Ridley et al. (1994), Sodowsky et al. (1994), Ottavi et al. (1994), and Thompson et al. (1994)', *Journal of Counseling Psychology*, 41: 162–5.

Helms, J.E. and Richardson, T.Q. (1997) 'How "multiculturalism" obscures race and culture as differential aspects of counselling competence', in D.B. Pope-Davis and H.L.K. Coleman (eds), *Multicultural Counseling Competencies*, Thousand Oaks, CA: Sage.

Jones, E.E. (1984) 'Some reflections on the Black patient and psychotherapy', *Journal of Clinical Psychology*, 37 (2): 62–5.

Kareem, J. (1992) 'The Nafsiyat Intercultural Therapy Centre: ideas and experience in intercultural therapy', in J. Kareem and R. Littlewood (eds), *Intercultural Therapy Themes, Interpretations and Practice*, London: Blackwell Scientific Publications.

Kareem, J. and Littlewood, R. (eds) (1992) *Intercultural Therapy: Themes, Interpretations and Practice*, London: Blackwell Scientific Publications.

Lago, C. and Thompson, J. (1996) *Race, Culture and Counselling*, Buckingham: Open University Press.

Lawrence, E. (1982) 'In the abundance of water the fool is thirsty: sociology and black "pathology"', in CCCS, *The Empire Strikes Back*, London: Hutchinson, pp. 95–142.

Littlewood, R. (1992) 'Towards an intercultural therapy', in J. Kareem and R. Littlewood, *Intercultural Therapy*, Oxford: Blackwell Scientific Publications.

Littlewood, R. and Lipsedge, M. (1997) *Aliens and Alienists: Ethnic Minorities and Psychiatry* (3rd edn), London: Routledge.

McLeod, J. (1993) *An Introduction to Counselling*, Buckingham: Open University Press.

Monks, P. and Martin, L. (1997) 'A deaf counselling trainee: can it work?', *Counselling*, 8 (4): 263–5. (See Chapter 27.)

Moodley, R. (1998a) '"I say what I like": frank talk(ing) in counselling and psychotherapy', *British Journal of Guidance and Counselling*, 26 (4): 495–508.

Moodley, R. (1998b) 'Cultural returns to the subject: traditional healing in counselling and therapy', *Changes, International Journal of Psychology and Psychotherapy*, 16 (1): 45–56.

Moodley, R. and Dhingra, S. (1998) 'Cross-cultural/racial matching in counselling and therapy: white clients and black counsellors', *Counselling*, 9 (4): 295–9. (See Chapter 82.)

Morrison, K. (1997) 'Researching the need for multicultural perspectives in counsellor training: a critique of Bimrose and Bayne', *British Journal of Guidance and Counselling*, 25 (1): 95–101.

Pankhania, J. (1996) 'Black feminist counselling', in M. Jacobs (ed.), *Jitendra: Lost Connections, in Search of a Therapist*, Buckingham: Open University Press.

Pedersen, P.B. (1985) *Handbook of Cross-Cultural Counseling and Therapy*, New York: Praeger.

Pedersen, P.B. (ed.) (1991) 'Multiculturalism as a fourth force in counseling' (Special Issue), *Journal of Counseling and Development*, 70: 4–250.

Pedersen, P.B. and Ivey, A.E. (1994) *Culture-Centred Counseling and Interviewing Skills*, Westport, CT: Praeger.

Ponterotto, J.G. (1988) 'Racial consciousness development among White counselors' trainees: a stage model', *Journal of Multicultural Counseling and Development*, 16: 146–56.

Pope-Davis, D.B. and Coleman, H.L.K. (eds) (1997) *Multicultural Counseling Competencies. Assessment, Education and Training and Supervision*, Thousands Oaks, CA: Sage.

Pope-Davis, D.B. and Liu, W.M. (1998) 'The social construction of race: implications for counseling psychology, *Counselling Psychology Quarterly*, 11 (2): 151–61.

Rack, P. (1982) *Race, Culture and Mental Disorder*, London: Tavistock Publications.

Ramirez, M., III (1991) *Psychotherapy and Counseling with Minorities: A Cognitive Approach to Individual and Cultural Difference*, Oxford: Pergamon Press.

Sabnani, H.B., Ponterotto, J.G. and Borodovsky, L.G. (1991) 'White racial identity development and cross-cultural counselor training: a stage model', *Counseling Psychologist*, 19: 76–102.

Said, E.W. (1978) *Orientalism*, London: Routledge & Kegan Paul.

Said, E.W. (1993) *Culture and Imperialism*, London: Chatto & Windus.

Sashidharan, S.P. (1986) 'Ideology and politics in transcultural psychiatry', in J.L. Cox (ed.), *Transcultural Psychiatry*, London: Croom Helm.

Sashidharan, S.P. (1990) 'Race and psychiatry', *Medical World*, 3: 8–12.

Shafi, S. (1998) 'A study of Muslim Asian women's experience of counselling and the necessity for a racially similar counsellor', *Counselling Psychology Quarterly*, 11 (3): 301–14.

Spivak, G.C. (1988) *In Other World*, London: Routledge.

Sue, D. (1997) 'Multicultural training', *International Journal of Intercultural Relations*, 21 (2): 175–93.

Sue, D.W. and Sue, D. (1990) *Counseling the Culturally Different: Theory and Practice* (2nd edn), New York: John Wiley & Sons.

Sue, D.W., Arredondo, P. and McDavis, R.J. (1992) 'Multicultural counseling competencies and standards: a call to the professional', *Journal of Counseling and Development*, 70: 477–86.

Thomas, A. and Sillen, S. (1972) *Racism and Psychiatry*, Secausus, NJ: Citadel.

Vontress, C.E. (1979) 'Cross-cultural counseling: an existential approach', *Personal and Guidance Journal*, 58: 117–22.

Vontress, C.E. (1985) 'Existentialism as a cross-cultural counseling modality', in P. Pedersen (ed.), *Handbook of Cross-Cultural Counseling and Therapy*, New York: Praeger.

Wheeler, S. (1996) *Training Counsellors: The Assessment of Competence*, London: Cassell.

Willett, C. (ed.) (1998) *Theorizing Multiculturalism*, Malden, MA: Blackwell Publishers.

Winnicott, D.W. (1971) *Playing and Reality*, London: Tavistock Publications.

Discussion issues

1 What do the terms transcultural, cross-cultural, intercultural and multi-cultural counselling mean? Do you think clients are aware of these concepts and their meanings?

2 Multicultural counselling seems to be used exclusively with black and ethnic minority clients. Is this appropriate in a multicultural society which should affirm gay, lesbian, disabled and working-class cultures as well? Explain?

3 All forms of counselling and psychotherapy ought to be multicultural. Discuss.

4 Training counsellors and psychotherapists for the twenty-first century should include issues appropriate to its time. What are they and how would a training course meet these needs?

89

Computer Therapeutics

Colin Lago

During the last two decades the development of computer-based systems has been extraordinarily rapid and widespread within society. Computers with their visual display units are as commonplace now in shops and offices as quills, ledgers and oil lamps would have been a hundred years ago!

Electronic mail and the Internet

This article has been driven, in part, by considerations that my colleagues and I have been engaged in recently, in trying to consider ways in which we might offer a counselling service to students on distant campuses of Sheffield University. Resources do not extend to the provision of a peripatetic counsellor travelling between sites, and unfortunately many students cannot afford either the time or expense to travel to visit our central service. One possible answer to this difficulty is to envisage a counselling response service using the technology of electronic mail.

Working within a university setting means that there exists a reasonable provision of computers available for students and staff usage, and many students now have their own electronic mail addresses. Specifically for counsellors and therapists there are 'units' of information stored about professional associations, discussion-based communications around particular theoretical issues (to which one may contribute), and indeed even support groups for clients for a whole range of psychological difficulties (Harris 1995).

Electronic mail (e-mail) offers new possibilities for direct communication between people across the world, through messages typed on the computer screen and transmitted to their electronic mail address. E-mail can be received and responded to immediately (in real time) or can be stored, until collected and responded to later (asynchronous time).

At the University of Sheffield we have evidence that students access psychological information that is presently available on the central university system, as well as use electronic mail to address enquiries of a personal nature (Shipton et al. 1995).

Elsewhere, the Samaritans already offer an electronic mail service to clients which apparently is very well used. A new national e-mail service related to men's health matters is soon to go on line (Culf 1996).

McLeod (1993) asserts that telephone counselling is the most used form of counselling. For many clients, then, the telephone will be a preferred way of eliciting help. Electronic mail is a further extension of the use of contemporary technology that has the potential to transmit and effect communications between helper and helped.

This chapter was first published in *Counselling*, Journal of the British Association for Counselling, vol. 7, no. 4, pp. 287–9 (1996). It is dedicated to the memory of Bethan Reeve, a valued friend and former Student Sabbatical Officer at the University of Sheffield.

The apparent potential of this new technology has far-reaching implications both in terms of its impact upon society, as well as how it might most appropriately be utilized for therapeutic communication. Certainly, it is urged that any new developments are monitored and researched carefully as to their efficacy, sensitivity and therapeutic potential.

Counselling relationships and e-mail

A substantial proportion of the theories of counselling and pshchotherapy lay considerable emphasis upon the relationship as a significant, if not the most significant, aspect of the therapeutic endeavour. The potential of relationship could be said to be diminished through the use of telephones in contrast to (live) interviews. Both parties, within the telephone encounter, are deprived of the visible, spatial and tactile possibilities that exist within a live counselling interview. Nevertheless, through concentrated listening both parties are able to pick up not only the spoken content of each other's statements but also all the clues and cues communicated through paralinguistic phenomena. The telephone relationship, though deprived of some of the major sensory areas necessary for human communication, nevertheless still retains this vital aural dimension.

By contrast, what sort of relationship do we have if I, as client, write to you (through e-mail) as a counsellor? How might we conceptualize this relationship in therapeutic terms? Also, recognizing that the majority of use of electronic mail will be carried out in asynchronous time, that is, I write to you today and you write back tomorrow or later, how long might it take for a relationship to develop?

The paradox of isolation and connection

A profound paradox seems to surround this activity. The user of electronic mail may communicate with others anywhere in the world and indeed do so over very personal matters. A form of connectedness and communication is thus established through the words on the screen. A recent legal case in the United States is even based upon the allegation by an aggrieved husband that his wife committed computer adultery with a man she never met (Slouka 1996). There are also several claims of people meeting and falling in love through the Internet (Billen 1996). Ultimately, however, despite the potential of such very intimate communications, both persons continue to be alone, in the physical sense, isolated from the world, sitting at their own computers. Slouka (1996) also asserts that there are many incidents of users being hurt emotionally by electronic communication.

The paradox can be thus expressed as follows; 'I have connected deeply with you psychologically and emotionally on my computer, yet I still remain isolated from you in every physical sense (no vision, no sound, no touch). It is very personal and not personal at all. You are ultimately words on a screen and a figure of imagination in my head! Yet I have told you things I've not shared with another person.'

For clients whose trust in persons has been considerably abused, the mechanism of electronic mail might prove extremely attractive. And if a sense of relationship exists for the client, is it to the computer itself or to the responding helper?

Typed language – the form of communication

A different language is a different form of life.

Frederico Fellini

The language used for electronic communication is reduced to words only, on a screen. All paralinguistic, non-verbal and cultural clues to communication are not available. Argyle (1975) cites research where 'no-vision' encounters were marked by greater formality, were more task-oriented, depersonalized and less spontaneous. They were experienced as more socially distant, and with less social presence (Rutter in Argyle 1975: 119). Rutter concludes that in the absence of visual cues, a greater focus is maintained on the communication task at hand. This particular finding might bode very well for the computer counselling process.

Both Billen (1996) and Slouka (1996) note the tendency of electronic mail writers to communicate more directly, more spontaneously, more frankly and abruptly. Discursive letter-writing styles do not hold sway. The messages become short, direct transmissions, not descriptive or conversational prose.

Dorothy Rowe has argued that the words we use determine what we do (1995). Words create metaphors and metaphors determine the framework in which we operate. All of this suggests that the counsellor offering an electronic mail response service will have to become a 'wordsmith' more than anything else.

This whole section asks what are the implications for therapeutic discourse in the wake of electronic communication? What are the connections between the language used in the communications and the thought, affect and actions of both participants? The use of computers changes and transforms language.

What do empathic, reflective, interpretive, instructive and congruent statements look like on a monitor screen? Also, how effective will they be?

The question of theory for e-mail counselling

The various sections detailed above, that is the nature of relationship, the paradox of isolation and intimacy and the restricted yet specialized forms of communication required of the medium pose considerable questions as to the nature of an appropriate underlying theory for the process. It might well be that an e-mail counselling approach can only simply communicate information in response to clients' questions or statements. However, as mentioned earlier, colleagues have already indicated that very personal communication can occur through this medium. Indeed, Kirschenbaum (1990: 114) cites research by Lindsley that provides empirical evidence for considerable patient improvement associated with interactions with a machine. Nevertheless, Kirschenbaum also concludes that 'trustworthiness' must be evident within the human–machine interaction for it to work effectively and therapeutically.

One theoretical idea that seems to have some potential in this domain is that of the pre-therapy work that has been developed in recent years by Gary Prouty (1990) in the USA and more recently by Dion Van Werde in Belgium (Mearns 1994).

The work of pre-therapy has taken as its starting point Rogers' first condition of the six necessary and sufficient conditions for therapeutic personality change to occur (1957). This condition states that for therapy to occur, 'it is necessary that the two persons (counsellor and client) are in psychological contact' (Rogers 1957: 96). This first condition has attracted very little attention historically, the common assumption being that psychological contact was automatic for two people in the same room. Prouty challenged this mistaken assumption and has been developing his 'pre-therapy' approach since the mid-1970s with client groups who experience difficulties in the establishment of contact with others, with 'reality' and with their own affective selves. This work has been applied with persons diagnosed as schizophrenic, retarded, suffering acute psychosis and with multiple personalities.

This does not infer or imply that users of e-mail counselling services will be suffering acute psychological states as medically defined above. Rather, it is argued here that the nature of establishing psychological contact with the client through e-mail will be a priority before other therapeutic work will become possible.

Staying within the theory of client-centred therapy, some of Rogers' other conditions, namely those of unconditional positive regard and congruence, will prove challenging to demonstrate because of the lack of non-verbal cues. Rogers' fifth condition, that the therapist strives for an empathic understanding of the client's internal frame of reference and then endeavours to communicate this experience to the client, may become a more important response mode as the relationship develops.

In being reduced to a words-only transaction, the client's perception of the counsellor's messages will be crucial in determining the extent to which they stay in contact to resolve their difficulties. The e-mail client has so much less to go on in their judgement of the counsellor, and this whole area of client perception, Rogers' sixth condition, may determine the extent to which therapy will continue.

The development of fantasy and counter-fantasy

Precisely because the form of e-mail communication determines that both participants type their messages into the vacuum of the machine, a potent opportunity exists for the development of fantasy, one to the other.

Rather more worrying, though, is the possibility that the development of the fantasized figure of the therapist by the client might become over-exaggerated and unrealistic. A psychotic tendency in the client might become exacerbated through this medium. The e-mail counsellor's sensitivity to this potential phenomenon must be well tuned. A practical point arising from this is the consideration that will need to be given, by services wishing to go on-line in offering an e-mail service, to the contact name they advertise. It is suggested here that perhaps that name is one that is short, gender-neutral and culturally appropriate. Gender-neutral names might include 'Sam' (Samuel, Samantha), 'Jo' (Joseph, Joanne) 'Les' (Lesley, Leslie) and so on. The name also should not be the name of one of the counsellors already in the service. These strategies might go some way towards offering primary safeguards against the personalization of fantasy figures by clients.

Ethical behaviour on e-mail

There is already a general and unwritten code of ethical behaviour on the Internet termed 'n'etiquette'. As e-mail counselling services begin to emerge, attention will have to be focused on the specialist construction of an ethical code for this work. Libel cases for 'flaming' another user (insulting) are already a known phenomenon in the United States and though it is hoped that counsellors would not knowingly be hurtful to clients through their messages, a considerable degree of latitude nevertheless remains within the verbal construction of messages that will require utmost care in their compositon.

The confidentiality of the system will be another huge area for concern and great care will have to be taken to prevent inappropriate and indeed deliberate breaking into the stream of communications.

Summing up

The general increase in usage of electronic forms of communication has paved the way for the emergence of counselling services on this medium. Being reduced to messages comprising printed words only between clients and counsellor, great attention to process and a redefinition of the relationship will be required.

This emerging field implicitly asks questions of existing theory. Do the existing theories of psychotherapy continue to apply, or do we need a new theory of e-mail therapy?

Themes of therapeutic (computer/therapist) competence are likely to include:

- the ability to establish contact;
- the ability to establish relationship;
- the ability to communicate accurately with minimal loss or distortion;
- the ability to demonstrate understanding and frame empathic responses;
- the capacity and resources to provide appropriate and supportive information. This might include reading lists and short relevant articles on a wide range of human concerns.

Computer communications might, at worst, exacerbate a psychological splitting away from humans for some clients who will seek refuge in intimate communications on the Internet.

At a theoretical level we might have to consider what these developments mean in terms of the self, of self-development, of self-actualization and interpersonal relations.

What good are therapy and education if they are not humanizing? The 'therapeuters'' task philosophically will be to facilitate, as best as possible, the personal and humanizing drives within each client.

Acknowledgements

The author is grateful to the following colleagues who have contributed, through various discussions, to the above article: Jean Willowes, Penny Copinger Binns, John Macauley, Bethan Reeves, Priscilla Kindrick, Safina Meah, Toni Wright and Tony Merry.

Update

A recent re-reading of the above chapter left me with the impression of how 'dated' (in one way) it seemed. This might be because, in the meantime, I have developed my own skills and knowledge a little more in relation to the computing world and feel somewhat more confident (though not necessarily more competent) than I did when I *penned* the article in 1996.

At that time, however, I can remember wondering why no one, to my knowledge, in the UK counselling field had written about this emerging medium. Counselling is not only about communication, but is often concerned with communicating about communication! Why, I wondered, were we as counsellors not communicating about this form of potential communication with clients?

The article certainly attracted some considerable interest from readers of *Counselling* and I found myself often being asked questions for which I had no answers. Somehow, it seemed, the article had touched a growing and very contemporary concern among both counsellors and those training in counselling. At the same time, it seemed that several well-established practitioners were throwing their hands up in horror at the prospect of electronic therapy, conveying that perhaps I had lost my way writing such a piece!

Any new medium of communication will always require consideration of its therapeutic potential. In the few years since the original publication (1996) an extraordinary increase in the ownership and regular usage of personal computers, right across the world and certainly within the UK, has occurred. Millions are now connected to the Internet and are using the very wide array of services and facilities it offers. E-commerce, already reasonably well established in the USA is expanding rapidly in the UK and some computer-system-based companies have already been sold at extraordinarily high prices, even before their markets are fully established!

The original article had been somewhat longer but had to be edited to a more appropriate length for the journal. It was with considerable satisfaction, then, that I read Peter Sanders' and Maxie Rosenfield's symposium of articles on this subject published in a special edition of the *British Journal of Guidance and Counselling* (1998). Alan Brice, Head of Student Counselling at the University of Newcastle, has also published an article concerned with these issues (1999).

A little while later and following on from an expression of my concern at an annual conference of the Association of University and College Counsellors, I was invited to constitute and chair a working party on the subject. The proceedings of the working party, after discussion between AUCC and BAC, were then used as the basis of a text now published by the British Association for Counselling with the title 'Counselling On-line' (1999). This publication explores, among other things, the particular concerns of security of messages, the establishment of e-mail counselling contracts and provides a range of other electronic sources that could be consulted. It was coincidentally published with a survey on the extent of and attitudes to on-line counselling among BAC members (Parker 1999). To my knowledge, there are now several post-graduate researchers in different institutions conducting contemporary research in this arena.

Some of the challenges originally proposed in the above chapter, of course, still obtain. Though not exactly in the e-mail therapy domain, there have now been cases of American and British students posting suicide messages on to discussion groups and causing very considerable concern to the security and welfare staff of their colleges who, having been informed, felt they had to locate and then visit the student's address to ascertain the veracity of their 'story'.

Such circumstances, which could easily be replicated on-line, are very anxiety-provoking indeed and might be enough to persuade some therapists not to work using this medium. The potential value, however, of this form of counselling, cannot be underestimated. Evidence from the Samaritans suggests that their e-mail service continues to increase in demand. Particular people might prefer to conduct their personal exploration/ therapy through this rather than a live medium – for example, people who are shy or extremely reticent, embarrassed and just not used to 'speaking' their troubles to another. Students on year-abroad schemes and employees of international companies outside the UK might all value the possibility of electronic therapy. Some counsellors agree to the use of this medium with on-going clients who have to be elsewhere for a period of time. In these cases, the already established therapeutic relationship can serve as a useful referent to the counsellor composing e-mail responses to the client's messages. This medium also might facilitate easier access to therapeutic services to particular user groups with certain disabilities, such as those with mobility difficulties or those with speech and hearing impairments (see Chapter 27).

Running somewhat parallel to the issues here has been the recent expansion of research into the efficacy of writing as a therapeutic tool. Though not exactly writing as defined by Gillie Bolton's research, counselling by electronic communication presently has to involve the client in the writing process and that, in itself, may have a therapeutic effect without any reply even being made (Bolton 1999) (see Chapter 14).

Technology is already available that will afford both visual and audio contact to be made between the counsellor and client and soon, therefore, communication through the typewritten word (the predominant concerns of this paper) may be overtaken by the challenges created by engaging with the client (both visually and aurally) via the computer when you both may be at opposite ends of the world!

In short, the technical innovations in this field continue to develop apace and the therapeutic world cannot afford to bury its collective head in the sand and ignore these developments. Certainly, there are many challenges still to be met, substantial research to be conducted to assess efficacy, and guidelines to be constructed to advise on appropriate, humane and ethical practices for the 'electronic therapeuter'. This broad field of application, like that of multicultural counselling, is really at the cutting edge of therapeutic development at the present time.

References

Argyle, M. (1975) *Bodily Communication*, London: Methuen.

BAC (1999) 'Counselling online: opportunities and risks in counselling clients via the Internet', Rugby: British Association for Counselling.

Becker, E. (1972) *The Birth and Death of Meaning*, Harmondsworth: Penguin.

Bolton, G. (1999) *The Therapeutic Potential of Creative Writing: Writing Myself*, London: Jessica Kingsley.

Billen, A. (1996) 'Kiss of the cyber woman', *Observer* Review, 11 February, p. 8.

Culf, A. (1996) 'BBC e-mail line to men's health', *Guardian*, 16 February, p. 8.

Dunbar, R. (1996) 'Grey natter', *The Times Higher Educational Supplement*, 26 January, p. 13.

Greenhalgh, T. (1995) 'Fenland city on the frontline', *The Times Higher Educational Supplement*, 9 June, p. xii.

Harris, S. (1995) 'Care in the (virtual) community', *Guardian*, 16 March, p. 4.

Kirschenbaum, H. (1990) *The Carl Rogers Reader*, London: Constable.

McLeod, J. (1993) *An Introduction to Counselling*, Buckingham: Open University Press.

Mearns, D. (1994) *Developing Person-Centred Counselling*, London: Sage.

Nealy, K. (1995) 'Suicide on the net', *Guardian* Weekend, 20 May, p. 11.

Parker, L. (1999) 'Counselling online: survey on the extent of attitudes to on-line counselling amongst 425 BAC members', Rugby: British Association for Counselling.

Prouty G.F. (1990) 'A theoretical evolution in the person-centred/experiential psychotherapy of schizophrenia and retardation', in G. Leitaer et al., *Client-Centred and Experiential Psychotherapy in the Nineties*, Leuven: Leuven University Press, 645–85.

Rogers, C.R. (1957) 'The necessary and sufficient conditions of therapeutic personality change', *Journal of Consulting Psychology*, 21 (2): 95–103.

Rowe, D. (1995) 'The uses and abuses of people', *Guardian* Weekend, 20 May, p. 11.

Shipton, G., Curson, J., McAuley, J. and Scott, P. (1995) W.I.S.H. – the Welfare, Information and Student Help computer programme, University of Sheffield, UK.

Slouka, M. (1996) 'Virtual anarchy', *Guardian*, 30 January, p. 2.

Discussion issues

1 List your particular concerns for the use of e-mail therapy, both from the perspective of a counsellor/therapist and from the position of being a prospective client.

2 List any advantages you can consider over the live therapeutic interview!

3 What criteria might you wish to include in drawing up (a) an ethical code of practice and (b) a set of 'n' etiquette guidelines to which electronic therapy should be subjected?

4 How could this field be researched as to efficacy, sensitivity, therapeutic intentions, etc.?

90

Counselling by e-mail

Steve Page

The purpose of the original paper was to explore contractual issues involved in working therapeutically via e-mail. It refers to a form of 'e-mail consultation' (BAC 1999: 11) and is hypothetical in as much as it has not, as yet, been tested in practice. I imagined a scenario in which a counsellor was located in a University Counselling Service and the client self-referred using an advertised e-counselling address. There are a number of ways of setting up an e-counselling relationship that have boundaries similar to a traditional counselling relationship. There might be a 'live' interaction at a specified time, or the counsellor might agree to respond to e-mail from a particular client once each week for a specified period of time.

I have deliberately gone for a somewhat different model in order to encourage thinking about what e-counselling might offer which face-to-face counselling cannot. This is to challenge the notion that e-mail offers a second-class service when face-to-face work is not practicable.

I present the contract below, with some comments interspersed. For the sake of brevity sections covering confidentiality, changing counsellor, data protection, and Codes of Ethics and Practice and complaints procedure have been omitted, as they are essentially the same as in a face-to-face counselling contract.

The hypothetical contract

Dear Jo,

Thank you for contacting the Counselling Service e-mail facility. You have requested counselling via e-mail and I want to introduce myself and to describe to you how I envisage this taking place.

My name is Steve and I am one of the counsellors working in this Service. I currently have a vacancy for an e-mail client which I am offering to you.

The purpose of counselling is to enable you to find ways to address difficulties that you are having and to find ways forward that are satisfying for you. We achieve this through a process of communication. You have an opportunity to describe what is troubling you and I will respond. I will not be telling you what to do but I shall try to understand what you tell me. I may ask you questions and I may suggest alternative ways of thinking about what is happening. I hope that you will respond to what I have said, as well as telling me more of what you are thinking and feeling.

This chapter was originally submitted as a background paper for the Association for University and College Counselling (AUCC) working party on On-line Counselling (BAC 1999). It was published in *Counselling*, Journal of the British Association for Counselling, vol. 11, no. 3, pp. 162–4 (2000).

Before you decide whether to start this process I need you to read the rest of this document which sets out how counselling will take place. In agreeing to work together as counsellor and client we are agreeing to the terms set out.

- This first section introduces the 'contract' and starts to define what we are entering into, as well as trying to set a friendly and clear tone of communication.

My availability

I set aside four hours of each working week when I respond to client e-mail messages. At the beginning of each working week I will send you a message confirming my availability during the coming two weeks. I will let you know of any holidays, or periods away for courses or conferences. If I am away unexpectedly then one of the administrators in the Counselling Service will send you a message about the change to my availability. Usually I will be able to respond to your messages within two to three days (three to four over a weekend). I read new messages at the next scheduled response session and cannot respond immediately to urgent messages that arrive outside of a response session.

- The response time is crucial in e-counselling. The e-client is particularly vulnerable to feeling left in suspense, awaiting a response to their last message. While this can have useful therapeutic consequences it is important that it is contained within an explicit commitment by the counsellor to a response time. At the same time it needs to be clear that the client's communications are held within clear boundaries and will not intrude upon the counsellor.

Identity

Whenever I send a message it will be me, Steve, who does so. I will always assume that any message I receive from you comes from you. If you allow anyone else to send messages on your behalf this will undermine what we are doing.

Length of messages

As a guideline I ask that you do not go above about three sides of A4 paper, although I recognize that there may be exceptions to this. Short messages are fine.

Frequency of messages

You are free to send messages as often as you wish. However I suggest that it is only in excepional circumstances that you send a message before I have responded to your last message, as this can become confusing.

In order for the communication between us to be active I expect you to communicate at least once a week, unless you tell me that you are planning to be away. If you do not communicate in a particular week I shall raise this with you. If you do not respond to that message within one week I shall take this as an indication that you are terminating the counselling and remove you from my e-mail client list. Should this happen we can restart when I have a vacancy, if this seems appropriate.

Safeguards

Although e-mail messages are somewhat vulnerable to interception, the risk is greatly reduced if we use an encryption system. I am sending you the encryption instructions separately.

- It is intended that encryption be dealt with in a future issue of *Counselling*.

Storing messages

I shall keep the messages that you send on disc and also on paper. When we bring the counselling to an end I shall wipe all messages on disc and keep the paper record for 7 years. I suggest that you keep a copy of this message so that you can refer back to these guidelines if necessary.

Ending counselling

There will come a point, typically after six to eight weeks when it is no longer appropriate to continue interaction at the level of once a week or more. At this point we may end communication or maintain a reduced level of contact. Under this arrangement you may continue to contact me when you wish to do so, and I make a commitment to respond briefly once a fortnight to any messages that you have sent. This can continue for a maximum period of 12 months.

Technology problems

If you experience technological difficulties in sending or receiving messages please contact our administrator. Similarly if we become aware of any problems with the technology at this end we will phone you to let you know.
    The contact details for the Counselling Service are:
Counselling Service
The University of Hull, Hull HU6 7RX
01482-465166

Completing a personal details form

If, having read the above groundrules, you want to start on the counselling process, please complete the next section, which is a form for recording your details. The information on the form will be kept on our confidential database and used to administer your use of the Service and for statistical purposes. When I receive the form from you I shall send you details of my availability for the next two weeks. If I do not receive a reply from you within seven days I shall assume that you have decided not to proceed and offer the e-mail client vacancy to someone else. If you have any questions that you need to ask please send them to me.

Best wishes, Steve.

Points to consider

This contract is intended to cover many of the areas where e-counselling differs from face-to-face counselling. It creates a structure for a workable counselling relationship and makes use of some of the benefits of this electronic form of communication. I originally included the option of requesting a face-to-face session, but have removed that clause as, on reflection, it seemed to be a potential source of confusion. A service such as that described in this contract would need a set of procedures and protocols, one of which would need to deal with how requests for other forms of contact (face-to-face, telephone or video linked) would be addressed.

At the University of Hull we are not, as yet, offering an e-counselling service, although some counsellors are using e-mail as an adjunct to face-to-face work. We are exploring the possibilities as the number of distance learning students increases, some using sophisticated web-based technology as their primary 'classroom'. In Higher Education it seems likely that such forms of electronic interaction with clients will become increasingly common as our student populations become more diverse and used to electronic forms of communication.

Reference

BAC (1999) *Counselling Online: Opportunities and Risks in Counselling Clients via the Internet*, Rugby: British Association for Counselling.

Discussion issues

1 What are the advantages and disadvantages of this form of counselling in comparison with face-to-face or telephone counselling?
2 If counselling by e-mail using this contract how would you deal with a request to have a face-to-face session?
3 Are there client issues that would particularly lend themselves to this form of counselling? Are there client issues for which you consider this form of counselling to be inappropriate?
4 How might it work to use e-mail alongside face-to-face contact with a client?

91

The Challenge of the Internet

Stephen Goss, Dave Robson, Nadine J. Pelling and Deborah E. Renard

This article introduces readers to some of the challenges to the counselling profession raised by the Internet. Possible uses are outlined and some pertinent issues are discussed. While example Web sites are noted, more comprehensive guides to the Internet's mental health related resources are provided by Kelley-Milburn and Milburn (1995), Grohol (1997), Morrison and Stamps (1998) and Pelling and Renard (1998), among others.

The introduction of technology into human communication, despite eventual acceptance as an everyday part of life, is often characterized by controversy. The advent of printing brought attempted suppression by the Church. In 1791 the telegraph was greeted with as mixed a response as that received by the Internet in the 1990s (Johnson 1997).

Over recent years the Internet has sometimes been presented as undesirable, undermining established ways of communicating. Yet it has also been viewed as a positive boon, set to revolutionize our lives by allowing us to contact anyone, for anything, at the click of a button. What has been termed 'technostress' (Weil and Rosen 1997) may be reduced by increased familiarity with computer applications (Mueller 1997), but for those not already among the cognoscenti, the Internet can seem a daunting, even alienating, prospect.

None the less, the burgeoning usage of the Internet is indisputably an emerging issue for the counselling profession (Lago 1996; Brooks 1997; American Psychological Association 1998; Johnson 1998). The Internet itself is no more than the vast network created by linking together computers throughout the world, and at present there are at least six ways it can directly assist counselling practice. Brief descriptive definitions of each are provided in Box 1.

Box 1

1 **Information** Above all, the Internet is a means of providing and obtaining information by contacting 'pages' of data known as 'Web sites'. Given the vast number of Web sites around the world, it is already a commonplace for commentators to note that the problem is not one of finding information, but of finding precisely the information needed and, once found, of ensuring that it is of good quality.

2 **Mailing and discussion lists** These allow any number of people with a common interest to exchange messages with everyone else on the same list. Participants may or may not be on-line simultaneously. Such groups may be set up and controlled by

continued

This chapter was first published in *Counselling*, Journal of the British Association for Counselling, vol. 10, no. 1, pp. 37–43 (1999).

one individual, an Internet service provider or once created they may have no controls at all. An excellent example is 'psych-couns' (available at http://www.mailbase.ac.uk) for those interested in the theoretical and research aspects of counselling.

3 **Letter-type e-mail** Perhaps the most commonly known means of using the Internet to communicate with others, electronic mail, or 'e-mail', is typed on a computer with suitable software and sent to a specified electronic address. Just like ordinary post, messages can be read and responded to at any time. The delay in delivery is usually a few seconds but it is not usually assumed that messages will be responded to right away as you cannot control when the recipient will switch on their computer to read it.

4 **Instant e-mail/chat systems** With prior agreement, of course, two or more people can be on-line at the same time and can send messages back and forth very quickly. Some Internet service providers have software to facilitate this which can be used to type and send messages so quickly as to stimulate verbal conversation, albeit restricted to the users' typing and literary ability.

5 **Video telephones** With ever-increasing quality and availability of the requisite technology this still fairly unusual use of the Internet is beginning to become increasingly widespread. Relatively high-grade computers and other equipment are needed. Participants can both talk to and see each other. The quality of connection depends on the systems used and varies from fuzzy pictures that change once every few seconds to near television-quality pictures and sound.

6 **Expert systems and independent software** It is also possible to use the Internet to access computer software and databases held elsewhere. A number of programs are already available that claim to be of help to users, sometimes entirely independently of any human operator.

Information and advertising

Increasing numbers of counselling organizations have Web sites offering descriptive information announcing their presence and outlining the therapies provided. However, they may also offer clients the opportunity to make direct contact by e-mail or even purchase services directly on a world-wide scale.

An advantage of computer-based information is the possibility of providing far greater quantities of information than leaflets or advertisements can generally accommodate, sometimes with the addition of sound, moving graphics or pictures. The BAC Web site (http://www.counselling.co.uk) is an example in which information is made available as an alternative to a large series of leaflets and booklets. Similarly, in the USA, the National Institute of Mental Health maintains a large, downloadable on-line catalogue of its publications (http://www.nimh.nih.gov/). Some of this information is of good quality, while some is questionable (Davison 1996; Impicciatore et al. 1997; Sacchetti et al. 1999). Web sites exist regarding a vast range of therapies, from Ericksonian (http://www.erickson.foundation.org) to 'cyber counselling' itself, as counselling via the Internet is sometimes known (http://www.centrefortheperson.org/ and http://onlinepsych.com/).

Indeed, at least in theory, Web sites could provide entire journals and books. An example is *The Qualitative Report* (http://www.nova.edu/ssss/QR/index.html), an on-line journal dedicated to qualitative research. The very ease with which information can be obtained on the Internet has created difficulties in making it as lucrative for publishers as their paper-based equivalents, with the result that it is more common for no more than summaries of texts to be made available.

A further advantage of the Internet is that by pressing a few buttons you can go from one Web site to another linked together because they contain related information. An example is the Mental Health Ring at http://www.gate/net/~rational/ring.html. A possible use of the Internet, but one which is rarely systematically attempted at present, could be the provision of detailed pre-counselling information for clients. Some models of counselling recommend the setting of pre-counselling tasks, which could be accessed over the Internet. Details of counsellors' backgrounds and qualifications can be listed and contractual details or complaints procedures set out, with links to further explanatory materials when appropriate.

Clearly, there are a number of advantages in providing information over the net. The BAC already requires such details to conform to the same standards as information provided in any other way (BAC Management Committee 1996: B.4.1, and B.4.2). As yet, however, there is no requirement for counsellors to account for the possibly very different interpretations of information when read in different parts of the world with different expectations of professional boundaries and different legal systems.

Mailing and discussion lists/groups, letter-type e-mail and instant e-mail

Joining a discussion list has been likened to subscribing to a magazine and it is about as easy to do (Pelling 1995; Hansen 1997). Participants may even agree to be on-line simultaneously, sometimes aiming to simulate therapy groups with many of the opportunities for self development, exploration, experimentation and feedback from others that one would expect in an ordinary therapy group.

Discussion groups, such as 'psych-couns' referred to in Box 1, are also used by counsellors to talk to each other regarding professional issues. The American Counseling Association (http://www.counseling.org/) has a link to the World Counseling Network, described as 'an interactive community designed specifically for the counseling profession'. Whether such support can be considered equivalent to supervision of professional work is, to date, a moot point. Certainly no one is yet proposing that it replace the requisite 'live' supervision sessions, but there is plenty of anecdotal evidence regarding the help provided by such groups. In no other way would it be possible to get opinions from professionals from so many different parts of the world so readily, although, of course, it is not always possible to guarantee the quality of responses, despite some very well-known leading practitioners participating in some discussions.

Increasingly, counsellors are using the Internet as a vehicle for soliciting research participants and collaborators, as well as clients for their services and colleagues for consultation. Geographical barriers are virtually removed. Some relatively inaccessible target populations can be researched and greater collaboration increases the feasibility of using more representative research samples and thus may even lead to a more valid and generalizable knowledge base. Despite problems proposed with collecting research information via the Internet, such information can be comparable to paper-based surveys (Hewson et al. 1996; Stones and Perry 1997; Kaye and Johnson 1999). The potential for Internet discussion groups to extend the academic and intellectual climate beyond the walls of universities, or the brief time when conferences are convened, may significantly strengthen the theoretical and research bases of counselling practice.

An advantage of the Internet for clients and practitioners alike is the access to experts for those in remote areas. In Australia vast distances have long hampered contact between health professionals and their clients, not least in the area of mental health. For some time the Internet has provided an easily used extension of the two-way radio already commonly used. Closer to home, counsellors in rural communities may face problems associated with serving a small population such as difficulties obtaining supervision locally in which they can discuss their clients without risk of identifying people with prior relationships with the supervisor.

Many companies or institutions based at more than one site have the opportunity to make considerable cost savings by reducing the number of journeys made by counsellors or, in some circumstances, even cutting the number of counsellors required to provide a certain level of service.

Anecdotal evidence reported by users of e-mail-based counselling services and self-help groups gathered over a period of three years by one of the current authors strongly suggests that some people do experience a noticeable degree of support and benefit, while others recommend caution:

> I am now 26 years old and have been going to councling since I was 15 ... [but] nothing has helped me like the internet has. talking to other survivors [of abuse] and the counclers here have been the greatest help. them not being able to see my face I can open up ... it has changed my life.
>
> (Personal communication with the author (Goss), 18.2.98)

> I realise that my written words are sometimes misperceived ... the time taken to get to know someone is much greater in person than online or e-mail. Its a different sensory realm and misunderstandings and jumps to conclusions are quicker to occur in e-mail than face to face.
>
> (Personal communication with the author (Goss), 13.2.98)

The ethics of counselling via the Internet seem to provoke highly polarized views (Marino 1996; Morrissey 1997; Adams 1998; Robson and Robson 1998). Senior members of the BAC have expressed the opinion that use of computers to communicate raises no additional ethical issues not already covered by the guidance issued for face-to-face work. On the other hand, the American Counseling Association has already issued special guidance expressing caution (Lee 1998), as has the American Psychological Association (http://www.apa.org/ethics/stmnt01.html).

There is a strong historical precedent for written therapeutic contacts from Freud onwards, and e-mail-based counselling services are already represented in the current counselling literature (e.g. Murphy and Mitchell 1998). Yet, in the USA when the National Board for Certified Counselors (NBCC) issued standards for counselling by e-mail (NBCC 1997), it was accused of legitimizing the relatively unknown area of counselling via the Internet too quickly (Morrissey 1997).

Confidentiality of anything sent over the Internet cannot be guaranteed. One e-mail counselling service asserts that 'unless you have reason to think that someone may be reading or hacking your e-mail I *honestly wouldn't worry*' (Sommers 1998, emphasis in the original). However, it is worth asking whether counsellors and clients would adequately understand the level of confidentiality any encryption method offers. Where services are paid for, usually by the exchange of credit card details, there are financial risks in addition to the problems of having someone access a detailed written record of your therapy. Indeed, Internet service providers may have legitimate reasons for accessing e-mail contents (when checking for viruses, for example) and such possibilities would have to be understood and accepted before informed consent to therapy could be given.

In those rare circumstances where codes of practice support the breaching of confidentiality, such as when a client is threatening suicide or homicide, peculiar questions arise, not least being reliable identification of the client's name and location. Furthermore, if the client is in a different country, with different local support systems, whom does the counsellor contact?

There are also dangers of people posing as someone they are not, whether as counsellors or clients. Van Gelder (1996) gives a vivid account of someone who assumed a convincing persona and encouraged other people to trust her (or him as it was eventually revealed). How can a counsellor ensure that they are not communicating with a minor who does not have the appropriate consent? How can clients ensure that someone who is advertising as a counsellor has the appropriate qualifications? What *are* the appropriate qualifications in a global marketplace? What would happen if there was a technical breakdown and the two parties could not communicate?

Turkle (1995) argues convincingly that the anonymity offered by e-mail relationships can have positive effects. It can allow people to express or experiment with aspects of themselves that are inhibited in everyday life. It has been reported that 'people are often much more open with their real feelings when they don't seem as directly accountable for them' (Klug 1998). Certainly a few cases are documented in which it has appeared possible for a client to reveal via e-mail details they felt unable to express face to face (e.g. Ridden 1998). It has also been suggested that men may find it easier to approach counselling via a technological means, raising the possibility of addressing the imbalance of male and female clients in most counselling situations (Bennet 1995).

Beneficence is a further ethical principle, which requires counsellors to enhance the client's well-being. This inevitably raises the question of clinical effectiveness when the communication is only at a textual level. At the time of writing the authors could find no empirical evidence of the effects of using computers to deliver counselling by any of the methods addressed in this article.

Again, views are highly divergent. Ainsworth (1997: 1) claims to have found general agreement that 'whatever this is, it is *not* psychotherapy in the traditional sense. ... These interactions over the internet are helpful for many people, but they will never replace the unique experience of forming a continuing face-to-face relationship with a psychotherapist', but goes on to suggest that 'whether or not this is "therapy", there is little doubt that these interactions can be therapeutic ... many people have been helped, some profoundly, by interacting with mental health professionals over the internet.'

A great many practitioners, and a majority of the current authors, take the view that the risks of counselling by e-mail probably outweigh the potential benefits, at least in most situations. The very foundations of successful therapy, basic rapport-building attending skills (e.g. Ivey 1998) have no functional equivalents in e-mail. Although electronic conventions can suggest a nod, smile or other facial expression,[1] and one can type minimal encouragers such as 'uh-huh' or 'I see – go on …', the same qualities of caring, interest or emotional shading that are subtly and easily conveyed when face to face are not demonstrated.

For example, the well-timed nod, the gentle smile of encouragement cannot be replicated. The closed body posture, downcast eyes, soft volume and a hesitant, slow rate of speech that might accompany a client's description of feeling 'OK' are unobservable. The power of silence and the flow and pacing of a counselling session are also disrupted when using e-mail, especially the non-instant letter-type. At best it is likely that the usual processes of counselling will be disrupted.

Skilful paraphrasing and summarizing of client concerns may be possible electronically but the level of skill is dependent on literary rather than verbal ability and far from all counsellors, or clients, may be able to express themselves with the requisite degree of accuracy and eloquence.

The ability to refer to a written record can assist in verbal tracking, focusing on particular aspects of a client's concerns, and can facilitate the counsellor's identification of the client's patterns of speech and styles of perceiving the world. However, the difficulty with which even gross deceptions can be seen through makes the client's experience of congruence, for example, particularly problematic.

Moreover, counselling via the Internet may even be actively iatrogenic. Dysfunctional behaviours may be reinforced. For instance, socially phobic individuals or those lacking in relationship skills may gravitate towards Internet counselling as a way of avoiding social encounters. Similarly, overly self-conscious and self-critical clients may struggle to rewrite their post to ensure 'perfection' and anxious clients may suffer while a response to their last missive is awaited.

Despite some standards for Internet counselling having been established (Bloom 1997, 1998), it is not certain how such standards could be enforced. Less obvious professional issues include questions regarding those who cannot afford Internet access and the technically or conventionally illiterate. For more detailed discussion of the ability of Internet counselling to be beneficial to clients the reader is referred to Pelling and Renard (2000).

Video links

With more in common with the usual telephone than a written letter, this form of computer-mediated interaction is one of those being experimented with at a number of sites around the world. Although access to the required equipment is currently very limited, the history of computer technology has been that prices have tended to fall rapidly as new and improved versions of both soft- and hardware become available.

In the UK, both Napier University and the University of the Highlands and Islands are currently looking at establishing the first pre-clinical and clinical trials of counselling via video link (Ross 2000) although other research is becoming increasingly widespread (e.g. Zeffert 2000).

With any of the uses of computers and the Internet mentioned in this article, a service that is required to provide counselling for a client group dispersed over a wide area is likely to save a great deal of money by reducing counsellors' (and clients') travelling time and might expect dramatically to increase access. Of course, for this to be a worthwhile venture, savings in costs must not be outmatched by a reduction in the benefits that might be expected from normal face-to-face counselling.

The experience of using live video contact as a means of establishing counselling currently receives scant attention in the literature. Counselling via the telephone has been accepted for many years, at least in the UK. The BAC Individual Counsellor Accreditation Management Group (ICAMG) takes the view that 'an application would be acceptable from a counsellor who is counselling by telephone, provided that person is meeting all the criteria' (ICAMG 1997) and although it is yet to be tested it might be that 'tele-counselling' via any medium that allows therapeutically significant relationships to be developed could be treated in a similar way.

This seems to suggest that counselling is possible via the Internet despite the fact that even with high quality sound and pictures many non-verbal cues are lost and the building of a relationship is, at best, altered by having one's only image of the other person framed behind glass and by the edges of a screen. Computer images tend to blur fast or large movements to some degree. If one person shifts their position without adjusting the camera angle they may be only partly visible at the other end, perhaps without realizing it.

However, it is certainly true that a great deal of the information that counsellors usually rely upon can be passed on via a video link. Early indications from experiments with video counselling suggest that it might be seen as lying part way between face-to-face and telephone work with the important caveat that both parties must be sufficiently comfortable with their image appearing on screen elsewhere to be able to express themselves freely. With increasing familiarity with the medium of video-phones it may well be that any hesitation over their use will disappear.

Expert systems and independent software

For clients

Computer systems to support the treatment of a variety of mental health problems have already been widely reported (Zarr 1984; Bloom 1992; Andrews et al. 1994; Marks et al. 1998). Promising outcomes have been reported for clients with phobic and obsessive-compulsive disorders, panic, non-suicidal depression and smoking cessation (Marks et al. 1998). Some systems have been developed for virtual reality, that is the construction of virtual environments to assist in therapy (Becker and North 1998; Neubeck and Neubeck 1998; Rizzo et al. 1998; Laszlo et al. 1999).

Randomized controlled trials of information supplied by 'expert' computer systems have also shown therapeutic effects (Robinson 1989; McConatha et al. 1995) and there are numerous self-help products of varying worth. However, Marks et al. suggest that 'the long-tantalizing promise of self-treatment systems that are effective with no human contact or supervision … has rarely been met yet' (1998: 6).

Quite a number of psychological tests can be accessed over the Internet and could be used by anyone interested in the profile of themselves provided by that particular measure. These may share a similar effect with computer-mediated counselling in that those who prefer not to approach a professional at all can utilize such things quickly, cheaply and, above all, anonymously and in complete privacy. However, a professional opinion is often needed for full interpretation.

While some systems are excellent, the potentially serious problem of unregulated quality, shared by all the uses of the Internet discussed here, is often evident in that some are difficult to see, may not be fully tested and lack even the most basic information needed to understand the raw scores they provide. It is rare, but perhaps should be much less rare, for such things to be provided with good quality information about their use, and clear guidance about when they should be administered by a suitably trained professional.

For counsellors and researchers

Of course, counsellors competent in the use of any particular test can make use of them over the Internet and many have the advantage of carrying out the requisite calculations automatically. Counsellors who wish to screen clients prior to or during counselling can make the tests available to their clients for use with the appropriate level of supervision and guidance and the possibility of harm is then minimized.

Although most are not made available over the Internet directly, so many computer products are now available we cannot mention more than a very few. Automated partial recognition of emotion from facial expression and gestures is already possible (Vanger et al. 1995). You can code session transcripts and even play audio or video recordings of the session as the analysis rolls past on the screen (Evans and Blake-Brennen 1996). Preliminary tests have even been made with a program that will scan pictures produced in art therapy sessions and provide a tentative diagnosis of the patient's condition with the suggestion that, for example, people with schizophrenia make greater use of a certain type and colour of line (Hacking and Foreman 1996).

Other services of use to counsellors and researchers alike include the increasing number of searchable databases. Competency in accessing bibliographic resources via the Internet is emerging as a critical research skill. Among others, 'Counsel.lit', produced by the Counselling in Primary Care Trust, provides access to 2,200 references to published material in that field (http://www.cpct.co.uk). In general, publishers of the main literature databases have not yet taken to providing access directly over the Internet because they still see better commercial prospects in selling the product as a whole to customers and libraries. However, we may not have to rely on their philanthropy for such things to become more widely available as financial transactions over the Internet will eventually become secure from fraud by third parties and a very large proportion of their market will eventually have Internet access.

Conclusions

Given the ever-changing state of technology and its applications, any predictions about the future of the Internet are likely to be out of date very rapidly. What is clear is that as those around us become more familiar with its uses it will be more and more useful for all of us to have at least some working knowledge of it. Access via an ordinary television set, removing the need to use a computer or keyboard altogether, is likely to be with us in the next few years and there is every reason to expect that the next generation will be as surprised at our hesitations over computer-mediated communication as we are now by the condemnation of the telegraph 200 years ago.

Computer technology changes notoriously fast and it may seem strange to develop statements that will almost certainly be out of date before they are out of print. However, it is necessary for the profession to put a stake in the ground at some point, albeit an arbitrary one, and take the most definitive stand it can regarding the possible uses and abuses of technology for the sake of supporting counsellors and, even more importantly, protecting clients against the unscrupulous or the incompetent, or those ignorant of the potential pitfalls. No such statement yet exists that applies to the UK.

Despite the difficulties, some counsellors will undoubtedly become involved in providing services via the Internet. The recommendation of the current authors is that clients might be well advised to be sceptical about counselling services offered through the Internet and that counsellors should think long and hard about the implications before using the Internet to communicate with clients, especially if providing counselling directly by any electronically mediated method (See Chapter 90).

Other counsellors may never integrate the Internet into their practice. However, as the influence of the Internet spreads, it is predictable that increasing numbers of clients will be coming to counselling with significant information and/or interaction experiences acquired through the Internet. At the very least, it behoves therapists to develop an understanding of the Internet environment in order to assist clients more appropriately in processing their experiences. A client may want to discuss a marital infidelity which occurs only in cyberspace: the therapist who cannot even grasp the concept is at a disadvantage.

Given that our profession has fought long and hard to establish itself as founded on counsellor skill and research, the public image of counselling will be greatly damaged if our activities are not based on clear, demonstrable evidence of effectiveness and propositions that are both theoretically and practically sound.

Note

1 For example, the best-known symbol for emotional expression (for 'emoticon' as they are sometimes know) is for happiness or a simple smile. Written as a colon, a hyphen and a close bracket thus :-) it is best understood by inclining one's head slightly to the left, whereupon it can be seen as a face on its side. Other emoticons include;-) for a wink, :-D for a laugh or to indicate a joke, #- o to indicate puzzlement, :-P for rudely sticking out one's tongue, and many more.

References

Adams, S.C. (1998) 'Concerns about counselling online' (on-line), available: http://www.counseling. org/ctonline/sr598/letter1_698.htm

Ainsworth, M. (1997) 'Terminology ... is this therapy?' (on-line), available: http://www.metanoia. org/imhs/isittx.htm

American Psychological Association (1998) 'Ethics committee issues statement on services by telephone, tele-conferencing and internet', *American Psychological Association Monitor*, 29 (1): 38.

Andrews, G., Unstun, T.B., Dilling, H. and Briscoe, M. (eds) (1994) *Computers in Mental Health*, 1, London: Churchill Livingstone/World Health Organization.

Becker, D. and North, M.M. (1998) 'The virtual Reality Therapy system: VRT-2002', *CyberPsychology and Behaviour*, 1 (4): 401–3.

Bennet, M. (1995) 'Why don't men come to counselling? Some speculative theories', *Counselling*, 6 (4): 310–13.

Bloom, B.L. (1992) 'Computer-assisted psychological intervention: review and commentary', *Clinical Psychological Review*, 12: 169–97.

Bloom, J.W. (1997) 'N.B.C.C. WebCounseling Standards', *Counseling Today Online*, available: http://www.counseling.org/ctonline/sr598/nbcc_standards.htm

Bloom, J.W. (1998) 'The ethical practice of Web counseling', *British Journal of Guidance and Counselling*, 26 (1): 53–9.

British Association for Counselling Management Committee (1996) *Code of Ethics and Practice for Counsellors*, Rugby: BAC.

Brooks, J.W. (1997) 'N.B.C.C. Bulletin from the Board', *Counseling Today*, 40 (5): 14.

Davison, K. (1996) 'The quality of dietary information on the World Wide Web', *Journal of the Canadian Dietetic Association*, 57 (4): 137–41.

Evans, R. and Blake-Brennen, A. (1996) 'IGOR: a demonstration and discussion of a multimedia computer tool for psychotherapy process research', presentation at the Thirteenth Annual Meeting of the Society for Psychotherapy Research (UK), Ravenscar, 26 March.

Grohol, J.M. (1997) *The Insider's Guide to Mental Health Resources Online*, New York: Guilford.

Hacking, S. and Foreman, D. (1996) 'The DAPA: a new way of comparing the pictures of psychiatric patients', presentation at the Thirteenth Annual Meeting of the Society for Psychotherapy Research (UK), Ravenscar, 26 March.

Hansen, J.T. (1997) 'Questions frequently asked about the internet for counselors', *Michigan Journal of Counseling and Development*, 25 (2): 17–19.

Hewson, C., Lautent, D. and Vogel, C. (1996) 'Proper methodologies for psychological and socio-logical studies conducted via the Internet', *Behaviour Research Methods, Instruments and Computers*, 28 (2): 186–91.

ICAMG (1997), extract of minutes from meeting of 5 December, item 97/64, by kind permission of Co-Chair of Individual Counsellor Accreditation Management Group.

Impicciatore, P., Pandolfini, C., Casella, N. and Bonati, M. (1997) 'Reliability of health information for the public on the World Wide Web: systematic survey of advice on managing fever in children at home', *British Medical Journal*, 314 (7098): 1875–9.

Ivey, A.E. (1998) *Intentional Interviewing and Counseling: Facilitating Client Development* (2nd edn), Pacific Grove, CA: Brooks/Cole.

Johnson, S. (1997) *Interface Culture*, San Francisco: Harper Edge.

Johnson, S. (1998) 'Therapy from long distance debated. Internet, telephone and mail counseling expected to grow', *San Jose Mercury News*, 9 April, p. 1.

Kaye, B. and Johnson, T. (1999) 'Research methodology: taming the cyber frontier: techniques for improving online surveys', *Social Science Computer Review*, 17 (3): 323–37.

Kelley-Milburn, D. and Milburn, M.A. (1995) 'Cyberpsych: resources for psychologists on the Internet', *Psychological Science*, 6 (4): 203–11.

Klug, E. (1998) e-mail to psycho-couns@mailbase.ac.uk 16 March.

Lago, C. (1996) 'Computer therapeutics', *Counselling*, 7 (4): 287–9. (See Chapter 89.)

Laszlo, J.V., Esterman, G. and Zabko, S. (1999) 'Therapy over the Internet', *CyberPsychology and Behaviour*, 2 (4): 293–307.

Lee, C. (1998) 'Counseling and the challenges of cyberspace', *Counseling Today Online*, April, available: http://www.counseling.org/ctonline/sr598/lee498.htm

Marino, T.W. (1996) 'Counselors in cyberspace debate whether client discussions are ethical' (on-line), available: http://www.counseling.org/ctonline/archives/ct0196a1.htm

Marks, I., Shaw, S. and Parkin, R. (1998) 'Computer-aided treatments of mental health problems', *Clinical Psychology: Science and Practice*, 5 (2): 151–70.

McConatha, J.T., McConatha, D., Deaner, S.L. and Dermigny, R. (1995) 'Computer based intervention for the education and therapy of institutionalized older adults', *Journal of Psychiatry*, XLI: 489–98.

Morrison, M.R. and Stamps, R.F. (1998) *The D.S.M.-IV Internet Companion*, London: W.W. Norton.

Morrissey, M. (1997) 'N.B.C.C. WebCounseling Standards unleash intense debate', *Counseling Today Online*, 40 (5) (on-line), available: http://www.counseling.org/cton-line.archives/ctl197/webcounseling.htm

Mueller, J.H. (1997) 'Test anxiety, self-efficacy and computer experiences', paper presented to the 50th Annual Meeting of the New Zealand Psychological Society, Massey, NZ, 1 September.

Murphy, L.J. and Mitchell, D.L. (1998) 'When writing helps to heal: e-mail as therapy', *British Journal of Guidance and Counselling*, 26 (1): 21–32.

NBCC (National Board for Certified Counselors) (1997) *Standards for the Ethical Practice of WebCounseling* (on-line), available: http://www.nbcc.org/wcstandards.htm

Neubeck, A.K. and Neubeck, B. (1998) 'Virtual reality as a support for psychodynamic treatment', *CyberPsychology and Behaviour*, 1 (4): 341–5.

Pelling, N. (1995) 'Counselling discussion groups on the Internet', *Counselling Today*, 38 (3): 51–2.

Pelling, N. and Renard, D. (1998) 'Integrating cyberspace into counselling practice and research', *Journal of the Michigan Counseling Association*, 21 (1): 5–12.

Pelling, N. and Renard, D. (2000) 'Counselling via the Internet: can it be done well?', *The Psychotherapy Review*, 2 (2): 68–72.

Ridden, G. (1998) 'Free in the Net: tutoring on e-mail', unpublished paper.

Rizzo, A., Wiederhold, B., Riva, G. and Van Der Zaag, C. (1998) 'A bibliography of articles relevant to the applications of virtual reality in the mental health field', *CyberPsychology and Behaviour*, 1 (4): 411–25.

Robinson, T.N. (1989) 'Community health behaviour change through computer network health promotion: preliminary findings from Stanford Health-Net', *Computer Methods and Programs in Biomedicine*, 30: 137–44.

Robson, D. and Robson, M. (1998) 'Intimacy and computer communication', *British Journal of Guidance and Counselling*, 26 (1): 33–41.

Ross, C. (2000) 'Counselling by video link', in *Counselling*, 11 (1): 28–9.

Sacchetti, P., Zvara, P. and Plante, M. (1999) 'The internet and patient education – resources and their reliability: focus on a select urologic topic', *Urology*, 53 (6): 1117–20.

Sanders, P. and Rosenfield, M. (1996) 'Counselling at a distance: challenges and new initiatives', *British Journal of Guidance and Counselling*, 26 (1): 5–10.

Sommers, D.I. (1998) *Mental Health Cyber-Clinic* (on-line), available: http://www.dcez.com/~davids/services.htm

Stones, A. and Perry, D. (1997) 'Survey questionnaire data on panic attacks gathered using the World Wide Web', *Depression and Anxiety*, 6: 86–7.

Turkle, S. (1995) *Life on the Screen: Identity in the Age of the Internet*, New York: Simon & Schuster.

Van Gelder, L. (1996) 'The strange case of the electronic lover', in R. Kling (ed.), *Computerisation and Controversy*, London: Academic Press.

Vanger, P., Hölinger, R. and Haken, H. (1995) 'Applications of synergetics in decoding facial expressions of emotion', in M. Bichsel (ed.), *International Workshop on Automatic Face- and Gesture-Recognition Proceedings*, Zurich.

Weil, M.M. and Rosen, L.D. (1997) *Technostress*, New York: Wiley.

Zarr, M.L. (1984) 'Computer-mediated psychotherapy: toward patient-selection guidelines', *American Journal of Psychotherapy*, 37: 47–62.

Zeffert, S. (2000) 'The efficacy of teleconsultation using interactive television for psychological counselling in the Highlands', unpublished research report cited in Ross 2000.

Discussion issues

1 How is the client–counsellor relationship affected by counselling via the Internet?
2 Should counselling via the Internet be seen as a distinct specialism with specific training requirements, ethical guidance, professional overseeing of quality assurance, etc.?
3 Does the faceless nature of text-based counselling make it free of racism and sexism, or does it make it more likely to ignore important cultural aspects of clients?
4 How can clients and counsellors assess the quality of information or therapy services offered over the Internet?

PART SIX

THE LAST WORD

Introduction to Part Six

The Reader finishes with an article by Ken Lewis, the former Chief Executive of BACP who has the last word. After setting the scene and the reasons for change within the former BAC, he considers the new future of the BACP.

92

Preparing the British Association for Counselling and Psychotherapy for a New Future

Kenneth J. Lewis

Place of The BACP *Counselling and Psychotherapy Reader*

When asked to write something to, as it were, 'round off' this *Reader* I was given two documents; first a list of the contents and secondly my predecessor's contribution from Volume I of the BAC *Counselling Reader*. I write, of course, as someone who is not a therapist but who believes that counsellors and psychotherapists are there to make a positive difference to the lives of others. Reading the list of contents I was immediately struck by the truly remarkable breadth of the contributions; but, on reflection, I should not have been so surprised. The issues, difficulties and problems encountered by individuals as they move through the stages of their lives can fairly be described as infinite in variety, and it is a remarkable tribute to the profession that counsellors and psychotherapists are regarded as having, at the very least, something useful to offer in so many dimensions.

I was also impressed that the *Reader* is playing its part in the removal of some, at least, of the preciousness with which some practitioners continue to regard their chosen model and towards opening up the debate about 'what works'. All too often I have listened to debate between practitioners where the client is seldom, or never, mentioned. If counselling and psychotherapy are to be given the credit they deserve and are capable of earning, then the needs of the client have to become of paramount importance. Without this client focus, it is my fear that the practitioner will become distracted from an attitude of curiosity for new approaches and techniques. Clearly, some of these 'new ways' will not stand rigorous scrutiny, but wilfully to ignore them in total risks stagnation for the profession on the one hand and clients not being helped as effectively as they could be on the other. If all this sounds too daring to think about, perhaps we should remind ourselves that Freud, Jung, and numerous others were pioneers in their time before they became founding figures in dealing with the workings of the mind. A useful tenet here that I frequently use is 'don't defend, explore'. If this also brings the needs of clients into more prominence and allows practitioners to be more effective, then it has to be seen as beneficial.

A good number of contributors have already dared to be controversial in their opinions, at some reputational risk, and I would certainly encourage this trend. Controversy often provides the catalyst to movement forward into developmental areas; given the complexity and breadth of the human experience, surely it cannot be that developments in counselling and psychotherapy are even close to being complete and the full understanding of the workings of the human mind achieved. Let me be clear that controversy and dissent are the most valuable tools available to us in moving counselling and psychotherapy forward and, provided that they are used with positive, constructive, intent, we should do all that we can to encourage their use.

Arrival and revival

Moving on to the development of BACP, my first duty is to acknowledge the role of my predecessor, Judith Baron, in leaving the Association in good heart and in a strong financial position; to have done so in the formative years of the organization which, in itself, presents a unique set of challenges to be met, is particularly noteworthy.

Coming into the role of Chief Executive at Christmas 1998, it seemed that the Board of Governors (formerly Management Committee) was ready to modernize the Association and that was the main reason for my being chosen. Since that time a systematic review of each of BACP's constituent parts has been, or is being, undertaken against a changing environment in the counselling and psychotherapy world, perhaps reflective of the maturity of the 'profession' – the quotation marks are used advisedly; more of that later. Counselling and psychotherapy have changed very significantly over the years and, to many, the pace of that change seems to be quickening as more and more is expected from practitioners and the Association. It would be an act of reckless bravery to predict the future in much more than overall terms and thus, with the full encouragement of the Board of Governors, I have embarked upon a strategy to bring agility to the Association. This will enable us, as with other organizations adopting a similar approach, to both act and react quickly to changes we believe to be desirable and to emergent events. The times when the Association could rely upon volunteers to 'get things done' are now coming to an end as members' needs and expectations increase and as the complexity of the items on the agenda also increases. It is for these reasons that the staff at Rugby now stands at 47 and will, undoubtedly, increase further. Early achievements, as a result of this approach, include a re-vamped journal, a new, comprehensive, Web site, an enhanced member benefits package, a full programme of regional consultations and a revised approach to accreditation.

All of this is set against the backdrop of the increasing prominence of the topic of regulation, which shows no sign of abating. The debate continues within the whole of the talking therapies upon the desirability and need for regulation and seems to be neatly polarized into two camps; vocation or profession. As a non-counsellor it would be folly for me to enter into the detail of this debate. However, I do have very definite views on the principles involved. It seems to me that the polarization runs the risk of not noticing how third parties, specifically government, view the issue. The paradigm which government brings, not surprisingly, is that of efficacy matched against cost and these twin drivers, coupled with an overt agenda of promoting the public interest, it seems, will prove pivotal in the way that the profession is regarded and how it will be dealt with. Under such circumstances, then, it would seem to be futile to resist the move towards an emphasis on standards and accountability and more responsible to contribute to the thinking of how this might be achieved to the benefit of the public and of practitioners generally. It is for this very reason that the Association has reviewed and modernized, for instance, its approach towards accreditation, to the codes of ethics and to research.

Going forward

Looking to the future, my personal hope and, dare I say it, ambition is that the Association continues further to develop its services to members and its position in leading the field of counselling and psychotherapy. The next year or two will see the Association making investments to bring these objectives about and put the Association into the position of organization of choice. Much has been contributed by members to BACP's development and much will be called upon as we move forward; the future will require that members' thoughts will be increasingly sought, with the delivery of their ideas and plans carried out by staff at Rugby. BACP is now of sufficient size and has sufficient skills in breadth and number to take itself towards the next step of being a truly professional organization; it is a debt due to members and a responsibility due to clients. In closing, I am conscious of how different these few paragraphs are from the final chapter of the BAC *Counselling Reader*, Volume I. My aspiration and guess is that the closing words to the BACP *Counselling and Psychotherapy Reader*, Volume III, will again be different and reflective of a more settled environment and mature organization but one which, nevertheless, continues to explore the boundaries which surround it.

Kenneth J. Lewis
Former Chief Executive

Notes on the Editors

Pat Milner is a Fellow of BACP. Former Features Editor of *Counselling*, she trained on the first British counselling course at Reading University and later as a Fulbright scholar at SUNY Buffalo, USA. A pioneer of school and university counselling, she was Founder Chair of the Association for Student Counselling (now AUCC), the oldest division of BACP. After working at Goldsmiths College, University of London, she became a Director of Dover Counselling Centre and Consultant Director of the Centre for Stress Management London. She is a choir member who sings with enthusiasm.

Professor Stephen Palmer, Ph.D., is founder Director of the Centre for Stress Management and Centre for Multimodal Therapy, London. He is Honorary Professor of Psychology in the Centre for Health and Counselling Psychology at City University, London, Visiting Professor at Middlesex University and Consultant Director of the New Zealand Centre for Rational Emotive Behaviour Therapy. He is a Fellow of BACP, former Managing Editor of *Counselling* and author or editor of over 20 books. His interests include jazz, art and walking.

Notes on the Contributors

Marie Adams has a private counselling and psychotherapy practice in South London. She is a founder member of the Cordia Counselling Group and is a trainer at the Metanoia Institute.

Peter L. Agulnik is a consultant psychiatrist.

Calvin Bell is a practitioner in cognitive analytic therapy, a community worker and international trainer in the field of domestic violence. He has considerable experience in working with men who harm. He is founder and Director of Ahimsa (previously the Plymouth EVERYMAN Centre) which provides psychosocial counselling for men who are violent and support services for their partners.

Irene Bloomfield is an Honorary Fellow of BAC and Leo Baeck College. She was formerly Principal Clinical Psychologist, psychotherapist and group therapist at University College Hospital, London, 1957–84, and co-founder and Clinical Director of the Raphael Centre, 1978–92.

Janet Boakes, a psychiatrist and group psychoanalyst, is a consultant psychotherapist at St George's Hospital, London, where she trains young doctors in basic counselling and psychotherapy skills. She is a Member of the Psychotherapy Executive Committee of the Royal College of Psychiatrists and of the Training Advisory Board of the London Marriage Guidance Council.

Gillie Bolton is Research Fellow in therapeutic creative writing and reflective writing for practitioners at Sheffield University Institute of General Practice, and is a steering committee member of the British Federation for Medical Humanities.

Tim Bond is Reader in Counselling and Professional Ethics at the University of Bristol. He researches ethical issues concerning counselling and other professional roles. He is a former chairperson of the British Association for Counselling and is a consultant to the Executive Council of the International Association for Counselling.

Judith M. Brech is Senior Associate Counsellor at the Isis Centre, Oxford.

Mary Burton is a chartered clinical psychologist and UKCP registered psychoanalytic psychotherapist with many years experience in private practice, the NHS, and supervision of counsellors in primary care. She is presently working on research with cancer patients.

Tomás Campbell is head of Clinical Health Psychology, Newham Community NHS Trust, London. He taught the first professional course in counselling in Zambia and helped Kara Counselling to set up its services.

William Campbell is Director of the Centre for Human Communication, at Manchester Metropolitan University.

Birgit Carolin, a BAC accredited counsellor, works in Cambridge in private practice and for Cruse Bereavement Care, counselling children and sixth-form college students. She is co-editor with Pat Milner of *Time to Listen to Children* (Routledge 1999).

Tashisho Chabala is a counsellor with experience in setting up and running support groups for PHIV in Africa.

David Clarke is Professor of Psychology at the University of Nottingham and Director of the Action Analysis Group. He is researching sequences of actions and events over time, including causes of road accidents and analysis of natural discourse.

Petruska Clarkson, Fellow of BAC, has almost 30 years' international experience with more than 150 professional publications (in 21 languages). She works at the Independent Centre for Qualitative Research in Psychotherapy Training, Supervision and Consultancy at PHYSIS, London.

Yvonne Craig, a retired qualified social worker, counsellor and magistrate, is an active mediator who has written widely on these subjects. She co-ordinates the Multi-Cultural Elder Mediation Project. Her Doctorate was on elder abuse.

Colin Crawford is a psychotherapist and lecturer in Applied Social Science at the Faculty of Social and Health Sciences and Education at the University of Ulster at Jordanstown.

Sheila Dainow, an experienced counsellor, supervisor, author and trainer, currently enjoys being an art student and delighted granny.

Angela Devlin, for 25 years a special needs teacher, is a full-time researcher, writer-broadcaster, lecturer and campaigner. Books include *Criminal Classes: Offenders at School* (Waterside 1995); *Anybody's Nightmare: The Sheila Bowler Story* (Taverner 1998); and *Going Straight: After Crime and Punishment* (Waterside 1999).

Graham Dexter is Associate Lecturer in counselling at the University of Hull, a freelance consultant in counselling and human resource management and a Master Practitioner in NLP. He currently specializes, with Janice Russell, in motivational profiling for use in counselling team building. They have co-authored numerous publications.

Shukla Dhingra is a person-centred counsellor at Loughborough University. Previously she held a number of posts in education as a teacher, language advisor, Head of Service for Multicultural Education and as Project Co-ordinator for Widening Access at Nottingham Trent University. Shukla has published papers in multicultural education, access to higher education, and has worked on a number of Open University teaching programmes.

Windy Dryden is Professor of Counselling at Goldsmiths College, University of London. He has written or edited over a 100 books.

Aisha Dupont-Joshua is a professional associate of the Nafsiyat Intercultural Therapy Centre, London, working privately with individuals, couples and families. She runs seminars and workshops on racial and cultural awareness as well as a counselling course at Lambeth College, London.

Ivan Ellingham is a chartered counselling psychologist who works for the Hertfordshire Partnership NHS Trust. He lectures on the counselling diploma courses at Harrow College and North Hertfordshire College.

Kim Etherington is a lecturer at the University of Bristol. She is a BAC accredited counsellor and recognized supervisor. Since completing a Ph.D. in 1995 Kim has written two books on issues related to male survivors and undertaken research in the subject area. In recent times she has become particularly interested in narrative methods of inquiry. She is also a proud grandmother and enjoys writing stories for her 'captive' and captivating audience – the grandchildren!

Peter Farrell is an holistic therapist studying for a degree in herbal medicine. He has a particular interest in grief and its effects on mental and physical health.

Colin Feltham is Senior Lecturer in Counselling at Sheffield Hallam University, Fellow of the British Association for Counselling and Psychotherapy, and co-editor of the *British Journal of Guidance and Counselling*. He is the editor, with Ian Horton, of the *Handbook of Counselling and Psychotherapy* (Sage 2000).

John Foskett, Fellow of BAC, is President of APSCC, emeritus chaplain to South London and Maudsley NHS Trust and a pastoral counsellor in private practice.

Cordelia Galgut is a BAC accredited counsellor, a supervisor, trainer and researcher. She has a private practice in East London.

Stephen Goss is Hon. Research Fellow at Strathclyde University Counselling Unit and a student counsellor at Napier University Student Support Services. He is also a counselling supervisor and Chair of the BAC Research and Evaluation Committee.

Andrew Grayson is a lecturer in psychology in the Centre for Human Development and Learning in the School of Education at the Open University, where he teaches developmental psychology and research methods. He is currently undertaking research in the area of communication disabilities and learning difficulties.

Jonathan Hales is a BAC accredited counsellor working in private practice, based in Brighton. He is also a supervisor and trainer specializing in person-centred counselling and solution-focused therapy.

Penny Henderson is a freelance counsellor, supervisor, trainer and consultant with a particular interest in the supervision of counsellors in general practice.

Peter Holmes is a counsellor and trainer seeking to integrate a person-centred way of working with an awareness of the psychodynamics of the counsellor–client relationship.

Zhijin Hou is a Ph.D. candidate of counselling psychology at the Chinese University of Hong Kong. She is an Associate Professor of Psychology at Capital Normal University, Beijing and a supervisor at the Women's Hotline, Beijing.

Richard House is a GP counsellor and co-editor of *Implausible Professions* (PCCS Books 1997). Formerly a supervisor, group facilitator and trainer, he is now an early years Steiner Waldorf teacher.

Patricia Hunt is a psychotherapist in psychoanalytic couple therapy, psychosexual counselling and individual therapy. She is also a trainer, supervisor, researcher and consultant in these fields.

Judi Irving is a chartered counselling psychologist sharing responsibility with Dave Williams for undergraduate and postgraduate counselling courses at the University of

Hull. She also teaches courses and workshops in Kuwait, Vienna (with Bosnian refugees), Singapore, Portugal and Khartoum.

Graham Curtis Jenkins worked as a GP and a paediatrician in the NHS for 30 years before taking up his present post as Director of the Counselling and Primary Care Trust.

Peter Jenkins is Senior Lecturer in Counselling Studies, University of Central Lancashire and a part-time student counsellor. He is author of *Counselling, Psychotherapy and the Law* (Sage 1997) and co-author with Debbie Daniels of *Therapy with Children* (Sage 2000).

Caroline Jones is a Fellow of BAC, former Chair of BAC Standards and Ethics Committee and a UKRC registered independent counsellor. A workplace counsellor, she works independently as a counselling supervisor.

David King is a Relate certified counsellor and an accredited counsellor with the Nottingham Counselling Centre, where he continues to practice in a voluntary capacity. A visiting therapist at the Nottingham Psychotherapy Unit and a counsellor in private practice, he is currently in training in psychoanalytic psychotherapy with the West Midlands Institute of Psychotherapy.

Sydney Klugman works as a senior art therapist at Broadmoor Special Hospital and as a lecturer in the Health Studies Department, Brunel University. His special interests are group work and the use of art in forensic psychiatry. He trained as an art therapist at Goldsmiths College, University of London.

Colin Lago Director of the Counselling Service at Sheffield University, is a Fellow of BAC and former Chair of both the RACE and Student Counselling divisions. His books include *Race, Culture and Counselling* (with Joyce Thompson), *The Management of Counselling Services* (with Duncan Kitchin), *On Listening and Learning: Student Counselling in Further and Higher Education* (with Geraldine Shipton) and, most recently, *Experiences in Relatedness: Groupwork and the Person-Centred Approach* (co-edited with Mhairi Macmillan). He is currently co-editing a book for Sage on counselling and anti-discriminatory practice (with Barbara Smith).

Pittu Laungani is an Honorary Senior Research Fellow at the University of Manchester. He is President of The Institute of Health Promotion and Education.

Arnold A. Lazarus is a Distinguished Professor Emeritus of Psychology at Rutgers University, New Jersey, and President of the Center for Multimodal Psychological Services in Princeton, New Jersey. He has written 16 books and over 200 professional articles, and is the recipient of numerous honours and awards – including Lifetime Achievement Awards from the California Psychological Association and the Association for Advancement of Behavior Therapy.

John Lees is a counsellor and supervisor. He is Senior Lecturer in Counselling, and Programme Leader for the M.Sc. in Therapeutic Counselling, at the University of Greenwich. He has edited books and written articles in the field.

Kenneth J. Lewis is Former Chief Executive of the British Association for Counselling and Psychotherapy.

Gui Rui Ling is Associate Professor and Director of the Student Counseling Centre, Capital Normal University, Beijing, China.

Pemma Littlehailes is an accredited counsellor, behavioural sexual therapist and trainer working in private practice. She is the author of a PR manual, *Up Front* (National Marriage Guidance Council).

Roger Litton is a Director of Smithson Mason Ltd (SMG), 31 Clarendon Road, Leeds LS2 9PA. SMG Professional Risks can be contacted on 0113 294 4042.

Del Loewenthal is Director of the M.Sc. in Counselling and Psychotherapy as a Means to Health, School of Educational Studies, University of Surrey.

Judith Longman is a publisher who edited the BAC journal, *Counselling*, from 1996–9.

Gordon Lynch lectures in Social and Pastoral Theology in the Theology Department of Birmingham University. He recently edited *Clinical Counselling in Pastoral Settings* (Routledge 1999).

Amelia Lyons is Head of the Department of Health and Social Care at University of Wales College, Newport, and a BAC recognized trainer. She is a member of the BAC Committee for Accreditation of Counselling Trainers and, since 1999, of the Higher Education Funding Council Wales (HEFCW) Quality Assessment Committee.

Billy McCullough is a Senior Lecturer and research co-ordinator in Social Work at the Faculty of Social and Health Sciences and Education at the University of Ulster at Jordanstown.

Catherine McKisack is currently enjoying a career break following several years working in specialist eating disorder clinics.

John McLeod is Professor of Counselling at the University of Abertay, Dundee. He is author of *An Introduction to Counselling* (Open University Press, 2nd edn, 1998), *Doing Counselling Research* (Sage 1994) and *Narrative and Psychotherapy* (Sage 1997).

Gladeana McMahon is a BAC Fellow, accredited counsellor and counselling supervisor, a BABCP accredited cognitive-behavioural psychotherapist and is UKCP and UKRC independent counsellor registered. She has written, co-authored or edited 16 books and is Associate Editor of *Counselling*, Managing Editor of *Stress News* and Associate Editor of the BABCP Newsletter.

Tony Makin has a Diploma in Disability Studies. Formerly Vice Chair of the BAC Committee for Disability Issues, he is on the executive of the Trade Union Disability Alliance (TUDA) and is a member of BCODP and GMCDP.

Gertrud Mander, BAC Fellow, is a supervisor on the Diploma in Advanced Psychodynamic Counselling, Westminster Pastoral Foundation, a supervisor for Counselling in Companies (WPF), and a psychotherapist, counsellor and supervisor in private practice. She is author of several papers on psychotherapy and counselling and of *A Psychodynamic Approach to Brief Therapy* (Sage 2000).

Lesley Marks works as a stress management trainer, a counsellor in private practice and a facilitator of support groups and workshops on a number of themes, including adoption.

David Martin is Senior Lecturer in the Centre for Human Communication, the Manchester Metropolitan University.

Linda Martin is a BAC accredited counsellor, BAC accredited counselling trainer, UKCP registered psychotherapist and is course leader, Advanced Diploma in Counselling, West Kent College, Tonbridge, Kent.

Alice Middleton founded SOBS (Survivors of Bereavement by Suicide), a national registered charity. She is happy to provide copies of her booklets *Grief in the Shadows*, and *Grief Coming out of the Shadows* (write to: 82 Arcon Drive, Hull, HU4 6AX).

Hugh Miller, Principal Lecturer in Psychology in the Department of Social Sciences at the Nottingham Trent University, specializes in teaching the psychology of design. His research is in the area of the social psychology of objects.

Pauline Monks has a private counselling practice, working with hearing and hearing-impaired clients. She presents workshops on deaf awareness and difference. She is studying TA psychotherapy.

Roy Moodley, a counsellor, psychotherapist, trainer in 'race' and ethnicity in therapy, was Assistant Director for Research and Development at Thomas Danby College, Leeds, and is now conducting research at the Centre for Psychotherapeutic Studies, University of Sheffield. He has published papers on 'race', counselling and psychotherapy, masculinity and management, and access to higher education.

Lyndsey Moon lectures in counselling psychology at Essex University where she is completing a PhD in the Sociology Department. She also works at a lesbian/gay/bisexual/alcohol counselling agency.

Lesley Murdin is a psychodynamic counsellor and psychoanalytic psychotherapist in London and Cambridge. She is head of training at WPF Counselling and Psychotherapy in Kensington. She has been on the editorial board of several journals and Chair of the Ethics Committee of UKCP. She is author of *How Much is Enough? Endings in Psychotherapy and Counselling* (Routledge 1999).

Maureen Murphy is a counsellor in private practice in Suffolk, working mainly with survivors of sexual abuse.

Michael Neenan is Associate Director of the Centre for Stress Management, London, a BABCP accredited cognitive behavioural therapist and a UKCP registered psychotherapist. His recent books include *Essential Cognitive Therapy* (Whurr 2000).

Richard Nelson-Jones is an author, psychotherapist and Director of the Cognitive-Humanistic Institute, Chiang Mai, Thailand. For over 20 years until 1997 he trained counsellors and counselling psychologists in British and Australian universities. He is a Fellow of BACP, BPS and APS.

John O'Brien At the time of writing the article was Director of an Anglo-American management consultancy, Creative Dimensions in Management (London and Philadelphia). While managing and training consultants in change management facilitation techniques, he also provides a personal mentoring and team-building service to senior executives. He has a small private practice in counselling and psychotherapy.

Bill O'Connell is a Senior Lecturer at the University of Birmingham Westhill where he is the Programme Leader for Counselling. He is a Fellow of BAC and a UKRC registered independent counsellor.

Steve Page is Head of Student Support Services at the University of Hull, with a counselling background in higher education, private practice and therapeutic community work. He is with V. Wosket co-author of *Supervising the Counsellor* (Routledge 1994, 2001) and author of *The Shadow and the Counsellor* (Routledge 1999).

Mary Parker is an experienced practitioner registered with AHPP and UKCP, and a BAC accredited supervisor with a large supervision practice. She runs workshops on case-study writing, note-taking and assessment and is a course consultant and external moderator.

Frank Parkinson, a clergyman and army chaplain for over 30 years, a Relate-trained counsellor and the author of four books, is a consultant and trainer on counselling and trauma.

Stephen Paul works as Principal Lecturer in Psychology at Leeds Metropolitan University. He currently co-ordinates counselling and psychotherapy courses and is course leader for B.Sc. (Hons) Counselling and Therapeutic Studies. He holds qualifications in counselling and psychotherapy.

Geoff Pelham is Course Leader for B.Sc. (Hons) Therapeutic Counselling at Leeds Metropolitan University. He is a BAC accredited counsellor and trainer. He has a private practice in both counselling and supervision.

Nadine Pelling is a Ph.D. candidate in counselling psychology at Western Michigan University who is currently finishing her predoctoral internship in Vancouver, Canada. She graduated in August 2000.

Raj Persaud is consultant psychiatrist at Bethlem and Maudsley Hospitals, London. Besides receiving numerous awards for his research and clinical work he was recently elected a fellow of University College London.

Deborah E. Renard is a Ph.D. student in the Department of Counselor Education and Counseling Psychology, Western Michigan University.

Cathy Richards is a chartered clinical psychologist working in the Young Peoples Unit in Edinburgh. When this article was first published she worked for the Student Support and Counselling Service at the University of Birmingham.

Susan Ridge is a research associate at Manchester Metropolitan University and professional counsellor for Mental Health Services at Salford.

Jane Robins is a tutor on a self-awareness option of the Certificate in Counselling Skills at Bristol University and works as a private counsellor.

Dave Robson is a Senior Lecturer in the Department of Computer Science at the University of Durham. He is a BAC accredited counsellor working for Relate.

Suzanna Rose is head of West Berkshire Traumatic Stress Service.

Peter Ross is Director of counselling at Reading University.

Janice Russell is associate lecturer in counselling, University of Hull, a freelance consultant in counselling and human resource management and a Master Practitioner in NLP (Neuro-Linguistic Programming). She is co-author with Graham Dexter of *The Differentiation Project: A Report to Lead Body on Similarities and Differences Between Advice, Guidance, Counselling, Counselling Skills and Befriending* (Department of Education 1992) and *Challenging Blank Minds and Sticky Moments in Counselling* (1998).

Christina Saunders is a BACP accredited and UKRC registered independent counsellor, who works in private practice with individuals and couples. She is also an affiliate counsellor with several EAPs, a supervisor and trainer in solution-focused therapy and personal development.

Mark Scoggins is a solicitor and a partner in Elborne Mitchell.

Gita Sheth is head of counselling for Kara Counselling and Training Trust and is a social worker by training. She established pre-test counselling services for people wishing to have antibody tests in Lusaka and is interested in using a group approach for sexual behaviour change.

Jackie de Smith is a counsellor and spiritual healer.

Ernesto Spinelli is the current Academic Dean of the School of Psychotherapy and Counselling at Regent's College, London. In recognition of his contributions to the profession, he was awarded a Personal Chair in Psychotherapy, Counselling and Counselling Psychology in 1998.

Gabrielle Syme, former BAC Chair, is a UKCP registered analytical psychotherapist, a UKRC registered independent counsellor who works in independent practice.

Kasia Szymanska is a chartered counselling psychologist and a UKCP registered psychotherapist. Associate Director at the Centre for Stress Management, London, and Senior Lecturer at the University of East London, she sees clients in a busy stress management unit in the City of London.

Lennox Thomas is a leading figure in intercultural therapy. Joint course director of the M.Sc. in Intercultural Therapy at University College Hospital and a visiting teacher at the Tavistock Centre, London, he works in private practice with individuals, couples and families.

Brian Thorne is Emeritus Professor of Counselling at the University of East Anglia, Norwich, and a Professor of Education in the College of Teachers. He is a Fellow of BACP.

Tuck-Chee Phung teaches social work in north-east Scotland. He has recently completed his training as a person-centred counsellor.

Moira Walker is former head of the University of Leicester Counselling Service, author of *Women in Therapy and Counselling* (OUP 1990), *Surviving Secrets – The Experience of Abuse for the Child, the Adult and the Helper* (OUP 1992) and editor of *Peta – a Feminist's Problem with Men* (OUP 1995), *Morag – Myself or Mother Hen* (OUP 1995) and *Hidden Selves* (with Jenifer Antony Black) (OUP 1999).

Margaret Ward was formerly a community psychiatric nurse at Godalming Health Centre, Surrey.

Sue Warren-Holland is a retired counsellor and counselling supervisor.

William West, lecturer in counselling studies at Manchester University, currently serves on the Research and Evaluation Committee of BAC and has written extensively on humanistic therapy, spirituality, supervision, and qualitative research. His latest book is *Psychotherapy and Spirituality* (Sage 2000).

Sue Wheeler is a Senior Lecturer in Counselling at the University of Birmingham and a counsellor and supervisor in private practice. She is the Director of the Professional Studies M.A., which promotes continuing professional development through the study of supervision and counsellor training, and supervises research students working on projects related to supervision, counsellor training, and delivery of counselling services. She is the author of several books including *Training Counsellors: The Assessment of Competence* (Cassell 1996) and *Supervising Counsellors: Issues of Responsibility* (Sage 2000). She is a BAC accredited counsellor and Fellow of BAC.

Diana Whitmore is Director of Development and Curriculum of the Psychosynthesis and Education Trust, and senior trainer and supervisor in psychosynthesis. She is on the UKCP National Register of Psychotherapists, is a BAC accredited supervisor, a founding board member of the Association of Accredited Psychospiritual Psychotherapists and a trustee of the Findhorn Foundation. She is author of numerous articles and two books: *Psychosynthesis and Education: A Guide to the Joy of Learning* (Turstone Press 1986) and *Psychosynthesis Counselling in Action* (Sage 1991).

Paul Wilkins is an academic working in the area of human communication and counselling and psychotherapy research, and a person-centred therapist, supervisor and psychodramatist. He is author of *Personal and Professional Development for Counsellors* (Sage 1996) and *Psychodrama* (Sage 1999).

David I. Williams, Senior Lecturer in psychology, is a chartered counselling psychologist, and Director of the Counsellor Training Unit at the University of Hull.

Index

INTELLECTUAL PROPERTY:
PATENTS, COPYRIGHT, TRADE MARKS
AND ALLIED RIGHTS

AUSTRALIA
LBC Information Services
Sydney

CANADA and USA
Carswell
Toronto

NEW ZEALAND
Brooker's
Auckland

SINGAPORE and MALAYSIA
Sweet & Maxwell Asia
Singapore and *Kuala Lumpur*